The Complete
Charity VAT Handbook

4th edition

Alastair Hardman
and Kate Sayer

dsc
directory of social change

Published by the Directory of Social Change (Registered Charity no. 800517 in England and Wales)

Head office: Resource for London, 352 Holloway Rd, London N7 6PA

Northern office: Suite 103, 1 Old Hall Street, Liverpool L3 9HG

Tel: 08450 77 77 07

Visit www.dsc.org.uk to find out more about our books, subscription funding websites and training events. You can also sign up for e-newsletters so that you're always the first to hear about what's new.

The publisher welcomes suggestions and comments that will help to inform and improve future versions of this and all of our titles. Please give us your feedback by emailing publications@dsc.org.uk.

It should be understood that this publication is intended for guidance only and is not a substitute for professional or legal advice. No responsibility for loss occasioned as a result of any person acting or refraining from acting can be accepted by the authors or publisher.

First published as *A Practical Guide to VAT for Charities* 1998
Second edition 2002
Third edition 2008
Reprinted 2011
Fourth edition published as *The Complete Charity VAT Handbook* 2016

ISBN 978 1 78482 015 2

British Library Cataloguing in Publication Data
A catalogue record for this book is available from the British Library

Cover and text design by Kate Bass
Typeset by Marlinzo Services, Frome
Printed and bound by Page Bros, Norwich

MIX
Paper from responsible sources
FSC
www.fsc.org
FSC® C023114

Contents

About the Directory of Social Change

The Directory of Social Change (DSC) has a vision of an independent voluntary sector at the heart of social change. The activities of independent charities, voluntary organisations and community groups are fundamental to achieve social change. We exist to help these organisations and the people who support them to achieve their goals.

We do this by:

- providing practical tools that organisations and activists need, including online and printed publications, training courses, and conferences on a huge range of topics;
- acting as a 'concerned citizen' in public policy debates, often on behalf of smaller charities, voluntary organisations and community groups;
- leading campaigns and stimulating debate on key policy issues that affect those groups;
- carrying out research and providing information to influence policymakers.

DSC is the leading provider of information and training for the voluntary sector and publishes an extensive range of guides and handbooks covering subjects such as fundraising, management, communication, finance and law. We have a range of subscription-based websites containing a wealth of information on funding from trusts, companies and government sources. We run more than 300 training courses each year, including bespoke in-house training provided at the client's location. DSC conferences, many of which run on an annual basis, include the Charity Management Conference, the Charity Accountants' Conference and the Charity Law Conference. DSC's major annual event is Charityfair, which provides low-cost training on a wide variety of subjects.

For details of all our activities, and to order publications and book courses, go to www.dsc.org.uk, call 08450 777707 or email publications@dsc.org.uk.

About the authors

Alastair Hardman is an author and advisor on charity taxation and accounting. After many years at the coalface of the voluntary sector running an organisation in North London, Alastair trained and qualified as a chartered accountant with Sayer Vincent. He helps charities to structure their affairs effectively for tax so that they can maximise their impact but also pay the right amount of tax.

Kate Sayer has specialised in charities since 1984. As a chartered accountant and partner in Sayer Vincent, she advises charities and social enterprises on a wide range of finance, tax, governance and management issues. Kate particularly enjoys training trustees and staff in charities to make finance and risk subjects more accessible. Kate teaches charity finance at Cass Business School and contributes to the leadership development programme for finance professionals.

Acknowledgements

The genesis of this book goes back a long way – to simple one-day courses at the Directory of Social Change that sought to explain VAT to charity staff and trustees. Based on those courses, Kate wrote the first edition of *A Practical Guide to VAT for Charities* in response to a huge demand for something that would simplify VAT for charities. Now re-named, this is a new edition but we have also substantially re-written the book and expanded the contents considerably to reflect the wide variety of activities undertaken by charities.

The authors would like to acknowledge the huge contribution made by Helen Elliott, partner in Sayer Vincent. Not only does Helen carefully check lots of draft chapters, but she also contributes practical points, ideas on how charities can manage their affairs better to cope with VAT and take advantage of the rules where possible. Her practical knowledge of doing this day to day helped both authors a great deal.

We are grateful to the Directory of Social Change for its support and patience, needed more than ever for this edition, as trying to make sure this was as up to date as possible was more difficult than ever.

Preface

Value Added Tax (VAT) was introduced in the UK in 1973. It is a transaction tax levied on sales of goods and services and operates throughout the European Union, although the rules vary from state to state. It is particularly the international aspects of VAT that have been changing in recent years as the EU seeks to harmonise taxation across the member states. This volume also updates earlier editions for all the case law and legislative changes that have been introduced. The book covers the relevant law and known cases up to July 2015.

We have attempted to bring together all the relevant aspects of VAT law to help charities and voluntary organisations as they grapple with this complex subject. However, we have to make choices about the aspects to cover and we have omitted some topics which are less commonly relevant to charities so that we can focus on areas such as fundraising. Charities undertaking commercial activities should remember to check the relevant law and VAT guidance before committing themselves irrevocably.

You also need to consider the interaction of VAT with other taxes and reliefs such as Gift Aid, business rates relief, corporation tax, stamp duty land tax and income tax. Case law is littered with examples of organisations that thought they had achieved a positive outcome for their VAT position only to discover that it had negative consequences for other taxes.

At Sayer Vincent, we believe that it is right to pay the correct amount of tax. We do not provide information to help people avoid paying the correct taxes. However, charities should maximise the value of their assets and apply their income for public benefit. And charities should not pay taxes unnecessarily. The purpose of our guidance is to provide information so that good decisions can be made to act both legally and in the best interests of the charity's beneficiaries.

Kate Sayer, Sayer Vincent

Foreword

The publication is a timely reference work for charities that navigates the diverse and often complex world of charity VAT.

Many people often mistakenly believe that charities do not pay VAT. They could not be more wrong – in particular, charities bear huge amounts of 'sticking' VAT on their essential expenditure, which have increased over the years as the standard rate has doubled. As Chairman of the Charity Tax Group (CTG), I spend countless hours navigating the legislation and guidance which appears to grow by the year.

It is important to note that charities do benefit from some very generous reliefs and these are laid out in great detail in the handbook. However, irrecoverable VAT is now estimated to cost the sector up to £1.5 billion each year. So, what is the solution? A full refund to charities of this irrecoverable VAT remains a long-term goal, although we recognise that in times of fiscal austerity a more incremental approach may be more successful. In recent times, the government has demonstrated willingness to look at VAT refunds afresh, prompted in part by confirmation by the European Commission that there is no European law obstacle (having used this excuse for many years previously). In addition to national museums and galleries, other charities including hospices, air ambulance providers and search and rescue organisations can all now claim VAT refunds.

In the 2015 Autumn Statement, two announcements really stood out: 1) that the government will be actively seeking a zero rate on sanitary products; and 2) that the government will allow sixth form colleges to convert to academies to avoid paying irrecoverable VAT. The former indicates that there may be room for negotiation on new zero rates (including possibly charity zero rates) in the ongoing European negotiations which presents both opportunities and threats. The latter demonstrates the distortions caused by the VAT system for organisations unable to recover their VAT and strengthens the case for VAT refunds for charities providing essential public services in competition with private and governmental suppliers. We will be pushing the government for serious consideration of further VAT refunds for charities to try and tackle these distortions and complexity.

In the meantime, core reference documents such as *The Complete Charity VAT Handbook* and CTG's forthcoming Charity Tax Map website are essential when it comes to policymaking. Knowing the law and how it must be implemented is crucial if we are to continue to prevent unintended consequences of VAT legislation and to seek proactive change to simplify the tax system for charities.

John Hemming, Chairman, Charity Tax Group

How to use this book

VAT REGISTRATION

For charities that are not registered for VAT, the need to be registered for VAT is usually an important consideration, especially if you know you already make or are about to make taxable sales. The need to register for VAT is explained in Chapter 2 'Registration and deregistration'.

VAT TYPES OF TRANSACTION

For all charities (registered and unregistered) determining the VAT status of its income streams can be challenging:

- The distinction between business and non-business income is covered in Chapter 4 'Business and non-business activities'.
- The key VAT exemptions are covered in Chapter 5 'Exempt activities' and Chapter 8 'Property' for the property-related exemptions.
- The key zero-ratings and reduced-ratings are covered in Chapter 6 'Zero and reduced rates' and Chapter 8 'Property' for the property-related zero-rating and reduced-rating reliefs.

ISSUES FOR VAT-REGISTERED ORGANISATIONS

For VAT-registered organisations there are some specific issues to deal with:

- Determining how much of the VAT incurred on purchases can be recovered. This is covered in Chapter 3 'Recovering VAT'.
- Special schemes, such as the Capital Goods Scheme and the non-business VAT refund schemes (for academy schools, hospices, etc.) are covered in Chapter 10 'VAT special schemes'.
- Handling the VAT returns and payment practicalities. This is covered in Chapter 12 'Operational aspects'.

FUNDRAISING ACTIVITIES

Chapter 7 'Fundraising' provides guidance on the VAT treatment of over 20 common types of fundraising activity including sales of advertising, fundraising events, corporate sponsorship, challenge events, charity shops, London Marathon and similar, merchandising, gifts in kind from businesses, and renting property.

CROSS-BORDER TRANSACTIONS

Chapter 9 'International aspects of VAT' covers the special VAT rules that apply if you sell goods or services to a foreign customer or purchase goods or services from a foreign supplier.

TECHNICAL ISSUES

The catch-all Chapter 11 'Other topics' deals with miscellaneous VAT issues including: transfer of a business as a going concern, membership subscriptions, single and multiple supplies, agency supplies, supplies of staff, supplies between connected parties, and the scope of the registrable entity.

CONTACTING HMRC, SOURCES OF FURTHER INFORMATION, ETC.

Chapter 14 'Further information' provides HMRC contact details, other useful links, how to check VAT numbers, territories of the EU, their VAT number formats, etc.

Table of cases

This list comprises more information than is in the main body of the book to assist any searches for additional details online. Information on VAT Tribunal cases is difficult to source and in some instances you will have more success searching for the LON/00/000-style reference rather than the VTD number.

UK

Court of Appeal (England and Wales)

Court of Session (Scotland)

First-tier Tribunal (Tax)

High Court of Justice (England and Wales)

Supreme Court

Upper Tribunal (Tax and Chancery Chamber)

VAT Tribunals

EUROPE
European Court of Human Rights

European Court of Justice

1 Overview of VAT

This chapter provides an overview of how Value Added Tax (VAT) works and the differences between non-business, exempt and taxable activities. It is divided into the following sections:

- 1.1 How VAT works
- 1.2 VAT types of transaction
- 1.3 Zero-rated activities

1.1 HOW VAT WORKS

VAT is a tax charged on certain **taxable supplies** (defined in 1.2.2). It is calculated as a percentage of the transaction price and added to the price charged to the customer. The added VAT is called **output VAT** (or **output tax**).

The price before VAT is added is called the **net price** and the price after output VAT is added is called the **gross price**. At the time of writing the standard rate of VAT in the UK is 20%. Businesses do not get to keep the output VAT they charge to their customers. It must be paid to HM Revenue & Customs (HMRC).

Example 1: Woodwork Ltd

Woodwork Ltd manufactures and sells chairs. It sells a chair for £100 plus VAT. The price charged to the customer is:

Net selling price	£100.00
Plus output VAT: 20% × £100	£20.00
Gross selling price	£120.00

Woodwork Ltd must pay the £20.00 output VAT to HMRC.

Businesses also incur VAT on the purchases they make. This is called **input VAT** (or **input tax**). Businesses are allowed to **recover** any input VAT they incur on purchases that are used in making their taxable supplies. They do this by **deducting** the input VAT incurred on the purchases from the output VAT due on the sales and paying only the balance over to HMRC.

Example 2: Woodwork Ltd

To make a chair, Woodwork Ltd purchases goods for £60 net. The gross cost to Woodwork Ltd is:

Net purchase price	£60.00
Plus input VAT: £60 × 20%	£12.00
Gross purchase price	£72.00

Woodwork Ltd can recover this input VAT by deducting it from the output VAT. It must pay to HMRC:

Output VAT	£20.00
Less input VAT	(£12.00)
VAT payable to HMRC	£8.00

If the input VAT is more than the output VAT, the balance is paid to the business by HMRC.

We can now see why the tax is called 'value added' tax. The amount of VAT payable to HMRC is the tax due on the value added.

The value added to the goods purchased for a chair by Woodwork Ltd is:

Selling price (net)	£100.00
Less purchase price (net)	(£60.00)
Value added	£40.00
VAT on value added: £40 × 20%	£8.00

For Woodwork Ltd, VAT simply passes through the business. The VAT it incurs on purchases can be recovered from HMRC, so it is not expenditure for Woodwork Ltd. The VAT it charges must be paid to HMRC, so it is not income for Woodwork Ltd. Woodwork Ltd is simply collecting tax on the value it adds and passing this to the government.

However, if the person purchasing the chair cannot recover the VAT they incur on purchases, the VAT charged on the chair is a cost to them. Individuals acting in a private capacity and businesses that are not registered for VAT with HMRC cannot recover the VAT they incur on purchases.

The cost of each chair to a private individual is £120 whereas the effective cost to a VAT-registered business is £100, if it can recover the £20 VAT charged by Woodwork Ltd.

1.2 **VAT TYPES OF TRANSACTION**

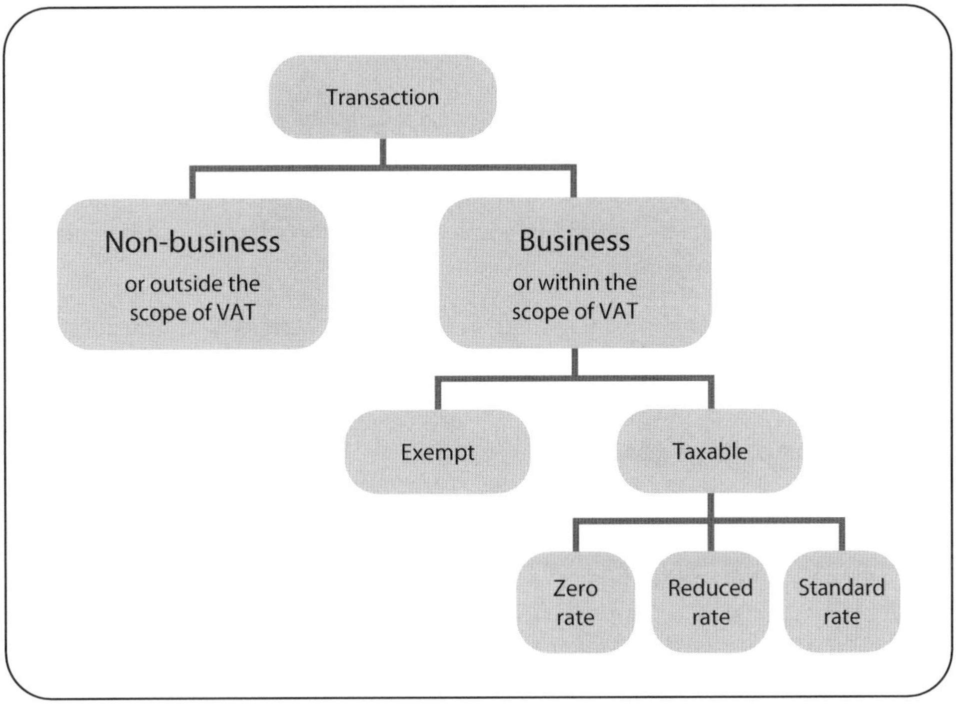

Fig. 1.1 VAT categories of transaction

1.2.1 **Business and non-business**

VAT is a tax that applies at the transaction level. However, not all transactions are subject to VAT. For a transaction to be subject to output VAT:

1. The transaction must be a **supply**. Supply means the provision of goods or services in return for **consideration**. Consideration is everything that is paid to the supplier in return for making the supply of goods or services.
2. The supply of goods or of services must be a **business supply**. This means that the supply is made in the course or furtherance of a business of the supplier's. Transactions for non-business purposes are **outside the scope** of VAT.

A transaction which meets these conditions is said to be **within the scope of VAT** or a **business supply**. A transaction which does not meet these conditions is referred to as **outside the scope of VAT** or **non-business**.

Examples of non-business transactions are:

- **Grants and donations** are not seen as consideration for a supply of goods or services provided the recipient does not provide goods or services in return for the grant or donation.
- **Giving away goods** for free or providing services for free is not normally seen as a supply on the basis that there is no consideration (though giving away goods or services for free can be *deemed* to be a supply, see 4.2 'Exceptions').
- **Supplies undertaken by individuals in a personal capacity** are not business supplies, for example an individual selling their home.

The distinction between **business** and **non-business activities** is considered in more depth in Chapter 4 'Business and non-business activities'.

1.2.2   Exempt and taxable supplies

Exempt supplies

By default all business supplies are taxable and output VAT must be charged to the customer at the appropriate rate of VAT. However, certain types of business supply are specifically exempted from VAT. These are referred to as **exempt supplies** and the activities that generate them as **exempt activities**.

Numerous activities of voluntary organisations are exempt and include business supplies of:

- education and vocational training;
- health and welfare services;
- cultural services;
- sports facilities;
- sales in connection with a qualifying fundraising event.

VAT is not charged on exempt supplies and generally VAT incurred in making exempt supplies cannot be recovered. In the UK, the exempt supplies are listed in Schedule 9 VAT Act 1994.

Exempt supplies are considered in Chapter 5 'Exempt activities'. Selling or renting real property (**land, buildings** and **civil engineering works** – see 8.6 'Property terms') is also normally an exempt supply though there are many exceptions. The land-related exemptions are considered in Chapter 8 'Property'.

Taxable supplies

If a business supply is not specifically exempted, then it is referred to as a **taxable supply**. An activity that generates taxable supplies is referred to as a **taxable activity**. If the total turnover from all taxable supplies exceeds a certain level (the **VAT Registration Threshold**), then an organisation must register for VAT with HMRC and start charging VAT on its taxable supplies. However, it can also recover the VAT incurred on purchases used in making the taxable supplies.

Common taxable supplies in the voluntary sector include:

- sales of donated goods;
- sales of bought-in goods/merchandising;
- supplies of food and catering;
- consultancy services;
- sales of advertising, use of logos and intellectual property rights, royalties, etc.;
- management/administration charges to subsidiaries;
- vehicle and equipment hire;
- some property rentals.

The requirement to register for VAT is explained in Chapter 2 'Registration and deregistration'. The rules for recovering VAT are explained in Chapter 3 'Recovering VAT'.

1.2.3 Rates of VAT

Three different rates of VAT are currently used in the UK:

- the standard rate (currently 20%): the default rate for taxable supplies;
- the reduced rate (currently 5%): applies to certain specific types of supply listed in schedule 7A VAT Act 1995;
- the zero rate (0%): applies to certain specific types of supply listed in schedule 8 VAT Act 1995.

The rate of VAT is multiplied by the net (VAT-exclusive) selling price to determine the amount of VAT to charge.

Reduced-rated and zero-rated supplies are considered in Chapter 6 'Zero and reduced rates'.

Examples: calculating the VAT due and gross price

Net price	Rate of VAT	VAT chargeable	Gross price
100.00	20%	£100 × 20% = £20	£100 + £20 = £120
100.00	5%	£100 × 5% = £5	£100 + £5 = £105
100.00	0%	£100 × 0% = £0	£100

VAT fractions

The VAT fraction is the number you must multiply the gross price by to get the amount of VAT included. There are different VAT fractions for different rates of VAT.

Examples: VAT fractions

Rate of VAT	VAT fraction	Gross amount	VAT included	Net amount
20%	1/6	£120	£120 × (1/6) = £20	£120 − £20 = £100
5%	1/21	£105	£1005 × (1/21) = £5	£105 − £5 = £100

See 12.1 VAT fractions and VAT rounding for more.

1.2.4 Recovering VAT

If a VAT-registered organisation has a mix of non-business, exempt and taxable activities, then all VAT incurred on purchases must be **attributed** to the different types of activity (the types being taxable, exempt and non-business) to determine if it is recoverable or not.

Attribution involves **directly allocating** VAT to one of the activity types wherever possible, then **apportioning** the remaining VAT between the different types of activity.

- **Direct allocation**: if a purchase is wholly used in (or for use in) a particular type of activity, then the VAT on that purchase is directly allocated to that activity type. For example, if a minibus is purchased wholly for hire (a taxable business activity), the VAT on the minibus purchase and running costs is allocated wholly to taxable activities.

- **Apportionment**: however, some purchases are not for use in one type of activity, for example a minibus purchased for hire and for use in a charity's exempt business activity of running a youth club. Here the purchase is for use in two types of activity. The VAT incurred on the minibus must be apportioned between taxable and exempt activities.

General organisational overheads ('support costs', 'governance costs', etc.) are also usually incurred for the benefit of all activities, for example general administration costs and the costs of setting up and running the legal entity such as audit fees and the costs of the AGM.

The VAT on mixed-use purchases and overheads must be pooled and that pool must then be apportioned between the activity types. There are special VAT rules as to how these apportionments must be carried out. These are explained in Chapter 3 'Recovering VAT'.

- The VAT on purchases that is attributed and apportioned to **taxable activities** is **recoverable**.
- The VAT on purchases that is attributed and apportioned to **exempt activities** is **not recoverable** unless it is below a certain level, in which case it is referred to as *de minimis* (see 3.1.11 'The *de minimis* test') and can be recovered.
- The VAT on purchases that is attributed and apportioned to **non-business activities** is **not normally recoverable**, though certain charities such as academy schools and hospices are eligible for **special non-business VAT refund schemes**. These special VAT refund schemes are covered in Chapter 10 'VAT special schemes'.

Example: the Advice Network

The Advice Network is registered for VAT and has three projects:

- **Project A** is a non-business activity entirely funded by a non-business grant. No VAT is charged to the grant provider. The total VAT on purchases attributed to Project A is £30,000. This VAT cannot be recovered and represents an expense for the Advice Network.
- **Project B** is an exempt educational service provided under a contract. No VAT is charged on the contract. The total VAT on purchases attributed to Project B is £20,000. This VAT cannot be recovered and represents an expense for the Advice Network (note: £20,000 is above the *de minimis* limit).
- **Project C** is a standard-rated contract for consultancy services. The total VAT on purchases attributed to Project C is £10,000. This can be recovered and does not represent an expense for the Advice Network.

1.2.5 **Residual VAT**

Where a purchase is used for a mix of activity types (taxable and exempt or non-business), there are special rules for determining how much of the VAT on that purchase can be recovered. VAT on purchases used for a mix of activities is referred to as **residual VAT**.

Example: the Advice Network

The Advice Network incurs VAT on overheads of £30,000. This must be apportioned between the activity types present (non-business, exempt and taxable). The VAT apportioned to taxable activities can be recovered, the VAT apportioned to non-business activities is irrecoverable and the VAT apportioned to exempt activities is also irrecoverable.

The apportionment rules are explained in Chapter 3 'Recovering VAT'.

1.3 **ZERO-RATED ACTIVITIES**

Zero-rated means that a supply is taxable, but at a zero rate of VAT. The effect is to add no output VAT to the sale price but any input VAT incurred by the activity can be recovered. Zero-rating applies to a limited range of supplies.

Zero-rated supplies include (at the time of writing) the sale of:

- printed books, booklets, leaflets, journals, periodicals, etc.;
- young children's sized clothing and footwear;
- some foodstuffs;
- goods donated by a charity.

Zero-rating is in many ways the ideal situation if your customers are private individuals or unregistered organisations and cannot recover the VAT they incur on purchases. The price charged to customers is not increased by VAT but all VAT incurred in making the zero-rated supplies can be recovered. If your customers are VAT-registered and can recover the VAT they incur on purchases, then being able to zero rate your supplies is less important. The net cost to the customer will be the same whether or not the supply is zero-rated or standard-rated.

It is important to appreciate the difference between exempt and zero-rated supplies. For both of these, no VAT is actually charged to customers. However, with zero-rated supplies, the VAT incurred on associated purchases can be recovered, while for exempt supplies the VAT incurred on associated purchases cannot be recovered, except under very limited circumstances (as explained above, when the VAT attributed to exempt activities is *de minimis*).

2 Registration and deregistration

This chapter covers:

- 2.1 **VAT registration**: when you must or may register for VAT
- 2.2 **VAT groups**: when you can register several organisations as one
- 2.3 **Deregistration**: when you must or may deregister for VAT
- 2.4 **Cross-border registration issues**: cross-border supplies can affect registration

2.1 VAT REGISTRATION

- You must register for VAT if your income from taxable supplies (see 1.2.2) has exceeded or is about to exceed the VAT Registration Threshold. This is referred to as mandatory VAT registration.
- You can also register voluntarily if you make, or will make, taxable supplies of any level. This is referred to as voluntary registration (see 2.1.3).
- You must deregister for VAT if you stop making taxable supplies altogether. This is referred to as mandatory deregistration.
- You can deregister for VAT voluntarily if your taxable turnover drops below the Deregistration Threshold. This is referred to as voluntary deregistration.

Income from taxable supplies excludes income from exempt supplies and non-business income. See 1.2 'VAT types of transaction' for the distinctions between non-business, exempt and taxable income.

2.1.1 VAT Registration and Deregistration Thresholds

The VAT Registration and Deregistration Thresholds are normally increased each year in the Chancellor's annual budget. Recent thresholds are listed overleaf.

From	To	Registration Threshold (£)	Deregistration Threshold (£)
1 April 2015		82,000	80,000
1 April 2014	31 March 2015	81,000	79,000
1 April 2013	31 March 2014	79,000	77,000
1 April 2012	31 March 2013	77,000	75,000
1 April 2011	31 March 2012	73,000	71,000
1 April 2010	31 March 2011	70,000	68,000
1 May 2009	31 March 2010	68,000	66,000
1 April 2008	30 April 2009	67,000	65,000
1 April 2007	31 March 2008	64,000	62,000
1 April 2006	31 March 2007	61,000	59,000
1 April 2005	31 March 2006	60,000	58,000

The Deregistration Threshold is normally £2,000 less than the Registration Threshold and the Registration Threshold normally increases by between £1,000 and £4,000 each year. The thresholds normally last from 1 April to the next 31 March; however, there can be exceptions (for instance 09/10 started on 1 May 2009). You can check the latest and historic thresholds on the gov.uk website (see Chapter 14 'Further information').

2.1.2 **Compulsory registration**

You are required to register for VAT if either of the following two conditions is met.

1. The 'past turnover' test

At the end of any calendar month, the value of taxable supplies in the last 12 calendar months has exceeded the VAT Registration Threshold. You must notify HMRC within 30 days of the end of the month in which the test is met and is registered from the first day of the second month.

Example: past turnover test

The VAT Registration Threshold for 2014/15 was £81,000 (see above table). Alpha Ltd started in business on 15 May 2014. Alpha's **taxable turnover** in the first few months of operation was:

	Taxable turnover in month (£)	Cumulative turnover at end of month (£)
May 2014	1,000	1,000
June 2014	10,000	11,000
July 2014	10,000	21,000
August 2014	20,000	41,000
September 2014	50,000	91,000

At the end of September Alpha had exceeded the Registration Threshold then in force (£81,000). Alpha must inform HMRC by 30 October 2014 and will be registered from 1 November 2014. This means that Alpha starts to charge VAT on supplies made on or after 1 November.

2. The 'future turnover' test

At any time, there are reasonable grounds for believing that the value of taxable supplies in the next 30 days alone will exceed the VAT Registration Threshold. You must notify HMRC within 30 days of being aware that the Registration Threshold will be exceeded in the following 30 days. The registration is effective from the date you became aware that the Registration Threshold would be exceeded.

Example: future turnover test

Beta Ltd has been running a business for several years, generating regular taxable sales of £3,000 per month (£36,000 per year). Beta's taxable turnover has stayed below the VAT Registration Threshold and the company has not registered for VAT voluntarily.

On 1 September 2014, Beta signed a taxable consultancy contract for £200,000. Under the terms of the contract an invoice for £100,000 was to be issued on 11 October 2014 and one for £100,000 on completion which took place at the end of November 2014. The Registration Threshold for 2014/15 was £81,000 (see table above).

On 12 September Beta knew that its taxable turnover in the next 30 days would be:

£3,000 + £100,000 = £103,000

As this was above the Registration Threshold Beta had to notify HMRC by 30 days from the end of the month in which the test is met. The test is met in September, so the end of the month is 30 September and Beta had to notify HMRC within 30 days of then, i.e. by 30 October 2014. Beta was registered from 12 September 2014.

In some situations, foreign purchases count towards your VAT Registration Threshold or can make you liable to be registered for VAT. See 2.4 'Cross-border registration issues'.

2.1.3 Voluntary registration

You can register for VAT voluntarily if:

1. you make or intend to make taxable supplies in the UK;
2. you make or intend to make supplies outside the UK that would be taxable if made in the UK.

You may be able to backdate a voluntary registration up to four years before the date of application. See 2.1.9 'Backdating voluntary registration'.

If you apply for registration on the basis of future intent, HMRC will need to be sure that you are in business and do genuinely intend making taxable supplies. HMRC may require evidence such as contracts, copy invoices showing investment for new activity or other appropriate evidence.

You can also register voluntarily in some other situations, for example see 2.4.3 'UK registration for relevant intra-EU acquisitions of goods'.

2.1.4 What counts towards your VAT Registration Threshold?

To calculate your taxable income:

- **Include**: income from business supplies that would be **taxable supplies** (standard-rated, reduced-rated or zero-rated supplies) if you were registered for VAT.
- **Exclude**: income that is **non-business** (grants, donations, legacies, bank interest, financial investment income, etc.).

- **Exclude** income that is covered by one of the **VAT exemptions** (education, welfare, cultural services, fundraising events, property rent, etc.).

Example: calculating your taxable turnover

Charity Gamma has received the following income in the last 12 months. Assume the Registration Threshold is £81,000:

Income	Amount (£)	VAT status	Taxable turnover (£)
Grants and public donations	500,000	Non-business	–
Sale of donated goods	50,000	Zero	50,000
Sale of bought-in goods	20,000	Standard/zero	20,000
Education fees (exempt)	20,000	Exempt	–
Rental income (exempt)	10,000	Exempt	–
Consultancy fees	3,000	Standard	3,000
Sale of publications	1,000	Zero/standard	1,000
Bank interest	1,000	Non-business	–
Totals	**605,000**		**74,000**

Taxable income arises from the sale of donated goods (zero-rated), publications and bought-in goods (zero- or standard-rated), and consultancy fees (standard-rated).Total taxable income is £74,000. This is below the VAT Registration Threshold (£81,000), so Gamma does not have to register yet. However, it should monitor the situation on a regular basis, as it is near to the Registration Threshold. Gamma should also check that it will not meet the 'future turnover' test. Gamma should also consider if it should register for VAT voluntarily as it makes substantial levels of zero-rated supplies.

For some supplies it is the margin (income less direct costs) that counts towards the VAT Registration Threshold.

This includes supplies under the various margin schemes (see Chapter 10 'VAT special schemes').

Income generated from the sale of capital assets such as buildings, equipment or vehicles is ignored unless it is an opted to tax supply of land or buildings that is not zero-rated (see 8.5 'Option to tax').

2.1.5   Exception from compulsory registration

You may be excepted from compulsory registration if:

- you meet the 'past turnover' test;
- you do not meet the 'future turnover test'; and
- you can satisfy HMRC that your taxable turnover in the following 12 months will be less than the VAT Deregistration Threshold.

You must tell HMRC that you have reached the VAT Registration Threshold within 30 days of the end of the month. You do not have to complete an application for VAT registration unless HMRC refuses exception from registration. If HMRC refuses, you will have to register for VAT and will be registered for the normal due date.

HMRC may be prepared to grant retrospective exception from registration if it receives an application for exception containing information which would have been available at that time, and would have led HMRC to grant exception from registration at the earlier date (*VATREG19150*).

2.1.6   Exemption from compulsory registration

You may be exempted from compulsory registration if all or most of your supplies will be zero-rated and you are able to persuade HMRC that your recoverable input VAT will normally be more than your **output VAT** (see 1.1), so you will be a net recoverer of VAT from HMRC.

This would normally be disadvantageous financially, as, if you were registered, HMRC would overall end up paying you money. However, there can be good reasons for taking advantage of this exemption, for example if the net amount of VAT involved is small but compliance costs are likely to be higher.

You must apply to HMRC for exemption from registration and must monitor your activities and notify HMRC as soon as there is any material change in your circumstances. A material change includes total output VAT exceeding recoverable input VAT in any 12-month period.

2.1.7 **Pre-registration VAT**

It is possible to claim for VAT that has been incurred prior to the date of registration. The claim should be made on the first VAT return but you can apply to HMRC for permission to claim on a later return.

The following can be claimed for:

- VAT incurred on goods that were purchased for the purpose of a taxable activity and are still 'on hand' at the date of registration, providing they were not purchased more than four years prior to registration. However, per HMRC (*VIT32000*), if the goods have been used before registration, the amount of VAT that can be recovered is correspondingly reduced. For example, if a van with an expected useful life of five years was purchased three years before registration, only two-fifths of the VAT incurred on the van can be recovered.
- VAT incurred on services supplied up to six months prior to the date of registration. The services must have been used for the purposes of a taxable business and not resupplied at the date of registration. The services will have been resupplied if they have been recharged to a business customer before the date of VAT registration
- For VAT registrations on or after 1 January 2011, VAT incurred on a capital item within the Capital Goods Scheme (CGS) up to ten years ago (land and buildings) or five years ago (other capital items). Capital items are (broadly) VAT bearing capital expenditure in excess of £250,000 on land, buildings or civil engineering works, or of £50,000 or more on an aircraft, ship, boat or other vessel, or a single computer. See 10.1.3 'Capital items'. There must have been an intention, at the time of the original purchase, to use the capital item wholly or partly to make taxable supplies. The VAT incurred is adjustable under the CGS and may be partially recoverable. See 10.1 'Capital Goods Scheme'

The six-month limitation on services can be a problem if high services costs were incurred more than six months before VAT registration, for example legal services incurred in setting up a business. See 2.1.9 'Backdating voluntary registration' below for a possible solution.

2.1.8 **Pre-incorporation VAT**

If a business is in the process of being incorporated, it cannot register for VAT because it does not yet exist and it will be unable to make payments, so it cannot incur its own pre-incorporation input VAT. However, HMRC accepts (*VAT Notice 700*, section 11.4) that pre-incorporation input VAT can be recovered if incurred by a member, officer or employee of the business and the VAT would be recoverable if incurred by the business.

The following conditions must all be met:

- The VAT incurred would be recoverable if the goods or services had been supplied to the person who is now registered for VAT.
- Goods or services were obtained or imported by a person who became a member, officer or employee of the body.
- That person was reimbursed for the full cost.
- That person was not a **taxable person** at the time of the supply or importation.

2.1.9   **Backdating voluntary registration**

If you are not yet registered for VAT, you can ask HMRC to backdate a voluntary VAT registration date by up to four years from the date of application.

This can be useful to enable recovery of input VAT you have incurred on services more than six months before. However, it does mean you will have to account for output VAT from the backdated date. You should ask for backdating at the time of your application for voluntary registration, as HMRC will not normally accept backdating when you are already registered for VAT.

2.1.10   **Applying for VAT registration**

The method by which you should register for VAT is subject to change and you should check the current gov.uk website for up-to-date information. At the time of writing, you can apply for VAT registration by completing an online registration form or downloadable form, and printing and posting it to HMRC. You can download the forms from the gov.uk website.

There are extra forms for partnership, group and divisional registrations, and if you wish to claim exemption or exception from registration, you have to send in a written application. HMRC aims to deal with applications within one month, though this can take longer, especially if HMRC has to carry out checks or if you have queries.

When HMRC has checked and agreed the registration it will send a registration certificate showing the VAT registration number, effective date of registration and the return periods to be used. From the point of registration onwards, you must charge your customers output VAT at the correct rate on your taxable supplies. You must also provide your VAT-registered customers with proper VAT invoices (see 12.4 'VAT invoices') and keep detailed VAT records (see 12.2 'Record-keeping').

If you do not receive your VAT registration details by your effective date of registration, you cannot issue valid VAT invoices even though you are registered for VAT and must charge VAT on your sales. You must issue invoices for the

VAT-inclusive amount but without showing the VAT as a separate item on the invoice. You must explain the situation to VAT-registered customers and tell them that you will send them a valid VAT invoice when your registration details are confirmed.

2.1.11   VAT returns and paying VAT

You must normally submit quarterly VAT returns online, and pay any VAT due to HMRC, within one month of the end of the VAT quarter.

However, there are a variety of simplified schemes for small businesses:

- Under the Annual Accounting Scheme a business with taxable turnover under £1.35 million can opt to make periodic VAT payments to HMRC on the basis of a single annual return.
- Various retail schemes, the Cash Accounting Scheme and the Flat Rate Scheme allow simplified accounting subject to varying conditions.

See Chapter 10 'VAT special schemes' for more on these schemes.

By default HMRC will tell you what quarter end to report to; however, you can request a quarter end, for example to coincide with your financial year end. Aligning the accounting year end and VAT year end can reduce the administrative burden of VAT, as the work done for one will often assist the other.

You can also request monthly VAT returns and you may have to pay VAT monthly under the payments on account scheme if your taxable turnover is sufficiently large (for more on this scheme see 12.6.3). Monthly VAT returns are advantageous from a cash flow perspective if you will normally make net recovery claims (recoverable input VAT exceeds output VAT due), though they are obviously a greater administrative burden. See 12.6 'The VAT return' for more on VAT returns and paying VAT.

2.1.12   Late registration

If you fail to register for VAT when you should have done, then you will be registered with effect from the date you should have been registered.

This is an exception to the normal four-year capping rule (see 12.6.8 'The capping rules'). HMRC can insist that you go back and account for undeclared output VAT (less recoverable input VAT) for up to 20 years. The first VAT return period is the period from the date you should have been registered to the first return due date.

You must account to HMRC for the output VAT which should have been charged to your customers from the date of registration onwards. The VAT has to be calculated and paid over as if you had registered on time, using the applicable VAT rate at the time of the supply. However, you can recover the input VAT you incurred in making the taxable supplies.

Unless the customer contract states that the customer must pay VAT on top of the amount already paid (and that is still enforceable), you may have to assume the amount paid was gross of VAT, at the applicable rate of VAT then in place. However, customers who are registered for VAT may be happy to receive and pay a VAT-only invoice for the VAT you should have charged.

The standard rate of VAT has changed several times in recent years (see 12.3.6 'Historic rates of VAT'), so you should take care to use the rate of VAT applicable at the **time of supply** (the point in time when a supply is regarded as taking place).

You will also have to pay a late registration penalty unless you can demonstrate that you have a reasonable excuse. See 12.9 'VAT penalties'. You will be able to recover the VAT on purchases that are attributable to the taxable activity, so this will offset the amount finally due to HMRC.

2.1.13   Transfer of a business as a going concern

If you take over a VAT-registered business as a going concern, then you must add that business's taxable turnover in the last 12 months to your taxable turnover in the last 12 months to see if you meet the Registration Threshold past turnover test.

You must do this at the point of transfer and during the first 12 months of operation. If the combined taxable turnover exceeds the Registration Threshold at the point of transfer, then you are compulsorily registered at the point of transfer. You must notify HMRC within 30 days of the transfer.

Example: transfer of a business as a going concern test

Tee Ltd is not registered for VAT. At the end of April 2014 its taxable turnover in the last 12 months was £30,000. On 3 May 2014 Tee takes over a VAT-registered business Vee Ltd which had taxable turnover of £70,000 for the 12 months to 30 April 2014.

At the point of transfer the VAT Registration Threshold was £81,000. The combined taxable turnover in the last 12 months was £30,000 + £70,000 = £100,000. This is greater than the Registration Threshold, so Tee must register for VAT with effect from 3 May and notify HMRC by 2 June.

In practice, it will often be advantageous to arrange a transfer of a business as a going concern (TOGC) so as to meet the conditions under which the transfer can be treated as **outside the scope** of VAT (see 1.2.1 'Business and non-business'). If a VAT-registered business is transferred, then for these conditions to be met, the acquirer must be registered for, or required to be registered for, VAT at the point of transfer. See 11.5 'Transfer of a business as a going concern' for more on the TOGC rules.

2.1.14 Divisional registration

A **body corporate** may apply for its separate divisions to be registered for VAT separately. Each division has its own VAT number and submits separate VAT returns, though the entire company still remains a single taxable person. This is done for administrative convenience

> **Bodies corporate** include companies, CIOs, industrial and provident societies, friendly societies, unincorporated associations, and corporations sole (see also 2.2.2 'Bodies corporate').

where it would be difficult for the company as a whole to submit a single VAT return within the required timeframe. All divisions must send in VAT returns for the same tax periods.

However, the conditions for divisional registration are onerous:

- The company as a whole must be fully taxable. This means that it must have no non-business activities and any exempt activities are *de minimis* (see 3.1.11 for the *de minimis* limits).
- The separate divisions must have their own accounting systems, operate from different geographical locations and supply different commodities or carry out different functions.
- HMRC must be satisfied that there would be real difficulty in submitting a single VAT return within the required timeframe.

See *VAT Notice 700/2* for more on divisional registration.

2.2 VAT GROUPS

Under certain circumstances bodies corporate may form a VAT group or join a VAT group with the VAT group being treated as one entity for VAT purposes.

There are several potential advantages to forming a VAT group:

- Most supplies between group members can be ignored for VAT purposes. This may result in a saving of VAT and simplified administration.

- The **representative member** is responsible for submitting a single VAT return for the whole group and dealing with the tax authorities on behalf of all group members. This will normally simplify administration.
- The taxable activity of some group members can improve VAT recovery in others as they are all now treated as one entity for VAT purposes – see Chapter 3 'Recovering VAT' for an explanation of VAT recovery.

There can also be disadvantages:

- Each group member is jointly and severally liable for any amounts owed to HMRC. This means that any group entity may become liable for the VAT debts of another, and this may apply to entities that have left a VAT group in respect of liabilities that arose whilst it was a member. If this occurs and there is a charity in the group this may give rise to a breach of trust if charity funds are applied for non-charitable purposes. The Charity Commission provides the following guidance on this issue:

> The registration of a 'VAT group' comprising a charity and its trading subsidiary or subsidiaries means that each entity within the group guarantees the settlement of the VAT liabilities of the other entities within the group. There is no objection in principle to the registration of a charity as part of a VAT group. But before doing so, trustees need to satisfy themselves that the overall benefits of group registration outweigh the risk of loss to the charity's assets, if those assets have to be used to settle a VAT liability of a trading subsidiary. In general, trustees must aim to ensure that all arrangements are demonstrably on commercial terms and for the benefit of the charity, and do not give rise to the difficulties mentioned above.
>
> CC35 *Trustees, trading and tax,* 2007, section D19

- The partial exemption *de minimis* limits (see 3.1.11 'The *de minimis* test') apply to the whole group, as do other fixed limits such as the limits for the voluntary disclosure of errors (see 12.6 'The VAT return'). You are also less likely to qualify for the Cash Accounting Scheme, Annual Accounting Scheme and other VAT simplifications targeted at small entities.
- If group entities have separate administrations, the quarter (or month) end procedures for getting VAT information to the representative member will need to be fairly efficient. In order to get information to the representative member on time, other group entities may have to set earlier deadlines than would normally apply. This may delay input VAT recovery if purchase invoices are not received or cannot be processed before the deadline.

2.2.1 **VAT grouping conditions**

For an entity to join a UK VAT group all of the following four conditions must be met:

1. The entity must be a body corporate (see 2.2.2) established in the UK or with a fixed establishment in the UK. Fixed establishment means (broadly) a permanent presence such as an office, warehouse or similar. See 9.7.5 'Place of belonging' for more on the meaning of fixed establishment.
2. All entities in the group must be under common control or one group member must control the rest. Control here has the standard Companies Act meaning; that is, control of 50% or more of the share capital or voting rights or the right to appoint or remove a majority of the directors. Control can be both direct and indirect, for example control of one company which controls another.
3. The entity must not be a member of any other VAT group.
4. An application must be made to HMRC for the entity to join or form a VAT group. HMRC may refuse the application on the grounds of protection of the revenue (see 2.2.5 'HMRC powers of exclusion').
5. For a **specified body**, the body must be permitted to join or be in a VAT group. This rule only applies if the group business turnover exceeds £10 million. See 2.2.3 'Specified bodies'.

Membership is effective from the date the application in condition 4 is received by HMRC, or such earlier or later time as HMRC may allow (see 2.2.4 'Group registration process').

HMRC accepts (*VGROUPS01550*) that group treatment is permitted where, as a result of the formation of the group, none of the members make taxable supplies outside the group. However, in consequence, the group will have no entitlement to recover any input VAT. In order to be eligible for group treatment in these circumstances, at least one of the members must be liable or eligible to be registered for VAT, if it were considered on its own outside the group. Even though the group makes no taxable supplies outside the group, it must be registered and must render returns (albeit nil returns) in the normal way.

See 9.7.6 'Cross-border VAT groups' for the implications of including a fixed establishment of a non-UK entity in a UK VAT group.

2.2.2 **Bodies corporate**

These include: limited companies (companies limited by guarantee or by share capital), Charitable Incorporated Organisations (CIOs), Scottish CIOs, companies established by Royal Charter or Act of Parliament, companies established under the law of another country, Industrial and Provident Societies, Registered Co-operative or Community Benefit Societies, Friendly Societies, Limited Liability Partnerships and a Corporation Sole (such as the Archbishop of Canterbury).

They exclude: charitable trusts, unlimited partnerships, sole traders.

2.2.3 **Specified bodies**

A body corporate in, or applying to join, a VAT group is blocked from joining or being in the VAT group if all the following apply:

- The VAT group business turnover exceeded £10 million in the previous year or is expected to exceed £10 million in the coming year.
- The body corporate concerned is partly owned by a third party, or it has a **relevant business activity** that is managed by a third party, or the body corporate is the sole general partner of a limited partnership. (See the definition of relevant business activity below.)
- The body corporate or limited partnership has a relevant business activity. This is broadly where it makes supplies to other group entities.

However, certain types of entity are exempted from these requirements and not blocked from joining a VAT group even if they meet the above three conditions. These types of entity include:

- charities;
- a body corporate that controls all the other VAT group members;
- a body corporate whose activities another body corporate is empowered by statute to control;
- a body corporate whose only activity is acting as a trustee of an occupational pension scheme.

> A **relevant business activity** is one where:
>
> 1. the business activity involves making supplies to other VAT group members;
> 2. the supplies carry VAT, or would carry VAT if the body corporate was not in the VAT group (i.e. they are not exempt, zero-rated or outside the scope of UK VAT);
> 3. the supplies are not merely incidental to the business activity; and
> 4. the VAT group cannot recover VAT in full on the supplies, or would not be able to do so if the body corporate was not in the VAT group.

HMRC provides a useful flowchart for deciding whether or not the specified body rules block an entity joining a VAT group at *VAT Notice 700/2*, section 3.12.9.

2.2.4 Group registration process

Companies seeking to form or join a VAT group must apply to HMRC.

When companies form a VAT group any previous VAT registration numbers are cancelled and a new one is provided for the group. All group members must use this. This VAT registration number remains, even when new members join the group or members leave the group. When members leave the group or the group is disbanded, the leaving members are issued with new VAT numbers.

At the time of writing, to form a VAT group you must apply using form VAT 1 (signed by the representative member), form VAT 50 (signed by the applicant company) and form VAT 51 for each company joining the group. Your application is provisionally effective from the date it is received by HMRC, and HMRC has 90 days in which to investigate the application and refuse it. HMRC states that it aims to reply within 15 days to confirm receipt of an application.

Backdated applications

HMRC has the power to accept backdated applications for the formation or membership of a VAT group; however, HMRC policy is to limit backdating to a maximum of 30 days except in cases of HMRC error or 'exceptional circumstances'. HMRC policy is (*VAT Notice 700/2*, sections 2.22–2.23):

> Can my application be backdated? Yes, but normally only up to 30 days prior to your application being received by us and only if it corresponds to the commencement of the current accounting period of either the existing VAT group or any of the companies forming, joining or leaving the VAT group So, if the commencement of the current accounting period is less than 30 days prior to your application being received by us, the maximum period of retrospection will be the beginning of that accounting period.

> Can I backdate my application for more than 30 days? Only in exceptional circumstances. Exceptional circumstances include: (i) if we lose your application and you can supply details of your original application and your attempts to follow it up (ii) if the delay was caused by lack of action on our part These examples are not exhaustive. However, we would not consider a failure to apply for grouping earlier because of ignorance or a misunderstanding on your part to be in itself an 'exceptional circumstance'. Neither would we would consider a situation where you simply find that in hindsight you could have arranged things to better effect if you had chosen to group earlier.

However, this policy was criticised by the First-tier Tribunal (*Copthorn Holdings v. Revenue & Customs* [2015] UKFTT 405) as being unbalanced, a high if not insurmountable bar and an unacceptable fettering of HMRC's discretion as set out explicitly in VAT legislation.

If an application is refused the group is treated as if it was never formed. Any returns or VAT treatments that were based on there being a VAT group must be corrected.

2.2.5 HMRC powers of exclusion

HMRC has the power to refuse an application and also the power to remove members from a VAT group if it considers it necessary for the protection of the revenue.

HMRC policy is that it will not normally use its revenue protection powers when it considers that the revenue loss follows from the normal operation of grouping. To assess this it will normally compare the result to what would happen if the group members were all one company. Where revenue losses go beyond this, HMRC is likely to use its revenue protection powers. See *VAT Notice 700/2* for full details of when HMRC will seek to apply these powers.

2.2.6 Intra-group exceptions

For VAT purposes, supplies between group members are usually ignored and supplies to or from outside the group are usually treated as made by or to the representative member. However, there are exceptions:

1. **VAT reliefs and exemptions**: in situations where the liability of a supply is determined by the status of the supplier or recipient, it is the status of the entity making or receiving the supply that counts, and not the status of the representative member or the group as a whole. For example, a supply of advertising is VAT zero-rated if it is made to a charity (see 6.2.3 'Advertising services). Where a charity is a member of a VAT group, it is the charitable status of the actual recipient of the advertising services that counts, not the status of the representative member.
2. **HMRC directions**: HMRC may direct that a particular intra-group supply is not ignored for VAT purposes if it considers this 'necessary for the protection of the revenue'. See *VAT Notice 700/1* for when HMRC will seek to apply this power.
3. **Transfers into a partly exempt VAT group**: if a partly exempt group acquires assets from a third party as part of a TOGC, there may be a requirement for the group to account for output VAT on those assets. See 11.5.7 'Transfers into a partly exempt VAT group'.

4. **Intra-group reverse charge**: if a VAT group includes a UK fixed establishment of a business established outside the UK, then in certain situations cross-border supplies within the group are not ignored. See 9.7.6 'Cross-border VAT groups'.
5. **Intra-EU supplies of goods**: transfers of goods to branches or group members in other EU states can be subject to VAT in some situations. See 9.6 'Intra-EU transfers of goods'.

2.2.7 Future of VAT grouping

In 2009 the European Commission (EC) issued a *Communication from the Commission to the Council and the European Parliament on the VAT group option* (EC 2009). EU law largely leaves it up to member states to lay down the detailed rules for VAT grouping. However, there are wide divergences between EU states and the EC sees it as essential that the grouping rules are applied more uniformly. The EC took the following view:

- As a matter of interpretation of EU VAT law, only businesses which make taxable supplies can join a VAT group. However, that view was rejected by the Court of Justice of the EU (CJEU or ECJ) in case C-86/11 *European Commission* v. *UK* [2011] where the court held that entities with no business activities can join a VAT group.
- Only business establishments (head offices) and fixed establishments (permanent branches) present in a group's EU state of registration can join the group. Fixed establishments outside the state must be excluded. This is in conflict with HMRC's current position, which is that once a business or fixed establishment of an entity joins a VAT group, the whole entity joins the group, including all its other businesses or fixed establishments, wherever they are located. See 9.7.6 'Cross-border VAT groups'.
- All activities of included establishments must be included in group activity and an entity can only be a member of one VAT group at any time.
- To join a group there must be financial, economic and organisational links between group members. The EC is of the opinion that all three links have to be met during the entire time a VAT group exists and that any member no longer fulfilling all three links should be required to leave the group.
- A VAT grouping scheme needs to be open to all sectors of economic activity in the member state which introduces such a scheme. The UK is potentially in breach of this requirement in limiting membership to corporate bodies.
- The VAT group's internal transactions do not exist for VAT purposes; they are outside the scope of VAT. The EC is of the opinion it follows from this that the VAT group option may also have cash flow advantages for businesses.

It seems likely that the EC will press for further alignment of national rules on VAT grouping and as a result the UK's VAT grouping rules are subject to change.

2.3   **DEREGISTRATION**

Deregistration means ceasing to be registered for VAT.

2.3.1   **Compulsory deregistration**

A VAT-registered business must deregister in each of the following circumstances:

- The business stops making taxable supplies and has no intention of making further taxable supplies.
- The business was registered on the basis of an intention to make taxable supplies but no longer intends making taxable supplies.
- The whole taxable activity is sold or transferred to another entity.
- The legal status of the business changes (see below).
- The business becomes part of a VAT group. The business loses its own VAT registration and joins that of the group. If it later leaves the group it does not get its old registration back.

Change of legal status

If a business becomes incorporated by setting up an incorporated body, transferring all of the assets and then closing down or making the old business dormant, the old business will have to deregister as it no longer makes taxable supplies. The incorporated body will have its own new VAT registration, though it can inherit the old business's in some circumstances (see 11.5 'Transfer of a business as a going concern').

2.3.2   **Voluntary deregistration**

A VAT-registered organisation may also deregister voluntarily if it can satisfy HMRC that:

1. Its taxable turnover in the next 12 months will fall below the **VAT Deregistration Threshold**. See 2.1 'VAT registration' for recent Deregistration Thresholds. You can check the latest Deregistration Threshold on the HMRC website (see 14.2 'HMRC website'), or
2. Its input VAT will normally exceed its output VAT and so it will be a net recoverer of VAT. The conditions are the same as those for exemption from registration (explained above).

For (1), the value to be compared to the VAT Deregistration Threshold is the expected net value of sales in the next 12 months, excluding any output VAT. However, if the net value is less than the threshold but the gross value (including output VAT) is more, then HMRC will require evidence that you will drop your prices by the VAT, as otherwise you would remain above the threshold.

2.3.3 **Repaying VAT on deregistration**

If, at the point of deregistration, you have any stock or fixed assets on hand on which you recovered input VAT, then you may have to repay part of this VAT to HMRC. You are deemed to supply the assets to yourself and have to account to HMRC for output VAT on that supply. However, if the total VAT due on all the assets is £1,000 or less, then it can be ignored and no VAT is repayable.

If you are transferring the business to another person under the TOGC rules then there is no deemed supply on deregistration. See 11.5 'Transfer of a business as a going concern'.

VAT is due on the following types of asset:

- Interests in land and buildings that would be standard-rated if you sold them, for example buildings that are opted to tax or new commercial property (see Chapter 8 'Property').
- Tangible goods on which you claimed input VAT when you bought them, for example unsold stock, plant, furniture, commercial vehicles, and computers.
- Tangible goods acquired VAT-free from a VAT-registered business under the TOGC rules.

If a capital item within its CGS **adjustment period** is on hand at deregistration, that triggers a final adjustment under the Scheme. See 10.1 'Capital Goods Scheme'.

VAT is not due on intangible assets such as patents, copyrights and goodwill, goods on which you did not recover any VAT and supplies that are zero-rated, for example a stock of printed books.

If any of the assets were acquired and held as non-business assets, then VAT is only due on the deemed disposal of the business portion. However, if a business asset was acquired partly for taxable and partly for exempt activities, so that a corresponding part of the input VAT incurred was treated as irrecoverable, there is no reduction in the value of the supply; the whole disposal value is subject to VAT.

Relevant stock and assets should be valued at the price you would expect to pay for them in their present condition. If this cannot be determined, they should be valued at the price you would expect to pay for similar items.

Example: repaying VAT on deregistration

At deregistration, business Delta had the following assets on hand. All assets were used wholly or partly in Delta's taxable activities and associated input VAT recovered:

Assets	Depreciated value (net) £
Zero-rated stock	5,000
Standard-rated stock	4,000
Office furniture and equipment	2,000
Delivery van (standard-rated)	7,000

No VAT is due on the zero-rated stock. The total value of the standard-rated stock, furniture, equipment and van is £13,000, so the output VAT due is £13,000 × 20% = £2,600. This is more than £1,000, so output VAT of £2,600 is payable to HMRC.

2.3.4   Recovering VAT incurred after deregistration

You cannot reclaim VAT on any goods you purchase after your registration was cancelled; however, you can claim relief for VAT on services supplied to you after your registration was cancelled, as long as these services relate solely to taxable business activities at the time you were VAT-registered. Any claim is subject to the four-year capping rule (see 12.6.8 'The capping rules'). You claim by completing HMRC form VAT 427 and sending it to HMRC.

2.4   CROSS-BORDER REGISTRATION ISSUES

The following cross-border registration issues are considered in this section (all from the perspective of a UK-established entity):

• supplying goods or services from the UK to non-UK customers;
• UK registration for purchases of certain cross-border services;
• UK registration for relevant intra-EU acquisitions of goods;
• UK registration for relevant disposals of goods.

2.4.1 Supplying goods or services from the UK to non-UK customers

Supplies of goods

If you make a taxable supply of goods (with delivery) from the UK to customers outside the UK the goods are by default considered sold in the UK and count towards your UK VAT Registration Threshold. However:

- If goods are sent outside the EU (exports) they can be zero-rated if the qualifying conditions are met; see 9.4 'Exports'.
- If the goods are sent to VAT-registered customers in other EU states you can zero rate them subject to the qualifying conditions being met, see 9.6 'Intra-EU transfers of goods'.
- If the goods are sent with delivery to unregistered customers in another EU state (for instance internet sales of goods to individuals), then if the total level of such sales to unregistered customers in that state goes above that state's **distance-selling threshold**, you must register for VAT in that EU state and charge that state's VAT on the sales to local customers. Distance-selling thresholds tend to be in the €30,000–€100,000 range. See 9.6.15 'Distance-selling'.
- There are special rules for (amongst others): goods installed or assembled in other EU states, goods purchased from one EU state but sent directly to another, transfers of own goods and call-off stock (stock put at the disposal of a third party to call for as required). See 9.6 'Intra-EU transfers of goods'.

Supplies of services

If you sell taxable services to non-UK customers, you must first determine the **place of supply** of those services. This is where, if subject to VAT, any output VAT is chargeable and due to the local VAT authority.

1. **If the place of supply is the UK**, the supply counts towards your UK VAT Registration Threshold and you charge UK VAT once registered.
2. **If the place of supply is outside the EU**, the supply is outside the scope of UK VAT and does not count towards your UK VAT Registration Threshold.
3. **If the place of supply is another EU state**, it does not count towards your UK VAT Registration Threshold; however, you may be required, or may be able, to register for VAT in the other EU state and charge that state's VAT.

The rules for determining the place of supply are explained in 9.7 'Cross-border services introduction'.

In scenarios 2 and 3 you can register for VAT in the UK voluntarily on the basis of making a supply that would be taxable if it had been made in the UK. This enables recovery of UK VAT incurred in making such supplies.

From 1 January 2015, sales of digital services to non-business customers in other EU states have been subject to VAT in that EU state. Digital services include sales of electronic products such as downloaded software, information, music, videos, recorded podcasts, games, etc. Non-business customers are individuals acting in a private capacity and entities with no business activities. There is a nil registration threshold for such supplies and all affected UK suppliers must either register for VAT in each EU state to which they make such supplies or register with HMRC for the special Mini One Stop Shop (MOSS) scheme. See 9.9 'The Mini One Stop Shop'.

2.4.2 UK registration for purchases of cross-border services

Purchases of services from foreign suppliers count towards your UK VAT Registration Threshold if:

- you have some business activities (so the supply is business to business (**B2B**)); and
- you purchase a **B2B general rule service** from a non-UK supplier.

The total value of such supplies counts towards your UK VAT Registration Threshold.

> **B2B general rule services** include consultancy services, management services, supplies of staff, advertising services, supplies of intellectual property rights and digital services.

Normally an invoice from an EU supplier will state 'subject to the **reverse charge**' or equivalent wording. However, some B2B services are only taxable in the UK under the **reverse charge** if the customer is registered for VAT in the UK, for example land-related services and event admissions (see 9.7.4 'Reverse charge' for more details). Receipt of such services does not count towards the customer's VAT Registration Threshold and it remains the supplier's responsibility to pay HMRC any UK output VAT due.

2.4.3 UK registration for relevant intra-EU acquisitions of goods

UK entities (business and non-business entities but not individuals acting in a private capacity) must register for VAT in the UK if they make **relevant acquisitions** of goods above the UK VAT Registration Threshold. Relevant acquisitions are goods purchased or otherwise acquired from VAT-registered businesses in other EU states and which are used, or are for use, in your non-business or exempt activities.

Goods purchased for use in taxable business activities are excluded, as the VAT chargeable on acquisition in the UK would be recoverable and so registration would have no purpose (the net payment to HMRC would be nil). The objective is to prevent organisations gaining a VAT advantage by purchasing goods from EU states with lower rates of VAT than the UK. Once registered, the EU supplier no longer adds their local VAT and the goods are liable for VAT in the UK at UK rates. See 9.6 'Intra-EU transfers of goods' for more on the acquisition of goods from VAT-registered suppliers in other EU states.

Registration test

You must register for VAT if the value of your relevant acquisitions meets either of the following tests:

- At the end of any calendar month, the total VAT-exclusive value of your relevant acquisitions in the period from 1 January before has exceeded the VAT Registration Threshold. You must notify HMRC within 30 days and will be registered from the first day of the month after next.
- At any time, there are reasonable grounds for believing the total VAT-exclusive value of relevant acquisitions in the next 30 days alone will exceed the VAT Registration Threshold. You must notify HMRC within 30 days and will be registered from the time the reasonable grounds arose.

In determining the value of relevant acquisitions, so much of the consideration as represents any liability of the supplier for VAT on the transaction, under the law of another EU state, is disregarded:

- **Exemption from registration**: you can be exempted from registration, with HMRC's agreement, if the goods are zero-rated under the UK rules.
- **Voluntary registration**: you can register voluntarily if you do or intend to make any level of relevant acquisitions. However, if you do or intend to make taxable supplies, you will be registered voluntarily for the taxable supplies rather than for the relevant acquisitions.
- **Cessation of registration**: you cease to be liable to be registered for relevant acquisitions if the value of relevant acquisitions in a whole calendar year did not exceed the VAT Deregistration Threshold and HMRC is satisfied the value of relevant acquisitions will not exceed the VAT Deregistration Threshold in the next calendar year. However, if you registered voluntarily, you must remain registered for the remainder of the calendar year of registration plus two full calendar years thereafter.

See *VAT Notice 700/1* for more on registration for relevant acquisitions.

2.4.4 UK registration for relevant disposals of goods

As explained in 9.2 'Recovering foreign VAT', a UK VAT-registered business may be able to claim back VAT incurred in other EU states in making its taxable supplies via a special EU VAT refund procedure (see 9.2.1 'EU VAT Refund Scheme').

In the same way as a business that is registered for VAT in another EU state may be able to claim a refund of UK VAT incurred in making its taxable supplies from HMRC, there is also a separate UK refund scheme for non-EU businesses to claim for UK VAT they incur in making taxable supplies.

> If a business that is not registered for VAT in the UK reclaims UK VAT on goods from HMRC via one of these UK refund schemes and then sells those goods as taxable supplies, the business is making a **relevant disposal** and must register for VAT in the UK. The business must notify HMRC within 30 days of the earlier of: the date of disposal, or the date on which there were reasonable grounds for believing that a relevant disposal would be made in the period of 30 days then beginning.

UK-established entities will normally be affected by this rule only if they acquire goods from a predecessor under the TOGC rules and the predecessor claimed VAT on those goods under one of the refund schemes:

- **Transfer of a business as a going concern**: if business assets on which UK VAT has been claimed via a UK VAT refund procedure are sold or otherwise transferred as a part of a TOGC, the sale or transfer is treated as neither a supply of goods nor of services and as such is outside the scope of VAT (see 11.5 'Transfer of a business as a going concern'). If a business sells goods where a predecessor under a TOGC claimed UK VAT on those goods under a UK refund procedure, then that is also a relevant disposal.
- **Effective date of registration**: the business is registered for VAT in the UK with effect from the date above. It must account to HMRC for UK output VAT on the disposal (though see below for zero-rated disposals). There is a nil registration threshold for relevant disposals, so any level of such disposal will trigger a liability to be registered for VAT in the UK.
- **Ceasing registration**: however, if a business is registered for VAT in the UK under this measure (and no other), it must notify HMRC within 30 days if it ceases or intends ceasing to make relevant supplies. If HMRC is satisfied the business has ceased to be liable to be registered for VAT in respect of relevant supplies, HMRC may cease registration.

- **Zero-rated supplies**: HMRC can exempt a business from liability to register for VAT for relevant disposals if the business satisfies HMRC that any such supplies are zero-rated.

3 Recovering VAT

This chapter explains the rules for determining how much of the VAT you incur on purchases can be deducted in the UK VAT return. It is divided into the following sections:

- 3.1 VAT recovery principles
- 3.2 Methods
- 3.3 General recovery issues

3.1 VAT RECOVERY PRINCIPLES

VAT that you can deduct in the UK VAT return is called **recoverable** or **deductible** and VAT that you cannot recover is called **irrecoverable** or **non-deductible**.

Recovering VAT means deducting VAT incurred on purchases from the **output VAT** (see 1.1) due to HMRC. You only have to pay over the net amount to HMRC, and if the amount of VAT you deduct exceeds the output VAT due, you receive a balancing payment from HMRC. Only VAT-registered organisations can recover the VAT they incur on purchases.

Please note that regarding:

- **Foreign VAT**: only UK VAT can be recovered in the UK VAT return. Foreign VAT must be claimed directly from the state concerned, see 9.2 'Recovering foreign VAT'.
- **Section 33 VAT refund schemes**: there are several VAT refund schemes that allow certain types of entity to make a claim to HMRC for VAT incurred in some or all of its non-business activities. These are (at the time of writing):
  - s. 33   the VAT refund scheme for local authorities;
  - s. 33a   the VAT refund scheme for national museums and galleries;
  - s. 33b   the VAT refund scheme for academy and free schools;
  - s. 33c/d the VAT refund scheme for certain charities (palliative care charities, air ambulance charities, search and rescue charities, medical courier charities and charities that support either of the last two).

  Eligible entities do not have to be registered for VAT to make a claim. See Chapter 10 'VAT special schemes' for the qualifying conditions for the various VAT refund schemes. This chapter covers principally the deduction/recovery of input VAT by VAT-registered organisations, but also includes comments on the implications of the s. 33 refund schemes where applicable.

- **Flat Rate Scheme**: under the Flat Rate Scheme, you do not have to record VAT incurred on most types of purchase. Instead you pay over to HMRC a flat rate percentage of the net value of business sales, calculated so as to allow for recoverable input VAT. There are different percentages for different business sectors. To qualify for the scheme your taxable turnover must be below £150,000. See Chapter 10 'VAT special schemes'.

3.1.1   Purchase VAT recovery steps

Purchase VAT is the term used in this chapter to describe the UK VAT you incur on all of your purchases. It includes:

- UK VAT charged by a UK-established and registered supplier;
- UK output VAT payable to HMRC on a **deemed supply** (see Chapter 4), for example on the change of use of a zero-rated building (see 8.3 'Property VAT reliefs');
- UK import VAT charged by HMRC on an import of goods from outside the EU;
- UK reverse charge VAT payable to HMRC on receipt of a reverse charge supply of services;
- UK **acquisition VAT** (see 9.6.1 'Acquisitions') payable to HMRC on an acquisition of goods from a VAT-registered supplier in another EU state.

See Chapter 9 'International aspects of VAT' for more on import VAT, reverse charge VAT and acquisition VAT.

To determine how much of the purchase VAT may be recovered it must be subdivided in the following order:

- **Step 1**: remove **blocked VAT**. Blocked VAT is always irrecoverable.
- **Step 2**: for the remaining purchase VAT, carry out direct attribution to the activity types: non-business, taxable, and exempt.
- **Step 3**: apportion any VAT that is left (**residual VAT**) between the activity types.

Then:

- the purchase VAT directly attributed and apportioned to **non-business activities** is irrecoverable, unless a section 33 VAT refund scheme applies;

- the purchase VAT directly attributed and apportioned to **exempt activities** is irrecoverable, unless the overall level of exempt activity is *de minimis*, in which case it is recoverable (see 3.1.11 'The *de minimis* test');
- the purchase VAT directly attributed and apportioned to **taxable activities** is recoverable.

Each of the three steps is explained in more detail below.

3.1.2 Step 1: Blocked VAT

VAT incurred on certain purchases is **blocked** so that it cannot be recovered. It includes:

- **VAT on business entertaining**: this means the provision, in the course of a business activity, of free entertainment to people who are not employees. Entertainment includes food, drink, accommodation and entrance to events. If entertainment is incidentally supplied to employees then the associated input VAT is also blocked, for example a restaurant meal for customers at which staff are present. But VAT incurred on business entertaining of overseas customers is not blocked if on a reasonable scale. See 12.10 'Blocked input VAT'.
- **VAT on certain cars**: VAT on the purchase of a car that will have some element of private use is blocked. If a car with private use is leased for more than ten days then there is a block on 50% of the VAT incurred. See 12.10 'Blocked input VAT'.
- **Builders' block**: builders, construction companies and property developers are blocked from recovering VAT on certain goods they sell with or install in buildings. See 8.6.14 'Builders' block'.

3.1.3 Step 2: Direct attribution

Having removed any blocked VAT, you directly attribute the remaining purchase VAT to the activity types (taxable, exempt, non-business) as far as possible. VAT on a purchase is directly **attributable** to an activity type if the purchased goods or services are used, or are to be used, wholly in activities of that type.

'Use' here refers to how the economic value of the goods or services is consumed. Direct project or activity costs of taxable, exempt and non-business activities in the accounting sense will normally be directly attributable to the corresponding VAT type of activity. However, there is an exception for costs incurred in generating unrestricted grants and donations, and (possibly) in managing financial investments and in generating other types of non-business income. These are looked through to see how the funds generated are actually used. See 3.1.13 'The *Children's Society* case'.

3.1.4   **Step 3: Apportion residual VAT**

The remaining purchase VAT represents VAT-bearing purchases that cannot be directly attributed to one of the activity types (taxable, exempt, non-business). Residual purchases can include:

- **Organisational overheads**: these are not directly attributable to any activity type but are incurred generally in support of all activities, for example the costs of central support, management, administration and governance costs.
- **Mixed-use purchases**: these are purchases that are directly attributable to two or more activity types, for example the purchase of a minibus that is used to transport members of a youth club (an exempt business activity) in the evenings and for commercial hire (a taxable business activity) during the day.

The purchase VAT incurred on residual purchases is referred to as **residual VAT**. Residual VAT must be apportioned between the activity types (non-business, exempt or taxable).

The apportionment must be carried out in the following order:

1. **Business/non-business method**: if you have non-business activities, then unless you use a **combined method** (see below), you must first apportion residual VAT between business and non-business activities. This apportionment is referred to as your business/non-business method. Any residual VAT apportioned to non-business activities is irrecoverable (unless an s. 33 refund scheme applies). Any residual VAT apportioned to business activities is input VAT or business VAT and goes forward to the next step.
2. **Partial exemption method**: if you have exempt activities, then unless you use a combined method, you must apportion the remaining purchase VAT between taxable and exempt activities. This apportionment is referred to as your partial exemption method. By default you must use the **standard partial exemption method** which is based on levels of VAT-exclusive turnover. However, it may be possible to use an alternative **special partial exemption method**.
3. **Combined method**: with effect from 1 January 2011, businesses can (with HMRC agreement) carry out a single apportionment between taxable and non-taxable activities (exempt and non-business activities) using a combined method. This ignores the distinction between non-business and exempt activities. This can be helpful where it is difficult to distinguish between the two. However, this is at the price of losing any *de minimis* recovery for small-scale exempt activities.

If there are taxable, exempt and non-business activities and a purchase is used for taxable and exempt activities but not for any non-business activities the associated purchase VAT is input VAT and so should go straight to the partial exemption apportionment, and not be put through the business/non-business apportionment.

3.2 'Methods' below explains the method rules in more detail with examples.

The purchase VAT directly attributed and apportioned to:

- non-business activities is referred to as **non-business VAT**;
- business activities is referred to as **input VAT** or **business VAT**;
- exempt activities is referred to as **exempt input VAT**.

Example: attribution and apportionment

Local Advice Organisation (LAO) receives a grant to fund a free advice service (a non-business activity), it rents out premises (an exempt activity) and charges for consultancy services (a taxable activity). LAO uses the relative levels of income to apportion residual VAT.

LAO has the following income and purchase VAT attribution:

Activity	Type/pool	Income (net)	% of total income	Purchase VAT direct attribution
Consultancy service	Taxable	£100,000	20%	£15,000
Premises rental	Exempt	£150,000	30%	£5,000
Free advice service	Non-business	£250,000	50%	£10,000
Overheads	Residual			£20,000
Total income		£500,000	100%	£50,000

The VAT directly attributed to taxable activity (£15,000) is recoverable in full. LAO apportions the residual VAT (£20,000) as follows:

To:		Apportionment
Taxable	20% × £20,000 =	£4,000
Exempt	30% × £20,000 =	£6,000
Non-business	50% × £20,000 =	£10,000
Total		£20,000

LAO can recover the purchase VAT directly attributed and apportioned to taxable activities, that is: £15,000 + £4,000 = £19,000.

LAO then checks if the VAT directly attributed and apportioned to exempt activity (£5,000 + £6,000 = £11,000) is *de minimis*; it is not (see 3.1.11). So the total irrecoverable VAT is £50,000 − £19,000 = £31,000.

3.1.5 Accounting systems

To implement VAT attribution and apportionment, your accounting systems will have to, as far as possible, link VAT on purchases to the type of activity incurring the expense – taxable, exempt, non-business or residual.

With a manual or spreadsheet ledger-based system, this could be achieved by using a 'VAT type' column to assign VAT on purchases into the different types.

Most commercial accounting systems provide a built-in VAT/sales tax system to deal with this. Some accounting systems provide add-on modules for carrying out the VAT recovery calculations. Others include facilities to help you analyse VAT, though you must carry out the apportionment calculations yourself. See 12.11 'Sage 50 T-codes' for an illustration of how to use Sage 50's T-codes to perform the VAT recovery calculations when there is a mix of taxable, exempt and non-business activities.

3.1.6 Claiming VAT

Even though the VAT on a purchase may be recoverable under the above principles, this does not mean that you can actually deduct it from the VAT you must pay over to HMRC. You must hold appropriate evidence, normally in the form of an original VAT invoice from the supplier or an HMRC VAT certificate for import VAT. Only when you have the required evidence can you make a claim to deduct the VAT.

See 12.4 'VAT invoices' for information on what must be included in a VAT invoice. See 12.5 'Claiming input VAT' for what alternative evidence HMRC will accept in the absence of a VAT invoice. In addition, there is a time limit for claiming; see 3.3 'General recovery issues: deadline for input VAT claims'.

3.1.7 **VAT returns**

The claim is normally made in the UK VAT return that all UK VAT-registered businesses must make periodically to HMRC. The UK VAT return has to be submitted electronically, though there are phone or paper options for a person for whom HMRC is satisfied that it is not reasonably practicable to make a return using an electronic return system for reasons of disability, age, remoteness of location or any other reason such as religious belief.

See 12.6 'The VAT return' for how to complete the VAT return.

3.1.8 **VAT reporting periods**

The period covered by a VAT return is referred to as the return's **VAT period**. The year and month of the end of the VAT period are usually used to reference the period, for example, quarterly return 03/15 means the three months to 31 March 2015.

By default you must submit quarterly VAT returns, although there are alternatives:

- **Monthly returns**: you may request monthly VAT returns. Monthly VAT returns can be advantageous from a cash flow perspective if you normally receive a VAT refund from HMRC, for example if you make mainly zero-rated supplies or mainly foreign supplies (**taxable supplies** outside the UK – defined in 1.2.2).
- **Single annual return**: organisations with taxable turnover under £1.35 million can submit just one annual VAT return under the Annual Accounting Scheme, though they must pay over VAT to HMRC more regularly. See 10.10 'Annual Accounting Scheme'.

A VAT-registered business claims on a particular VAT return for all purchase VAT that becomes claimable in the return's VAT period. For a particular purchase, this is normally when you either pay or receive a VAT invoice.

If you do recover any of the VAT, then that VAT recovery may become adjustable dependent on actual use of the purchase – see 3.1.14 'Adjusting initial VAT recovery'.

3.1.9 **Longer period**

When you first register for VAT you are given a VAT year end to report to. By default this is 31 March, 30 April or 31 May, though you can ask HMRC to give you a different year end, for example to align with your financial year end. The **longer period** or **VAT year** is the period of one year between one VAT year end and the next.

Where you incur exempt input VAT you must calculate the value of recoverable input VAT on a provisional basis in each VAT return, using the VAT recovery principles outlined above. However, you must also adjust that calculation at the end of every longer period. This correction process is known as the **annual adjustment**.

The longer period is normally the same as your VAT year. However, it can be different:

1. **Registration period**: if, when you first register for VAT, you have exempt activities, then your first longer period is the period from your registration date to the end of the day before the start of your first full VAT year. Your subsequent longer periods are then your VAT years.
2. **First longer period**: if you start exempt activities after VAT registration, your first longer period runs from the start of the VAT period in which you first incur exempt input VAT to the end of the day before the start of your next full VAT year.
3. **Last longer period**: if you deregister for VAT, your final longer period runs from the day after the end of your last VAT year to the date of deregistration.

Examples: longer period

- **Registration period**: Charity A carries out exempt and taxable activities. It registers for VAT on 15 August 2015 and has a VAT year end of 31 March. Its first longer period runs from 15 August 2015 to 31 March 2016. Its next longer period is 1 April 2016 to 31 March 2017
- **First longer period**: Charity B is registered for VAT with a year end of 31 March and quarterly VAT periods. It commences VAT-exempt activities on 15 August 2015. Its first longer period runs from 1 July 2015 to 31 March 2016. Its next longer period is 1 April 2016 to 31 March 2017
- **Last longer period**: Charity C is registered for VAT with a year end of 31 March. It deregisters with effect from 15 August 2015. Its final longer period runs from 1 April 2015 to 15 August 2015.

3.1.10 **The annual adjustment**

The annual adjustment repeats the quarterly/monthly recovery calculation but using the totals for all of the quarters or months. It is carried out at the end of the longer period. Any difference from the VAT recoverable under the quarterly/ monthly calculations is either paid to or recovered from HMRC:

- If the VAT recoverable in the annual adjustment is greater than the sum of the amounts treated as recoverable in each quarter, then the difference can be claimed from HMRC.
- If the VAT recoverable in the annual adjustment is less than the sum of the amounts treated as recoverable in each quarter, then the difference must be paid to HMRC.
- If the VAT recoverable in the annual adjustment is equal to the sum of the amounts treated as recoverable in each quarter, there is no adjustment to be made.

You can make this adjustment in either the last VAT return of the longer period or the first VAT return of the next longer period. This adjustment is not an error and does not incur penalties or interest.

However, there is no need to carry out an annual adjustment if there is only one VAT reporting period in your longer period, for example if you have just registered for VAT, and your registration period is less than three months.

Example: annual adjustment

Charity X submits quarterly VAT returns and carries out the following VAT recovery calculations:

Quarter	1	2	3	4	**Total**
VAT claimed	£1,200	£1,400	£1,100	£1,100	£4,800

It carries out an annual adjustment and calculates that the recoverable VAT for the whole year is £4,900. It can deduct the difference £4,900 - £4,800 = £100 in its annual adjustment. It claims £100 from HMRC in either the last VAT return for the longer period or the first VAT return for the subsequent longer period.

If it had calculated the recoverable VAT for the whole year as £4,700, it would have had to pay the difference £4,800 - £4,700 = £100 to HMRC.

3.1.11 **The *de minimis* test**

The *de minimis* test will only be met if the level of exempt activity is very small, so voluntary organisations with substantial levels of exempt activity (for example exempt education, health or care service providers) will normally be able to dispense with this step and simply assume that the *de minimis* test fails.

If the overall level of exempt activity is very small, then the exempt input VAT is recoverable. The *de minimis* test can be applied each VAT period or it may be assumed to apply each VAT period and corrected in the annual adjustment, subject to the conditions set out below. However, there is no *de minimis* test if you have agreed a **Combined Method** with HMRC (see 3.2 'Methods').

The *de minimis* test comprises three conditions. If one or more of the conditions is satisfied, then you are *de minimis* for the period concerned. The tests for quarterly VAT returns are:

Condition 1

■ Total input VAT is less than or equal to £1,875; and
■ The turnover on exempt supplies is less than or equal to the turnover on taxable supplies.

Condition 2

■ Total input VAT less input VAT directly attributable to taxable activities is less than or equal to £1,875; and
■ The turnover on exempt supplies is less than or equal to the turnover on taxable supplies.

Condition 3

■ Exempt input VAT is less than or equal to £1,875; and
■ Exempt input VAT is less than or equal to 50% of total input VAT.

If VAT returns are submitted monthly, the figure of £1,875 above is replaced with £625 and for a 12-month longer period annual adjustment it is replaced with £7,500. For a longer period that is not 12 months, the figure to use is £625 multiplied by the number of whole or part months in the longer period.

Example: *de minimis* test

Charity W carries out the following apportionment in quarter 1:

	Taxable (£)	Exempt (£)	Non-business (£)	Total (£)
Turnover (ex. VAT)	12,000	8,000	30,000	50,000
Directly attributable VAT	1,000	800	4,000	5,800
Apportioned residual VAT	1,200	800	3,000	5,000
Total VAT on purchases	2,200	1,600	7,000	10,800

First calculate input VAT and exempt input VAT:

Input VAT = £2,200 + £1,600 = £3,800

Exempt input VAT = £1,600

Then apply the conditions:

- **Condition 1** fails as total input VAT (£3,800) is more than £1,875
- **Condition 2** fails as total input VAT less VAT directly attributable to taxable activities is £3,800 - £1,000 = £2,800, which is more than £1,875
- **Condition 3** succeeds as exempt input VAT (£1,600) is less than £1,875 and is less than 50% of total input VAT (50% × £3,800 = £1,900)

So charity W is *de minimis* in quarter 1 on Condition 3

Up to March 2010 there was only one *de minimis* condition (condition number 3 above). Conditions 1 and 2 were introduced on 1 April 2010. The idea is that conditions 1, 2 and 3 are in order of difficulty of calculation. You check condition 1 first. If that is met you are *de minimis* for the period and you do not need to check the other conditions. If condition 1 is not satisfied, you check condition 2 and so on. However, this approach is designed for commercial businesses without non-business activities.

3.1.12 Assuming *de minimis*

If you were *de minimis* in the previous year's annual adjustment, and you expect total input VAT in the current VAT year to be less than or equal to £1 million, then you can assume you are *de minimis* in each VAT period of the current longer period.

You then apply the *de minimis* test to the longer period results in the annual adjustment. If it turns out that you were not *de minimis* for the longer period, you must repay the exempt input VAT you assumed to be recoverable in each VAT period and you may not assume you are *de minimis* in the next longer period. If you assume you are *de minimis* in the first VAT period then you must assume you are *de minimis* in every VAT period of the current longer period.

3.1.13 The *Children's Society* case

The High Court case *Church of England Children's Society* v. *Revenue & Customs* [2005] EWHC 1692 (Ch) established the 'Children's Society principle' that where you incur VAT on the costs of raising general unrestricted donations (in the Society's case, agency costs for a committed giver scheme), then the VAT incurred on those fundraising costs can be treated as residual if the proceeds raised are used to support all of the activities of the organisation.

In the *Children's Society* case, the donations were used for the general purposes of the Society and as such they were seen as benefitting all types of activity (non-business, taxable and exempt), so they were themselves treated as residual. For many voluntary organisations, overheads are the most difficult cost to fund so they are often supported by unrestricted donations wherever possible.

In *Business Brief 19/05* HMRC accepts this principle, setting out the following 'way forward':

> Where funds are raised solely for a restricted charitable purpose involving wholly non-business activities, the VAT incurred on raising those funds is not input tax and is not recoverable.

> Conversely, where the funds raised are used wholly to support the making of business supplies, all of the VAT incurred on fundraising costs can be treated as input tax. The recovery of this input tax will depend upon whether these business supplies are taxable or exempt. Where fundraising input tax is wholly attributable to the making of taxable supplies by the charity, it can be recovered in full, subject to the normal rules. On the other hand, where fundraising input tax is wholly attributable to the making of exempt supplies by the charity, none of it will be recoverable, subject to the partial exemption de-minimis limits.

> So where a charity which has non-business and business activities incurs VAT on fundraising costs and the funds raised support various activities of the charity, the VAT incurred can only be recoverable input tax to the extent that the funds raised will support taxable business supplies. In practice this means that VAT incurred on fundraising costs must first be subject to an initial business/non-business apportionment to determine how much of the VAT incurred may be treated as

input tax. Then, in circumstances where the charity has exempt business activities, this input tax is further subject to the partial exemption rules.

In some cases, a charity's existing business /non-business apportionment method and partial exemption method will produce a fair and reasonable basis by which input tax can be recovered. However, where this is not the case, HMRC will consider proposals for alternative methods. If exceptional circumstances exist, HMRC may allow alternative methods to be applied retrospectively, provided it is fair and reasonable for the charity as a whole.

See 3.3.4 'Effect of the *Children's Society* case' for an assessment of the impact of this case on business/non-business methods.

Investment management costs

In *Revenue & Customs* v. *University of Cambridge* [2015] UKUT 305 (TCC), the Upper Tribunal (Tax) accepted the University's argument that the *Children's Society* principle applies to investment management costs incurred in managing a portfolio of financial investments. This acceptance was on the basis that the non-business investment income and gains (see 13.32 '*Wellcome Trust*' for why these are non-business receipts) support all the activities of the University. HMRC argued that as the investment management costs did not burden the prices of taxable supplies (all the costs being covered by the non-business income and gains) they were not cost components of those supplies and hence not overheads. However, this was rejected. The Tribunal's conclusion was:

> The question to be asked in this case is whether the University's investment activity through the Fund was carried out for the benefit of the University's economic (business) activity in general. If so, the costs of that activity form part of the University's overheads and are therefore, as such, component parts of the price of its products. The University incurred costs in relation to an activity, namely investment, which was outside the scope of VAT. Accordingly, there were no supplies of investments to which the input transactions could be attributed. The FTT [First-tier Tribunal] found that the investment activity was not an activity carried out for its own sake but for the benefit of the University's economic (business) activity in general. It follows that the costs associated with that investment activity were part of the University's overheads and, as such, (partly) deductible...

At the time of writing, HMRC has announced it is seeking leave to appeal this decision to the Court of Appeal.

3.1.14 **Adjusting initial VAT recovery**

For most purchases VAT is recovered when incurred or when the VAT invoice is received based on the intended use of the purchase. If the purchase is residual, its VAT recovery is then corrected as necessary in the annual adjustment. The purchase is then considered 'consumed' as far as the VAT system is concerned with no further adjustment being made. There are, however, various exceptions to this rule, where the initial VAT recovery must or may be revisited, after the annual adjustment has taken place. These include:

- the Capital Goods Scheme;
- the payback/clawback rules;
- mixed private/business use assets;
- VAT not paid.

See below for more on each exception.

Capital Goods Scheme (CGS)

If you purchase, create or improve a **capital item** then you must adjust the initial VAT recovery for any changes in the use of that item for the next nine longer periods (land and buildings items), or four longer periods (other capital items).

Capital items are, with effect from 1 January 2011:

- Land on whose acquisition its owner incurs VAT-bearing capital expenditure of £250,000 or more.
- A building, a part of a building, a civil engineering work or a part of a civil engineering work on whose acquisition, construction, refurbishment, fitting out, alteration or extension (including construction of an annexe) its owner incurs VAT-bearing capital expenditure of £250,000 or more.
- An aircraft, a ship, a boat or other vessel on whose acquisition, construction, manufacture, refurbishment, fitting out, alteration or extension its owner incurs VAT-bearing capital expenditure of £50,000 or more.
- An individual computer or single item of computer equipment on whose acquisition its owner incurs VAT-bearing capital expenditure of £50,000 or more.

See 10.1 'Capital Goods Scheme' for more on the CGS.

Payback/clawback rules

If VAT is recovered on the basis of an intended use but the actual use is different (or the intention changes), then the initial VAT recovery may have to be adjusted under the **payback/clawback rules**. See 3.3.7 'Payback/clawback rules'.

Mixed-use assets

Where a business acquires an asset for mixed taxable and private or non-organisational use (use for purposes outside those of the organisation), then the 'Lennartz Treatment' may be possible. The business can recover all of the VAT incurred on the asset on purchase but then accounts for output VAT on any private or non-organisational use of the asset when it occurs. The output VAT charge in effect repays some of the VAT initially recovered. However, this treatment is not available for non-business activities carried out by voluntary organisations within their objects. See 3.3.11 'Lennartz Treatment'.

VAT not paid

If you receive supplies and claim purchase VAT on those supplies but have not paid for them by six months after the payment became due, then you must repay the claimed input VAT to HMRC in your next VAT return. See 12.5.6 'Unpaid supplier invoices'.

3.2 METHODS

Every organisation that has a mix of taxable activities and exempt or non-business activities (or both) must decide how residual VAT is to be apportioned between the different types of activity. The way this apportionment is carried out is referred to as a **method**. There are three types of method:

● The **business/non-business method**
● The **partial exemption method**
● The **combined method**

3.2.1 The business/non-business method

The business/non-business method is used to apportion residual VAT between business and non-business activities after first having discarded any blocked VAT.

If you do not have any non-business activities, there is no need for a business/non-business method. Nor is there a need if you can claim under a section 33 scheme and have no business activities.

Insignificant non-business activity

Where non-business activity is regarded as insignificant, HMRC officers may use their discretion to allow a waiver of the business/non-business apportionment. HMRC provides the following guidance at *VBNB31000*:

> Where non-business use is regarded as insignificant HMRC may use its discretion to allow a waiver of apportionment. There is no statutory de minimis level in terms of a monetary or percentage figure. It is a matter of judgment whether the benefit in terms of revenue is outweighed by the administration cost to the business and the cost to the Department in checking that an apportionment has been carried out.

If HMRC decides to allow a waiver of apportionment HMRC will write to the business and tell it that the arrangement applies only for as long as the existing low level of non-business use is kept up. If the extent of non-business use goes up to a significant level the business will need to make an apportionment.

Business recovery rate

The usual approach to the business/non-business method is to first derive a **business recovery** rate or percentage which is then applied to the amount of residual VAT in the period, to determine the amount of residual VAT that is apportioned to business activities. The business recovery percentage should be rounded to two decimal places (for example 25.125% rounds to 25.13%).

Example: business/non-business method

Charity B uses a staff cost-based business/non-business method. In quarter 1 the cost of staff working in non-business activities is £100,000 and the cost of staff working in business activities is £25,000. Its residual VAT for the quarter is £20,000.

$$\text{Business recovery percentage} = \frac{£25,000}{£25,000 + £100,000} \times 100\% = 20\%$$

Residual VAT apportioned to business activity = 20% × £20,000 = £4,000. Residual VAT apportioned to non-business activity = £20,000 − £4,000 = £16,000. The latter is irrecoverable.

There is no 'standard' business/non-business method and there is no requirement to obtain the prior approval of HMRC for the method you use or for any change in the method used. However, it must be 'fair and reasonable' and you must be able to justify it to HMRC if asked. 'Fair and reasonable' means that it results in residual VAT being attributed to business activities to the extent that the associated purchases are, or are to be, used in making business supplies. HMRC may reject a business/non-business method on the grounds that it does not provide a fair and reasonable result or that it is incapable of independent verification.

Annual adjustment

There is no mandatory requirement to carry out an annual adjustment for a business/non-business method. However, a business/non-business method may have to include an annual adjustment in order to be fair and reasonable, and

HMRC generally expects this where a business/non-business method is operated in conjunction with a partial exemption method. If a partial exemption annual adjustment is carried out it is usually straightforward also to incorporate a business/non-business annual adjustment.

Provisional business recovery percentage

An advantage of carrying out an annual adjustment is that it should generally be possible to use a provisional business recovery percentage in each VAT period based on that derived in the last long period annual adjustment, subject to correction in the current longer period annual adjustment, in a similar way to that permitted for the standard partial exemption method (see 3.2.2 'The standard partial exemption method'). Such an approach may be preferable or even necessary, for example if an income-based business/non-business method is used but a major non-business grant is received annually.

HMRC approval

From 1 January 2011 HMRC can formally approve a business/non-business method of apportionment as long as there is no element of private use and as long as you have not incurred any exempt input VAT in the current VAT year or the previous VAT year (or registration period if newly registered for VAT). If you have exempt activities, HMRC can approve the use of a combined method covering both your business/non-business calculation and your partial exemption calculation, but HMRC will not approve separate business/non-business and special partial exemption methods. See 3.2.7 'The combined method'.

Basis for methods

Business/non-business methods are commonly based on the levels of income generated by business and non-business activities, the number of staff or cost of staff working in the different activities, or the floor areas occupied by the different activities. Many of the considerations applicable to non-business and 'special' partial exemption methods are similar, and these are examined in 3.3.1 'Choosing methods'. Many organisations using the standard (income-based) partial exemption method use an income-based business/non-business method as well.

Section 33 recovery schemes

If a section 33 refund scheme recovery scheme applies, the purchase VAT apportioned to non-business activities can be reclaimed.

3.2.2 **The standard partial exemption method**

The standard partial exemption method is a two-step process. It takes an amount of residual input VAT and apportions it between taxable and exempt activities.

Step 1

Calculate the **partial exemption recovery percentage** for the period (VAT period or longer period) as follows:

$$\frac{\text{Partial exemption}}{\text{recovery percentage}} = \frac{\text{Taxable turnover}}{\text{Taxable turnover} + \text{Exempt turnover}} \times 100\%$$

Taxable turnover excludes output VAT. Both amounts exclude particular types of supply (see 3.2.4 'Excluded supplies').

Rounding

The partial exemption recovery percentage is rounded up to the nearest whole per cent (for example, 25.125% is rounded to 26%), unless (for VAT periods beginning on or after 1 April 2005) the total amount of residual input VAT is more than £400,000 per month on average, in which case it is rounded to two decimal places.

Provisional recovery rate

With effect for VAT periods beginning on or after 1 April 2009, you can either calculate the partial exemption recovery percentage afresh every VAT period, using the values of taxable and exempt supplies in that period, or, provided you incurred exempt input VAT in the previous longer period, you can use the partial exemption recovery percentage calculated in your previous annual adjustment on a provisional basis in each VAT period of the current longer period, subject to correction in the annual adjustment for the current longer period.

Step 2

The rounded partial exemption percentage is then applied to the amount of residual input VAT in the period in order to apportion it between taxable and exempt activity as follows:

| Residual input VAT apportioned to taxable activity | = | Partial exemption recovery percentage | × | Residual input VAT for the period |

| Residual input VAT apportioned to exempt activity | = | Residual input VAT for the period | − | Residual input VAT apportioned to taxable activity |

For the annual adjustment, the residual input VAT for the period is the total of the VAT on residual purchases in each quarter, after having removed any blocked VAT and any VAT apportioned to non-business activities in the business/non-business method.

Example: the standard partial exemption method

Children's Help Centre is registered for VAT and has a mix of taxable and exempt activities. It uses the standard partial exemption method. In VAT quarter 4 its residual input VAT is £2,000 and its sales were £200,000 taxable and £170,000 exempt.

The apportionment of residual input VAT is as follows:

$$\text{Partial exemption recovery percentage} = \frac{£200,000}{£200,000 + £170,000} \times 100\% = 54.05\%$$

Round up to nearest whole per cent: 55%

Residual input VAT apportioned to taxable activity = 55% × £2,000 = £1,100

Residual input VAT apportioned to exempt activity = £2,000 − £1,100 = £900

The standard method therefore apportions the £2,000 residual input VAT as £1,100 to taxable activities and £900 to exempt activities.

3.2.3 Use-based standard partial exemption method

With effect from 1 April 2009 an organisation may opt to operate a 'use-based' standard partial exemption method in the following longer periods:

- In its registration period – the period running from the date of registration to the day before the start of the first full VAT year.
- In the first VAT year after the registration period, provided it did not incur exempt input VAT in the registration period.
- In any VAT year, provided it did not incur exempt input VAT in the previous VAT year.

Once the eligible longer period has finished the organisation must switch to the normal turnover-based standard partial exemption method as described above.

In a use-based method residual input VAT is apportioned on the basis of actual use or intended use of the purchases concerned, rather than on the basis of turnover. In effect the organisation is allowed to use a special partial exemption method during the eligible period without prior HMRC approval. This can be useful if substantial start-up costs are being incurred in advance of any sales, so a turnover-based method would not provide a fair attribution of residual VAT.

3.2.4 Excluded supplies

In calculating the value of supplies under the standard partial exemption method, certain supplies must be excluded. These include:

- Sales of capital business assets, for example sales of used office equipment and furniture and sales of business premises.
- Incidental financial or real estate transactions, for example sales of investment properties.
- The value of reverse charge supplies of services received from abroad. See 9.7 'Cross-border services introduction' for reverse charge services.
- The value of taxable or exempt supplies made from branches located outside the UK. See 3.3.13 'Foreign and specified supplies' for more on how supplies from foreign branches are dealt with.

3.2.5 Special partial exemption methods

Any partial exemption method that does not strictly use the value of taxable and exempt supplies to apportion residual input VAT is a **special partial exemption method** (also referred to as a 'partial exemption special method' or 'PESM') and must normally be approved by HMRC. HMRC may also direct you to use a special partial exemption method.

You may have to adopt a special partial exemption method if the standard partial exemption is not fair or reasonable. You may also be permitted to adopt a special partial exemption method on the grounds that it gives a more accurate result than the standard method or that it is easier to implement, for example because it ties in with how you manage the organisation. See 3.3.1 'Choosing methods'.

A special partial exemption method should result in a fair and reasonable apportionment of input VAT. Here, 'fair and reasonable' means that it results in input VAT being recovered to the extent that it is used in making taxable supplies (or other supplies that carry a right of recovery). The method must also avoid ambiguities and situations in which interpretation is unclear, and it must be capable of being verified by HMRC without undue difficulty. Use is not limited to physical use. The assessment of use must be made having regard to economic reality, in the light of the observable terms and features of the business.

The underlying approach for special partial exemption methods is normally the same as in the standard partial exemption method, in that a partial exemption recovery percentage is first calculated, with that percentage then being rounded and applied to the residual input VAT for the period. However, a different cost driver is normally used to calculate the partial exemption recovery percentage.

Example: the special partial exemption method

Charity H agrees with HMRC a special partial exemption method based on the staff cost spent on different activities. Staff submit detailed timesheets and the charity uses them to bill clients. The staff cost of taxable activities in quarter 1 is £100,000 and the staff cost of exempt activities is £120,000. The residual input VAT is £10,000.

$$\text{Partial exemption recovery percentage} = \frac{£100,000}{£100,000 + £120,000} \times 100\% = 45.45\%$$

(rounded to 2 decimal places, see below)

Residual input VAT apportioned to taxable activity = 45.45% × £10,000 = £4,545. Residual input VAT apportioned to exempt activity = £10,000 − £4,545 = £5,455

Rounding

The partial exemption recovery percentage should generally be rounded to two decimal places. Before 1 April 2005 it was permissible to round the recovery percentage generated by an output-based special partial exemption method up to the nearest whole percentage (as described above for the standard method). Any such method agreed before 1 April 2005 is still valid, though as soon as the method is modified this advantage is lost.

Excluded supplies

The value of excluded supplies (see 3.2.4 'Excluded supplies') must also be excluded from any calculation under a special partial exemption method.

No longer fair

If a special method becomes unfair or unreasonable, for example due to a change in circumstances, then you must serve HMRC with a **Special Method Override Notice** and account for an appropriate correction in your annual adjustment. See 3.2.9 'The Special Method Override Notice'.

Pre-1 April 2005 HMRC approval

Before 1 April 2005 it was possible for HMRC to give verbal or de-facto approval of a special partial exemption method and such verbal or de-facto approvals may still be effective, though it may be difficult to get HMRC to accept such approval unless you have clear and convincing evidence.

Post-1 April 2005 HMRC approval

From 1 April 2005 all new or revised special partial exemption methods must be approved under a formal written agreement with HMRC and, from 1 April 2007, you must make a written declaration that, to the best of your knowledge and belief, the method will result in a fair and reasonable attribution of VAT to taxable supplies. HMRC can serve a notice to recover any over-claimed VAT in the previous four years (but not earlier than the start of the method) in the event that:

- the method is found to be unfair or unreasonable;
- the method results in an over-recovery of VAT; and
- the person making the declaration knew or ought to have known this when making the declaration.

An application for a new special method or for a change to a special method or to stop using a special method should be made in writing to HMRC. If applying for a new special method, you should provide full details of the proposed method, explain why it is fair and reasonable and provide the above written declaration. HMRC may ask you to provide a worked example of the method using actual figures. HMRC provides a template declaration in *VAT Notice 706*.

Records

Some special methods may require you to keep specific records. For example, if your method is based on staff time spent on different activities, you will have to keep records of how much time staff spend on different activities. HMRC will generally refuse methods that use records that are kept only for the purposes of the method. However, if records are kept for other purposes as well, they may be acceptable.

Backdating

HMRC will not normally consent to a special partial exemption method being backdated before the start of the longer period of application. However, it may be prepared to do so in the following circumstances (*PE3110*):

- The business was not aware that it was partly exempt and recovered all of its input VAT, but the standard partial exemption method does not give a fair and reasonable result.
- The business has been unknowingly operating an unapproved special method, but that method gives a fair and reasonable result.

HMRC has the power to approve a backdated special method; so if HMRC refuses to agree backdating, it may be possible to establish that it has acted wholly unreasonably in refusing to do so.

3.2.6 Sectorised methods

HMRC can approve the use of a sectorised special partial exemption method, provided separate accounts are kept for each sector. HMRC can also require the keeping of separate accounts for each sector and the use of a sectorised method.

Sectorisation usually applies to large businesses which are split into divisions, with each division carrying out distinct activities, making a mix of taxable and exempt supplies and incurring its own residual costs. In such a scenario it is possible to agree with HMRC that you can carry out separate residual recovery rate calculations for each sector's residual input VAT.

Sectors refer to distinct types of business activity and not to geographical areas. If you sectorise you must sectorise all business activities fairly and reasonably, and each sector must include all of the instances of that particular type of business activity.

In the VAT Tribunal case *University of Glasgow* [2006] VTD 19885, the University adopted, with HMRC's agreement, a sectorised method that included a sector for its sports facilities and a separate sector for its halls of residence. Both sectors made a mix of taxable and exempt supplies. It subsequently asked HMRC to approve an amendment to create a separate sector for a particular sports facility with a particularly high level of taxable activity. HMRC refused and the Tribunal held that HMRC was within its rights to do so. It was neither fair nor reasonable to cherry pick the particular facility while ignoring the University's general activities within the sports facility sector. An example of appropriate sectorisation was its halls of residence as that covered a complete sector of provision.

3.2.7 The combined method

Combined methods became available from 1 January 2011 and were designed to simplify VAT recovery calculations by removing any need to distinguish between non-business and exempt activities. However, they cannot be used if the non-business activity includes private activity. With a combined method the distinction is between taxable and non-taxable activities, the latter including non-business and exempt activities. The combined method recovery percentage should be rounded to two decimal places.

Example: the combined method

C is a care charity. Most of its staff work on non-business or exempt care activities; however, it also runs several charity shops (taxable sales). C has agreed with HMRC a combined method based on the number of full-time equivalent staff working in the different types of activity (excluding core staff). It has agreed that this can be calculated on an annual basis.

In its VAT year to 31 March 2016 it has a total of 100 full-time equivalent staff: 70 working in the care services, 10 working on retail sales and 20 core staff. Its residual VAT for the year is £120,000.

$$\text{Combined method recovery rate} = \frac{10}{(10 + 70)} \times 100\% = 12.5\%$$

Residual VAT apportioned to taxable activity = 12.5% × £120,000 = £15,000

Advantages and disadvantages of combined methods

A combined method will clearly be helpful in situations where it is difficult to distinguish between non-business and exempt activities. However, they come with a few disadvantages:

- There is no *de minimis* 'allowance' for exempt input VAT, so if you are *de minimis* or hover around the *de minimis* limits, you might lose out financially. However, this is unlikely to be a problem for organisations with a substantial level of exempt activity.

- There are many valuable VAT reliefs that are given specifically for charity non-business activities (see Chapter 6 'Zero and reduced rates' generally and 8.3 'Property VAT reliefs'). It may be to your advantage to carry on making the distinction so that you are clear on what your business and exempt activities are so that you can take advantage of the reliefs available. However, it may also be possible to make the distinction whilst also using a combined method.
- A combined method must be formally agreed with HMRC in writing as for special partial exemption methods (see above), as must any changes to the method. By using separate partial exemption and business/non-business methods, even though the special partial exemption method (or any change thereto) requires HMRC agreement, the non-business method (or any change thereto) does not. You therefore retain flexibility over how your business/non-business apportionment is carried out and you do not need to obtain HMRC approval for any changes to the method.
- If you are eligible for one of the section 33 reclaim schemes, you will have to carry out separate business/non-business and partial exemption apportionments, the latter if applicable.

3.2.8 The standard method override

You must make an input VAT adjustment in your annual adjustment if all of the following conditions are met:

1. The standard partial exemption method does not provide an attribution of residual input VAT that reflects the actual or intended use of residual business purchases.
2. Total residual input VAT is more than £50,000 in a 12-month longer period or more than £25,000 in a 12-month longer period if the organisation is a member of a corporate group (unless all corporate group members are members of the same VAT group). The £50,000 and £25,000 figures are adjusted proportionately for longer periods that are not 12 months.
3. The difference between the results produced by the standard method and one based on actual use is more than £50,000 or more than the higher of £25,000 and 50% of the residual input VAT (excluding any attributed to non-business activities).

The amount of the adjustment is the difference identified in condition 3.

Where residual input VAT exceeds £50,000 per year or £25,000 per year for members of a corporate group (as above), HMRC advises all businesses to consider their position. HMRC states (at *PE1450*):

When does the standard method reflect use?
The standard method provides for a fair and reasonable deduction on the basis of use (but not intended use) where residual inputs are used:

- to make supplies in the same period in which the inputs are incurred;
- in proportion to the values of supplies made in the period; and
- to make all of the supplies whose values are included in the standard method pro rata calculation.

Where based on a fair and reasonable assessment of the facts the above questions are answered in the affirmative, a use-based calculation will not be needed for inputs actually used.

3.2.9 The Special Method Override Notice

If HMRC considers that a special partial exemption method is not fair and reasonable, it can serve a Special Method Override Notice. The notice allows HMRC to impose an immediate override on the results of the special method until a replacement method is implemented. A notice served by HMRC will usually specify how the partial exemption calculation should be performed in the period until a new method is agreed.

The organisation can also serve a Special Method Override Notice on HMRC if its special partial exemption has become unfair or unreasonable, for example due to the introduction of new activities or changes in activities. The organisation should write to HMRC explaining that it is serving a Special Method Override Notice, the date from which it takes effect, and the reasons why the result of the current special method does not fairly and reasonably reflect actual use of purchases.

Once a notice has been served you must, for each VAT return period beginning on or after the date specified in the notice, carry out the following calculations in your annual adjustment:

- determine the amount of deductible VAT using your current special method;
- determine the amount of deductible VAT in accordance with the use of purchases in making taxable supplies; and
- account for any difference between these amounts.

If the date specified in the notice falls part way through your tax year or longer period, you must carry out these calculations at the year end in relation to the part of the year falling after the date specified in the notice, excluding the part before.

3.3 GENERAL RECOVERY ISSUES

3.3.1 Choosing methods

Organisations generally implement special partial exemption methods when the standard method does not produce a fair and reasonable apportionment, or when there is a special method that is administratively easier to use and that also provides a fair and reasonable apportionment or where a special method produces a fairer apportionment than the standard method.

Choosing a special method because it ties in with how you manage your organisation or how you cost projects is a perfectly reasonable and valid approach, so long as it also provides a fair and reasonable attribution of VAT. There are, however, many situations in which the standard method does not provide a fair and reasonable result, so a special method is required however you manage the finances.

The standard method assumes that each pound of taxable sales and each pound of exempt sales incurs the same level of VAT-bearing residual expense. Likewise, an income-based business/non-business method assumes that each pound of business income and each pound of non-business income incurs the same level of VAT-bearing residual expense. Situations in which this might not be the case include:

- One type of activity is subsidised and the other is not, for example by block grants or public donations.
- One type of activity produces high-value sales but these incur, on a transaction-by-transaction basis, no more VAT-bearing residual costs than do low-value sales generated by a different type of activity.
- One type of activity makes heavy use of volunteers and so requires a lower level of income than another type which makes little use of volunteers.
- There is a significant timing difference between the receipt of supplies and the associated sales, for example where sales are made in one VAT year but the associated costs were incurred in a different VAT year.

3.3.2 Partial exemption frameworks

HMRC has agreed a series of 'partial exemption frameworks' with representative bodies in certain sectors setting out agreed approaches to VAT recovery and covering when and why special partial exemption methods are likely to be needed in the sector. They are aimed at allowing special partial exemption methods to be agreed which are fair and consistent with the minimum of time and costs to both parties. Frameworks are regularly updated to ensure that they remain accurate and current. The frameworks at the time of writing are:

- **Higher Education Framework**, agreed with the British Universities Finance Directors' Group and the University Funding Councils via the Higher Education Funding Council for England;
- **Housing Associations Framework**, agreed with the Housing Federation, the Scottish Federation of Housing Associations and Community Housing Cymru;
- **NHS Bodies Framework**, agreed with the Health Finance Managers Association;
- **Insurance Framework**, agreed with the Association of British Insurers.

3.3.3 Income-based business/non-business methods

Many organisations use the turnover-based standard partial exemption method in conjunction with an income-based business/non-business method. A typical income-based non-business method is:

$$\text{Business recovery percentage} = \frac{\text{Business income}}{\text{Business income} + \text{Non-business income}} \times 100\%$$

This business recovery percentage is then applied to the residual VAT to split it between input VAT (which goes into the partial exemption calculation) and non-business VAT (irrecoverable unless a section 33 recovery scheme applies).

However, there are dangers with such a method that may result in an unfair attribution of residual VAT:

1. *Children's Society* **case**. See 3.3.4 'Effect of the *Children's Society* case'.
2. **Passive income**. Some passive non-business income such as deposit interest may incur little or no generation of VAT-bearing residual costs, so its inclusion in the denominator (bottom half) would be distortive.
3. **Distortive receipts**. Inclusion of some types of receipt would be highly distortive, by analogy with the excluded transaction rules for partial exemption (see 10.9.5 'Excluded transactions'). For example, inclusion of large one-off operational or investment property sales would likely be distortive, over- or under-attributing the amount apportioned to business activities. If large legacies are received occasionally these may also need to be excluded (though see also 3.3.4 'Effect of the *Children's Society* case' for an alternative approach for legacy income and bank interest). Large restricted grants may need to be excluded if they are received and then passed on intact with minimal associated residual VAT-bearing costs.
4. **Subsidised activities**. Some activities may be taxable but subsidised, for example a taxable trade subsidised by a start-up grant. If income really is an

appropriate driver for how residual costs are used, this non-business income may have to be included in business activities.

5. **Non-business activities with no income**. If there are substantial non-business activities that are funded wholly from the profits made on business activities, then an income-based method will completely miss the non-business activity. For example, if a charity generates all of its income by letting out property on a commercial basis and uses the proceeds to provide free accommodation to the homeless, then the charity is likely to be using a substantial part of its residual costs in supporting the non-business activity; however, an income-based method would assign all of the residual VAT to business activity on the basis that the only income is business.

3.3.4 Effect of the *Children's Society* case

The *Children's Society* case (see 3.1.13) suggests that VAT incurred on fundraising costs incurred in generating unrestricted donations used to support the general activities of a charity is residual VAT and partly recoverable. The *Revenue & Customs* v. *University of Cambridge* [2015] case suggests that the same principle applies to VAT incurred in managing a portfolio of financial investments.

This suggests that the associated donation/investment income should be omitted from the denominator (bottom half) of any income-based business/non-business apportionment formula on the basis its inclusion would assign the donations' share of residual VAT to wholly irrecoverable, when it should be residual. The same principle more clearly applies to cost-based methods (as illustrated by the *Oxfam* case below).

However, what matters is how the donations are actually used. This is illustrated by the VAT Tribunal case *Oxfam* [2008] VTD 20752. Oxfam used an HMRC-agreed expenditure-based business/non-business method:

$$\text{Business recovery rate} = \frac{\text{exclusive business expenditure}}{\begin{array}{c}(\text{exclusive business expenditure} + \\ \text{exclusive non-business} \\ \text{expenditure})\end{array}} \times 100\%$$

Oxfam argued (and HMRC did not dispute) that the result of the *Children's Society* case was that fundraising costs should be removed from exclusive non-business expenditure. However, HMRC's objection was that this did not produce a fair and reasonable result. The effect of removal was to increase the business recovery rate from 75% to 85%, whereas evidence (annual accounts and marketing materials) suggested that 80% of the donations were used to support Oxfam's non-business activities. The Tribunal found against Oxfam on the basis that it had failed adequately to show that the change would be fair and reasonable. Oxfam then sought to argue before the High Court (*Oxfam* v.

Revenue & Customs [2009] EWHC 3078 (Ch)) that it had a legitimate expectation that HMRC would be bound by the agreement. The High Court first decided that the First-tier Tribunal did have jurisdiction to hear this particular legitimate interest claim (for which see 12.8.5 'Legitimate expectation'), but then rejected Oxfam's legitimate expectation claim. In its opinion HMRC's conduct in rejecting the agreed method after the mutual change of understanding as a result of the *Children's Society* case was that of a responsible public authority mindful of its duties to the Exchequer and at the same time acting fairly to the citizen.

3.3.5 Basis for non-business and special partial exemption methods

Non-business and special partial exemption methods are commonly based on the following factors.

1. Activity income

This method uses the levels of business and non-business income to apportion residual VAT between business and non-business activities. This method is commonly used in conjunction with the income-based standard partial exemption method. However, it can be problematic. See 3.3.3 'Income-based business/non-business methods'.

2. The number of full-time equivalent staff employed in the different areas of activity

When used as a non-business method, the proportion of residual VAT attributed to business activities is the number of staff working in business activities divided by the number of staff working in business and non-business activities. When used as a partial exemption method, the recoverable proportion is the number of staff working in taxable activities divided by the number of staff working in business activities. If this is a special partial exemption method or a combined method you will have to agree with HMRC how core staff are dealt with.

The staff numbers method assumes that each member of staff incurs roughly the same amount of VAT-bearing residual cost. This might be appropriate where most of the organisation's work is carried out by staff and the residual costs incurred by each member of staff are roughly equal or indistinguishable. Areas where this might be problematic include: substantial use of volunteers, in which case volunteer numbers may have to be included, and large numbers of people working part time, in which case staff full-time equivalents might be more appropriate.

3. The staff cost of different areas of activity

This is broadly the same as using the number of staff but may be easier to implement in a financial system, as figures for staff costs are likely to be more readily available. It assumes that higher-paid staff incur proportionately more VAT-bearing residual cost than lower-paid staff, but it does allow for full-time staff incurring more VAT-bearing residual costs than part-time staff.

4. The staff time spent in different areas of activity

This is broadly equivalent to using the number of full-time equivalent staff but allows for staff working flexibly across different activities. It will be necessary to keep records of how much time staff spend working in different activities, for example staff timesheets. HMRC may reject the method if the only reason the staff time records are kept is for VAT purposes. However, where staff timesheets are kept for apportioning staff costs to projects for billing, management or statutory accounting purposes, then HMRC may be prepared to accept staff time as appropriate. If volunteer time is also significant, this may have to be included.

5. The floor area occupied by different activities

If VAT-bearing premises costs such as maintenance, heating, lighting, cleaning, etc. form a major part of residual costs and if activities occupy clearly defined areas, using the floor area occupied by different activities may be appropriate. You will have to consider how areas such as corridors, entrance halls, services and facilities are dealt with. If areas are used differently at different times, you may have to carry out another apportionment for those areas, for example based on area occupied multiplied by time occupied.

6. The levels of expenditure incurred in different areas of activity

This method assumes that VAT-bearing residual costs are incurred in proportion to the level of direct expenditure on activities. HMRC provides the following comments on expenditure-based methods (*VBNB33000*):

> When there is little directly attributable expenditure these methods give a misleading result and should not be used. An example of this would be where most of the tax incurred is non-attributable. When this happens there is unlikely to be sufficient information for the apportionment to be reliable.

> Expenditure based methods are also not appropriate if the ratio of attributable expenditure is likely to be different from the extent of business use of the non-attributable goods and services.

> For example, a charity with mostly non-business expenditure may buy a computer system to make taxable supplies of publications. It might only use the computer

incidentally for non-business activities. When this happens, an expenditure based method could lead to an apportionment that understates the business purpose behind the computer purchase.

7. Transaction counts

This method (when used as a business/non-business method) uses the numbers of business transactions versus the number of non-business transactions. It assumes that all business and non-business activities are transaction-based and that each transaction incurs roughly the same amount of VAT-bearing residual cost. HMRC provides the following comments on transaction-based methods (*VBNB33000*):

> A common difficulty with such methods is that non-business activities often do not involve recordable transactions. In contrast the business activities will involve making charges and making distinct, recordable supplies. In such cases a transactions based method can lead to an unfair result. HMRC staff will not automatically dismiss transaction based methods. However, we will want to be sure that they are founded on a valid indicator of business and non-business activity.

8. Other activity-level statistics

Other activity-level statistics include, for example, the number of users or user visits.

9. Combinations of methods

A combination of the above methods may be appropriate.

3.3.6 Methods and VAT groups

Where different organisations are members of the same VAT group (see 2.2 'VAT groups') there is a single entity for VAT purposes, and therefore, unless a sectorised method is appropriate and approved by HMRC, a single business/non-business method and a single partial exemption method must be applied across the group. The *de minimis* test is also applied across the group.

When determining whether any supplies are incidental (and should therefore be excluded from any method calculations – see 3.2.4 'Excluded supplies') the group entities must be considered separately. For example, the incidental sale of a building by one group entity does not have to be included even if the entity is in the same VAT group as a separate entity that trades in property.

3.3.7 **Payback/clawback rules**

It is the actual use of purchased goods or services that matters for determining whether the VAT is deductible. However, a determination of use must be made at the time the VAT is incurred on the purchase, so that determination may have to be on the basis of intention as to use.

If the activity is aborted and no use is made of the purchase, then the initial attribution of any VAT incurred on the abortive purchases stands and no adjustment is possible if the purchase is not used to make any supply.

If the actual use is different from the intended use, or if there is a change in intention as to use, a correction must be made under the payback/clawback rules. The rules only apply if the change is from one of type (A) to one of the list in the corresponding column (type B):

Type A: Intended use	Type B: First actual use or revised intention
Taxable	Exempt, non-business* or residual
Residual	Exempt or non-business*
Exempt or non-business*	Residual or taxable
Residual	Taxable

*Non-business included for purchases on or after 1 January 2011 only.

However, the payback/clawback rules are time-limited. They only apply if the change of intention or actual use occurs within six years of the beginning of the VAT period of initial deduction. The payback/clawback adjustment must be carried out in the VAT return for the period in which the first use occurred or the intention changed. The payback/clawback adjustment is not an error, does not need to be separately reported to HMRC and does not give rise to penalties or interest.

3.3.8 **Deadline for input VAT claims**

Under-claimed input VAT cannot be claimed more than four years after the due date of the return for the period in which the VAT was chargeable, though if you could not claim at that time because you did not hold an appropriate VAT invoice, the four-year time limit runs from the due date of the return in which the VAT invoice was received.

Errors resulting in an over-claim of input VAT cannot be corrected more than four years after the end of the VAT period in which the input VAT was over-claimed.

See 12.6.6 'Errors and mistakes' for more on the capping rules for claims and errors.

3.3.9 Who can reclaim input VAT?

To be able to deduct input VAT, a business must pay the input VAT concerned and it must use or intend to use the associated purchase in its own taxable activities. If a business pays VAT on goods or services used wholly by another entity, it cannot recover the VAT. For example:

1. **Third party's legal costs**: when a business loses a legal dispute and pays the other party's legal costs, those legal costs are not supplies to the loser but supplies to the winner. The loser cannot recover the associated VAT.
2. **Third-party consideration**: if a fully taxable business must pay for a consultant's report commissioned by and used exclusively by a third party (for example a report to a bank in order to obtain a loan), then the supply of consultancy services is to the bank and the business cannot recover the VAT it must pay. Even if the business has a right to a copy of the report, that does not make the consultant's supply to the business.

However, it is acceptable for a business to recover VAT incurred in running an independently constituted funded pension scheme, see 3.3.10 'Funded pension schemes'.

3.3.10 Funded pension schemes

A funded pension scheme is one in which the employer and employees' pension contributions are vested in separate trustees who may be individuals or corporate bodies. The pension fund is normally separate and distinct from the employer's business.

HMRC has long accepted that the employer can treat the VAT incurred on certain fund management costs as its own input VAT and recover accordingly. For most affected employers this will mean treating it as residual VAT. HMRC states (*VAT Notice 700/17*, section 2.2)

> What pension scheme activity forms part of my business activities? The management of your own employee pension scheme is a part of your normal business activities. If you are a VAT registered employer, and set up a pension fund for your employees under a trust deed, the VAT incurred in both setting up the fund and on its day-to-day management is your input tax. This applies even where responsibility for the general management of the scheme rests (under the

trust deed) with the trustee, or the trustees pay for the services supplied. A clear distinction is, however, made between 'management' and 'investment' costs.

Before 25 November 2014 HMRC insisted that only VAT on management and administration costs can be recovered by the employer (audit, accountancy and legal advice, etc.), but not on investment management services. If a combined service was provided, HMRC permitted 30% to be treated as for management and administration (*VAT Notice 700/17*, section 2.7). However, on 25 November 2014, following a decision by the CJEU (PPG Holdings), HMRC announced in *Revenue & Customs Brief 43/14*:

> HMRC accepts that there are no grounds to differentiate between the administration of a pension scheme and the management of its assets, therefore there is no longer a need for any administrative simplification to deal with supplies involving both elements. In each case the employer will potentially be able to deduct input tax if it receives the supply of services. . . .

> HMRC will not accept that the VAT incurred in relation to a pension scheme is deductible by an employer unless there is contemporaneous evidence that the services are provided to the employer and, in particular, the employer is a party to the contract for those services and has paid for them. . . .

> If an employer receives a taxable supply of administration and investment management services and recharges them to the pension scheme, that recharge is consideration for an onward taxable supply. VAT is due accordingly. This amount is potentially deductible by the pension scheme to the extent that it is engaged in taxable business activities.

HMRC further clarified in *Revenue & Customs Brief 08/15*, in reply to queries concerning tripartite contracts between a scheme manager, employer and fund:

> Given the unique nature of these DB [Defined Benefit] pension arrangements HMRC accepts that tripartite contracts can be used to demonstrate that the employer is the recipient of a supply of DB pension fund management services. An employer may therefore be able to deduct VAT incurred on these services in line with its residual recovery position where, as a minimum, the contract with the service provider evidences that:
>
> - the service provider makes its supplies to the employer (albeit that the contract may recognise that, in the particular regulatory context in which DB schemes operate, the service provider may be appointed by, or on behalf of, the pension scheme trustees)
> - the employer directly pays for the services that are supplied under the contract
> - the service provider will pursue the employer for payment and only in circumstances where the employer is unlikely to pay (for example, because it has gone into administration) will it recover its fees from the scheme's funds or the pension scheme trustees

- both the employer and the pension scheme trustees are entitled to seek legal redress in the event of breach of contract, albeit that the liability of the service provider need not be any greater than if the contract were with the pension scheme trustees alone and any restitution, indemnity or settlement payments for which the service provider becomes liable may be payable in whole to the pension scheme trustees for the benefit of the pension scheme (for example in circumstance where the scheme is not fully funded)
- the service provider will provide fund performance reports to the employer on request (subject to the pension scheme trustees being able to stipulate that reports are withheld, for example where there could be a conflict of interest)
- the employer is entitled to terminate the contract, although that may be subject to a condition that they should not do so without the pension scheme trustees prior written consent (this can be in addition to any right that the pension scheme trustees may have to terminate the contract unilaterally)

In addition to the above, evidence that the pension scheme trustees agree that it is the employer who is entitled to deduct any VAT incurred on the services will reduce the potential for disputes.

3.3.11 Lennartz Treatment

Where a VAT-registered organisation assigns capital goods wholly or partly to its business assets, recovers VAT on the asset or part, and subsequently, within the economic life of those goods, puts that asset or part, permanently or temporarily, to a private use, or to use for purposes outside those of the organisation, there is a **deemed supply** of the asset by the business on which output VAT is due (see 4.2 'Private use of business goods'). This is referred to as the 'Lennartz Treatment'.

The advantage of assigning a mixed taxable/private use asset wholly to business assets is that it gives a VAT cash flow advantage. Instead of the VAT being only partly recoverable when incurred, all of the VAT incurred can be recovered upfront but is then repaid as output VAT over the life of the asset as private use occurs.

The Lennartz Treatment is named after a court case in which the Court of Justice of the EU (CJEU or ECJ) decided that when a business acquires an asset for mixed taxable and private use (in Mr Lennartz's case, a car) the business can assign as much or as little of the asset to its business assets as it likes, including assigning it wholly to its business assets, however little the level of actual taxable use intended.

Before 2008 the Lennartz Treatment was generally considered to apply to business assets put to any non-business use, including the non-business activities of a charity. HMRC accepted that charities and voluntary organisations could use the Lennartz Treatment for certain tangible assets put to a mix of taxable and non-private non-business use. However, the CJEU case C-515/070 *Vereniging Noordelijke Land-en Tuinbouw Organisatie* v. *Staatssecretaris van Financiën* [2009] ECR I-00839 made a distinction between three mutually exclusive types of non-business use of an asset:

1. **Private use**: use for the private purposes of the business owners, staff or volunteers, for example an architect constructing a building which is partly their own living accommodation (private use) and partly an office (business use).
2. **Use outside the purposes of the organisation**: use for purposes that are not private but are outside the purposes of the organisation. HMRC accepts that such use will be rare for most charities and voluntary organisations.
3. **Use within the purposes of the organisation**: use for the non-business purposes of an organisation but excluding private use and excluding use outside the purposes of the organisation. This will include most if not all non-business activities of charities and other voluntary organisations.

The CJEU then decided that the Lennartz Treatment only applies to the first two; it does not apply to the third. This decision therefore excludes most non-business use of business assets by charities and other voluntary organisations from the scope of the Lennartz Treatment.

UK law was changed with effect from 1 January 2011. With effect from this date the Lennartz Treatment is restricted to private use and non-organisational use (1 and 2 above) of business assets that are not **immoveable property** (see 8.6 'Property terms'), ships, boats or aircraft. Changes in non-private non-business use (3 above) and immoveable property, ships, boats and aircraft are now dealt with by restricting the initial VAT recovery to the level of taxable use in the VAT year of acquisition and, for capital items, under an extended CGS (to include non-private non-business use).

However, HMRC permits organisations that adopted the Lennartz Treatment before 1 January 2011 either to carry on the Lennartz adjustments or totally unwind them and apply the correct treatment as above, subject to the normal four-year time limit for correcting errors (*Revenue & Customs Brief 02/10*).

3.3.12 **Free admissions or membership**

In *Imperial War Museum* [1992] VTD 346/92 the public were charged for admission to the museum (a business activity) but school parties were admitted free, and anyone was admitted free on Fridays. HMRC argued that the free admissions were a separate non-business activity; however, the VAT Tribunal found there to be a single business activity of supplying museum admissions and that the provision of the free admission was an act performed in the course of the conduct of that one business.

The *Imperial War Museum* decision was followed in *British Dental Association* v. *Revenue & Customs* [2010] UKFTT 176 (TC) where free membership was offered to students as a way of attracting dentists to membership at the training stage. Very few students would join, while at university, if there was a membership fee, and it would then be very difficult to recruit them once they had left university and taken up practice anywhere in the country. The First-tier Tribunal found that the Association conducted only one business; it did not, in the normal usage of the phrase, conduct any distinct activity that might be a non-business activity; and the provision of free membership was a commercially sensible introductory offer made entirely for business purposes, and made to foster the Association's one and only business, and thus made in the course of that business.

3.3.13 Foreign and specified supplies

Foreign supplies are supplies of services that are made outside the UK that would be taxable if made in the UK.

Specified supplies are supplies of financial or insurance services supplied to persons belonging outside the EU or directly related to an export of goods or the making of arrangements for these specified supplies.

UK VAT incurred in making foreign and specified supplies can be recovered in the UK VAT return. From 1 April 2009 such supplies must be dealt with as follows for the purposes of the standard partial exemption method:

1. The turnover on specified supplies is excluded in the partial exemption recovery percentage calculation. Input VAT wholly or partly relating to specified supplies is ring-fenced and recovered on the basis of the use of the purchases in making UK taxable and foreign and specified supplies.
2. The turnover on foreign supplies made from UK establishments is included in the partial exemption recovery percentage calculation; however, the turnover on foreign supplies from non-UK establishments is excluded from the partial exemption recovery percentage calculation and recovered on the basis of use of the purchases in making UK taxable and foreign and specified supplies.

3.3.14 Banding system for cathedrals and churches

There is an informal arrangement between HMRC and the Churches Main Committee for apportionment of residual VAT. This allows cathedrals and churches that are tourist attractions and receive substantial business income to claim part of the VAT which is not directly attributable to a business or non-business activity via a banding system.

This includes VAT incurred on repairs or upkeep to the cathedral or church itself. It also includes VAT incurred on all associated buildings, apart from domestic accommodation, within its curtilage.

Whether VAT can be recovered on domestic accommodation depends on why the person who uses it is engaged. It also depends on whether they work on business or non-business activities. None of the VAT can be recovered if the person is engaged for religious purposes. An apportionment of VAT will have to be agreed if the occupant is a lay person engaged on some business activities.

The banding system has four bands. These are:

- **Band A (90%)**: to apply where there are significant entry charges to all main areas;
- **Band B (65%)**: to apply where there is no entry charge but there are high numbers of visitors. Also there is significant taxable income such as from entry charges to other areas such as a crypt, museum or tower, or lettings for concerts;
- **Band C (45%)**: to apply where there is no entry charge and insignificant taxable income from entry charges for other areas. But there are a reasonable number of visitors generating income from other sources, for example the book/souvenir shop;
- **Band D (25%)**: to apply where there are no entry charges or only a few small charges, small numbers of visitors and little taxable income.

HMRC states that it should be simple to identify cathedrals and churches falling within Bands A and D. The majority of queries will be over Bands B and C. Where HMRC thinks that the business activities show that the cathedral or church clearly falls above Band C it will normally apply Band B. See VIT45600 for more on the agreement.

4 Business and non-business activities

This chapter is divided into the following sections:

- 4.1 **Basic rules** covering the meanings of supply, business, etc.
- 4.2 **Exceptions** to the basic rules: **deemed supplies**, deemed non-supplies, etc.
- 4.3 **Non-business activities** commonly undertaken by voluntary organisations

For VAT purposes income is divided into business income which is **within the scope** of VAT and non-business income which is **outside the scope** of VAT (see figure 4.1).

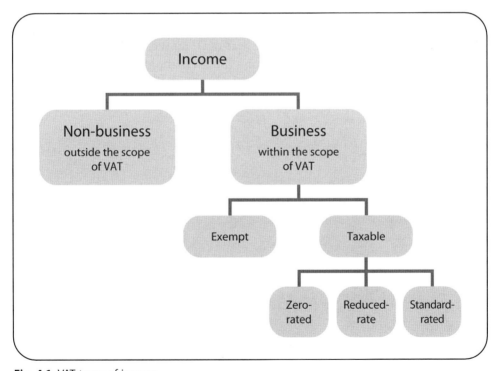

Fig. 4.1 VAT types of income

4.1 **BASIC RULES**

Currently the UK's VAT system is a part of an EU-wide taxation system set out mainly in the Principal VAT Directive (Directive 2006/112/EC). EU states are obliged to implement the EU's VAT system, with the UK implementation being primarily in the VAT Act 1994.

The Court of Justice of the EU (CJEU or ECJ) is the final arbiter in any dispute relating to the interpretation of VAT law. Cases on the interpretation of VAT law can be referred to the CJEU by UK courts and tribunals but not directly by claimants. Most CJEU cases go first to the Advocate General who issues an opinion, with the CJEU then providing its own ruling or decision.

Some of the cases referred to in italics below are summarised in Chapter 13 'Cases'.

4.1.1 **The scope of output VAT**

This chapter considers the scope of **output VAT** (see 1.1), that is, when output VAT is potentially due to HMRC in respect of a transaction. Such a transaction is said to be 'within the scope of VAT' or a 'business supply'.

> Output VAT applies at a transaction level. Subject to exceptions (see 4.2 'Exceptions'), for a transaction to be within the scope of VAT or a business supply it must meet all three of the following conditions:
>
> 1. The transaction must be a **supply**.
> 2. The supply must be of **goods** or of **services**.
> 3. The supply of goods or of services must be a **business supply**.
>
> If one or more of the conditions is not met then the transaction is said to be **non-business** or **outside the scope of VAT**. No output VAT is due on the transaction. These conditions amount to a series of tests that must be applied to determine if a transaction is within the scope of VAT.

See the separate sections below for more on each test. Please note that regarding:

- **Economic activity**: EU law uses the term **economic activity** where UK law uses the term **business activity**.
- **Exempt supplies**: some business supplies are within the scope of VAT but are specifically exempted from VAT. Key exemptions for voluntary organisations are explained in Chapter 5 'Exempt activities' and Chapter 8 'Property'.
- **Place of supply**: for VAT purposes business supplies are deemed to take place at a particular location (the **place of supply**) at a particular point in time (the

time of supply). If the place of a business supply is outside the UK, then the supply is outside the scope of UK output VAT, though it is still a business supply as far as the VAT system is concerned. As VAT is an EU-wide tax system, if the place of supply is another EU state, then output VAT may be due in that state. See Chapter 9 'International aspects of VAT' for more on determining the place of supply.

- **Import VAT**: import VAT is a special type of VAT that is due upon bringing goods into the territory of the EU. The scope of import VAT is different. All imports, whether by businesses or by private individuals, can be liable for import VAT. See 9.5 'Imports'.

4.1.2   Test 1. The transaction must be a supply

A supply is an exchange transaction in which one party (**the supplier**) provides an independent party (**the customer**) with goods or services in return for a **consideration**.

The meaning of goods or services is considered in test 2. The key aspect of test 1 is that the goods or services are provided 'in return for' the consideration.

The **consideration** for the goods or services is everything that is given to the supplier in return, by whomsoever. Consideration:

- can be paid by the customer or by a third party;
- can be paid in parts by different parties;
- does not have to be monetary; it can include payment by way of barter, part-exchange and the granting of rights or the acceptance of constraints or limitations;
- can be by way of certain types of grant or subsidy.

The customer does not have to personally receive the economic benefit of the goods or services; it can be provided to a third party (the **true beneficiary** of the supply), for example care provided to a third party under a local authority care contract. However, case law has established the following basic principles that apply to **supplies**:

1. **No consideration**: if goods or services are provided for free, with no consideration paid to the supplier in return, the goods or services are not seen as being supplied (see 13.14 '*Hong-Kong Trade Development Council*'). However, see also 4.2 'Exceptions'. If VAT was recovered on purchasing the goods or services their disposal for free can be a deemed business supply.

2. **Direct link:** there must be a direct link between the goods or services provided and the consideration received in order for the consideration to be in return for the goods or services (see 13.1 '*Apple and Pear Development Council*'). An indirect link is not enough, and 'insufficiently intense' or 'contaminated links', where the amount of consideration depends on factors other than the level of supply, can also fail this test (see 13.7 '*EC* v. *Finland*').

3. **Reciprocal performance:** there must be a legal relationship between the supplier and the customer pursuant to which there is reciprocal performance. The consideration is the amount that is actually received by the supplier in return for the goods or services (see 13.26 '*R. J. Tolsma*').

4. **Quantifiable consideration:** non-monetary consideration must be capable of being valued monetarily. There is no supply if any purported non-monetary consideration is unquantifiable. Non-monetary consideration is valued subjectively (i.e. from the perspectives of the transacting parties), and not according to objective criteria (for example by reference to market rates) (see 13.6 '*Dutch Potato* case').

5. **Agreed payment:** in order to determine if a particular payment is, wholly or partly, consideration for particular goods or services, it is necessary to determine if, at the time of the payment, the supplier and customer had agreed that the whole or a part (whether identifiable or not) of the payment would constitute the value given in return for the goods or services (see 13.17 '*Kuwait Petroleum*').

6. **Independent parties:** a transaction is a supply only if it takes place between at least two independent and separately identified parties. An entity does not make a supply when it charges its own branch for services rendered (decided in case C-210/04 *Ministero dell'Economia e delle Finanze and Agenzia delle Entrate* v. *FCE Bank plc* [2006] ECR I-02803) and an employee does not make a supply of their work as employee to their employer, as the employee is not independent of their employer. In the case C-276/14 *Gmina Wrocław* v. *Minister Finansów* [2015] the CJEU decided that, in order to determine if a person acts independently in carrying out an economic activity, it is necessary to check whether that person performs the activities in their own name, on their own behalf and under their own responsibility, and whether they bear the economic risk associated with carrying out those activities.

4.1.3 Test 2. It must be a supply of goods or of services

If you determine that your transaction is a supply, you must also check that the supply is of goods or of services. If it is not a supply of goods or of services then the transaction is outside the scope of VAT.

Supply of goods

A **supply of goods** is the **transfer** of the right to dispose of tangible property as owner. Supplies of gas and electricity through transmission networks are treated as supplies of goods. In UK VAT law, the grant, assignment or surrender of the freehold or a long lease in land or buildings is treated as a supply of goods. Long lease means broadly a lease exceeding 21 years (not less than 20 years in Scotland). The supply of a short lease or of a licence to occupy is a supply of services. See 8.6.2 'Freeholds leases and licences to occupy' for more.

> **Goods** are tangible property such as vehicles and animals.

Transfer does not refer to transfer of legal title in accordance with contract or property law but covers any transfer of goods by one party which empowers the other party actually to dispose of those goods as if the other party were their owner (see 13.3 '*Auto Lease Holland*'). An economic substance over legal form approach applies and goods are seen as being supplied between the persons who have actual economic possession and use of the goods. Goods provided under hire purchase agreements and finance leases are treated as supplies of goods.

Supply of services

A supply of services is a supply that is not a supply of goods.

At first sight this suggests that all supplies are supplies of goods or supplies of services. However, that is not the case:

1. **No goods or service provided for consideration**: some exchange transactions are not capable of being a supply of goods or of services for a consideration despite the fact that something of substance is provided by one party to another in return for monetary payment. An example is the issue of a new share by a company seeking to raise capital (see 13.16 '*Kretztechnik*').
2. **No consumption**: as VAT is a tax on consumption, anything that is supplied must be capable of being consumed. Goods are deemed to be consumed when the actual right to dispose of the goods as owner is transferred. However, for services something has to be provided that is capable of being consumed. For example, in the *Landboden-Agrardienste* case (see 13.18) a farmer was given compensation for agreeing not to harvest at least 20% of his potato crop. The court decided that as this did not give rise to any consumption, it could not be a supply.
3. **Deemed supplies and deemed non-supplies**: economic reality is overridden in some situations. Some actual supplies are deemed not to be supplies and some non-supplies are deemed to be supplies. These exceptions to the normal supply rules can include giving away goods for free, making private use of

goods, making private use of services and selling a business. See 4.2 'Exceptions'.

4. **Packaged supplies**: if you supply goods and services together as a package, then you must consider the single/multiple supply tests to determine if you are, for VAT purposes, seen as supplying goods or services or both. See 11.3 'Single and multiple supplies'.

4.1.4   Test 3. It must be a business supply

If you decide that you are making a supply of goods or of services (or both) you must then decide if the supply is a **business supply**.

There is a difference between UK law and EU VAT law at this point.

1. UK law

Under UK law a supply is a business supply if it is made by a person 'in the course or furtherance of any business carried on by' that person (VAT Act 1994, s. 4(1)).

So if you make a supply of goods or of services, but it is not in the course or furtherance of a business you carry on (i.e. it is a **non-business activity**), then that supply is outside the scope of VAT. If it is in the course or furtherance of a business you carry on (i.e. if it is a **business activity**), then it is a business supply. UK case law has established the **business tests** to help establish whether an activity is business or non-business. See 4.1.5 'Business tests'.

However, you only charge VAT on a business supply if you are a **taxable person**. In UK law a taxable person is a person who is registered for, or liable to be registered for, VAT. This is different from the EU law term where 'taxable person' can include unregistered persons.

2. EU law

The Principal VAT Directive defines the scope of output VAT to comprise supplies of goods or of services made by a taxable person when they **act as such**:

- **Taxable person**: in EU law taxable person is defined to mean 'any person who, independently, carries out in any place any economic activity, whatever the purpose or results of that activity'.
- **Economic activity**: see 'Meaning of economic activity' below.
- **Acts as such**: a taxable person 'acts as such' when they carry out an economic activity.
- **Independently**: the requirement for the economic activity to be carried out independently excludes the services an employee provides to an employer and

(in most situations) excludes activities within a single legal entity, for example supplies between two branches of a single business.

- **In any place**: if a person carries out an economic activity in one place, they are a taxable person in any place.
- **Whatever the purpose or results of the activity**: this means that the activity is considered per se (in itself or objectively) without regard to its purpose or result (*EC* v. *Netherlands*, see 13.9). An activity carried out for some other purpose besides profit can be an economic activity, though the absence of a profit motive can be a contributing factor in determining whether or not an activity is economic.

Meaning of economic activity. The CJEU approach to assessing if an activity is economic is to see if the activity fits into either or both of the following two categories:

1. any activity of producers, traders or persons supplying services, including mining and agricultural activities and activities of the professions;
2. the exploitation of tangible or intangible property for the purposes of obtaining income therefrom on a continuing basis.

The above definition of a taxable person is over-ridden to include any person who, on an occasional basis, supplies a **new means of transport** (see VAT Act 1994 s. 95) which is dispatched or transported to a destination within the EU.

Case law establishes various principles for applying these tests:

- To be within either of these categories an activity must be permanent and carried out in return for remuneration (see 13.12 '*Götz*'). These are necessary but not sufficient conditions. One-off and occasional supplies are not normally considered permanent and hence are not normally seen as constituting an economic activity, but occasional supplies of a new means of transport can be seen as an economic activity.
- To see if an activity falls within the first category, an objective assessment must be made without regard to its purpose or result (see 13.9 '*EC* v. *Netherlands*'). However, the activity must be capable of being carried out by economic operators (see 13.15 '*Hutchison 3G*').
- For the second category, exploitation refers to all transactions, whatever their legal form, by which it is sought to obtain income from the property in question on a continuing basis (see 13.31 '*van Tiem*'). However, it excludes such exploitation for a purpose other than obtaining income therefrom on a continuing basis, for example where the purpose is to carry out a statutorily imposed duty (see 13.15 '*Hutchison 3G*'). This is so even if the activity constitutes exploitation of property and actually generates income on a continuing basis.

4.1.5 **Business tests**

The UK case law **business tests** first appeared in their present form in the 1978 Court of Session case *Morrison's Academy* (see 13.22) in which the renting of accommodation to school pupils was found to be a business activity. The court put forward various tests which were later refined in the 1981 High Court case *Lord Fisher* (see 13.20). The *Lord Fisher* case considered whether contributions made by friends and family towards the costs of a shooting party were consideration for business supplies.

The **business tests** are:

1. Is the activity a serious undertaking earnestly pursued?
2. Is the activity pursued with reasonable continuity?
3. Is the activity substantial in amount?
4. Is the activity conducted in a regular manner and on sound and recognised business principles?
5. Is the activity predominantly concerned with the making of supplies to consumers for consideration?
6. Does the activity consist of supplies of a kind which, subject to differences of detail, are commonly made by those who seek to make profit from them?

The tests are not intended as a checklist but more as a series of questions to ask about an activity in order to gain a general impression of its objective nature. The second and third tests (continuity and scale) cannot in themselves determine the status, as a non-business activity can have continuity and scale (see, for example, the *Wellcome Trust* decision (section 13.32) in which the sale of a substantial volume and value of shares was held to be non-business). However, the second and third tests are factors that can contribute to a determination that a business activity exists.

The fifth 'predominant concern' test does not relate to the subjective aim or purpose pursued, but to the inherent objective nature of the activity. If that objective nature is economic then it is a business activity. However, if that objective nature is no more than something else, then it is non-business. In the *Lord Fisher* case (see 13.20) the court held that business activities exclude any activity, such as the shoot in question, which is no more than an activity for pleasure and social enjoyment. In the *Yarburgh Children's Trust* case (see 13.33) the judge doubted that a parent-run charity playgroup operated on a break-even basis could be anything more than the charity carrying out its charitable functions. This was because the activity lacked any business or economic content.

For a case where the CJEU gets close to the UK's business tests approach in deciding if an activity is business, see the *Rēdlihs* case in 4.1.7 below and 13.24.

4.1.6 **Non-business assets**

The HMRC guidance on capital assets (*VAT Notice 706/2*, section 5.1) explains that HMRC accepts that if a business also has non-business activities, it can opt to acquire and hold assets outside the VAT system:

> You may make a choice, when acquiring an asset, to exclude all or part of it from your business's assets, by holding it privately or as a non-business asset. If such an option is made, the excluded element never forms part of your business assets. The option is only available if you have private or non-business activities. If all or part of an asset is excluded from your business assets because you hold it for private or non-business use, the costs and related VAT are also excluded from the VAT system... the related VAT is always non-deductible and will not benefit from adjustment if taxable use increases.

4.1.7 **Sale of non-business assets**

When a business sells a non-business asset the sale can be within or outside the scope of VAT. Two CJEU cases, C-291/92 *Finanzamt Uelzen* v. *Dieter Armbrecht* [1995] ECR I-02775 and C-263/11 *Ainārs Rēdlihs* v. *Valsts ieņēmumu dienests* [2012], illustrate the range of options.

In the *Armbrecht* case, the CJEU held that a taxable person is not precluded from retaining part of an item of property amongst their private assets and excluding it from the VAT system. The taxable person must, however, throughout their period of ownership of the property, demonstrate an intention to retain it amongst their private assets. This makes it possible for a taxable person to choose whether or not to integrate into their business part of an asset which is given over to their private use. See also 13.2.

In the *Rēdlihs* case Mr Rēdlihs purchased a forest for his personal use. A storm subsequently blew down some of the trees. Mr Rēdlihs sold the fallen trees, making 37 separate supplies of timber over a period of 9 months. The question was whether this was an economic activity. The CJEU left the matter for the referring court to decide based on the facts but proposed the following approach:

1. Is the subject matter suitable only for economic exploitation?
2. Is the subject matter subject to economic exploitation by economic operators and if so are the circumstances similar to the circumstances in which the corresponding economic activity is usually carried out?
3. Does the supplier take active steps by mobilising resources similar to those deployed by a producer, a trader or a person supplying services?

4. The actual length of the period over which the supplies took place, the number of customers and the amount of earnings are also factors which, forming part of the circumstances of the case as a whole, may be taken into account, with others.
5. The fact that a person acquired the tangible property to meet their own personal needs does not preclude that property from being subsequently used for the purposes of the exercise of an economic activity.

See also 13.24.

4.1.8 Public bodies

Activities and transactions engaged in as a public authority by states, regional and local government authorities and other bodies governed by public law are regarded as non-business, even where they collect dues, fees, charges, etc. and would otherwise be regarded as business activities. Activities engaged in as a public authority are those engaged under the special legal regime applicable to the authority concerned and exclude activities pursued under the same legal conditions as those that apply to private businesses.

However, the following exceptions are treated as business activities:

1. Activities listed in Annex I to the Principal VAT Directive, provided that those activities are not carried out on such a small scale as to be negligible. The listed activities include: the supply of telecoms services; supplies of water, gas, electricity and thermal energy; port and airport services; passenger transport; the supply of new goods manufactured for sale; the organisation of trade fairs and exhibitions; and the running of staff shops, cooperatives, industrial canteens and similar institutions.
2. Activities or transactions whose treatment as non-business **would lead to significant** distortions of competition. In case C-288/07 *Revenue & Customs* v. *Isle of Wight Council* [2008] EWHC (Ch) ECR I-07203, the CJEU decided that the expression 'would lead to' encompasses not only actual competition, but also potential competition, provided that the possibility of a private operator entering the relevant market is real, and not purely hypothetical. The word 'significant' is to be understood as meaning that the actual or potential distortions of competition must be more than negligible.

4.2 EXCEPTIONS

There are many exceptions to the basic VAT rules. The exceptions covered in this section are:

1. disposal of business goods for no consideration;
2. change of use of business goods;

3. non-business use of services;
4. sales to connected parties;
5. HMRC directions: sales to unregistered sellers.

Other situations are covered in other chapters. These include:

- **Change of use of zero-rated buildings**: the construction or purchase of certain buildings is zero-rated dependent on the intended use. If actual use changes from that intended then a **deemed supply** can take place on which output VAT is due. See 8.3.13 'Change of use rules'.
- **Deregistration**: the retention of business assets on deregistration on which VAT has been recovered is a deemed supply. See 2.3 'Repaying VAT on deregistration'.
- **Self-build construction services**: there is a deemed self-supply for self-build constructions where the value of the labour element is £100,000 or more. See 8.3.12 'Self-supply of construction services'.
- **Removal of goods from one EU state to another**: there can be a deemed supply when goods are moved from one EU state to another, including within the same legal entity, see 9.6.9 'Removals'.

4.2.1   Disposal of business goods for no consideration

The disposal of business goods for no consideration is a deemed business supply of goods if VAT was wholly or partly recovered on the goods. However, there are the following exceptions and special rules:

- **Non-business goods**: there is no deemed supply for disposals of non-business goods for no consideration as no VAT is recoverable on the purchase of non-business goods.
- **Small-value business gifts**: there is no deemed supply for small-value business gifts. Business gift means that a gift of goods made in the course or furtherance of a business. Small value means the cost of all business gifts to the same person in any period of 12 months that includes the date of the gift is not more than £50. Business gifts to different individuals having the same employer are not treated as gifts made to the same person.
- **Business samples**: there is no deemed supply for business samples given away for free. A sample is a specimen of a product which is intended to promote the sales of that product and which allows the characteristics and qualities of that product to be assessed.
- **Valuation of the supply**: the value of the deemed supply is the consideration payable for identical or similar goods, or if that cannot be ascertained, the cost of the goods
- **Zero-rated gifts**: a gift of goods by a business to a charity for sale, letting or export is zero-rated (see 6.3.2 'Sale of donated goods'), so no output VAT is due on such gifts. An export of goods (to a place outside the EU) by a charity

for no consideration is deemed to be a zero-rated supply (see 6.3.1 'Export of goods by a charity'). Therefore no output VAT is due on such exports but associated UK input VAT costs can be recovered. If a gift of zero-rated goods such as qualifying printed matter is a deemed supply, it is a deemed zero-rated supply (*Church of England Children's Society* [2004] VTD 18633).

4.2.2 Private use of business goods

If business goods on which VAT has been wholly or partly recovered are put to a temporary private use, there is a deemed supply of services on which output VAT is payable to HMRC. The VAT on the deemed supply is irrecoverable. However, this rule does not apply to:

- any interest in land;
- a building or a part of a building;
- a civil engineering work;
- any goods incorporated or to be incorporated into a building or civil engineering work;
- any ship, boat or other vessel; or
- any aircraft.

If such items fall within the Capital Goods Scheme (CGS) (see 10.1 'Capital Goods Scheme'), then the CGS deals with the VAT recovery adjustment. Otherwise the extent of business use is determined in the year of acquisition and that initial VAT recovery then remains fixed.

4.2.3 Non-business use of services

If VAT was recovered on services which are then put to a non-business use, there is a deemed supply on which output VAT is due. The value of the deemed supply is the cost to the business of supplying the services. However, there are the following exceptions and concessions:

- **Part non-business use**: there is no deemed supply if VAT was only partly recovered under a business/non-business apportionment.
- **Minor or occasional changes of use and small-value gifts**: HMRC accepts that (*Business Brief 17/94*) minor or occasional changes of use can be ignored and that in practice most deemed supplies of services will occur where the change of use is permanent. HMRC also accepts that private or non-business use of services akin to business gifts attracts the same treatment as business gifts (see above) and that there is no deemed supply on services that are fully depreciated or where the output VAT on deemed supplies of the service exceeds the VAT, as has proved not to be **attributable** to business use (see 3.1 'VAT recovery principles').

4.2.4 Sales to connected parties

Where goods or services, on which VAT has been recovered, are supplied at less than their open market value to a connected party, and the connected party cannot recover all of the VAT incurred on the supply, then HMRC may, at its discretion, deem the supply to be at open market value for VAT purposes. Any output VAT due to HMRC is calculated as a percentage of the open market value rather than on the net amount actually paid.

4.2.5 HMRC direction: sales to unregistered sellers

Where a business supplies goods to unregistered sellers, for onward sale by those sellers, then HMRC has the power to direct that the value of the business's supplies for VAT purposes is the open market value of the goods rather than the actual consideration received.

HMRC uses this power where school photographs are sold to parents by unregistered schools. If the photographer sells the photographs to the school at a discount to the final retail price charged to parents, and if the total value of sales by the photographer to the school and/or other registered persons for re-sale exceeds £50,000 per annum, HMRC policy is to issue a notice of direction requiring the photographer to account for VAT on the retail selling price (*VTAXPER72000*)

4.3 NON-BUSINESS ACTIVITIES

This section examines common activities of voluntary organisations from a business/non-business perspective.

4.3.1 Grants, donations, contributions and subsidies

Most grants from public bodies and grant-giving charities, public donations, legacies and other bona fide gifts received by charities and other voluntary organisations are not consideration for any supply and so are non-business income.

This is subject, however, to the requirement that the funds are not paid subject to any condition that the recipient makes a supply of goods or services. If a grant is paid subject to the condition that a supply is made, then the grant is potentially, consideration for that supply. In *Landboden-Agrardienste* (1997) the Advocate General explained the distinction between 'subsidies' (i.e. grants, etc.) and consideration:

> The [VAT] Directive makes only limited provision for taxation of subsidies. [It] includes in the taxable amount 'subsidies directly linked to the price' of supplies.

Thus, a subsidy will be included in the taxable amount if it is paid subject to the condition that the recipient makes a supply of goods or services. For example, a support measure whereby a farmer receives a certain sum for each product sold forms part of the consideration for the supply. On the other hand, subsidies that are more remote from particular supplies and intended more generally to improve the undertaking's economic position do not form part of the basis of assessment. Examples of such subsidies include subsidies for the purchase of assets, for covering losses and for the restructuring of an undertaking...

One might, with some justification, take the view that there is little, if any, point in imposing VAT on subsidies. By doing so a public authority simply claws back money which has been granted by itself or by another public authority; in the latter case taxation of subsidies amounts to a rather circuitous — and costly — way of reallocating revenue between public authorities. National taxation of Community subsidies would, for example, represent no more than a diversion of resources from the Community budget to that of a Member State.

4.3.2 Service level agreements

A grant-making charitable trust may achieve its objects through the work funded by its grants. However, this does not turn the grant into consideration for a supply. Administrative conditions attached to grants, such as the need to meet service standards or to complete returns or provide details of how the grant was spent, do not constitute a supply by the recipient charity to the grant-maker.

However, if a grant is paid subject to the condition that the recipient makes a supply of goods or services, it will be a supply – see 4.3.7 'Subsidies directly linked to the price of a supply'.

4.3.3 Parental contributions

In *Sheiling Trust* [2006] VTD 19472, parents were asked to make contributions towards a school's costs and a table of indicative contributions was provided. The evidence was that about half of the parents contributed the indicative average amounts, and the balance contributed more or less, with a significant number of parents contributing nothing in terms of payment, though many contributed substantially in other ways, such as by volunteering. The VAT Tribunal decided that this was not a business supply of education for the suggested contributions.

4.3.4 Contracts

A contract (under applicable UK or other law) normally creates the reciprocity necessary for a supply. Most contracts set out binding conditions under which something will be done (or not done) in return for a consideration. However, this does not automatically mean that the contract is a business supply:

- What is provided for the consideration must be a supply of goods or of services, so a contract not to do something, for example a contract under which a farmer agrees not to harvest potatoes, would not be a supply (see 13.18 '*Landboden-Agrardienste*').
- It must be a business supply in order for it to be within the scope of VAT, so it must pass the business tests. Contracts with public bodies and uncommercial contracts can fail the business tests in some situations. See 4.3.10 'Playgroups, nurseries, crèches and similar' and 4.3.11 'Government and local authority contracts'.
- HMRC accepts that public interest grants received by a lead partner on behalf of a consortium of charities can be passed on from the lead partner to the other partners under contract but treated as a non-business sharing of a grant in some situations, see 4.3.5 'Collaborative grant-funded projects'.
- Contracts executed as deeds do not always require a consideration, so they may be non-business on the basis of the *Hong-Kong Trade Development Council* case (see 13.14).
- There are several HMRC concessions or practices that might apply to allow treatment of contractual income as non-business, for example see 4.3.12 'The 15% welfare services concession', and 4.3.13 'Advertising in charity publications'.

4.3.5 **Collaborative grant-funded projects**

In *Revenue & Customs Brief 10/13* HMRC states:

> HMRC has been made aware that a significant amount of research is collaborative – indeed, this seems common in the case of research council funding. Collaborative research is where several bodies (typically universities or other eligible bodies) get together to apply for grant funding to undertake a research project. It is not uncommon for one of the applicants to be shown as the head or lead body which deals primarily with the funding body including receiving funding which is passed to other applicant bodies for their contribution to the project. For ease, contracts are often concluded only in the name of the funding body and the lead research body even though this is a collaborative project.

> HMRC will accept that in such cases of collaborative research, all research services provided by each of the bodies involved in the project are outside the scope of VAT, even if the funding may be passed on by the lead research body to others and that only the lead research body is party to the contract with the funding body.

> HMRC may ask for evidence that research bodies are participating in collaborative research; the best evidence of that will be the original application for funding

which would, in many cases, show who all the collaborative partners are. However, HMRC will accept any alternative evidence that clearly demonstrates that the bodies concerned were participating in collaborative research . . .

Situations where the funding will be outside the scope of VAT include:

- research which is funded for the 'general public good' and there is no direct benefit for the funding body
- research which is funded for the general public good and is either not expected to generate any intellectual property (IP), or if it does then any reports or findings will be freely available to others
- where there is a 'collaborative' agreement between different research institutions where all parties to the grant are named on the application
- where the funding flows through one named party – and they act purely as a conduit passing on the funds to others involved in the research project – the funding remains outside the scope of VAT

Where funding is provided to a named party for research that will either generate IP to be exploited by the funder and/or is not for the public good and they subsequently decide to sub-contract some of the research to an eligible body (for example a university), the initial funding to the named party (assuming an eligible body) will be taxable consideration for a supply.

It is difficult to see why this principle should not apply more widely than to collaborative research projects, for example by including Department for International Development (DFID) funded collaborative aid projects and similar.

At the time of writing, HMRC has been approached regarding the VAT statuses of aid contracts with DFID and between DFID-funded partners. HMRC appears sympathetic to the view that these are non-business in the same way. However, there is as yet no formal acceptance of this by HMRC.

4.3.6   Grants in support of business activities

If an activity is business then receipt of a grant as subsidy for the activity will not necessarily stop the activity from being wholly a business activity and thus will not necessarily block full recovery of VAT on purchases attributable to the activity.

Examples are a start-up grant to support a taxable business activity, grants for the purchase of assets, and grants for covering losses and for restructuring costs. The grant may be outside the scope of VAT, but if the funded activity is taxable the VAT on the inputs is recoverable, including on the costs of applying for the grant.

4.3.7   **Subsidies directly linked to the price of a supply**

Grants can be subject to VAT if they are a 'subsidy directly linked to the price of a supply'. This usually occurs where a third party, usually a public body, subsidises a specific supply so as to reduce the cost of that supply to a final consumer. This includes where the third party pays for the supply in full, so that the cost to the final customer is nil. The subsidy may be expressed as a fixed amount per sale made or as a percentage of the price charged to each qualifying customer or as a percentage of the cost of goods or services provided free of charge. In effect the third party is paying a part or the whole of the consideration for the supply.

This is illustrated by the CJEU case C-353/00 *Keeping Newcastle Warm Ltd* v. *Customs & Excise* [2002] ECR I-05419. Keeping Newcastle Warm was a business providing energy efficiency advice to local residents. It received a government grant of £10 for every piece of energy-saving advice it gave. The CJEU held the grant to be part of the consideration for the supply of energy advice. The Advocate General in the case drew a distinction between subsidies that were directly linked to a supply (as in this case), which could be consideration for a supply, and global subsidies which would generally not constitute consideration for a supply. Thus block grants are treated as a   general subsidy of operating costs, even though such subsidies may have the overall effect of reducing prices. To be caught by the subsidies rule, there must be a direct link between a subsidy-qualifying sale and the subsidy such that when the sale has occurred there is a right to the subsidy. The subsidy must have the effect of reducing the price that would otherwise be charged to the customer.

In *Landboden-Agrardienste* (1997) the Advocate General explained the problem that the inclusion of subsidies directly linked to the price of a supply as consideration for a business supply creates for the VAT system:

> the [VAT] Directive stipulates that subsidies received by a taxable person which are 'directly linked to the price' of the supplies made by that person must be included in the taxable amount as components of the prices paid by third parties.

> While it is relatively easy to decide straight away that subsidies are 'directly linked to the price' when their amount is determined either by reference to the selling price of the goods or services supplied, or in relation to the quantities sold, or again in relation to the cost of goods or services supplied to the public free of charge, it is extremely difficult to decide in the case of other types of subsidy such as deficit subsidies or operating subsidies, which are paid with the aim of improving a firm's economic position and which are granted without specific reference to any price.

> The absence of any substantial difference between these two types of subsidy (those 'directly linked to the price' are usually also aimed at improving a firm's

position), together with the fact that a Member State can convert a subsidy of the first type into a subsidy of the second type, illustrate the fragility of a distinction based on purely formal criteria (the manner in which the subsidy is granted) and thus the inadequacy of the Directive in this respect. Nevertheless the treatment of subsidies in the Directive may be seen to conform to the general rule that there should be a direct link between a supply and the consideration given. It might also be justified on the ground that subsidies granted with reference to specific supplies are likely to have a more direct impact on competition. Superficially at least, there seems to be a greater case for treating such subsidies as part of the price paid by (or on behalf of) the consumer.

4.3.8 Making errors in the VAT treatment of grants and contracts

Long-standing HMRC policy was to take a pragmatic approach when a charity has made errors and to inhibit penalties and interest when the charity had taken reasonable steps to establish the VAT status (*V1–9 Charities*, section 10.2):

10.2 What if a charity has incorrectly treated funding as an outside the scope grant?

You will need to consider the correct liability of the supply being made by the charity. If the supply is taxable then it may be appropriate for you to assess the charity for the tax due on the supplies made, which the charity can in turn charge on to the funder.

However, before assessing you should carefully consider all the papers available regarding the funding. The responsibility is on the charity, as the supplier, to determine the VAT liability of the supply.

This guidance has since been reduced to the first two paragraphs quoted above (at *VCHAR10000*), though the final two paragraphs may still be relevant where the error was made prior to March 2015:

This is not always a straightforward task. You may find that the charity has made reasonable enquiries of the funder in an attempt to establish whether they are making a supply, but has effectively been misled by the funder or the funder has been less than helpful. For example, the funder may have insisted that the monies are a 'grant' or specifically said in accompanying contracts or paperwork that the funding is either exempt from VAT or outside the scope.

You should also consider other factors, such as whether the charity is VAT registered and is likely to have had access to appropriate professional advice, and whether the charity has charged VAT in respect of other funding agreements it has with Government. If you conclude that the charity took reasonable steps to establish the supply position you should take a pragmatic approach and ensure that you inhibit any interest and penalties on any assessment you may raise. If you are in any doubt please contact the Charities Policy Team for advice.

4.3.9 **Goods and services provided free of charge**

Goods and services provided genuinely free of charge by charities and voluntary organisations in furtherance of their objects are unlikely to be considered supplied for consideration on the basis of the CJEU decision in the *Hong-Kong Trade Development Council* case (see 13.14). Examples include rescue at sea, ambulance services, first aid, emergency relief goods, religious ceremonies, free education, free goods and services for the poor and free admission to a museum or gallery.

However, the provision of goods or services for free can also be business supply, for example:

- if VAT is recovered on goods or services that are provided for free, there may be a deemed supply on which output VAT is due when they are given away. See 4.2 'Exceptions'.
- The provision of free services can be ancillary to a business activity, in which case VAT incurred on the free goods or services is recoverable if the activity is taxable. For example, if a museum or gallery provides free entrance offers as a trade promotion or if a professional association provides free or reduced-rated membership to students or trainees to encourage later membership, the free activity is not a separate non-business activity, see 3.3.12 'Free admissions or membership'.
- A business can give away free small-value promotional business goods and business samples without losing VAT recovery on those goods. See 4.2.1 'Disposal of business goods for no consideration'.
- Where a charity provides goods free of charge to a destination outside the EU, for example as aid or disaster relief, it is deemed to be a zero-rated business activity. This allows the charity to recover all associated input VAT. See 6.3.1 'Export of goods by a charity'.

4.3.10 **Playgroups, nurseries, crèches and similar**

The High Court case *Customs & Excise* v. *Yarburgh Children's Trust* [2001] EWHC 2201 (Ch) concerned a co-operatively run charitable playgroup whose fees were subsidised. The High Court held that this was not a business activity and that an intention to trade at a profit is not an essential feature of a business, but it is relevant to the consideration of whether a charity can seriously be regarded as doing anything more than the carrying out of its charitable functions. In the *St Paul's Community Project* case a Sure Start playgroup charging subsidised fees of £85–£95 per place per week was held to be non-business on a similar basis. HMRC set out their position on charity-run playgroups, nurseries, crèches and similar in *Business Brief 02/05*:

> The Court found that the intrinsic nature of the enterprise was not the carrying on of a business, identifying the distinguishing features as the social concern for

the welfare of disadvantaged children, lack of commerciality in setting fees and the overall intention simply to cover costs. Customs do not agree that these features point to the activities being non-business because we consider that the charity is making supplies of services for consideration in much the same way as a commercial nursery. However, taking into account all the circumstances in this case, Customs have decided not to appeal further. This means Customs will now accept that the provision of nursery and crèche facilities by charities, along the same lines as those in Yarburgh Children's Trust and St Paul's Community Project Ltd, is not a business activity for VAT purposes.

At the time of writing, *Business Brief 02/05* is still in force, so HMRC should accept that the provision of playgroups, nurseries, crèches, parent and toddler clubs, etc. by a charity is non-business where the above three conditions are all met; that is, that there is a social concern for the welfare of disadvantaged children, a lack of commerciality in setting fees and the overall intention is simply to cover costs.

4.3.11 Government and local authority contracts

In several cases the tribunals have decided that services provided under contract to local authorities, and regional and central government are non-business:

In *Donaldson's College* [2005] VTD 19258, a charity operated a school for deaf and hearing-impaired children. It was funded 35% by fees charged to each child's local authority and 65% by a block grant from the Scottish government. The Tribunal decided that the services were not provided to the local authority, the entire exercise being for all practical purposes controlled by central government.

Similar decisions were reached in *Quarriers 1* [2008] VTD 20660 and *Quarriers 2* [2008] VTD 20670. The first concerned supplies of epilepsy assessment services under contract to health boards in Scotland and the second charges made to local authorities for places at a residential school for children with severe emotional difficulties.

4.3.12 The 15% welfare services concession

HMRC provides the following concession (*VAT Notice 701/1*, section 5.18.2):

Charities that provide welfare services at significantly below cost, to distressed persons for the relief of their distress, may treat these supplies as non-business and outside the scope of VAT. 'Significantly below cost' means subsidised by at least 15%, and the subsidy must be available to everyone. The charity must be providing the service to the distressed individual, and not a local authority.

By 'distressed' we mean someone who is suffering pain, grief, anguish, severe poverty, etc. An example of a non-business welfare service would be a night shelter for the homeless where a nominal charge of £1 per bed per night is made by the charity. However, the cost to the charity of providing the shelter might be £10 per bed per night.

This concession was introduced in 1973 when VAT was introduced as a result of charity concerns about its potential impact on welfare services that, while not supplied free, are supplied at significantly below cost. At the time such welfare services were standard-rated, the VAT exemptions for welfare services only being introduced later. It was agreed that supplies by charities of welfare services, at significantly below cost, to distressed persons for the relief of their distress would be regarded as non-business and the concession has been in place ever since.

Local authority contracts

HMRC provides the following guidance on the exclusion of local authority contracts (*VCHAR3540*):

Charities often provide welfare services such as day centres, meals on wheels, etc., under contract to local authorities. Charities will often tender for such work in competition with commercial providers. Where there is a contractual relationship between a charity and a local authority for the provision of services the supply is always to the local authority. This would always be a business activity. This is the case even if the supply to the local authority is made below cost.

Intent to subsidise

The main point on which HMRC will need to be satisfied is that there is deliberate policy to subsidise welfare supplies by at least 15%. The subsidy should not be achieved as a result of circumstance or unintentionally (*VCHAR3580*).

Availability

In order to qualify as a non-business activity HMRC will need to be satisfied that the subsidised services are available equally to all distressed persons. The subsidy must be available not only to those people who cannot afford to pay the full rate but also to those who can afford to do so. In addition, it must not be applied conditionally, for example, only during spells of very cold weather or only to persons living in a certain area or a person of a certain age (*VCHAR3600*).

Calculation of cost

The cost should be calculated to include all out-of-pocket expenses incurred by a charity in providing the welfare services. It should exclude (*VCHAR3560*):

- All capital expenditure on buildings: inclusion of these values would distort the cost of making the welfare supplies.
- Notional charges for depreciation: these are not actual charges incurred.
- The creation of financial reserves, contingency funds, etc.: these are not actual charges.
- No account should be taken of what it would cost a commercial organisation to provide the same service. Therefore the fact that a charity may benefit from using unpaid volunteer labour means that the cost of providing the service is less. What is important is the actual cost, not the commercial value.
- Similarly donated goods for use in the provision of welfare services should not be included, as they cost nothing.

Uncertainty

If a charity is unsure if it will meet the 15% subsidy level, HMRC would suggest that at the start of its financial year the charity should calculate, by reference to its projected income and expenditure figures, whether or not it expected to break even, or to what extent it expected to subsidise the operation. The outcome of this calculation would enable the charity to decide if it could expect to be engaged in a business or non-business activity for the coming year. HMRC would accept that the outcome would be valid for the whole financial year.

Application for zero-rating reliefs

HMRC accepts that the concession can increase charities' entitlement to reliefs linked to non-business activity (*VCHAR3520*). See in particular the zero-rating reliefs for qualifying buildings, 8.3 'Property VAT reliefs'.

4.3.13   Advertising in charity publications

HMRC provides the following concession (*VAT Notice 701/1*, section 5.2):

> Charities sometimes sell advertising space in their own brochures, programmes, annual reports or similar. The sale of such advertising space is a business activity and is normally standard-rated (the sale of such space can be zero-rated if supplied to another charity). However, if 50% or more of the total adverts in a publication are clearly placed by private individuals the charity can treat all the sums received as donations and outside the scope of VAT.
>
> What is a private advertisement? A private advertisement makes no reference to a business. An example of a private advertisement is one that says 'Good wishes from (or 'space donated by') John and Susan Smith'; but not those with otherwise similar wording taken out by say, 'John and Susan Smith, Grocers, 49 High Street, Anytown'.

4.3.14   Minimum and suggested donations

Benefits freely given to solicit or acknowledge donations are not supplies as long as a minimum donation is not specified. For example, if at a charity open day people are told that they may help themselves to tea and cakes in return for a donation, with no minimum donation specified, there is no supply of the tea or cakes as there is no consideration, and any donations made are outside the scope of VAT.

Where benefits are provided to the donor conditional on the donation being at or above a specified minimum, the minimum donation amount is likely to be seen as consideration for the benefits offered: any donation that is above the minimum donation is seen as a genuine donation that is outside the scope of VAT.

In the case *Glasgow's Miles Better Mid-Summer Ball* [1989] VTD 4460, a voluntary organisation put on a ball in aid of a hospice. The organisation printed application forms for tickets which stated 'Please supply tickets at *£50 for the Mid-Summer Ball'. The asterisk referred to a line of very small print at the foot of the form which stated '*Price indication only. For VAT purposes the entrance fee is £20. The balance of £30 represents a minimum voluntary donation in aid of hospice funds.'

The Tribunal decided that the ordinary person, looking casually at the ticket or at the application form, would take the purchase price to be £50 and would not get the impression that entrance could be obtained for less. The whole £50 was therefore consideration for the ticket and not a donation. The Tribunal accepted that, if the price on the ticket had been £20, with the footnote indicating a hope that the purchaser would voluntarily donate at least a further £30, the consideration would have been accepted as being £20 with a donation of £30.

4.3.15   Trivial benefits for donation

HMRC accepts that negligible benefits provided in return for donations can be ignored, for example low-value stickers, badges, flags, etc. (*VCHAR3400*). Providing such tokens have no intrinsic value and are low-cost, HMRC does not regard the payment as consideration for the supply of the token. However, if a minimum or fixed price is required before a token is given, such a payment is regarded as the consideration for the supply of the token.

4.3.16   Free updates

In the case *Church of England Children's Society* [2004] VTD 18633, the VAT Tribunal held that, on the facts, a regular supporters' newsletter offered to committed givers was not goods supplied in return for any part of the committed givers' donations. The £5 monthly direct debit by the committed giver was a gift with a promise by the charity to send them the free newsletters so that they could monitor how their gift had been spent. Following the CJEU decision in *Kuwait Petroleum* (see 13.17), there was, at the time of donation, no evidence of any bargain between the parties that the donation would be wholly or partly consideration for the newsletters.

4.3.17 *De minimis* benefits for Gift Aid

The Gift Aid rules allow charities and Community Amateur Sports Clubs to give low-value benefits to donors without affecting their ability to claim Gift Aid on the donations. In addition, some donor benefits can be ignored for Gift Aid purposes. However, there are no similar arrangements for VAT. If a donor has to make a set 'minimum donation' to secure a specified package of benefits, that includes more than purely trivial benefits, then, in principle, the donation is consideration for the benefits and VAT potentially applies to the whole minimum donation amount.

This is illustrated by the case *Customs & Excise* v. *Tron Theatre* [1994] STC 177 in which a charity set up a 'sponsor a seat' scheme whose brochure indicated that, in return for a minimum donation of £150, a sponsor would receive a benefit package comprising a personalised brass plaque displayed on a theatre seat; acknowledgement of the donation in the theatre foyer; a commemorative limited edition print; and priority booking for two gala evenings. Many sponsors did not know or care about the benefits and thought that their value was about £5. The Court of Session held that the motives of the supplier or the recipient of a supply were not relevant and it was of no consequence if there was an element of overcharging or of donation in the sum which was paid; the consideration for the supply of benefits was the amount of money which had to be paid in order to receive them. It was irrelevant that the motive of the sponsors was to increase the company's funds by including a large element of donation in the consideration which had to be paid.

Despite this case, HMRC accepts that names on seat plaques and names on donor boards can be ignored as nominal membership benefits in some situations – see 11.4 'Membership subscriptions'.

In *Serpentine Trust Ltd* v. *Revenue & Customs* [2014] UKFTT 876 (TC) an art gallery operated a supporter scheme in which pre-set packages (benefactor, patron, etc.) of substantive benefits were offered each for a specified minimum donation. The minimum donation was designed to fit within the Gift Aid donor benefit limits, including, for some levels of supporter, the 5% cap on benefits for donations above £1,000. Donor benefits included: free invitations to private views, a monthly online Art Tour; advance notice to purchase limited edition prints; priority bookings and various acknowledgements as a benefactor. The benefits were held to be supplied for the minimum donation.

4.3.18   Gift Aid split payment treatment

If a benefit value exceeds the Gift Aid donor benefit limits, then for Gift Aid purposes HMRC (2013, *Charities: detailed guidance notes*, chapter 3, s. 3.25.1) accepts that a donor can 'buy the benefit', so a part of their payment is consideration for the benefits and the balance is a Gift Aidable donation. This is subject to two conditions:

- the benefit can be purchased separately; and
- the donor is aware of the value of the benefit at the time the donation is made.

In *VAT Notice 701/1*, section 5.2, HMRC accepts that if a patron or supporter pays more than a minimum amount you can treat the excess as a donation and outside the scope of VAT as long as the patron or supporter is aware that scheme benefits are available for a given amount, and that anything in excess of that amount is a voluntary donation. This should be explicit in the patron or supporter scheme literature.

4.3.19   Membership subscriptions

An HMRC extra-statutory concession (*VAT Notice 48*, section 3.35, known as ESC 3.35) allows the consideration payable for membership subscriptions charged by non-profit membership bodies to be treated as apportioned according to the VAT treatment of each of the benefits provided. For example, the provision of qualifying printed matter is zero-rated and the provision of an eligible educational course is VAT exempt. In this apportionment nominal benefits can be ignored. Nominal benefits include:

- simple acknowledgements of support in the form of membership badges, flags or stickers; and
- listing of names in a programme or on a theatre seat or entrance.

HMRC also accepts (*VAT Notice 701/5*, section 5.3) that a membership body may treat part of a subscription as a voluntary payment or donation if either:

- all the substantive benefits provided are available to non-members at no charge or more cheaply than the subscription; you should ignore any nominal benefits;
- some or all of the substantive benefits are exclusive to members and you are able to demonstrate that the amount paid is higher than the amount that the subscriber would normally have to pay for similar goods or services.

See 11.4 'Membership subscriptions' for more on the VAT treatment of membership subscriptions.

4.3.20 Investment income and gains

Several court cases have established that the passive generation of investment income and gains from shares, bonds and other forms of financial investment by a charity or other voluntary organisation is a non-business activity. See 13.32 'Wellcome Trust' and 13.10 'Fanfield and Thexton'.

4.3.21 Secondment of staff

By concession (*VAT Notice 701/1*, section 5.17) HMRC accepts that supplies of staff from one not-for-profit organisation to another (excluding public bodies) can be treated as non-business; therefore any charges made for the staff are outside the scope of VAT. See 11.1 'Supplies of staff'.

4.3.22 Non-returnable deposits

The VAT status of non-returnable deposits depends on whether or not they count towards payment for an ultimate supply. If the deposit counts towards the final consideration for any supply, then the VAT status of the deposit follows that of the supply. If a non-returnable deposit is taken and the customer defaults, so that there is no supply, then the forfeited deposit is not consideration for any supply and is therefore outside the scope of VAT (see 13.28 'Société Thermale d'Eugénie-les-Bains').

4.3.23 Insurance claims

Claim payments by insurance companies are compensation for the loss suffered and are outside the scope of VAT. If the loss was suffered on non-business or exempt activities, on which VAT is irrecoverable, the irrecoverable VAT should form part of the claim.

4.3.24 Compensation and damages

Most compensation and damages payments amount to a financial settlement of losses caused by the breach of an agreement or the infringement of rights. As such, there is no supply and so the compensation payment is outside the scope of VAT. However, compensation agreements can sometimes include the granting of rights by one party to the other, in which case any settlement may comprise partly or wholly consideration for the supply of the rights.

4.3.25   **Fines and penalties**

HMRC accepts that fines and penalties levied for a breach of contract or agreement are not consideration for a supply; however, excess charges, calculated within the terms of the agreement, are consideration for a supply of the extra services. Following a case involving the VAT treatment of penalties and excess charges levied in car parks (*Bristol City Council* [2004] VATTR 1766), HMRC issued *Revenue & Customs Brief 57/08* clarifying the distinction:

> We now accept that there is a difference between the situation where the contract under which parking is supplied allows for an extension of the original terms, for which additional consideration will be payable, and the situation where the driver is not permitted to extend the original terms and a penalty for breach of contract ensues if this in fact happens. Thus, where a car park operator makes an offer of parking under clear terms and conditions, setting punitive fines for their breach, the fines constitute penalties for breaching the contract, rather than additional consideration for using the facilities. Consequently, they are outside the scope of VAT.

4.3.26   **Disbursements**

A payment by an **agent** (see 11.2) on another person's behalf is called a disbursement, for example where a conveyancing solicitor pays for a search fee. The agent records the disbursement as a debtor (amounts receivable), and when a compensating amount is received, that receipt does not count as income but is used to settle the debt. As such, the receipt is outside the scope of VAT in the hands of the agent. See 11.2.4 'Disbursements'.

5 Exempt activities

The following VAT exemptions are covered in this chapter:

Exemptions in the public interest
- 5.1 Education and vocational training
- 5.2 Health and welfare
- 5.3 Cultural services
- 5.4 Sports and physical education
- 5.5 Subscriptions to public interest bodies
- 5.6 Cost sharing groups
- 5.7 Fundraising events
- 5.8 Public postal services

Other exemptions
- 5.9 Insurance services
- 5.10 Betting, lotteries and other forms of gambling
- 5.11 Sale of business goods on which VAT was wholly irrecoverable

Further exemptions include **supplies of land and buildings** and **the leasing or letting of immovable property** – see Chapter 8 'Property' for more on these exemptions.

Scope of the exemptions

The VAT exemptions covered in this chapter are all set out in EU law (mainly in Articles 132 to 135 of the Principal VAT Directive) and must be implemented by the UK. The UK implementation is in section 9 of VAT Act 1994.

The case law of the Court of Justice of the EU (CJEU or ECJ) has established broad principles that apply to the various VAT exemptions. The terms used to describe the exemptions ('education', 'sport', 'insurance services', etc.) are independent concepts of EU law. They must be interpreted consistently throughout the EU in order to avoid divergences in the application of VAT from one EU state to another. They must be interpreted strictly, since they constitute exceptions to the general principle that VAT is to be levied on all business supplies. Nevertheless:

1. any interpretation must be consistent with the objectives pursued by the exemptions. The broad objective of the exemptions in the public interest is to

encourage certain public interest activities by relieving the final consumer of the burden of VAT;

2. the exemptions must comply with the requirements of the principle of fiscal neutrality, that is, supplies that meet the same needs of a customer should receive the same VAT treatment; and

3. the requirement of strict interpretation does not mean that the terms used should be construed in such a way as to deprive the exemption of its intended effect.

Direct effect

The Principal VAT Directive can take precedence over UK law; this is referred to as EU law having **direct effect**. The CJEU ruled in case C-8/81 *Ursula Becker* v. *Finanzamt Münster-Innenstadt* [1982] ECR 53 that in the absence of duly adopted implementing measures, individuals and organisations may invoke provisions of the Principal VAT Directive which are unconditional and sufficiently precise, against all UK legislation which does not conform with it. Individuals and organisations may also invoke provisions of the Principal VAT Directive if they lay down rights which can be enforced against the UK government.

This principle has been used on several occasions to establish that some of the UK's implementations of the VAT exemptions are too narrow:

- In the *Horizon College* case (C-434/05 *Stichting Regionaal Opleidingen Centrum Noord-Kennemerland/West-Friesland (Horizon College)* v. *Staatssecretaris van Financiën* [2007] ECR I-04793), the CJEU ruled that (contrary to UK law) supplies closely related to an exempt supply of education do not have to be for the direct use of a person receiving VAT-exempt education in order to be exempt from VAT. See 5.1 'Education and vocational training'.
- In the *Canterbury Hockey* case (see 5.4.3 'Persons taking part in sport'), the CJEU ruled that UK law cannot limit the sporting exemption to supplies to individuals.
- In case C-495/12 *Revenue & Customs* v. *Bridport & West Dorset Golf Club Ltd* [2013] UKUT (TCC), the CJEU ruled that the UK could not impose a minimum three-month membership requirement before the sporting exemption applied to subscriptions to membership sports clubs. See 5.4 'Sports and physical education'. This requirement was removed from UK law with effect from 1 January 2015.
- In *Revenue & Customs* v. *British Film Institute* [2014] UKUT 370 (TCC), the Upper Tribunal ruled that the UK cannot limit the cultural exemption to particular types of admission (though at the time of writing HMRC has appealed this decision to the Court of Appeal and the matter has been referred to the CJEU). See 5.3 'Cultural services'.

- In *Loughborough Students' Union* v. *Revenue & Customs* [2013] UKUT 517 (TCC), the Upper Tribunal questioned whether the UK's fundraising exemption rules are too restrictive in requiring the exemption to be limited to events that are primarily for raising funds and promoted as such, though at the time of writing the matter is still before the courts. See 5.7 'Fundraising events'.

In light of these problems, when considering the VAT exemptions it is sometimes necessary to consider the wording of the EU law as well as the UK law. For this reason each section below sets out the EU law as well as the UK law and considers some of the differences.

Exemptions in the public interest

When supplied by non-public bodies, EU member states may restrict the following exemptions in the public interest to supplies of such services by particular **eligible bodies** as defined by the member state:

- hospital and medical care;
- welfare and social security work;
- protection of children and young persons;
- education and vocational training;
- subscriptions to public interest bodies;
- sports and physical education;
- cultural services;
- fundraising events put on by any of the above types of eligible body.

EU member states may subject eligible bodies to one or more of the following conditions:

- The bodies in question must not systematically aim to make a profit, and any surpluses nevertheless arising must not be distributed, but must be assigned to the continuance or improvement of the services supplied. In the UK this condition applies (partly) for the purposes of the education exemption, the cultural exemption, the sporting and public interest body subscription exemptions.
- Those bodies must be managed and administered on an essentially voluntary basis by persons who have no direct or indirect interest, either themselves or through intermediaries, in the results of the activities concerned. In the UK this condition applies for the purposes of the cultural exemption.
- Those bodies must charge prices which are approved by the public authorities or which do not exceed such approved prices or, in respect of those services not subject to approval, prices lower than those charged for similar services by commercial enterprises subject to VAT. This condition is not currently applied in the UK.

- The exemptions must not be likely to cause distortion of competition to the disadvantage of commercial enterprises subject to VAT. This condition applies in the UK for the purposes of the fundraising and cost sharing exemptions.

5.1 EDUCATION AND VOCATIONAL TRAINING

EU law

The Principal VAT Directive exempts the following transactions:

- Article 132(1)(i) the provision of children's or young people's education, school or university education, vocational training or retraining, including the supply of services and of goods closely related thereto, by bodies governed by public law having such as their aim or by other organisations recognised by the member state concerned as having similar objects.
- Article 132(1)(j) tuition given privately by teachers and covering school or university education.

UK law

VAT Act 1994 (Schedule 9, Part II, Group 6) exempts:

- the provision of education or vocational training by an eligible body;
- research supplied by one eligible body to another (to 31 July 2013 only);
- supplies closely related to the above;
- private tuition;
- examination services;
- government-funded education and vocational training;
- youth club facilities.

Each exemption is considered below. References to HMRC guidance are, unless otherwise stated, to *VAT Notice 701/30.*

5.1.1 Eligible body

Some of the UK education exemptions only apply when the supplier or customer is an eligible body. Eligible body, for the purposes of the education exemption, means a body of any of the following six types:

(a) **Recognised schools**: a school recognised in UK law, including LEA, independent, grant maintained, community, foundation and voluntary schools, academies and free schools.
(b) **Universities**: a UK university, and any college, institution, school or hall of such a university.
(c) **Further and higher education bodies**: these include a further education corporation, a designated institution for the purposes of Education Act 1992

(and Welsh or Scottish equivalents), a university receiving statutory financial support and other statutorily defined bodies.

(d) **Public bodies**: certain public bodies (government departments, local authorities, and 'any body which acts under any enactment or instrument for public purposes and not for its own profit and which performs functions similar to those of a Government department or local authority').

(e) **Certain non-profit-making bodies**: these are any bodies which meet both of the following conditions:

   (i) **Profit-distributing condition**: they are precluded from distributing and does not distribute any profit it makes; and

   (ii) **Ring-fencing condition**: they apply any profits made from educational supplies to the continuance or improvement of such supplies.
   Educational supplies are supplies of education, vocational training, closely related supplies, examination services, grant-funded education and vocational training and youth clubs.

   See below for more on these two conditions.

(f) **Other bodies**: an organisation providing teaching of English as a foreign language (EFL); however, the exemption only applies to the tuition in EFL.

Profit-distributing condition

Charities and other voluntary organisations which are precluded from distributing profits in their governing documents should qualify for this condition if they do not actually distribute any profits. However, HMRC will look for disguised distributions. HMRC states (*VATEDU39700*):

> Any profit (the eligible body) does make must be reinvested in the education it supplies. By this we mean that the profits are used to support the range of education supplied. Profit from, for example, art courses can be used to support courses other than art.

> We are aware of arrangements whereby bodies that would ordinarily make profit from educational courses argue that they meet the terms of (e) above because such sums are passed to associated companies through charges such as rent or management charges, or alternatively, because such profits are covenanted to a parent company. We do not agree with either argument...

Ring-fencing condition

If educational activities overall, including apportioned support costs, make a loss or break even over the medium to long term then this condition is presumably satisfied, as there are no profits to be applied; similarly if educational activities have to be subsidised by other activities or sources of funding. Profit determination can presumably be made on a full cost recovery basis and/or on the basis of figures from the statutory accounts.

University institutions

VAT Information Sheet 03/10 sets out HMRC's policy on when a separately registered company is a college, institution, school or hall of a university. HMRC sees three key 'themes' that should be present:

- There must be a close relationship between the university and the company. In the case of a university-owned/controlled company this is always likely to be present.
- The company must provide university-level education leading to a qualification awarded by the parent university or a nationally recognised body. This would include so-called 'closed' university-level courses that are intended to lead to a qualification; that is, the fact that access to the courses may be restricted, priced 'commercially' or run at a profit is not determinative of their status in this context.
- If students on the course are registered/enrolled with the parent university, are subject to its rules and regulations, and are awarded qualifications by it (with the implication that the university monitors, quality assures and validates the company's courses), it is likely that the company is acting as an institution, school or hall of a university and is therefore an eligible body.

HMRC's view is that a university-owned/controlled company with close academic links to its parent university that is delivering university-level education leading to a qualification is likely to be, de facto, acting as a college or an institution of the university. The absence of formal recognition as such a body, or the fact that it may trade with a view to profit does not exclude that company from that classification.

CJEU case law on eligible bodies

In case C-319/12 *Minister Finansów* v. *MDDP sp. z o.o. Akademia Biznesu sp. komandytowa* [2013] the CJEU held that eligible bodies for the purposes of the education exemption are restricted to bodies whose aim is the provision of children's or young people's education, school or university education, vocational training or retraining, including the supply of services and of goods closely related thereto. The CJEU held that Poland, in allowing the exemption of supplies of education by any type of supplier, had exceeded its authority. An education eligible body must have the required educational aim, and it must either be a public body or another type of organisation recognised as having an educational aim by the member state concerned.

5.1.2 **Education**

The provision by an eligible body of education is VAT exempt. The VAT Act 1994 does not define education; however, HMRC defines it as follows (*VAT Notice 701/30*, section 5.1):

What does the term 'education' cover?

Education means a course, class or lesson of instruction or study in any subject, regardless of when and where it takes place.

- Education includes: lectures; educational seminars; conferences and symposia; recreational and sporting courses; and distance teaching and associated materials. If a separate charge is made for registration, this is part of the provision of education.
- Education does not include admission to events such as: plays; concerts; sports meetings; and exhibitions.

HMRC provides the following example (*VAT Notice 701/30*, section 5.2) from the sports sector, identifying the distinction as being between charges for classes that are led and directed, which are education, as opposed to charges for classes that are merely supervised, which are not education (however, these may be VAT exempt in their own right, see 5.4 'Sports and physical education').

If the supplier is:	And:	Then it is a:
running a gymnasium	supplying instruction in the use of equipment and warming-up techniques and assessing a person when he or she first enrols	supply of education
	charging the person to use the gym in a separate session where no instruction takes place	charge for admission
running a swimming pool	staff are on hand primarily to coach	supply of education
	staff are on hand primarily to satisfy health and safety and insurance requirements	charge for admission

CJEU case law on the meaning of education

Article 132(1)(i)–(j) of the Principal VAT Directive defines three types of education which qualify for exemption:

1. children's or young people's education;
2. school or university education; and
3. vocational training or retraining.

In the *Horizon College* case, the CJEU held that the educational activities referred to include two elements that must both be present:

- the transfer of knowledge and skills between a teacher and students; and
- the organisational framework of the establishment concerned; this means the whole framework of facilities, teaching materials, technical resources, educational policy and organisational infrastructure within the specific educational establishment in which those teachers work.

However, the extent of the organisational framework required may vary and be fairly minimal in the case of distance learning. In *Revenue & Customs* v. *The Open University* [2015] UKUT 263 (TCC), the Upper Tribunal asked itself what degree of organisational framework has to be found in order to satisfy the educational aim. It answered as follows:

> It seems clear that the mere provision of course materials with an educational content for use by other educational institutions would not suffice... If, on the other hand, distance learning materials were provided as self-contained courses, together with appropriate back-up material, in a way that was suitable for home study without the mediation of another educational institution, the position might well be different. The education would then be provided directly, and the lack of a conventional educational infrastructure would not necessarily be fatal. Indeed, if this were not so, bodies such as the Open University itself might have difficulty in satisfying the educational aim, but nobody suggests that to be the case. In short, I consider that it would be a mistake to apply the Horizon College test in a mechanical fashion, and the organisational framework that is required will vary according to the type of education that is being provided.

In case C-445/05 *Werner Haderer* v. *Finanzamt Wilmersdorf* [2007] ECR I-04841, a case concerning pottery classes provided in an adult education institute, the CJEU held that the concept of school or university education is not limited only to education which leads to examinations for the purpose of obtaining qualifications or which provides training for the purpose of carrying out a professional or trade activity, but includes other activities which are taught in schools or universities in order to develop pupils' or students' knowledge and skills, provided that those activities are not purely recreational. The Advocate General stated, in reference to pottery classes:

> there must of course be a defining line between exempt tuition and purely recreational activities of no educational value, but any subject or activity in which

instruction is commonly given in schools or universities must in my view fall within the scope of the exemption, regardless of whether it follows a strictly defined programme or curriculum.

Making education taxable

Eligible bodies sometimes seek to avoid VAT exemption by supplying education from a separate profit-distributing entity, for example a charity's trading subsidiary. This is usually done where the customer does not mind VAT being added to the contract price (for example where the customer is a public body, local authority or fully taxable business) in order to improve VAT recovery for the supplier. There are, however, several risks with this approach:

1. Such an arrangement is potentially notifiable to HMRC as a Listed Scheme (listed scheme 8. Education and training by a non-eligible body). See 10.15 'Listed and hallmarked schemes'. There are penalties for failure to notify use of a Listed Scheme on time.
2. If the essential aim of the scheme is to obtain a VAT advantage then it can potentially be unwound by HMRC using the *Halifax* case principles (see 10.14.1).
3. As explained above, HMRC is likely to see a university-controlled company as an eligible body in its own right.
4. The arrangement may simply not work if the separate profit-distributing entity is a 'shell'. In the case *Revenue & Customs* v. *Robert Gordon University* [2008] ScotCS CSIH 22, the University transferred some of its courses to a separate subsidiary (Univation) in order to make the supply of education a taxable supply. The customer (the Scottish Executive) could reclaim this VAT. The University aimed to cross-charge its own educational costs to Univation, as a taxable supply of 'resources and facilities', thereby rendering the VAT incurred on those costs recoverable. However, HMRC successfully argued that what the University supplied to Univation was itself education, as the University remained for all practical purposes in control of the staff, the provision of the courses, the monitoring of performance and staff discipline, the examination of the students, the awarding of their diplomas, the provision of the social and environmental services, and the preparation of the students for registration.

   The Court agreed, finding that there was no material difference between the situations before and after the Univation arrangement was entered into. The interposition of Univation in the chain of control, even if it had involved substantial as distinct from purely nominal intervention in management, did not alter the characterisation of the University's supply. In the Court's opinion, what the University supplied to Univation was education, just as much as was the supply the University made to the Scottish Executive prior to the arrangements with Univation. The result was that the input VAT incurred by the University in making its exempt supply of education to Univation was irrecoverable.

5.1.3 Vocational training or retraining

EC Implementing Regulation 282/1011 defines vocational training or retraining to include:

> instruction relating directly to a trade or profession as well as any instruction aimed at acquiring or updating knowledge for vocational purposes, regardless of the duration of a course

Vocational training is defined in UK legislation to mean: training, retraining or the provision of work experience for:

(a) any trade, profession or employment; or
(b) any voluntary work connected with:
  (i) education, health, safety, or welfare; or
  (ii) the carrying out of activities of a charitable nature.

Vocational training can include on-the-job training, classroom-type courses and other forms of instruction aimed at acquiring or updating knowledge for vocational purposes. However, it does not include consultancy designed to improve the efficiency or smooth running of the whole organisation, which should be standard-rated. Individual counselling is also excluded from this category, although it may be exempt if it is part of a training package or as a supply of welfare services (for which see 5.2.4 'Welfare services').

5.1.4 Research

UK law exempted the supply of research by one eligible body to another up to 31 July 2013.

The definition of **eligible body** with regard to research is the same as for education and vocational training above. This exemption was withdrawn for all written contracts not entered into by 1 August 2013 (see 'Transitional arrangements' below). This was after the European Commission objected that this UK exemption is not included in the Principal VAT Directive's list of exemptions.

Meaning of research

The HMRC guidance on research (*VATEDU37000*) states:

> **What is research?** Research means original investigation undertaken in order to gain knowledge and understanding. A supply is one of research whenever the activities are directed towards increasing areas of knowledge or understanding. It

is the intention at the beginning of a project that will determine whether the supply qualifies as research. If the intention is to progress understanding, the supply is one of research. On the other hand, research means more than simply confirming existing understandings...

Borderline areas In the absence of any legal definition of research, there are bound to be borderline cases where you cannot easily categorise the precise nature of the activity – for example, in distinguishing between research and consultancy. Although the availability of research funds can be a useful indicator that a project is research, you cannot always rely on this. Therefore, if you examine a contract but find that it does not give a sufficiently clear indication of the activity to enable you to decide whether it is research or consultancy, you should accept the eligible body's own categorisation, unless there are clear and compelling reasons to do otherwise.

Transitional arrangements

There is a transitional arrangement for supplies of research made under a written contract entered into before 1 August 2013 (whether or not work under these contracts has commenced by that date). The exemption can continue to apply to supplies within the scope of the contract as at 31 July 2013. HMRC provides the following guidance on these transitional arrangements in *VAT Information Sheet 11/13*:

If the contract is extended or varied (whether or not the consideration payable is increased) on or after 1 August 2013 then payments for these new or changed supplies will be standard-rated. Supplies relating to the contract as it stood at 31 July 2013 will remain exempt.

Some minor variations will not affect the liability of the original contract. This might include one or more of:- (i) Changing the supplier of a subcontracted service, (ii) Changing the order the contract is performed in, (iii) Minor changes to the delivery time of the contract and milestones (less than three months) providing there is no additional consideration. This list is not exhaustive but the changes involved must have only very minor impact of delivery of the contract as agreed at 31 July 2013.

However, substantial variations may include one or more of the following:- (i) Increases the length of the contract (over three months), (ii) Payment of additional consideration, (iii) Requirement for new or additional tests to be performed, (iv) Changes to the product or topic on which research is being carried out. Again, this list is not exhaustive as the impact needs otherwise to be determined on a case-by-case basis but the changes involved will impact on delivery of the contract as at 31 July 2013.

5.1.5 **Supplies closely related to the above**

UK law

A supply of any goods or services is VAT exempt if it meets all of the following conditions:

1. it is closely related to an exempt supply of education or vocational training (the principal supply);
2. it is supplied by or to the eligible body making the principal supply;
3. it is provided for the direct use of the pupil, student or trainee receiving the principal supply; and
4. where the supply is to the eligible body making the principal supply, it is made by another eligible body.

Examples of closely related supplies are accommodation, catering, transport, school trips and field trips for school pupils. In *VATEDU52000* HMRC accepts that food and drink supplied at or below cost to pupils from a tuck shop or vending machine run by a school takes on the same liability as the education.

Excluded supplies

In *VATEDU51600* HMRC states that it does not accept the following as being closely related supplies subject to the overriding principle that supplies of catering by an eligible body to its pupils, students or trainees are closely related:

- supplies to staff (including tutors on summer schools) and to other non-students;
- sales of goods from school shops, campus shops and student bars (subject to the above exception for supplies of catering to pupils, students or trainees);
- sales from vending machines to staff and visitors;
- sales of goods not needed for regular use in class;
- separately charged laundry and other personal services;
- sales of school uniforms and sports clothing;
- admission charges (other than for taking part in sports activities), for example admission to plays, concerts, dances, sporting venues, exhibitions, museums and zoos (though see the *Brockenhurst College* case below);
- administration and management services;
- commission for allowing sales by outside organisations at an educational establishment; and
- sales by a sole proprietor or partnership in connection with private tuition.

Grant-funded education

HMRC accepts that if the eligible body provides non-business education then supplies that are closely related to the non-business education are themselves non-business, as long as they are sold at or below cost (see 10.5 'Academies and free schools').

Supplies of teaching staff

If the school or educational institution supplies teaching staff to another educational institution, then this may qualify for exemption as a closely related supply, but not a supply of education. In the *Horizon College* case, the CJEU held that the making available, for **consideration** (see 1.2.1), of a teacher to an educational establishment in which that teacher temporarily carries out teaching duties under the responsibility of that establishment, may constitute a transaction that is exempt from VAT on the basis that it is a supply of services closely related to education, if such a teacher placement is a means of better enjoying the education deemed to be the principal service, provided that:

- both that principal service and the placement which is closely related to it are provided by eligible bodies;
- that placement is of a nature and quality such that, without recourse to such a service, there could be no assurance that the education provided by the host establishment and, consequently, the education from which its students benefit, would have an equivalent value; and
- the basic purpose of such a placement is not to obtain additional income by carrying out a transaction which is in direct competition with commercial enterprises liable for VAT.

The CJEU also held that it is not necessary for the closely related supply to be directly to the pupils or students.

Catering provided by student unions

HMRC provides the following concession in *VAT Notice 709/1*, section 5.5:

> If you are a student union and you are supplying catering (including hot take-away food) to students both on behalf, and with the agreement, of the parent institution, as a concession you can treat your supplies in the same way as the parent institution itself. This means that you can treat your supplies as exempt when made by unions at universities, and other institutions supplying exempt education, and outside the scope of VAT when supplied at further education and sixth form colleges.

> This means that most supplies of food and drink made by the union, where the food is sold for consumption in the course of catering, will be exempt. For example, food and drink sold from canteens, refectories and other catering outlets

(excluding bars), plus food and drink sold from vending machines situated in canteens and similar areas.

However, it does not cover food and drink sold from campus shops, bars, tuck shops, other similar outlets and certain vending machines. Further the concession does not cover any other goods or services supplied by the student unions.

Training cafes and student shows

In *Revenue & Customs* v. *Brockenhurst College* [2014] UKUT 46 (TCC), the Upper Tribunal found that charges made to members of the public for meals prepared by catering students as a part of their course and for entrance to concerts and performances put on by performing arts students as part of their courses were VAT exempt as supplies closely related to an exempt supply of education. The Tribunal avoided having to find that the UK law requirement for direct use (point 3, p. 114) by the pupil or student is incompatible with the Principal VAT Directive by considering that the requirement for direct use denotes no more than a need for the goods or services to be for the direct benefit of the student and that, in this respect, it does not matter that the supplies are consumed by third parties.

However, in *Revenue & Customs Brief 39/14* HMRC announced its intention to appeal this decision and that there is no change to HMRC's policy that such supplies are outside the scope of the educational exemption because they are enjoyed by third parties not in receipt of education. This policy will not be reviewed until the Court of Appeal releases its judgment.

Supplies to eligible bodies

HMRC's position on supplies to eligible bodies is in *VATEDU53200*:

If the supply is made by...	then it...
an educational institution such as a school, college or university which is an eligible body	may not charge VAT on the closely related goods and services it provides direct to the pupils, students and trainees of other schools, colleges or universities that are also eligible bodies
an eligible body other than a school, college or university	should charge VAT on the closely related goods and services it provides unless relief is available elsewhere

5.1.6 **Private tuition**

UK law

The supply of private tuition, in a subject ordinarily taught in a school or university, by an individual teacher acting independently of an employer, is VAT exempt.

To be private tuition, an individual teacher must supply education or training in a personal capacity or as a member of a partnership, on their own account and at their own risk. The subject matter of the course must be taught in a number of schools or universities on a regular basis. Various First-tier Tribunal cases have held that courses in transcendental meditation, belly dancing, morris dancing, yoga and ballroom dancing are not courses in a subject ordinarily taught in a school or university.

HMRC accepts (*VATEDU40200*) that, for the purposes of this exemption that it is irrelevant whether the individual teacher:

- delivers the instruction to one person or to a group;
- contracts with an individual, or with an organisation that makes an onward supply of the educational services; or
- works under a franchise agreement that allows him or her to use the teaching methods, name or trading style of another person or organisation.

The following are excluded from the private tuition exemption:

- supplies of tuition carried out by employees;
- supplies of tuition carried out by agency staff.

5.1.7 **Examination services**

UK law exempts the following supplies:

1. a supply of examination services by an eligible body;
2. a supply of examination services to an eligible body;
3. a supply of examination services to a person receiving exempt or non-business education or vocational training.

Examination services are defined to include:

1. the setting and marking of examinations;
2. the setting of educational or training standards;
3. the making of assessments; and
4. other services provided with a view to ensuring that educational and training standards are maintained.

In the VAT Tribunal case *RM Education plc* [2009] VTD 20911, RM supplied IT services ('e-marking') to an examination board. The Tribunal decided that RM's services were too remote and not sufficiently closely linked to education to be examination services. The Tribunal held that each of the above four categories should be considered separately, and that the final category of other services must be construed as its own distinct residual category but coloured by the nature of the services described in the first three categories. The fourth category does not stretch to any service provided with a view to maintaining educational standards but is restricted to those services that are closely related to education with a view to maintaining educational standards.

Exam fees

HMRC accepts that when schools receive payments from pupils or parents and pass them on to examination boards they can treat them as disbursements (*VAT Notice 701/30*, section 7.3).

School inspections

HMRC also accepts that the services of school inspections are exempt if they are made by or to an eligible body (*VAT Notice 701/30*, section 7.4).

5.1.8 Government-funded education and vocational training

UK law

Supplies of education or vocational training are VAT exempt if the supplier is contracted or subcontracted to provide the education or vocational training and the consideration for the service is ultimately funded by:

- the Education Funding Agency or predecessors;
- the Skills Funding Agency;
- the National Council for Education and Training for Wales;
- a Local Enterprise Company; or
- the European Social Fund under a scheme approved by the Department for Education.

The supplier does not have to be an eligible body for VAT exemption to apply and can be a profit-making concern. Exemption also extends to goods and services that are essential to the provision of the education or vocational training if the goods or services are provided directly to the person receiving the education or training.

5.1.9 **Youth club facilities**

UK law

The provision of facilities by:

(a) a youth club or an association of youth clubs to its members; or
(b) an association of youth clubs to members of a youth club which is a member of that association

– is VAT exempt.

The HMRC guidance on youth clubs is in *VAT Notice 701/35*. The following information is summarised from the June 2011 edition.

> For VAT purposes, a youth club is defined as a club –
>
> (a) that is established to promote the social, physical, educational or spiritual development of its members;
> (b) whose members are mainly under 21 years of age; and
> (c) which:
>   (i)   is precluded from distributing and does not distribute any profit it makes; and
>   (ii) applies any profits made from its educational supplies (including supplies of youth facilities) to the continuance or improvement of such supplies.

In *Hastings & Rother YMCA* [1986] VTD 2329, the VAT Tribunal held that a youth club is an organisation that provides recreational, educational, social or cultural activities for members who are mainly, but not necessarily exclusively, under 21 years of age. The Tribunal found that Hastings & Rother YMCA was a youth club. However, in *Haggs Castle Golf Club* VTD 13653 the VAT Tribunal rejected a claim that membership subscriptions to the junior section of a golf club were exempt as a supply of youth club facilities. The Tribunal held that the exemption cannot be extended to a youth or junior section of a senior club.

HMRC sees a youth club as having to meet all of the following conditions in order to exempt its supplies of facilities:

● Its members are mainly under 21 of age.
● It has been established to promote the social, physical, educational or spiritual development of its members.
● It provides a range of activities.
● It has its own constitution and is able to produce its own accounts.

● It cannot and does not distribute any profit and it applies any profit made to provide or enhance the youth service to its members. A youth club must not use any of its income to subsidise any outside activity.

HMRC applies the *Haggs Castle Golf Club* decision and sees youth sections of larger organisations such as sports clubs, cultural societies and environmental groups as not being youth clubs in the VAT sense unless they meet the above criteria. In addition a single activity club such as a junior rugby club is not a youth club even if its members are mainly under 21 years of age.

Facilities

HMRC sees **facility** as meaning the provision of an amenity or service that enables an activity to be carried out. HMRC examples are:

Facility	*Not a facility*
● A shop	● Selling items from the shop
● Fitness centre	● Aerobics class
● Internet café	● Surfing the web
● Library	● Hire of videos and DVDs or use of photocopier
● Access to student union bar through payments of union subscriptions	● Purchase of alcohol and food from a student union bar

HMRC then provides the following guidance:

1. If you are a youth club then the facilities you supply to members are exempt when:
    ● provided in return for their subscriptions; or
    ● for an additional payment, provided the facilities are directly related to the club's ordinary activities.

2. If you are an association of youth clubs, then the facilities you supply to:
    ● youth clubs that are members of the association are exempt when provided in return for subscriptions, affiliation fees or similar payment;
    ● members of individual youth clubs are exempt when provided to a member of a youth club which is part of the association of youth clubs; and the facilities are of a type that would be exempt if provided by a youth club.

HMRC regards the following supplies as not being covered by the exemption:

(a) supplies to non-members; or

(b) supplies not commonly provided by a youth club to its members, such as: food and drink sold; overnight accommodation similar to the type provided by a hotel; purely recreational holidays; and fundraising events where tickets are sold to the public (unless otherwise exempt).

5.2 **HEALTH AND WELFARE**

EU law

The Principal VAT Directive makes a number of exemptions under the 'health and welfare' heading:

Article 132(1)(b) hospital and medical care and closely related activities undertaken by bodies governed by public law or, under social conditions comparable with those applicable to bodies governed by public law, by hospitals, centres for medical treatment or diagnosis and other duly recognised establishments of a similar nature

Article 132(1)(c) the provision of medical care in the exercise of the medical and paramedical professions as defined by the Member State concerned

Article 132(1)(d) the supply of human organs, blood and milk

Article 132(1)(e) the supply of services by dental technicians in their professional capacity and the supply of dental prostheses by dentists and dental technicians

Article 132(1)(g) the supply of services and of goods closely linked to welfare and social security work, including those supplied by old people's homes, by bodies governed by public law or by other bodies recognised by the Member State concerned as being devoted to social wellbeing

Article 132(1)(h) the supply of services and of goods closely linked to the protection of children and young persons by bodies governed by public law or by other organisations recognised by the Member State concerned as being devoted to social wellbeing;

Article 132(1)(k) the supply of staff by religious or philosophical institutions for the purpose of the activities referred to in points (b), (g), (h) and (i) and with a view to spiritual welfare. (i) refers to the provision of education or vocational training [see 5.1 'Education and vocational training'].

UK law

UK law exempts supplies of:

1. medical care by a registered medical professional;
2. medical or surgical treatment in a hospital or medical centre;
3. the provision of a deputy for a registered medical practitioner;
4. welfare services, including spiritual welfare services;
5. ambulance services;
6. human body parts.

Each of these categories is considered below.

5.2.1   Medical care by a registered medical professional

A supply of medical care by a registered medical professional is VAT exempt.

The main HMRC guidance on the exemption for supplies of professional medical care is in *VAT Notice 701/57* (referred to below).

Registered medical professionals

HMRC accepts that all of the following are registered medical professionals when they are enrolled or registered on the appropriate statutory register:

- medical practitioners;
- nurses, midwives and health visitors;
- dentists, dental hygienists, dental therapists, dental nurses, clinical dental technicians, dental technicians, orthodontic therapists;
- optometrists, dispensing opticians, osteopaths, chiropractors, pharmacists;
- professionals registered under the Health Professions Order 2001. These professionals are: arts therapists, biomedical scientists, chiropodists/podiatrists, clinical scientists, dieticians, hearing aid dispensers, occupational therapists, operating department practitioners, orthoptists, paramedics, physiotherapists, practitioner psychologists, prosthetists and orthotists, radiographers, and speech and language therapists, but will also include any medical care professionals added to the Order at a future date.

Medical care by persons who are not enrolled or registered as above qualifies for exemption if the services are wholly performed or directly supervised by a person who is so registered or enrolled.

Medical care

HMRC's position is that a supply of services must meet two conditions to be a supply of medical care by a registered medical professional:

- the services must be within the profession in which the supplier is registered to practise; and
- the primary purpose of the services is the protection, maintenance or restoration of the health of the person concerned.

HMRC accepts the following as medical care (*VAT Notice 701/57*, section 2.3):

- health services provided under the following types of contract – General Medical Services (GMS), Personal Medical Services (PMS), Alternative Provider Medical Services (APMS), Primary Care Trust Medical Services (PCTMS), General Dental Services (GDS) and Personal Dental Services (PDS);

- sight testing and prescribing by opticians (only in England, Wales and Northern Ireland) and primary eye examinations and secondary eye examinations (only in Scotland); enhanced eye health services; laser eye surgery;
- hearing tests;
- treatment provided by osteopaths and chiropractors;
- nursing care provided in a patient's own home; and
- pharmaceutical advice.

However, HMRC does not accept that the following are medical care: services not aimed at the prevention, diagnosis, treatment or cure of a disease or health disorder, such as paternity testing and the writing of articles for journals; services directly supervised by a pharmacist; general administrative services such as countersigning passport applications and providing character references; supplies of health professional staff, except where they are treated as being exempt from VAT under the nursing agencies' concession (see below).

Supplies of goods

If you provide medical care that is exempt from VAT, any supply of bandages, drugs, medicines or prostheses, administered or applied to the patient in the course of the treatment is also VAT exempt. If the goods are separable from any supply of medical care, see Chapter 6 'Zero and reduced rates' for zero-rating reliefs on prescription charges and aids for disabled persons.

Nursing agencies' concession

By concession HMRC accepts that nursing agencies (or employment businesses that provide nurses and midwives, as well as other health professionals) may exempt the supply of nursing staff and nursing auxiliaries supplied as a principal to a third party. See 11.1 'Supplies of staff' for the terms of the concession.

5.2.2 Medical or surgical treatment in a hospital or medical centre

The supply of care or medical or surgical treatment and, in connection with it, the supply of any goods, in any hospital or state-regulated institution, is VAT exempt. The supplier must be a hospital or state-regulated institution and the supply must be of care or medical treatment or surgical treatment, or ancillary to or closely related to such a supply.

The HMRC guidance on the exemption for medical or surgical treatment is in *VAT Notice 701/31*.

CJEU case law

The aim of the exemption is to reduce the cost of medical care and to make that care more accessible to individuals (decided in case C-45/01 *Christoph-Dornier-Stiftung für Klinische Psychologie* v. *Finanzamt Gießen* [2003] ECR I-12911). Such services are exempted when provided in a hospital environment (case C-86/09 *Future Health Technologies Ltd* v. *Revenue & Customs* [2010] ECR I-05215). Medical care covers services that are intended to diagnose, treat or cure diseases or health disorders or to protect, maintain or restore human health (decided in cases C-91/12 *Skatteverket* v. *PFC Clinic AB* [2013] and C-106/05 *L.u.P. GmbH* v. *Finanzamt Bochum-Mitte* [2006] ECR I-05123). The therapeutic purpose of the medical care should not necessarily be interpreted narrowly. The CJEU has held that it is consistent with the aim of reducing healthcare costs to include examinations or preventive medical treatment even when it is clear that the person concerned is not suffering from any disease or health disorder (case C-212/01 *Margarande Unterpertinger* v. *Pensionsversicherungsanstalt der Arbeiter* [2003] ECR I-13859).

Hospital or state-regulated institution

HMRC accepts the following as qualifying institutions (*VAT Notice 701/31*, section 2.1):

- hospitals;
- a hospice or nursing home which is approved, licensed or registered under the relevant social legislation, or exempted from obtaining such an approval or registration by the relevant legislation.

An institution may be qualifying regardless of whether its activities are carried out on a charitable or commercial basis.

HMRC states that supplies made by a qualifying institution are exempt when both of the following conditions are met (*VAT Notice 701/31*, section 2.2):

- the supply consists of care or medical or surgical treatment in connection with the health of the beneficiary; and
- this care or treatment is provided under the terms of an approval, licence, registration or an exemption from registration under the appropriate social legislation.

Care or medical or surgical treatment

HMRC accepts that the following are supplies of care or medical or surgical treatment (*VAT Notice 701/31*, section 2.3):

- performing medical or surgical procedures with the aim of protecting, maintaining or restoring the health of an individual;
- nursing sick or injured patients in a hospital, hospice or nursing home.

Closely related and ancillary supplies

HMRC accepts that the following supplies are ancillary or closely related to an exempt supply of medical or surgical treatment and as such also exempt:

- other state-regulated institutions providing diagnostic services or services helping to enable another health professional or health institution to make a diagnosis, for example, pathology laboratories or scanning units (*VAT Notice 701/31*, section 2.3);
- meals and accommodation provided to in-patients, residents or other care beneficiaries (*VAT Notice 701/31*, section 2.3);
- supplies of food and drink (but not alcohol) from trolleys, canteens and shops to patients (*VAT Notice 701/1*, section 5.6);
- supplies of meals and accommodation to a relative staying in hospital with a sick child (*VAT Notice 701/31*, section 2.12).

EU case law on closely related activities

Closely related activities include: the transfer of a blood sample, by the laboratory which took it, to another laboratory for the purpose of analysis (decided in case C-76/99 *European Commission* v. *France* [2001] ECR I-00249). The supply of telephone services, the hiring out of televisions to in-patients by hospitals and the supply of beds and meals to people accompanying in-patients may amount to closely related activities, provided that the supply is essential to achieve the therapeutic objects sought by the hospital and the medical care, and the basic purpose of the supply is not to obtain additional income through transactions which are in direct competition with those of commercial enterprises subject to VAT (decided in case C-394/04 *Diagnostiko & Therapeftiko Kentro Athinon-Ygeia AE* v. *Ypourgos Oikonomikon* [2005] ECR I-10373).

Exclusions

HMRC does not accept that the following qualify for exemption (*VAT Notice 701/31*, section 2.4):

- Any service that is not provided under the terms of an approval, licence, registration or exemption from registration, granted under the appropriate social legislation.
- Any service provided to a person other than an in-patient, resident or other beneficiary of care or treatment. This includes any supply made to visitors, though where a qualifying institution supplies accommodation and meals to a relative staying in a hospital or hospice with a sick child, those supplies are exempt.
- Any goods or services that are separable from care or treatment provided within the institution. For example, charges made for the use of telephones.

5.2.3 The provision of a deputy for a registered medical practitioner

UK law exempts the provision of a deputy for a person registered in the register of medical practitioners or the register of medical practitioners with limited registration.

In the case *Rapid Sequence Ltd* v. *Revenue & Customs* [2013] UKFTT 432 (TC), the First-tier Tribunal held that this exemption does not apply to supplies of medical staff by an employment agency and that, in order to conform with the Principal VAT Directive, this exemption should be read as 'the provision of medical care services provided by a deputy for a person registered in the register of medical practitioners or the register of medical practitioners with limited registration'.

5.2.4 Welfare services

EU law

EU law exempts:

- Article 132(1)(g): the supply of services and of goods closely linked to welfare and social security work, including those supplied by old people's homes, by bodies governed by public law or by **other bodies recognised by the member state concerned** as being **devoted to social well-being** (see below);
- Article 132(1)(h): the supply of services and of goods closely linked to the protection of children and young persons by bodies governed by public law or by other organisations recognised by the member state concerned as being devoted to social well-being;
- Article 132(1)(k): the supply of staff by religious or philosophical institutions for the purpose of the activities referred to in Articles 132(1) (b), (g), (h) and (i) and with a view to spiritual welfare.

Note: (i) refers to the provision of education or vocational training.

Other bodies recognised by the member state concerned

The term is sufficiently broad to include private profit-making entities (decided in case C-498/03 *Kingscrest Associates Ltd and Montecello Ltd* v. *Customs & Excise* [2005] ECR I-04427).

Devoted to social well-being

In case C-594/13 *'go fair' Zeitarbeit OHG* v. *Finanzamt Hamburg-Altona* [2015] BFH, the CJEU held that:

> it is for the national authorities, in accordance with EU law and subject to review by the national courts, to take into account a number of factors in order to determine which bodies must be recognised as 'devoted to social well-being'....

Such factors include the existence of specific provisions, be they national or regional, legislative or administrative, or tax or social security provisions, the general interest of the activities of the taxable person concerned, the fact that other taxable persons carrying on the same activities already have similar recognition, and the fact that the costs of the supplies in question may be largely met by health insurance schemes or other social security bodies.

UK law

UK law exempts a supply of **welfare services** and a supply of goods provided in connection with welfare services, by any of the following:

(a) **a charity**: for the meaning of charity see 6.1.1;
(b) **a state-regulated private welfare institution or agency** (see below);
(c) **a public body**: a local authority, government department or non-departmental public body (see 5.3.1 'Public body').

> **Welfare services** means services which are directly connected with:
>
> (a) the provision of **care, treatment or instruction** designed to promote the physical or mental welfare of elderly, sick, distressed or disabled persons; or
> (b) the **care or protection of children and young persons**; or
> (c) the provision of **spiritual welfare services** by a religious institution as part of a course of instruction or a retreat, not being a course or a retreat designed primarily to provide recreation or a holiday.

See the sections below for more on each category. In the case of welfare services supplied by a state-regulated private welfare institution, the exemption includes only those services in respect of which the institution is regulated.

Supplies of accommodation or catering are specifically excluded from exemption unless they are ancillary to the provision of care, treatment or instruction.

State-regulated private welfare institution or agency

State-regulated private welfare institution or agency means an institution or agency approved, licensed, registered or exempted from registration by any Minister or other authority pursuant to a provision of a public general Act, other than a provision that is capable of being brought into effect at different times in relation to different local authority areas. Approval, licensing and registration bodies include the Care Quality Commission, Scottish Commission for Regulation of Care, Care and Social Inspectorate of Wales, Northern Ireland

Regulation and Quality Improvement Authority, OFSTED and any similar regulatory body.

Care, treatment or instruction

Care, treatment or instruction means that a supply of services which is directly connected with the provision of care, treatment or instruction designed to promote the physical or mental welfare of elderly, sick, distressed or disabled persons is VAT exempt. The care, treatment or instruction must relate to one or more specified persons who are elderly, sick, distressed or disabled.

HMRC accepts (*VAT Notice 701/2*, section 2.1) that care, treatment or instruction can include:

- personal or nursing care, including assistance with bathing, dressing, toileting and other personal hygiene;
- general assistance and support with everyday tasks such as form-filling, letter reading/writing, bill-paying;
- certain **routine domestic tasks** (see below);
- counselling;
- looking after or supervising vulnerable people;
- support or instruction designed to develop or sustain a person's capacity to live independently in the community;
- protection, control, guidance or companionship that is required to meet an individual's personal or domestic needs; and
- residential care, including accommodation, board and other services provided to residents as part of a care package.

Routine domestic tasks

HMRC accepts (*VAT Notice 701/2*, section 2.1.2) that routine domestic tasks such as housework, simple odd jobs, shopping and collecting a prescription or pension can be care, treatment or instruction when all of the following conditions are met:

- the recipient of the service is an elderly, sick, distressed or disabled person;
- an assessment of the recipient's health condition, medical needs and ability to perform each task has been carried out by an appropriately trained person – such as a medical or health professional or any person with relevant training or experience in social work or social care;
- this assessment has shown that the recipient is unable to carry out the tasks safely or adequately or without significant pain or discomfort and that this inability presents a risk to their health or welfare;
- a record of each assessment is maintained by the supplier of the service; and
- the service provided is a routine domestic task that the majority of the population would expect to carry out for themselves and which is required to

keep a household going. This excludes specialist services such as non-essential gardening, decorating and other house maintenance including re-roofing, plumbing and electrical services.

Care or protection of children and young persons

The care or protection must relate to one or more specific children. HMRC accepts (*VAT Notice 701/2*, section 2.2) that this can include:

- care provided in a children's home;
- day-care services such as those provided by a nursery, playgroup or after-school club, but excluding activity-based clubs such as dance classes;
- the placement of a child with foster carers by a fostering agency;
- the assessment of families to be included on the at-risk register;
- the care, support and protection of looked-after children; and
- the training and assessment of prospective adopters by an adoption agency.

Spiritual welfare services

Spiritual welfare services means services which are directly connected with the provision of spiritual welfare by a religious institution as part of a course of instruction or a retreat, not being a course or a retreat designed primarily to provide recreation or a holiday.

Also exempt is the not-for-profit supply of goods and services incidental to the provision of spiritual welfare by a religious community to a resident member of that community in return for a subscription or other consideration paid as a condition of membership.

HMRC accepts (*VAT Notice 701/2*, section 2.3.2) that the following may qualify:

- spiritual counselling of an individual;
- guided exploration of spiritual needs and development; and
- discussion, meditation, prayer or worship sessions.

However, HMRC does not accept that the following qualify for VAT exemption:

- any supply made by a body other than a religious institution or community;
- any supply that is not made as part of an organised retreat or course of instruction provided by a religious institution;
- conferences or retreats when the predominant purpose is not spiritual welfare;
- educational courses in theology, or similar subjects, where the predominant purpose is to expand knowledge of spiritual matters rather than to provide spiritual welfare and meetings to discuss theology or aspects of Church doctrine. However, these are potentially eligible for exemption as supplies of education.

5.2.5 Ambulance services

The supply of transport services for sick or injured persons in vehicles specially designed for that purpose is VAT exempt.

5.2.6 Human body parts

Supplies of the following human body parts or products are VAT exempt: blood, products for therapeutic purposes derived from human blood, human (including foetal) organs or tissue for diagnostic or therapeutic purposes or medical research.

5.3 CULTURAL SERVICES

EU law

EU law exempts (Article 132(1)(n)): the supply of certain cultural services, and the supply of goods closely linked thereto, by bodies governed by public law or by other cultural bodies recognised by the member state concerned.

UK law

UK law exempts the supply by a **public body** or by an **eligible body** of a right of admission to:

(a) a museum, gallery, art exhibition or zoo; or
(b) a theatrical, musical or choreographic performance of a cultural nature.

The main HMRC guidance on the cultural services exemption is in *VAT Notice 701/47*. The information below is summarised from the September 2011 edition, unless otherwise indicated.

5.3.1 Public body

A public body is a local authority, a government department or a non-departmental public body listed in the 1995 edition of the Office of Public Services publication, *Public Bodies*.

A supply of a right of admission in categories (a) or (b) above by a public body is excluded from exemption if exemption would be likely to create distortions of competition such as to place a commercial enterprise carried on by a taxable person at a disadvantage.

A supply of a right of admission in category (b) above is exempt only if the performance is provided exclusively by one or more public bodies, one or more eligible bodies or any combination of public bodies and eligible bodies.

5.3.2 **Eligible body**

An eligible body for the purposes of the cultural services exemption is a body that is not a public body and which meets each of the following conditions:

1. it is precluded from distributing, and does not distribute, any profit it makes;
2. it applies any profits made from its cultural supplies to the continuance or improvement of the facilities made available by means of the supplies;
3. it is managed and administered on a voluntary basis by persons who have no direct or indirect financial interest in its activities.

1. Profit distribution

A body whose governing documents preclude it from distributing surpluses of income over expenditure to its members, shareholders or any other party (other than in the event of a liquidation or cessation of activities), and which as a matter of fact does not distribute any profit, will normally be accepted as having satisfied this condition.

2. Application of profits

All profits arising from exempt admission fees must be:

- used for the continuance or improvement of the facilities made available to the fee-paying public by payment of the exempt admission fees; or
- applied in connection with the making of related cultural supplies such as research or conservation projects.

If profits are applied to any other activities of the body than those above, the body is not eligible for exemption. In practice many cultural bodies have expensive facilities to maintain, so meeting this condition is not usually a problem.

3. Managed and administered on an essentially voluntary basis

This is the key test and one that is the source of much dispute. The test is the UK's implementation of the third condition in Principal VAT Directive Article 133 (see 'Exemptions in the public interest' in the introduction to this chapter). Under EU law the body must be managed and administered on an essentially voluntary basis by persons who have no direct or indirect interest, either themselves or through intermediaries, in the results of the activities concerned. The UK implementation omits the word 'essentially' and also the 'through intermediaries' requirement. However, HMRC and the UK courts accept that UK law must be read as importing these requirements.

Case law suggests that this test must be interpreted as follows:

Step 1

It is first necessary to identify the persons who carry out the management and administration of the body. In case C-267/00 *Customs & Excise* v. *Zoological Society of London* [2002] EWHC (QB) ECR I-03353, the CJEU drew a distinction between:

- the **persons who take the decisions of last resort** (see below) concerning the policy of the body and carry out the higher supervisory tasks; and
- the persons who implement those decisions.

> The CJEU ruled that **the persons who take the decisions of last resort** are the members of the body who are designated in accordance with its constitution to direct it at the highest level. That is, the trustees or company directors, as well as other persons who, without being designated by the constitution, do in fact direct it in that they take the decisions of last resort concerning the policy of that body, especially in the financial area, and carry out the higher supervisory tasks (i.e. shadow directors and similar).

Step 2

Having identified the persons who carry out the management and administration of the body, it is then necessary to establish if they carry out that role on 'an essentially voluntary basis'. In the *Zoological Society of London* case, the Advocate General said:

> the requirement... that management and administration be conducted on an essentially voluntary basis is to be interpreted as meaning that substantially all the management and administration... of the body in question must be conducted by unremunerated persons. However, the fact that paid staff intervene in such activities occasionally or in a peripheral manner, or that nominal or token payments are made to the persons responsible for management and administration, is not contrary to that requirement.

So all trustees, company directors and shadow directors must be unremunerated in respect of their role as trustees, directors and shadow directors, though nominal or token payments to such persons will not block this requirement.

In *Bournemouth Symphony Orchestra* v. *Revenue & Customs* [2006] EWCA Civ 1281, the salaried managing director was paid to act as a trustee and take decisions of last resort and thus blocked this requirement from being met. However, a paid member of the orchestra was elected by the orchestra members to attend board meetings and take decisions of last resort in order to represent their interests. Even though that person was remunerated, they were not remunerated for taking decisions of last resort; so their role on the board was essentially voluntary and they did not, in themselves, block this requirement from being met.

In *Loughborough Students' Union* [2013] the Union argued that sabbatical officers paid two-thirds of the market rate for the job were working essentially as volunteers. The Tribunal rejected this. The facts showed that the sabbatical officers did take decisions of last resort and their salary was clearly more than a nominal amount or contribution towards out-of-pocket expenses. The salaried sabbatical officers were therefore not volunteers and blocked this requirement from being met.

Step 3

It is then necessary to establish that the trustees/company directors, etc. have no direct or indirect interest, either themselves or through intermediaries, in the results of the activities concerned.

In *Longborough Festival Opera* v. *Revenue & Customs* [2006] EWHC 40 (Ch) a trustee guaranteed the deficits of the Festival. The High Court held that this requirement is directed at potential enrichment and is not designed to preclude participation in management by persons who for the benefit of the cultural body assume responsibility for a liability of the body and accordingly risk impoverishment. The High Court also took the view that a body is not disqualified as a result of this requirement because it legally can and in fact does enter into commercial contracts with a trustee, director or shadow director so long as the contract does not confer any interest in the body's results or profits.

5.3.3 **Qualifying cultural services**

The UK restricts the cultural exemption to rights of admission to:

(a) a museum, gallery, art exhibition or zoo; or
(b) a theatrical, musical or choreographic performance of a cultural nature.

HMRC's position is set out in *VAT Notice 701/47*, section 2.3:

> 2.3 What is the definition of a museum, gallery, art exhibition or zoo? This has to be judged by reference to the normal everyday meaning of the words, taking into account indicative evidence such as the nature of the collections, objects, artefacts,

site and exhibits on show for example. However, for the avoidance of doubt, a botanical garden does not qualify for exemption.

2.4 What is meant by a theatrical, musical or choreographic performance of a cultural nature? Each event has to be judged on its individual merits. However, where live performances of stage plays, dancing or music are considered to be cultural (as they generally are) they will qualify for exemption.

Various UK cases have decided the following do not qualify as any of the above:

- A right of admission to a botanical garden on the basis that it is not a museum of living plants (*Trebah Garden Trust* [2000] VTD 16598).
- A right of admission to a film show on the basis that it is not a live performance (*Chichester Cinema* [2004] VTD 19344 and *Corn Exchange Newbury* [2007] VTD 20268).

However, the following have been found to qualify:

- In *Wildfowl & Wetlands Trust* v. *Revenue & Customs* [2013] UKFTT 423 (TC), a wildfowl/wetland site was found to be a zoo, which was defined as a place where wild animals are kept for breeding, study or exhibition to the public.
- In *Loughborough Students' Union* v. *Revenue & Customs* [2012] UKFTT 331 (TC), HMRC did not dispute that events of the type organised by the Union (live music, balls, discos, dances, etc.) are 'theatrical, musical or choreographic performance of a cultural nature'. The judge stated: 'There is no suggestion that performances of a cultural nature are restricted to what might be termed high culture and so any performance which is musical or choreographic will be capable of qualifying'.

5.3.4 The *British Film Institute* case

The UK restrictions are on the basis that the Principal VAT Directive states that exemption applies to 'certain cultural services' and this therefore gives the UK the right to restrict the scope of the cultural services that qualify for exemption. However, in the case *British Film Institute* v. *Revenue & Customs* [2013] UKFTT 72 (TC), the First-tier Tribunal rejected this approach on the basis of various CJEU decisions on the exemptions in the public interest. It held that the term 'cultural services' has an independent EU-wide meaning and a member state cannot restrict it to particular types of cultural services, in the same way that member states cannot restrict the meaning of sport to football but not basketball (see *EC* v. *Spain* below in 5.4 'Sports and physical education').

At the time of writing, the Upper Tribunal (Tax) has approved the First-tier Tribunal's decision though HMRC has appealed the decision to the Court of Appeal which has agreed to refer the matter to the CJEU.

5.4 **SPORTS AND PHYSICAL EDUCATION**

EU law

Article 132(1)(m) exempts the supply of certain services closely linked to sport or physical education by non-profit-making organisations to persons taking part in sport or physical education.

In case C-124/96 *European Commission* v. *Spain* [1998] ECR I-02501, the CJEU decided that placement of the word 'certain' is unfortunate, as 'certain' does not restrict the scope of 'services closely linked to sport or physical education' but states that, of all supplies of services closely linked to sport or physical education, only those supplied by non-profit-making organisations to persons taking part in the sport or physical education qualify for exemption. As such, it is not open to an EU member state to, for example, exempt services closely linked to football but not services closely linked to basketball.

UK law

UK law exempts the following:

1. **Non-profit competition fees**: the grant of a right to enter a competition in sport or physical recreation where the consideration for the grant consists of money which is to be allocated wholly towards the provision of a prize or prizes awarded in that competition.
2. **Competition fees charged by eligible bodies**: the grant, by an eligible body established for the purposes of sport or physical recreation, of a right to enter a competition in such an activity.
3. **Supplies of services closely linked to sport by an eligible body**: the supply by an eligible body to an individual of services closely linked with and essential to sport or physical education in which the individual is taking part. At the time of writing the CJEU has decided that the UK implementation of item 3 above is wrong in that supplies to non-natural persons can qualify for exemption in some situations. See the *Canterbury Hockey* case in 5.4.3 'Persons taking part in sport' for more on this decision.

The main HMRC guidance on the sporting exemption is in *VAT Notice 701/45*. The information below is summarised from the August 2011 edition, unless otherwise stated.

135

5.4.1 Services closely linked to sport or physical education

Three conditions must each be met for a supply of services to be exempt:

(a) The services supplied must be **closely linked and essential to sport or physical education**.

(b) The supplier must be an eligible body for the purposes of the sporting exemption.

(c) The customer is a natural person taking part in sport or an organisation, but the true beneficiary of the supply is one or more natural persons taking part in sport.

Closely linked and essential to sport or physical education

HMRC accepts that the following are supplies closely linked with and essential to sport or physical education (*VAT Notice 701/45*, section 3):

- provision of playing area, for example, court, pitch or green fees;
- use of changing rooms, showers and playing equipment, trolley and locker hire, and storage of equipment essential to sport;
- use of multi-sport playing facilities;
- sports club membership subscriptions and joining fees covering active participation in sport;
- playing, competing, refereeing, umpiring, judging, coaching or training but not attending as a spectator or involvement in administration;
- match fees charged by an eligible body for use of the playing facilities; and
- mooring, hangarage and use of workshop facilities but not the use of parts, or the services of an engineer.

However, HMRC does not accept that supplies of the following are capable of being services closely linked to sport or physical education: accommodation; catering, gaming machines; social functions; transport; social or non-playing membership subscriptions; admission charges for spectators; parking charges; charges to use saunas, tanning machines and similar; and charges for activities that do not amount to sport or physical recreation, such as chess, card games and dominoes. See the following section, however, for whether or not contract bridge is a sport.

Meaning of sport or physical recreation

At 3.2 of *VAT Notice 701/45* HMRC accepts that a wide range of activities are sport or physical recreation including: angling; archery; ballooning; billiards and snooker; bowls; canoeing; caving; dance; darts; martial arts; equestrian; exercise and fitness; field sports; flying (including model flying activities in which competence is dependent on physical skill or fitness); gliding; golf; ice-skating; motor sports; mountaineering; movement and dance; rambling; roller skating; rowing and sailing; shooting; skiing; surfing; table tennis; and yoga. If an activity is not included in HMRC's list then you can write to HMRC (see Chapter 14 'Further information') with full details of the activity and HMRC will consider whether the activity is a sport within the meaning of the sports exemption.

In *English Bridge Union Ltd* v. *Revenue & Customs* [2014] UKFTT 181 (TC), the First-tier Tribunal accepted HMRC's contention that for an activity to qualify as sport or physical education, it must involve physical activity as opposed to purely mental activity. The Tribunal therefore rejected the Union's claim that contract bridge is a sport. However, at the time of writing, the matter has been appealed to the Upper Tribunal which has agreed to refer the matter to the CJEU. This is on the basis that several other EU states accept 'mind sports' such as bridge as qualifying sporting activities for the purposes of the sporting exemption.

5.4.2 Eligible body

The UK imposes the following conditions on eligible bodies for the purposes of the sporting exemption:

(a) The body must be precluded from distributing any profit it makes, or is allowed to distribute any such profit by means only of distributions to a non-profit-making body.
(b) The body applies any profits it makes from its supplies of services closely linked to sport or physical education for one or more of the following purposes:
  (i) the continuance or improvement of any facilities made available in or in connection with the making of such supplies;
  (ii) the purposes of a non-profit-making body.
(c) The body is not subject to 'commercial influence'.

Non-profit-making bodies exclude local authorities, government departments and non-departmental public bodies. See 5.4.4 'Leisure Trusts'.

Condition (c) is anti-avoidance legislation introduced with effect from 1 January 2000. The aim of condition (c) is to prevent a profit-making body setting up a non-profit-making eligible body in order to benefit from the VAT exemption whilst extracting profits via the provision of **relevant supplies** to the eligible body.

Relevant supplies are:

(i) a licence to occupy sports facilities;
(ii) supplies of management and administration services; or

(iii) the supply of any goods or services for a consideration in excess of what would have been agreed between parties entering into a commercial transaction at arm's length.

However, condition (c) does not block situations where relevant supplies are made by a charity or local authority to an eligible body. See *VAT Notice 701/45*, section 5 for detailed HMRC guidance on the commercial influence condition.

5.4.3 Persons taking part in sport

Up to the *Canterbury Hockey* case (C-253/07 *Canterbury Hockey Club* v. *Revenue & Customs* [2008] EWHC (Ch) ECR I-07821), HMRC's view was that natural persons alone are capable of taking part in sport, and that, consequently, only services supplied directly to such persons may be exempted. The CJEU agreed that only natural persons can take part in sport. However, the CJEU rejected HMRC's approach as being too narrow on the grounds that such an interpretation would defeat the exemption's objective, which is to encourage participation in sport. The CJEU held that, in the context of persons taking part in sport, this includes services supplied to corporate persons and to unincorporated associations, provided that those services are closely linked and essential to sport, that they are supplied by an eligible body and that their true beneficiaries are persons taking part in sport.

Following this decision HMRC accepted in *Revenue & Customs Brief 15/10* that the ruling means that some supplies which were previously regarded as standard-rated may now be exempt from VAT if the services are closely linked and essential to sport and the true beneficiaries are individuals taking part in sport. From 1 September 2010 HMRC policy is the following:

- Supplies made to commercial profit-making organisations do not meet the true beneficiary test and will not fall within the exemption for supplies of services closely linked and essential to sport.
- The letting of sports facilities to a club for the direct use of its members is exempt if the club is non-profit-making. Otherwise it will be taxable.

5.4.4 Leisure trusts

Local authorities are specifically precluded from being eligible bodies, so their supplies of sports facilities are VAT standard-rated (though supplies of licences to occupy sports facilities by local authorities can benefit from the 24-hour or series of lettings rules – see 8.2.2 'Sports facilities'). There are thus potential VAT advantages in hiving off leisure services into separate charitable trusts in order to render the supply VAT exempt. In addition, if a separate leisure trust runs all the facilities, benefitting from a peppercorn lease from the council, any VAT on capital expenditure on the facilities incurred by the council is potentially recoverable under section 33 of the VAT Act 1994 (see Chapter 10 'VAT special schemes'). There are also other potential tax advantages for local authorities in the splitting of services in this way; for example, mandatory (80%) charity rates relief is funded by central government.

Leisure trust management agreements

In *Edinburgh Leisure* [2004] VTD 18784, a local authority leased its leisure facilities to a separate charitable trust for a peppercorn rent. The trust received funding from the local authority under a contract which required the funds to be used exclusively for the purpose of running the leisure facilities. HMRC claimed that the funding was a grant and the trust claimed that it was consideration for a taxable supply of the service of operating the facilities. The Tribunal agreed with the trust, finding there to be a direct link between the service supplied and consideration received under a binding legal agreement.

HMRC/CIPFA MOU

HMRC and the Chartered Institute of Public Finance and Accountancy (CIPFA) have agreed a Memorandum of Understanding (MOU) that sets out the agreed VAT treatment of local authority-supported leisure facilities, including the treatment of contracted-out local authority leisure facilities. The agreement is in the *HMRC Government and Public Body* manual at *VATGPB8520*. Where leisure facilities are run by an independent party such as a leisure trust, the MOU identifies three potential scenarios:

- An independent party manages local authority-owned facilities under a management agreement with the local authority, with the independent party supplying leisure facilities to end users as principal. This is a standard-rated supply of management services by the independent party to the local authority.
- An independent party acts as **agent** in managing leisure facilities for a local authority. The local authority provides the leisure facilities to end users as **principal** (for the meanings of agent and principal see 11.2 'Agency supplies'). The independent party's supply of agency services to the local authority is standard-rated. Consideration for the independent party's supply can include amounts retained from takings.
- An independent party runs its own leisure facilities with support from the local authority. Here, any local authority funding is likely to be a non-business grant.

Membership schemes

In *Basingstoke & District Sports Trust Ltd* [1995] VTD 13347, the VAT Tribunal held that privilege cards did not amount to a membership scheme, since the concept of membership involves an element of participation or belonging which is absent in the case of a privilege card. Following this case HMRC announced in *Business Brief 3/96* that it accepted that where a body does not operate a full membership scheme (i.e. where members do not have voting rights or any form of control over the management of the centre), sporting and physical education services provided are exempt from VAT subject to the normal conditions. This applies irrespective of whether users are called 'members' for the purpose of obtaining discount on use of the facilities.

All-inclusive leisure passes

Some leisure passes offer access to sports facilities (gym, courts, pool, etc.) but also to non-sports facilities such as a sauna. HMRC policy on such all-inclusive leisure passes is at *VAT Notice 701/45*, section 3.5.9:

> In most cases, the typical consumer who purchases an all-inclusive package will have access to a range of facilities at the leisure centre. Usually most of these facilities would, if supplied individually, be exempt as services closely linked with and essential to sport or physical education in which the individual is taking part, (e.g. use of swimming pools, courts, pitches showers, changing rooms, etc.). Therefore, in cases where the predominant reason for purchasing an all-inclusive package is to use the range of available sports facilities, the single supply is exempt. If the predominant reason a typical consumer purchases an all-inclusive package is to make use of standard-rated facilities (e.g. use of a sauna) the single supply is standard-rated.

5.4.5 Sports competitions

Entry fees to competitions in sport or physical recreation organised by anyone are exempt, providing the entry fee is entirely used to provide the prizes. In addition, eligible bodies established for the purposes of sport or physical recreation can exempt entry fees to competitions. The sports that can be included are extended in this case to include greyhound/pigeon racing and clay pigeon shooting. Local authorities are not within this definition as they are not established for the purposes of sport or physical recreation.

5.4.6 Letting sports facilities

The letting of land or buildings involves the grant of an exclusive right to occupy the land or buildings. The grant of a right to use a shared sports facility (for example, a right to use a golf course, ice rink or swimming pool) during a shared use session is not an exclusive right to occupy and so is not capable of being a letting of land or buildings. However, the letting of the whole or a defined part of a sports facility is capable of being an exclusive right to occupy, for example where a charity hires a specific lane of a swimming pool for a sponsored swim.

Most supplies of exclusive licences to occupy sports facilities are VAT standard-rated; however, exclusive licences to occupy sports facilities are VAT exempt in some situations. See 8.2.2 'Sports facilities'.

5.5 SUBSCRIPTIONS TO PUBLIC INTEREST BODIES

EU law

EU law Article 132(1)(l) exempts the supply of services, and the supply of goods closely linked thereto, to their members in their common interest in return for a subscription fixed in accordance with their rules by non-profit-making organisations with aims of a political, trade union, religious, patriotic, philosophical, philanthropic or civic nature, provided that this exemption is not likely to cause distortion of competition.

UK law

UK law exempts the supply to its members of **qualifying goods and services** (see below) in return for a membership subscription by non-profit-making bodies of the following types:

(a) trade unions;
(b) professional associations;
(c) associations for the advancement of knowledge or the fostering of professional expertise;
(d) representational trade associations;
(e) other public interest bodies: these are bodies which have objects which are in the public domain and are of a political, religious, patriotic, philosophical, philanthropic or civic nature.

See 5.5.3 to 5.5.7 below for more on each category.

Public interest membership bodies also include organisations and associations the membership of which consists **wholly or mainly** of constituent or affiliated associations of the above categories.

See 5.5.4 'Professional associations' for the definition of 'wholly or mainly'.

Qualifying goods and services

To qualify for exemption goods or services provided in return for a membership subscription must be:

● referable only to the aims of the organisation;
● available without payment other than a membership subscription; and
● not a right of admission to any premises, event or performance to which non-members are admitted for a consideration.

The following membership benefits are therefore excluded from exemption:

- Any right of admission to any premises, event or performance, to which non-members are admitted for a consideration. If you put on an event or provide premises to which members gain free access, but for which non-members must pay, then that benefit is excluded from exemption (though it may, of course, qualify for exemption in its own right as a supply of education, culture, sports facilities, etc.).
- Any membership benefit which is only available by payment in addition to the membership subscription, for example a discount.
- Goods and services unconnected to the aims of the organisation. Some membership bodies purchase commercial packages of member benefits such as discounts at restaurants and hotel chains. Such benefits are likely to be seen as being unconnected to the organisation's aims and therefore excluded from exemption.

Where particular membership benefits are excluded from exemption HMRC's position is that the subscription must be apportioned between benefits qualifying for exemption and other benefits with VAT being accounted for on any standard-rated or reduced-rated benefits. See 11.4.2 'Apportioning membership subscriptions'.

The main HMRC guidance on this exemption is in *VAT Notice 701/5*, the October 2013 edition of which is referred to below.

5.5.1 Zero-rating of particular membership benefits

Non-profit-making public interest membership bodies can take advantage of extra-statutory concession 3.35 (*VAT Notice 48*, section 3.35) to treat their membership subscription as (in effect) a multiple supply of the benefits concerned. Benefits such as printed journals, magazines and annual reports can then be zero-rated in preference to exemption. See 11.4.2 'Apportioning membership subscriptions' for more on this concession and apportioning membership subscriptions. At *VTUPB7000* HMRC explains the history of this treatment:

> Between 1973 and 31 December 1977, subscriptions to trade unions were outside the scope of VAT and trade/professional/vocational associations could choose between taxable and outside-the-scope treatment. The ability to zero rate certain supplies to members was therefore not a major issue during that period. When the 1989 version of VAT Leaflet 701/33 was issued in May 1989, the passage stating that traders could zero rate the element of the subscription attributable to identifiable zero-rated benefits was accidentally omitted. An erratum slip was issued in June 1989, which (appearing separately) drew attention to the possibility of such treatment. It also created an impression that the treatment was something not previously possible.

In fact, the capacity to zero rate a proportion of the subscription in respect of identifiable zero-rated supplies to members has always been available. Publication of the fact was initially via Notice 701 VAT: Scope and Coverage. The 1973 and 1975 versions of the notice, and a 1977 supplement to it, stated that if any supply falls within the terms of both the Schedule of zero-rated items and the Schedule of exempt items, the supply is zero-rated. The 1976 and 1979 versions specifically stated that zero-rating took precedence over exemption.

At *VTUPB7000* HMRC accepts that a public interest membership body can in principle backdate an apportionment of the subscription between zero-rated and exempt. In considering any such claim, the crucial element will be the extent to which the trader was aware of the availability of zero-rating over the past period being claimed.

5.5.2 **History of the exemption**

UK law (s. 94 VAT Act 1994) deems the provision by a club, association or organisation, for a subscription or other consideration, of the facilities or advantages available to its members, to be a business supply. Prior to 1 January 1978, this deeming excluded subscriptions to trade unions, whose subscriptions were outside the scope of VAT. Subscriptions to trade, professional and vocational associations had the option of being treated as taxable or outside the scope of VAT.

With effect from 1 January 1978, following the introduction of the exemption for subscriptions to public interest bodies in the EU's Sixth Directive, exemptions were introduced into UK law for subscriptions to trade unions, and trade, professional and vocational associations. However, there was also a deemed non-business treatment for subscriptions to a body which had objects in the public domain and of a political, religious, philanthropic, philosophical or patriotic nature, if the subscription obtained no facility or advantage for the subscriber other than the right to participate in its management or receive reports on its activities.

As HMRC explains at *VTUPB1300*, it had been anticipated that exemption would not extend to associations of employers and the self-employed because the majority of these had opted to be taxable prior to 1 January 1978. However, as a result of much lobbying and protest from these bodies, the exemption was extended to professional associations and learned societies where membership was directly or necessarily connected with the members' professions or employments. This extension of the exemption still excluded employers and some other influential interest associations, so item (d) was added to the group. This provided exemption for representational bodies on the basis that such bodies performed functions comparable to those of trade unions proper.

By 1999 it had become clear that the UK exemption was still too narrow, in particular in excluding public interest civic bodies, so the item (e) exemption for 'bodies which have objects which are in the public domain and are of a political, religious, patriotic, philosophical, philanthropic or civic nature', essentially replicating the Principal VAT Directive, was added with effect from 1 December 1999. At the same time, the non-business treatment was removed from subscriptions to such bodies providing no more than the right to participate in its management or receive reports on its activities.

5.5.3 Trades unions

Under UK law exemption applies to the membership subscriptions of 'a trade union or other organisation of persons having as its main object the negotiation on behalf of its members of the terms and conditions of their employment'.

Trade union has the meaning assigned to it by section 1 of the Trade Union and Labour Relations (Consolidation) Act 1992:

> an organisation (whether temporary or permanent)—
>
> (a) which consists wholly or mainly of workers of one or more descriptions and whose principal purposes include the regulation of relations between workers of that description or those descriptions and employers or employers' associations; or
> (b) which consists wholly or mainly of—
>> (i) constituent or affiliated organisations which fulfil the conditions in paragraph (a) (or themselves consist wholly or mainly of constituent or affiliated organisations which fulfil those conditions), or
>> (ii) representatives of such constituent or affiliated organisations,
>
> and whose principal purposes include the regulation of relations between workers and employers or between workers and employers' associations, or the regulation of relations between its constituent or affiliated organisations.

In case C-149/97 *Institute of the Motor Industry* v. *Customs & Excise* [1998] ECR I-07053, the CJEU held that:

> The expression trade-union... means specifically an organisation whose main object is to defend the collective interests of its members whether they are workers, employers, independent professionals or traders carrying on a particular economic activity and to represent them vis-à-vis the appropriate third parties, including the public authorities. Thus, a non-profit-making organisation whose main object is to defend and represent the collective interests of its members satisfies the criterion of exercising an activity in the public interest, which is the basis of the exemptions set out in Article 132(1)(l) of the Directive, in so far as it provides its members with a representative voice and strength in negotiations with third parties.

5.5.4 **Professional associations**

Under UK law exemption applies to membership subscriptions of 'a professional association, membership of which is **wholly or mainly** restricted to individuals who have or are seeking a qualification appropriate to the practice of the profession concerned'.

Wholly or mainly

HMRC's broad position is that **wholly or mainly** means 75% or more (*VAT Notice 701/5*, section 11.8). However, HMRC implies that it may accept percentages below this (*VTUPB4300*):

> There is no tribunal or court precedent for what proportion of the membership satisfies the wholly or mainly criterion. However, our policy is to interpret the phrase as being significantly nearer 100% than 50% of the membership; and we regard any association with a membership comprising 75% or more individuals as satisfying the criterion.

Individuals who have or are seeking a qualification

The membership must be wholly or mainly restricted to individuals who have or are seeking an appropriate qualification. This will include trainees, qualified members and retired qualified members. However, it will exclude: corporate members and unqualified members who are not seeking an appropriate qualification. HMRC accepts that the existence of any restriction can be judged by what actually happens in practice, so if the membership is in fact composed of 'wholly or mainly' of such persons, it meets this condition (*VAT Notice 701/5*, section 11.8).

Professional association

Professional association means an association of professional persons as generally understood by the term. HMRC states (*VAT Notice 701/5*, section 11.6):

> There is no legal definition of a profession. However VAT tribunal and court decisions have restricted the meaning of the words 'profession' and 'professional' to occupations generally understood to be a profession. Factors in judging whether an occupation is generally understood to be a profession include:
>
> - the nature and status of the activity and those engaged in it
> - whether the exercise of the activity requires a qualification
> - whether the persons carrying out the activity are bound by a code of conduct
> - whether the activity entails having a distinctive and broad base of knowledge from which a person may subsequently diversify into more specialised areas

- the nature of the association's aims and objectives
- the actual activities carried out by it

These criteria are neither fixed nor exhaustive. This means for example that some occupations not currently regarded as professions may acquire that status in the future.

In *Institute of Leisure and Amenity Management* [1988] STC 602, concerning an association for managers in the leisure and amenity industries, the High Court judge stated:

> The skill or technique concerned, management of leisure facilities, is one relevant to the particular industry and not, as in the case of the traditional professions, a skill or technique of general application although of course the traditional professions do have specialist as well as general professional bodies. The industry – and I use the word in a neutral sense – provides a focal point for the association. The fact that the association was set up to serve the needs of a particular industry, the leisure industry, makes it more difficult, in my judgment, to regard it as a professional body as compared with a body serving all those with a skill or technique of general application.

Similar decisions were reached in respect of the *Committee of Directors of Polytechnics* v. *Customs & Excise* [1992] STC 873, *Association of Payroll and Superannuation Administrators* [1990] VTD 7009, *Institute of Legal Cashiers and Administrators* [1993] VTD 12383, and *Association of Reflexologists* [1994] VTD 13078. In the latter case the Tribunal held that reflexology was not a 'profession', on the basis that there is not sufficient general acceptance of reflexology as a subject for the practice of it to be generally regarded as a profession. However, in *Institute of Shipbrokers* [1996] VTD 15033, the VAT Tribunal accepted that the Institute of Shipbrokers was a professional association on the basis of the degree of expertise required, the setting of exams which involved a substantial intellectual element and the Institute's maintenance of standards of conduct.

5.5.5 Associations for the advancement of knowledge or the fostering of professional expertise

Under UK law exemption applies to the membership subscriptions of 'an association, the primary purpose of which is the advancement of a particular branch of knowledge, or the fostering of professional expertise, connected with the past or present professions or employments of its members'. The association must restrict its membership wholly or mainly to individuals whose present or previous professions or employments are directly connected with the purposes of the association.

Wholly or mainly

As for professional associations (listed in 5.5.4 'Professional associations'), HMRC's broad approach is to see 'wholly or mainly' as meaning 75% or more of the membership must be qualifying individuals.

Primary purpose

In *Bookmaker's Protection Association (Southern Area) Ltd* v. *Customs & Excise* [1979] VATTR 215, the VAT Tribunal took the view that the primary purpose of the Association was what its directors and members considered to be the most important matter it is seeking to achieve or doing in return for membership subscriptions. The Tribunal found that the Association's main activity was advising and helping its members in their day-to-day business. This was not 'for the advancement of a particular branch of knowledge, or the fostering of professional expertise'. However, in *Revenue & Customs* v. *European Tour Operators' Association* [2012] UKUT 377 (TCC), the Upper Tribunal rejected this approach, stating: 'the relevant enquiry is an objective one, to be answered primarily by an examination of the stated objects and the actual activities of the body in question. The subjective views of the members or officers may throw some light on this enquiry, but they cannot be elevated into a diagnostic test'.

Advancement of a branch of knowledge

In *British Institute of Cleaning Science* [1985] VTD 1981, the VAT Tribunal judge said in respect of the phrase 'advancement of a branch of knowledge':

> I would give those words a narrow, rather than a wide meaning. I would not regard cleaning, even referred to as science of cleaning, as a particular branch of knowledge. To my mind these words refer to a branch of science or the art in a sense in which an academic would employ it. The words are not 'the advancement of knowledge about a particular subject', but 'the advancement of a particular branch of knowledge'.

In *Permanent Way Institution* [2001] VTD 17746, the VAT Tribunal found that an association of railway track inspectors had as its primary purpose the advancement of a particular branch of knowledge – that concerned with the acquisition and exchange of technical and general knowledge relating to the design, construction, inspection and maintenance of railway track.

In *British Association for Counselling* [1993] VTD 11855, the VAT Tribunal found that counselling was not a profession for the purposes of the professional associations exemption (see 5.5.4). However, it accepted that the primary purpose of the Association was the advancement of a particular branch of knowledge connected with the past or present professions or employments of its members, largely on the basis of the academic content of the Association's publications and courses.

Fostering of professional expertise

HMRC's position is that 'professional expertise' is restricted to expertise connected with what is generally understood to be a profession (*VAT Notice 701/5*, section 11.13). However, in *Rixml Org Ltd* v. *Customs & Excise* [2004] VTD 18717, the VAT Tribunal stated:

> Our interpretation... is that professional expertise can apply equally to a profession as such or to any employment requiring expertise whether or not it is a profession in the ordinary sense. Indeed the reference to the employments of an association's members as an alternative to their profession makes it very clear that expertise is not restricted to professions as such.

Similarly in *Institute of Information Security Professionals* v. *Revenue & Customs* [2009] UKFTT 365 (TC), the First-tier Tribunal found that, though the Institute was not a professional association, the intention of the Institute was to foster professional expertise within that employment in order that in time it may be recognised as a profession. If Parliament had intended that fostering of professional expertise can only be met by a body that has members who are members of a profession it could have said so. The Tribunal found that, taking all the evidence together, the Institute's primary purpose was to advance the professionalism of information security practitioners and thereby the professionalism of the industry as a whole and, as such, the Institute's subscriptions qualified for VAT exemption.

5.5.6 Representational trade associations

A representational trade association is defined as an association, the **primary purpose** of which is to make representations to the government on legislation and other public matters which affect the business or professional interests of its members. The association must restrict its membership **wholly or mainly** to individuals or corporate bodies whose business or professional interests are directly connected with the purposes of the association.

For the meaning of primary purpose, see 5.5.5 'Associations for the advancement of knowledge or the fostering of professional expertise'. For the meaning of wholly or mainly, see 5.5.4 'Professional associations', though for representational trade associations, qualifying members include corporate bodies.

HMRC's position is that a representational trade association must satisfy all the following criteria (*VAT Notice 701/5*, section 11.15):

1. the association's primary purpose is to 'make representations to the Government';
2. representations 'to the Government' are to the UK government;
3. the representations must relate to legislation or public matters affecting the members' business or professional interests;

4. the members are 'wholly or mainly individuals or corporate bodies whose business or professional interests are directly connected with the purposes of the association' – you should use the 75% criterion (see professional associations above) in applying the 'wholly or mainly' criterion.

In *British Association of Leisure Parks Piers & Attractions Ltd* v. *Revenue & Customs* [2011] UKFTT 662 (TC), the First-tier Tribunal found that, though lobbying was one of the Association's objects, it could not properly be described as its primary purpose which was found to be generally assisting and promoting the interests of its members through its promotion of safe practice, dissemination of information, training, lobbying, facilitating networking, etc. Even though the Tribunal accepted that the chief executive had spent 70% of his time on lobbying in recent years, that was not the case in previous periods and it rejected the idea that the primary purpose could be determined by which object makes the greatest demand on resources at a particular point in time.

In *European Tour Operators' Association* v. *Revenue & Customs* [2011] UKFTT 88 (TC) and *Revenue & Customs* v. *European Tour Operators' Association* [2012] UKUT 377 (TCC), both Tribunals considered HMRC's condition (2) above to be wrong in that it excludes representations to EU institutions and other EU governments. The Upper Tribunal also drew a distinction between the primary 'purpose' of the association, which has to be lobbying, and the 'purposes' to which the business or professional interests of its members are connected. Those purposes can be other than lobbying. The Upper Tribunal found that a direct connection with all the purposes of the Association taken together will satisfy the membership requirement, though 'whether a direct connection with just one of the ancillary purposes, viewed in isolation, would also suffice is far less clear'.

5.5.7 **Other public interest bodies**

Under UK law other public interest bodies are bodies which have objects which are in the public domain and are of a **political**, **religious**, **patriotic**, **philosophical**, **philanthropic** or **civic** nature.

Objects

All of the body's principal objects may have to fall within one or more of the above categories. In *United Grand Lodge of England* v. *Revenue & Customs* [2014] UKFTT 164 (TC), the First-tier Tribunal stated

> It seems to us that the Directive does not make it a condition for exemption that the aims of the body must fall exclusively into one of the listed categories. Thus a body whose aims were partly religious and partly patriotic could qualify. That

follows from the use of the plural 'aims'. But it is not enough that some of its aims, or some part of its aims fall within one or more of the listed categories because the requirement is that the nature of the aims falls within those categories. Unless the principal part of those aims falls within one or more listed categories, its aims would not have the requisite nature. That requires in our view that the remainder of those aims are minor, insignificant or incidental, or ancillary to aims of the requisite character.

In the public domain

This means that the benefits conferred by the objects must be directed outside the particular organisation and beyond the members themselves to the general community.

HMRC definitions

HMRC defines the above terms as follows (*VAT Notice 701/5*, section 12.2):

- **Political** aim includes campaigns for or against legislative and constitutional changes or campaigns in local and central government elections.
- **Religious** aim includes all denominations and creeds, old and new, that command a following.
- **Patriotic** aim means to do good work for the benefit of a nation state or for those who have served their country and their dependants.
- **Philosophical** aim means the advancement of a particular way of thinking but which is not of a political or religious nature. They are very similar to learned societies in that they are of an academic nature.
- **Philanthropic** means to do good work for the direct benefit of the general community or a particular section of the community or designed to promote the well-being of mankind.
- **Civic** aims promote rights and duties of citizens in matters of public interest and public affairs.

Religious

In *United Grand Lodge of England* v. *Revenue & Customs* [2014], the First-tier Tribunal adopted the description of religion set out by Lord Toulson in *R. (Hodkin)* v. *Registrar-General of Births, Deaths and Marriages* [2013] UKSC 77:

I would describe religion in summary as a spiritual or non-secular belief system, held by a group of adherents, which claims to explain mankind's place in the universe and relationship with the infinite, and to teach its adherents how they are to live their lives in conformity with the spiritual understanding associated with the belief system. By spiritual or non-secular I mean a belief system which goes beyond that which can be perceived by the senses or ascertained by the application of science... Such a belief system may or may not involve belief in a supreme being, but it does involve a belief that there is more to be understood about mankind's nature and relationship to the universe than can be gained from the senses or from science. I emphasise that this is intended to be a description and not a definitive formula.

Philanthropic

In *Rotary International* [1991] VATTR 177 the Tribunal adopted the *Shorter Oxford Dictionary* definition of philanthropy which is 'Love towards mankind; practical benevolence towards men in general; the disposition to promote the well-being of one's fellow men' and philanthropic means 'Characterised by philanthropy; benevolent, humane'.

Civic

In *Expert Witness Institute* v. *Customs & Excise* [2001] EWCA Civ 1882, 'civic' was defined as 'of, pertaining or proper to citizens' and the requirement that a body has objects which are of a civic nature means that the body must have objects which promote the relationship of citizens, not among themselves, but with the state of which they are citizens. The Court of Appeal found that the Institute's stated objective which was 'the support of the proper administration of justice and the early resolution of disputes through fair and unbiased expert evidence' was in the public domain and civic in nature.

5.6 **COST SHARING GROUPS**

EU law

The Principal VAT Directive Article 132(1)(f) exempts:

> the supply of services by independent groups of persons, who are carrying on an activity which is exempt from VAT or in relation to which they are not taxable persons, for the purpose of rendering their members the services directly necessary for the exercise of that activity, where those groups merely claim from their members exact reimbursement of their share of the joint expenses, provided that such exemption is not likely to cause distortion of competition.

The objective of the measure is to allow small and medium-sized entities to obtain the same economies of scale that larger entities obtain.

UK law

The UK did not enact this exemption until 17 July 2012 when it added a new group (group 16) to the VAT exemptions listed in section 9 VAT Act 1994. This exempts:

1. the supply of services by an independent group of persons where each of the following conditions is satisfied:
   (a) each of those persons is a person who is carrying on an activity ('the relevant activity') which is exempt from VAT or in relation to which the person is not a taxable person (i.e. exempt or non-business activities);
   (b) the supply of services is made for the purpose of rendering the members of the group the services directly necessary for the exercise of the relevant activity;
   (c) the group merely claims from its members exact reimbursement of their share of the joint expenses; and
   (d) the exemption of the supply is not likely to cause distortion of competition.

The exemption applies to supplies of services only, not to supplies of goods. As such, it can be used for supplies of staff, advice services, research, intellectual property rights, digital supplies and so on, but not for bulk purchase schemes for goods such as bulk equipment and materials purchases.

At the time of writing there are no detailed VAT regulations for this exemption. See 'The Luxembourg case' below as to why. The main HMRC guidance is in *VAT Information Sheet 07/12* (issued 24 August 2012). Unless otherwise stated, references to HMRC statements are references to this Information Sheet.

5.6.1 Cost sharing group conditions

As HMRC sees it, there are five conditions that a supply of services must meet in order to be VAT exempt as a 'qualifying CSG supply'.

1. There must be an 'independent group of persons' (a Cost Sharing Group or CSG) supplying services to persons who are its 'members'.
2. All the members must carry on an activity that is exempt from VAT or one which is not a business activity for VAT purposes.
3. The services supplied by the CSG, to which the exemption applies, must be 'directly necessary' for a member's exempt and/or non-business activities.
4. The CSG merely claims from each member exact reimbursement of their share of the joint expenses.
5. The application of the exemption to the supplies made by the CSG to its members is not likely to cause a distortion of competition.

Each condition is considered below.

1. There must be an 'independent group of persons' (a Cost Sharing Group or CSG) supplying services to persons who are its 'members'

The CSG must be legally separate from each of its members; otherwise it cannot make supplies to its members. Each CSG must have two or more members otherwise it is not a group of persons. Organisations can be members of more than one CSG if they so choose. The CSG must be established, owned and operated by the members for their cooperative benefit and be independent of any ownership, control or influence outside the membership. If the members agree one or more members can hold more than 50% of the shares. No shares can be held by any person who is not a member of the CSG.

2. All the members must carry on an activity that is exempt from VAT or one which is not a business activity for VAT purposes

HMRC imposes a 5% entry criterion. This means, a member cannot join unless they have (or will have within 12 months) at least 5% exempt plus non-business activity. If the level of exempt plus non-business activity drops below 5% the member must leave. All members must also actually receive qualifying exempt supplies from the CSG or have a realistic and genuine intention to do so. If they cease to receive qualifying CSG supplies for a period of more than 12 months then HMRC will presume (subject to being shown to be wrong) that an intention to receive such supplies had ceased and, therefore, the member will cease to be eligible for membership of the CSG going forward.

3. The services supplied by the CSG, to which the exemption applies, must be 'directly necessary' for a member's exempt and/or non-business activities

HMRC's interpretation is that directly necessary means directly **attributable** (see 3.1.3 'Step 2: Direct attribution') to the exempt and/or non-business activities in the partial exemption sense (see 3.1 'VAT recovery principles'). This means that CSG services used for mixed/residual activities do not qualify for exemption. However, 'on an optional simplification basis', where a member of a CSG has low levels of taxable activity, all the supplies they receive from a CSG will be regarded by HMRC as 'directly necessary' for the exempt and/or non-business activities. A low level of taxable activity for the purposes of this test is less than 15%, so, where a member of a CSG has exempt and/or non-business activities that form 85% or more of their total activities, all the supplies they receive from their CSG will be regarded as 'directly necessary'. The member will be entitled to receive all of their supplies from the CSG exempt for as long as their level of exempt and/or non-business supplies remains at 85% or more.

4. The CSG merely claims from each member exact reimbursement of their share of the joint expenses

HMRC expects a CSG to have a clear audit trail demonstrating how this condition is met. HMRC accepts that allowable expenses for the CSG include amounts required to meet anticipated future expenditure and depreciation in the value of the CSG's assets. HMRC states:

> Provided the CSG can demonstrate that the exact reimbursement rule has been met over a reasonable period of time, running a deficit or surplus (provided any surplus is held for future use by the CSG for the specific benefit of its members) will not affect the use of the exemption. CSGs can demonstrate whether the exact reimbursement test has been met or not by using normal accounting techniques and the judgement can be made over a period of time that is reasonable given the nature and context of the supplies being made.

In *West of Scotland Colleges Partnership* (see 5.6.2 below) the First-tier Tribunal decided the 'exact reimbursement' condition is a strict one and it is for the CSG to demonstrate that it is met.

5. The application of the exemption to the supplies made by the CSG to its members is not likely to cause a distortion of competition

HMRC states (*VAT Information Sheet 07/12*, section 51)

> A CSG is a cooperative self-supply arrangement. It is not a commercial outsourcing arrangement therefore it does not exist or compete in a market. As long as all the conditions of the exemption are met, particularly that it can only supply its members on a direct reimbursement basis, that is, it self-supplies at cost, there should be little question of the exemption distorting a market and therefore little question of failing to meet this condition.

5.6.2 Case law

The Advocate General in the *Taksatorringen* case (case C-8/01 *Assurandør-Societetet acting on behalf of Taksatorringen* v. *Skatteministeriet* [2003] ECR I-13711) stated:

> There are two fundamental requirements that must be met in order to qualify for an exemption. First, the independent external service provider must consist only of operators carrying out an activity which is exempt from, or not subject to, VAT. Secondly, it is essential that the group does not exist for purposes of gain, in the sense that it only charges its members for expenses incurred by it in order to meet their requirements, and makes no profit whatsoever out of doing so. This means that the group must be entirely transparent and that, from an economic point of view, it must not have the characteristics of an independent operator seeking a customer base in order to generate profits.

In case C-407/07 *Stichting Centraal Begeleidingsorgaan voor de Intercollegiale Toetsing* v. *Staatssecretaris van Financiën* [2008] ECR I-09615, the Netherlands government argued that 'claim from its members exact reimbursement of their share of the joint expenses' refers to services supplied to all the members of the group and not to services supplied to one member of it, so the latter cannot qualify for exemption. The CJEU rejected this. Such a restriction of the scope of the exemption is not supported by the purpose of that provision. The CJEU held that the services are capable of being covered by the exemption, even if those services are supplied to one member or to a subset of the members.

In *West of Scotland Colleges Partnership* v. *Revenue & Customs* [2014] UKFTT 622 (TC), a group of further and higher education colleges set up a CSG to help them find new sources of funding. In the initial year subscriptions were equal. In the next year an increase was tapered in relation to the size of the particular college. HMRC disputed that this met the 'exact reimbursement condition' (see 5.6.1 'Cost sharing group conditions' condition 4). The Tribunal found that the exact reimbursement condition is a strict one and that it was for the Partnership to prove that it has been met. The Partnership was unable to provide sufficient evidence that its fee structure resulted in exact reimbursement and the Tribunal accordingly found that the conditions for exemption had not been met.

5.6.3 **CSGs and VAT groups**

HMRC accepts that one or more members of a VAT group can join a CSG and also that the CSG itself can be a member of a VAT group:

- **Member in a VAT group**: HMRC accepts that a VAT group member can be a member of a CSG. However, even though supplies by the CSG to the member are deemed to be to the VAT group's representative member, the VAT group is looked through when considering CSG supplies. So it is the actual CSG member that must meet the CSG entry criteria and that must receive the supplies wholly or 85% or more for its non-business or exempt activities. Supplies from the CSG that go to other VAT group members are not covered by the cost sharing exemption, unless the other VAT group member is also a member of the CSG.
- **CSG in a VAT group**: HMRC accepts that a CSG can be a member of a VAT group, provided the normal VAT grouping conditions are met. These (broadly) are that all members must be corporate bodies controlled by one another (directly or indirectly) or subject to common control. See 2.2 'VAT groups' for more on the VAT group conditions.

- **CSG and member in the same VAT group**: HMRC accepts that this is possible. HMRC states:

> For example if the controlling entity of the VAT group was also a CSG member and had over 50% of the shareholding of the CSG (with the remaining shareholding spread between the other CSG members) the CSG would meet the control condition to be a member of the VAT group.

HMRC also accepts that in principle a CSG member can supply services to the CSG. However, HMRC warns that if such supplies are used as a mechanism to artificially inflate costs in order to extract a profit from the supplies made by the CSG then they will fail to meet the 'exact reimbursement' condition and will be treated as fully taxable.

5.6.4 Cross-border CSGs

HMRC accepts that members of a UK-established CSG can themselves be established in other EU member states and similarly a UK-established business or organisation can be a member of a CSG established in another EU member state.

However, cross-border CSGs are likely to be problematic since (as explained in Chapter 9 'International aspects of VAT') if the place of supply of a service is another EU state, that state's VAT-exemption rules apply and, as illustrated by the Luxembourg case below, there are substantial variations between EU member states in the implementation of the cost sharing exemption.

5.6.5 The Luxembourg case

The EC has commenced infringement proceedings against Luxembourg on the basis that its implementation of the cost sharing exemption is flawed. The EC objects to the Luxembourg implementation on three grounds, one of which is that members can join a CSG if taxable activities do not exceed 30% of their annual turnover (or 45% under certain conditions). This gives rise to the question of whether HMRC's '85%' test (see 5.6.1 'Cost sharing group conditions' condition 3) is possible, as it permits CSG treatment if taxable activity remains below 15%.

HMRC will monitor these proceedings and consider whether or not any changes are necessary to the guidance. Should changes prove to be necessary, then transitional arrangements, as far as possible, will be put in place to facilitate an orderly move to the revised position.

5.7 **FUNDRAISING EVENTS**

EU law

EU law exempts in Principal VAT Directive Article 132(1)(o):

> the supply of services and goods, by eligible organisations in connection with fundraising events organised exclusively for their own benefit, provided that exemption is not likely to cause distortion of competition. Member States may introduce any restrictions necessary to prevent distortion of competition, in particular as regards the number of events or the amount of receipts which give entitlement to exemption.

The eligible organisations are the following bodies whose supplies qualify for VAT exemption in the public interest:

- Article 132(1)(b): hospitals, centres for medical treatment or diagnosis and other duly recognised establishments of a similar nature (see 5.2.2 'Medical or surgical treatment in a hospital or medical centre');
- Article 132(1)(g): eligible suppliers of welfare and social security work, including old people's homes, bodies governed by public law and other bodies recognised by the member state concerned as being devoted to social well-being (see 5.2.4 'Welfare services');
- Article 132(1)(h): eligible suppliers of services and of goods closely linked to the protection of children and young persons (see 5.2.4 'Welfare services');
- Article 132(1)(i): eligible suppliers of children's or young people's education, school or university education, vocational training or retraining (see 5.1.2 'Education' and 5.1.3 'Vocational training or retraining');
- Article 132(1)(l): non-profit-making membership organisations with aims of a political, trade union, religious, patriotic, philosophical, philanthropic or civic nature (see 5.5 'Subscriptions to public interest bodies');
- Article 132(1)(m): eligible suppliers of services closely linked to sport or physical education (see 5.4 'Sports and physical education');
- Article 132(1)(n): eligible suppliers of cultural services (see 5.3 'Cultural services').

UK law

UK law exempts supplies at three types of fundraising event:

1. Fundraising events organised by one or more charities

The supply of goods and services by a charity in connection with an event:

(a) that is organised for charitable purposes by a charity or jointly by more than one charity;
(b) whose primary purpose is the raising of money; and
(c) that is promoted as being primarily for the raising of money.

2. Fundraising events organised by a qualifying body

The supply of goods and services by a **qualifying body** (see 5.7.1 Qualifying bodies) in connection with an event:

(a) that is organised exclusively for the body's own benefit;
(b) whose primary purpose is the raising of money; and
(c) that is promoted as being primarily for the raising of money.

3. Fundraising events organised jointly by one or more charities and a qualifying body

The supply of goods and services by a charity or a qualifying body in connection with an event:

(a) that is organised jointly by a charity, or two or more charities, and the qualifying body;
(b) that is so organised exclusively for charitable purposes or exclusively for the body's own benefit or exclusively for a combination of those purposes and that benefit;
(c) whose primary purpose is the raising of money; and
(d) that is promoted as being primarily for the raising of money.

Excluded supplies

Items (1) to (3) above do not include the following excluded supplies:

- supplies at events where participants are supplied with accommodation that is not incidental to the event itself (see 5.7.10 'Challenge events');
- supplies at some events where more than 15 events of the same kind are held at the same location (see 5.7.7 'Limitation on the number of events');
- any supply the exemption of which would be likely to create distortions of competition such as to place a commercial enterprise carried on by a taxable person at a disadvantage (see 5.7.8 'Primary purpose and promotion').

The main HMRC guidance on the exemption for qualifying fundraising events is at www.gov.uk/government/publications/charity-fundraising-events-exemptions which is the HMRC guidance referred to below unless otherwise stated.

5.7.1 Qualifying bodies

These are:

- qualifying public interest membership bodies: trades unions; professional associations; associations for the advancement of knowledge or the fostering of professional expertise; representational trade associations; and bodies which have objects which are in the public domain and are of a political, religious, patriotic, philosophical, philanthropic or civic nature (see 5.5 'Subscriptions to public interest bodies');

- an eligible body for the purposes of the exemption for sports and physical education whose principal purpose is the provision of facilities for persons to take part in sport or physical education (see 5.4 'Sports and physical education');
- an eligible body for the purposes of the exemption for cultural services (see 5.3 'Cultural services').

5.7.2 Charity subsidiaries

In the UK exemptions (1) and (3) above, 'charity' is deemed to include a body corporate that is wholly owned by a charity, provided:

- the body has agreed in writing (whether or not contained in a deed) to transfer its profits (from whatever source) to a charity; or
- the body's profits (from whatever source) are otherwise payable to a charity.

At *VCHAR9400* HMRC states:

> We will accept that for the purposes of this exemption, the transfer of profits condition is met when: (i) the arrangements are compatible with charity law, (ii) profits are paid to the charity, (iii) the only profit retained annually by the subsidiary is not subject to Corporation Tax, (iv) the profit is retained for development which has the clear aim of increasing funds going to the charity, and (v) the subsidiary is not involved in any abuse or avoidance. This approach may be reviewed if the amount of profits eligible for Corporation Tax relief changes or abuse occurs.

All taxable profits retained after Gift Aid will normally be subject to Corporation Tax so it is difficult to see when condition (iii) would apply. The original HMRC guidance on this point (at section 9.4 of *V1–9*) was framed in terms of the retained profits falling within the pre-2006 nil band for Corporation Tax (£10,000 divided by the number of associated companies). However, this nil band was abolished with effect from 1 April 2006.

5.7.3 Goods and services exempted

The exemption covers all supplies made 'in connection with' a qualifying fundraising event including: admissions, sales at the event such as catering and merchandise; sponsorship of the event; the letting out of land for stalls and stands; and the sale of advertising in an event brochure.

Option to tax overridden

In *Southport Flower Show* v. *Revenue & Customs* [2012] UKFTT 244 (TC), a charity licensed trade stands at a qualifying fundraising event; however, the charity claimed that the option to tax overrode the exemption for supplies in connection with the event. The Tribunal dismissed the charity's appeal. The option to tax did not alter the fact that the supply of the trade stands was 'in connection with' a qualifying fundraising event and therefore VAT exempt.

5.7.4   Zero-rated sales

Sales that qualify for zero-rating can be zero-rated in preference (by virtue of VAT Act 1994 section 30(1)), for example:

● printed programmes;
● children's clothing;
● supplies of advertising to charities;
● auction lots comprising goods donated to a charity for sale.

However, auction lots comprising bought-in goods, bought-in services and donated services (for example, a donated restaurant meal) are not covered by the zero-rating and so their sale is VAT exempt unless they qualify for zero-rating in their own right, for example an auction lot comprising a bought-in hamper of zero-rated foodstuffs.

5.7.5   Sales after the event

Goods and services sold after the event do not qualify for VAT exemption, unless they are sold at another qualifying event, for example surplus stock and video recordings of the event.

5.7.6   Meaning of event

UK legislation defines event as including an event accessed (wholly or partly) by means of electronic communications. HMRC defines an event as follows:

> An 'event' is an incident with an outcome or a result. This means that activities of a semi-regular or continuous nature, such as the frequent operation of a shop or bar, cannot therefore be an event. The relief is not intended to exempt normal trading activities from VAT.

See 5.7.7 'Limitation on the number of events' for the types of event HMRC accepts as different kinds of event.

Events within events

HMRC accepts that it is possible for a qualifying fundraising event to take part at another qualifying or non-qualifying event (*VCHAR9300*):

> Sometimes a charity may be able to organise an exempt fund-raising event in association with a different event (which may or may not be an exempt fund-raising event in its own right). An example might be a national sporting event where the charity plans to have a marquee and hold an auction of sporting memorabilia. The charity can use the fund-raising exemption as long as the event it is organising meets all the other conditions of the fund-raising exemption.

5.7.7 Limitation on the number of events

There must be not more than 15 events of the same kind in the same location in the body's financial year. However, kinds of events whose aggregate gross takings at any location do not exceed £1,000 per week can be ignored when assessing the 15 limit. This means that small-scale events such as coffee mornings and jumble sales should be able to be omitted in counting the 15 limit.

If the financial year is not 12 months, the 15 limit is adjusted proportionately (on a day basis). If the 15 limit is exceeded then none of the events (including the 15 already put on) qualify for VAT exemption.

Same kind of event

HMRC accepts the following as different kinds of event:
- a ball, dinner dance, disco or barn dance;
- a performance – such as concert, stage production, and any other event which has a paying audience;
- the showing of a film;
- a fete, fair or festival;
- a horticultural show;
- an exhibition – such as art, history or science;
- a bazaar, jumble sale, car boot sale, or a good-as-new sale;
- sporting participation (including spectators), such as a sponsored walk or swim;
- a sporting performance;
- a game of skill, a contest, or a quiz;
- participation in an endurance event;
- a fireworks display;
- a dinner, lunch or barbecue;
- an auction of bought-in goods.

> HMRC (2011), *Fundraising events: exemption for charities and other qualifying bodies*, section 3.3).

In *Newsvendors Benevolent Institution* [1996] VTD 14343 a charity claimed that a festival dinner, a race day and a carol concert were all of the same kind. The VAT

Tribunal held that they were not like events, as the events were intrinsically dissimilar with no quality inherent in the nature of the events which is common to all.

Series of events

HMRC's position is that, where an event, such as a concert, is repeated on successive evenings each performance is a separate event and counts towards the 15 limit. However, a single event which takes place at the same location for more than one day, such as a golf tournament, is accepted as one event.

Same location

HMRC does not accept that the following are separate locations (HMRC 2011, *Fundraising events: exemption for charities and other qualifying bodies*, section 3.5):
- car boot sales each held in different, but adjacent fields;
- events held in different cinemas, theatres or concert halls within the same building.

Online auctions

For online auctions HMRC's position (*VCHAR9300*) is that an auction taking place over several days is a single event if: (i) there is a specified closing date; (ii) bidding closes at this date; and (iii) goods are not sold before the closing date. When these conditions are not met, the sale of each item (or lot) would be a separate event.

5.7.8 Primary purpose and promotion

UK law specifies that the primary purpose of a qualifying fundraising event must be the raising of money and that it must be promoted as such. However, these requirements are absent from the Principal VAT Directive and there is therefore a question as to whether these requirements of UK law are beyond the UK's legal authority. The Principal VAT Directive specified that EU states may impose any restrictions necessary to prevent distortions of competition, but it is not clear that these two restrictions are necessary to prevent distortions of competition, especially given the UK exemption specifically excludes from exemption any supply the exemption of which would be likely to create distortions of competition.

In the case *Loughborough Students' Union (LSU)* v. *Revenue & Customs* [2012], the First-tier Tribunal (Tax) (FTT) found no evidence that the Union's Freshers' and Graduation Balls were promoted as being primarily for the raising of money, and rejected exemption on this basis. The publicity disclosed that profits would go to the Union but the FTT considered that this is not the same as disclosing that the primary purpose of the events was to raise money. The Union appealed to the Upper Tribunal (Tax) (UTT) in *Loughborough Students' Union* v. *Revenue & Customs* [2013] (partly) on the basis that the FTT had failed to consider its argument that the UK law requirements are *ultra vires*. The UTT remitted the case to the FTT for a decision on the issue which it considered to be essentially one of fact – do the restrictions as to purpose and promotion prevent distortion of competition in LSU's case? At the time of writing the FTT's decision is awaited.

5.7.9 Commercial fundraising events

Events that are not organised by a charity, a qualifying charity trading subsidiary or other qualifying body do not qualify for exemption. For example, a fundraising event organised by a private company with proceeds donated to charity.

5.7.10 Challenge events

Fundraising events do not qualify for exemption if they include provision of:
- a package of both travel and accommodation; or
- bought-in accommodation; or
- more than two nights' accommodation from a charity's own resources.

This exclusion means that challenge-type events, where participants are provided with bought-in accommodation, or a package of travel and accommodation, will not qualify for VAT exemption.

See 7.8 'Challenge events'.

5.8 PUBLIC POSTAL SERVICES

EU law

Principal VAT Directive Article 132(1)(a) exempts the supply by 'the public postal services' of services other than passenger transport and telecommunications services, and the supply of goods incidental thereto.

UK law

UK law exempts the supply of public postal services (and incidental goods) by a **universal service provider** (USP). Public postal services means any postal services which the USP is required to provide in the discharge of a **specified condition**.

For more on specified conditions and downstream services see 5.8.3 'Upstream and downstream services').

Specified conditions refer to conditions specified in or via the Postal Services Act 2011. Exemption also applies to services a USP provides to allow access to their network which are required to be provided by a specified condition, such as **downstream services**.

5.8.1 Universal Service Providers (USPs)

This exemption must be read in conjunction with the EU Postal Directive (97/67/EC) which establishes common rules concerning the provision of a universal postal service within the EU by USPs. EU States must ensure that users enjoy the right to a universal postal service involving the permanent provision of a postal service of specified quality at all points in their territory at affordable prices for all users. USPs must guarantee one local clearance and one delivery to the home or premises of every natural or legal person every working day and not less than five days a week, save in circumstances or geographical conditions deemed exceptional. Each member state must adopt the measures necessary to ensure that the universal service includes as a minimum the clearance, sorting, transport and distribution of postal items and postal packets up to set weights and services for registered items and insured items.

Exempt Royal Mail Services

At the time of writing the UK Royal Mail is the sole UK USP and Royal Mail's exempt public postal services are:

UK
- 1st and 2nd Class (stamps, online, franking, account)
- Special Delivery Guaranteed™ (stamps and franking)
- Royal Mail Signed For™ (if purchased with a VAT-exempt service)
- Keepsafe™ (personal and business)

International
- International Standard
- International Economy
- International Signed and International Tracked & Signed
- All HM Forces Mail (BFPO)

Inbound Mail
- Redirections within UK (personal and business)

Royal Mail 2015, 'Information on VAT and postal services'

Notably excluded from exemption are individually negotiated bulk mail agreements and Business Mail type services which all bear standard-rated VAT. See 5.8.3 'Upstream and downstream services'.

5.8.2 The *TNT Post* case

Before 2010 UK law exempted a much wider range of Royal Mail services; however, the exemption was restricted from 2010 as a result of the CJEU's decision in case C-357/07 *TNT Post UK Ltd* v. *Revenue & Customs* [2009] EWHC (QB) ECR I-03025. In this case the CJEU held that the public postal services referred to in the Principal VAT Directive exemption refer to the actual organisations which engage in the supply of the services to be exempted. It follows that the public postal services must be regarded as operators, whether they are public or private, who undertake to supply postal services which meet the essential needs of the population and therefore, in practice, to provide all or part of the universal postal service in a member state, as defined in Directive 97/67.

However, the CJEU also stated that, contrary to the UK government's position, it may not be inferred that all the services supplied by the public postal services are exempted, regardless of their intrinsic nature. The services exempted are those that the public postal services carry out as such by virtue of their status as public postal services. The exemption is not to apply to specific services dissociable from the service of public interest, including services which meet special needs of economic operators. Individually negotiated services cannot be regarded as exempted, as by their very nature, those services meet the special needs of the users concerned.

Following this decision the UK law was changed with effect from 31 January 2011.

5.8.3 Upstream and downstream services

Upstream services

Upstream services are the collection of sorted and unsorted mail from collection points, the provision of mechanised and manual sorting services (for unsorted mail), and processing and delivery to a Royal Mail regional depot.

Downstream services

Downstream services are delivery of collected and sorted mail between regional depots and delivery from a regional depot to the addressees (the 'final mile').

In the UK Royal Mail is currently the dominant provider of downstream services; however, commercial operators compete in the upstream market. Upstream service providers are also entitled to access Royal Mail's downstream services by law and this downstream access service is covered by the UK's VAT exemption.

Downstream service access (DSA) providers provide an upstream service (which includes collection, sorting and delivery to Royal Mail) coupled with an agency agreement with Royal Mail under which the DSA provider acts as its customers' **agent** (see 11.2) in obtaining Royal Mail downstream services. This means that Royal Mail's exempt supply of downstream access services is direct to the customer and covered by the VAT exemption. Standard-rated VAT is only charged on any upstream component. As the downstream access is normally the most expensive component (by a factor of ten plus), this potentially represents a considerable saving for organisations that purchase bulk mail services but cannot recover all of the related VAT.

5.8.4 Supplies of goods with delivery

The exemption in this section applies where postal services are provided by a USP. If you arrange for Royal Mail delivery of goods, then there are various options:

1. If your contract with your customer is for delivered goods and you arrange for delivery of the goods by Royal Mail with Royal Mail acting as your agent in delivering the goods, you are making a single supply of delivered goods taking on a single VAT status.
2. If delivery is an optional extra and as such a separate supply of delivery services, then, as you are not a USP, your supply of delivery services is standard-rated.
3. HMRC accepts (*VAT Notice 700/24*, section 3.4) that direct mail providers (posting a client's mail to listed addresses) can treat Royal Mail charges as a disbursement for VAT purposes, provided the following conditions are all met:

    * the provider meets the general disbursement requirements (see 11.2.4 'Disbursements');
    * the provider's responsibility for the mail ceases when it is accepted for safe delivery by Royal Mail; and
    * the provider passes on any Royal Mail discount or rebate in full or, if it obtains the discount or rebate from posting various clients' mail at the same time, it apportions it fairly between them.

5.9 INSURANCE SERVICES

EU law

Principal VAT Directive Article 135(1)(a) exempts insurance and reinsurance transactions, including related services performed by insurance brokers and insurance agents.

In the *Card Protection Plan* case (see 11.3.3 'Single/multiple supply case law') the CJEU defined an insurance transaction as an undertaking by an insurer, in return for prior payment of a premium, to provide the insured, in the event of materialisation of the risk covered, with the service agreed under the insurance contract.

UK law

UK law exempts:

1. insurance transactions and reinsurance transactions;
2. the provision by an insurance broker or insurance agent of insurance intermediary services.

The main HMRC guidance on insurance services is in *VAT Notice 701/36*, the February 2013 edition of which is referred to below.

5.9.1 **Block policies**

Voluntary organisations sometimes hold a block insurance policy and sell the insurance to third parties. For example, a sports body may hold a block policy that covers purchasing members against injury or third-party liability whilst taking part in the sport concerned. Or a charity hiring out its premises for events may provide an optional insurance package for hirers.

If the insurance is optional it is treated as a sale of insurance for VAT purposes and is VAT exempt, even though the membership body is not itself the insurer. The membership body is acting as principal in this arrangement, so the whole premium receivable is exempt income.

A block insurance policy will normally name the business taking out the policy as the 'Policyholder', with the 'Persons Insured' shown as the customers of the policyholder. Sometimes the contract will name the 'Persons Insured' as the business taking out the policy and its customers, without actually naming each individual customer. HMRC defines the key characteristics of a block policy as follows (*VAT Notice 701/36*, section 2.5.1):

- there is a contract between the block policyholder and the insurer which allows the block policyholder to effect insurance cover subject to certain conditions;
- the block policyholder, acting in their own name, procures insurance cover for third parties from the insurer;
- there is a contractual relationship between the block policyholder and third parties under which the insurance is procured; and
- the block policyholder stands in place of the insurer in effecting the supply of insurance to the third parties.

5.9.2 **Services of insurance intermediaries**

The provision by an insurance broker or insurance agent of the services of an insurance intermediary is VAT exempt where those services:

(a) are related (whether or not a contract of insurance or reinsurance is finally concluded) to an insurance transaction or a reinsurance transaction; and

(b) are provided by that broker or agent in the course of their acting in an intermediary capacity.

Services of an insurance intermediary are:

(a) **introductory services**: the bringing together, with a view to the insurance or reinsurance of risks, of (i) persons who are or may be seeking insurance or reinsurance, and (ii) persons who provide insurance or reinsurance;

(b) **preparatory work**: the carrying out of work preparatory to the conclusion of contracts of insurance or reinsurance;

(c) **claims handling**: the provision of assistance in the administration and performance of such contracts, including the handling of claims;

(d) **collecting premiums**: the collection of premiums.

However, the following services are excluded:

- the supply of any market research, product design, advertising, promotional or similar services;
- the collection, collation and provision of information for use in connection with market research, product design, advertising, promotional or similar activities;
- valuation or inspection services.

Where a person provides exempt insurance intermediary services, the person's commission is the exempt turnover for partial exemption purposes.

5.9.3 Introductory services

It can be difficult to distinguish introductory services (which qualify for exemption) from advertising (which does not qualify for exemption). HMRC accepts that an insurance intermediary is providing introductory services where they are playing an active part in the sale of the insurance and the following three criteria are met (*VAT Notice 701/36*, section 8.3.1):

- they are paid per successful take-up of an insurance policy;
- they are targeting their own customer base; and
- the intermediary endorses the product or the insurer.

In *Revenue & Customs* v. *Trader Media Group Ltd* [2009] EWHC 999 (Ch) and *Revenue & Customs* v. *Insurancewide.com* [2010] EWCA Civ 422, Trader Media operated a website where a member of the public could click a button labelled 'get a quote'. Clicking the button led through to a Trader Media branded form that was actually operated by a third party (BISL). The form was prepared by and submitted to BISL which returned several quotes from different insurance companies within a few minutes. The user could click on one of the insurance offers if they wished to purchase that product. If the user took out one of the insurance contracts offered, Trader Media was paid a commission by the insurer.

All communications between the users were done on Auto Trader branded e-mails sent by BISL.

HMRC argued that Auto Trader was just supplying advertising services; however, the High Court and Court of Appeal both rejected this and accepted that Auto Trader was doing enough to be supplying introductory services. The High Court defined an introducer as 'one who, by reason of his relationship with two or more individuals or groups of individuals, is able to put two or more of those individuals or groups in contact with each other with a view to their forming, in the future, a commercial relationship, in these cases a relationship of insurer and insured'. It is not necessary for the introducer to have a direct relationship with both customer and insurer as long as they are part of a chain of introduction communicating between customer and insurer.

Following this case HMRC issued *Revenue & Customs Brief 31/10* in which it accepted that insurance introductory services will be exempt from VAT when a provider is doing much more than acting as a 'mere conduit' through which a potential customer is passed to a provider. This can be demonstrated by all of the following four conditions being met:

1. The services are provided by someone engaged in the business of putting insurance companies in touch with potential clients or more generally acting as an intermediary between the two parties (although this may not necessarily be their principal business activity).
2. The business provides the means (that is, by way of an internet 'click through' or some other form of introduction) by which a person seeking insurance is introduced to a provider of insurance or to another intermediary in a chain leading to an insurance provider.
3. That introduction takes place at the time a customer is seeking to enter into an insurance contract (although in some instances an insurance contract may not actually go on to be finally concluded).
4. The introducer also plays a proactive part in putting in place the arrangements under which that introduction is effected.

For the purposes of condition 4 above, evidence that the introducer has been proactive in putting in place the arrangements under which the introduction is effected could, for example, take the form of some or all of the following:

- active endorsement of the insurer or the insurance product;
- involvement in the selection of the insurance products and/or providers;
- involvement in the process under which the insurance contract is entered into, even though the intermediation of the contact itself is undertaken by a third party (for example, by having input into what questions should be asked of the prospective insured or the design of the third party's website);
- negotiating a special rate for the insurance product/s on behalf of its customers or membership base;

- some form of assessment of the customer's requirements so that they are directed to the most appropriate insurer for them.

5.10 BETTING, LOTTERIES AND OTHER FORMS OF GAMBLING

EU law

Principal VAT Directive Article 135(1)(i) exempts betting, lotteries and other forms of gambling, subject to the conditions and limitations laid down by each member state.

UK law

UK law exempts (VAT Act 1994 Sch. 9 Group 4):

1. the provision of any facilities for the placing of bets;
2. the provision of any facilities for the playing of any games of chance for a prize;
3. the provision of any facilities for the playing of dutiable machine games, but only to the extent that the facilities are used to play such games, and the takings and payouts in respect of those games are taken into account in determining the charge to machine games duty;
4. the granting of a right to take part in a lottery.

Exemptions (1) and (2) exclude:

- admission to any premises;
- the provision by a club of such facilities to its members as are available to them on payment of their subscription but without further charge;
- the provision of a relevant gaming machine.

The value of the exempt supply is the full amount of the stakes or takings, less any money paid out in winnings or, if the prizes are goods, their cost (including VAT). However, you must not deduct any betting or gaming duty payable.

5.10.1 Games of chance

A game of chance is defined to exclude a sport but includes:

- a game that involves both an element of chance and an element of skill;
- a game that involves an element of chance that can be eliminated by superlative skill; and
- a game that is presented as involving an element of chance.

A person plays a game of chance if they participate in a game of chance:

- whether or not there are other participants in the game, and
- whether or not a computer generates images or data taken to represent the actions of other participants in the game.

HMRC's position (*VAT Notice 701/29*) is that games of chance include:

- pure games of chance – such as dice or roulette, where the result cannot be influenced by the player; or
- chance and skill combined, such as whist or rubber bridge, where the player either cannot eliminate chance or can only do so by exercising superlative skill;
- participation and session charges made for the right to take part in a game or series of games of bingo are also VAT exempt with effect from 27 April 2009.

However, they exclude games of pure skill such as chess or duplicate bridge.

Meaning of playing games of chance

In *Revenue & Customs* v. *Sportech* [2014] UKUT 398 (TCC), the Upper Tribunal explained this as a composite phrase as follows:

> A 'game' is an activity which ordinarily is an end in itself, conducted under rules which provide a specific outcome such that it can be said that a player has won or lost (or, where there is more than one player, drawn). Part of the objective of a game is to 'win': and the game itself represents some form of contest. In a commercial game (i.e. one that a participant pays to play) the rules will be set out or referred to in the governing contract. Otherwise are to be found in the external rules to which a participant submits or (in games with more than one player) to which the parties agree to submit.

> 'Playing' a game involves (a) the player doing something which causes a change in existing circumstances and (b) the player thereafter interacting with the changed circumstance or responding to another player's interaction with the changed circumstance.

> In a typical 'game of chance' (this is neither a definition nor a comprehensive description) (a) the rules provide for some event occurring after the start of the game randomly to influence its outcome to a significant degree (in the same way as a bet or a gamble turns on the occurrence of an uncertain event, being what the Gaming Act 1968 called 'the chances in the game'); and (b) the effect produced by the uncertain outcome of the random element is one of the purposes of the game.

5.10.2 Dutiable machine games

From 1 February 2013, a new excise duty, Machine Games Duty was introduced. Where Machine Games Duty is chargeable, no VAT is due on the machine game takings as the supplies are VAT exempt.

5.10.3 Lotteries

The sale of lottery tickets is VAT exempt. However, the exempt turnover (for VAT return and partial exemption purposes, etc.) is the gross proceeds from the ticket sales less the amount of cash prizes given and less the cost, including VAT, of goods given as prizes.

If a retailer sells lottery tickets as an agent for either a lottery management company or promoter, the commission that they receive is consideration for an exempt service of selling lottery tickets to the public, so the commission is itself exempt income.

5.11 SALE OF BUSINESS GOODS ON WHICH VAT WAS WHOLLY IRRECOVERABLE

If a business acquires goods and the VAT incurred on those goods was wholly irrecoverable on the basis that they were used wholly for VAT-exempt activities (not carrying a right of recovery), then if the goods are subsequently sold by the business, the subsequent sale is VAT-exempt.

A supply of goods is VAT exempt if each of the following conditions is satisfied:

(a) the supplier, or a **predecessor** has incurred or will incur input VAT on the goods used for the supply;

(b) the only such input VAT is **non-deductible input VAT**; and

(c) the supply is not a supply of opted to tax land or buildings.

The goods used for the supply are the goods supplied and any goods used in the process of producing the supplied goods so as to be comprised in them.

Non-deductible input VAT is input VAT which:

- ignoring the *de minimis* rule (see 3.1.11), is not and will not become attributable to a taxable supply or a supply carrying a right of recovery (foreign and specified supplies); or
- is blocked (business entertainment, motor cars, etc.).

Non-deductible input VAT excludes VAT which has been refunded under the following sections of the VAT Act 1994:

- s. 33 (local authorities, etc.), s.33a (national museums and galleries), s. 33b (academy schools), s. 33c/d (hospices, search and rescue charities, etc.);
- s. 39 (refunds of VAT to non-EU businesses);
- s. 41 (government departments).

A person is a **predecessor** of the supplier if they transferred goods to the supplier under the transfer of a business as a going concern (TOGC) rules.

Note that:

- if VAT was partly recoverable on the basis that the goods were for mixed table and exempt use, then condition (b) above is not met and the sale is (unless otherwise exempted) a taxable supply;
- if the goods are acquired and held as non-business assets, then their sale is outside the scope of VAT (see 4.1.7 'Sale of non-business assets').

6 Zero and reduced rates

This chapter is divided into the following sections:

- 6.1 Introduction to zero-rating
- 6.2 Zero-rated supplies *to* charities
- 6.3 Zero-rated supplies *by* charities
- 6.4 General zero-rated supplies
- 6.5 Reduced-rated supplies

Section 6.1 covers issues common to many of the zero-and reduced-rating reliefs, such as the meaning of charity and definition of disabled person. Section 6.2 then considers when supplies to charities and other specific types of voluntary organisation are zero-rated. A charity or voluntary organisation does not need to be registered for VAT to obtain these reliefs. Section 6.3 then considers the scenarios in which supplies by charities are zero-rated because they are by charities. Section 6.4 considers the general zero-rating reliefs, that apply broadly without restriction on the supplier or customer. Section 6.5 considers all the reduced-rating reliefs in one place. Within each section the reliefs are listed alphabetically.

6.1 INTRODUCTION TO ZERO-RATING

Zero-rating means that a supply is taxable, but at a zero rate of VAT (0%). For the supplier, the price charged to the customer is not increased by VAT, but the costs of making the sale are reduced by being able to recover associated input VAT.

Zero-rating is normally considered to be very desirable if sales are made to private individuals or to organisations that cannot recover all the VAT they incur on their purchases.

VAT is charged on reduced-rated supplies at 5% (2015/16 rate). Input VAT incurred in making the reduced-rated supply is recoverable. This is clearly not as beneficial as zero-rating; however, if customers cannot fully recover the VAT they incur on purchases, it is also clearly better than standard-rating.

6.1.1 **Meaning of charity**

For supplies on or after 1 April 2012 a special definition of charity is adopted for VAT (and most other tax) purposes. An entity must meet four conditions to qualify for charity-specific VAT reliefs.

The four conditions are:

1. It must be established for charitable purposes only. Charitable purposes are the England and Wales definitions in section 2 of the Charities Act 2011.
2. It is subject to the control of a relevant UK court (the High Court or Court of Session) in the exercise of its jurisdiction with respect to charities, or any other court in the exercise of a corresponding jurisdiction under the law of a relevant territory. Relevant territories were originally the member states of the EU, Iceland and Norway, but Lichtenstein was added with effect from 31 July 2014.
3. It has complied with any requirement to be registered with a charity regulator such as the Charity Commission, Office of the Scottish Charity Regulator or the Charity Commission for Northern Ireland and any equivalents in a relevant territory.
4. Its managers are fit and proper persons to be managers of the organisation. Managers are defined as 'the persons having the general control and management of the administration of the organisation'. This is the same as the definition of charity trustee used in section 177, Charities Act 2011. HMRC provides non-statutory guidance on what it sees as being the meanings of 'managers' and 'fit and proper' (available on gov.uk). This condition is treated as met if HMRC considers that the failure to meet this condition has not prejudiced the charitable purposes of the organisation, or it is just and reasonable in all the circumstances for the condition to be treated as met.

6.1.2 **Certificates**

Some of the zero-rating and reduced-rating reliefs are only applicable if and when the customer has provided the supplier with a certificate of eligibility. The certificate should be provided in writing and before the **time of supply** (the point in time when a supply is regarded as taking place), though in some situations HMRC permits suppliers to accept belated certificates (see 8.3.8 'Certificates').

Certificates are required for:

- some of the property-related zero-rating and reduced-rating reliefs covered in Chapter 8 'Property';
- the lifeboat-related reliefs explained in 6.2.8 'Boats, lifeboats and ships';

- **relevant goods** under the HMRC concession, see 6.2.13 'Relevant goods';
- Motability schemes: HMRC form *VAT1615A* must be provided to the supplier, see 6.2.12 'Motor vehicles'.

6.1.3 **Declarations**

For other reliefs there is no statutory obligation on the customer to provide the supplier with a formal certificate; however, if the goods are purchased from a UK supplier, HMRC expects the supplier to obtain written confirmation that the customer qualifies for relief and that any qualifying conditions are met.

HMRC states (*VAT Notice 701/6*, section 8.2):

> The supplier is responsible for ensuring that all the conditions for zero-rating are met. We recommend that suppliers obtain a written declaration of eligibility from each customer who claims entitlement to VAT relief. Such a declaration should contain sufficient information to demonstrate that the conditions for the relief are fulfilled. The declaration should be separate, or clearly distinguishable from, any order form or invoice against which the goods or services are supplied. A customer signing an order should not automatically be signing a declaration of eligibility for VAT relief.

HMRC provides example declarations in the Notice.

Incorrect declarations

Where a customer provides an incorrect declaration, and where a supplier, despite having taken all reasonable steps to check the validity of the declaration, nonetheless fails to identify the inaccuracy and in good faith makes the supplies concerned at the zero rate, or a reduced rate, by extra-statutory concession HMRC will not seek to recover the tax due from the supplier (*VAT Notice 48*, section 3.11).

6.1.4 **Disabled persons and invalids**

Several of the reliefs in this chapter are restricted to goods and services that are for or relate to 'handicapped persons' or to 'invalids'. For the term handicapped person this book (and some of the HMRC guidance) generally uses the term 'disabled person'.

Handicapped person

The statutory definition of a handicapped person for VAT purposes is 'a person who is chronically sick or disabled'; so a disabled person includes a person who is chronically sick.

HMRC's position (*VAT Notice 701/7*, section 3.2) is that a person is chronically sick or disabled if he/she is a person:

- with a physical or mental impairment which has a long-term and substantial adverse effect upon his/her ability to carry out everyday activities;
- with a condition which the medical profession treats as a chronic sickness, such as diabetes; or
- who is terminally ill.

HMRC does not accept that the following are chronically sick or disabled:

- a frail elderly person who is otherwise able-bodied;
- any person who is only temporarily disabled or incapacitated, such as with a broken limb.

However, HMRC does accept that if a parent, spouse or guardian acts on behalf of a chronically sick or disabled person, the supply is treated as being made to that chronically sick or disabled person. One potential problem with HMRC's approach is that several of the reliefs are for 'invalids' which, in the normal English usage, includes a person who is injured but the impact may not be long-term or result in a chronic sickness.

Invalid

There is no statutory definition of the term 'invalid'. A dictionary definition is 'a person made weak or disabled by illness or injury' (OUP 2015).

6.1.5 **Priority of zero-rating**

Sometimes a supply can qualify as both zero-rated and reduced-rated or exempt. In such situations zero-rating takes precedence over other possible treatments (VAT Act 1994 s. 30(1)).

6.1.6 **Production of zero-rated goods**

A supply of services which consist of applying a treatment or process to another person's goods is zero-rated if by so doing zero-rated goods are produced.

This includes where the processed goods would be zero-rated if supplied to the customer by a person applying the treatment or process. For example, binding loose papers into a book is zero-rated. However, HMRC does not accept that re-binding an existing book is zero-rated, as new zero-rated goods are not being produced. This zero-rating relief is most commonly encountered in the production of zero-rated books and printed matter and is considered further in 6.4 'General zero-rated supplies'.

6.1.7 **Zero-rating law**

The Principal VAT Directive (*2006/112/EC*) prohibits EU states from applying zero-rating to any supplies not specifically zero-rated by the Directive. However, Article 110 of the Principal VAT Directive permits member states which, at 1 January 1991, were applying a zero rate (or reduced rate lower than 5%) to ineligible supplies, to continue to zero rate or reduce rate those supplies. But these Article 110 zero and reduced rates must be in accordance with EU law and must have been adopted for clearly defined social reasons and for the benefit of the final consumer.

In the CJEU case C-416/85 *European Commission* v. *UK* [1988] ECR 3127, the EC challenged the UK on the basis that many of its Article 110 zero-rating reliefs were not adopted for clearly defined social reasons and for the benefit of the final consumer. Reliefs challenged included the zero-rating of food, general construction services and water and sewerage services.

The CJEU held that the final consumer is the person who acquires goods or services for personal use and bears the VAT, as opposed to a person who acquires them for a business activity. It follows that, having regard to the social purpose, the term final consumer can be applied only to a person who does not use the zero-rated goods or services in the course of a business activity. However, the provision of goods or services at a stage higher in the production or distribution chain which is nevertheless sufficiently close to the consumer to be of advantage to them must also be considered to be for the benefit of the final consumer.

The CJEU accepted that the UK's zero-rating of food, water and sewerage services was adopted for clearly defined social reasons and for the benefit of the final consumer. It accepted the same in respect of construction services for housing but not for the construction of (the then zero-rated) industrial and commercial buildings. The UK's zero-rating rules were amended as a result.

The *Talacre* case

Case C-251/05 *Talacre Beach Caravan Sales Ltd* v. *Customs & Excise* [2006] EWCA Civ ECR I-06269 establishes that the article 110 zero-rating reliefs are frozen in time: they cannot be expanded but only contracted. The CJEU held that Article 110 amounts to a standstill clause intended to prevent social hardship likely to follow from the abolition of the reliefs concerned. Having regard to that purpose, the content of the national legislation in force on 1 January 1991 is decisive in ascertaining the scope of the supplies allowed to retain relief.

However, some zero-rating reliefs are built into the VAT system, for example:

- the export of goods;
- the removal of goods to a VAT-registered EU customer;

- the special zero-ratings for **privileged persons** (defined in 6.4.11 'Privileged persons in other EU states');
- the reliefs for charity exports of goods;
- reliefs for lifeboats, boats, ships, etc.

As these are features of the VAT system and required by the Principal VAT Directive, the Article 110 limitations do not apply.

6.1.8 Future of zero-rating

At the time of writing there is discussion at the EU level of whether or not the VAT system should be simplified by abolishing or substantially reducing the zero- and reduced-rating reliefs and many of the VAT exemptions also. This is in the interests of a simpler VAT system and a broader tax base.

The discussion is ongoing, though the UK government has announced in its 2015 summer budget that legislation will be introduced specifying that, for the duration of the 2015/20 Parliament, the standard rate can be no higher than 20% and that the reduced rate can be no higher than 5%. The legislation will also prevent supplies specified in Schedule 7A (reduced-rated supplies) and Schedule 8 (zero-rate supplies) from being removed.

6.1.9 Imports and acquisitions

If qualifying goods are imported from outside the EU then the import is also zero-rated or reduced-rated, though a declaration of eligibility must be provided to HMRC at the point of importation. There are also some specific VAT reliefs for imports of goods by charities – see 9.5.6 'Import VAT exemptions'.

If qualifying goods are acquired from another EU state by a VAT-registered charity then the charity may zero rate or reduced rate the acquisition provided proof of eligibility is retained. No proof of eligibility need be provided to the overseas supplier (*VAT Notice 701/6*, section 7.2).

If the charity is not registered then the EU supplier may charge VAT in the EU state of supply if there are no similar reliefs available in that state. This VAT cannot be recovered from HMRC.

6.2 ZERO-RATED SUPPLIES TO CHARITIES

Certain goods and services are zero-rated when supplied to a charity or other qualifying body or purchased for donation to a charity or other qualifying body and any qualifying conditions are met. It does not matter whether the purchaser is VAT-registered or not.

If a supplier has incorrectly charged VAT within the last four years, you can ask them to issue a VAT-only credit note and refund the VAT, though HMRC will not make refunds of VAT directly to customers.

6.2.1 Access works for disabled persons

The following supplies to a charity are zero-rated:

1. **Ramps**: constructing a ramp or ramps for the purpose of facilitating a disabled person's entry to or movement within any building. Includes: the raising of a floor level to match that of another existing floor level so as to remove a step or steps; the reduction of the angle of an incline; or the creation of a slope.
2. **Widening doorways or passages**: the widening of doorways or passages for the purpose of facilitating a disabled person's entry to or movement within any building.
3. **Washrooms and lavatories**: providing, extending or adapting a washroom or lavatory for use by disabled persons in a building, or any part of a building, used principally by a charity for charitable purposes where such provision, extension or adaptation is necessary to facilitate the use of the washroom or lavatory by disabled persons. Washroom means a room containing a lavatory or washbasin (or both) but not containing a bath or shower or cooking, sleeping or laundry facilities. A lavatory is a room containing a toilet and possibly, but not always, a washbasin.
4. **Bathrooms**: providing, extending or adapting a bathroom for use by disabled persons in residential accommodation, or in a day-centre where at least 20% of the individuals using the centre are disabled persons, where such provision, extension or adaptation is necessary by reason of the condition of the disabled persons. Bathroom includes a shower room.
5. **Lifts**: the supply to a charity providing a permanent or temporary residence or day-centre for disabled persons of services necessarily performed in the installation of a lift for the purpose of facilitating the movement of disabled persons between floors within that building. In *Friends of the Elderly* [2008] VTD 20597, the VAT Tribunal found that services of architects and the supply of a feasibility report were 'services necessarily performed in the installation of a lift' and as such qualified for zero-rating.
6. **Associated goods**: also zero-rated are any goods supplied in connection with the above supplies.
7. **Restoring space**: for items (1) to (4) above, HMRC states (*VAT Notice 701/7*, section 6.5):

   where economy and feasibility dictate that you have constructed or extended in the course of a zero-rated supply, and have occupied space which was previously part of another room then you may also zero rate the service of restoring that room elsewhere in the building to its original size. This is because the work is essential to providing the service to your disabled customer.

6.2.2 **Adaptation of goods**

The supply to a charity of services of adapting any goods to suit the condition of a disabled person is zero-rated. The adapted goods must be made available to a disabled person, by sale or otherwise, by the charity.

If the goods are adapted prior to their supply to the charity, an apportionment must be made to determine the value of the supply of adaptation services which qualify for zero-rating. This assumes that the whole of the goods do not qualify for zero-rating under any other option outlined in this chapter.

See also 6.2.4 'Aids for disabled persons' and 6.2.13 'Relevant goods'.

6.2.3 **Advertising services**

Advertising and closely related services are zero-rated when supplied to a charity. This includes supplies of advertising services by one charity to another.

Initially the scope of this relief was restricted to newspaper advertising, but zero-rating has since been extended. To qualify, the advert must be placed in third-party media and not targeted at selected individuals. So advertising on a charity's own website or in its own publications does not qualify.

Advert types

The zero-rating applies to all types of advertising by charities, including recruitment advertisements, attracting new members, pupils or students, advertising events, raising awareness or fundraising. All forms of media are allowed, including third-party-owned billboards, cinema, TV, radio, newspapers, magazines, the sides of vehicles, internet advertising and advertising on third-party-owned goods such as calendars, clothing, diaries and beer mats. However, the media that contain the advertising must be third-party-owned, so, for example, a charity's own advertising on its own website or T-shirts does not qualify.

Design services

If the advert itself is zero-rated then so are any services of design and production of the advert, along with any closely related goods such as photographs.

Declarations

In order to zero rate the invoice, the supplier must be satisfied that it is a supply of advertising to a charity. HMRC recommends that charities give suppliers a declaration that the conditions for zero-rating have been met. HMRC provides a template declaration in *VAT Notice 701/58*.

Excluded advertising services

Zero-rating is not available in the following situations:

1. Where the advertising is targeted at identified individuals, for example personally addressed letters, direct marketing and telesales. However, it may be possible for individual items of the promotional material used to be zero-rated, see 6.4.1 'Books and printed matter'. However, adverts in specialist publications targeted at an open group of persons can qualify for zero-rating. For example, in *Sussex County Association of Change Ringers* (*VTD 14116*) the VAT Tribunal accepted that an advert in a specialist bell-ringing periodical qualified for zero-rating.
2. Where the advertisement appears in a charity's own magazine, noticeboard, calendar or other publication or on the charity's own website and where the charity prepares its own advertisements in-house.
3. Where the supply is not directly to a charity, for example where the supply is to a trading subsidiary or to a recruitment agency placing the advertisement on behalf of a charity. See the comments in 11.2 'Agency supplies' for agency supplies of advertising to a charity.

Pay per click adverts

In *Revenue & Customs Brief 25/10* HMRC accepts that 'pay per click' adverts qualify for zero-rating. HMRC accepts that PPC-sponsored links appearing on search engine websites are advertisements and qualify for zero-rating when supplied to a charity. It follows that the supply of copyright and design services associated with such sponsored links falls within the zero-rating.

However, HMRC regards services supplied by copywriters and designers for the purpose of search engine optimisation (structuring a website so that it contains as many keywords as possible) as not qualifying for relief. HMRC considers that these services entail the optimisation of the charity's own website, and so are specifically excluded.

6.2.4   **Aids for disabled persons**

Charities can zero rate the purchase of certain **qualifying goods** if the goods are made available to one or more disabled persons for their **personal or domestic use**. The charity can make the qualifying goods available by selling them to a disabled person, gifting them to a disabled person or making them available for use by a disabled person. For the meanings of qualifying goods and personal or domestic use, see below.

Qualifying goods

Qualifying goods are:

1. medical or surgical appliances;
2. electrically or mechanically adjustable beds;
3. devices for sitting over or rising from a sanitary appliance;
4. chair-lifts or stair-lifts;
5. hoists and lifters;
6. adapted motor vehicles;
7. other equipment and appliances;
8. parts and accessories designed solely for use in or with the above goods;
9. adapted boats.

See opposite for more on each option.

As explained at 6.1.4 'Disabled persons and invalids', the legislation uses the term 'invalid' for some of these reliefs and this term is not defined. Oxford Dictionaries online defines this term as 'a person made weak or disabled by illness or injury' (OUP 2015).

Personal or domestic use

Domestic use means use in a disabled person's home or relating to the family relations of a disabled person. Personal use means use by a disabled person in person. However, the relief does not extend to qualifying goods for the business use of one or more disabled persons.

Excluded supplies

Except for invalid wheelchairs or invalid carriages, zero-rating does not apply if qualifying goods are provided or paid for (partly or wholly) in accordance with any agreement, arrangement or understanding (whether or not legally enforceable) to which any of the following is or has been a party other than as the supplier:

● a statutory Health Authority, Health Board, NHS Trust, NHS Foundation Trust, Primary Care Trust; or
● any hospital, nursing home or other institution which provides care or medical or surgical treatment and which is required to be approved, licensed or registered or would be so required if not exempt.

However, for these bodies, qualifying goods (and a much wider range of other goods) can be zero-rated as **relevant goods**. See 6.2.13 'Relevant goods'.

1. Medical or surgical appliances

These are medical or surgical appliances designed solely for the relief of a severe abnormality or severe injury.

These can include: artificial joints, artificial limbs, artificial respirators, heart pacemakers, invalid wheelchairs, leg braces, neck collars, specialist clothing, specialist footwear and wigs.

2. Electrically or mechanically adjustable beds

These are electrically or mechanically adjustable beds designed for invalids. For the meaning of invalid see 6.1.4 'Disabled persons and invalids'.

HMRC provides the following guidance (*VRDP06500*):

Most adjustable beds have:

- adjustable head and back hinged panel;
- adjustable foot and knee hinged panel;
- slats/supports with individual suspension whose rigidity can be individually adjusted to suit the user's needs.

Beds designed for invalids must also have

- adjustable height from the floor to assist:
  (a) raising from the bed to a standing position; or
  (b) moving from the bed to a wheelchair; and
- be capable of being slotted into a cot frame or fitted with cot sides.

We would expect beds designed for invalids to have other features that are designed to assist with movement, treatment, safety and/or relief from bed sores and pain.

3. Devices for sitting over or rising from a sanitary appliance

These are commode chairs and stools, devices incorporating a bidet jet and warm air drier and frames, and other devices for sitting over or rising from sanitary appliances.

HMRC provides the following guidance (*VRDP33000*, item 2(c)):

In essence, the relief is for attachments which enable a disabled person to get on or off a toilet, usually from a wheelchair. The toilet will also be eligible for zero-rating if part of a single supply with the qualifying attachments.

Products not eligible for zero-rating

- bed pans; or
- bed pan washers

are standard-rated.

4. Chair-lifts or stair-lifts

These are chair- or stair-lifts designed for use in connection with invalid wheelchairs, even if the invalid is not in a wheelchair when using them. (For the meaning of invalid see 6.1.4 'Disabled persons and invalids'.) HMRC provides the following guidance (*VRDP13000*, item 2(d)):

Chair lift

A chair lift is a platform conveyed along a rail up or down the stairs, normally to carry a wheelchair.

Stair lift

A stair lift conveys the individual between floors, often to a wheelchair at either end. It must be designed in such a way as to be able to transfer the individual easily from the wheelchair to the lift for zero-rating to apply. It is not the same as the shaft lifts that operate in offices or tower blocks.

Which lifts are eligible for VAT relief?

The lifts which qualify include stair-lifts and chair-lifts which:

- are fitted with a bracket to enable the wheelchair to be moved with the lift; or
- enable a disabled person to transfer to the lift from one wheelchair and transfer to another wheelchair at the other end.

While the lift has to be capable of conveying a wheelchair bound disabled person up and down stairs or from one level to another, the law does not require the disabled person to be seated in the wheelchair when using the lift.

5. Hoists and lifters

These are hoists and lifters designed for use by **invalids**. (For the meaning of invalid see 6.1.4 'Disabled persons and invalids'.) HMRC provides the following guidance (*VRDP19000*, item 2(e)):

Eligible hoists and lifters

Examples of qualifying hoists include hoists for lifting any of the following:

- wheelchairs into motor vehicles;
- people in or out of the bed;
- people in or out of the bath; or
- people on and off the lavatory.

The zero rate applies to the types of lifting chairs and seats which:

- are often operated by automatic button; and
- enable disabled people who need assistance to move from a seated to a standing position.

Are recliner chairs eligible for zero-rating?

Only recliner chairs which have a seat raising and lowering feature are eligible for VAT relief. The seat must be capable of raising a person from a seated position to a standing position and lowering a person from a standing position to a seated position.

Are transfer boards eligible for zero-rating?

Transfer boards and similar items used to transfer a person from a trolley to a bed are not lifting devices. They are not eligible for VAT relief under item 2(e).

6. Adapted motor vehicles

These are motor vehicles designed or substantially and permanently adapted for the carriage of a person in a wheelchair or on a stretcher and of no more than 11 other persons. See 6.2.12 'Motor vehicles'.

7. Other equipment and appliances

These are other equipment and appliances designed solely for use by a disabled person.

General purpose goods that may be of particular use to disabled persons are not covered, for example ordinary orthopaedic mattresses. Also excluded are: hearing aids (except hearing aids designed for the auditory training of deaf children); dentures; spectacles and contact lenses. However, the following are included: clothing, footwear and wigs; invalid wheelchairs and invalid carriages; renal haemodialysis units, oxygen concentrators; artificial respirators and other similar apparatus. For everyday goods adapted to suit the condition of a disabled person, see 6.2.2 'Adaptation of goods'.

HMRC's stated position (*VAT Notice 701/7*, section 4.5) is that in order for goods to be 'designed solely for use by a disabled person' the original intention of the designer must have been to produce goods designed solely to meet the needs of persons with one or more disabilities. It is therefore only the designer or manufacturer who is able to determine whether the goods qualify for zero-rating. However, this interpretation was rejected by the Upper Tribunal in *Revenue & Customs* v. *The British Disabled Flying Association* [2013] UKUT 162 (TCC), which held that the goods must be designed solely for use by a disabled person at the time of the sale that is to be zero-rated, not at the point of original manufacture.

8. Parts and accessories

These are parts and accessories designed solely for use in or with goods described in sections 1–7 above.

HMRC provides the following guidance (*VRDP39000*, item 2(h)):

> Examples of parts and accessories eligible for zero-rating are:
>
> - the foot rest for a wheelchair could be zero-rated because it clearly has no use other than in connection with the wheelchair and so passes the 'designed solely' test; and
> - a replacement lever for a chair lift.
>
> Examples of parts and accessories not eligible for zero-rating are:
>
> - standard batteries supplied for use in an invalid scooter; and
> - a mobile phone supplied for use in a qualifying vehicle.

9. Adapted boats

These are boats designed or substantially and permanently adapted for use by disabled persons. See 6.2.8 'Boats, lifeboats and ships'.

6.2.5 Air ambulances

The supply of an air ambulance to an **eligible body** (defined in 6.2.13) qualifies for zero-rating as 'relevant goods', as do repairs and spare parts for qualifying air ambulances.

HMRC also accepts that the supply of an air ambulance with pilot can be treated as a single supply of relevant goods and zero-rated as long as the supply is being made to an eligible body and the supply is being paid for using charitable or voluntary contributions. See 6.2.13 'Relevant goods'.

VAT refund scheme for air ambulance services

From 1 April 2015 charities which provide an air ambulance service under arrangements with a relevant NHS body, the Secretary of State or a Welsh Minister are able to claim for non-business VAT under the new section 33c refund scheme. See 10.6 'Charity VAT refund scheme'.

6.2.6 Alarm systems

The supply to a charity of an alarm system is zero-rated if it is for making it available to disabled persons (by sale or otherwise) for domestic or their personal use. The alarm system must be designed to be capable of operation by a disabled person, and it must be designed to enable a disabled person to alert directly a specified person or a control centre.

A specified person or control centre is a person or centre who or which (i) is appointed to receive directly calls activated by the alarm system, and (ii) retains information about the disabled person to assist them in the event of illness, injury or similar emergency.

Also zero-rated is the supply of services necessarily performed by a control centre in receiving and responding to the calls from the alarm system.

6.2.7 Blind and partially sighted persons

Charities working with blind and partially sighted persons can zero rate a variety of magnetic tape-related equipment used to assist the blind or severely disabled persons.

Spectacles and contact lenses cannot be zero-rated. However, special low-vision aids will qualify for zero-rating. Included are custom-made spectacle-mounted low-vision aids and closed-circuit video magnification systems capable of magnifying text and images.

Radios and tape players bought by a charity for free loan or rental to blind people are zero-rated.

6.2.8 Boats, lifeboats and ships

There are several options for zero-rating boats and ships including:

- boats adapted for use by disabled persons, see below;
- lifeboats and lifeboat station repairs, dredging, cliff stabilisation, etc., see below;
- qualifying ships, see 6.4.13 'Ships and works on ships';
- houseboats, see 6.4.8 'Houseboats'.

Boats adapted for use by disabled persons

The supply to a charity or to an eligible body of a boat designed or substantially and permanently adapted for use by disabled persons is zero-rated (see 6.2.13 'Relevant goods' for the definition of eligible body). The zero-rating covers boats for the personal or domestic use of disabled persons and boats to transport disabled persons. HMRC states (*VAT Notice 701/7*, section 4.4):

> to qualify for relief, a boat should include all or most of the following features: a ramp for wheelchairs; lifts and level non cambered surfaces to accommodate wheelchair movements; specialised washing and lavatory facilities accessible to

disabled people; specially equipped galley and sleeping areas and steering facilities designed for use by disabled people; handrails; and wheelchair clamps.

Also zero-rated are services of repair or maintenance of such boats but not parts or accessories for such boats. HMRC used to permit, by concession, the zero-rating of parts and accessories designed or adapted for use in or with qualifying boats. This concession was withdrawn with effect from 1 January 2012. VAT zero-rating is, however, still available for the supply of parts and accessories that are used in connection with repairs or maintenance to qualifying boats, and parts and accessories that are included as part of a single supply of a qualifying boat.

See also 6.2.12 'Motor vehicles' for HMRC proposals to modify this relief with effect from 1 April 2016.

Lifeboats

The supply to a charity providing rescue or assistance at sea of any lifeboat is zero-rated. A lifeboat is any vessel used or to be used solely for rescue or assistance at sea.

Also zero-rated are:

- repair and maintenance of lifeboats;
- carriage equipment designed solely for the launching and recovery of lifeboats including the repair and maintenance thereof;
- tractors for the sole use of the launching and recovery of lifeboats including the repair and maintenance of;
- winches and hauling equipment for the sole use of the recovery of lifeboats including the repair and maintenance of;
- the construction, modification, repair or maintenance of slipways used solely for the launching and recovery of lifeboats;
- the supply of spare parts or accessories for use in or with lifeboats or slipways;
- the supply of equipment that is to be installed, incorporated or used in a lifeboat and is of a kind ordinarily installed, incorporated or used in a lifeboat;
- the supply of fuel where the fuel is for use in a lifeboat.

For all such zero-rated supplies the charity must give the supplier a certificate stating the name and address of the recipient and that the supply is of a description specified above.

Lifeboat station repairs, dredging, cliff stabilisation, etc.

In *Royal National Lifeboat Institution* v. *Revenue & Customs* [2009] UKFTT 39 (TC), a charity sought to rely on the broader zero-rating provided by Article 148 of the Principal VAT Directive. This zero rates:

(a) the supply of goods for the fuelling and provisioning of vessels used for rescue or assistance at sea;

(b) the supply, modification, repair, maintenance, chartering and hiring of such vessels;

(c) the supply, hiring, repair and maintenance of equipment incorporated or used therein; and

(d) the supply of services other than those referred to in point (c), to meet the direct needs of the vessels referred to in point (a) or of their cargoes.

RNLI argued that services to meet the direct needs of lifeboats include alterations, improvements, repairs and maintenance to lifeboat stations and other services such as dredging of harbours and the maintenance of cliff hoists. The First-tier Tribunal concluded that a service meets a need if it is directly connected with that need and satisfies it in whole or in part. It is not necessary for it to extinguish the need. It found that the repair and maintenance of lifeboat stations did not meet a direct need, so they were not zero-rated. In so far as alterations make for the speedy or speedier launch of a lifeboat, they meet the direct need of the craft to be able to get to the sea quickly and so qualify for zero-rating. Likewise, it found that cliff stabilisation did not qualify but dredging did.

6.2.9 **Buildings**

There is a variety of zero-rating reliefs for the sale of, construction of or works on 'qualifying buildings' and qualifying parts of buildings. Qualifying buildings include:

- **dwellings**: a dwelling broadly comprises self-contained living accommodation;
- **relevant charitable purpose buildings**: these are buildings used by a charity for non-business activities or as a **village hall or similarly** (see 8.6.7) in providing social or recreational activities for a local community;
- **relevant residential purpose buildings**: these are broadly children's homes, care homes, residential hospices, monasteries, nunneries, residential accommodation for pupils, students and members of any of the armed forces.

See 8.3 'Property VAT reliefs' for more on these reliefs and on the meanings of dwelling, relevant charitable purpose and relevant residential purpose.

6.2.10 **Goods connected with collecting donations**

By HMRC concession (*VAT Notice 48*, section 3.3 and *VAT Notice 701/58*, section 5) various goods connected with collecting donations are zero-rated if supplied to a charity.

They include the following items:

1. **Collecting envelopes** which ask for donations of money, and stewardship and similar envelopes used by religious and other organisations in their planned giving schemes.
2. **Pre-printed appeal letters** that are primarily aimed at seeking money for the charity.
3. **Envelopes used to send out appeal letters** and envelopes for forwarding donations to the charity; provided each type is over-printed with an appeal request related to that contained in the letter, or is distinguishable from the charity's usual stationery.
4. **All types of boxes and receptacles used for collecting money**: these qualify providing they comply with all the following conditions. They must (a) be secure, that is, capable of being sealed, for example by tamper evident sticker, tape or lock; (b) clearly be charity collecting boxes for a named charity; and (c) either bear the name of the charity, for example by indelible printing or embossing or having raised letters, or allow for the charity name to be added later.
5. **Collecting buckets**: general purpose buckets of the kind available from hardware stores are not covered by the concession. However, the following will qualify for relief: specially designed tamper proof bucket lids with tamper evident stickers making them suitable for a charity donation; bucket-shaped receptacles, which cannot be used for anything except collecting donations of money; bucket packs for assembly consisting of bucket, money-collecting top and tamper evident seals and labels.
6. **Lapel stickers, emblems and badges** which are to be given free as an acknowledgement to donors of money, have no intrinsic value and are low-cost to the charity will qualify. Low-cost means 'considerably less than £1 per unit'. The relief is restricted to small items designed to be worn on clothing, of a kind that were traditionally attached to the lapel. Included are paper stickers, ribbons, artificial flowers (if these are used as a symbol of the charity) and metal pins and badges. Large items for decorating buildings, vehicles, monuments, etc. are not eligible for relief even if these are just bigger versions of a lapel badge.
7. **Parts for badges, etc.**: if a charity buys identifiable constituent parts, which it will assemble into badges in-house, these come within the concession.

6.2.11 **Medicines and medicinal products**

The following are zero-rated:

1. The supply to a charity, providing care or medical or surgical treatment for human beings or animals, or engaging in medical or veterinary research, of a **medicinal product** or **veterinary medicinal product** where the supply is solely for use by the charity in such care, treatment or research.
2. The supply to a charity of a **substance** directly used for synthesis or testing in the course of medical or veterinary research.

The definitions of medicinal product or veterinary medicinal product were amended with effect for supplies on or after 14 August 2012. The effect is to reduce the scope of products that can be zero-rated under this relief to substances and to exclude certain 'articles', which were previously covered.

Medicinal product from 14 August 2012

The meaning of medicinal product was narrowed with effect from 14 August 2012 to include only substances. From this date medicinal product means:

(a) any substance or combination of substances presented as having properties of preventing or treating disease in human beings; or
(b) any substance or combination of substances that may be used by or administered to human beings with a view to (i) restoring, correcting or modifying a physiological function by exerting a pharmacological, immunological or metabolic action, or (ii) making a medical diagnosis.

Veterinary medicinal product

Veterinary medicinal product means:

(a) any substance or combination of substances presented as having properties for treating or preventing disease in animals; or
(b) any substance or combination of substances that may be used in, or administered to, animals with a view either to restoring, correcting or modifying physiological functions by exerting a pharmacological, immunological or metabolic action, or to making a medical diagnosis.

Substance

HMRC states that (*VAT Notice 701/1*, section 6.1.4):

> A 'substance' can be natural or artificial, and can be in solid or liquid form or in the form of a gas or vapour. If the substance is purchased in the form of gas the zero-rating will also apply to the cylinder rental.

Medicinal product before 14 August 2012

Medicinal product before 14 August 2012 meant: any substance or article (not being an instrument, apparatus or appliance) which is for use wholly or mainly in either or both of the following ways:

- by being administered to one or more human beings for a medicinal purpose; or
- as an ingredient in the preparation of a substance or article which is to be administered to one or more human beings for a medicinal purpose.

Medicinal purposes were as defined in Medicines Act 1968:

- treating or preventing disease;
- diagnosing disease or ascertaining the existence, degree or extent of a physiological condition;
- contraception;
- inducing anaesthesia;
- otherwise preventing or interfering with the normal operation of a physiological function, whether permanently or temporarily, and whether by way of terminating, reducing or postponing, or increasing or accelerating, the operation of that function or in any other way.

Substance meant as defined in section 132 Medicines Act 1968 which is 'any natural or artificial substance, whether in solid or liquid form or in the form of a gas or vapour'.

In *Pasante Healthcare* [2006] VTD 19724 the VAT Tribunal accepted that condoms supplied to West Pennine Brook Advisory Centre for use in its provision of sexual health advice and contraception services to young people qualified for zero-rating on the grounds that condoms are an article (but not a substance) administered to one or more human beings for a medicinal purpose.

6.2.12 **Motor vehicles**

The following types of motor vehicle can be zero-rated if the qualifying conditions are met:

1. adapted motor vehicles for charitable use;
2. adapted motor vehicles for personal or domestic use;
3. qualifying motor vehicles (designed or substantially and permanently adapted);
4. care buses and minibuses;
5. ambulances;
6. Motability scheme.

See below for more on each relief.

1. Adapted motor vehicle for charitable use

Wheelchair adapted motor vehicles such as minibuses and buses can qualify for zero-rating as relevant goods. See 6.2.13 'Relevant goods'.

2. Adapted motor vehicles for personal or domestic use

The supply to a charity of a motor vehicle which is designed or substantially and permanently adapted for the carriage of a person in a wheelchair or on a stretcher and of no more than 11 other persons is zero-rated if the charity is purchasing the vehicle for making it available to a disabled person (by sale or otherwise) for their personal or domestic use.

Also zero-rated are parts and accessories designed solely for use with the vehicle and services or repair or maintenance of the vehicle. For the meaning of personal or domestic use, see 6.2.4 'Aids for disabled persons'. For the meaning of substantially and permanently adapted, see the following section 'Qualifying motor vehicles'.

3. Qualifying motor vehicles

The supply of a **qualifying motor vehicle** to a charity for making available for the domestic or personal use of a disabled person who usually uses a wheelchair or who is usually carried on a stretcher, is zero-rated. Also zero-rated is the supply to a charity of a service of repair or maintenance of such qualifying motor vehicles.

A **qualifying vehicle** is a motor vehicle that is not capable of carrying more than 12 persons (including the driver) that is either:

- designed or substantially and permanently adapted to enable the disabled person to enter, and drive or be otherwise carried in, the motor vehicle; or
- by reason of its design, or being substantially and permanently adapted, includes features whose design is such that their sole purpose is to allow a wheelchair used by a disabled person to be carried in or on the motor vehicle.

HMRC provides the following guidance (*VRDP29300*):

> The vehicle must provide the necessary space and facilities for a disabled person to be transported in reasonable safety and comfort. The vehicle must also be adapted to carry the disabled person whilst in their wheelchair/stretcher.

If the vehicle is intended to carry a disabled person in a wheelchair, (either as driver or passenger) it will require a permanently fitted hoist or ramp, so that the disabled person can get in or out of the vehicle while sitting in the wheelchair.

Changes to zero-rating of qualifying vehicles

On 30 June 2014 HMRC issued a consultation on amending this zero-rating relief and also the zero-rating relief for adapted motor vehicles for personal or domestic use (see relief number 2 above) and boats for use by disabled persons (see 6.2.8 'Boats, lifeboats and ships') on the basis of concerns that the relief was being abused.

The government announced in December 2014:

> The Government will proceed with reform of the relief. Legislative changes will be made to limit VAT relief to one adapted motor vehicle, purchased for the personal use of a disabled wheelchair user, in any three year period. However, provision will also be made to allow more than one vehicle in exceptional circumstances. The Government will define 'substantially' and 'permanently' in the legislation but there will be no minimum cost of adaptation rule.

> Motor vehicle suppliers will be required to submit details of zero-rated sales to HMRC. HMRC will work with the sector to establish the easiest method for suppliers to provide this information. Use of eligibility declarations will be mandatory and penalties will be introduced for the provision of false declarations.

> References to 'stretcher users' will remain in the legislation.... Issues regarding boats will be explored with the sector to see if the same legislative concepts that apply to both motor vehicles and boats can be aligned without detriment to disabled people and boat suppliers.

> Legislative changes will be taken forward in Finance Bill 2016. New guidance and procedures will be introduced alongside the legislation. The guidance will clarify that users of lower limb prosthetics are entitled to relief, explain the new procedures and provide further information about what constitutes a 'substantially and permanently' adapted motor vehicle.

> *HMRC 2014, VAT relief on substantially and permanently adapted motor vehicles for disabled wheelchair users* (consultation outcome)

4. Care buses and minibuses

The supply of a vehicle with 7 to 50 seats for use by an eligible body providing care for blind, deaf, mentally handicapped or terminally sick persons mainly to transport such persons is zero-rated. Eligible bodies include hospitals, care institutions, research institutions, rescue and first-aid organisations. The vehicle does not have to be adapted for wheelchairs. See 6.2.13 'Relevant goods'.

5. Ambulances

The supply of an ambulance to or for an eligible body is zero-rated. Eligible bodies include hospitals, care institutions, research institutions, rescue and first-aid organisations. Ambulances include air and sea ambulances. See 6.2.13 'Relevant goods'.

6. Motability scheme

The letting on hire of a motor vehicle for a period of not less than three years to a disabled person in receipt of certain allowances is zero-rated. The lessor's business must consist predominantly of the provision of motor vehicles to such persons. Also zero-rated is the first sale of the vehicle which had been let on hire, where the sale constitutes the first supply of the vehicle after the end of the period of letting. A charity Motability has been set up to run this scheme.

The disabled person must give the supplier an HMRC certificate (*VAT1615A*) to confirm eligibility. The disabled person must be in receipt of any of the following:

- a disability living allowance high-rate mobility component;
- a personal independence payment enhanced mobility component;
- an armed forces independence payment; or
- a war pensioner's mobility supplement.

See www.motability.co.uk for more on the Motability scheme.

6.2.13 **Relevant goods**

The following supplies are zero-rated:

- A **qualifying supply** of **relevant goods**.
- Supplies of repairs, maintenance and spare parts for relevant goods owned or in the possession of an eligible body.

Relevant goods are:

1. medical, scientific, computer, video, sterilising, laboratory or refrigeration equipment for use in medical or veterinary research, training, diagnosis or treatment;
2. ambulances;
3. parts or accessories for use in or with goods described in (1) or (2) above;
4. aids for disabled persons;
5. adapted motor vehicles;

6. vehicles with more than 6 but fewer than 51 seats for use by an eligible body providing care for blind, deaf, mentally handicapped or terminally sick persons mainly to transport such persons;

7. telecommunication, aural, visual, light enhancing or heat detecting equipment (not being equipment ordinarily supplied for private or recreational use) solely for use for the purpose of rescue or first-aid services undertaken by a charitable institution providing such services.

Each of these categories is considered in the sections 1–7 starting on p. 202. The main HMRC guidance on relevant goods is in *VAT Notice 701/6*, the August 2014 edition referred to below (unless otherwise stated).

Qualifying supplies are any of the following:

(a) The supply of relevant goods to an eligible body which pays for them with funds provided by a charity or from voluntary contributions.

(b) The supply of relevant goods to an eligible body which is a charitable institution providing care or medical or surgical treatment for disabled persons.

(c) The supply of relevant goods for donation to a nominated eligible body where the goods are purchased with funds provided by a charity or from voluntary contributions. The donor must either be a charity or not have contributed in whole or in part to the funds for the purchase of the goods.

(d) By HMRC extra-statutory concession (*VAT Notice 48*, section 3.19), the supply of relevant goods to a charity:

    (i) whose sole purpose and function is to provide a range of care services to meet the personal needs of disabled persons; or

    (ii) which provides transport services predominantly to disabled persons.

For more on this concession see 'Relevant goods concession' below.

Hire of relevant goods

Options (a), (b) and (c) above include the letting on hire of relevant goods and references to purchase or ownership are deemed to include references respectively to their hiring and possession.

Repair and maintenance of relevant goods

The repair and maintenance of relevant goods owned or possessed by an eligible body and supplies of goods in connection with repairs or maintenance (such as spare or replacement parts) can also be zero-rated, provided that:

- the repairs, maintenance or spare parts are paid for with funds provided by a charity or from voluntary contributions; and
- where the owner of goods repaired is not a charity, the owner has not contributed in whole or in part to those funds.

Eligible bodies

Eligible bodies comprise:

- hospitals whose activities are not carried on for profit;
- research institutions whose activities are not carried on for profit;
- charitable institutions providing care or medical or surgical treatment for disabled persons in a 'relevant establishment' (see below for the meaning of relevant establishment);
- charitable institutions providing rescue or first-aid services;
- by extra-statutory concession, a charity whose sole purpose and function is to provide a range of care services to meet the personal needs of disabled persons;
- by extra-statutory concession, a charity which provides transport services predominantly to disabled persons;
- assorted public health bodies.

See 'Relevant goods concession' below for information on this extra-statutory concession.

At the time of writing the assorted public health bodies are: a Strategic Health Authority or Special Health Authority in England; a Health Authority, Special Health Authority or Local Health Board in Wales; a Health Board in Scotland; a Health and Social Services Board in Northern Ireland; the Common Services Agency for the Scottish Health Service, the Northern Ireland Central Services Agency for Health and Social Services or the Isle of Man Health Services Board; a National Health Service trust established under Part I of the National Health Service and Community Care Act 1990 or the National Health Service (Scotland) Act 1978; a Primary Care Trust established under section 16A of the National Health Service Act 1977.

Example: rescue or first aid

In *Isabel Medical Charity* v. *Customs & Excise* [2003] VTD 18209, a charity set up an online database for medical professionals to help them accurately diagnose and treat disease. The charity claimed its purchases of computer equipment and software were relevant goods supplied to 'a charitable institution providing rescue or first-aid services'. The Tribunal rejected this. Rescue means removal from physical danger such as rescue from shipwreck or fire. It does not extend to a metaphorical meaning such as deliverance from harm or evil, rescue from disease, or rescue from bankruptcy.

Relevant goods concession

Following a change in the law in 1997 certain types of charity lost their eligibility to zero rate relevant goods, so an extra-statutory concession (*VAT Notice 48*, section 3.19) was introduced to ensure that their reliefs were retained. The charities eligible for relief under this concession are charities:

(a) whose sole purpose and function is to provide a range of care services to meet the personal needs of disabled persons (of which transport might form a part); or

(b) which provide transport services predominantly to disabled persons.

The text of section 3.19 is:

VAT: supplies of 'relevant goods' to charities

Where 'relevant goods' of a kind described in note (3) to Group 15 of the Value Added Tax Act 1994 are supplied to a charity:

(a) whose sole purpose and function is to provide a range of care services to meet the personal needs of handicapped people (of which transport might form a part), or

(b) which provides transport services predominantly to handicapped people,

then by concession, the supply of those goods will be zero rated, as will the repair and maintenance of those goods and the supply of any further goods in connection with that repair and maintenance.

'Handicapped' means chronically sick or disabled.

In order to be eligible for this concession, a charity must demonstrate that it meets the requirements of sub-paragraphs (a) or (b) above by way of:

- its aims and objectives [which may be an extract from the constitution]
- its publicity and advertising material
- its documents which it has issued for the purpose of obtaining funding from a third party such as a local authority
- its day to day operations, and
- any other evidence that may be relevant [for example an analysis of passengers carried over a representative period]

In order to be eligible for this concession, a charity must issue a certificate to the supplier claiming eligibility for relief and where required it must attach documentary evidence to support the claim covering the conditions listed above. See *VAT Information Sheet 08/98* for detailed guidance.

Relevant establishment

This means either:

- a day-centre, other than a day-centre which exists primarily as a place for activities that are social or recreational or both; or
- an institution which is statutorily approved, licensed or registered or statutorily exempted from such.

The majority of the persons who receive care or medical or surgical treatment in the relevant establishment must be disabled persons and the relevant goods must be for use in the relevant establishment or for use in providing medical care to disabled persons in their own homes.

HMRC examples of the first category of day-centres are physiotherapy centres for disabled children or charitable establishments which run daily rehabilitation or training classes for disabled adults. For the second category HMRC examples are residential care institutions such as nursing homes for disabled adults or residential homes for disabled children.

In *Revenue & Customs* v. *The British Disabled Flying Association* [2013] UKUT 162 (TCC), a charity provided opportunities for disabled persons to experience and participate in aviation using adapted aircraft. The Upper Tribunal accepted that the charity was a charitable institution providing care for disabled persons but held that the care was not provided in a relevant establishment. The Tribunal held that since the care has to be provided in a relevant establishment the context implies that it must be a physical place such as a building or premises but excluding aircraft.

Funds provided by a charity or from voluntary contributions

As explained above in 'Qualifying supplies', two types of qualifying supply depend on how they are paid for:

(a) the supply of relevant goods to an eligible body which pays for them with funds provided by a charity or from voluntary contributions;

(b) the supply of relevant goods for donation to a nominated eligible body where the goods are purchased with funds provided by a charity or from voluntary contributions. The donor must either be a charity or not have contributed in whole or in part to the funds for the purchase of the goods.

Option (b) above extends the zero-rating relief for relevant goods to purchases by 'friends of'-type bodies, which are not themselves eligible bodies but will donate the good to a nominated eligible body and where the funds are provided by a charity or from voluntary contributions.

HMRC explains these requirements as follows (*VCHAR14950*):

> Charitable funds are those which are held by a charity and can derive from any number of fund-raising sources. Voluntary contributions are similar but do not necessarily have to be held by a charity. For example, a commercial company might collect contributions from its staff which it uses to buy a piece of medical equipment for a charity. This would qualify as having been purchased with voluntary contributions.

> An important point is that 100% of the funding must be from funds provided by a charity or from voluntary contributions. If the charity only makes a contribution towards the cost of purchasing equipment, or if the level of voluntary contributions needs to be supplemented by an eligible body's own funds, the supply of goods does not qualify for zero-rating.

A more detailed description of relevant goods is given below.

1. Medical, scientific, etc. equipment

The equipment must meet two conditions:

1. It must be medical, scientific, computer, video, sterilising, laboratory or refrigeration equipment; and
2. The equipment must be for use in medical or veterinary research, training, diagnosis or treatment. HMRC accepts that equipment meets this test if it is mainly for such use. By 'main' HMRC means 'real, substantial and continuing' (*VAT Notice 701/6*, section 4.3).

By extra-statutory concession (*VAT Notice 48*, section 3.25) HMRC accepts that this category includes human resuscitation training models acquired for use in first-aid training in either or both cardiopulmonary resuscitation and defibrillation techniques. Resuscitation training model means a model which includes a head and torso designed for use in the training of cardiopulmonary resuscitation or defibrillation techniques.

In *Customs & Excise* v. *David Lewis Centre* [1995] STC 485, the High Court found that, in order to be identified as medical or scientific equipment, the equipment must have some specialised feature identifying and limiting its use to the specified field and should not be capable of being used for other purposes. It is necessary to consider the goods at the time of the supply and decide whether, against that background, the goods could be described as the specified equipment giving those words their normal everyday meaning.

In *Research Establishment* [2005] VTD 19095 the VAT Tribunal noted that this zero-rating was originally restricted to 'medical or scientific equipment solely for use in medical research, diagnosis or treatment' but was later expanded to include computer, video, sterilising, laboratory and refrigeration equipment, and the word 'solely' was removed. In the Tribunal's view the removal of the word 'solely' leaves the use of the equipment as a question of fact.

The HMRC definitions of the terms equipment, medical equipment, scientific equipment, etc. are in *VAT Notice 701/6*, section 4.2. The subsequent sections provide these definitions.

Equipment:

Equipment is articles designed or used for a specific purpose. It will usually be durable, although certain disposable items, such as syringes that are designed to be used once only, may still be equipment. The following items are not equipment:

- bulk materials such as liquids, powders, sheets, pellets, granules
- clothing (other than specialist medical equipment such as surgical masks, gowns and gloves)
- consumables such as chemical reagents, fuel, ink, medicines, oil, paper, and cleaning and sterilising fluids

See also 6.2.11 'Medicines and medicinal products' for other zero-rating reliefs.

Medical equipment:

Medical equipment is equipment that has features or characteristics that identify it as having been designed for a medical (including dental) purpose or function, such as the diagnosis or treatment of patients. This covers a wide range of goods, from simple items like bandages and tongue depressors, to complex machinery such as x-ray machines and scanners. General use items used to equip a medical facility, such as a television purchased for use in a hospital ward, are not medical equipment

In *Medical & Dental Staff Training* [2001] VTD 17031, HMRC argued that artificial heads used in dentists' training were not medical equipment on the basis that the heads were training equipment, not medical equipment for use in training. However, in practice actual patient casts were often used by trainers to plan and practise the dental treatment to be performed later. The VAT Tribunal held that HMRC's distinction between training and medical equipment could not be made and allowed the appeal. In *Anglodent* [2000] VTD 16891, the VAT Tribunal decided that artificial human heads, for use in training dentists, were medical equipment.

Scientific equipment:

Scientific equipment is equipment designed to perform a scientific function. This includes precision measuring equipment and analytical equipment such as thermometers, weighing machines and spectrometers. Equipment that is not designed to perform a scientific function, but merely works on a scientific principle, is not scientific equipment.

Computer equipment:

Computer equipment includes computer hardware such as servers, screens, keyboards, and disks. Machinery or other equipment that is either operated by computer or has computerised components, is not computer equipment.

For computer software HMRC states:

Computer software is zero-rated when purchased by an eligible body solely for use in medical research, diagnosis or treatment. Zero-rating does not apply to computer software or programs that are purchased:

- for a purpose other than medical research, diagnosis or treatment
- by a person, body or organisation other than an eligible body – even if the software is purchased for donation to an eligible body

Video equipment:

This includes video recording and playback equipment.

Sterilising equipment:

This includes autoclaves and other specialised equipment using steam or other high temperature processes. Microwave ovens and other cooking appliances are not sterilising equipment, even if they can be used to sterilise. Sterilising fluid is not equipment.

Laboratory equipment:

This includes equipment that is designed for use in a laboratory, such as: test tubes and other laboratory glassware; Bunsen burners; fume cupboards; microtomes; cryostats; laboratory benches; specialised sinks and catch pots. The following are not laboratory equipment:

- ordinary cupboards, lockers, seats and other furniture, even when these are used to equip a laboratory
- bulk materials such as liquids, powders, sheets, pellets, granules; general purpose items used to equip a laboratory
- consumables such as chemical reagents, medicines, and cleaning and sterilising fluids

In *Clinical Computing Ltd* [1983] VTD 121 the VAT Tribunal decided that a specialist laboratory ventilation system designed to allow precise control of room temperature, humidity and air pressure qualified as laboratory equipment.

Refrigeration equipment

This includes all cooling and freezing equipment, whether designed for industrial, domestic or any other purpose.

2. Ambulances

HMRC states (section 4.4):

An ambulance is an emergency vehicle used for transporting sick and injured people or animals. This includes specially equipped air ambulances or watercraft. To qualify for zero-rating as an ambulance, the vehicle must have the following features:

- the front and both sides must bear permanently fitted signs indicating that the vehicle is an ambulance
- in the case of an ambulance for transporting human patients, adequate door space for the loading of a patient on a stretcher
- seating to the rear of the driver (or pilot) for at least one attendant
- one or more stretcher that, with its handles extended, measures at least 1.95 metres, together with permanent fittings to hold this stretcher in position. This size specification applies only to ambulances that transport human patients. For ambulances that transport animals, any reasonable lifting or carrying equipment is acceptable

Air ambulances

At *VCHAR6000* HMRC accepts that a helicopter or airplane meeting the above conditions qualifies as an **air ambulance**. HMRC also accepts that the supply of an air ambulance with pilot can be treated as a single supply of relevant goods and zero-rated as long as:

- the supply is being made to an eligible body; and

- the supply is being paid for using charitable or voluntary contributions. However, NHS funds are not charitable funds and a supply that is only part funded by charitable funds or voluntary contributions will not qualify for relief. The supply of air ambulances to commercial organisations is standard-rated, and this includes the supply of an air ambulance to a charity's trading subsidiary.

3. Parts or accessories

These are parts or accessories for use in or with ambulances and medical, scientific, etc. equipment.

HMRC states (section 4.5):

> Parts are integral components without which the equipment is incomplete. Accessories means optional extras that are not necessary for the equipment to operate in its normal course, but are used to: improve the operation of the equipment; or enable the equipment to be used, or used to better effect, in particular circumstances. This would cover, for example, a printer for use with a computer; a specially designed camera for use with a microscope; and a rack for holding test tubes. Items that are not parts or accessories include: items that have independent uses, such as television sets; accessories to accessories; and generic bulk substances, such as liquids, powders, sheets, pellets and granules.

In *Royal Midland Counties Home for Disabled People* [2002] STC 395, the High Court accepted that an electricity generator was an accessory for use with medical equipment.

4. Aids for disabled persons

These are qualifying goods as explained in 6.2.4 'Aids for disabled persons' and comprise:

1. medical or surgical appliances;
2. electrically or mechanically adjustable beds;
3. devices for sitting over or rising from a sanitary appliance;
4. chair-lifts or stair-lifts;
5. hoists and lifters;
6. adapted motor vehicles;
7. other equipment and appliances;
8. parts and accessories designed solely for use in or with the above goods; and
9. adapted boats.

5. Adapted motor vehicles

An adapted motor vehicle is a motor vehicle with up to 50 seats (including seats for the driver and any crew) which is designed or substantially and permanently adapted for the safe carriage of a specified minimum number of disabled persons in wheelchairs:

Number of seats in vehicle	Minimum number of wheelchair spaces
up to 16	1
17–26	2
27–36	3
37–46	4
47–50	5

There must also be either a fitted electrically or hydraulically operated lift or, in the case of vehicles with fewer than 17 seats, a fitted ramp to provide access for a passenger in a wheelchair.

6. Vehicles with 7–50 seats

These vehicles do not need to be adapted. However, they must be for use by an eligible body providing care for blind, deaf, mentally handicapped or terminally sick persons mainly to transport such persons.

7. Rescue equipment

HMRC states:

> Rescue equipment that is eligible for zero-rating includes: image intensifiers, heat seekers and similar specialist equipment used to locate casualties; flares used to illuminate large areas for search purposes; and two-way radios that are pre-calibrated to the emergency frequency. General-use items such as mobile phones and pagers; binoculars; torches; searchlights; and loudhailers are not zero-rated, even when they are purchased for use by a rescue or first aid charity.

In *Severnside Siren Trust Ltd* [2000] VTD 16640, the VAT Tribunal accepted that early warning sirens designed to alert the public to industrial accidents were rescue equipment.

6.3 ZERO-RATED SUPPLIES BY CHARITIES

The following supplies are zero-rated when (and only when) made by a charity or other type of organisation as indicated. In addition, the supplies described in 6.4 'General zero-rated supplies' will be zero-rated when made by any type of organisation.

6.3.1 **Export of goods by a charity**

The export of goods by a charity is a deemed zero-rated business activity. Goods are exported when they are sent to a destination outside the EU. It does not matter if the goods were purchased or donated.

The result is that VAT incurred in exporting aid goods can be recovered on the basis that it is **attributable** (see 3.1.3) to a deemed zero-rated supply, even if the goods are given away for free. This can include VAT incurred on costs of purchasing aid goods, modifying them, warehousing costs, packing, transport and delivery. Even if a charity has no other business activities it can register for VAT and recover VAT incurred in the deemed zero-rated supplies. For a list of the various territories that are not outside the EU see 14.4 'VAT in other EU states'.

If exports are sold commercially then they can be zero-rated under the normal export rules, though proof of export must be obtained and retained, see 9.4 'Exports'.

However, the following are not exports of goods:

- the export of services, for example the services of engineers and doctors;
- goods sent to destinations inside the EU, including the UK.

See also 6.4.5 'Export-related services'.

6.3.2 **Sale of donated goods**

A **profits-to-charity person** is a person who has agreed to transfer to a charity the profits from supplies of the goods or a person for whom the profits are otherwise payable to a charity.

The sale or hire by a charity or a **profits-to-charity person** of goods donated to it for sale or letting is zero-rated.

The sale or letting must take place as a result of the goods having been made available for purchase or hire to the general public or to two or more **specified persons**, and the sale or letting must not take place as a result of any arrangements entered into by the supplier, customer or donor, before the goods were made available for sale or letting.

A **specified person** is a person who is chronically sick or disabled or a person entitled to any one or more of certain specified benefits. At the time of writing these are: income support; housing benefit; council tax benefit; an income-based jobseeker's allowance, working tax credit; universal credit and any element of child tax credit other than the family element.

The following sales of donated goods can be zero-rated:

- sales of donated goods in charity shops, and, provided the profits-to-charity person condition is met, charity shops operated by charity trading subsidiaries;
- sales and auctions at fundraising events;
- sales at online auctions;
- sales at jumble sales, car boot sales, etc.

Sale to the general public or specified persons

The goods may be new or second-hand, but must be donated for the purpose of a sale or hire by the charity or profits-to-charity person and should be available for purchase or hire by the general public or by two or more specified persons.

The inclusion of specified persons means that charities or their subsidiaries may restrict sales to disabled persons and/or to those on means-tested benefits, for example in schemes whereby recycled furniture is sold at low prices.

Rags and scrap

By extra-statutory concession (*VAT Notice 48*, section 3.21) HMRC also allows zero-rating of the sale of donated goods that are in a poor condition and unwanted donated goods such as electrical items to scrap merchants and similar.

Excluded supplies

The relief only applies to goods, not services. It cannot apply to land and buildings. It does not apply to donated raffle prizes, though it does apply to donated auction items. The goods must be donated for the purpose of a sale or hire, and not for the charity's own use.

Work on goods

The goods can be cleaned or repaired as long as this does not alter their structure or original use. However, if the donated goods are converted or used to make other goods for sale the derived goods do not qualify; for example, if a painting is donated and used to make prints for resale.

Pre-arranged sales

Pre-arranged sales will not be eligible for zero-rating. Likewise, an arrangement by the donor of the goods with the charity or a purchaser will exclude the sale from the scheme. Thus zero-rating will not apply to schemes where the charity collects used goods such as toner cartridges from businesses and then sells them on to one pre-arranged purchaser.

Retail Gift Aid Scheme

This is an HMRC-approved scheme under which a charity or its trading subsidiary sells donated goods as an **agent** (see 11.2) of the donor in order to be able to claim Gift Aid on the sale proceeds. See 7.22 'Retail Gift Aid Scheme' for more on the Retail Gift Aid Scheme.

VAT position of a business donor

If a business has recovered VAT on goods that it subsequently gives away, then that giving away may amount to a **deemed supply** of the goods by the donor on which **output VAT** is due to HMRC (see the Glossary for definitions). See also 4.2.1 'Disposal of business goods for no consideration'. However, if the goods are donated to a charity for sale, hire or export, then that deemed supply is zero-rated, and the donor does not have to actually account for any output VAT on the deemed supply.

6.4 GENERAL ZERO-RATED SUPPLIES

6.4.1 Books and printed matter

The supply of **qualifying printed matter** is zero-rated.

> **Qualifying printed** matter is:
>
> - books, booklets, brochures, pamphlets and leaflets;
> - newspapers, journals and periodicals;
> - children's picture books and painting books;
> - music (printed, duplicated or manuscript);
> - maps, charts and topographical plans;
> - covers, cases and other articles supplied with any of the above and not charged for separately.

However, zero-rating excludes: plans or drawings for industrial, architectural, engineering, commercial or similar purposes.

Zero-rating covers:

- outright sales of qualifying printed matter;
- hire or loan: the transfer of possession of qualifying printed matter;
- undivided shares: the transfer of an undivided share of qualifying printed matter.

To qualify for zero-rating, an item must pass two tests:

(a) Its physical description must meet one of the above categories. It is the nature of the item, not the method of production, which determines whether it is zero-rated. For example, a newsletter produced by photocopying would still qualify for zero-rating.

(b) Its function is primarily that of the ordinary understanding of a book, booklet, brochure, etc. For example, a book of carpet samples physically resembles a book but its function is not that ordinarily understood of a book, booklet, etc.

Connected supplies

Under **anti-avoidance** legislation zero-rating does not apply if a supply of qualifying printed matter is connected to a supply of services made by another supplier and the two would be a single supply of standard-rated, reduced-rated or exempt services if made by the same supplier. The anti-avoidance affects supplies of qualifying goods on or after 19 July 2011.

> The **anti-avoidance** was introduced to counter broadcast companies selling print listings magazines via a separate group company. This was done to zero rate the magazines when they would be standard-rated as an ancillary element of a single supply of broadcast service if provided by the same entity.

Electronic publications

Publishing by electronic means does not fall within the zero-rating. This includes publishing by CD, the internet or email, cassette or video, though talking books for the blind are the subject of a separate zero-rating allowance and certain supplies of welfare information or advice are reduced-rated (see 6.5.10 'Welfare advice and information').

Brochures and pamphlets

Brochures usually consist of several sheets of reading matter fastened or folded together, not necessarily bound in covers. Pamphlets are similar, but usually comprise material of a political, social or intellectual nature.

HMRC accepts that (*VAT Notice 701/10*, section 3.2) single-sheet brochures and wallet-type brochures designed with a flap may be zero-rated provided they: convey information, and contain a substantial amount of text, with some indication of contents or of the issuing organisation, are not primarily designed to hold other items, and are supplied complete.

Stationery and forms

Items that contain significant areas for completion or detachment are not considered to be zero-rated printed matter but standard-rated stationery.

The following items will usually not qualify for zero-rating: posters, diaries and calendars, stationery postcards and greeting cards, commercial plans or drawings, globes and similar, badges, bingo cards, book covers supplied separately, bookmarks, business cards, calendars, certificates, folders, invitation cards, tickets, membership cards, photographs and printed pictures, questionnaires, waste paper, wrapping paper. However, these items may qualify for zero-rating if supplied as part of a package of advertising services or as goods connected with collecting donations and supplied to a charity. See the 'The package test' below.

Where printed matter contains areas for completion or areas to be detached and returned, HMRC will accept (*VAT Notice 701/10*, section 3.4) that items are not primarily intended for completion or detachment if 25% or less of their total area consists of: (a) areas which are blank and available for completion, or (b) parts to be detached and returned. Whatever the area for completion, a publication which is designed to be returned whole after completion is always standard-rated.

Leaflets

A leaflet is considered to be either ephemeral in nature or designed to accompany some other product or service. It should be a single sheet not larger than A4 primarily intended to be held in the hand for reading by individuals (rather than for hanging up for general display). It has to convey information and be complete in itself. It should contain a significant proportion of text, and at least 50 copies should be produced so that it can be generally distributed. A leaflet may also be up to A2 in size provided it is printed on both sides, folded down to A4 size or smaller and meets all the other conditions.

Supplies connected with producing zero-rated printed matter

Services involved in producing zero-rated printed matter are themselves zero-rated if they result in the production of new zero-rated goods. A printer with a contract to supply zero-rated goods may zero rate any preparation work, such as design and typesetting, and any post-production work, such as folding, inserting into envelopes and wrapping. It can therefore be advantageous to arrange for all services to be provided by the printer and then invoiced as one zero-rated supply. However, if an organisation purchases component supplies separately, only those that result in the production of zero-rated goods may be zero-rated. For example, if layout and design services are purchased separately, they will be standard-rated.

HMRC concessions for printed matter

HMRC provides the following concessions (*VAT Notice 701/10*, sections 6.5–6.7):

1. The package test

Where you supply a package consisting entirely of items printed on paper or card, you have a choice. You can account for VAT by apportionment between the standard-rated and zero-rated elements or you can apply the **package test**. For this purpose, a package is a collection of items printed on paper or card usually enclosed in some sort of wrapper. The articles must physically form a package and have a common link in that they are intended to be used together.

> The **package test** operates as follows: if the package contains more zero-rated than standard-rated items, the package as a whole can be zero-rated. If there are more standard-rated items, the package as a whole is standard-rated. Where there are equal numbers of zero-rated and standard-rated items, the liability of the package is decided by the costs of the goods. If the zero-rated elements of the package cost more, the whole package is zero-rated and vice versa.

In the event that the standard- and zero-rated elements cost exactly the same amount, apportionment should be applied. The outer envelope in which the package items are enclosed is not taken into account in the count, but a reply-paid envelope counts as a standard-rated item. If any item in the package is not printed on paper or card the package test cannot be applied.

2. Package test for charities

A charity can treat some items connected with collecting monetary donations as zero-rated for the purposes of the package test (see above). The following are zero-rated items: letters appealing for donations, printed envelopes for use with appeal letters, money-collecting envelopes, money-collecting boxes made of card. However, stickers are standard-rated. If any items are not made of paper or card the package test cannot be used.

3. Promotional items in magazines

If you link a cover-mounted item such as a sachet of perfume or a CD to a magazine, you can treat it as zero-rated if the following conditions are met: (a) you do not make a separate charge for it, (b) issues with cover-mounted items are sold at the same price as those without, and (c) the cost to you of the cover-mounted item or items included in any individual issue does not exceed

20% of the total cost to you of the combined supply (excluding VAT), and £1 (excluding VAT).

This linking of goods can take place at any point in the distribution chain (for example, distributor or retailer). If at the point of linkage the supply satisfies the terms of this concession, it becomes a single zero-rated supply and will continue to be a single supply throughout the chain.

Printed matter supplied together with other services

If the supply of printed matter is ancillary or incidental to another supply, then its VAT treatment will normally follow that of the other supply. Examples include translation services and reports by consultants, though if extra copies are provided and charged as such then these may be zero-rated.

Where printed matter is supplied as part of a package of education for a single fee, then the single/multiple supply tests (see Chapter 11 'Other topics') must be used to determine whether there is a single supply of education or a mixed supply of education and printed matter.

If zero-rated printed matter is the only supply received in return for a membership subscription, then the whole subscription will be zero-rated. Where other supplies are received in return for a subscription to certain non-profit-making bodies the subscription may be apportioned between the various supplies involved, with the part relating to the zero-rated supply of printed matter being zero-rated. See 11.4 'Membership subscriptions'.

Direct marketing

VAT Notice 700/24, section 3 sets out HMRC's policy on zero-rating in situations where a printer supplies a package of services such as design, production, distribution, marketing management or analysis. This states that the following services may be treated as ancillary to the supply of zero-rated printed matter when they are supplied by the person who has the contract to supply the completed printed matter:

- the creative design, drafting and preparation of printed matter;
- the printing of direct mail packs using pre-sorted or unsorted data provided by the printing supplier's customer, so that the mail packs include names, addresses, postcodes and barcodes;
- the printing of direct mail packs and correction of data supplied by the printing supplier's customer – data correction includes only: (i) amendment in accordance with Royal Mail address format guidance; (ii) amendment to comply with the requirements of the Mail Preference Service; and (iii) removal of 'gone-aways' and the deceased.

When any of the services listed below (or other marketing-related services) are supplied with printed matter as a single supply, then that single supply is standard-rated as a supply of direct marketing services. Where the printed matter and any services are supplied separately, then that may comprise multiple supplies and each component is taxed according to its VAT liability. Example services that block zero-rating are:

● posting or arranging the posting of customer mail such as publicity, advertising material or promotional goods to many recipients, including unaddressed mail (known as door drops);
● analysis or manipulation of data (either provided by the customer or sourced directly) for strategic or marketing reasons – for example, to target direct mail at specific groups based on geography, socio-economic factors or gender of recipients;
● purchase or rental of third-party mailing lists, including for amalgamation with customer's own lists;
● analysis of own and customer data to produce reports on campaign results and advice on strategy.

However, HMRC does accept that when supplying printed matter a supplier may treat mail charges by mail operators as a disbursement for VAT purposes provided the following conditions are all met:

● the supplier meets the general disbursement requirements (see 11.2.4 'Disbursements');
● the supplier's responsibility for the mail ceases when it is accepted for safe delivery by the mail company;
● the supplier passes on any discount or rebate from the mail company to the supplier's clients in full or, if the supplier obtains the discount or rebate from posting various clients' mail at the same time, the supplier apportions it fairly between them.

Library services

The hire or loan of qualifying printed matter is itself zero-rated. So a hire charge for a book is zero-rated. Also zero-rated are any excess use charges, though penalties for failure to keep to the hire agreement are **outside the scope of VAT** or **non-business** (see also 4.3.25 'Fines and penalties').

However, this does not mean that charges for general library and information services are zero-rated. In the VAT Tribunal case *UU Bibliotech Ltd* [2006] V19764, a university (UU) transferred its libraries to a subsidiary company (UUB) with the subsidiary then supplying 'library services' to UU. It argued that those services are partly or wholly zero-rated as a supply of the hire of qualifying printed matter. UU's students obtained access to and use of a wide range of media and support under the agreement including: access to books and periodicals; the right to loan books; access to e-media such as CD ROMs, electronic databases, electronic journals, internet, email and other library materials such as slides, tapes and microfiche; staff advice and support; access to study areas; and many other benefits. The VAT Tribunal decided that UUB was not supplying UU with the hire or loan of books but with a standard-rated supply of learning resources.

6.4.2 Caravans

With effect from 6 April 2013:

1. The sale of a new caravan is zero-rated if it is longer than 7 metres or wider than 2.55 metres, and is manufactured to BS 3632:2005. This requirement is directly linked to the 2005 version of the British Standard and changes to that standard will not affect the VAT liability of caravans, unless further changes are made to the VAT legislation.
2. The sale of a second-hand caravan is zero-rated if it is longer than 7 metres or wider than 2.55 metres, was occupied before 6 April 2013 and meets BS 3632:2005 or an earlier version of that standard. Earlier versions of the standard were published in 1963, 1970, 1981, 1989 and 1995.
3. The sale of a new or second-hand caravan is reduced-rated if it is longer than 7 metres or wider than 2.55 metres, and is not manufactured to BS 3632:2005.
4. The sale of any other caravan is standard-rated.

If the sale of a caravan is zero-rated, so also is (a) the lease of it under a long-term leasing agreement under which the lessee is free to transport it to a place of their own choosing; (b) the loan of it without making a charge; and (c) a deemed supply resulting from any private use of the caravan.

Excluded from zero-rating are any removable contents such as tables, chairs, mattresses, seat cushions, fridges, carpets and washing machines. However, goods of a kind ordinarily incorporated by builders as fixtures in a new dwelling qualify for zero-rating, for example sinks, baths, WCs, fixed partitions and water heaters.

Note that:

- the provision of a pitch for a caravan on a holiday/leisure site is standard-rated unless the pitch is occupied by an employee of the site operator as their principal private residence;
- the provision of a pitch for a caravan for restricted periods is standard-rated;
- the provision of a pitch for a caravan on other sites is VAT exempt (for example on a site where the caravan can be lived in throughout the year);
- the supply of accommodation in a caravan that is sited on a park advertised or held out for holiday use and let to a person as holiday accommodation is standard-rated;

- the supply of accommodation in a caravan that is on a site designated by the local authority as for permanent residential use, and let to a person as residential accommodation is VAT exempt.

6.4.3 **Clothing and footwear**

Most supplies of clothing and footwear are standard-rated; however, the following are zero-rated:

- young children's clothing and footwear;
- children's uniforms;
- protective boots and helmets;
- clothes donated to a charity for sale;
- exports of clothes.

The hire or loan of a zero-rated item of clothing or footwear is also zero-rated, as is the hire of roller skates, ice skates and similar items if the foot size criteria are met.

See below for more on each zero-rating.

Young children's clothing and footwear

The supply of articles designed as clothing or footwear for young children and not suitable for use by older children or adults is zero-rated.

HMRC generally accepts that items below specified garment or foot sizes are designed for young children and not suitable for older persons. HMRC publishes tables of eligible sizes (*VAT Notice 714*, section 4.2). If a garment is designed to stretch, its maximum stretch size must not exceed specified limits.

Fur exclusion

There are restrictions on garments containing fur. Zero-rating excludes articles of clothing made wholly or partly of **fur skin**, except: headgear; gloves; buttons, belts and buckles; any garment merely trimmed with fur skin unless the trimming has an area greater than one-fifth of the area of the outside material or, in the case of a new garment, represents a cost to the manufacturer greater than the cost to them of the other components.

> **Fur skin** means any skin with fur, hair or wool attached except: rabbit skin; woolled sheep or lamb skin; and the skin, if neither tanned nor dressed, of bovine cattle (including buffalo), equine animals, goats or kids (other than Yemen, Mongolian and Tibetan goats or kids), swine (including peccary), chamois, gazelles, deer or dogs.

Children's uniforms

HMRC policy on children's uniforms is as follows (*VAT Notice 714*, section 6.1).

> If you supply garments under a specific agreement with a school catering exclusively for pupils under 14 years of age you may be able to apply the zero rate beyond the garment measurements... The garments must be unique to that school by design, such as a prominent badge or piping in school colours, and held out for sale as being for that school only. If these conditions are met, you may apply the zero rate irrespective of garment size.

> The same principles apply to clothing items which form the uniform of other children's organisations catering exclusively for the under 14s, such as Beavers and Brownies. These may be zero-rated irrespective of size provided they're: designed exclusively for the organisation; worn only by under 14s; and clearly identifiable to the organisation. Zero-rating doesn't apply to items which may also be worn by older groups such as Scouts.

Protective boots and helmets

The item must conform to British, EU or equivalent safety standards. Qualifying items include motorbike and cycling helmets and the hire or loan of such items. However, protective boots and helmets are standard-rated when supplied to an organisation for use by its employees.

Clothes donated to a charity for sale

The sale of clothing or footwear donated for sale by a charity or a profits-to-charity person is zero-rated.

See 6.3.2 'Sale of donated goods'.

Exports of clothes

The export of clothing and footwear of all types by a charity is zero-rated. 'Export' means sending to a destination outside the EU. See 6.3.1 'Export of goods by a charity'.

6.4.4 **Export of goods**

A supply of any type of tangible moveable goods is zero-rated if all the following conditions are met:

- The supply involves the goods being exported from a location in the UK to a location outside the EU.
- The goods physically leave the UK within certain time limits (normally three months from the tax point of the supply but extended to six months in some situations).
- The supplier retains adequate evidence of export.

Also zero-rated is work on goods that are for export. All of the following conditions must be met for zero-rating to apply:

- The goods on which the work is to be carried out, must have been obtained, acquired within, or imported into the EU for the purposes of being worked on.
- The goods must not be used in the UK between the time of leaving the supplier's premises and exportation.
- On completion of the work, the goods are intended to be, and in fact are, exported from the EU either: (i) by you, the supplier of the service (or someone acting on your behalf), or (ii) if your customer belongs outside the EU, by your customer (or someone acting on your customer's behalf).

See 9.4 'Exports' for more on the zero-rating of exports. See also 6.3.1 'Export of goods by a charity' for a separate zero-rating relief for exports of goods by charities.

6.4.5 **Export-related services**

The supply of services consisting of the making of arrangements for:

(a) the export of any goods to a place outside the EU;
(b) a supply of work on goods for export to a place outside the EU; or
(c) any supply of services which is made outside the member states.

– is zero-rated, though this excludes VAT-exempt insurance and financial services, for which see below.

The UK zero rate only applies where the place of supply of the above services is the UK. For more on determining the place of supply services see Chapter 9 'International aspects of VAT'.

VAT-exempt insurance and financial services supplied to a person who belongs outside the EU or which are directly linked to an export of goods outside the EU are VAT exempt with a right to deduct attributable input VAT. The effect is the same as zero-rating. See 3.3.13 'Foreign and specified supplies'.

6.4.6 **Food and drink**

For VAT purposes, food includes drink. The supply of the following items is zero-rated:

- food of a kind used for human consumption;
- animal feeding stuffs;
- seeds or other means of propagation of plants comprised in items 1 or 2;
- live animals of a kind generally used as, or yielding or producing, food for human consumption.

However:

- there are 'exceptions' and some 'exceptions to the exceptions';
- 'supplies in the course of catering' do not qualify for zero-rating.

Exceptions and exceptions to the exceptions

The exceptions (standard-rated) and the exceptions to the exceptions (zero-rated) are:

1. Frozen products

- **Exceptions (standard-rated)**: ice cream, ice lollies, frozen yoghurt, water ices and similar frozen products, and prepared mixes for making such products.
- **Exceptions to exceptions (zero-rated)**: yoghurt unsuitable for immediate consumption when frozen.

2. Confectionery

- **Exceptions (standard-rated)**: all forms of confectionery including chocolates, sweets and biscuits; drained, glacé or crystallised fruits; and any item of sweetened prepared food which is normally eaten with the fingers.
- **Exceptions to exceptions (zero-rated)**: cakes or biscuits other than biscuits wholly or partly covered with chocolate or some product similar in taste and appearance. Drained cherries and candied peels.

3. Alcoholic beverages

- **Exceptions (standard-rated)**: alcoholic beverages chargeable with any duty of excise specifically charged on spirits, beer, **wine** or **made-wine** and preparations thereof.

4. Other beverages

- **Exceptions (standard-rated):** other beverages (including fruit juices and bottled waters) and syrups, concentrates, essences, powders, crystals or other products for the preparation of beverages.
- **Exceptions to exceptions (zero-rated):**
  - tea, maté, herbal teas and similar products, and preparations and extracts thereof;
  - cocoa, coffee and chicory and other roasted coffee substitutes, and preparations and extracts thereof;
  - milk and preparations and extracts thereof; and
  - preparations and extracts of meat, yeast or egg.

4A. Sports drinks

- **Exceptions (standard-rated):** sports drinks that are advertised or marketed as products designed to enhance physical performance, accelerate recovery after exercise or build bulk, and other similar drinks, including (in either case) syrups, concentrates, essences, powders, crystals or other products for the preparation of such drinks.

5. Snacks

- **Exceptions (standard-rated):** any of the following when packaged for human consumption without further preparation, namely, potato crisps, potato sticks, potato puffs, and similar products made from the potato, or from potato flour, or from potato starch, and savoury food products obtained by the swelling of cereals or cereal products; and salted or roasted nuts other than nuts in shell.

6. Pet foods

- **Exceptions (standard-rated):** pet foods, canned, packaged or prepared; packaged foods (not being pet foods) for birds other than poultry or game; and biscuits and meal for cats and dogs.

7. Brewing and winemaking products

- **Exceptions (standard-rated):** foodstuffs which are canned, bottled, packaged or prepared for use: (a) in the domestic brewing of any beer; (b) in the domestic making of any cider or perry; or (c) in the domestic production of any wine or made-wine.

> In the Alcoholic Liquor Duties Act 1979, **wine** is defined as 'any liquor which is of a strength exceeding 1.2% and which is obtained from the alcoholic fermentation of fresh grapes or of the must of fresh grapes, whether or not the liquor is fortified with spirits or flavoured with aromatic extracts'. **Made-wine** means 'liquor which is of a strength exceeding 1.2% and which is obtained from the alcoholic fermentation of any substance or by mixing a liquor so obtained or derived from a liquor so obtained with any other liquor or substance but does not include wine, beer, black beer, spirits or cider'. Mead is an example of a made wine.

Supplies in the course of catering

These are excluded from zero-rating. A supply of anything in the course of catering includes:

(a) any supply of it for consumption on the **premises** on which it is supplied; this includes meals and drinks of all types (hot or cold) for consumption in cafes, restaurants, bars, hotels, inns, etc.;

(b) any supply of **hot food** for consumption off those premises; this includes supplies of hot takeaway food, but not cold takeaway food.

Premises

With effect for supplies on or after 1 October 2012 premises on which food is supplied are defined to include any area set aside for the consumption of food by that supplier's customers, whether or not the area may also be used by the customers of other suppliers. So consumption of food and drink in gardens, outdoor seating areas, standing areas and shared consumption areas in shopping centres and similar are all treated as consumption on the premises, but if cold food is taken away from any dedicated consumption area, for example to public areas, home, a workplace desk, etc. then cold takeaway food can be zero-rated though hot takeaway food is still standard-rated.

Hot food

With effect for supplies on or after 1 October 2012 **hot food** means food which (or any part of which) is hot at the time it is provided to the customer and:

- has been heated for the purposes of enabling it to be consumed hot;
- has been heated to order;
- has been **kept hot** after being heated;

- is provided to a customer in packaging that retains heat (whether or not the packaging was primarily designed for that purpose) or in any other packaging that is specifically designed for hot food; or
- is advertised or marketed in a way that indicates that it is supplied hot.

> Something is **hot** if it is at a temperature above the ambient air temperature, and something is **kept hot** after being heated if the supplier stores it in an environment which provides, applies or retains heat, or takes other steps to ensure it remains hot or to slow down the natural cooling process.

Ancillary and closely related supplies of catering

A supply of catering can take on a different VAT status when it is a part of a broader package of supplies:

- Supplies of meals to school pupils and students can be closely related to the overall supply of education and follow the VAT status of the education. See 5.1 'Education and vocational training' for exempt supplies of education and 10.5 'Academy and free schools' for non-business education (academy and free schools).
- Supplies of meals to residents in a hospital, care home, or at a lunch club in a day care centre for the elderly, etc. can be closely related to the supply of care and follow its VAT status. See 5.2 'Health and welfare'.
- Supplies of catering at a qualifying charity fundraising event may be VAT exempt. See 5.7 'Fundraising events'.

Catering contracts

Catering contracts can take on a variety of VAT statuses. HMRC provides the following guidance (*VAT Notice 709/1*, section 2.2):

1. **Catering concession**: a licence to occupy a specific kitchen and restaurant area is an exempt licence to occupy (unless the landlord has opted to tax the premises). This is the case even if the grant includes use of kitchen or catering equipment.
2. **Cold food for customer preparation**: if the customer must prepare the food themselves before it can be consumed, this is not a supply in the course of catering. This will apply whether the food is delivered to, or collected by, the customer. For these purposes, 'preparation' includes: thawing frozen food cooking food reheating pre-cooked food and arranging food on serving plates.

3. **Sandwich delivery**: if you take sandwiches, or other items of food and drink, to buildings in order to sell them, but have no contract or agreement to do so, this is not a supply in the course of catering and you can zero-rate any item that is eligible.

4. **Event catering**: if you are supplying the food under a contract, for example to cater for an event, you are making a supply in the course of catering and all your supplies will be standard-rated.

5. **Grocery items sold from catering outlets**: provided these items are in the same form as when sold by a grocer or supermarket, and are clearly not intended for on-premises consumption, you do not have to treat them as being made in the course of catering. Examples of items that are clearly not intended for on-premises consumption include packets of tea, packaged coffee granules, powder, beans, etc., sugar, loaves of bread and cartons of factory sealed milk.

6. **Packed lunches**: where you provide packed meals as an incidental to an event or a function, such as for coach parties or race meetings, the meals are supplied in the course of catering and should be standard-rated. If you run a hotel or similar establishment and you supply bed and board (including packed meals) at an inclusive price, you should treat the whole supply as standard-rated. Where however, you supply a packed meal over and above your supply of accommodation and a separate charge is made, then provided it is for consumption off your premises, it can be zero-rated.

6.4.7 **Freight transport services**

The transport of goods from a place within the UK to a place outside the EU (or vice versa) is zero-rated to the extent that the services are performed in the UK. Also zero-rated are:

1. the supply of services of transport, handling and storage of goods, when they are supplied in connection with a journey from the place of importation to their destination either within the UK or within another EU member state (to the extent that those services are supplied in the UK);

2. the supply of services of transport, handling and storage of goods, when they are supplied in connection with a journey from their origin either within the UK or within another member state to the place of export (to the extent that those services are supplied in the UK).

See 9.8.9 'Transport of goods'.

6.4.8 **Houseboats**

The sale or hire (for towing away to a mooring of the customer's choosing) of a houseboat is zero-rated. A houseboat is a floating decked structure which:

- is designed or adapted for use solely as a place of permanent habitation; and
- does not have the means of, and which is not capable of being readily adapted for, self-propulsion.

Any removable contents are excluded from zero-rating (see 6.4.2 'Caravans'). The supply of accommodation in a houseboat is also excluded from zero-rating.

6.4.9 **Passenger transport**

Passenger transport services are supplied when a vehicle, ship or aircraft is provided, together with a driver or crew, for the carriage of passengers. This may also include any incidental services (see below). If a vehicle, ship or aircraft is hired without a driver or crew or a ship or aircraft is provided under charter arrangements, this is a hire of goods, not passenger transport. The following passenger transport services are zero-rated:

1. **Transport in passenger-carrying vehicles**: the transport of passengers in any vehicle, ship or aircraft designed or adapted to carry not less than ten passengers (including driver and crew). If the vehicle has been adapted to cater for the special needs of people with disabilities, for example to carry wheelchairs, then the number of persons that could have been carried but for that adaptation is used. If the vehicle has been adapted for another reason, for example to carry luggage, then the spaces lost are not ignored.
2. **Post Office transport**: the transport of passengers by a Universal Service Provider. Universal Service Provider means a person who provides a universal postal service (within the meaning of Part 3 of the Postal Services Act 2011) or part of such a service, in the UK. See 5.8 'Public postal services' for more on Universal Service Providers and postal services.
3. **Scheduled flights**: the transport of passengers on any scheduled flight. A scheduled flight is one that runs either according to a published timetable or so regularly or frequently as to constitute a recognisable systematic series of flights.
4. **Cross-border transport**: the transport of passengers from a place within to a place outside the UK or vice versa, to the extent that those services are supplied in the UK.
5. **Designated travel services**: the supply of a **designated travel service** to be enjoyed outside the EU, to the extent to which the supply is so enjoyed. See 10.2 'Tour Operators' Margin Scheme (TOMS)'.

However, the following are excluded from zero-rating:

1. **Places of entertainment, etc.:** the transport of passengers in any vehicle to, from or within: (a) a place of entertainment, recreation or amusement; or (b) a place of cultural, scientific, historical or similar interest, by the person, or a person connected with them, who supplies a right of admission to, or a right to use facilities at, such a place.
2. **Airport transport:** the transport of passengers in any motor vehicle between a car park (or land adjacent thereto) and an airport passenger terminal (or land adjacent thereto) by the person, or a person connected with them, who supplies facilities for the parking of vehicles in that car park.
3. **Pleasure flights:** the transport of passengers in an aircraft where the flight is advertised or held out to be for the purpose of: (a) providing entertainment, recreation or amusement; or (b) the experience of flying, or the experience of flying in that particular aircraft, and not primarily for the purpose of transporting passengers from one place to another.

If the supply of passenger transport is zero-rated, then incidental supplies may also be zero-rated, even if there is a separate charge. 'Incidental supplies' include the transport of accompanied luggage and pets, seat reservations and airport charges. Charges for car parking, cycle storage and left luggage are always standard-rated.

See also 6.5.1 'Cable-suspended passenger transport'.

6.4.10 Prescription goods

The supply of prescription goods is zero-rated. The following conditions must all be met:

1. The goods must be qualifying goods. Qualifying goods are any goods designed or adapted for use in connection with any medical or surgical treatment except hearing aids, dentures, spectacles and contact lenses.
2. The goods must be dispensed to an individual for that individual's personal use.
3. The dispensing must be on the prescription of an appropriate medical practitioner.
4. The dispensing must be by a registered pharmacist or equivalent.
5. The goods must not be supplied for use for patients while in hospital or in a similar institution or administered, injected or applied by health professionals to their patients in the course of medical treatment. Such goods are covered by the VAT exemptions for supplies of hospital care or of professional medical services – see 5.2 'Health and welfare'.

6.4.11 **Privileged persons in other EU states**

Sometimes a **privileged person** in another EU state can zero rate a supply that would otherwise be standard-rated or reduced-rated in the UK.

> **Privileged persons** include:
>
> - diplomatic missions such as embassies, high commissions and consulates;
> - the institutions of the EU including the European Atomic Energy Community, the European Central Bank and the European Investment Bank;
> - international organisations: these are organisations established by treaty between sovereign governments and the subsidiary bodies of such organisations, for example the United Nations and its various subsidiary organisations and NATO;
> - visiting NATO armed forces: the forces must be visiting another EU state;
> - the armed forces of the UK stationed in Cyprus pursuant to the Republic of Cyprus's Treaty of Establishment.

Goods

HMRC accepts (*VAT Notice 725*, section 14.4) that a supply of goods to a privileged person qualifies for zero-rating if:

1. The customer gives you a certificate of entitlement.
2. The goods are for the official use of an embassy; a high commission; a consulate; an international organisation; a NATO visiting force; or a British armed force contingent based in Cyprus, or for the personal use of a member of staff of one of these bodies.
3. You, or a forwarder acting on your behalf, must remove the goods to an official address of the embassy, high commission, consulate, international organisation or force in another EU member state or in one of the Sovereign Base Areas in Cyprus. If your customer is a British embassy or high commission in another member state, you may consign goods to the Foreign and Commonwealth Office for delivery through diplomatic channels. You must obtain and keep proof of the removal of the goods from the UK to the customer's address in the host country. Proof of posting is sufficient.
4. If the supply is for a contingent of British forces in Cyprus or its staff, or for a NATO visiting force in Germany or its staff, the order must be placed by an Official Procurement Agency for the force, such as the NAAFI or a regimental purchasing officer.

If these conditions are not met the supply must be treated as though the goods have been dispatched to a private individual in the EU and UK VAT charged where appropriate.

Services

HMRC also accepts (*VAT Notice 725*, section 14.5) that a supply of services to a privileged person qualifies for zero-rating if:

1. You receive a certificate of entitlement.
2. The supply of services is made to an international organisation, a NATO visiting force, or a British force in Cyprus, for the official use of the force or organisation.
3. The person placing the order is based in an office of the force or international organisation in an EU member state other than the UK.
4. A supply of services to British forces must in addition satisfy the following conditions:
   - the service must consist of training, software development, a supply of staff, or goods forwarding;
   - for training, the trainees must all be members of a British contingent based in an EU member state other than the UK, or members of British forces Cyprus;
   - for software development, the software must be for the use of the force, and not for use in the UK;
   - for a supply of staff, the staff must work exclusively for the force in the visiting force's host country or in a Sovereign Base Area in Cyprus; and
   - if the service is goods forwarding, the goods must all be forwarded to or from the force's premises in the other member state or in a Sovereign Base Area in Cyprus.

EC Sales List

Qualifying supplies of goods or services should be omitted from the EC Sales List. In general, qualifying supplies of goods are not regarded as distance sales and do not count towards distance-selling thresholds. Exceptionally supplies to Germany do count towards your distance-selling threshold in that country (*VAT Notice 725*, section 14.9).

6.4.12 **Removal of goods**

Tangible moveable goods are removed from the UK when they are taken from a location in the UK to a location in another EU state. Removals between VAT-registered businesses qualify for zero-rating as follows:

1. The supplier must obtain the customer's VAT registration number (in the EU state of acquisition) and show this on its VAT invoice together with the customer's two-letter country prefix code.

2. The supplier must check that the customer's VAT registration number is valid and retain evidence of this check for at least six years.
3. The goods must have physically left the territory of the UK for a destination in another EU state within the requisite time limit, normally three months.
4. The supplier must obtain evidence of removal of the goods within the requisite time limit and retain this for at least six years.

See 9.6.10 'Zero-rating removals' for more on this zero-rating.

6.4.13   Ships and works on ships

The supply, repair or maintenance of a qualifying ship is zero-rated as is the modification or conversion of a qualifying ship, provided that when so modified or converted it will remain a qualifying ship. Also zero-rated are:

- the supply of parts and equipment, of a kind ordinarily installed or incorporated in, and to be installed, or incorporated in the propulsion, navigation or communication systems or the general structure of a qualifying ship;
- the supply of life jackets, life rafts, smoke hoods and similar safety equipment for use in a qualifying ship;
- the supply of services wholly performed in the UK under a charter of a qualifying ship except where the services supplied under such a charter consist wholly of any one or more of the following: transport of passengers, accommodation, entertainment or education.

A qualifying ship is any ship of gross tonnage of not less than 15 tonnes which is neither designed nor adapted for use for recreation or pleasure. Qualifying ships can include passenger-carrying ships, barges, fishing vessels, large houseboats (Dutch barges) and similar. There is a separate relief for un-propelled houseboats, see 6.4.2 'Caravans' and 6.4.8 'Houseboats'.

It is the design or adaptation of the ship that matters, not its actual or intended use. HMRC states (*VAT Notice 744C*, section 2.4)

> You need to consider the nature of the vessel's design. To be a qualifying ship it must be designed for commercial purposes or to be used for permanent residential living by the owner. If your ship does not have any features that indicate a commercial design (such as a cargo hold, commercial fishing equipment, or the ability to convey large numbers of passengers) or of permanent residential living then it is not a qualifying ship

For registered ships the gross tonnage of a ship is as ascertained under the Merchant Shipping Acts. For unregistered ships HMRC provides a formula for calculating the gross tonnage. See *VAT Notice 744C*, section 2.10.

6.4.14 Training for overseas governments

By HMRC concession (*VAT Notice 741A*, section 8.2), training services supplied in the UK to overseas governments can be zero-rated if the following conditions are met:

1. the services must be used by the foreign or overseas government for the furtherance of its sovereign activities (that is, not for business purposes); and
2. you must obtain and retain a written statement from the foreign or overseas government concerned, or its accredited representative, certifying that the trainees are employed in furtherance of its sovereign activities.

Foreign or overseas government includes overseas government officials, public servants and members of organisations such as the armed forces, the police, the emergency services and similar bodies answerable to the government concerned.

The relief does not apply if:

- The training services are received for business purposes. It therefore excludes the training of personnel from government-owned industries or sponsored commercial organisations such as state airlines or nationalised industries.
- The training services are exempt from VAT. See 5.1 'Education and vocational training' for the VAT exemption for education and vocational training.

6.4.15 Water and sewerage services

The following supplies are zero-rated.

The supply of water

The supply of water is zero-rated unless it is for use in connection with a relevant industrial activity. Relevant industrial activities are manufacturing, construction, mining, energy and water supply.

The following are excluded from zero-rating:

- distilled water, deionised water and water of similar purity;
- deliberately heated water; however, naturally occurring hot water (arising from hot springs, etc.) is zero-rated and supplies of hot water for heating may be eligible for reduced-rating (see 6.5.5 'Fuel and power'); and
- mineral, table and spa waters in bottles or similar containers held out for sale as a beverage. However, ordinary water, of a kind usually supplied by water mains, supplied in bottles as a drought alleviation or other emergency measure can be zero-rated.

Sewerage services

These are services of:

- reception, disposal or treatment of foul water or sewage in bulk; and
- emptying of cesspools, septic tanks or similar receptacles, but excluding emptying in connection with a relevant industrial activity.

6.5 REDUCED-RATE SUPPLIES

EU law

EU states are permitted to apply one or two reduced rates of not less than 5% to a range of items specified in the Principal VAT Directive. These include:

- supplies of natural gas, electricity and district heating;
- certain importations and supplies of works of art, collector's items and antiques (see 6.5.7 'Imported works of art, antiques and collector's items');
- supplies of live plants and other floricultural products including bulbs, roots, cut flowers, ornamental foliage and wood for use as firewood;
- items listed in Annex III to the Principal VAT Directive.

However, reduced rates may not be applied to electronically supplied services (for the definition of which see 9.8.6 'Electronically supplied services'). EU states are also permitted to carry on applying reduced rates to goods and services not listed above, provided they were in place at 1 January 1991. There are also many special reduced-rating rules for particular EU states. EU states may restrict reduced-rating to concrete and specific aspects of the items listed above (see 11.3 'Single and multiple supplies').

UK law

The UK has implemented the reduced rates set out below using, at the time of writing, a rate of 5% VAT. The property-related reduced rates are covered in 8.3 'Property VAT reliefs'.

6.5.1 Cable-suspended passenger transport

With effect from 1 April 2013, the transport of passengers by means of a cable-suspended chair, bar, gondola or similar vehicle designed or adapted to carry not more than nine passengers is reduced-rated. However, this excludes the transport of passengers to, from or within:

- a place of entertainment, recreation or amusement; or
- a place of cultural, scientific, historical or similar interest,

by the person, or a person connected with that person, who supplies a right of admission to, or a right to use facilities at, such a place.

6.5.2 Children's car seats

Supplies of children's car seats are reduced-rated. Child means a person aged under 14 years. The following are children's car seats: a safety seat; a related base unit for a safety seat; the combination of a safety seat and a related wheeled framework; a booster seat; and a booster cushion.

6.5.3 Contraceptive products and women's sanitary products

Supplies of contraceptive products and supplies of women's sanitary products are reduced-rated. Supplies of such products on prescription are zero-rated, and where contraceptive products are fitted, injected or implanted by a health professional there is a single supply of exempt medical care.

6.5.4 Energy-saving materials

The following supplies are reduced-rated:

- supplies of services of installing **qualifying energy-saving materials** in **qualifying residential accommodation**; and
- supplies of qualifying energy-saving materials by a person who installs those materials in qualifying residential accommodation.

Any incidental work such as minor building work is also reduced-rated.

Qualifying energy-saving materials

Qualifying energy-saving materials are:

(a) insulation for walls, floors, ceilings, roofs or lofts or for water tanks, pipes or other plumbing fittings;
(b) draught stripping for windows and doors;
(c) central heating system controls (including thermostatic radiator valves);
(d) hot water system controls;
(e) solar panels;
(f) wind turbines;
(g) water turbines;
(h) ground source heat pumps;
(i) air source heat pumps;
(j) micro combined heat and power units; and
(k) boilers designed to be fuelled solely by wood, straw or similar vegetal matter.

Qualifying residential accommodation

Qualifying residential accommodation is:

- a building, or part of a building, that consists of a dwelling or a number of dwellings; or
- a building, or part of a building, used for a relevant residential purpose; or
- a caravan used as a place of permanent habitation; or
- a houseboat.

See 8.6 'Property terms' for the meanings of dwelling and relevant residential purpose.

Separately purchased materials

If the materials are purchased and installed separately neither the materials nor the installation services qualify for reduced-rating. If the materials are installed as part of a zero-rated construction, they may be zero-rated; however, if they are installed as a part of a wider standard-rated installation (for example, central heating system controls installed as a part of a complete central heating system installation), then no reduced-rating applies (see the *AN Checker* case in 11.3 'Single and multiple supplies').

EC infringement proceedings

In case C-161/14 *European Commission* v. *UK* [2015], the CJEU decided that the UK's reduced-rating for qualifying supplies of energy-saving materials as set out above is too broad and must be limited to:

- installations that comprise the provision, construction, renovation and alteration of housing, as part of a social policy;
- installations that comprise the renovation and repairing of private dwellings but excluding situations where the energy-saving materials account for a significant part of the value of the services supplied.

In August 2015 HMRC released *Revenue & Customs Brief 13/15* in which the UK government announced that it is considering the implications of the decision. But if there are to be any legislative changes, they will not be implemented before Finance Act 2016. Until then, supplies of the installation of energy savings materials will continue to be reduced-rated and any changes will only apply to future supplies and not to supplies already made.

Relevant charitable purpose buildings

Before 1 August 2013 the installation of energy-saving materials in a building intended for use solely for a relevant charitable purpose also qualified for reduced-rating; however, this was withdrawn with effect from that date. HMRC announced in *Revenue & Customs Brief 26/12* that where work has commenced for the installation of energy-saving materials before 1 August 2013, the reduced-rate will continue to apply to the whole installation even if part of that installation is performed after that date.

History

This reduced-rating was first introduced with effect from 31 October 2001 and comprised items (a)–(g) above. (h) was added with effect from 1 June 2004, (i) and (j) from 7 April 2005 and (k) from 1 January 2006.

6.5.5 **Fuel and power**

Eligible supplies of fuel or power for **qualifying use** are reduced-rated.

Eligible supplies

Eligible supplies of fuel or power are supplies of:

(a) coal, coke or other solid substances held out for sale solely as fuel;
(b) coal gas, water gas, producer gases or similar gases;
(c) petroleum gases, or other gaseous hydrocarbons, whether in a gaseous or liquid state;
(d) fuel oil, gas oil or kerosene;
(e) electricity, heat or air-conditioning.

Eligible supplies include supplies of mains gas and electricity, solid fuels such as coal, wood logs and peat, cylinder gas and fuel oils such as kerosene, but not petrol or diesel. Fuel supplied to a charity providing rescue at sea for use in a lifeboat is zero-rated (see 6.2.8 'Boats, lifeboats and ships'). Batteries are excluded but electricity from a mobile generator is included if the supplier operates the equipment and charges for the power supplied.

Qualifying use

Qualifying use means:

1. For use by a charity other than in the course or furtherance of a business.
2. For use in:
    - a building, or part of a building, that consists of a dwelling or number of dwellings;
    - a building, or part of a building, used for a relevant residential purpose (see 8.6.9 'Relevant residential purpose' for the definition of this);
    - self-catering holiday accommodation;
    - a caravan; or
    - a houseboat (see 6.4.8 'Houseboats' for the meaning of houseboat).

3. *De minimis* use (see 3.1.11). This includes:
   - piped gas not exceeding 150 therms a month (4,397 kilowatt hours a month);
   - electricity not exceeding 1,000 kilowatt hours a month;
   - any quantity of wood, peat or charcoal not intended for sale by the recipient;
   - a supply of not more than 2,300 litres of fuel oil, gas oil or kerosene;
   - a supply of liquefied petroleum gas in cylinders where each cylinder weighs less than 50 kg and either the number of cylinders supplied is at most 20 or is not intended for sale by the recipient;
   - a supply of liquefied petroleum gas (not in cylinders) to a person at any premises where the recipient is not able to store more than 2 tonnes of such gas.

Part-qualifying use

Where there is a supply partly for qualifying use (see 1 and 2 above) and partly not, if at least 60% of the goods are supplied for qualifying use, the whole supply is treated as a supply for qualifying use. In any other case, an apportionment must be made to determine the extent to which the supply is a supply for qualifying use.

Certificates

Energy suppliers may ask for a certificate to confirm the intended use of supplies.

Connection charges

Before 1 January 2012, by concession first-time connection charges made by the supplier of fuel and power for a qualifying use were zero-rated. The concession was withdrawn with effect from 1 January 2012. From that date, the treatment of one-off charges for the first-time connection to gas and electricity is as follows:

1. If the supply of the connection and provision of the utility is made by the same person (or by members of the same VAT group) the connection charge will follow the treatment of the utility.
2. If the supplies are not made by the same person or if, at the time of connection, the supplier of the utility has not been determined, the connection charge will be standard-rated irrespective of who eventually provides the utility.
3. The first-time connection of a new dwelling or relevant residential or relevant charitable purpose building to the gas or electricity mains supply is zero-rated if the connection is made as part of the construction of the building. See Chapter 8 'Property'.

4. Works in connection with the means of providing fuel and power as part of the renovation or alteration of empty residential premises, or of the conversion of premises to a different residential use may be reduced-rated see Chapter 8 'Property'.
5. Grant-funded connection or reconnection to a mains gas supply relating to a qualifying person's sole or main residence is reduced-rated. See 6.5.6 below.

6.5.6 Grant-funded heating and security equipment

The following supplies to **qualifying persons** (see below) are reduced-rated to the extent that the **consideration** for the supply (everything that is paid to the supplier in return for making the supply of goods or services) is, or is to be, funded by a grant made under a relevant government grant funding scheme:

1. **Heating appliances**: supplies to a qualifying person of any services of installing heating appliances in the qualifying person's sole or main residence, and supplies of heating appliances made to a qualifying person by a person who installs those appliances in the qualifying person's sole or main residence. Heating appliances means any of the following: (a) gas-fired room heaters that are fitted with thermostatic controls; (b) electric storage heaters; (c) closed solid fuel fire cassettes; (d) electric dual immersion water heaters with factory-insulated hot water tanks; (e) gas-fired boilers; (f) oil-fired boilers; (g) radiators.
2. **Mains gas connections**: supplies to a qualifying person of services (including associated goods) of connecting, or reconnecting, a mains gas supply to the qualifying person's sole or main residence.
3. **Central heating systems**: supplies to a qualifying person of services of installing, maintaining or repairing a central heating system in the qualifying person's sole or main residence and supplies of goods whose installation is necessary for the installation, maintenance or repair of the central heating system.
4. **Renewable source heating systems**: supplies to a qualifying person of services of installing, maintaining or repairing a renewable source heating system in the qualifying person's sole or main residence and supplies of goods whose installation is necessary for the installation, maintenance or repair of the system. Renewable source heating system means a space or water heating system which uses energy from: (a) renewable sources, including solar, wind and hydroelectric power; or (b) near-renewable resources, including ground and air heat.
5. **Qualifying security goods**: supplies to a qualifying person of services of installing qualifying security goods in the qualifying person's sole or main residence and supplies of qualifying security goods made to a qualifying person by a person who installs those goods in the qualifying person's sole or main residence. Qualifying security goods means any of the following:

(a) locks or bolts for windows; (b) locks, bolts or security chains for doors; (c) spy holes; (d) smoke alarms.

Qualifying person

A person to whom a supply is made is a qualifying person if at the time of the supply they are either: (i) aged 60 or over; or (ii) in receipt of one or more of the following benefits – child tax credit (other than the family element), council tax benefit, disability living allowance, disablement pension, housing benefit, income-based job seeker's allowance, income support, war disablement pension, personal independence payment, armed forces independence payment, working tax credit, or universal credit.

6.5.7   Imported works of art, antiques and collector's items

Strictly these goods are standard-rated and not reduced-rated. However, they are subject to a 'reduced-value' rule so that output VAT is due on a percentage of the selling price and not the full selling price. The effect is that the item is purchased reduced-rated.

To qualify for the reduced-value rule, an item must meet all of the following conditions:

1. The item must be imported from a country outside the EU. The reduced-value rule applies to the import VAT due on the item. See Chapter 9 'International aspects of VAT' for more on import VAT. Import VAT is normally due on the purchase price of the item, all other taxes and duties, levies, incidental expenses such as commission (but excluding certain auctioneer's commissions), packing, transport and insurance.
2. The item must not have been exported from the UK in the period of 12 months ending with the date of import in circumstances where the exportation and subsequent importation were effected to obtain the benefit of the reduced-value rule.
3. The item must be an **eligible work of art, antique** or **collector's item**. See below for the definitions of eligible works of art, antiques and collector's items.

Please note that there are parallel though not identical reliefs from Customs Duties.

Eligible collector's items

Eligible collector's items are any collection or collector's piece that is of zoological, botanical, mineralogical, anatomical, historical, archaeological, palaeontological, ethnographic, numismatic or philatelic interest.

A collector's piece is of philatelic interest if:

1. it is a postage or revenue stamp, a postmark, a first-day cover or an item of pre-stamped stationery; and
2. it is franked or (if unfranked) it is not legal tender and is not intended for use as such.

For historic items HMRC says (*VAT Notice 702*, section 11.4):

> An article which is not 100 years old may be eligible for the scheme under this heading if it is of historical significance because of its uniqueness, or by having a direct association with an historical person or event, or is a rare example marking an important change in technical or artistic development in a particular field. Items, which were mass-produced or are merely the products of a bygone age, are unlikely to be eligible.

Eligible works of art

These are:

(a) any mounted or unmounted painting, drawing, collage, decorative plaque or similar picture that was executed by hand;
(b) any original engraving, lithograph or other print which: (i) was produced from one or more plates executed by hand by an individual who executed them without using any mechanical or photomechanical process; and (ii) either is the only one produced from the plate or plates or is comprised in a limited edition;
(c) any original sculpture or statuary, in any material;
(d) any sculpture cast which: (i) was produced by or under the supervision of the individual who made the mould or became entitled to it by succession on the death of that individual; and (ii) either is the only cast produced from the mould or is comprised in a limited edition. The edition must be limited so that the number produced from the same mould does not exceed eight; or the edition comprises a limited edition of nine or more casts made before 1 January 1989 which HMRC has directed should be treated as a limited edition;
(e) any tapestry or other hanging which: (i) was made by hand from an original design, and (ii) either is the only one made from the design or is comprised in a limited edition. The edition must be limited so that the number produced from the same design does not exceed eight;
(f) any ceramic executed by an individual and signed by them;
(g) any enamel on copper which: (i) was executed by hand; (ii) is signed either by the person who executed it or by someone on behalf of the studio where it was executed; (iii) either is the only one made from the design in question or is comprised in a limited edition; and (iv) is not comprised in an article

of jewellery or an article of a kind produced by goldsmiths or silversmiths. The edition must be limited so that the number produced from the same design does not exceed eight; and each of the enamels in the edition is numbered and is signed by the above person;

(h) any mounted or unmounted photograph which: (i) was printed by or under the supervision of the photographer; (ii) is signed by the photographer; and (iii) either is the only print made from the exposure in question or is comprised in a limited edition so that the number produced from the same exposure does not exceed 30; and each of the prints in the edition is numbered and is signed by the photographer.

The following do not qualify as works of art:

(a) any technical drawing, map or plan;
(b) any picture comprised in a manufactured article that has been hand-decorated; or
(c) anything in the nature of scenery, including a backcloth.

The above goods are eligible for the margin scheme for second-hand goods, for which see 10.13 'Margin Schemes'.

Eligible antique

This is any antique, not being an **eligible collector's item** or an **eligible work of art**, that is more than 100 years old.

6.5.8 Mobility aids for the elderly

The following are reduced-rated:

1. the installation of **mobility aids** for use in **domestic accommodation** by a person who, at the time of the supply, is aged 60 or over;
2. the supply of mobility aids by a person installing them for use in domestic accommodation by a person who, at the time of the supply, is aged 60 or over.

Mobility aids means any of the following: (a) grab rails; (b) ramps; (c) stairlifts; (d) bath lifts; (e) built-in shower seats or showers containing built-in shower seats; (f) walk-in baths fitted with sealable doors.

Domestic accommodation means a building, or part of a building, that consists of a dwelling or a number of dwellings.

6.5.9 **Residential conversions and renovations**

Certain works of renovation to residential property and renovation or alteration of qualifying residential premises are reduced-rated. See Chapter 8 'Property'.

6.5.10 **Welfare advice and information**

A supply of **welfare advice or information** by a charity, or a **state-regulated private welfare institution or agency**, is reduced-rated. (See 5.2 'Health and welfare' for the meaning of 'state-regulated private welfare institution or agency'.) The reduced-rating covers welfare advice or information supplied via CDs, DVDs, posters, websites, etc., though advice or information provided via printed books, booklets, leaflets, etc. will qualify for zero-rating as explained above.

> **Welfare advice or information** means advice or information which directly relates to: (a) the physical or mental welfare of elderly, sick, distressed or disabled persons, or (b) the care or protection of children and young persons.

However, the following supplies are excluded:

- Supplies that would be exempt supplies of education or vocational training if they were made by an eligible body. See 5.1 'Education and vocational training' for the meanings of these terms.
- Supplies of goods, unless the goods are supplied wholly or almost wholly for the purpose of conveying the advice or information. See below.
- Supplies of advice or information provided solely for the benefit of a particular individual or according to their personal circumstances. However, such supplies may qualify as VAT-exempt welfare services, see 5.2 'Health and welfare'.

HMRC provides the following advice (*VAT Notice 701/2*, section 6.4) on supplies via goods:

> The reduced rate applies to supplies of goods made wholly or almost wholly for the purpose of giving welfare advice or information (i.e. at least 90% of the purpose of any goods used must be for conveying welfare advice or information). Examples include a video advising the elderly on safety in the home, or a DVD featuring advice for children on dealing with bullying. The inclusion on such goods of incidental information, for example, an appeal for donations or information on the charity's objects, will not affect the reduced rate. Goods that have an independent use and also carry incidental welfare advice, such as a mug or tee shirt bearing a slogan, are not covered by the reduced rate.

It is arguable that reduced-rating cannot apply to digital supplies of welfare advice or information (for example electronic databases or publications) due to their exclusion from reduced-rating by the Principal VAT Directive (see the start of 6.5 'Reduced-rate supplies'). However, HMRC does not appear to take this view.

7 Fundraising

This chapter looks at the following fundraising activities that charities and other voluntary organisations commonly undertake:

- 7.1 Admission fees
- 7.2 Advertising
- 7.3 Affinity credit cards
- 7.4 Auctions
- 7.5 Barter arrangements
- 7.6 Bingo and games of chance
- 7.7 Cause-related marketing
- 7.8 Challenge events
- 7.9 Christmas and other greeting cards
- 7.10 Consultancy services
- 7.11 Corporate events
- 7.12 Corporate sponsorship
- 7.13 Donations
- 7.14 Financial investments
- 7.15 Fundraising events
- 7.16 Gifts in kind from businesses
- 7.17 London Marathon and similar
- 7.18 Lotteries and raffles
- 7.19 Merchandising
- 7.20 Recycled goods
- 7.21 Renting property
- 7.22 Retail Gift Aid Scheme
- 7.23 Sale of donated goods
- 7.24 Shops
- 7.25 Supporter schemes

7.1 ADMISSION FEES

This section considers admission fees in the context of fundraising; however, there are several VAT exemptions for admission fees to sports facilities and cultural facilities such as theatres, galleries, museums, zoos, etc. For these exemptions see Chapter 5 'Exempt activities'.

Charities and certain other non-profit bodies will usually be able to arrange admission fees to fundraising events so that they are covered by the special VAT exemption for fundraising events, and so admission fees in this situation will be VAT exempt. See 7.15 'Fundraising events'. However, some events are excluded from the exemption:

- Events involving travel and/or accommodation such as challenge events – see 7.8 'Challenge events'.
- Events which the charity is not itself organising, for example a business arranging its own staff fundraising day where the proceeds are donated to charity or groups of charity friends organising a coffee morning and donating the proceeds to charity. The donation received by the charity is **outside the scope** of VAT.

- Commercial fundraising events – see 7.17 'London Marathon and similar'. However, HMRC does accept charities can organise their own qualifying fundraising event at a separately organised event (see 5.7.6 'Meaning of event').

If you only suggest an amount that may be given for admission, this can be treated as a donation, but you would have to allow free admission to anyone who asked for it.

You may also charge an admission fee that is simply enough to cover the direct costs of the event and then invite donations in addition. VAT then has to be accounted for on the admission fees only (assuming not VAT exempt as above). Again, you would have to admit someone who only paid the admission fee.

7.2 ADVERTISING

Voluntary organisations sometimes sell advertising in printed publications, and their own websites, letterheads, billboards, noticeboards, stationery and similar. Generally, the sale of advertising is standard-rated, with a few exceptions:

- The sale of advertising to a charity is zero-rated (see 6.2 'Zero-rated supplies to charities').
- Advertising in the programme or brochure for a qualifying fundraising event will be seen as part of the income from the event and will therefore be exempt. See 7.15 'Fundraising events'.
- In *VAT Notice 701/1*, section 5.2, HMRC accepts that if 50% or more of the total adverts in a publication are clearly placed by private individuals the charity can treat all the sums received as donations and outside the scope of VAT. A private advertisement makes no reference to a business. An example of a private advertisement is one that says 'Good wishes from (or 'space donated by') John and Susan Smith'; but not those with otherwise similar wording taken out by say, 'John and Susan Smith, Grocers, 49 High Street, Anytown'.
- HMRC accepts that the grant of a space for a third party to erect an advertising hoarding and sell advertising themselves is a licence to occupy land and as such VAT exempt subject to any option to tax. See 8.4 'Leases and lettings'.

7.3 AFFINITY CREDIT CARDS

These are credit cards carrying a charity name and logo. Under a typical charity affinity credit card arrangement the credit card company has limited use of the charity's name and logo, mailing list and some assistance in the recruitment of the charity's members and supporters to become subscribers to the card. The charity usually receives a fixed payment on first use of the card and an agreed percentage of all retail spending thereafter.

In *VAT Notice 701/1*, section 8, HMRC accepts that charities may treat income from affinity credit cards as follows, as long as they are not acting as an intermediary between the card provider and the applicant. This treatment only applies to income from affinity credit cards and does not extend to any other financial products.

Subject to the agreements between the charity and card provider being structured in a qualifying manner, the bulk of the monies received by a charity from the card provider can be treated as outside the scope of VAT.

- At least 20% of the initial payment is to be treated as the **consideration** (everything that is paid to the supplier in return for making the supply) for the standard-rated business supplies by the charity.
- The remaining 80% or less of the initial payment, and all subsequent payments based on turnover, are outside the scope of VAT.

To benefit from this treatment there must be two separate agreements:

- One agreement, between the charity (or its trading subsidiary) and the card provider should provide for the supply by the charity (or its trading subsidiary) of the necessary marketing and publicity services, access to membership lists and other promotional activity for the card (marketing services). These supplies are taxable at the standard rate.
- A second and separate agreement between the charity and the card provider should provide for contributions to be made by the card provider in respect of the use only of the charity's name and/or logo. Contributions made under this agreement can be treated as outside the scope of VAT.

7.4 **AUCTIONS**

Charity auctions at a qualifying fundraising event will be covered by the overall exemption for all income at the event (see 7.15 'Fundraising events'), unless any goods being sold in the auction qualify for zero-rating in their own right (for example, printed books) or are donated for auction, in which case they can be zero-rated if the auction is open to the general public or two or more specified persons (see 6.3.2 'Sale of donated goods'). An auction can itself be a fundraising event, as can an online auction.

7.5 **BARTER ARRANGEMENTS**

If one party (A) provides another party (B) with goods or services and in return B provides A with goods or services, then this is what is known as a barter arrangement. Each part of the arrangement is potentially subject to VAT as a separate supply with the gross (VAT-inclusive) considerations for each being netted off against each other:

- Supply 1 is the supply of goods or services by A to B.
- Supply 2 is the supply of goods or services by B to A.

The values of the two supplies must be assumed to be the same as they are provided in return for each other. The value is therefore the subjective value agreed by the parties, and it is advisable to explicitly state the agreed value in any contract in case of query or dispute by HMRC.

7.6 BINGO AND GAMES OF CHANCE

As explained in 5.10 'Betting, lotteries and other forms of gambling', there is a specific VAT exemption for income raised from betting, lotteries and other forms of gambling (games of chance). This includes bingo, race nights, sweepstakes, lotteries, etc. but excludes games of skill (such as chess and contract bridge).

The total amount charged to play is VAT exempt. For the organiser, the value of the exempt supply is the net proceeds after deducting the VAT-inclusive cost of cash or goods given as prizes. With effect from 27 April 2009 participation and session charges made for the right to take part in a game or series of games of bingo are also accepted as VAT exempt.

If any sort of game is played at a qualifying fundraising event, then participation fees will be VAT exempt; see 7.15 and 5.8 'Fundraising events'.

7.7 CAUSE-RELATED MARKETING

Cause-related marketing is really sponsorship in reverse – a business values a charity's brand and pays the charity a fee for the use of its name and/or logo. This is a supply of intellectual property rights and is standard-rated for VAT. If the charity also supplies other services such as advertising and promotion then the single/multiple supply rules should be applied to determine the VAT status, see 11.3 'Single and multiple supplies'.

The charity may receive donations in addition to the licence fee. The donations will be outside the scope of VAT, but the arrangement must make it clear that the donations are separate (see 7.12 'Corporate sponsorship').

7.8 CHALLENGE EVENTS

Challenge events usually involve participants undertaking some activity for which they have raised sponsorship. They can range from a local walk or run, to cycling across a desert or undertaking the Three Peaks Challenge. The sponsor usually understands that all proceeds, after costs, will be donated to the specified charity.

In order to determine the VAT statuses involved, the first thing to consider is who is organising the event. The organiser is the person who is making the arrangements for the participants and assuming the risks and responsibilities should anything go wrong. There are two options:

- the charity or its subsidiary or a connected entity is the organiser;
- an independent third party is the organiser.

7.8.1   Charity as organiser

If a charity or its trading subsidiary or a connected entity is the organiser, the next thing to consider is if the participant must raise or pay any specific amount before they are allowed to participate in the event, for example a deposit, booking fee, or a required amount of fundraising.

If no specific amount must be paid and this is a realistic possibility, then all sponsorships received should be able to be treated as outside-the-scope donations.

If participants must pay a mandatory amount before they are permitted to take part, then HMRC sees that as consideration for a supply of participation in the event.

If the event is a qualifying fundraising event (see 7.15 'Fundraising events'), then the mandatory fee is VAT exempt. This would cover, for example, entry fees for self-organised fun runs and walks where participants are not provided with any sleeping accommodation or facilities. Any sponsorship donations received above the entry fee would be outside the scope of VAT.

The usual reason why self-organised challenge events do not qualify for the fundraising exemption is because bought-in sleeping accommodation is provided to participants. In this case the mandatory charge is likely to fall within the Tour Operators' Margin Scheme (TOMS). This is explained in more detail in 10.2 'Tour Operators' Margin Scheme (TOMS)'. In summary:

- The margin on the event (mandatory charges less VAT-inclusive costs of bought-in services resupplied to participants) is subject to VAT.
- This margin is zero-rated if the event takes place wholly outside the EU and standard-rated if the event takes place entirely within the EU (including within the UK). If the event takes place partly in the EU and partly outside, an apportionment can be made.

Charities putting on their own events involving travel and accommodation should be aware that there is consumer protection legislation covering such events, restricting such things as the way the event is promoted, and introducing licensing and bonding requirements for air flights. There may also be significant personal risks involved for participants. Partly for these reasons charities putting on challenge events (especially ones involving foreign travel and accommodation) usually use or engage specialist suppliers who are experienced in organising and putting on such events, so the event falls into the next category.

7.8.2 Third-party organiser

No arrangement between charity and organiser

If a third party is the organiser, for example a commercial travel company, and the participant deals solely with the travel company, with no prior agreement between the charity and travel company, then the charity is not supplying anything in return for whatever amount it receives, so the amount received is an outside-the-scope-of-VAT donation.

Arrangement between charity and organiser

If there is an arrangement between the charity and travel company, then the charity will usually be acting as a **disclosed agent** for the travel company. This means the supply of the event is directly between the event organiser and the participant, with the charity acting as the event organiser's **agent** (see 11.2) in promoting the event, recruiting and supporting participants and in handling payments from the participants.

HMRC accepts (*VAT Notice 701/1*, section 10.2) that a charity will be acting as a **disclosed agent** of a specialist travel company if:

- both the charity and the specialist company have agreed that the charity will act as the company's agent;
- the charity discloses the name of the principal (the specialist company), for example in the event terms and conditions and on all tickets issued; and
- the charity is not taking any significant commercial risk in relation to the event (for example, the charity does not have any financial liability should something go wrong).

The charity usually receives the participant's sponsorship payments and pays over set amounts to the travel company on a schedule, retaining any payments in excess of what must be paid to the travel company. The charity is seen as supplying agency services to the organiser. The charity's commission is the mandatory charge received from the participant less the amount that must be paid to the organiser. That commission is VAT standard-rated income (assuming the organiser is in the UK, if not see 9.8.14 'Intermediary services').

HMRC example: charity acting as agent

A charity promotes a challenge event where participants will walk the Great Wall of China. The charity uses the services of a specialist company VAT registered in the UK and acts as its disclosed agent. The specialist company puts together the package of travel, accommodation, itinerary and guide. The charity promotes the event to its supporters. The charity asks participants to pay a non-returnable booking fee of £250 before allocating them a place. The charity asks participants to raise sponsorship of £3,000. The charity insists that 50% of the sponsorship target (£1,500) is paid to the charity by the participant 8 weeks before departure date.

So, the participants pay the charity £1750 (£250 booking fee + £1,500 sponsorship) before the charity allows them to take part in the challenge event. This is the cost of the event and constitutes a supply for VAT purposes made by the specialist company.

The charity, acting as a disclosed agent, has agreed with the specialist company that it will receive a commission of £550, and it invoices the specialist company for this amount plus £110 VAT as the commission is taxable at the standard rate. This VAT of £110 is due from the charity as output tax (and can be reclaimed by the specialist company as input tax). In practice, the charity can retain the commission and VAT (£660) from the amount collected from the participant and passes what remains to the specialist company.

As the charity has made a taxable supply it can reclaim any UK input tax it has incurred in promoting the event (subject to normal VAT reclaim rules).

Any further money raised by the participant and passed on to the charity is a donation and is outside the scope of VAT provided it is not consideration for other goods or services.

VAT Notice 701/1, section 10.3

7.9 CHRISTMAS AND OTHER GREETING CARDS

The sale of paper or electronic greeting cards is standard-rated, unless:

- the sale is at a qualifying fundraising event – it can then qualify for exemption;
- the cards are donated for sale – then the sale is zero-rated.

7.10 **CONSULTANCY SERVICES**

The provision of advice to other organisations and persons is by default standard-rated, though if:

1. the advice involves education or training it may be covered by the VAT exemption for education (see 5.2 'Education and vocational training');
2. the supply is of **welfare advice or information** by a charity or state-regulated private welfare institution, the supply is VAT reduced-rated.

> **Welfare advice or information** means advice or information which directly relates to:
>
> ■ the physical or mental welfare of elderly, sick, distressed or disabled persons; or
> ■ the care or protection of children and young persons.
>
> However, it excludes advice related to a specific individual. See 6.5.10 'Welfare advice and information' for more on this reduced-rating.

3. Advice or information related to the welfare of a specific individual may qualify for VAT exemption, see 5.3 'Health and welfare'

7.11 **CORPORATE EVENTS**

Companies may organise an event in order to raise funds for charity, or a charity may organise an event for a company, for example race days or events at major sporting events.

If the company organises an event and states that it intends to donate the money raised to a charity, and the charity is not responsible for the financial arrangements, then the charity merely receives a donation after the event, which is outside the scope of VAT.

If the charity organises the event it is likely to be a qualifying fundraising event and, as such, exempt. However, you do need to fulfil the criteria of fundraising events. So, for example, it should be clear that the event is for raising funds for your charity. Corporate events that are sold as a team-building exercise may fall outside the scope of the fundraising event definition and may be standard-rated supplies. See 5.8 'Fundraising events'.

7.12 **CORPORATE SPONSORSHIP**

Corporate sponsorship is a term that is used to cover a wide variety of arrangements. It is always necessary to consider what each party is providing to the other:

- If the sponsor is receiving only insignificant benefits in return for a sponsorship payment then the payment may in effect be a donation that is outside the scope of VAT. HMRC's stated position (*VAT Notice 701/41*, section 2.2) is that the following benefits can be treated as insignificant:
  - giving a flag or sticker;
  - naming the donor in a list of supporters in a programme or on a notice;
  - naming a building or university chair after the donor;
  - putting the donor's name on the back of a seat in a theatre.
- If the sponsor is a business receiving substantial benefits in return for its sponsorship payment then it is likely to be seen as a supply of goods or services for consideration and the normal VAT rules apply. HMRC regards the following as substantial benefits (*VAT Notice 701/41*, section 2.1):
  - naming an event after the sponsor;
  - displaying the sponsor's company logo or trading name;
  - participating in the sponsor's promotional or advertising activities;
  - allowing the sponsor to use your name or logo;
  - giving free or reduced price tickets;
  - allowing access to special events such as premieres or gala evenings;
  - providing entertainment or hospitality facilities;
  - giving the sponsor exclusive or priority booking rights.
- If you provide a package of benefits then it may be necessary to apply the single/multiple supply rules to determine the VAT status of the supply. See 11.3 'Single and multiple supplies'.
- If the sponsorship is of a qualifying fundraising event, then the supply is exempt as a supply in connection with the event. See 7.15 'Fundraising events'.
- HMRC accepts that sponsorship can be split between consideration for the benefits and a donation (*VAT Notice 701/41*, section 2.3):

  2.3 Mixed sponsorship and donation. Provided it is entirely separate from your sponsorship agreement, you are not required to account for VAT on any donation or gift you might also receive from a sponsor. However, it must be clear that any benefits your sponsor receives are not conditional on the making of the donation or gift.

- Sponsorship of the type where an individual undertakes an activity entirely at an independent business's cost and initiative and colleagues, friends and relatives support the effort by making donations to a nominated charity will be outside the scope of VAT donations for the charity, assuming that the charity is not doing anything in return for the monies given.

7.13 **DONATIONS**

Charities use a variety of methods to raise donations including street collections, regular envelope collections in churches, telephone fundraising, direct mail, house-to-house collections and many more. The basic VAT principle here is that money freely given to a charity with no expectation of goods or services in return is outside the scope of VAT, as it is not a consideration for any supply. If the charity is required to provide any service in return for the donation then it is not freely given and you need to consider whether VAT should apply.

HMRC accepts (*VCHAR9200*) that lapel stickers, emblems and badges may be given free as an acknowledgement to donors, providing they have no intrinsic value. Providing such tokens have no intrinsic value and are low-cost, HMRC does not regard the payment as the consideration for the supply of the token. HMRC would normally regard low-cost to be less than £1 per token. However, if a minimum or fixed price is required before a token is given, such a payment is regarded as the consideration for the supply of the token. The value of the supply would be either the fixed or a minimum price. Any amount above the minimum price can be treated as a donation.

See 4.3.17 'De-minimis benefits for Gift Aid' for the VAT implications of offering donors more substantial benefits but below the Gift Aid donor benefit limits.

Purchases directly relating to collecting donations may be residual (see 3.1.13 '*Children's Society* case'), but a charity may be able to reduce its VAT burden still further by purchasing goods at zero rates of VAT. Collecting tins, lapel badges and fundraising advertisements and literature will qualify for zero-rating. See 6.2.10 'Goods connected with collecting donations' for more information about the goods that qualify for zero-rate relief in this way.

7.14 **FINANCIAL INVESTMENTS**

Income from financial investments such as shares, bonds, interest income, etc. is likely to be outside the scope of VAT in the hands of a charity or other voluntary organisation carrying on the investment activity in order to raise funds for its primary purposes. See 4.3.20 'Investment income and gains'.

7.15 **FUNDRAISING EVENTS**

Charities, wholly owned charity subsidiaries and various other qualifying bodies can treat all supplies made 'in connection with' a qualifying fundraising event as VAT exempt. Exemption covers admissions; sales at the event such as catering and memorabilia; sponsorship of the event; the letting out of land for stalls and stands; and the sale of advertising in an event brochure. However, if a supply would qualify for zero-rating (for example children's clothing or the sale of donated goods) it can be zero-rated in preference. See 5.8 'Fundraising events' for more on the VAT exemption for fundraising events.

Meaning of event

Events include an event on the internet, participatory events such as golf days, gala dinners, premiere nights, dinner dances and any other events organised for a fundraising purpose.

Challenge events

Self-organised events such as walks, marathons or cycle rides can also be included in the exemption as long as no or very limited overnight accommodation is provided.

7.16 GIFTS IN KIND FROM BUSINESSES

If a business donates goods on which it has recovered VAT, then the business is deemed to supply those goods in donating them (see 4.2.1 'Disposal of business goods for no consideration'), so it has to account for any **output VAT** due on the cost of the goods. However, if the business donates the goods to a charity for sale, hire or export, that **deemed supply** by the business is zero-rated (for definitions, see the Glossary).

If the charity sells or hires the donated goods, then this will be a zero-rated supply by the charity, provided the conditions are met (see 7.23 'Sale of donated goods'). The export of the donated goods will also be a deemed zero-rated supply by the charity, see 6.3 'Zero-rated supplies by charities' for more.

If the goods are used for the charity's own activities, then there are no VAT consequences for the charity, but the company donating the goods may have to account for the VAT under the self-supply rules. If the business provides goods or services in return for advertising or promotion of its name, or for any other goods or services, then this amounts to a barter arrangement and is subject to VAT under the normal rules (see 7.5 'Barter arrangements').

7.17 LONDON MARATHON AND SIMILAR

Commercially organised events such as the London Marathon do not qualify for the fundraising exemption as they are organised by non-qualifying for-profit entities, even though so much fundraising takes place for qualifying not-for-profit entities through such marathons.

So supplies of places (bonds, etc.) to and by charities do not qualify for VAT exemption and are VAT standard-rated. If a charity charges a registration fee or entry fee to a participant, then this is subject to VAT. If the charity goes further and insists that the participant raises a minimum amount of sponsorship, then this too will be subject to VAT. However, HMRC accepts (*VAT Notice 701/1*, section 5.9.3) that these amounts can be outside the scope of VAT and treated as donations if the charity only asks the participant to 'pledge' an amount of sponsorship.

Charities usually buy 'gold-bond' places in the London Marathon – and these are subject to VAT. Charging VAT on the registration fee enables the charity to recover this VAT in full. Similar arrangements may apply for other marathons or events organised on a similar basis, i.e. by a commercial body.

In addition, the charity should not provide substantial benefits. In relation to events such as marathons, HMRC accepts that charities may provide the following which will not count as substantial benefits (*VAT Notice 701/1*, section 5.9.3):

- provision of free training and health advice;
- a free t-shirt, running vest or similar that clearly portrays the charity the individual is taking part on behalf of;
- free massages and support for physical well-being during the event;
- free pre-event meeting, which may include free professional advice or support, a simple meal, energy drinks and encouragement from the charity and other participants; and
- free post-event meeting, which may include medical treatment or advice, changing facilities, light refreshments and gives the charity the opportunity to thank participants.

Provision of free travel or accommodation and other benefits or 'gifts', such as bikes or watches, are benefits. If a charity provides such benefits the amount raised by the participant will be taxable at the standard rate. Some charities offer prizes to top fundraisers. These are not benefits for VAT purposes and do not affect the VAT treatment of income from participants.

7.18   LOTTERIES AND RAFFLES

The sale of lottery or raffle tickets is exempt from VAT. For the organiser, the value of the exempt supply is the net proceeds after deducting the VAT-inclusive cost of cash prizes and goods given as prizes. If you receive donated raffle prizes, then you cannot make the sale of the raffle tickets zero-rated as a sale of donated goods.

Many charities organise fundraising that amounts to a lottery or raffle, because there is a prize distributed on the basis of chance. For example, 'guess the name of the teddy bear' is considered a lottery as there is normally more chance than skill in guessing the correct name and winning the prize.

Lotteries are covered by gambling legislation and may have to be registered or licensed.

7.19 MERCHANDISING

Generally, bought-in goods sold by a charity to raise funds will be standard-rated, unless covered by a zero-rating or at a qualifying fundraising event. So mugs, T-shirts, pens and other items will be standard-rated, even if they have the charity's name and logo on them. Goods sold at a fundraising event will be covered by the exemption for the event, unless the goods are zero-rated in preference, such as books or children's T-shirts. The sale of donated goods can be zero-rated – see 7.23 'Sale of donated goods'.

7.20 RECYCLED GOODS

A number of schemes exist whereby charities can collect used printer cartridges, used mobile telephones or other equipment and then sell these to companies which will recycle the goods. Even though the charity is collecting donated goods, these arrangements are not qualifying zero-rated sales of donated goods if there is a contract to sell to one purchaser. These supplies are taxable at the standard rate.

Similar arrangements may exist for the collection of old clothes, shoes, books and so on. If the charity is collecting the goods to be sold on to a specific third party, then the sale is a taxable supply at the standard rate.

7.21 RENTING PROPERTY

Property here refers to immoveable real property such as land and buildings. By default rental income is VAT exempt; however:

- if you opt to tax the property, the rental income is VAT standard-rated unless the hirer **disapplies** your option to tax, in which case the rental income remains VAT exempt (see 8.5 'Option to tax' and 8.5.1 'Disapplications');
- rental income for certain types of property is VAT standard-rated, for example hotel accommodation, parking facilities, sports facilities and facilities for the storage of goods, though there are exemptions and special situations (see 8.2 'Exceptions to the basic property rule' and 8.4 'Leases and lettings');

- if you rent stalls at a qualifying fundraising event, the rental income is VAT exempt even if you have opted to tax the property (see 7.15 'Fundraising events' and 5.8 'Fundraising events');
- if you lease or let property for a peppercorn rent then the rental activity is outside the scope of VAT.

7.22 RETAIL GIFT AID SCHEME

Only monetary donations qualify for Gift Aid, so a charity cannot claim Gift Aid on a donation of goods. However, the Retail Gift Aid Scheme (RGAS) is an HMRC-approved way of Gift Aiding monetary proceeds from the sale of personal goods donated by UK Income Tax/Capital Gains Tax-paying individuals. With effect from 6 April 2013 RGAS works as follows:

1. The charity or its trading subsidiary enters into a written agreement under which they act as agent of the donor in selling the donor's personal goods. The donor also signs a Gift Aid declaration in favour of the charity.
2. The donor gives personal goods to the charity or its trading subsidiary. The goods remain the property of the donor until sold, so the charity/subsidiary must have some way of identifying the goods as belonging to the donor, for example via labels attached to the goods. It must be clear to potential customers that the charity/subsidiary is selling the goods on behalf of the donor and not the charity.
3. After the donor's goods are sold, the charity notifies the donor and gives the donor 21 days in which to claim the proceeds (less any selling commission charged). If the donor does not claim the proceeds within the 21-day period, the proceeds less any commission can be considered Gift Aided to the charity.
4. Under the 'standard method' the donor must be notified before Gift Aid can be claimed on any sale. Under 'Method A' or 'Method B' the charity/trading subsidiary does not have to notify the donor until total sales proceeds for that donor in any tax year (6 April – 5 April next) go over a pre-set limit. The pre-set limit is at most £100 for method A (charity-operated shops) and at most £1,000 for method B (trading subsidiary-operated shops). All donor notifications under the standard method or methods A or B must use HMRC template wording.
5. Under methods A or B the donor must be able to opt to receive an annual statement showing net sales proceeds in any tax year. The donor will need this if they wish to claim higher rate or additional rate Income Tax relief on their Gift Aided donations.

7.22.1 **VAT treatment of sales**

The sale of goods under RGAS is no longer the sale by a charity or its subsidiary of goods donated to it for sale, as they are not donated to it, so the sale no longer qualifies for zero-rating as such. Instead the sale is a sale by the charity/subsidiary as a disclosed agent for the donor. As explained in 11.2 'Agency supplies', the sale is treated as a supply by the donor to the end customer and, if a commission is charged to the donor, a separate supply of agency services by the charity/subsidiary to the donor.

Provided the goods are personal goods belonging to an individual and provided that the individual's sales do not amount to a business activity for the individual, the sale of the goods is outside the scope of VAT (see 4.1.7 'Sale of non-business assets'). So no output VAT is chargeable on the sale on behalf of the donor.

7.22.2 **Charging a commission**

The sale of goods as agent is seen by HMRC as a non-business activity for the charity/subsidiary unless the charity/subsidiary makes a charge for its agency sales activity. Treating the sales as a non-business activity would restrict VAT recovery on shop running costs as such costs would be partly used for a non-business activity. So it will normally be advantageous to charge a commission in order to retain VAT recovery on shop costs.

This commission can potentially be structured as:

- a seller's commission charged to the donor for the service of selling their goods;
- if the agency sales are made by a subsidiary, a commission charged to the charity for the service of generating Gift Aid donations for it. However, option (2) alone will not render the agency sales a business activity if the charity and subsidiary are VAT-grouped.

The usual approach is to charge the donor a selling commission. Assuming that the charity/subsidiary is registered for VAT, this commission is standard-rated and the charity/subsidiary must pay the output VAT due on the commission to HMRC when the sale is made. The gross commission (including VAT) is deducted from the sale proceeds and the balance is eligible for Gift Aid.

> ## Example: sales commission charged to donor
>
> Charity ABC operates the RGAS and sells an item under the scheme for £10. The charity charges scheme members a gross (VAT-inclusive) selling commission of 5%. Assume the standard rate of VAT and basic rate of Income Tax are both 20%.
>
> The gross commission is 5% × £10 = 50p
>
> The VAT due on the gross commission is 1/6 × 50p = 8p (see 12.1 'VAT fractions and VAT rounding')
>
> The charity's net commission is 50p − 8p = 42p
>
> The donor's proceeds eligible for Gift Aid are £10 − 50p = £9.50
>
> The Gift Aid claimable on the proceeds is 25% × £9.50 = £2.38 (with Income Tax at 20%, Gift Aid is 25% of the donation amount)

7.22.3 Rate of commission

There is obviously an incentive to keep any commission charged to the donor as low as possible in order to maximise the Gift Aid reclaimable, though if a substantial number of donors do retain sales proceeds, it will be important to ensure that losses are avoided; so the commission rate will have to be set reasonably.

Any charges for the supply of agency services must be sufficient to render the agency selling activity a business activity. HMRC states

> Commissions charged by charities or their trading subsidiaries must be set at a reasonable rate to cover the costs of operating the scheme. Charities may be asked by HMRC to explain how they've set their commission rates. Because the agency arrangement for selling goods on behalf of an individual is a business activity, commissions charged are a consideration for a taxable supply and VAT must be accounted for at the standard rate. If the commissions charged do not reflect the real costs of acting as agent to sell goods on behalf of individuals, it will not constitute a business for VAT purposes. Under these circumstances any VAT incurred on costs associated with the agency arrangement will not be recoverable by the charity or subsidiary trading company.
>
> HMRC 2013, *Charities: detailed guidance notes*, chapter 3, s. 3.42.18

HMRC does not specify a minimum rate of commission. Charging a commission rate to cover the marginal or direct costs of operating RGAS is one obvious option, though an activity does not have to be profit-making in order to be a business, so the rate could potentially be set lower. As HMRC expects charities/subsidiaries to provide a rationale for the commission rate set, it would make sense to monitor the costs of running RGAS and to set the commission rate based on these costs.

If RGAS is operated by a non-VAT-grouped subsidiary, charging the charity a commission for generating Gift Aid donations is also a possibility. This could help keep the donor commission low, enabling more of the sales proceeds to be Gift Aided whilst maintaining overall coverage of the costs of running RGAS.

7.22.4 Donations from businesses

Donations of goods from businesses should generally be excluded from RGAS:

- **Company donations**: monetary donations from companies and other incorporated bodies (Industrial and Provident Societies, Friendly Societies, Royal Charter companies, etc.) are not eligible for a Gift Aid refund claim, so there is no point (from the charity's perspective) in putting donations of goods from incorporated entities through RGAS.
- **Sole trader and partnership donations**: donations from sole traders and UK partnerships (including limited liability partnerships) can potentially be Gift Aided. However, if the goods are sold as a disclosed agent of a sole trader or partnership which recovered VAT on the goods, their sale is a taxable supply by the sole trader/partnership and output VAT will have to be deducted from the proceeds (unless the goods are zero-rated, for example as printed books), thereby negating much of the advantage to be gained from claiming Gift Aid on the proceeds (HMRC 2015, *Charities: detailed guidance notes*, chapter 3, s. 3.10.3).

If you can establish that the sole trader/partnership incurred VAT on the goods, but that VAT was wholly irrecoverable, then an agency sale is VAT exempt for the sole trader/partnership (see 5.11 'Sale of business goods on which VAT was wholly irrecoverable') and the advantage from putting through RGAS is the same for individual donations. However, establishing this with evidence sufficient to satisfy HMRC may be difficult, so in general the most straightforward option is likely to be to completely exclude business donations from RGAS.

7.23 SALE OF DONATED GOODS

The sale by a charity of goods donated to it for sale is zero-rated. The goods can be of any type (except land or buildings). Zero-rating extends to sales by a **profits-to-charity person** – that is, a person who has agreed to pay any profits from the sale to a charity. This can include a charity's trading subsidiary.

The goods may be new or second-hand, but must be donated for the purpose of a sale or hire and should be available for purchase by the general public. So sales through charity shops are zero-rated, but also sales at fundraising events open to the public, such as auctions. Charities or their subsidiaries may also sell donated goods to the disabled and those on means-tested benefits. This will help the schemes whereby recycled furniture is sold at low prices to those in need, as no VAT has to be charged.

See 6.3.2 'Sale of donated goods' for more on this zero-rating. See also 7.22 'Retail Gift Aid Scheme'.

7.24 SHOPS

Donated goods sold in a shop are zero-rated, but bought-in goods are standard-rated, unless they are covered by another zero-rating, such as books or children's clothing. See 7.23 'Sale of donated goods' for more on the zero-ratings for donated goods.

7.25 SUPPORTER SCHEMES

Many charities run supporter schemes (Friends, Patrons, Gold Members, etc.) as a means of raising funds. These are frequently structured as a specified minimum 'donation' with a package of benefits structured to be either:

1. within the Gift Aid donor benefit limits so that the whole minimum donation can be Gift Aided;
2. eligible for the Gift Aid 'split payment treatment' so that part of the payment is payment for the benefits and part a Gift Aidable donation.

See 4.3.17 'De-minimis benefits for Gift Aid' and 4.3.18 'Gift Aid split payment treatment' for more on the VAT treatment of these two options. For VAT the broad position is that any minimum amount the donor must pay to obtain the benefits is consideration for a supply, and any optional donation above the minimum is an outside-the-scope-of-VAT donation.

Extra statutory concession 3.35

In practice, HMRC officers have sometimes accepted that the extra-statutory concession 3.35 (*VAT Notice 48*, section 3.35) applies to treat payments under supporter or patron schemes as, in effect, multiple supplies for VAT. This means that, rather than assuming a single VAT status, the minimum donation can be split between a zero-rated component for benefits that comprise printed matter or other zero-rated supplies, an exempt component for exempt benefits and a standard-rated component for the rest. However, at the time of writing it appears that HMRC is denying use of this concession to supporter schemes that do not provide voting rights or a say in the management of the organisation. In such a situation, the single/multiple supply rules (see 11.3 'Single and multiple supplies') must be applied to determine the VAT status of the minimum donation (or HMRC's denial of the use of extra-statutory concession 3.35 is successfully challenged).

8 Property

This chapter is divided into the following sections:

- 8.1 Property supply rules
- 8.2 Exceptions to the basic property rule
- 8.3 Property VAT reliefs
- 8.4 Leases and lettings
- 8.5 Option to tax
- 8.6 Property terms

8.1 PROPERTY SUPPLY RULES

In this chapter **property** refers to all types of immoveable real property. These are usually subdivided into land, buildings and civil engineering works. A **supply of property** is a supply of the freehold of, a lease of or a licence to occupy property. See 8.6 'Property terms' for the definitions of freehold, lease, licence to occupy, buildings and civil engineering works.

There are five general VAT rules for supplies of property:

1. **Basic property supply rule**: the default position is that a supply of property is VAT exempt.
2. **Special types of property**: the main exceptions to this default position are covered in 8.2 'Exceptions to the basic property rule' and are for supplies of special types of property such as: new or incomplete commercial buildings, hotel accommodation, sports facilities, car parking facilities and goods warehouses. Supplies of these special types of property are normally standard-rated, though they can be exempt in some situations.
3. **Option to tax**: if a supplier has **opted to tax** a property, then that supplier's supplies of that property become VAT standard-rated, that is, unless the supplier's option to tax is **disapplied** for a particular supply of the property, in which case that supply is unaffected by the supplier's option to tax. Some supplies are disapplied automatically (such as supplies of **dwellings**) and some only if the supplier is given a 'disapplication certificate' (for instance, supplies of **relevant charitable purpose** buildings). See 8.5 'Option to tax'.

4. **Property reliefs**: some supplies of qualifying property and some supplies of building works that create or renovate qualifying property are zero-rated or reduced-rated. Qualifying property includes **relevant charitable purpose** buildings, **relevant residential purpose** buildings and buildings that are designed as one or more **dwellings**. See 8.3 'Property VAT reliefs'.
5. **Transfer of a business as a going concern**: if property is transferred in accordance with the transfer of a business as a going concern (TOGC) rules, then that property transfer is outside the scope of VAT. Selling a building with a sitting tenant can be a TOGC, even if the property is only partially tenanted. See 11.5 'Transfer of a business as a going concern'.

For the definition of bold terms see 8.6 Property terms.

8.2 EXCEPTIONS TO THE BASIC PROPERTY RULE

There are many exceptions to the above default property supply rule for special types of property. The exceptions covered below are for supplies of:

- new **non-qualifying buildings** and civil engineering works;
- sports facilities;
- facilities for the storage of goods;
- vehicle parking facilities;
- accommodation in hotels, hostels and similar.

Other exceptions include supplies of: camping and caravanning facilities; holiday accommodation; hairdressing facilities; residence restricted dwellings; and the right to occupy a box, seat or other accommodation at a sports ground, theatre, concert hall or other place of entertainment. However, for the latter see 5.4 'Cultural services'.

8.2.1 New non-qualifying buildings and civil engineering works

The supply of the freehold of an incomplete or new non-qualifying building or civil engineering work is VAT standard-rated. This exception only captures freehold sales; the sale of a lease or licence to occupy a new building or civil engineering work is exempt subject to any option to tax.

- **Non-qualifying building**: non-qualifying building is a building that is not a dwelling, not a relevant charitable purpose building and not a relevant residential purpose building. See 8.6 'Property terms' for the definitions of these terms.
- **Civil engineering work**: these are built structures that are fixed in or to the ground that are not buildings, for example roads, running tracks and artificial sports pitches. See 8.6 'Property terms'.

- **Complete and incomplete**: a building is completed at the earlier of when the architect issues a certificate of practical completion and when the building is first fully occupied. A civil engineering work is completed at the earlier of when the engineer issues a certificate of completion and when the work is first fully used.
- **New**: a building or civil engineering work is new for three years from the date of completion.

8.2.2 Sports facilities

The letting of sports facilities is standard-rated with two exceptions:

1. the let is for a continuous period of use exceeding 24 hours; or
2. all of the following six conditions are satisfied:
   (a) the hirer is a school, a club, an association or an organisation representing affiliated clubs or constituent associations;
   (b) the letting is for a series of ten or more periods;
   (c) each period is in respect of the same activity carried on at the same place;
   (d) the interval between each period is not less than one day and not more than 14 days;
   (e) consideration is payable by reference to the whole series and is evidenced by written agreement;
   (f) the hirer has exclusive use of the facilities.

If either condition (1) or condition (2) is satisfied, the letting is VAT exempt. However, if the supplier has opted to tax the sports facility and the option to tax is not disapplied, the letting is VAT standard-rated even if conditions (1) or (2) are satisfied.

Lettings

Letting excludes a non-exclusive right to use a sports facility in conjunction with others, for example the right to share use of a golf course, swimming pool or skating rink. However, such a right may be VAT exempt in its own right if the supplier is an **eligible body** for the purposes of the exemption for sports and physical education – see 5.4.2 'Eligible body'. If the whole of the sports facility, or a defined part of the facility, is let with exclusive use, then that can constitute the letting of a sports facility, for example the letting of a specific lane of a swimming pool or letting of a cordoned off area of an ice rink.

Sports facilities

HMRC provides the following guidance on the meaning of sports facility (*VAT Notice 742*, section 5.2):

> What is a sports facility? Premises are sports facilities if they are designed or adapted for playing any sport or taking part in any physical recreation, such as swimming pools, football pitches, dance studios and skating rinks. Each court or pitch (or lane in the case of bowling alley, curling rink or swimming pool) is a separate sports facility. General purpose halls, such as village or church halls, which merely have floor markings are not themselves classed as sports facilities and the letting of such halls is exempt even when let for playing a sport. Similarly, school halls or similar (but not gymnasiums) are treated as exempt providing it is the bare hall that is provided. However, if equipment such as racquets and nets are provided along with the hall the supply is of standard-rated sports facilities.

24-hour use condition

Where there is a single let of a sports facility for a continuous period of over 24 hours to the same person, and that person has exclusive control of the facility throughout the period, the supply will be exempt (subject to any option to tax) regardless of the status of the person receiving the supply (*VATLP19400*).

Schools, clubs, associations, etc.

HMRC provides the following guidance (*VATLP19400*):

> **What is a club or association?** Clubs and associations may be unincorporated or incorporated associations, unincorporated or incorporated members' clubs, employees' or trade union social clubs, proprietary clubs or service messes. In its simplest context individual teams can be treated as clubs, provided that they conduct their affairs in the same manner. This would mean entering into formal agreements with the owner of the sports facilities, collecting subscriptions from members and so forth. It is also possible to allow committees and teams being part of the main club to individually be treated as clubs in their own right, provided that they conduct their affairs as if they were a club.

> **What is a school?** A school is an institution that provides statutory education (primary or secondary) required by the Education Act 1996. For example, the hire of a dance studio to a comprehensive school would qualify for exemption (provided the other conditions are met). But a dance studio hired by a 'Dance School', which makes supplies of dance tuition to members of the public in return for payment, would not qualify for exemption since a 'Dance School' is not an educational institution providing primary or secondary education.

Same activity and place

For condition (2c) above, HMRC accepts that this condition is met where a different pitch, court or lane is used (or a different number of pitches, courts or lanes), as long as these are at the same establishment (*VAT Notice 742*, section 5.4).

Period interval

The meaning of the condition in (2d) above 'the interval between each period is not less than one day' is ambiguous. Does it mean:

1. the hires must be on separate days; or
2. the interval between the starts of each hire must be not less than 24 hours; or
3. the interval from the end of one hire period to the start of the next must be not less than 24 hours; or
4. something else?

HMRC's policy (*VATLP19300*) is that it means (2); however, in the case *Polo Farm Sports Club* [2007] VTD 20105, the VAT Tribunal disagreed on the basis that the natural meaning of 'interval between' excludes the hire periods before and after the interval between. The Tribunal preferred meanings (1) or (3) and between the two it preferred (1), though the distinction did not matter in the case. However, HMRC has not changed its interpretation following this decision and HMRC's position is helpful as school/club hires tend to be at the same time of the day.

8.2.3 **Facilities for storing goods**

With effect from 1 October 2012 the lease or letting of **facilities for the self-storage of goods** is VAT standard-rated, though with some exceptions, including charity non-business use. The freehold sale of a storage facility is not affected and follows the basic property rules set out at 8.1 'Property supply rules'.

> **Facilities for the self-storage of goods** means the use of a **relevant structure** for the storage of goods by the person to whom the supply of facilities is made.
>
> **Relevant structure** means the whole or part of:
>
> (i)   a container or other structure that is fully enclosed; or
> (ii) a unit or building.

Relevant structures include fixed containers but not containers in use to provide freight transport services. If the customer does not itself use the relevant structure for the storage of goods but permits (without creating a supply) another person to do so (for example by providing free use or a peppercorn lease or let), then the customer is deemed to be using the relevant structure for the storage of goods.

Determining use

It is the supplier's responsibility to establish how their property is being used. HMRC provides the following guidance (*VAT Information Sheet 10/13*):

> In most cases, the use of the space will be clear from the nature of the facilities and the agreements you have entered into with your customer. However, in some instances, facilities may be suitable for a variety of uses. In such cases, suppliers are advised to obtain confirmation from the customer of how the customer is using the space, in writing where possible, and to retain it with their VAT records.

> In addition to periodic reviews, businesses letting out property and space may wish to insert clauses in leases specifying that the customer must tell them if they either start or stop using the facilities for storage, or permit a third party to do so and include provisions as to the VAT consequences.

Excluded supplies

The following supplies of storage facilities are excluded from standard-rating under this rule and follow the basic rules above:

1. **Live animals**: the leasing or letting of facilities for the storage of live animals.
2. **Charities**: where the hirer is a charity which uses the facilities solely for non-business activities. HMRC accepts that the term 'solely' can incorporate a *de minimis* element of business use (see 8.6.6 'Meaning of solely').
3. **Ancillary storage**: where the relevant structure is part of a building, if its use for the storage of goods by the customer is ancillary to other use of the building by the customer. HMRC provides the following examples (*VAT Information Sheet 10/13*):

> A retailer rents a high street shop which includes a stockroom. In some cases, the storage area may be greater than the retail space. However, the commercial reality is that the premises are being used as a shop. The rent payable is accordingly exempt unless the landlord has an effective option to tax.

> A delivery service uses a warehouse to sort and process mail. Whilst it could be said that the mail is temporarily stored in the premises, the reality is that the facility is used as a postal depot. The rent payable is exempt unless the landlord has an effective option to tax.

4. **Capital Goods Scheme (CGS) and connected persons**: if all of the following conditions are met, then a lease or let by business A to business B is not caught by these rules:

    - Business A supplies a lease or licence to occupy a relevant structure to business B which uses the relevant structure to store goods.
    - Business A and business B are connected.
    - The relevant structure is a CGS **capital item** within its **adjustment period** for business A.

See 10.1 'Capital Goods Scheme' for details of the CGS.

8.2.4 Parking facilities

The lease or letting of facilities for parking a vehicle is standard-rated. The freehold sale of such facilities follows the basic VAT rules set out above.

Vehicle parking facilities are property that is either designed or adapted for parking vehicles, or provided specifically for parking vehicles. Parking facilities include garages, car parks and spaces in them, parking bays, taxi ranks, bicycle storage facilities, and land that is let specifically for the construction of a garage or for parking vehicles.

If a parking facility is specifically designed or adapted for parking vehicles (for example a garage or car park) then its leasing or letting is standard-rated even if it is used for some other purpose such as storing goods, unless the lease or licence of the facility specifically excludes the parking of vehicles.

If land is specifically provided for the parking of vehicles, for example under a term in the planning consent, conveyance or contract, then the supply of land is standard-rated unless any supply of parking facilities is either incidental to the main use of the land or closely linked to it. Incidental uses include use for a market or car boot sale, the exhibition of vehicles, or a travelling circus or fair.

Ancillary parking facilities

Where a supply of parking facilities is closely linked to another supply of property, its VAT treatment follows the VAT status of that supply. The letting of a garage or parking space provided with a dwelling is exempt, and the letting of parking spaces provided with commercial premises follows the VAT status of the commercial premises. To be regarded as being closely linked to the supply of property the parking facility must be near to the property and supplied for use with that property.

Right to buy

The rules on parking facilities can be a problem for right-to-buy properties. If a tenant exercises their right to buy and purchases the freehold of their property but continues to rent a garage, the supply of the garage is standard-rated because it is no longer closely linked to the supply of the property.

8.2.5 **Hotels and hostels**

The provision in a hotel, inn, boarding house or similar establishment of:

(a) sleeping accommodation and accommodation in rooms which are provided in conjunction with sleeping accommodation; or

(b) accommodation in rooms for the purpose of a supply of catering

is standard-rated, subject to the **reduced-value rule**. The freehold sale or the long-term lease of an entire hotel, inn, boarding house or **similar establishment** follows the basic property rules set out above.

> **Similar establishment** means premises in which there is provided furnished sleeping accommodation, whether with or without the provision of board or facilities for the preparation of food, which are used by or held out as being suitable for use by visitors or travellers. Similar establishments can include B&Bs, private clubs, hostels and halls of residence (under certain circumstances, for example if let out during holiday periods for use by visitors or travellers) and serviced houses or flats for use by travellers and visitors.
>
> **Reduced-value rule**. Where an individual stays in hotel accommodation or similar for more than 28 days consecutively, then, from the 29th day on, VAT should be charged on the non-accommodation element of the charge only, that is, the element that relates to meals, service charges and other facilities that are provided. The facilities charge must be at least 20% of the (net) value of the charge for accommodation and facilities. The accommodation element does not become VAT exempt and so there is no restriction of input VAT recovery. In effect the accommodation element becomes zero-rated.

If an inclusive charge is made it must be apportioned between the supply of accommodation and the supply of other facilities and services. To do this, you must calculate the amount of the charge that is for meals, drinks and other goods and services, and also treat at least 20% of the remainder as being for facilities. However, if the true value of the facilities is more than this, you must charge VAT on the true amount.

Example: reduced-value rule

The normal charge for one night's stay in a hotel is £100 + VAT, of which the meal element is £40 + VAT. The reduced-value charge is calculated as follows:

The charge for accommodation and facilities is £100 - £40 = £60 net. At least 20% of this must be treated as being for the supply of facilities, i.e. 20% × £60 = £12 net. The charge for accommodation is £60 - £12 = £48 net. The reduced-value charge is:

	Net	VAT
Accommodation	£48	Nil
Facilities	£12	£12 × 20% = £2.40
Meals	£40	£40 × 20% = £8.00
Totals	£100	£10.40

The reduced-value charge is therefore £110.40 and is applied from the 29th day onwards.

HMRC extra-statutory concession

Normally the departure and later return of a guest will break a period of stay. Breaks are treated as terminating a period of stay unless the guest can return at any time and continue their occupancy of the room, or a similar room, as if they had never vacated it (HMRC 2014, *Withdrawal of extra statutory concessions: Technical note and call for evidence*, 31 January).

Long-stay contracts

Under the reduced-value rule, the supply does not have to be paid for by the guest. In the VAT Tribunal case *Afro Caribbean Housing Association* [2006] VTD 19450, the housing association provided hostel accommodation for asylum seekers under contract to the British Refugee Council. HMRC argued that, for the reduced-value rule to apply, the accommodation must be occupied by the recipient of the services. The VAT Tribunal found that there was no such requirement and so the reduced-value rule applied to the supply to the British Refugee Council.

Hostels for the homeless

Some voluntary organisations run hostels or other establishments that share some of the characteristics of a hotel, for example hostels for the homeless or for asylum seekers. They may supply the accommodation under contract to a third party, for example a government department or agency. HMRC provides guidance on the subject in the Land and Property manual at *VATLP11400* The following scenarios can be distinguished:

1. If the accommodation is provided free of charge and funded by grants, donations, reserves, etc. it is likely to be a non-business activity. If a fee is charged for the accommodation but the fee is heavily subsidised by grants, donations, etc., the activity may also be non-business. See 4.1 'Basic rules'.
2. If the accommodation is provided as an incidental, ancillary or closely related part of another activity such as education or care, its VAT status will generally follow that of the other activity. Hostels providing long-term accommodation with a substantial element of personal care may amount to a single VAT-exempt supply of welfare. See below, 'Hostel cases'.
3. If accommodation is block-booked in a commercial hotel, B&B or similar, which also provides accommodation on the open market, then HMRC sees that as always being a supply of hotel accommodation and as such standard-rated subject to the reduced-value rule.
4. Accommodation provided in multi-occupancy dwellings together with a package of goods and services such as the cleaning of rooms, provision of bed linen, food parcels and a live-in manager or 24-hour staff presence is seen by HMRC as being hotel-type accommodation which is standard-rated subject to the reduced-value rule.
5. Accommodation in multi-occupancy dwellings with minimal additional goods and services and no permanent on-site staff presence is seen by HMRC as a VAT-exempt supply of furnished living accommodation. This can include the provision of food vouchers and services not normally provided by hotels such as transportation to the hostel, advice on medical and other emergency services and translation services.

Hostel cases

In *Dinaro Ltd* [1999] VTD 17148, a hostel for the homeless only accepted people with mental health problems for whom they provided a high degree of care and supervision. The VAT Tribunal found that the hostel was not similar to a hotel or inn, and there were three main elements in establishing the dissimilarity: the selectivity exercised over the choice of residents, the high degree of care and supervision for all the inhabitants and the emphasis on a family concept for all those who were residents.

In *North East Direct Access* v. *Customs & Excise* [2003] VTD 18267, the organisation provided accommodation, meals and supervised personal care for homeless men, many of whom had a high level of need and had lived at the hostel for many years. The VAT Tribunal nevertheless found that the main supply was of accommodation and food and the supply of care was ancillary. The case was distinguished from *Dinaro* by the fact that there was a lesser degree of selectivity exercised over the choice of residents, the care requirements of residents varied widely and there was no emphasis on a family concept or any other particular philosophy.

8.3 PROPERTY VAT RELIEFS

These reliefs are available to VAT-registered customers and customers that are not VAT-registered. They work by reducing the amount of VAT you must pay for your property-related purchase. The reliefs considered below are:

1. qualifying new buildings – zero-rating;
2. residential conversions – zero-rating;
3. substantially reconstructed protected buildings – zero-rating;
4. DIY builders and convertors VAT refund scheme – zero-rating;
5. qualifying residential conversion works – reduced-rating;
6. residential renovations and alterations – reduced-rating.

The reliefs broadly aim to zero rate or reduce rate the creation or renovation of residential property and, to a lesser extent, charity non-business-use property, including in the latter village halls and similar community-use buildings. They work via a variety of routes. For example, the zero-rating relief for qualifying new buildings (relief 1) zero rates the supply of construction services to a charity that creates its own qualifying new building and also zero rates the first freehold or long-lease sale of a qualifying new building by a property developer.

8.3.1 Terminology

These reliefs require the use of specific VAT terms which are explained in more detail in 8.6 'Property terms'. These include the following key terms.

Qualifying building: this means a relevant charitable purpose building, a relevant residential purpose building, or one or more dwellings

Relevant charitable purpose building: this means a building (or a part of a building) that is, at the time of the supply for which relief is claimed, intended solely for use by a charity for:

- non-business activities; or
- as a **village hall or similarly** (see 8.6.7) in providing social or recreational facilities for a local community.

Relevant residential purpose building: this means a building (or a part of a building) that is, at the time of the supply for which relief is claimed, intended for use solely as:

- a children's home, a residential care home, a hospice, a monastery or nunnery, or any other institution which is the sole or main residence of at least 90% of its residents; or
- residential accommodation for students, school pupils, or members of any armed forces;
- but excluding use as a hospital, prison, hotel or similar.

Dwelling: this is self-contained living accommodation that has no internal access to any other dwelling (apart from doors for emergency use only). Its separate use or disposal must not be prohibited by a covenant or planning consent or similar. If required, statutory planning consent must have been granted for any works and they must have been carried out in accordance with that consent.

Use: use here refers to the use of the building made by its occupier, for example if a business lets a building to a charity that occupies and uses the building solely for its non-business activities, then that building is a relevant charitable purpose building despite the fact that it is owned and commercially let by a business.

Solely: the entirety of occupational use of the building or part must be for relevant residential or charitable purposes. For example, if a charity intends to use a part of a building for mixed business and non-business activities, then the use of that part does not qualify as relevant charitable purpose (unless it qualifies as village hall or similarly). However, HMRC does accept that a *de minimis* level of up to 5% business use can be ignored.

Construction services: these are any services related to the construction other than the services of an architect, surveyor or any person acting as a consultant or in a supervisory capacity. They include work on the building itself prior to completion, and any other works that are closely connected to the construction of the building such as demolition, site clearance and landscaping included in the planning consent.

Major interest and long lease: a major interest in property is the freehold interest or a long lease in that property. In England, Wales and Northern Ireland a long lease is a tenancy for a **term certain** (see 8.6.2) exceeding 21 years. In Scotland it is the lessee's interest under a lease for a period of not less than 20 years.

Building materials are goods of a description ordinarily incorporated by builders in a building of that description or its site, but subject to various exclusions such as for carpets and carpeting materials.

8.3.2 **Qualifying new buildings**

The following supplies are zero-rated:

1.1 The first grant by a person constructing a qualifying new building of the freehold of or a long lease in, or in any part of, the building or its site.

1.2 The supply in the course of the construction of a qualifying new building of any services related to the construction other than the services of an architect, surveyor or any person acting as a consultant or in a supervisory capacity.

1.3 The supply of building materials to a person to whom the supplier is supplying services within (1.2) above which include the incorporation of the materials into the building or its site.

Part qualifying buildings

If only a part of a new building is qualifying, a corresponding part can be zero-rated. A fair and reasonable apportionment of the contract price should be made. See 8.3.9 'Apportionment for part qualifying buildings'.

New building

New building means any of the following:

(a) Complete new building

A complete new building is created. Any existing building or buildings on the site of the new building must be demolished completely to ground level. The retention of cellars, basements and the slab at ground floor level is permitted. The retention of a façade (or if on a corner, a double façade) is permitted if this is a condition or requirement of statutory planning consent or similar permission. For terraced properties, the retention of a party wall is permitted if it forms part of a neighbouring property that is not being developed. The constructed building must not be:

- the conversion, reconstruction, or alteration of an existing building;
- any enlargement of or extension to an existing building (unless (b) below applies);
- an **annexe** to an existing building (unless (c) below applies).

If any pre-existing structures on site are not buildings (for example a single wall), then they may not have to be demolished and in some cases the courts have allowed parts of existing buildings to be maintained without blocking the constructed building being 'new'. For example, in *Revenue & Customs* v. *Astral Construction Ltd* [2015] UKUT 21 (TCC), the Upper Tribunal accepted that a care home constructed around and incorporating a redundant church was a new building and not an enlargement of or extension to an existing building.

(b) Added dwelling(s)

The new building is a dwelling or dwellings and is wholly the result of the enlargement or extension to an existing building. The new dwelling or dwellings must be wholly within the enlargement or extension and zero-rating only applies to the extent that any works create such a new dwelling or dwellings.

(c) Relevant charitable purpose annexe

The new building is a **qualifying annexe** to an existing building or buildings and is intended for use solely for a relevant charitable purpose. An annexe is broadly a building that is ancillary to another building (or buildings) but has minimal physical integration with that building (or buildings) and is visually distinct. See 8.6 'Property terms' for the meaning of annexe. A **qualifying annexe** is an annexe that meets both of the following conditions:

(i) It is capable of functioning independently from the existing building or buildings. It should have all the facilities necessary to function as designed without reliance on the existing building or buildings and be capable of being separately locked and secured when not in use. This includes (where necessary to function as designed) adequate toilet, kitchen, heating and other facilities and services.

(ii) The only or the main access to the annexe is not via the existing building or buildings and the only or the main access to the existing building or buildings is not via the annexe. In other words, the existing building and the annexe must each have their own separate entrances and not via each other.

First sales

This must be the first sale by the person constructing the new building of the freehold or a long lease; subsequent freehold and long-lease sales are not covered by the zero-rating. However, intervening use of property for granting short leases and licences to occupy does not block a later freehold or long lease from being zero-rated, but might create VAT recovery problems for the initial construction costs. See 8.3.11 'House builders'. In *Business Brief 23/06* HMRC accepts that a zero-rated first grant occurs even where the value of the first grant does not represent full equity in the property, such as in shared ownership schemes run by housing associations.

Long leases

If the supply is a long lease, then if a lease premium is payable, only that premium is zero-rated. If there is no premium payable but periodic rental payments are due, then only the first rental payment qualifies for zero-rating.

Person constructing

HMRC provides the following guidance on the identity of the 'person constructing' (*VAT Notice 708*, section 4.5):

> You are a 'person constructing' a building if, in relation to that building, you are acting as, or you have, at any point in the past, acted as:
>
> - a developer – you physically constructed, or commissioned another person to physically construct, the building (in whole or in part) on land that you own or have an interest in, or
> - a contractor or subcontractor – you provided construction services to the developer or another contractor for the construction of the building, sub-contracting work as necessary

HMRC accepts (*VAT Notice 708*, section 4.5.2) that where a developer takes over and finishes a partly completed building, both the first and second developers have 'person constructing' status because they have both been involved in physically constructing the building. If the developer is a member of a VAT group, the group is looked through to see the person who actually developed the building.

Subcontractors and certificates

For the relevant charitable and residential purpose zero-ratings, only construction services supplied to the person who supplies the zero-rating certificate qualify for zero-rating. Supplies by a subcontractor to a main contractor do not qualify. However, if a main contractor engages subcontractors to carry out work on the project, the main contractor can recover the VAT charged by the subcontractors on the basis that those supplies are cost components of its zero-rated supply. For works on a new dwelling there is no requirement to hold a certificate, so subcontractors can also zero rate invoices to a main contractor if the qualifying conditions are met. See 8.3.8 'Certificates'.

Professional services

The services of an architect, surveyor or any person acting as a consultant or in a supervisory capacity, including the services of quantity surveyors, engineers and project managers, are specifically excluded from zero-rating. However, HMRC accepts that they can be zero-rated via a 'design and build contract'; see 8.3.10 'Design and build contracts'.

Residence restrictions

A dwelling does not qualify for zero-rating under (1.1) above if the person purchasing the interest is not entitled to reside there throughout the year, or is prevented from residing in the accommodation throughout the year by the terms of a covenant, statutory planning consent or similar. This often happens with holiday homes.

Change of use

If a new building (or part) is zero-rated on the basis of intended relevant charitable purpose or relevant residential purpose use, but that use changes within the first ten years, then some of the VAT initially saved through zero-rating may have to be paid back to HMRC. See 8.3.13 'Change of use rules'.

Builders' block

If a freehold or long lease sale by a property developer is zero-rated under (1.1) above, then the property developer is blocked from recovering VAT on any goods that are incorporated into the building or its site but are not building materials. See 8.6.14 'Builders' block'.

8.3.3 Residential conversions

The following supplies are zero-rated:

2.1 The first grant by a person converting a non-residential building or a non-residential part of a building into a building designed as a dwelling or number of dwellings or a building intended for use solely for a relevant residential purpose, of a major interest in, or in any part of, the building, dwelling or its site

2.2 The supply to a **relevant housing association** in the course of conversion of a non-residential building or a non-residential part of a building into a building or part of a building designed as a dwelling or a number of dwellings or intended for use solely for a relevant residential purpose of any services related to the conversion other than the services of an architect, surveyor, or any person acting as a consultant or in a supervisory capacity

> **Relevant housing association** means a private registered provider of social housing, or a Registered Social Landlord.

2.3 The supply of building materials to a housing association by a supplier of residential conversion services within (2.2) above which include the incorporation of the materials into the building or its site

Non-residential building or part of a building

A building or a part of a building is non-residential if:

(a) it is neither designed nor adapted for use as a dwelling or number of dwellings or for a relevant residential purpose; or

(b) it is designed or adapted for such use but was constructed more than ten years before the sale (2.1) or before commencement of conversion works (2.2) and no part of it has, in that ten years, been used as a dwelling or for a relevant residential purpose;

(c) for (2.2), no part of the building is being used as a dwelling or for a relevant residential purpose during the conversion works.

The additional dwelling requirement

If the conversion is of a non-residential part of a building and that part already contains a residential part, and the conversion is into a dwelling or dwellings, then to qualify for zero-rating, the result of the conversion must be to create an additional dwelling or dwellings. In *Customs & Excise* v. *Jacobs* [2005] EWCA Civ 930, the Court of Appeal held this requirement to mean that what is being converted must end up with more dwellings that it had before conversion. However, HMRC's position (*Business Brief 22/05* on the basis of an earlier VAT Tribunal case *Calam Vale* [2001] VTD 16869) is that this requirement means that if a dwelling derives wholly or partly from a residential part, zero-rating is not available.

The case *Alexandra Countryside Investments Ltd* v. *Revenue & Customs* [2013] UKFTT 348 (TC) concerned a pub converted into two semi-detached dwellings. Each dwelling contained a part of what had been the pub manager's flat. HMRC argued that zero-rating was not available as each dwelling was not created wholly from non-residential parts of the pub. However, the Tribunal rejected this and accepted zero-rating on the basis of the *Jacobs* test; that is, that before conversion the building had contained one dwelling and after conversion it contained two.

Certificates

If the result of the conversion is a relevant residential purpose building, for relief (2.1) the purchaser must give the convertor a zero-rating certificate to this effect. For reliefs (2.2) and (2.3), the housing association must give the supplier of conversion services a zero-rating certificate. HMRC provides model certificates to use in *VAT Notice 708*.

Ignored use

HMRC accepts (*VAT Notice 708*, sections 5.3.4 and 6.3.4) that the following use can be ignored for the purposes of the ten-year rule in the non-residential condition (b) above: illegal occupation by squatters, occupation by guardians, and use that is not residential in nature, such as storage for a business. A guardian is a person who is installed in a property by the owner or on behalf of the owner to deter squatters and vandals. He or she may pay a low rent on terms that fall short of a formal tenancy. Alternatively, he or she may be paid to occupy the property. A guardian is to be distinguished from a caretaker or housekeeper who lives permanently in the property. Property occupied by a caretaker or housekeeper is likely to be furnished throughout.

The following comments in relief 1 above also apply to these reliefs: change of use rules, builders' block, residence restrictions, first sales, long leases, person constructing, subcontractors and professional services.

8.3.4 **Substantially reconstructed protected buildings**

The first sale of a **major interest** in a **substantially reconstructed protected building** by its developer is zero-rated.

There are five conditions that must all be satisfied for zero-rating to apply:

1. The sale must be the first sale of a freehold or a long lease (major interest) in the building following its substantial reconstruction.
2. The sale must be made by the developer of the building. This is a person with an interest in the building who commissions its substantial reconstruction.
3. The building must be Grade I, Grade II* or Grade II listed (or Scottish or Northern Ireland equivalents) or a scheduled monument. Buildings within the curtilage of a listed building, such as outhouses or garages which, although not fixed to the building, form part of the land and have done so since before 1 July 1948, are treated for planning purposes as part of the listed building. Unlisted buildings in conservation areas, or buildings included in a local authority's non-statutory list of buildings of local interest, are not protected buildings for the purposes of VAT.
4. The building must be substantially reconstructed. A building is substantially reconstructed when the reconstructed building incorporates no more of the original building (that is to say, the building as it was before the reconstruction began) than the external walls, together with other external features of architectural or historic interest.
5. At the time of supply, the building must be:
   - designed to remain as or become a dwelling or number of dwellings; or
   - intended for use solely for a relevant charitable purpose; or
   - intended for use solely for a relevant residential purpose; or
   - a combination of these.

See 8.6 'Property terms' for the meanings of **relevant charitable purpose**, **relevant residential purpose**, **solely** and **dwelling**. For dwellings there is no requirement that statutory planning consent was obtained for use as a dwelling. This is because most protected buildings will have been constructed before statutory planning consent for new properties was introduced.

Apportionment

If a developer sells a substantially reconstructed listed building that will only partly be put to a qualifying use, then a corresponding portion of the contract price can be zero-rated.

Certificates

If the building is intended for use solely for a relevant charitable or residential purpose following purchase, the purchaser must give the developer a zero-rating certificate. See 8.3.8 'Certificates'.

Transitional measures

Before 1 October 2012 this relief was wider, using a less strict definition of substantial reconstruction and also zero-rating 'approved alterations' to protected buildings. As a transitional measure to 1 October 2015 zero-rating is still available under the pre-October 2012 rules provided:

- for approved alterations – the supply is made pursuant to a written contract entered into, or a relevant consent applied for, before 21 March 2012. Relevant consent means listed buildings consent or equivalent.
- for substantial reconstructions – at least 10% (measured by reference to cost) of the reconstruction of the protected building was completed before 21 March 2012.

Change of use

The change of use rules do not apply to buildings zero-rated under this zero-rating relief.

Builders' block

See 8.6.14 'Builders' block'.

8.3.5   **DIY builders and converters VAT refund scheme**

This scheme allows persons carrying out qualifying self-build projects to benefit from some of the same reliefs outlined above.

Qualifying works are:

(a) the construction of a building designed as a dwelling or number of dwellings;

(b) the construction of a building for use solely for a relevant charitable or residential purpose; and

(c) a residential conversion.

There are two situations in which a person can make a claim for VAT incurred on construction or conversion materials and works:

4.1 Where a person carries out qualifying works, the carrying out of the works is lawful and otherwise than in the course or furtherance of any business, and VAT is chargeable on the supply, acquisition or importation of any building materials which, in the course of the works, are incorporated into the building or its site.

4.2 Where a person carries out a residential conversion by arranging for any of the work of conversion to be carried out by a contractor, the carrying out of the conversion by the person is lawful and otherwise than in the course or furtherance of any business, the contractor is not acting as an architect, surveyor or consultant or in a supervisory capacity, and VAT is chargeable on services consisting in the work done by the contractor. See 8.6 'Property terms' for the meanings of **relevant charitable purpose, relevant residential purpose, dwelling** and **building materials**. See 8.3.3 'Residential conversions' for the meaning of **residential conversion**. Services of builders for (a) and (b) should qualify for zero-rating in their own right under the relief for qualifying new buildings above.

A claim for any VAT described in (4.1) or (4.2) above must be made to HMRC within the three months after completion of the building by completing the relevant claim form. Claims cannot be made before completion. Form VAT431NB must be used for building constructions and form VAT431C for residential conversions. The claimant must send the following with the completed form:

- A **certificate of completion** obtained from a local authority or such other documentary evidence of completion of the building as is satisfactory to HMRC. HMRC will accept any of these as evidence that the work is finished:

  (i) a certificate or letter of completion from the local authority for Building Regulations purposes or otherwise;

  (ii) a habitation certificate or letter from the local authority – or in Scotland, a temporary certificate of habitation;

  (iii) a valuation rating or Council Tax assessment; or

  (iv) a certificate from your bank or building society with the following wording: 'This is to certify that the . . . . Bank/Society released on . . . . (date) the last instalment of its loan secured on the dwelling/building at . . . . because it then regarded that building as complete.'

- An **invoice** showing the registration number of the person supplying the goods, whether or not such an invoice is a VAT invoice, in respect of each supply of goods on which VAT has been paid which have been incorporated into the building or its site.
- In respect of imported goods which have been incorporated into the building or its site, documentary evidence of their importation and of the VAT paid thereon.
- Documentary evidence that planning permission for the building had been granted.
- A certificate signed by a quantity surveyor or architect that the goods shown in the claim were or, in their judgement, were likely to have been, incorporated into the building or its site. In practice, HMRC will accept copies of approved plans of the external elevations and internal layout plans of all floors in lieu of this.

8.3.6 Qualifying residential conversion works

Supplies of building services, and supplies of building materials by the builder, are reduced-rated if **qualifying conversion works** are being carried out.

Qualifying conversion works are any of the following:

5.1 **A changed number of dwellings conversion**: the conversion of premises consisting of a building or a part of a building where, after conversion, the premises contain a different number of single household dwellings (greater than zero) than before, and no part of the premises being converted contains the same number of single household dwellings (whether zero, one or more) as before. A single household dwelling means a dwelling designed for occupation by a single household.

5.2 **A house in multiple occupation conversion**: the conversion of premises consisting of a building or a part of a building where before conversion the premises do not contain any multiple occupancy dwellings and after conversion the premises being converted contain only one or more multiple occupancy dwellings. However, this excludes conversion to multiple occupancy dwellings for relevant residential use. Multiple occupancy dwelling means a dwelling that is designed for occupation by persons not forming a single household.

5.3 **A special residential conversion**: a non-relevant residential purpose building, buildings or parts of buildings are converted into a relevant residential purpose building or buildings. However, if the intention is to use the building or buildings for an institutional purpose, the building, buildings or parts of buildings must form the entirety of an institution used for that purpose. The customer must give the builder a certificate stating that the conversion is a special residential conversion.

See 8.6 'Property terms' for the meanings of dwelling and relevant residential purpose. Institutional purposes are uses (a)–(c) and (f)–(g) in the definition of relevant residential purpose.

Consents

To qualify, any necessary statutory planning consent or building-control consent must have been granted.

Qualifying works

Qualifying works include: works to the fabric of the building, site works for utilities, waste disposal, drainage or security and associated building materials. Qualifying works exclude the incorporation or installation as fittings of any goods that are not building materials. See 8.6.13 'Building materials' for the definition of building materials.

8.3.7 Residential renovations and alterations

A supply of **qualifying building services** and associated building materials (by the builder) is reduced-rated if **qualifying residential premises** are being renovated or altered.

To be **qualifying residential premises** a building (or part) must meet all of the following conditions:

(a) The premises are a single household dwelling, a multiple occupancy dwelling or a building or a part of a building which, when last lived in, was used for a relevant residential purpose. Single household dwelling means a dwelling designed for occupation by a single household. Multiple occupancy dwelling means a dwelling that is designed for occupation by persons not forming a single household. For the meaning of relevant residential purpose, see 8.6.9 'Relevant residential purpose'.

(b) The premises have not been lived in for at least two years before the date the works commenced. A single household dwelling can also qualify if the dwelling was empty for at least two years up to re-occupation, no renovation or alteration works were carried out during that period and the works are being carried out by the person re-occupying the property

(c) If the premises, when last lived in, were used for a relevant residential purpose, then the premises must also be used for a relevant residential purpose after the works are finished and the supplier must be provided with a certificate. Where a number of buildings are renovated or altered at the same time and will be used together as a unit for a relevant residential purpose after the works are finished, then all the buildings are treated as relevant residential purpose use.

Consents

To qualify, any necessary statutory planning consent or building control consent must have been granted.

Qualifying works

Qualifying works include: works to the fabric of the building, site works for utilities, waste disposal, drainage or security and associated building materials. Qualifying works exclude the incorporation or installation as fittings of any goods that are not building materials. See 8.6.13 'Building materials' for the definition of building materials.

8.3.8 **Certificates**

Model certificates

HMRC provides model zero-rating and reduced-rating certificates to use in *VAT Notice 708*.

Time of issue

You should issue your certificate before your supplier makes their supply, though HMRC will allow your supplier to adjust their VAT charge on receipt of a belated certificate provided that you can demonstrate to the supplier that at the time of the supply you had an intention that the building will be used in the way being certified, and all other conditions for relief are met (*VAT Notice 708*, section 16.6). However, a supplier cannot make an adjustment if they are limited by the 'four-year cap'. If the certificate only zero rates or reduce rates a percentage of the contract cost involved, it should state the percentage zero-rated or reduced-rated.

Penalties

If you issue an incorrect certificate you are liable to a penalty which is calculated as the difference between the amount of VAT which would have been charged had the certificate been correct and the amount of VAT actually charged. However, no penalty is due if the person issuing the certificate can satisfy HMRC or a tribunal that they have a reasonable excuse for having issued an incorrect certificate. See 12.6.5 'Reasonable excuse'.

The same penalty applies to incorrect certificates disapplying an option to tax, see 8.5 'Option to tax'.

8.3.9 Apportionment for part qualifying buildings

HMRC accepts that the term 'solely' in the reliefs above incorporates a 5% *de minimis* level of non-qualifying use. This means that, for example, if a charity constructs a building it intends to use 95% or more for its non-business activities with the rest of the use for business activities, then it can ignore the *de minimis* business use and zero rate all eligible supplies of construction services. See 8.6.6 'Meaning of solely'.

If the whole building is not intended for use 95% or more for qualifying use but identifiable parts of the building are (for example particular floors or rooms), then a corresponding portion of the construction costs can be zero-rated.

Where a building must be apportioned between the qualifying use areas and non-qualifying use areas the method of apportionment can be on any basis that is fair and reasonable. Potential apportionment bases include:

- hours of use for the different types of activity;
- floor area assigned to the different types of activity;
- the numbers of users of the different types of activity;
- staff numbers or cost of staff working in the different types of activity.

In *VAT Information Sheet 13/10* HMRC states that it will consider any calculation to be 'fair' provided that it accurately reflects the extent that the building is used for a qualifying purpose and it can be carried out and checked without undue difficulty or cost. HMRC provides (amongst many others) the following examples of potentially acceptable approaches to apportionment:

Time apportionment. A school hall is available for (qualifying) use by the school five days a week, 42 weeks a year from 8.30 am to 4.30 pm. Every Friday evening during term time, from 7.00 pm to 9.00 pm, the hall is made available for non-qualifying use. A representative period would be a week during term time. The total time that the hall is available for use during a week is 42 hours (8 hrs × 5 days + 2 hrs on a Friday).

The total time that the hall is available for qualifying use is 40 hours (8hrs × 5 days). Percentage qualifying use = 40/42 × 100 = 95.24. So the whole use can be treated as qualifying.

Floor area method. A new village hall has an area of 200 square metres. One room of 15 square metres is rented out for use exclusively as a post office and cannot be used for village hall activities.

Percentage qualifying use = 185/200 × 100 = 92.5

Qualifying use is less than 95% therefore the building is not eligible for the zero rate under this method. However, the part of the building that is being used for village hall activities (the 92.5%) is eligible for the zero rate.

Staff number method. A research laboratory employs 275 full-time staff but no specific area or member of staff is used exclusively on non-business research. It is therefore not possible to use any of the methods quoted above. Of the 275 staff employed, 75 work 90% of the time on non-business work, 150 are researchers engaged 75% of the time on non-business research and the remaining 50 staff provide technical and administrative support equally to the researchers.

Full-time equivalent of staff engaged on non-business research = $(75 \times 90\%)$ + $(150 \times 75\%) = 67.5 + 112.5 = 180$

Therefore the percentage of researchers' time that is spent on non-business research is $180 \div 225 = 80$. Since the support staff equally support the researchers, 80% of their time must also be spent on non-business work. Percentage qualifying use = 80. Qualifying use < 95% therefore the building is not eligible for the zero rate using this method.

Cost based. A research laboratory will be used for a mixture of commercial and non-commercial research. There is no difference in the ways that the two types of research are carried out. Commercial clients will pay 3% of the research costs. Percentage qualifying use = 97. Qualifying use > 95% therefore the building is eligible for the zero rate.

Extra-statutory concession 3.29

HMRC used to accept that up to 10% non-qualifying use could be ignored (*VAT Notice 48*, section 3.29). This concession was abolished with effect from 30 June 2010 but has enduring effect for those that relied on it to zero rate a supply. See 8.3.13 'Change of use rules'.

8.3.10   **Design and build contracts**

The principle behind design and build contracts is that a single person or entity contracts to provide both the construction/building services and the professional services (architects, surveyors, consultants, project managers, etc.). The single person or entity then makes a single zero-rated or reduced-rated supply of 'design and build' services to the parent entity. This single person or entity can be a subsidiary company set up to act as lead contractor, purchasing separately the services of builders, architects, surveyors, consultants and supervisors. The subsidiary may be charged standard-rated VAT by its subcontractors but it can recover this on the basis that it is using those services to make a single zero-rated or reduced-rated supply to the parent entity.

At the time of writing there is a question over whether this approach is acceptable, given that such costs are explicitly excluded by the legislation. HMRC's position is to broadly accept that design and build contracts can be effective for zero-rated supplies, including via a subsidiary design and build company. HMRC states (*VAT Notice 708*, section 3.4):

> **Design and build**: Here the building client engages a contractor to carry out both the design and construction elements of the project. Where it is clear in the contract that any services of architects, surveyors or others acting as a consultant or in a supervisory capacity are no more than cost components of the contractors supply and are not specifically supplied on to the customer, then the whole supply can be treated as being eligible for the zero rate.

> **Project/construction management**: Here the building client engages an external consultant to plan, manage and co-ordinate the whole project including establishing competitive bids for all elements of the work, with the successful contractors being employed directly by the building client. Management fees paid by the building client to the consultants are standard-rated.

> **Management contracting**: This system can take various forms. Normally the building client first appoints a professional design team and engages a management contractor to advise them. If the project goes ahead, the management contractor will act as the main contractor for the work (engaging 'works contractors' to carry out work to him as necessary). His preliminary advisory services are then treated in the same way as his main construction services. If the project does not go ahead, his preliminary advisory services are standard-rated.

Assignments to a design and build subsidiary

In *Community Housing Association (CHA)* v. *Revenue & Customs* [2009] EWHC 455 (Ch), a VAT-registered housing association set up a design and build subsidiary (Ventures) and assigned to Ventures all construction projects in hand charging as consideration what it had paid in respect of professionals' fees on those projects. CHA then claimed the input VAT charged by the professionals, on the basis that, under the clawback rules, its original intention as to use of the professional services had changed from exempt (letting dwellings) to standard-rated (the resupply to Ventures). The High Court accepted that the arrangement was effective. In *Revenue & Customs Brief 57/09* HMRC accepts the High Court's decision but warned that the mere raising of invoices and passing of funds between companies does not automatically create supplies.

8.3.11 **House builders**

In *Information Sheet 07/08* HMRC accepts that house builders, who would normally construct dwellings and sell zero-rated major interests, but who could not sell due to a market downturn, could, in order to preserve full VAT recovery on construction costs, grant long leases to a connected company which let out the dwellings. HMRC accepts that this is not an abusive scheme. HMRC makes the following statement:

> For a scheme to be abusive, it must (as well as having the essential aim of saving VAT) produce a result contrary to the purpose of the VAT legislation. HMRC believe that Parliament intended that the construction of new dwellings should be relieved from VAT. The first grant mechanism introduced by Parliament does achieve this but it relies on the assumption that there will always be a grant of a major interest around the time the dwelling is complete, so ensuring deduction of VAT on all appropriate costs.

> In HMRC's view, the arrangement set out above does not produce a result contrary to the purpose of the legislation, but rather ensures that a transaction of the kind Parliament envisaged will actually take place at the appropriate time. That view rests on the assumption that the purpose of the zero-rating provisions associated with new dwellings is to relieve fully from VAT the provision of precisely that – new dwellings. That means that all the costs (save on blocked goods such as washing machines, carpets, etc.) associated with producing a new house should either not carry VAT, or carry VAT that is deductible in full.

8.3.12 **Self-supply of construction services**

Where a business uses its own employees to construct or extend a building or civil engineering work for the purposes of its own business use then it can be deemed to supply construction services to itself. This rule applies where a business, in the course or furtherance of a business and for the purpose of that business, performs any of the following services other than for consideration:

(a) the construction of a building; or
(b) the extension or other alteration of, or the construction of an annexe to, any building such that additional floor area of not less than 10% of the floor area of the original building is created; or
(c) the construction of any civil engineering work; or
(d) in connection with any such services as are described in sub-paragraph (a), (b) or (c) above, the carrying out of any demolition work contemporaneously with or preparatory thereto.

If the open market value of those services is £100,000 or more, and the services are not zero-rated, then those services are treated as both:

- supplied to the business for the purpose of that business; and
- supplied by the business in the course or furtherance of it.

When valuing the supply you must include demolition work carried out at the same time or in preparation for any of the building work but exclude goods and materials, and services that would be zero-rated if supplied by a VAT-registered person.

8.3.13 Change of use rules

The change of use rules apply where all the following conditions are met:

- A building or a part of a building was zero-rated under: the zero-rating relief for qualifying new buildings or the zero-rating relief for residential conversions.
- The zero-rating was on the basis of intended relevant charitable or residential purpose use.
- Within ten years of completion, actual use of that building or part changes from relevant charitable or residential purpose use or the entire interest in building or part is disposed of.
- The zero-rated building or part was not designed as a dwelling or dwellings.
- The change is the first such change of use for the building or part.

In such a situation, there is a **deemed supply** of that building or part of it by the customer to itself:

The supply by the customer to itself is VAT standard-rated. If the customer is registered for VAT, the customer must account for **output VAT** to HMRC on the deemed supply. If the customer is not registered for VAT, this may cause the customer to have to register for VAT. (For definitions, see the Glossary.)

The supply is also received by the customer from itself. If the customer is VAT-registered (or becomes VAT-registered as a result of the deemed supply) the output VAT due on the supply is also the customer's purchase VAT. This is recoverable by the customer subject to the normal VAT recovery rules, so:

- if the change of use is to a taxable activity, the VAT is recoverable;
- if the change of use is to an exempt activity the VAT is irrecoverable (subject to de minimis rule) and
- if the change of use is to a mixed activity, the VAT is residual.

If the deemed purchase is a capital item for the purposes of the CGS, then the CGS operates to adjust the initial VAT recovery, though a special modification applies, see Chapter 10 'VAT special schemes'.

The change of use rules were changed with effect for buildings completed on or after 1 March 2011.Buildings completed before 1 March 2011 must be adjusted under the **Pre-1 March 2011 rules**. Buildings completed on or after 1 March 2011 must be adjusted under the **1 March 2011 and later rules**.

1 March 2011 and later change of use rules

The value of the deemed supply and the output VAT due to HMRC are given by the following formulae:

$$Value\ of\ deemed\ supply = \frac{(120 - Z)}{120} \times C \times Y \times V$$

$$Output\ VAT\ due\ to\ HMRC = Value\ of\ deemed\ supply \times R$$

Where:

Z = number of complete months between completion and date of change of use

C = change in the percentage of qualifying use of the building

$$Y = \frac{(Standard\ rate\ of\ VAT\ applicable\ at\ the\ time\ of\ zero\text{-}rating)}{(Standard\ rate\ of\ VAT\ applicable\ at\ change\ of\ use)}$$

V = Value of original zero-rated supply

R = standard rate of VAT applicable at change of use

Example: change of use rules from 1 March 2011

Charity X constructs a new four-storey building completed on 1 June 2011 and zero-rating qualifying construction costs of £10 million on the basis of intended relevant charitable purpose use.

On 1 June 2013 (24 months later) the charity changes one floor (25%) to taxable business use. The standard-rates of VAT at 1 June 2011 and 1 June 2013 were 20%.

Value of deemed supply = (120 − 24)/120 × 25% × (20/20) × £10 million = £2 million

Output VAT due = £2 million × 20% = £400,000

This can be recovered as input VAT as the change of use is to taxable activity. The value of the deemed supply is above the CGS adjustment threshold (£250,000) so the deemed supply of the floor to Charity X (by itself) is a capital item adjustable under the CGS.

Extra-statutory concession 3.29

Before 1 July 2009, HMRC provided an extra-statutory concession (*VAT Notice 48*, section 3.29) that permitted up to 10% of non-qualifying use to be ignored as *de minimis*, provided the calculation of the level of use was as set out in section 3.29. In addition, in *Revenue & Customs Brief 29/07*, HMRC accepts that if this concession was used to zero rate a building (or part) then any change in the use of that building (or part) that was not anticipated at the time that zero-rating was obtained under the concession could be ignored for the purposes of the change of use rules.

HMRC withdrew extra-statutory concession 3.29 with effect from 1 July 2009, though for a transitional period of one year (to 30 June 2010) organisations could choose to either use the existing concession 3.29 or rely on their revised interpretation of the meaning of 'solely' as permitting up to 5% non-qualifying use to be ignored (see 8.6.6 'Meaning of solely'). Organisations that obtained zero-rating under section 3.29 are still able to rely on *Revenue & Customs Brief 29/07* and ignore changes of use.

HMRC also states in *Revenue & Customs Brief 29/07*: 'This change may also affect the position of any charity that obtained zero-rating under Group 5, Schedule 8 of the VAT Act 1994, rather than the ESC [extra-statutory concession]. In the event of any change of use of their building, the charity should contact HMRC for further advice.'

Pre-1 March 2011 change of use rules

If extra-statutory concession 3.29 (*VAT Notice 48*, section 3.29) was not or could not be relied on or the above statement in *Revenue & Customs Brief 29/07* is not applicable, then the pre-1 March 2011 change of use rules were as follows:

Disposals

If the zero-rated building or a zero-rated part of the building is disposed of (freehold, lease or licence to occupy), then the VAT treatment of the disposal is as follows:

- If the interest is no longer intended for use solely for a relevant residential or charitable purpose, VAT must be charged on the disposal consideration at the standard rate. If the building was only partly zero-rated then an apportionment must be made. If you are not registered for VAT, this may cause you to have to register.
- If the interest is still intended for use solely for a relevant residential or charitable purpose, then you must consider if any of the above reliefs apply. If not, the disposal is exempt.

Change of own use

If the interest in the property is retained but the balance of qualifying and non-qualifying activities undertaken in the building changes, then the VAT treatment of the disposal is as follows: any increase in non-qualifying use is a deemed standard-rated self-supply and output VAT must be accounted for. This output VAT is, however, **deductible** to the extent that the change of use is **attributable** to **taxable supplies** (for definitions see the Glossary). The formula for calculating the value of the deemed supply is:

$$\text{Output VAT due} = \frac{(10 - N)}{10} \times \text{VAT originally saved by zero-rating}$$

Where N is the number of whole years since the day the building was completed for which the building or part concerned has been used for a relevant charitable purpose or a relevant residential purpose.

Example: Change of use without disposal

A charity paid £1 million net for a new building zero-rating 50%. The standard rate of VAT at the time was 17.5%. After four years' use the qualifying use drops to 40% (standard rate of VAT is now 20%). Extra-statutory concession 3.29 was not used.

VAT originally due on the 10% change is 10% × £1 million × 17.5% = £17,500

The output VAT due is £17,500 × (10 − 4)/10 = £10,500

The value of the deemed supply is £10,500/20% = £52,500

The £10,500 output VAT is recoverable as input VAT if the change of use relates to taxable activity. If the change of use relates to residual activity it is residual VAT.

8.4 LEASES AND LETTINGS

EU law

The Principal VAT Directive exempts 'the leasing or letting of immovable property', though it excludes from exemption:

(a) the provision of accommodation in hotels, holiday camps, camp sites and similar;
(b) the letting of premises and sites for parking vehicles;

(c) the letting of permanently installed equipment and machinery;

(d) the hire of safes.

EU member states are also permitted to make other exclusions. The UK uses this option to make further exclusions such as facilities for storing goods (see 8.2 'Exceptions to the basic property rule').

EU case law

The leasing or letting of immoveable property is an independent concept of EU law and its scope is not determined according to English or Scottish property law (or any other EU state's property law). In case C-284/03 *Belgian State* v. *Temco Europe SA* [2004] ECR I-11237, the CJEU gave the following guidance on determining whether a supply is a letting of immoveable property for VAT:

> In numerous cases, the Court has defined the concept of the letting of immoveable property ... as essentially the conferring by a landlord on a tenant, for an agreed period and in return for payment, of the right to occupy property as if that person were the owner and to exclude any other person from enjoyment of such a right.

> While the Court has stressed the importance of the period of the letting in those judgments, it has done so in order to distinguish a transaction comprising the letting of immovable property, which is usually a relatively passive activity linked simply to the passage of time and not generating any significant added value, from other activities which are either industrial and commercial in nature, or have as their subject-matter something which is best understood as the provision of a service rather than simply the making available of property, such as the right to use a golf course, the right to use a bridge in consideration of payment of a toll or the right to install cigarette machines in commercial premises.

> The actual period of the letting is thus not, of itself, the decisive factor in determining whether a contract is one for the letting of immovable property, even if the fact that accommodation is provided for a brief period only may constitute an appropriate basis for distinguishing the provision of hotel accommodation from the letting of dwelling accommodation.

> In any event, it is not essential that that period be fixed at the time the contract is concluded. It is necessary to take into account the reality of the contractual relations. The period of a letting may be shortened or extended by the mutual agreement of the parties during the performance of the contract. Furthermore, while a payment to the landlord which is strictly linked to the period of occupation of the property by the tenant appears best to reflect the passive nature of a letting transaction, it is not to be inferred from that that a payment which takes into account other factors has the effect of precluding a 'letting of immovable property', particularly where the other factors taken into account are

plainly accessory in light of the part of the payment linked to the passage of time or pay for no service other than the simple making available of the property.

Lastly, as regards the tenant's right of exclusive occupation of the property, it must be pointed out that this can be restricted in the contract concluded with the landlord and only relates to the property as it is defined in that contract. Thus, the landlord may reserve the right regularly to visit the property let. Furthermore, a contract of letting may relate to certain parts of a property which must be used in common with other occupiers. The presence in the contract of such restrictions on the right to occupy the premises let does not prevent that occupation being exclusive as regards all other persons not permitted by law or by the contract to exercise a right over the property which is the subject of the contract of letting.

It is [necessary] to consider all the circumstances surrounding [the transaction] in order to establish its characteristics and to assess whether it can be treated as a 'letting of immovable property'. It is also [necessary] to establish whether the contracts, as performed, have as their essential object the making available, in a passive manner, of premises or parts of buildings in exchange for a payment linked to the passage of time, or whether they give rise to the provision of a service capable of being categorised in a different way.

8.4.1 **HMRC examples**

HMRC provides the following examples of what it sees as being exempt licences to occupy land (*VAT Notice 742*, section 2.6):

- the provision of a specific area of office accommodation, such as a bay, room or floor, together with the right to use shared areas such as reception, lifts, restaurant, rest rooms, leisure facilities and so on;
- the provision of a serviced office but only where the use of phones, computer systems, photocopiers, etc. is incidental to the provision of office space;
- granting a concession to operate a shop within a shop, where the concessionaire is granted a defined area from which to sell their goods or services;
- granting space to erect advertising hoardings;
- granting space to place a fixed kiosk on a specified site, such as a newspaper kiosk or flower stand at a railway station;
- hiring out a hall or other accommodation for meetings or parties and so on (but not wedding or party facilities where the supplier does more than supplying accommodation, for example by assisting with entertainment and arranging catering); the use of a kitchen area, lighting and furniture can be included;
- granting a catering concession, where the caterer is granted a licence to occupy a specific kitchen and restaurant area, even if the grant includes use of kitchen or catering equipment;

- granting traders a pitch in a market or at a car boot sale; or
- granting a specific space for the installation of a 'hole in the wall' cash machine (ATM).

The following are HMRC examples of supplies that are not exempt licences to occupy land (*VAT Notice 742*, section 2.7):

- the rental by a hairdressing salon of chair spaces to individual stylists, unless a clearly demarcated area is provided (such as a floor or whole salon) and no other services;
- the hire of tables in nail bars to self-employed manicurists;
- providing another person with access to office premises to make use of facilities, such as remote sales staff away from home having access to photocopiers and the like at another office;
- allowing the public to tip rubbish on your land;
- storing someone's goods in a warehouse without allocating any specific area for them;
- granting of an ambulatory concession, such as an ice cream van on the sea front or a hamburger van at a football match;
- allowing the public admission to premises or events, such as theatres, historic houses, swimming pools and spectator sports events;
- wedding facilities (including, for example, use of rooms for a ceremony, wedding breakfast and evening party);
- hiring out safes to store valuables; or
- granting someone the right to place a free-standing or wall-mounted vending or gaming machine on your premises, where the location is not specified in the agreement.

8.4.2 Peppercorn rents

Letting out or leasing a property for a peppercorn rent or premium is normally seen as a non-business activity for the provider. However, leasing for a peppercorn in conjunction with other substantial supplies, such as under some PFI contracts, is likely to be a part of a business supply.

8.4.3 Payments connected to leases and licences

Premiums and rental payments

Premiums and rental payments are VAT exempt, unless the lessor (person supplying a lease) or licensor (person supplying a licence) has opted to tax the property and that option to tax is not disapplied, in which case the payments are VAT standard-rated.

Lease inducements

Where a landlord pays an inducement to the tenant to take-up a lease (often referred to as a reverse premium), the payment will be outside the scope of VAT unless it is directly linked to a specific benefit supplied by the tenant to the landlord in return for the inducement payment, in which case it will follow the VAT status of the supply provided by the tenant. Situations in which an inducement payment would be taxable include agreeing to undertake repair or improvement work or acting as an anchor tenant. An anchor tenant is a prestige tenant that will attract other tenants.

Rent-free periods

A rent-free period given by a landlord is outside the scope of VAT unless something is supplied by the tenant to the landlord in return, in which case its VAT status follows that of the supply by the tenant.

Assignments

If a third party pays a tenant to assign a lease, then the tenant makes a supply of property in return for consideration. This supply is VAT exempt unless the tenant has opted to tax the property and the tenant's option to tax is not disapplied, in which case the supply is VAT standard-rated.

Reverse assignments

If a tenant pays a third party to take the lease then the third party makes a supply of services to the tenant in return for consideration. This is a standard-rated supply by the third party as the third party is not supplying property to the tenant.

Surrenders

If a landlord pays a tenant to surrender a lease before the lease term has expired, then that is an exempt supply of property by the tenant to the landlord, unless the tenant has opted to tax the property and the tenant's option to tax is not disapplied, in which case it is standard-rated.

Reverse surrenders

If a tenant pays a landlord to take back a lease then that is treated by law as an exempt supply by the landlord, unless the landlord has opted to tax the property and the landlord's option to tax is not disapplied, in which case the supply is standard-rated.

Dilapidation payments

Dilapidation payments may be charged by the landlord to the tenant at or near the end of a lease. Such payments are a claim for damages by the landlord and are not consideration for a supply. They are therefore outside the scope of VAT.

8.4.4 **Service and other charges**

As well as charging rent, landlords often recharge costs for additional facilities and services in the form of a service charge. Service charges commonly relate to maintenance of the fabric of the building; insurance; cleaning, maintenance and heating of common areas; reception services; communal heating, water and similar.

General rule for service charges

If the lease agreement specifies that the landlord will provide such additional services and the tenant must pay for such services via a specified service charge, then in general the VAT status of the service charge follows that of the rental payments. Charges for separately metered services (such as water, gas and electricity) and services that are optional are seen as consideration for separate supplies that assume their own independent VAT statuses. If the landlord handles payments to third parties on behalf of tenants, then such payments are usually seen as supplies directly by the third party to the tenant.

Insurance

If the landlord is the policyholder for the buildings insurance, but recharges the tenant under a lease term, such payments will follow the VAT status of the rent. If the tenants are the policyholders, with the landlord collecting payments and passing them on to the insurer, such payments are treated as disbursements by the landlord.

Rates

May be the responsibility of the landlord and recharged to tenants. Again, if this is in the lease, it will fall into the same VAT category as the rent. If the tenant is responsible for the rates, then the landlord is likely to be acting as **agent** (see 11.2) in collecting rates and paying them over on behalf of tenants, and the associated charge will be outside the scope of VAT.

Gas, electricity, heating, water, etc.

If the landlord makes a separate charge for un-metered supplies used by tenants, such charges follow the VAT status of the rent. If the landlord operates a secondary meter, and charges tenants based on actual use, the charges are consideration for separate supplies and follow their natural VAT statuses. See 6.5.5 'Fuel and power' and 6.4.15 'Water and sewerage services' for the VAT treatment of supplies of fuel, power, water and sewerage services.

Telephone lines

Telephone lines in the name of the landlord which are then recharged to the tenants are a supply of standard-rated services.

Reception services

Reception services which are not discretionary and are part of the lease agreement will fall into the same VAT category as the rent, even when charged separately. If they are an optional additional service then they will be standard-rated.

Photocopying and other support services

Photocopying and other support services will generally be standard-rated, as charges will usually be an optional extra and charges made based on usage. If an all-inclusive rental is charged, however, then the whole amount may be exempt, though see 8.4.5 'Active v. passive lets'.

Management charges

Management charges by the landlord for collecting service charges and managing the property are part of the main property supply and therefore follow the VAT category of the rent.

8.4.5 Active v. passive lets

An 'active let' occurs where a right to occupy property is supplied together with other services as part of the same bargain and, for the typical customer:

- the right to occupy the property is not an aim in itself but a means of better enjoying the other services; or
- the right to occupy and other services form, objectively, a single, indivisible service which it would be artificial to split and that cannot be characterised as the making available, in a passive manner, of premises in exchange for a payment linked to the passage of time.

An example of the first scenario is the hire of a recording studio. The typical customer's objective is not to occupy property but to gain use of the recording equipment.

The second scenario is illustrated by the case *Best Images* v. *Revenue & Customs* [2010] UKFTT 175 (TC). This case concerned two halls in a building used for Indian weddings, let out on a commercial basis. There was no sleeping accommodation. Catering was arranged directly between the customer and an independent caterer, the caterer usually being one of those recommended by the hall owner. The hall owner also guided the customer to various other suppliers (caterers, flowers, music, Indian dancers, etc.); the hall owner and/or his wife were present and assisted at the weddings. The following were provided: bar staff (but not waitress or serving staff), tables and chairs, cleaner and security staff. The customer expected these additional services for the price paid. The First-tier Tribunal concluded that it would be artificial to split the additional services from the provision of the premises. These were so closely linked that they constituted a single supply. The additional services provided added value and were not simply for the better enjoyment of the hall; they were not merely ancillary to the use of the hall. The conclusion was that the hall owner was not providing the passive activity of letting land but providing to his customers help and support both before and during the event. This went beyond merely providing the key to the door.

8.4.6 Letting rooms for events and meetings

Where organisations let out rooms on a regular and commercial basis for events, parties, conferences, meetings, etc. it can be difficult to know whether additional services have gone over the line between active and passive lets. HMRC provides the following helpful guidelines for the hotel sector (*VAT Notice 709/3*, section 4) in connection with rooms provided for weddings, parties, conferences, etc.

4.1 Accommodation used for catering

If you provide accommodation in a room within a hotel, inn, boarding house or similar establishment for the purpose of catering, your supply is standard-rated whatever the length of let. This is the case regardless of whether the catering supplied by you or by another person...

If you supply a room that is not for the purpose of a supply of catering such as for a conference, your supply is exempt, provided you have not opted to tax.

4.2 Accommodation and catering supplied to employees

If you supply your employees with accommodation or food and drink, in your establishment and they pay for it, the payments are treated as including VAT and you must account for it on your VAT return. Where employees pay for meals and so on from their pay including under a salary sacrifice arrangement employers must account for VAT from 1 January 2012 on such supplies unless they are zero-rated. Subject to the normal rules, the employer can continue to recover the VAT incurred on related purchases.

4.3 Other accommodation and services

Other supplies of accommodation such as hiring a room for a meeting, or letting of shops and display cases are generally exempt, but you may choose to standard-rate them by opting to tax.

If you make an exempt supply such as providing a room for a meeting or a conference and you provide minimal refreshments such as tea, coffee and biscuits, the room and the incidental catering will be treated as a single exempt supply. But, if you serve substantial refreshments such as a meal or buffet, the catering should be treated as a separate supply and you must account for VAT based on the normal charges you would make for such catering.

Where a meeting room is supplied, together with meal(s) and overnight accommodation in return for an inclusive charge, each element is treated as a separate supply. The catering and the overnight accommodation are taxable, while the supply of the meeting room is exempt unless you have made an option to tax. Any additional goods or services which are separately charged for are standard-rated (for example, catering, car parking, use of equipment and licensed bars).

4.4 Wedding packages

If you supply a package of wedding services (including, for example, use of rooms for a ceremony, wedding breakfast and evening party), this is a single standard-rated supply, regardless of whether the catering is supplied by you or someone else.

8.4.7 Letting office space and spaces for exhibition stands

HMRC provides the following guidance (*VATLP06130*):

Licence to occupy an office including use of telephones, computer system, photocopiers, etc. [This is a] leasing or letting of immovable property (exempt unless licensor has opted). The provision of the other facilities is incidental to the predominant supply of office accommodation. However if the licensee has the right to choose what services he wants and pays for them separately there may be two supplies: an exempt supply of land (the office); and a taxable supply of services.

Licence to occupy office space, including the provision of secretarial services, such as typing, photocopying, mail sorting, etc. [This is a] standard-rated supply of office services. The inclusion of secretarial type services will normally result in the supply being characterised as the provision of 'office services' and not the making available of property. See *Pethericks & Gillard Ltd* (VTD 20564) which supports such treatment.

Hire of space for exhibition stand. [This is a] standard-rated supply. There is likely to be a package of services, but even if minimal additional services are provided, HMRC consider this to be a standard-rated supply because the predominant aim of the agreement is to participate in an exhibition and benefit from the publicity of the event.

8.5   OPTION TO TAX

An option to tax is a formal declaration made by a business in relation to one or more specific properties (land, buildings or civil engineering works) that henceforth that business's supplies of that property will, by default, be VAT standard-rated rather than VAT exempt. **Supplies of the property** means supplies of the freehold of, a lease in or a licence to occupy the property.

The option to tax must be notified in writing to the HMRC Option to Tax Unit (see 14.1 'Contacting HM Revenue & Customs' for contact details) and HMRC provides a form with which to do so. If you are not sure if you have already opted to tax a property you can contact the HMRC Option to Tax Unit to enquire.

Effect of the option to tax

If a person exercises the option to tax a property, and a supply is then made of that property by that person (or by a **relevant associate** of that person – broadly a person in the same VAT group – see below) at any time when the option to tax has effect, then the supply does not fall within the general exemption for supplies of property and is VAT standard-rated.

Disapplication

This is subject to the condition that the option to tax is not **disapplied** in respect of that supply. If an option to tax is disapplied for a specific supply, then it has no effect on the VAT status of that supply. See 8.5.1 'Disapplications' for the scenarios in which an option to tax can be disapplied.

Scope of the option to tax

An option to tax only applies to one or more specific properties, so any new building, acquired or constructed outside the curtilages of the existing set of opted to tax properties, is not normally covered. However, as many businesses wish to automatically opt to tax all new property acquisitions, the **Real Estate Election** was introduced. This allows a business to automatically opt to tax each new property acquisition as it occurs. If the business does not wish particular properties to be opted to tax, they can be excluded on a case-by-case basis.

HMRC guidance

The main HMRC guidance on the option to tax is in *VAT Notice 742A*. Some of this notice has statutory force.

8.5.1 **Disapplicatons**

A supplier's option to tax over a specific property is 'disapplied' (or rendered ineffective) in various situations. Some options are disapplied automatically and some only when a 'disapplication certificate' is provided to the supplier. The disapplication scenarios covered here are:

- dwellings and relevant residential purpose buildings;
- residential conversions;
- charities;
- housing associations;
- land supplied to an individual for construction of a dwelling;
- anti-avoidance: developers of land, etc.

HMRC can issue penalties for incorrect or invalid disapplication certificates. See 8.3.8 'Certificates'.

Dwellings and relevant residential purpose buildings

An option to tax has no effect on any grant of a building or part of a building if the building or part of the building is designed or adapted, and is intended, for use:

(a) as a dwelling or number of dwellings; or
(b) solely for a relevant residential purpose.

For the meanings of **dwelling**, **solely** and **relevant residential purpose**, see 8.6 'Property terms'.

HMRC guidance

HMRC recommends that suppliers retain evidence to show that the building is intended for use as a dwelling or dwellings. HMRC provides the following guidance for relevant residential purpose buildings (*VAT Notice 742A*, section 3.3):

> Your option to tax will not apply if you supply a building, or part of a building that is designed or adapted for use for a Relevant Residential Purpose (such as a nursing home) and the purchaser or tenant informs you before you make your supply that it is intended for use solely for a Relevant Residential Purpose. Whilst there is no requirement for a formal certificate to be given, we strongly

recommend that you obtain confirmation of the intended use in writing and retain it with your VAT records.

Where part of a building is intended for use solely for a Relevant Residential Purpose and part is not, your option to tax will not apply to the part to be used for a Relevant Residential Purpose, but only where the different functions are to be carried out in clearly defined areas. In these circumstances the value of your supply should be fairly apportioned between the exempt and taxable elements.

Residential conversions

An option to tax has no effect in relation to any grant of a building (or a part of a building) if the recipient certifies that the building (or part) is intended for use:

(a) as a dwelling or number of dwellings; or
(b) solely for a relevant residential purpose.

The recipient of the supply must give a completed certificate VAT1614D to the person making the grant ('the seller'):

1. before the price for the grant to the recipient by the seller is legally fixed, for example by exchange of contracts, letters or missives, or the signing of heads of agreement; or
2. if the seller agrees, at any later time before the seller makes the supply. However, any supplies made before the certificate is given is not affected by the certificate.

The recipient may give the certificate to the seller only if the recipient:

- intends to use the building or part of the building as a dwelling or number of dwellings, or solely for a relevant residential purpose; or
- intends to convert the building or part of the building with a view to it being used as a dwelling, dwellings or for a relevant residential purpose; or
- is a **relevant intermediary**: a person who intends to dispose of the relevant interest to a third person and that third person gives a VAT 1614D certificate to the relevant intermediary.

See *VAT Notice 742A*, section 3.4 for relevant conversion intentions and relevant intermediaries. See 8.6 'Property terms' for the definitions of **dwelling, solely** and **relevant residential purpose**.

Charities

An option to tax has no effect on any grant made to a person in relation to a building or part of a building intended by the person for use:

(a) solely for a relevant charitable purpose; but
(b) not as an **office**.

Use for a relevant charitable purpose means use by a charity for non-business activities or use by a charity as a **village hall or similarly** in providing social or recreational facilities for a local community. See 8.6 'Property terms' for definitions of **solely**, **relevant charitable purpose**, **village hall or similarly**.

> **Office.** HMRC provides the following guidance on the meaning of 'office' (*VATLP22320*):
>
> > 'Office' is not defined... but HMRC's interpretation is that office used in this context means use for the administrative functions of the charity that are similar to those carried out in other organisations, such as personnel, payroll and general administration of the charity as a whole. For example, a building used as the administrative headquarters of a charity is considered an 'office', unlike a charity call centre set up solely for the purpose of collecting voluntary donations.

HMRC advice for sellers

HMRC provides the following guidance for landlords and vendors (*VAT Notice 742A*, section 3.5):

> Where part of a building is intended to be used solely for a Relevant Charitable Purpose (other than as an office) and part is not, your option to tax will not apply to the part used for a Relevant Charitable Purpose, provided that the different functions are carried out in clearly defined areas. In these circumstances the value of your supply should be fairly apportioned between the exempt and taxable elements.

Certificate

There is no template certificate for relevant charitable purpose disapplications; however, it is advisable to provide a written certificate to the supplier before the supply takes place, specifying the percentage disapplied if appropriate. Suitable wording for a certificate might be:

> I certify that, in accordance with VAT Act 1994 schedule 10 paragraphs 7 and 33, xx.xx% of [property description] is intended by [charity name] for use solely for a relevant charitable purpose but not as an office.

Sellers may require some evidence to support any disapplication. HMRC provides the following guidance on certificate formats (*VATLP22320*)

> A charity might ask you whether HMRC has provided a certificate for them to complete in order to disapply the option. To date, we have not provided a

certificate for this purpose. Our longstanding policy, which has been agreed with representatives of the charity and property sectors, is that it is sufficient for the charity to inform the vendor/landlord of the intended use, before the supply is made, in order to disapply the option (if the charity does not inform the vendor/landlord, the option to tax applies). However, we strongly recommend that the charity informs the vendor/landlord in writing and that the vendor/landlord retains this written confirmation. Some charities choose to use an adapted version of the certificate in section 17, *Notice 708 Buildings and construction* for this purpose.

Charities should note that disapplication of a supplier's option to tax may be disadvantageous. For example, if the supply contract specifies that the stated price is inclusive of any VAT, then the contract price will remain the same whether or not the supplier's option to tax is disapplied. If, without disapplication, the VAT charged would be wholly or partly recoverable, then the charity would be better off not disapplying the option to tax.

Housing associations

An option to tax has no effect in relation to the supply of any freehold of, lease in or licence to occupy land made to a **relevant housing association** if the association certifies that the land is to be used (after any necessary demolition work) for the construction of a building or buildings intended for use:

Relevant housing association means a private registered provider of social housing or a registered social landlord under Part 1 Housing Act 1996 or Welsh, Scottish or Northern Ireland equivalents.

(a) as a dwelling or number of dwellings; or

(b) solely for a relevant residential purpose.

The association must give a completed certificate VAT 1614G to the person making the grant ('the seller'):

• before the price for the grant to the recipient by the seller is legally fixed, for example exchange of contracts, by missives or letters, or the signing of heads of agreement; or

• if the seller agrees, at any later time before the seller makes a supply to which the grant gives rise. However, the certificate does not affect supplies made before the certificate is given.

Land supplied to an individual for construction of a dwelling

An option to tax has no effect in relation to any grant made to an individual if:

(a) the land is to be used for the construction of a building intended for use by the individual as a dwelling; and

(b) the construction is not carried out in the course or furtherance of a business carried on by the individual.

No certificate is required. This scenario includes cases where the purchaser intends to engage a builder to carry out the construction work on their behalf.

Anti-avoidance: developers of land, etc.

The purpose of the anti-avoidance is broadly to prevent businesses from gaining a cash flow advantage by structuring property developments via a separate connected entity that has opted to tax the property. The HMRC guidance explains that the anti-avoidance measure disapplies an option to tax on a supply if three conditions are all met at the time of the grant (*VAT Notice 742A*, section 13.2). The grantor is the person supplying the property and the grantee is the person receiving the supply of property:

1. The property is, or is expected to become, a capital item for the purposes of the Capital Goods Scheme, either for the grantor, a person treated as the grantor or the grantee. Persons treated as the grantor are persons connected to the grantor, a person who has provided finance for the development and persons connected to a person who has provided finance for the development.
2. It is the intention or expectation of the grantor or the person treated as the grantor or a person responsible for financing the grantor's acquisition or development, that the building will be occupied by them or a person connected with them.
3. The person occupying the property will be doing so less than 80% for eligible purposes. Eligible purposes are making taxable business supplies, occupation by a local authority (or other s. 33 body) for its non-business activities or occupation by a government department (including NHS bodies, etc.), but not by an academy school, hospice, search and rescue charity, etc.

See 10.1 'Capital Goods Scheme' for more on the meaning of capital item and the scheme in general. There are two exemptions from this rule:

- **The 10% rule for development financiers**: if the person in occupation is not the grantor or a person connected to the grantor, the anti-avoidance rule can be ignored if there is no intention or expectation at the time of the grant that the development financier (or a person connected to a development financier) will occupy more than 10% of any building (or part of a building) included in the grant at any time during the grantor's Capital Goods Scheme (CGS) adjustment period.
- **The 2% rule for grantors**: if the person in occupation is the grantor or a person connected to the grantor the anti-avoidance rule can be ignored if there is no intention or expectation at the time of the grant that the grantor (or a person connected to a grantor) will occupy more than 2% of any building (or

303

part of a building) included in the grant at any time during the grantor's CGS adjustment period.

The conditions are not satisfied where the person occupies any land included in the grant which is not a building. However, the occupation of land that falls within the curtilage of the building or is used for parking vehicles can be disregarded as long as such occupation is ancillary to that of the building.

The proportion of a 'relevant building' occupied is to be calculated using the recommended practices set out in the current version of *RICS Property Measurement* (RICS 2015; formerly the *Code of Measuring Practice*). The following parts of the building must be excluded: any part which is not available for exclusive occupation; any part intended primarily for use for vehicle parking; any part which is land forming part of the curtilage of the building.

8.5.2 Permission to opt to tax

If you have not made any exempt supply of the property within the last ten years you can opt to tax a property without having to meet HMRC's automatic permission conditions or obtain HMRC's permission. However, if you have made, or intend to make, any exempt supplies of the land or buildings within the ten years prior to the date you wish your option to take effect, you will need HMRC's written permission to opt to tax unless you meet one or more of the automatic permission conditions set out in section 5.2 of *VAT Notice 742A*.

At the time of writing you (broadly) have automatic permission if any of the following four conditions are met:

1. **Mixed-use development**: it is a mixed-use development and the only exempt supplies have been in relation to the dwellings.
2. **No prior recovery**: you do not wish to recover any input tax in relation to the land or building incurred before your option to tax has effect, and the consideration for your exempt supplies has, up to the date when your option to tax is to take effect, been solely by way of rents or service charges and excludes any premiums or payments in respect of occupation after the date on which the option takes effect. The only input tax relating to the land or building that you expect to recover after the option to tax takes effect must be on overheads, such as regular rental payments, service charges, repairs and maintenance costs. If you expect to claim input tax in relation to refurbishment or redevelopment of the building you will not meet this condition.
3. **Incidental supplies**: the exempt supplies have been incidental to the main use of the land or building. For example, where you have occupied a building for taxable purposes the following would be seen as incidental to the main use and the condition would be met: (i) allowing an advertising hoarding to be

displayed; (ii) granting space for the erection of a radio mast; or (iii) receiving income from an electricity sub-station. The letting of space to an occupying tenant, however minor, is not incidental.

4. **No special arrangement**: you may opt to tax if you satisfy the first (outputs) requirement and (if applicable) the second (inputs) requirement.

First (outputs) requirement

You do not intend or expect that any supply which will be taxable as a result of your making your option to tax will either:

1. be made to a person connected with you; or
2. arise from an agreement under which you or another person has made or will make an exempt supply in respect of a right to occupy the property, where the right begins or continues after the date on which the option takes effect.

You may disregard condition (1) if the person connected with you is expected to be entitled to credit or refund of at least 80% of the VAT chargeable on the supply. For the purposes of condition (2) you may ignore permissible exempt supplies. These are supplies for which the consideration solely represents legal and/or valuation costs reimbursed under the agreement for the grant, or supplies where:

(i)   the consideration is provided by way of regular rents and/or service charges; and
(ii) the consideration relates to a period of occupation of the property and that period ends no later than 12 months from the date on which the option first takes effect; and
(iii) no opted supply, other than an opted supply relating solely to the same period of occupation as an exempt supply under point (ii) above, will be reduced in value as a result of the consideration payable for these exempt supplies.

Second (inputs) requirement

This requirement applies if you have been or expect to be entitled to credit for any part of the input tax incurred on your capital expenditure on the property as being wholly or partly attributable to supplies that are taxable supplies by virtue of your option to tax. Where this requirement applies you must not intend or expect to use any part of the capital expenditure for either of the following purposes:

1. making exempt supplies which do not confer a right to credit for input tax; or
2. for private or non-business purposes, other than purposes giving rise to a right to a refund of VAT on the supplies under sections 33, 33a or 41(3) of the VAT Act 1994.

You may disregard condition (1) if any the following apply:

(a) all the exempt supplies concerned are supplies which fulfil any of the following descriptions:

   (i) supplies capable of disapplication and made to a person who is not connected to you;

   (ii) permissible exempt supplies (see the first inputs requirement for the definition of permissible exempt supplies);

   (iii) financial services which are incidental to one or more of your business activities.

(b) you make exempt supplies, but intend or expect that the input tax incurred on your capital expenditure on the property that is attributed to those exempt supplies, including any subsequent adjustments to initial input tax deduction, will not exceed £5,000;

(c) you expect to be entitled to full credit for all the input tax incurred on your capital expenditure on the property as a result of the application of section 33(2) of the VAT Act 1994 (*de minimis* rules for local authorities, etc.).

An application for permission to opt to tax must be made on form VAT1614H and must contain the information requested on that form.

8.5.3 Exclusion of a new building from an option to tax

If you construct a new building on land that you have opted to tax (and the new building is not within the curtilage of an existing building) you may exclude the new building (and land within its curtilage) from the effect of the option to tax by notifying HMRC of the exclusion on form VAT1614F. If you decide to do this, the new building will be permanently excluded from the effect of your existing option to tax. But you may, if you wish, make a fresh option to tax in the future, subject to obtaining permission from HMRC if necessary.

The earliest time that you can exclude a building from the effect of an option to tax is when construction begins. Construction of a building begins when it progresses above the level of the building's foundations. Exclusion has effect from the earliest of the following times:

- when a grant of an interest in the building is first made;
- when the new building, or any part of it, is first used; or
- when the new building is completed.

Notification must be made after construction has begun and, normally, within 30 days of the date the exclusion has effect. A longer period may be allowed in exceptional circumstances.

8.5.4   **Relevant associates**

An option to tax made by a member of a VAT group is generally binding upon all members of the same VAT group. The other members of the VAT group are the member's 'relevant associates'. If you are a relevant associate, you must normally charge VAT on any supplies you make of the opted property, even, in some situations, after you have left the VAT group.

Becoming a relevant associate

You become a relevant associate if:

- you are in the same VAT group as the opter when the option first has effect;
- you are in the same VAT group as the opter at any later time when the opter has an interest in the opted property; or
- you are in the same VAT group as another relevant associate of the opter when that relevant associate has an interest in the opted property.

Ceasing to be a relevant associate

You can cease to be a relevant associate by:

1. meeting the statutory conditions; or
2. meeting HMRC's automatic permission conditions; or
3. obtaining HMRC's permission.

1. **Statutory conditions**: you must meet all of the following conditions:

   - you are no longer in the VAT group in which you became a relevant associate;
   - you do not hold any interest in the opted property;
   - you have not disposed of the opted property on terms that may require the purchaser to make additional payment in the future. Such payment is often referred to as an 'overage' and can be contingent on such things as the purchaser obtaining planning permission; and
   - you are not 'connected' with any person who is the opter or relevant associate and who holds an interest in the land.

   If you meet all of these conditions, you automatically cease to be a relevant associate from the time that all four conditions are met. There is no need for you to notify HMRC or to seek HMRC's permission.

2. **HMRC automatic permission conditions**: you must meet all of the conditions specified in section 6.3.5 of *VAT Notice 742A* and notify HMRC on form VAT1614B.
3. **Permission**: permission should be sought by completing form VAT1614B and must contain the information requested on that form.

8.5.5 Land and buildings covered

An option to tax has effect in relation to the particular property specified in the option, subject to the following conditions:

- If an option to tax is exercised in relation to a building, or part of a building, the option has effect in relation to the whole of the building and all the land within its curtilage.
- If an option to tax is exercised in relation to any land, but is not exercised by reference to a building or part of a building, the option is nonetheless taken to have effect in relation to any building which is (or is to be) constructed on the land as well as in relation to land on which no building is constructed.
- Buildings linked internally or by a covered walkway, and complexes consisting of a number of units grouped around a fully enclosed concourse, are treated as a single building. But buildings which are linked internally are not treated as a single building if the internal link is created after the buildings are completed, and buildings which are linked by a covered walkway are not treated as a single building if the walkway starts to be constructed after the buildings are completed. Covered walkway does not include a covered walkway to which the general public has reasonable access.
- A building includes: an enlarged or extended building; an annexe to a building; and a planned building.

Before 1 March 1995, slightly different rules applied to determine the scope of an option to tax. These rules will still apply if, before 1 March 1995, you opted to tax agricultural land, or units within a parade, precinct or complex (such as a row of shops or a retail precinct). If you have any queries about the scope of an option to tax exercised before 1 March 1995 in relation to agricultural land or a parade, precinct or complex you can contact the HMRC Option to Tax Unit (see 14.1 'Contacting HM Revenue & Customs')

8.5.6 Effective date

An option to tax has effect from the start of the day on which it is exercised, or the start of any later day specified in the option. An option to tax cannot be backdated, though HMRC can accept a backdated notification, as explained below.

8.5.7 Notification requirements

An option to tax has effect only if:

(a) notification of the option is given to HMRC within 30 days of the day on which the decision to opt to tax was made; and

(b) notification is given together with such information as HMRC may require.

HMRC recommends that a decision to opt to tax a property is recorded in writing, for example by being recorded in the minutes of a board meeting. HMRC can accept a belated notification beyond the 30 day deadline. HMRC states (*VAT Notice 742A*, section 4.2):

> We will normally accept a belated notification if:
>
> - you provide direct documentary evidence that the decision was made at the relevant time (e.g. copies of correspondence with third parties referring to the option to tax), or
> - you provide evidence that output tax has been charged and accounted for and input tax claimed in accordance with the option; and a responsible person (such as a director) provides a written declaration that the decision to opt was made at the relevant time and that all relevant facts have been given.
>
> We might accept a belated notification in other circumstances. This will depend on the facts of your case.

HMRC provides form VAT1614A for notifying an option to tax which is available on gov.uk. Using the form should help ensure that you provide all the information required by HMRC. HMRC aims to acknowledge receipt of a notification within 15 working days, although this is not necessary for the option to tax to have legal effect. You should not delay charging VAT just because you have not received HMRC's acknowledgement.

8.5.8 Real Estate Elections

A Real Estate Election (REE) is a formal decision to opt to tax all future property acquisitions. It has to be notified to HMRC. If you make a REE, you will be treated as if you have made an option to tax in relation to every property in which you subsequently acquire an interest, subject to the exceptions below.

Each property you acquire will be treated as separately opted, with effect from the time of acquisition. Each of these options is capable of being revoked under the six-month cooling-off rule if the conditions for revocation are met and as requiring permission from HMRC to opt to tax if permission to opt to tax the property is required (for which see 8.5.2).

For a REE to have legal effect, you need to notify the REE itself to HMRC but once you have made a REE, there is no need for you to notify HMRC of an option to tax each time you acquire an interest in a property. You will, however, need to keep records and provide HMRC with information if it is requested.

For existing properties, if you have already opted the property, that option continues in place; however, if you have already disposed of a property that old option is revoked in some circumstances. See *VAT Notice 742A*, section 14.

8.5.9 Revoking an option to tax: six-month cooling-off period

An option to tax any property exercised by any person ('the taxpayer') may be revoked with effect from the day on which it was exercised if:

(a) the time that has lapsed since the day on which the option had effect is less than six months; and

(b) the taxpayer has not used the land since the option had effect;

(c) no tax has become chargeable as a result of the option;

(d) there is no relevant TOGC;

(e) notification of the revocation is given to HMRC on form VAT1614C; and

(f) any conditions which HMRC may specify are met.

The HMRC conditions are set out in section 8.1.2 of *VAT Notice 742A*; alternatively you can seek HMRC's permission. Where HMRC grants permission it may impose conditions. The conditions set out in the VAT Notice are:

1. neither the person who exercised the option to tax ('the opter') nor any relevant associate of the opter has recovered 'extra property input tax'; extra property input tax means input tax attributable to supplies which, if made at a time when the option has effect, would be taxable supplies by virtue of the option;

2. by virtue of the revocation, the opter and all relevant associates of the opter would be liable to account to [HMRC] for all of the extra property input tax they have recovered; or

3. extra property input tax has been recovered entirely on one capital item and amounts to less than 20% of the total input tax incurred on that item; 'Capital item' means a capital item for the purposes of the Capital Goods Scheme.

8.5.10 Revocation of option – lapse of six years since having a relevant interest

An option to tax is automatically revoked where the opter has not held an interest in the opted building or land for a continuous period of six years commencing at any time after the option to tax took effect. The revocation is automatic and no notification is required.

However, an option to tax is not revoked in any of the following scenarios:

1. Where the opter or a relevant associate of the opter has sold the property on terms that may require the purchaser to make additional payment after the revocation date – for example under an overage agreement.

2. Where before the revocation date a relevant associate of the opter in relation to the opted property left the opter's VAT group and at the time of leaving any of the following applied:

    (i) the relevant associate had an interest in the property;

(ii) the relevant associate had, prior to leaving the VAT group, disposed of an interest on terms that might have required the purchaser to make additional payment at a later date; or

(iii) the relevant associate was connected to the opter or another relevant associate of the opter and that person had an interest in the property.

3. Where, at the revocation date, a relevant associate of the opter in relation to the opted property is a member of the same VAT group and either currently holds an interest in the property or has held one during the previous six years.

8.5.11 Revocation of option: lapse of more than 20 years

An option to tax any land exercised by any person ('the taxpayer') may be revoked if the time that has lapsed since the day on which the option had effect is more than 20 years and either:

(i) the conditions set out in a public notice by HMRC are met; or
(ii) HMRC's permission is sought and obtained.

HMRC provides form VAT1614J which must be used to notify a 20-year revocation. HMRC's conditions are as follows (*VAT Notice 742A*, section 8.3). Either condition 1 must be met or all of conditions 2 to 5 must be met:

1. **The relevant interest condition**: Neither the taxpayer nor any relevant associate connected with the taxpayer has a relevant interest in the building or land at the time when the option is revoked, and, if the taxpayer or a relevant associate of the taxpayer has disposed of such an interest, no supply for the purpose of the charge to VAT in respect of the disposal –
   (i) is yet to take place; or
   (ii) would be yet to take place if one or more conditions (such as the happening of an event or the doing of an act) were to be met.
   'Relevant interest in the building or land' means an interest in, right over or licence to occupy the building or land (or any part of it).

2. **The 20 year condition**: The taxpayer or a relevant associate connected with the taxpayer held a relevant interest in the building or land: after the time from which the option had effect, and more than 20 years before the option is revoked.

3. **The capital item condition**: Any land or building that is subject to the option at the time when it is revoked does not fall, in relation to the taxpayer or a relevant associate connected with the taxpayer, for input tax adjustment as a capital item under part 15 of the Value Added Tax Regulations 1995 (Capital Goods Scheme).

4. **The valuation condition**: Neither the taxpayer nor any relevant associate connected to the taxpayer has made a supply of a relevant interest in the building or land subject to the option in the ten years immediately before

revocation of the option that: (i) was for a consideration that was less than the open market value of that supply, or (ii) arose from a relevant grant.

5. **The pre-payment condition**: No part of a supply of goods or services made for consideration to the taxpayer or a relevant associate connected with the taxpayer before the option is revoked will be attributable to a supply or other use of the land or buildings by the taxpayer more than 12 months after the option is revoked.

8.6 PROPERTY TERMS

8.6.1 Land, buildings and civil engineering works

- **Land** is an area of the surface of the Earth including land under water.
- **Immoveable property** includes any structure fixed in or to the ground. It can include structures fixed to walls, trees, etc.
- A **building** is a built structure fixed in or to the ground that encloses space and has a roof. It excludes structures such as a wall around a cemetery, an outdoor skate park and easily moveable structures such as a tent or marquee, though sheds fixed to concrete bases that can be moved only with difficulty are buildings.
- **Civil engineering works** are other types of built structure fixed in or to the ground including walls, roads, bridges and constructed outdoors sports or recreational facilities such as an outdoor skate park, running track or tennis court.

8.6.2 Freeholds, leases and licences to occupy

In English property law, the **freehold** of property is the most complete interest in property that can be held (outside the Crown). Freehold means the outright ownership of property for an unlimited period of time.

A **lease** is a grant of a right of exclusive possession of property for a **term certain**. Exclusive possession means that the tenant has the ability to exercise the rights of the owner, in particular the right to exclude any person from the property, though a landlord can reserve the right to inspect, carry out repairs, etc. A lease must also have consideration, though this does not have to be monetary and it can be for a peppercorn rent. Consideration for the grant of a lease can comprise an upfront **premium** and/or periodic payments of **rent**.

> **Term certain** means broadly that the maximum duration of the lease must be ascertainable at its commencement.

A **long lease** is:

- in England, Wales and Northern Ireland: a tenancy for a term certain exceeding 21 years;

- in Scotland: the lessee's interest under a lease for a period of not less than 20 years.

A **short lease** is a lease that is not a long lease. This includes a lease that is terminable at will or after a short notice period.

A **major interest** in property is the freehold or a long lease in the property.

A **licence to occupy** is a limited permission to occupy property. It is a permission that does not create any transferable interest in the property for the licensee.

8.6.3 Qualifying and non-qualifying buildings

Qualifying buildings are any of the following:

1. A **relevant charitable purpose building** is one that is (at the time of the supply concerned) intended for use solely for a **relevant charitable purpose**.
2. A **relevant residential purpose building** is one that is (at the time of the supply concerned) intended for use solely for a relevant residential purpose.
3. A **dwelling** is self-contained living accommodation that meets various physical and legal requirements.

A **non-qualifying building** is a building that is not a qualifying building. See below for the meanings of **intended for use**, **solely**, **relevant charitable purpose**, **relevant residential purpose** and **dwelling**.

8.6.4 Intended for use

For relevant charitable and relevant residential purpose buildings, it is the intended use at the tax point of the supply that counts. However, if subsequent use is different, some of the VAT saved by zero-rating may have to be repaid to HMRC (see 8.3.13 'Change of use rules').

8.6.5 Meaning of 'use'

Use in this context means the occupational or physical use of the building, not its economic use. If a landlord lets occupation of a building to a tenant, then the occupational use of the building is the tenant's use, not the landlord's letting.

In *Customs & Excise* v. *St Dunstan's Educational Foundation* [1999] STC 381, a charitable foundation leased a sports hall to a fee-paying charitable school for free. The Court of Appeal held that the word 'use' in this context does not include the activity of leasing a building, so the use of the building was the fee-paying school's (business) use, not the Foundation's free (non-business) lease.

8.6.6 **Meaning of solely**

Solely means that the building or part must be intended for use wholly for relevant charitable or residential purposes. So a building (or part) intended for use partly for relevant charitable or residential purposes and partly for some other purpose or purposes is not eligible for zero-rating.

However, a *de minimis* level of non-qualifying use can be ignored. HMRC, in *VAT Information Sheet 08/09*, accepts that the term 'solely' incorporates a *de minimis* level of non-qualifying use of up to 5%, calculated on any basis that is fair and reasonable.

Before 1 July 2010 HMRC provided an extra-statutory concession (*VAT Notice 48*, section 3.29) that permitted up to 10% of non-qualifying use to be ignored as *de minimis*. If this concession was used to zero rate a building or part, it can still be relied on. See 8.3.13 'Change of use rules'.

8.6.7 **Relevant charitable purpose**

Use for a relevant charitable purpose means use by a charity in either or both the following ways:

(a) otherwise than in the course or furtherance of a business; or
(b) as a village hall or similarly in providing social or recreational facilities for a local community.

Option (a) refers to use by a charity for non-business activities. See Chapter 4 'Business and non-business activities' for the meaning of non-business activity.

Options (a) and (b) are alternatives, so business use is permissible under option (b) – the **village hall** option. See the next section, 8.6.8.

8.6.8 **'Village hall or similarly'**

Use as a 'village hall or similarly' refers to use of buildings, such as traditional village halls, community centres, church halls, scout or guide huts and multi-purpose use buildings attached to charitable playing fields and recreation grounds, to provide social or recreational facilities for a local community.

In *Customs & Excise* v. *Jubilee Hall Recreation Centre* [1999] STC 381, the judge explained the purpose of the 'village hall option' (sub-para (b)) as follows:

> the plain purpose of sub-para (b) was in my judgment to extend the relief in sub-para (a) to the case where a local community is the final consumer in respect of the supply of the services, including the reconstruction of a building, in the sense that the local community is the user of the services (through a body of trustees or a management committee acting on its behalf) and in which the only economic

activity is one in which they participate directly; the obvious examples are the bring-and-buy or jumble sale, the performance of a play by local players and the like. On a strict construction, any economic activity carried on by somebody outside the local community even to raise money for the maintenance of a village hall (by, for example, letting the village hall at a commercial rate) would be outside sub-para (b)...

Sub-paragraph (b) is intended to cover economic activities which are an ordinary incident of the use of a building by a local community for social, including recreational, purposes. The village hall is the model or paradigm of that case.

HMRC provides the following guidance in *VAT Notice 708*, section 14.7.4:

Village halls and similar buildings

A building falls within this category when the following characteristics are present:

- there is a high degree of local community involvement in the building's operation and activities, and
- there is a wide variety of activities carried on in the building, the majority of which are for social and/or recreational purposes (including sporting).

NB: Users of the building need not be confined to the local community but can come from further afield. Any part of the building which cannot be used for a variety of social or recreational activities cannot be seen as being used as a village hall.

The term 'similar' refers to buildings run by communities that are not villages but who are organised in a similar way to a village hall committee. It does not include buildings that provide a range of activities associated with village halls but who are not organised on these lines. In order to be similar to a village hall, a charity would have trustees who are drawn from representatives of local groups who intend to use the hall. The trustees would therefore be made up of individuals from say the Women's Institute, the Bridge Club, the Amateur Dramatics Society, etc. The building would be hired out to the local community for a modest fee for use by a range of local clubs and groups, and also for wedding receptions, birthday parties, playgroups and other leisure interests. Whilst, the size, and level of provision and facilities will be decided by the local community, we would at the very least expect the principal feature of a village hall to be a large multi-purpose hall where members of different households can meet to undertake shared activities.

The emphasis for a village hall should be on promoting the use of the facilities for the benefit of the whole community rather than for the benefit of one particular group. An important characteristic is that the building must be available for use by all sectors of the community. It must therefore be capable of meeting the social and recreational needs of the local community at large and not be predominantly confined to a special interest group. It should also be arranged on a first come first served basis and no single group should have priority over all the others.

On the other hand, a building designed for a particular sporting activity, for example, a cricket pavilion or football clubhouse and ancillary facilities is not seen as being similar to a village hall. Whilst these types of buildings are often made available to the wider community; this would be required to fit in around the sports club's usage. In essence it would be the sports club who would determine how the building was to be used and not the wider community.

Buildings that are not typically seen as being similar to village halls are: community swimming pools; community theatres; membership clubs (although community associations charging a notional membership fee can be excluded); or community amateur sports clubs.

Buildings that are seen as being similar to village halls when the characteristics noted above are present: scout or guide huts (please note that where scout or guide huts are used purely for scouting and guiding activities, they are not being used as village halls but neither are they being used for business purposes); sports pavilions; church halls; community centres; and community sports centres.

However, case law suggests the zero-rating is rather wider than the HMRC guidance suggests.

In *Sport In Desford* [2005] VTD 18914, the VAT Tribunal found that the construction of a sports clubhouse qualified for zero-rating. The clubhouse comprised a fitness room, a squash court, two small kitchens, a function room, a bar, changing rooms and showers, stores, and a multi-use dance studio. The VAT Tribunal decided it is not necessary for the activities to encompass the same mix of activities as one would expect to find in a village hall. The essence of the test of similarity is to distinguish between, on the one hand, community buildings where the supply in reality is to the community as such, and, on the other hand, buildings which are commercial operations.

In *New Deer Community Association* v. *Revenue & Customs* [2014] UKFTT 1028 (TC), a charity replaced a small changing pavilion attached to a football pitch with a larger one, comprising two changing rooms plus showers, toilets, facilities for referees, a lobby, a kitchen and a small meeting room. By the time of the case the pavilion was finished and had been used by a variety of local groups. The First-tier Tribunal decided that only the kitchen and meeting room had the multi-use ability required to be 'use as a village hall or similarly'. The changing rooms and lobby were not practical for varied use and, as they were single purpose, they did not qualify.

However, in *Caithness Rugby Club* v. *Revenue & Customs* [2015] UKFTT 378 (TC), the First-tier Tribunal decided the entire construction of a clubhouse by a charitable rugby club qualified for zero-rating on the basis its use was in fact 90% by the local community for social or recreational activities and only 10% by the rugby club for its own activities. The clubhouse comprised four changing rooms, a main hall, a kitchen/bar area, toilets, an officials' room, a store room and a boiler room. Contrary to HMRC's position, the fact that the clubhouse was not owned, organised and administered by the local community did not prohibit zero-rating, nor did the fact there was occasional use by commercial organisations or persons from outside the local area. In the context of a rural area such as Caithness, the First-tier Tribunal considered the geographic size of a local community may be significantly larger than in an urban area.

8.6.9 Relevant residential purpose

Use of a building for a relevant residential purpose means use of that building as:

(a) a home or other institution providing residential accommodation for children;
(b) a home or other institution providing residential accommodation with personal care for persons in need of personal care by reason of old age, disablement, past or present dependence on alcohol or drugs or past or present mental disorder;
(c) a hospice;
(d) residential accommodation for students or school pupils;
(e) residential accommodation for members of any of the armed forces;
(f) a monastery, nunnery or similar establishment; or
(g) an institution which is the sole or main residence of at least 90% of its residents.

However, use of a building for a relevant residential purpose excludes use as:

• a hospital, prison or similar institution or
• a hotel, inn or similar establishment.

Hospices

At the time of writing HMRC's guidance (*VCONST15300*) states that a hospice building only falls within the meaning of 'relevant residential purpose' to the extent that it contains residential accommodation. Day hospices that do not provide residential accommodation are not used for a 'relevant residential purpose'. However, day hospice buildings may qualify for zero-rating under the relevant charitable purpose option (see above).

It is understood that HMRC has agreed that a hospice building can qualify as relevant residential purpose as long as it contains at least one patient bed, that is, non-residential areas can be ignored if this condition is met. However, this policy change has not yet been announced publicly.

Buildings constructed together

Where a number of buildings are constructed at the same time and on the same site and are intended to be used together as a unit solely for a relevant residential purpose, then each of those buildings is to be treated as intended for use solely for a relevant residential purpose.

For example, if student accommodation and a separate ancillary laundry building are constructed at the same time, then the construction of the laundry building also qualifies for relief. However, if the laundry building is constructed separately, it is not student accommodation in and of itself, and so does not qualify.

Distinction between homes, institutions and residential accommodation

The above building types divide into two groups:

- institutional buildings – homes, institutions and establishments, – see (a), (b), (c), (f) and (g) under 8.6.9;
- residential accommodation – see (d) and (e) under 8.6.9.

HMRC explains the distinction as follows (*VCONST15130*):

> With residential accommodation, relief is limited to living space inclusive of leisure and recreational facilities (such as library, games room) and ancillary facilities (for example, storage, boiler room). Residential accommodation may offer fewer or more amenities than those present in a dwelling, and can be simply overnight accommodation… At its barest, 'residential accommodation' can comprise simply of sleeping accommodation… This must always be present before accepting that accommodation is residential.

> Although the extent of the residential accommodation can be much broader, such as including kitchen and eating areas, such facilities aren't residential accommodation when provided on their own.

> In contrast, a home or institution may consist of more than the residential accommodation, and can include recreational and occupational facilities and administration areas. For example, a residential care home for the elderly may include a hairdressing salon or a handicrafts room. Thus, more can be relieved as a home or institution than the residential accommodation because it is the home or institution that qualifies for relief and not simply its residential element.

Home or institution

In *Wallis Ltd* v. *Customs & Excise* [2002] UKFTT V18012, the VAT Tribunal rejected HMRC's suggestion that 'institution' refers to an organisation or body as follows:

> In item (g) 'institution' must be referring to a building: a society or organisation cannot be the main residence of its residents. In items (a) and (b) the term must

also be referring to a building; the 'use' is that of a building. In all those cases institution refers to buildings of a certain type, namely buildings used by an organisation or a body; they could be described as institutional buildings.

Student accommodation in the Higher Education Institution (HEI) sector

Under a 1990 agreement (the 'CVCP concession'), HMRC allowed HEIs to ignore vacation use of the building when determining if a building is to be used solely for a relevant residential purpose. This concession is withdrawn with effect from 1 April 2015; however, HEIs with student accommodation which has been zero-rated as a result of using the concession can continue to rely on the concession when determining whether there has been a change in the use of the building for the purposes of the change of use rules (*Revenue & Customs Brief 14/14*).

Student dining halls

In the 1997 version of *VAT Notice 708* HMRC allowed dining rooms and kitchens to be zero-rated as residential accommodation for students and school pupils if they were used 'predominantly' by the living-in students. Although this is not included in later issues, this concession is still in existence. The dining room and/or kitchen must be owned by the educational establishment and not a third party. The concession allows the construction of dining halls to be zero-rated if constructed at the same time as student accommodation and if residents in that student accommodation make up at least 50% of the users of the dining hall. This concession is withdrawn with effect from 1 April 2015. Accommodation providers with dining halls which have been zero-rated as a result of using the concession can continue to rely on the concession to determine whether there has been a change in the use of the building for the purposes of the change of use rules (*Revenue & Customs Brief 14/14*).

Hotels and similar

In *Capernwray Missionary Fellowship of Torchbearers* v. *Revenue & Customs* [2014] UKFTT 626 (TC), the First-tier Tribunal considered that hotels, inns and similar establishments are places to which people resort generally for a short time because of work or for a holiday.

Relevant residential purpose and dwellings

HMRC accepts (*VAT Information Sheet 02/14*) that a building can be both intended for use solely for a relevant residential purpose and designed as a dwelling or dwellings (see below for the meaning of designed as a dwelling). In such a situation the change of use rules do not apply if there is a change from relevant residential use within the first ten years of use, as the change of use rules do not apply to buildings designed as dwellings.

8.6.10 Dwellings

To be 'designed as a dwelling or dwellings' a building must meet all of the following four conditions:

1. The building consists of self-contained living accommodation. To be self-contained, the accommodation must contain all the facilities that are normally associated with a dwelling, such as access to a public highway, sleeping, washing, toilet and cooking facilities, though cooking facilities can be limited, for example to a fridge, kettle, and microwave. Where essential facilities are shared with another dwelling or lacking, this will prevent it from being self-contained.
2. There is no provision for direct internal access from the dwelling to any other dwelling or part of a dwelling. Internal fire doors for use in an emergency only are allowed.
3. The separate use, or disposal of the dwelling, is not prohibited by the term of any covenant, statutory planning consent or similar provision. This condition precludes most annexes, self-contained extensions and accommodation attached to property such as caretakers' flats. However, the condition does not preclude restriction on the type of occupant, for example by age, disability or occupation, nor does it preclude the ability to dispose of the freehold whilst being restricted as to disposal of leases.
4. Statutory planning consent has been granted in respect of that dwelling and its construction or conversion has been carried out in accordance with that consent. This condition is dropped in the case of the zero-rating provisions for protected buildings (see 8.3.4 'Substantially reconstructed protected buildings'), as in many cases the building will have been constructed before statutory planning consent was introduced.

The Town and Country Planning (Use Classes) Order 1987 puts uses of land and buildings into various categories known as 'Use Classes'. Dwellings will normally fall into use classes C3 Dwellinghouses and C4 Houses in multiple occupation. In *Revenue & Customs Brief 47/11* HMRC accepts that extra care accommodation classified as C2 (residential institutions) can qualify as 'designed as a dwelling' if conditions (1) to (4) above are met. Extra care accommodation is self-contained flats, houses, bungalows or maisonettes that are sold or let with the option for the occupant to purchase varying degrees of care. It does not apply to accommodation where the occupant needs care or supervision of a type typically provided by an institution.

If statutory planning consent is not required, or if the planning authority advises that no such consent is required, then condition (d) is met. In *Sally Cottam* [2007] VTD 20036, the VAT Tribunal said, in relation to conversion works that did not require statutory planning consent:

> we note that there is no suggestion that the present conversion was carried out in an unauthorized manner. This leaves only the question of whether planning permission was granted in respect of Greengage Cottage. The words of [condition (d)] do not, as we read them, require the works of conversion to have been the subject of a formal planning application resulting in the issue of a consent notice. Properly understood, those words mean that so long as, by virtue of the statutory planning regime, consent has been granted, the condition is satisfied. The nature of the consent is left to the circumstances of the conversion. Where, as here, the conversion is carried out in pursuance of the relevant Planning Act or a general consent and the Act and/or on the strength of an assurance by the planning authority that the statutory regime allows conversion without further formality, then we think that the [condition (d)] will have been satisfied.

8.6.11 **Annexes**

An annexe is a supplementary structure to another building or buildings that either has no integration or only tenuous integration with the existing building or buildings. It should be visually distinct from and not an enlargement of or extension to an existing building or buildings. In *Abercych Village Association* [2008] VTD 20746, the VAT Tribunal explained the distinction between extensions, enlargements and annexes as follows:

> In MacNamara [1999] VTD 16032 the tribunal described the scheme of (the law) thus: 'The scheme of the (law) is to exclude from the expression 'construction of a building' a series of building works. (The law) deals with these in descending order of their degree of integration with the existing building. Conversions, reconstructions and the alterations of existing buildings, the most closely integrated, are excluded. Enlargements of existing buildings are then excluded... Then come annexes which, as a matter of principle, are also excluded...'

> This description... shows that what is being excluded from zero-rating are works which are integrated into the existing building. That pattern is carried on into (annexes): it is only those annexes which are sufficiently un-integrated which can escape into zero-rating.

> In the same paragraph the tribunal gave its views on the meanings of enlargement, extension and annexe:... the word enlargement connoting structural work producing an overall increase in size or capacity. The word 'extension' in relation to an existing building refers... to building work which provides an additional section or wing to that existing building; the degree of association is one stage less than with enlargements. The term 'annexe' connotes something which is adjoined but either not integrated with the existing building or of tenuous integration.

In *Cantrell (t/a Foxearth Lodge Nursing Home)* v. *Customs & Excise Commissioners* [2000] EWHC (Admin) 283, the annexe tests were explained as follows:

> The two stage test for determining whether the works carried out constituted an enlargement, extension or annexe to an existing building is well established. It requires an examination and comparison of the building as it was or (if more than one) the buildings as they were before the Works were carried out and the building or buildings as they will be after the Works are completed; and the question then to be asked is whether the completed Works amount to the enlargement of or the construction of an extension or annexe to the original building...

> It is necessary to examine the pre-existing building or buildings and the building or buildings in course of construction when the supply is made. What is in the course of construction at the date of supply is in any ordinary case (save for example where a dramatic change is later made in the plans) what is subsequently constructed.

> Secondly the answer must be given after an objective examination of the physical characters of the building or buildings at the two points in time, having regard (inter alia) to similarities and differences in appearance, the layout, the uses for which they are physically capable of being put and the functions which they are physically capable of performing.

> The terms of planning permissions, the motives behind undertaking the works and the intended or subsequent actual use are irrelevant, save possibly to illuminate the potential for use inherent in the building or buildings.

Note that even if a building is a new annexe, it must meet two further conditions before zero-rating applies. See 8.3.2 'Qualifying new buildings'.

8.6.12 **Construction and building services**

These are any services related to the construction or other qualifying building works other than the services of an architect, surveyor or any person acting as a consultant or in a supervisory capacity. They include the services of builders, snagging works, and any other service closely connected to the construction of the building.

HMRC accepts (*VAT Notice 708*, section 3.3) that closely connected services can include: demolition, providing or improving access, ground works (including the levelling and drainage of land), site clearance, security, mains and services connections, site access works (such as roads, footpaths, parking areas, drives and patios), construction of boundary features such as walls, fences and gates, the provision of soft landscaping within the site of a building (such as the application of topsoil, seeding with grass or laying turf).

HMRC would not see the planting of shrubs, trees and flowers as normally being 'closely connected...' except to the extent that it is detailed on a landscaping scheme approved by a planning authority under the terms of a planning consent condition. This does not include the replacement of trees and shrubs that die, or become damaged or diseased.

HMRC examples of work (summarised from *VAT Notice 708*, sections 3.3.5/6) that is unconnected to the construction of a building are:

- the provision of on-site catering;
- the cleaning of site offices;
- landscaping (other than the landscaping described above);
- the provision of outdoor leisure facilities for a dwelling such as tennis courts and swimming pools (although the provision of a playground at a school would qualify as it is needed for the school to be used);
- works outside the site of the building (other than those described above), including where that work is carried out under a 'planning gain' agreement with a planning authority;
- site investigation or demolition work that is carried out before planning permission for the construction of a building that qualifies for the zero rate has been granted;
- services for a building (water, electricity) installed on land which is to be sold as building land where it is not clear that the construction of a building that qualifies for the zero rate will take place shortly afterwards;
- work that is delayed until after the building is complete owing to an insufficiency of funds.

8.6.13 **Building materials**

Building materials are goods of a description ordinarily incorporated by builders in a building of that description or its site. The incorporation of goods in a building includes their installation as fittings. However, building materials:

- *Exclude* finished or prefabricated furniture, *but include* finished or prefabricated furniture designed to be fitted in kitchens.
- *Exclude* materials for the construction of fitted furniture, *but include* materials for the construction of fitted kitchen furniture.
- *Exclude* electrical or gas appliances, *but include* an electrical or gas appliance which is:
  (i)   designed to heat space or water (or both) or to provide ventilation, air cooling, air purification, or dust extraction; or
  (ii) intended for use in a building designed as a number of dwellings and is a door-entry system, a waste disposal unit or a machine for compacting waste; or

(iii) a burglar alarm, a fire alarm, or fire safety equipment or designed solely for the purpose of enabling aid to be summoned in an emergency; or

(iv) a lift or hoist.

- *Exclude* carpets or carpeting material.

If goods are incorporated that are not building materials, then the service of incorporation is zero-rated; however:

- if the builder is supplying construction services – the supply of the goods themselves is VAT standard-rated;
- if a property developer is supplying a zero-rated major interest in the property – the developer is blocked from recovering VAT on the goods via the **builders' block** – for which see 8.6.14 'Builders' block'.

If goods are supplied with a building but not installed (for example free-standing furniture) the goods are regarded as a separate supply.

Meaning of incorporated

HMRC's position (*VAT Notice 708*, section 13.3) is that an article is incorporated in a building or its site when it is fixed in such a way that its fixing or removal would either require the use of tools or result in either the need for remedial work to the fabric of the building (or its site), or substantial damage to the goods themselves. HMRC examples of incorporated materials are built-in, wired-in or plumbed-in appliances such as boilers or wired-in storage heaters but exclude appliances that are merely plugged in, and moveable furniture such as sofas, tables and chairs. However, HMRC does accept that topsoil, trees, shrubs, turf, grass seed and plants are capable of being incorporated.

8.6.14 **Builders' block**

If a freehold or long-lease sale by a property developer is zero-rated, then the developer is blocked from recovering VAT on any goods that are incorporated into the building or its site but are not building materials. However, any necessary installation services qualify for zero-rating.

9 International aspects of VAT

This chapter is divided into the following sections:

- 9.1 Introduction
- 9.2 Recovering foreign VAT
- 9.3 Cross-border goods introduction
- 9.4 Exports
- 9.5 Imports
- 9.6 Intra-EU transfers of goods
- 9.7 Cross-border services introduction
- 9.8 Place of supply of services rules
- 9.9 The Mini One Stop Shop (MOSS)

9.1 INTRODUCTION

This chapter considers the VAT treatment of cross-border supplies. Cross-border supplies occur where the customer and supplier are in different nation states. The UK is treated as a single state for VAT purposes, see 9.1.1 'Territories of the UK and EU'.

As explained in 4.1 'Basic rules', VAT is an EU-wide taxation system that all EU member states must adopt. Under this system a transaction-level tax (VAT) is collected on certain types of transaction by EU VAT authorities. Any VAT that becomes due to an EU VAT authority does so where and when a **chargeable event** occurs. So far this book has only considered one type of chargeable event, that is, the liability to account for **output VAT** (see 1.1) to an EU VAT authority that occurs when a **taxable supply** is made by a taxable person (see 1.2.2). There are several complications for cross-border transactions:

1. Determining where a supply takes place. Supplies of goods and services are deemed to take place at a particular location (the **place of supply**) at a particular time (the **time of supply**). The place of supply is where, if output VAT is due on a supply, it is due:

   - If the place of supply is outside the EU – the transaction is **outside the scope** of UK or EU output VAT, and no output VAT is due to any EU VAT authority.
   - If the place of supply is the UK, any output VAT due is UK output VAT due to the UK VAT authority (HMRC) under the UK's VAT rules.

- If the place of supply is another EU state, any output VAT due is that state's output VAT due to that state's VAT authority under that state's VAT rules.

2. Two further types of chargeable event can occur for goods (but not for services), generating two new types of liability to account for VAT:

  - **Import VAT** can become due to an EU VAT authority when and where goods are imported into the EU from outside the EU. See 9.5 'Imports'.
  - **Acquisition VAT** can become due to an EU VAT authority when and where goods are acquired in one EU state from a supplier in another EU state. See 9.6 'Intra-EU transfers of goods'.

3. The rules for determining the place of supply are different for goods and for services. The VAT rules for cross-border supplies of goods, acquisitions and imports are explained in sections 9.3 to 9.6 below. The VAT rules for cross-border supplies of services are explained in sections 9.7 to 9.9 below.

9.1.1 Territories of the UK and EU

The UK

For VAT purposes, the territory of the UK comprises:

Included territory	Excluded territory
England	Channel Islands (Alderney, Jersey, Guernsey, Sark and Herm)
Scotland	
Wales	Gibraltar
Northern Ireland	British Overseas Territories (Bermuda, British Virgin Isles, Cayman Islands, Falkland Islands, Turks & Caicos, etc.)
Isle of Man	

The excluded territories are outside the EU, for VAT purposes, except for the UK Sovereign Base Areas of Akrotiri and Dhekelia in Cyprus which are treated as part of Cyprus for VAT. Though the Isle of Man is not part of the UK, there is a taxation agreement between the UK and Isle of Man and the two territories are regarded as one for most VAT purposes. The Channel Islands are not in the EU for VAT purposes, but they are in the EU for Customs Duty purposes. Goods can circulate within the EU Customs Union without Customs Duties being levied.

The EU

At the time of writing the EU comprises 28 states all of which have adopted the EU VAT system:

Joined	EU state (with two letter state prefix code in brackets)
1957	Belgium (BE), France (FR), Italy (IT), Luxembourg (LU), Netherlands (NL), Germany (DE)
1973	Denmark (DK), Ireland (IE), UK (GB)
1981	Greece (GR)
1986	Portugal (PT), Spain (ES)
1995	Austria (AT), Finland (FI), Sweden (SE)
2004	Cyprus (CY), Czech Republic (CZ), Estonia (EE), Hungary (HU), Latvia (LV), Lithuania (LI), Malta (MT), Poland (PL), Slovakia (SK), Slovenia (SI)
2007	Bulgaria (BU), Romania (RO)
2013	Croatia (HR)

In the same way that for VAT purposes the UK includes and excludes various of its territories, other EU states include and exclude specific territories. See 14.4 'VAT in other EU states' for guidance on which territories the EU includes and excludes for VAT purposes and for state specific information.

9.2 RECOVERING FOREIGN VAT

VAT charged by a supplier in another EU state cannot be recovered through the UK VAT return. Instead, it must be claimed directly from the tax authorities of the supplier's EU state:

- If you are registered for VAT in that state, you reclaim it by completing a local VAT return.
- If you are not registered for VAT in that country then you may be able to claim for the VAT to be refunded under the EU VAT Refund Scheme.

9.2.1 **EU VAT Refund Scheme**

This scheme is for businesses established and registered for VAT in one EU state to make a refund claim for VAT incurred in another EU state. There is a different procedure for claims by non-EU businesses.

Refund Scheme claims are made online and by reference to calendar years which are referred to as 'refund periods'. You must meet all of the following conditions to make a claim for a 'refund period':

1. You must be VAT-registered in an EU member state. This state is referred to as the Member State of Registration (MSR). For UK VAT-registered and established businesses the MSR will be the UK.
2. Throughout the claim period you must not be registered or liable to be registered for VAT in the state in which the VAT is incurred, and you must not have in that state your business establishment or a fixed establishment from which business transactions were effected, or, if no such business or fixed establishment existed, your domicile or normal place of residence. For the meaning of business and fixed establishment see 9.7.5 'Place of belonging'.
3. Throughout the claim period you must not make any supplies in that state other than freight transport services related to the international carriage of goods or a supply of services where the customer must account for VAT under the reverse charge (see 9.7.4 'Reverse charge') or a supply of goods where the customer must account for **acquisition VAT** (see 9.6 'Intra-EU transfers of goods').
4. The VAT must be recoverable under the EU state's rules. Many EU states apply different rules to the UK for commonly incurred types of expense such as accommodation, travel and subsistence costs. When you submit an online claim you must analyse the claim by a set of pre-defined purchase types (fuel, accommodation, etc.) The online portal will ask further questions if more detailed local rules apply.
5. You comply with any evidence requirements. You may have to attach scanned invoices or other evidence to support claims. The online portal will advise you if this is required.

Claim deadline

The claim period is a calendar year. Claims must be made within nine months of the end of the calendar year in which the VAT was incurred.

Minimum claim amount

The minimum amount you can claim varies between EU states, but is generally €400 for claims of more than three months but less than a year, or €50 for claims for a whole year or the period between your last claim and the end of the year

Claim procedure

With effect from 1 January 2010 a new claims procedure was implemented. Where the MSR is the UK claims must be made via your online HMRC Government Gateway account. You must submit a separate claim for each suppler state concerned.

Claims processing

Once the refunding EU state receives the claim, it must normally be processed within four months and, if approved, repaid within ten working days. If further information is requested the processing period can be extended up to a maximum of eight months. If these time limits are exceeded then interest will be paid.

9.2.2 Recovering VAT incurred outside the EU

Most countries outside the EU implement some form of sales tax system and many of these accept direct claims for refund of sales tax incurred by foreign businesses, though you must seek country-specific guidance as the regimes vary considerably.

For example, Goods and Services Tax (GST) charged by the state of Jersey is potentially refundable if all of the following conditions are met:

- you are not registered in Jersey for GST and you do not have to, or cannot, register for GST in Jersey;
- you do not have a place of business or a residence in Jersey, and you do not make any sales in Jersey;
- your business is a registered 'taxable person' under a similar indirect tax scheme to Jersey; and
- your own country operates a similar refund scheme which is available to Jersey businesses.

States of Jersey (2015), 'Overseas businesses and GST refunds'

9.3 CROSS-BORDER GOODS INTRODUCTION

VAT legislation uses particular terms to describe cross-border transfers of goods:

- **Exports** are goods taken from a place within the EU to a place outside the EU, from the perspective of the person who exports them (the **exporter**).
- **Imports** are goods brought within the EU from a place outside the EU, from the perspective of the person who imports them (the **importer**).
- **Acquisitions** are goods brought within the territory of an EU state from the territory of another EU state, from the perspective of the person who acquires the goods (the **acquirer**).
- **Removals** or **dispatches** are goods taken from the territory of one EU state to the territory of another EU state, from the perspective of the **dispatcher** of the goods.

For goods there are potentially three chargeable events when VAT can become payable to an EU VAT authority:

- When a **taxable supply of goods** occurs **output VAT** becomes due to an EU VAT authority if the **place of supply** is in the EU. The output VAT is due to the VAT authority of the state of supply. See 9.3.1 'Place of supply of goods' for the place of supply of goods.
- When a **taxable import of goods** occurs **import VAT** becomes due to an EU VAT authority. Imports by businesses, entities with no business activities and private individuals can be subject to import VAT though there are many exemptions, including some specifically for imports by charities. See 9.5 'Imports'.
- When a **taxable acquisition of goods** occurs **acquisition VAT** becomes due to an EU VAT authority. This happens where goods are acquired by a VAT-registered business in one EU state from a VAT-registered business in another. See 9.6 'Intra-EU transfers of goods'.

9.3.1 Place of supply of goods

If goods are not dispatched or transported, the place of supply is the place where the goods are located at the time when the supply takes place.

If the goods are dispatched or transported (by the supplier, the customer or a third party), the place of supply is where the goods are located at the time when dispatch or transport of the goods to the customer begins.

This means that by default goods sent from the UK, or collected by a non-UK customer in the UK, are supplied in the UK and any UK output VAT due is due to HMRC. However, there are many exceptions to these basic rules, including:

- **Distance sales**: sales with delivery to unregistered customers in another EU state above that state's distance-selling threshold are subject to a special place of supply rule. The place of supply becomes the customer's state, see 9.6.15 'Distance-selling'.
- **Installed or assembled goods**: where goods dispatched or transported by the supplier, by the customer or by a third person are installed or assembled by or on behalf of the supplier, the place of supply is the place where the goods are installed or assembled.
- **Goods sold on ships, planes or trains**: where goods are supplied on board ships, aircraft or trains during the section of a passenger transport operation effected within the EU, the place of supply is the point of departure of the passenger transport operation.
- **Supplies of gas through a natural gas system, of electricity and of heat or cooling energy through heating and cooling networks**: these are supplied where consumed, unless the supply is to a taxable energy dealer in which case the place of supply is where the dealer has established its business or has a fixed establishment from which the goods are supplied or, in the absence of such a place of business or fixed establishment, the place where it has its permanent address or usually resides.

Time of supply of goods

By default a supply of goods occurs when there is a transfer of the right to dispose of tangible property as owner. However, there are variations to this. The time of supply rules for cross-border supplies of goods are explained in the following sections:

- For exports, in 9.4.1 'Selling goods'.
- For imports, in 9.5.1 'Place and time of import'.
- For acquisitions, in 9.6.4 'Time of acquisition'.
- For removals, in 9.6.13 'Time of supply of removals'.

9.3.2 **EORI number**

The Economic Operator Registration and Identification (EORI) scheme was implemented in the EU with effect from 1 July 2009. It provides a common unique ID for 'economic operators' across the EU that is recognised by all EU states and is used when goods are subject to customs checks on crossing the external borders of the EU.

If you are registered for VAT your EORI number is your VAT registration number prefixed with 'GB' and followed by three numbers, 000 if not in a VAT group and 000, 001, etc. for each member of a VAT group.

All businesses established in the EU require an EORI number if they are involved in business activities covered by EU customs legislation. In particular you will require an EORI number if you import goods from outside the EU and want to reclaim any of the import VAT or if you export business goods or export goods and are registered for VAT.

HMRC advises (HMRC 2014, *Economic Operator Registration and identification scheme: supporting guidance*) application as soon as you become aware that you will be involved in customs-related activities and when all details required on your application are available. Applications can take up to three working days to process. You will be able to use your EORI number 24 hours after receiving your notification from HMRC.

For non-economic operators who are not required to obtain an EORI number there are special 'dummy' EORI codes you can use without having to apply for an EORI number. Full details about EORI including the EORI application forms can be found on the gov.uk website. There are separate applications for VAT-registered businesses and unregistered applicants.

9.4 **EXPORTS**

In VAT terminology, goods sent from the UK to a destination outside the EU are called 'exports'.

9.4.1 **Selling goods**

Where goods are sold to a non-EU customer and the place of supply is the UK, then, provided the goods physically leave the UK within specified time limits (normally three months), and you satisfy HMRC's evidence requirements, the supply is zero-rated. An overseas customer is an individual or organisation that is not UK-resident, not registered for VAT in the UK, and does not have a business or fixed establishment in the UK from which taxable supplies are made.

There are two types of export:

- **Direct exports**: where the supplier or supplier's **agent** (see 11.2) is responsible for delivering the goods to the non-EU customer. This includes postal deliveries where the delivery service is acting as agent for the supplier.
- **Indirect exports**: where the customer or an agent of the customer collects the goods from the UK supplier and then takes them outside the EU. This includes situations where the customer instructs a delivery service to collect the goods.

The conditions for zero-rating **direct exports** are:

- the goods are taken out of the UK within the specified time limits;
- evidence of export is obtained within specified time limits and retained for at least six years. See 9.4.2 'Evidence of export' for what constitutes acceptable evidence of export;
- you comply with the law and the conditions of *VAT Notice 703*.

The conditions for zero-rating **indirect exports** are:

- the overseas customer exports the goods within the specified time limits;
- the overseas customer obtains and gives you valid official or commercial evidence of export as appropriate within the specified time limits and you keep this and supplementary evidence of export for at least six years;
- the goods are not used between the time of leaving your premises and export, except where specifically authorised by HMRC;
- you comply with the law and the conditions of *VAT Notice 703*.

Time limits

The time limits within which the goods must be taken out of the UK and within which the evidence of export must be obtained are by default three months. However, they are extended to six months for:

- supplies of goods involved in processing or incorporation prior to export;
- thoroughbred racehorses (subject to conditions to be found in *VAT Notice 700/57*).

Conditions not met

If any of these conditions for zero-rating direct or indirect exports are not met, then VAT must be charged as if the goods were supplied in the UK. The actual sale price is assumed to be the gross selling price inclusive of any VAT due. If evidence of export is not obtained within the time limits, then you should account for any VAT due in the next VAT return, though if evidence of export is later obtained, you can then recover this.

Time of supply of an export

In most cases the time of supply of an export will be the earlier of either the date you (i) send the goods to your customer or your customer takes them away, or (ii) receive full payment for the goods. Deposits and progress payments have the same VAT liability as the final supply.

9.4.2 **Evidence of export**

You must obtain either official evidence of export or commercial evidence and back this up with supplementary evidence.

Official evidence of export

Official evidence of export is evidence as produced by HM Customs systems, for example Goods Departed Messages generated by the National Export System (NES) (see 9.4.6 'UK export procedures').

Commercial evidence

This includes: authenticated sea-waybills. PIM/PIEX International consignment notes, master air-waybills or bills of lading, certificates of shipment containing the full details of the consignment and how it left the EU, or International Consignment Note/Lettre de Voiture International (CMR) fully completed by the consignor, the haulier and the receiving consignee, or Freight Transport Association (FTA) own account transport documents fully completed and signed by the receiving customer. Photocopy certificates of shipment are not normally acceptable as evidence of export, nor are photocopy bills of lading, sea-waybills or air-waybills (unless authenticated by the shipping or airline).

Supplementary evidence

Supplementary evidence includes: the customer's order; sales contract; inter-company correspondence; copy of export sales invoice; advice note; consignment note; packing list; insurance and freight charges documentation; evidence of payment, and/or evidence of the receipt of the goods abroad.

See *VAT Notice 703* for detailed HMRC guidance on acceptable types of evidence for different shipping routes.

9.4.3 Selling goods to an overseas customer established in the UK

Where you supply goods for export outside the EU, and your customer has an establishment in the UK from where they make taxable supplies, you may zero rate the supply as a direct export, provided:

- you or your representative arranges for the goods to be sent directly to a non-EU country;
- the overseas delivery address for the goods is shown on the invoice even if the invoice is made out or sent to the address of the UK establishment, or a UK Shared Service Centre for administrative reasons; and
- the conditions, time limits and evidential requirements for direct exports are met.

But where your customer or their representative arranges for the goods to be exported outside the EU, this is an indirect export. As the customer is established in the UK, it is not an 'overseas person' for VAT zero-rating purposes. This means that the conditions for zero-rating an indirect export are not met and the supply cannot be zero-rated as such. VAT is due at the appropriate UK rate.

9.4.4 Export of goods by a charity

UK law treats the export of any goods by a charity to a place outside the EU as a deemed business supply by the charity made in the UK. See 6.3.1 'Export of goods by a charity'.

In Article 146(1)(c) the Principal VAT Directive mandatorily exempts from VAT 'the supply of goods to approved bodies which export them out of the EU as part of their humanitarian, charitable or teaching activities outside the EU'. Member states may grant this exemption by means of a refund of the VAT.

Aid sent to a destination inside the EU does not qualify. If aid goods are sent to a destination in the EU, see 9.6.17 'Humanitarian aid'.

9.4.5 Transfer of own goods abroad

If goods are transferred outside the EU for use in a non-business activity, then, unless the organisation transferring the goods is a charity (in which case the transfer is deemed to be zero-rated), **attributable** (see 3.1.3) UK input VAT is not **deductible**. Even if the goods are to be used wholly for a non-business activity, they may need to be declared to Customs and valid proof of export should be retained.

335

If goods are sent outside the EU for a project and then imported back into the UK in substantially the same condition as when they left, then a special returned goods import VAT exemption applies, see 9.5.6 'Import VAT exemptions'.

9.4.6 **UK export procedures**

There are a variety of ways for making exports of goods from the UK:

Postal exports

You must complete and affix a customs declaration, (*CN22* or *CN23*) Preference Certificates or similar documentation must be attached to the outside of the package and clearly identified before posting. For commercial items a commercial invoice must accompany the package. If you are a VAT-registered business you will need to obtain and keep a Certificate of Posting to support the zero-rating of your supply and to discharge your liability to Customs charges on goods temporarily imported into the UK.

Fast Parcel Operators

The NES Express Industry MOU offers a bulk export process to facilitate the express movement of goods. The MOU arrangements require the express/fast parcel operator to fulfil specific roles and conditions set out by HMRC.

Humanitarian aid

The UK puts into practice a recommendation of the World Customs Organisation aimed at speeding up the forwarding of relief consignments in the event of disasters. In the case of exports, the recommendation provides for official certification of lists of the contents of relief consignments and the securing of goods under Customs Seal to aid the passage of the goods. Action is taken by HMRC under these arrangements only at the request of exporters or their agents. The arrangements do not affect normal customs export documentation. Pre-entry, export licensing or other export restrictions requirements continue to apply. However, HMRC advises its own staff (*EXPP8250*):

> In cases when humanitarian goods are presented for export without a licence and there is no evidence of a deliberate attempt to evade the controls, you should normally only detain the goods until the exporter obtains a licence, rather than moving to seizure. On each occasion the exporter or agent is to make a formal application to Customs at the port for the certification and sealing of the goods to be exported. The exporter is to supply a list of the goods to be exported, clearly indicating the place and organisation to which the consignment is being sent.

It is the exporter's responsibility to ensure that a sufficient number of copies of the list are provided for delivery to customs authorities in the countries of transit and destination. Consignments of goods (e.g. second-hand clothing and bedding) to countries which although they have not suffered a recent disaster are undergoing a period of hardship or economic difficulty should be expedited but should not circumvent normal freight controls.

The procedures covering Disaster relief arrangements should be followed where requested by the exporter or their representative.

Merchandise in baggage

Where goods are accompanied in personal baggage, you must make a Customs export declaration via the CHIEF system (see 'The NES' below) before arriving at the port/airport, though in some circumstances a form C88/ESS may be used. If an officer is not in attendance you must use the red phone at the export point to speak to an officer and follow the instructions given. To support your claim for the VAT zero-rating of your goods, you need official evidence that the goods have left the EU.

The National Export System (NES)

The National Export System (NES) is the UK's system for processing exports. Data is entered into the HMRC CHIEF computer system at the four stages of an export:

1. **Export declaration**: you must make an electronic export declaration prior to the shipment of the goods. This can be via web, email or XML, though you must apply for a 'CHIEF badge' (authority to use the CHIEF system) using form PA7 before you can access the system. There is a simplified declaration procedure for low-value items (under £800).
2. **Presentation**: this is notification of the arrival of the goods at the required location for Customs control. An electronic 'arrival' message is sent to CHIEF by an authorised CHIEF Loader. Where there is no electronic link to CHIEF, HMRC can perform the role of Loader and input the arrival message. Requests for a manual submission of the arrival message should be made on a form C160.
3. **Customs clearance**: when the goods are 'arrived' on CHIEF and on acceptance of the arrival message, CHIEF re-examines, re-validates and risk assesses the data in the declaration. CHIEF will then allocate one of various routes for the goods to take. Some of these require supporting documentation and/or the goods to be examined before **Permission to Progress** (P2P) is granted. P2P means that the CHIEF Export entry has been cleared and the goods may now be loaded on to the means of transport for export. This message is sent to the person submitting the export declaration.

4. **Departure message**: once the means of transport upon which the goods were loaded has left the UK a Departure message must be submitted to CHIEF by an authorised CHIEF Loader, though, where no commercial departure facilities are available, traders can submit form C1602 to the National Clearance Hub. The departure message updates the Export status on CHIEF to 'ICS60' meaning 'Departed'. Once the Departure message has been accepted by CHIEF, it will send copies of the Movement Departure Advice (S8) to the persons who input the declaration (the Submitting Trader). The CHIEF entry status then changes to 'SOE8'.

9.4.7   Retail export scheme

The retail export scheme is a voluntary scheme that allows UK retailers to zero rate sales of 'eligible goods' to an 'overseas visitor' in 'qualifying circumstances'. The retailer charges VAT as normal at the point of sale, but also provides the customer with a VAT reclaim form (VAT 407). When the customer leaves the EU, they must produce the form and the goods to a customs officer (UK or EU but not non-EU) then stamping the form if they are satisfied. The customer must produce for the customs officer the goods and purchase receipt for the goods. The customer then sends the stamped form back to the retailer to claim their VAT refund. For full details of the scheme, see *VAT Notice 704*.

9.5   IMPORTS

An import occurs when and where goods are brought into the EU from outside the EU. A special type of VAT, **import VAT**, is payable when goods are imported. Potentially any import of goods by anyone can be caught, though there are important exemptions and exclusions. In the UK, import VAT must normally be paid before goods can clear UK Customs, though there are prepayment schemes and for small-value postal imports it may be able to be paid on delivery. Import VAT is charged at the applicable UK rate, so goods that qualify for zero-rating or reduced-rating in the UK also qualify for zero-rating or reduced-rating on import.

9.5.1   Place and time of import

The import occurs where and when the goods are brought into the EU, though if goods are not entered into free circulation but placed under a special **suspensive regime** (see 9.5.8 'Suspensive regimes'), the place and time of import is where and when the goods cease to be covered by that regime.

9.5.2 Chargeable amount

The UK procedure for calculating the chargeable amount of an import is set out in detail in *Notice 252*. In outline:

1. By default the value is the total of:
   - the **Customs Value** of the goods, which is, if the goods are sold, the price paid or payable by the buyer to the seller;
   - any Customs Duty, Excise Duty, levy or other charges payable on importation into the UK;
   - all incidental expenses such as commission, packing, transport and insurance costs incurred up to the goods' first destination in the UK, and all such incidental expenses where they result from transport to a further place of destination in the EU if that place is known at the time of importation.

2. If there is no sale the Customs Value is based on the Customs Value of identical goods exported to the EU at or about the same time as the goods to be valued. Identical goods are goods produced in the same country as those being valued. They must also be the same in all respects, such as physical characteristics, quality and reputation. Minor differences in appearance do not matter.

3. If there are no identical goods the Customs Value is based on the Customs Value of similar goods exported to the EU at or about the same time as the goods to be valued. Similar are goods which differ in some respects from the goods being valued but they must be produced in the same country, be able to carry out the same tasks and are commercially interchangeable.

4. If there are no similar goods there are a variety of other methods for valuing however the rules are complex. See HMRC *Notice 252*.

9.5.3 C79 certificates

You need to hold official evidence of VAT paid on import before you can recover the import VAT as input VAT. The normal evidence is the monthly C79 certificate issued by HMRC. At the time of writing HMRC aims to send a monthly C79 certificate of import VAT paid. It is important to quote the correct VAT number or EORI number when paying import VAT in order for it to appear on the C79 certificate.

9.5.4 VAT groups

If goods are imported by a member of a VAT group, the goods are treated as having been imported by the representative member of the group, unless the import VAT treatment depends on the status of the importer, in which case it is the latter that matters.

339

9.5.5 **Payment of import VAT**

Unless the goods are placed under Excise warehousing or one of the special customs arrangements listed in *VAT Notice 702/9*, the payment of any import VAT due must normally be made either at the time of importation, or be deferred under the 'deferment scheme', provided you or your agent are approved to use the scheme. The goods will not normally be released from Customs until the import VAT has been paid.

Deferment scheme

Under this scheme import VAT and Customs Duties are paid by direct debit monthly in arrears, on the 15th of the following month (or if the 15th is not a working day, the next working day after). The importer must provide HMRC with a bank, building society or insurance company guarantee on HMRC form *C1201*. The guarantor must agree to cover each and every sum deferred up to an overall maximum amount in any calendar month.

Simplified Import VAT Accounting (SIVA)

Businesses must be authorised to operate SIVA. Approved businesses are able to benefit from a reduction in the level of financial guarantee required to operate a deferment account by not having to provide security for any deferred import VAT charges. This may mean that where the only charges going through a deferment account are import VAT, no guarantee is required at all. Customs and excise duties must still be fully secured.

Postal imports

At the time of writing the procedures for postal imports are as follows. Under international postal agreements the sender must complete a customs declaration (form *CN22* or *CN23*) which in most cases should be fixed to the package. The declaration includes a description of the goods, the value and whether they are gifts or commercial items. Under Customs law, you as the importer are legally responsible for the information on the declaration. If no declaration is made, or the information is inaccurate, the package may be delayed while the UK Border Force makes further enquiries, or in some cases the package and its contents may be returned to the sender or seized.

Charges are calculated by Border Force officers at the postal depots where the packages are received. Import VAT is then charged at the same rate that applies to similar goods sold in the UK (subject to the exceptions below).

If delivery is valued at under £2,000 and is via Royal Mail, you are provided with several options for payment and Royal Mail will inform you of the options available and the amounts payable when they contact you. A postcard or letter is usually delivered to your address, detailing the amount due and the options available for payment. Once payment has been made, the package may be collected from the post office or if you have paid online/by phone you can arrange for it to be delivered. Details of the charges, including the Royal Mail or Parcelforce Worldwide handling fee, will be shown separately on a label affixed to the package which should be retained as evidence of payment.

If the value of the package is over £2,000 or it is for a particular customs regime, you will be sent a customs declaration form (*C88* or *C160*) which you must complete and return to the Border Force at the Postal Depot before your package can be delivered. You should not send any payment with this form unless asked to do so; however, if there are any charges due you will be required to pay them to the Border Force before your goods can be released.

9.5.6 Import VAT exemptions

The following goods are exempt from import VAT (and in many cases Import Duty also). In the event of query or dispute contact the HMRC National Import Reliefs Unit (see 14.1 'Contacting HM Revenue & Customs').

Returned goods

If you re-import your own goods in the same state as they were exported, you need not pay import VAT provided:

- the goods were last exported from the EU by you or on your behalf; and
- any import VAT chargeable on the goods was accounted for or paid and neither has been, nor will be reclaimed; and
- the goods were not exported with a view to avoiding or abusing the normal VAT supply rules by using Returned Goods Relief.

The goods must also meet conditions 2–5 in the checklist for Customs duty Returned Goods Relief in section 5 of *Notice 236*. This relief is intended primarily to avoid import VAT having to be paid and reclaimed, perhaps several times, for example, on goods taken outside the EU on approval and brought back unsold or on tools and equipment returned after use outside the EU.

Imports by charities, etc.

The following imports by charities are exempt from import VAT.

- **Goods for the needy**: **basic necessities** obtained without charge for distribution free of charge to the needy by a **relevant organisation**. Relevant organisation means a state organisation or other approved charitable or philanthropic organisation. Basic necessities means food, medicines, clothing, blankets, orthopaedic equipment and crutches, required to meet a person's immediate needs
- **Fundraising goods**: goods donated by a person established abroad to a relevant organisation for use to raise funds at occasional charity events for the benefit of the needy. HMRC states (*VAT Notice 317*, section 2.4) 'An occasional charity event normally means any event held not more than four times a year by any one organisation.'
- **Equipment and office materials** donated by a person established abroad to a relevant organisation for meeting its operating needs or carrying out its charitable aims.
- **Disaster relief goods**: goods imported by a relevant organisation for distribution or loan, free of charge, to victims of a disaster affecting the territory of one or more member states. This includes goods imported by a relevant organisation for meeting its operating needs in the relief of a disaster affecting the territory of one or more member states. These reliefs apply only where the EC has made a decision authorising relief for the goods
- **Goods for disabled persons**: articles donated to and imported by a relevant organisation for supply to blind or other physically or mentally handicapped persons and which are specially designed for the education, employment or social advancement of such persons, including spare parts, components or accessories and including tools for its maintenance, checking, calibration or repair. 'Relevant organisation' means an approved organisation principally engaged in the education of, or the provision of assistance to, blind or other physically or mentally handicapped persons.

Works of art, antiques and collector's pieces

Works of art and collector's pieces imported by approved museums, galleries or other institutions for a purpose other than sale are exempt from import VAT. This applies only where the goods are:

- of an educational, scientific or cultural character; and
- imported free of charge or, if for a **consideration** (everything that is paid to the supplier in return for making the supply), are not supplied to the importer in the course or furtherance of any business.

Works of art, antiques and collector's items imported by any person may qualify for VAT reduced-rating – see Chapter 6 'Zero and reduced rates'.

Low-value consignment relief

Commercial consignments (goods you have purchased from outside the EU) of £15 or less are free from Customs Duty and import VAT. This does not include alcohol, tobacco products, perfume or toilet waters. In addition, commercial consignments sent to the UK from the Channel Islands do not benefit from any relief of import VAT with effect from 1 April 2012. At the time of writing there is an EC proposal to completely abolish this relief.

Small-value gifts

Small-value gifts are goods sent as a gift that are under £36 in value (£40 before 1 January 2013) and are exempt from import VAT. Customs Duty is payable if the value of the goods is over £135 but is waived if the amount of duty calculated is less than £9. To qualify as a gift:

- the Customs declaration must be completed correctly;
- the gift must be sent from a private person outside the EU to a private person(s) in this country;
- there is no commercial or trade element and the gift has not been paid for either directly or indirectly by anyone in the UK;
- the gift is of an occasional nature only, for example for a birthday or anniversary.

Capital goods

Import VAT exemption applies to capital goods and equipment imported by a person for the purposes of a **taxable activity** (an activity that generates **taxable supplies**) they have ceased to carry on abroad and which they have notified HMRC is to be carried on by them in the UK. This is subject to the condition that the goods:

- have been used in the course of the business for at least 12 months before it ceased to be carried on abroad;
- are imported within 12 months of the date on which such business ceased to be carried on abroad, or within such longer period as HMRC allows; and
- are appropriate both to the nature and size of the business to be carried on in the UK.

Promotion of trade

The following items related to the promotion of trade are exempt from import VAT:

- articles of no intrinsic commercial value sent free of charge by suppliers of goods and services for the sole purpose of advertising;
- samples of negligible value of a kind and in quantities capable of being used solely for soliciting orders for goods of the same kind;
- printed advertising matter, including catalogues, price lists, directions for use or brochures, which relate to goods for sale or hire by a person established outside the UK;
- goods to be distributed free of charge at an event, as small representative samples, for use or consumption by the public;
- goods imported solely for the purpose of being demonstrated at an event and goods imported solely for the purpose of being used in the demonstration of any machine or apparatus displayed at an event;
- paints, varnishes, wallpaper and other materials of low value to be used in the building, fitting out and decoration of a temporary stand at an event;
- catalogues, prospectuses, price lists, advertising posters, calendars (whether or not illustrated), unframed photographs and other printed matter or articles advertising goods displayed at an event, supplied without charge for the purpose of distribution free of charge to the public at such event.

Goods for testing or research

Goods imported for the purpose of examination, analysis or testing to determine their composition, quality or other technical characteristics, to provide information or for industrial or commercial research are exempt from import VAT.

Health goods and products

VAT exemption applies to the following items related to health goods and products:

- animals specially prepared for laboratory use and sent free of charge to a relevant establishment;
- biological or chemical substances sent to a relevant establishment;
- human blood and products for therapeutic purposes, derived from human blood, human (including foetal) organs or tissue for diagnostic or therapeutic purposes or medical research.

Graves and funerals

For graves and funerals, import VAT exemption applies to:

- remains of the dead;
- goods imported by an approved organisation for use in the construction, upkeep or ornamentation of cemeteries, tombs and memorials in the UK which commemorate war victims of other countries;
- flowers, wreaths and other ornamental objects, imported without any commercial intent by a person resident abroad, for use at a funeral or to decorate a grave.

Inheritances

Property acquired as an inheritance by an EU resident or by a non-profit-making company established in the EU are exempt from import VAT. However, this excludes: alcoholic drinks, tobacco and tobacco products; stocks of raw materials and finished or semi-finished products; tools of trade; commercial vehicles; livestock and stocks of agricultural products which are more than what are required to meet a family's normal needs; goods bought from the executor of the estate; and goods bought or received as a gift from the person who legally inherited them.

UN goods

Certain audio-visual goods produced by the UN or a UN organisation including holograms for laser projection, multi-media kits, materials for programmed instruction, films of an educational, scientific or cultural character, etc. are exempt from import VAT.

Miscellaneous

VAT exemption also applies to the following items:

- material relating to trademarks, patterns or designs and supporting documents and applications for patents, imported for the purpose of being submitted to bodies competent to deal with protection of copyright or industrial or commercial patent rights;
- objects imported for the purpose of being submitted as evidence, or for a like purpose, to a court or other official body in the UK;
- photographs, slides and stereotype mats for photographs, whether or not captioned, sent to press agencies and publishers of newspapers or magazines;
- recorded media, including punched cards, sound recordings and microfilm, sent free of charge for the transmission of information;
- any honorary decoration conferred by a government or head of state abroad on a person resident in the UK and imported on their behalf;

- any cup, medal or similar article of an essentially symbolic nature, intended as a tribute to activities in the arts, sciences, sport, or the public service, or in recognition of merit at a particular event, which is either: (a) donated by an authority or person established abroad for the purpose of being presented in the UK, or (b) awarded abroad to a person resident in the UK and imported on their behalf.

9.5.7 Claiming charity import VAT exemptions

HMRC provides the following advice (*VAT Notice 317*, section 3):

Goods in accompanied baggage

These must be declared at the Customs Red channel or Red point when you arrive. You should produce evidence to satisfy HMRC that all the conditions of the relief are met. HMRC suggests that you carry a letter from a responsible official of your charitable or philanthropic organisation stating that the organisation will meet the conditions of the relief. The letter should also describe the goods, state how they will be used and whether the goods are donated or purchased. If HMRC is not satisfied you will have to provide financial security (normally a cash deposit or banker's guarantee) to cover the duty and VAT. HMRC will discharge this when you prove that the goods qualify for relief. Where the value of the goods is over £600, HMRC will require a formal import declaration

Goods imported as freight

You must claim relief by completing an import declaration on a Single Administrative Document (SAD: form C88). You can get an import agent to do this. You will need to use one of the special Customs Procedure Codes (CPCs) for use in box 37 of the SAD:

- CPC 40 00 C20: for basic necessities imported from outside the Customs Union, goods to be used or sold at charitable events imported from outside the Customs Union, equipment and office materials imported from outside the Customs Union.
- CPC 49 00 C20: for basic necessities imported from the Special Territories or countries having a Customs Union with the EU, goods to be used or sold at charitable events imported from the Special Territories or countries having a Customs Union with the EU, equipment and office materials imported from the Special Territories or countries having a Customs Union with the EU.

Goods imported by post

Ask the sender to write clearly on the package and its accompanying international Customs declaration (*CN22* or *CN23*): 'CHARITY ITEMS: RELIEF CLAIMED'. If HMRC needs more information it will send you a simplified form to complete. If satisfied, HMRC will then release the goods for delivery free of duty and VAT.

Claiming retrospectively

HMRC may accept a belated claim and repay the appropriate charges, subject to the application (on form *C285*) being received by HMRC within three years from the date you were notified of the debt, usually the date of the customs declaration or post clearance demand note (*C18*). The three-year time limit can only be extended if you can provide evidence that you were prevented from making a claim within the three years as a result of unforeseeable circumstances or *force majeure.*

9.5.8 **Suspensive regimes**

The special suspensive regimes for import VAT include:

1. Customs Warehousing

Under Customs Warehousing the payment of import duties and/or VAT is suspended or delayed for imports which are stored in premises or under an inventory system authorised as a Customs Warehouse. Import VAT only becomes due when the goods are removed from the warehouse to free circulation. Import VAT is normally payable together with any Customs Duty or Excise Duty suspended by the person removing the goods.

2. IP suspension

The inward processing (IP) regime provides relief to promote exports from the EU and assist EU processors to compete on an equal footing in the world market. Duty is relieved on imports of non-EU goods which are processed in the EU and re-exported, providing the trade does not harm the essential interests of EU producers of similar goods. Under **IP drawback** you must pay the import VAT at the time of entry. However, under **IP suspension**, the payment of import VAT is suspended and only becomes due if you subsequently divert the goods to free circulation.

3. Temporary admission (TA)

TA allows total or partial relief from import duties on a range of goods imported from outside the EU; providing they are intended for re-export within a specified time, usually a maximum of two years.

4. Processing under Customs Control (PCC)

PCC is a trade facilitation measure intended to encourage processing in the EU by allowing certain raw materials or components to be imported under duty suspension arrangements. After processing, the finished products may be declared to free circulation at a lower value. Import VAT is similarly suspended until the goods are processed and declared to free circulation

5. Transit arrangements

Transit is a customs procedure which allows you to move goods within the customs territory of the EU without the payment of import duties and other charges until they reach their final destination.

- The **external transit procedure** (**T1**) allows the movement of mainly non-EU goods within the customs territory of the EU without their being subject to import duties or import VAT and other charges or to commercial policy measures.
- The **internal transit procedure** (**T2** or **T2F**) allows the movement of EU goods from one point to another within the customs territory of the EU to pass through the territory of a non-EU country without any change in their customs status. Any goods you place under external transit have the customs duty and import VAT suspended. Goods placed under internal transit may have the import VAT suspended in particular circumstances (such as the T2F procedure for movements to/from special territories).

6. Onward Supply Relief

Any goods that you import under IP suspension, PCC, TA or Customs Warehousing arrangements, imported in the course of an onward supply to a taxable person in another member state may be put into Free Circulation in the UK without the payment of import VAT. VAT is accounted for on the supply/ acquisition by the purchaser in the EU country of destination.

9.5.9 Goods from the Isle of Man

Under the special VAT regime between the UK and Isle of Man, goods removed from the Isle of Man to the UK are not treated as an import into the UK provided that either of the following apply:

- any import VAT due has been accounted for in the Isle of Man;
- if the goods were relieved of import VAT in the Isle of Man, the conditions of the relief are still applicable.

9.6   INTRA-EU TRANSFERS OF GOODS

> Goods are referred to in this section as acquired in an EU state when they are sent from the territory of one EU member state (the member state of **dispatch**) to the territory of another EU state (the member state of **acquisition**). The customer is the **acquirer** and the supplier is the **dispatcher**. The goods themselves are referred to as 'removals' or 'dispatches' by the dispatcher, and 'acquisitions' by the acquirer.

Supplies of goods to privileged persons

Supplies of goods to privileged persons in other EU states attract a special VAT treatment and can be zero-rated under conditions similar to those for exports. Privileged persons include organisations established by international treaty such as the UN and its subsidiary bodies, embassies, consulates, and NATO armed forces in other EU states. See 6.4.11 'Privileged persons in other EU states'.

9.6.1   Acquisitions

An acquisition of goods in the UK by a UK-based customer from a VAT-registered supplier in another EU state can be subject to UK acquisition VAT. This is a special type of VAT that is reported in box 2 on the UK VAT return. The person who is liable for the acquisition VAT is the UK customer.

UK acquisition VAT is chargeable if all of the following conditions are met:

1. The customer acquiring the goods is registered for VAT in the UK (or the goods are excise goods or a **new means of transport**).
2. The goods are acquired in the course or furtherance of a business activity of the customer's or in the course of any activity (business or non-business) carried out by an organisation. This formulation excludes acquisitions by individuals acting in a private capacity.
3. The acquisition is not already taxed in the UK or elsewhere in the EU (see 9.6.19 'Triangulation').
4. The acquisition is not an exempt acquisition. An acquisition of goods is exempt if the goods are acquired in pursuance of an exempt supply.
5. The supplier is registered for VAT in the EU state of dispatch.
6. The supply is a taxable supply for the supplier in their EU state. Intra-EU transfers of own goods can be a deemed business supply, so the same entity can be dispatcher and acquirer (see 9.6.9 'Removals').

7. The supply is not one of the margin scheme supplies (second-hand goods, works of art, collector's items or antiques, for which see Chapter 10 'VAT special schemes') or various others (such as supplies of gold to central banks).

9.6.2 Consideration amount

The consideration for the acquisition is the amount actually paid, including any discount. If goods are transfers within the same legal entity, the consideration is the cost value of the goods at the time of the transfer. If the supplier and customer are connected, the consideration value is less than the open market value of the goods, and the acquirer cannot fully recover the acquisition VAT, then HMRC may direct that the acquisition value is taken to be the open market value of the goods.

If the consideration is not in UK sterling, it must be converted to sterling using the UK market selling rate at the time of the acquisition. As an alternative you may use the period rate of exchange published by HMRC for customs purposes and you may apply to HMRC to use some other rate (*VAT Notice 725*, section 8.5).

9.6.3 Rate of acquisition VAT

The rate of VAT is the rate that would apply if the goods were purchased from a UK supplier. HMRC accepts that a charity can zero rate acquisition VAT in the same way as for a UK supplier, see 6.2 'Zero-rated supplies to charities'.

9.6.4 Time of acquisition

The time of acquisition is the earlier of either:

1. the fifteenth day of the month following the one in which the goods were sent; or
2. the date your supplier issued their invoice to you.

9.6.5 Reporting acquisitions

Add the acquisition VAT to Box 2 of the UK VAT return and any recoverable part of this to Box 4. Include the VAT-exclusive value of the acquisition in Boxes 7 and 9. If you are required to complete an Intrastat Return for arrivals, include on the Intrastat Return (see 9.6.18 'Intrastat Return').

9.6.6 Place of acquisition

By default the place of acquisition is the EU state in which transport of the goods ends. However, for an exception, see 9.6.19 'Triangulation'.

9.6.7 **VAT groups**

If goods are acquired by a member of a VAT group, the goods are treated as having been acquired by the representative member of the group, unless the acquisition VAT treatment depends on the status of the acquirer, in which case it is the latter that matters.

9.6.8 **Registering for relevant acquisitions**

If an unregistered organisation (but not a private individual acting in a private capacity) makes **relevant acquisitions** above the UK's Acquisition Threshold it must register for VAT in the UK. Relevant acquisitions are goods acquired for a VAT-exempt or non-business activity. The goods must be supplied by a VAT-registered business in another EU state in the course of that supplier's business. See 2.4.3 'UK registration for relevant intra-EU acquisitions of goods'.

9.6.9 **Removals**

A removal or dispatch of goods from the UK occurs when goods are sent from the UK to another EU state. If there is not already a business supply on removal of business goods from the UK, then there is (subject to exceptions as outlined below) a deemed business supply of those goods when removed from the UK if all of the following conditions are met:

1. The goods are business assets of the dispatcher.
2. The goods are removed from the UK in the course or furtherance of a business activity of the dispatcher.
3. The goods are removed by or under the direction of the dispatcher.
4. The removal is to another EU state.

This deeming rule can apply if the goods are transferred other than as a supply, for example where goods are transferred within the same entity such as transfers between different branches of a business. If the corresponding acquisition is by a VAT-registered business, the removal can be zero-rated providing any qualifying conditions are met. See 9.6.10 'Zero-rating removals'.

However, there are many exceptions to this deeming rule, including the following:

- **Installed or assembled goods**: see 9.6.21 'Installed and assembled goods'.
- **Temporary transfers**: see 9.6.16 'Transfers of own goods'.
- **Distance-selling**: in some situations a supply is treated as taking place in the customer's state, see 9.6.15 'Distance-selling'.
- **Supplies on board a ship, an aircraft or a train**: these are treated as supplied at the place of departure.

- **Loops**: where the removal is to another part of the same EU state via another, for example, goods sent from England to Northern Ireland via the Republic of Ireland, the supply is not seen as intra-EU.
- **Call-off stock**: this means goods transferred by the supplier to another EU state, to be held for calling off by an individual customer. See 9.6.20 'Consignment and call-off stock'.
- **Returns**: goods sent for valuation or repair and which will be returned afterwards.
- **Gas or electricity networks**: the removal of gas through a natural gas system situated within the territory of an EU state or any network connected to such a system; electricity; or heat or cooling supplied through a network. The place of such supplies is the EU state of removal.
- **Disposals for free**: if business goods on which VAT has been recovered are given away for free, there is a deemed business supply of those goods on disposal. This 'business disposal' deeming overrides the 'removal deeming' to create any necessary business supply.

9.6.10   Zero-rating removals

The conditions for zero-rating a supply from the UK to a customer who is registered for VAT in another EU state are set out in tertiary legislation (where a VAT Notice has the rule of law) in *VAT Notice 725*, section 4. The up-to-date wording of the notice should be referred to. The broad approach is:

1. The supplier must obtain the customer's VAT registration number (in the EU state of acquisition) and show this on its invoice together with the customer's two-letter country prefix code.
2. The supplier should check that the customer's VAT registration number is valid and retain evidence of this check for at least six years. See 14.3 'Checking VAT numbers'.
3. The goods must have physically left the territory of the UK for a destination in another EU state within the requisite time limits. See 9.6.11 'Time limits for removal'.
4. The supplier must obtain evidence of removal of the goods within the requisite time limits and retain this for at least six years. See 9.6.14 'Evidence of removal'.

9.6.11   Time limits for removal

In all cases the time limits for removing the goods and obtaining valid evidence of removal begin from the time of supply, and are:

- three months (including supplies of goods involved in groupage or consolidation prior to removal); or
- six months for supplies of goods involved in processing or incorporation prior to removal.

Time limits not met

If the goods do not leave the UK within the time limits or if the evidence requirements are not met within the time limits, the goods should be treated as if supplied to a UK customer and UK VAT charged as appropriate (for example printed matter would be zero-rated). If the goods are subsequently removed from the UK and/or you later obtain evidence showing that the goods were removed, you may zero rate the supply and adjust your VAT account for the period in which you obtain the evidence. This is provided that the goods have not been used in the UK before removal, unless specifically authorised (*VAT Notice 725*, section 16.13).

9.6.12   UK reporting of removals

The supplier must report the sale in Boxes 6 and 8 of the UK VAT return The supplier must report the sale on the UK EC Sales List. See 12.7 'The EC Sales List'. If the supplier is required to complete Intrastat Returns for removals, the supply must be included on that. See 9.6.18 'Intrastat Return'.

9.6.13   Time of supply for removals

The tax point for a supply of goods to a VAT-registered customer in another EU state is the earlier of either:

- the fifteenth day of the month following the one in which the goods are dispatched; or
- the date a VAT invoice is issued for the supply.

If you receive payment in advance of invoicing or delivery, this does not create a tax point for the intra-EU supply. However, you must issue a VAT invoice to your customer for the amount paid to you within 30 days of receipt and the date of issue of the VAT invoice will be the tax point for the payment. Where you issue a series of invoices relating to the same supply of goods, the time limit for obtaining valid evidence of removal begins from the date of the final invoice.

9.6.14   Evidence of removal

The documents you use as proof of removal must clearly identify the following: the supplier, the consignor (where different from the supplier), the customer, the goods, an accurate value, the mode of transport and route of movement of the goods, and the EU destination. Vague descriptions of goods, quantities or values are not acceptable. A combination of the following documents must be used to provide clear evidence that a supply has taken place and the goods have been removed from the UK (*VAT Notice 725*, section 5.1):

- the customer's order;
- inter-company correspondence;

- copy sales invoice;
- advice note;
- packing list;
- commercial transport documents;
- details of insurance or freight charges;
- bank statements as evidence of payment;
- receipted copy of the consignment note as evidence of receipt of goods abroad;
- any other documents relevant to the removal of the goods in question which you would normally obtain in the course of your intra-EU business.

Evidence for postal removals

Goods sent by post may be zero-rated if they are sent directly to a customer who is registered for VAT in another EU state, and you hold the necessary evidence of posting. The receipted forms listed below, plus the Parcelforce Worldwide statement of account or parcel manifest listing each parcel or multi-parcel, will provide evidence of removal.

- **Letter post or airmail**: a fully completed certificate of posting form presented with the goods, and stamped by the Post Office.
- **Post Office SmartPost**: if the parcel is taken to a post office, the counter clerk will provide you with a printed proof of shipment from the Post Office SmartPost system. You should keep this printed proof of shipment as your evidence of removal.
- **Couriers and fast parcel services**: Most courier and fast parcel operators do not issue separate certificates of shipment. The invoice for moving goods from the UK, which bears details of the unique airway bill numbers for each shipment, represents normal commercial evidence of removal. In addition, many express companies are able to offer a track and trace service via their websites where the movement of goods can be traced through to the final destination. This information can be printed and also be used to confirm removal from the UK. see *VAT Notice 725*, section 5 for more information.

9.6.15 Distance-selling

Distance sales are sales of goods, made in the course of a taxable business activity, to unregistered customers in other EU states where the supplier or an agent of the supplier is responsible for the delivery of the goods.

Where a UK supplier starts to make distance sales, UK VAT is charged at the rates that would apply if the sales had been made to customers in the UK. The sales are not included in Box 8 (EC Sales) on the VAT return, although they are included as part of UK sales on the return (Boxes 1 and 6).

When the total annual VAT-exclusive value of sales to customers in any particular EU state reaches that state's **distance-selling threshold**, the UK supplier must register for VAT in that state and then charge local VAT on those sales and complete a local VAT return. The place of supply of the supply to the end customer switches to the other EU state.

Distance-selling thresholds (at the time of writing) are:

€35,000	Austria, Belgium, Cyprus, Estonia, Finland, Greece, Hungary, Ireland, Italy, Latvia, Lithuania (from 1 January 2015), Malta, Portugal, Slovakia, Slovenia, Spain
€100,000	France*, Germany, Luxembourg, Netherlands
Others	Bulgaria: 70,000 BGN; Croatia: 270,000 HRK; Czech Republic: 1,140,000 CZK; Denmark: 280,000 DKK; Poland: 160,000 PLN; Romania: 118,000 RON; Sweden: 320,000 SEK; UK: £70,000

* In October 2015, France announced it is to lower its distance selling VAT threshold from €100,000 to €35,000 from 1 January 2016.

Businesses may also register voluntarily in the destination state before the distance-selling threshold is reached. The sales are then included in Box 8 of the UK VAT return. The business must also notify HMRC by writing or by phoning the VAT Helpline.

To assess if a threshold has been breached, the total net value (excluding VAT) of distance sales from the last 1 January to customers in an EU state must be compared to that EU state's distance-selling threshold. If the value of sales goes over the threshold you are then required to register for VAT in that state and start charging VAT on all subsequent distance sales to that state. You remain liable to be registered for VAT in that state in accordance with that state's distance-selling rules. This normally includes any calendar year where the threshold was exceeded in the previous calendar year.

Future changes to distance-selling

In the *Digital Single Market Strategy for Europe*, the EC (2015) announced its plan to extend the Mini One Stop Shop (MOSS) reporting regime used for certain cross-border digital services to tangible goods ordered online both within and outside the EU. Instead of having to declare and pay VAT to each individual EU state where its customers are based, businesses would be able to make a single declaration and payment in their own member state. See 9.9 'The Mini One Stop Shop (MOSS)'.

9.6.16 **Transfers of own goods**

If business goods are transferred from one EU state to a branch of the same legal entity located in another EU state the removal from the first EU state can be a deemed business supply of those goods in the EU state of removal (see 9.6.9 'Removals'). However, this does not include the temporary transfer of goods abroad, see 'Conditions for temporary transfer of goods' below.

Both branches registered for VAT

If both branches are registered for VAT in their respective states, then, providing the zero-rating conditions are met, the dispatching branch zero rates the removal and the acquiring branch charges itself acquisition VAT.

Acquiring branch not registered for VAT

If the acquiring branch is not registered for VAT locally, but the dispatching branch is VAT-registered in its EU state, the dispatcher must charge its country's VAT on the removal (subject to the local distance-selling thresholds – see above). This VAT is irrecoverable for the dispatching branch. However, if the acquiring branch subsequently registers for VAT in the state of acquisition, and that registration is backdated to include the period when the goods were transferred, HMRC accepts (*VATSM4320*) that the **deemed supply** may be retrospectively zero-rated subject to:

(i)   possession of satisfactory documentary evidence that the goods have left the UK;
(ii) inclusion of the value of the deemed supply on a current EC Sales List; and
(iii) acquisition VAT having been accounted for on the goods in the member state of arrival.

Some member states will only register businesses from a current date, in which case the business should obtain written confirmation from the tax authorities in the member state concerned that they will not allow retrospective registration. Subject to this confirmation, and meeting the further conditions set out above, the supply may be zero-rated.

Dispatching branch not registered for VAT

If the dispatching branch is not registered for VAT, no VAT is chargeable by either branch, though the sending branch may need to register locally if the value of its UK supplies exceeds the local VAT Registration Threshold and the receiving branch may need to register for VAT locally subject to the local registration rules.

Conditions for temporary transfer of goods

The goods must be either (*VAT Notice 725*, section 10):

- transferred temporarily to another member state in order to make a supply of services there. You must not have a place of business in the member state to which the goods are temporarily transferred. You must have a specific contract to fulfil, and you must intend to return the goods to the member state from which they were dispatched. This can apply to tools and equipment which you take to another member state to use there. It also applies to goods that are loaned or leased to somebody in another member state; or
- transferred to another member state for temporary use there. The goods must be eligible for temporary importation relief if they were imported from outside the EU and they must remain in the other member state for no longer than two years.

Although these transfers of your own goods are not treated as supplies for VAT purposes, you still need commercial evidence that the goods left the UK and have later returned. You must also maintain a register of temporary movements of goods

Register of temporary movements of goods

HMRC explains (*VAT Notice 725*, section 16.9)

> If you are a taxable person and you move goods to, or receive goods from, other Member States on a temporary basis, you must keep a register of temporary movements of goods. The register need not be kept in any particular format but it must be readily available for all goods temporarily moved to and from the UK and include in the register all goods moved between the UK and other Member States where they are to be returned within a period of two years after their first removal or receipt. It would also be advisable to include any goods for which you are not sure of the date of return.

9.6.17 Humanitarian aid

If humanitarian aid is provided within the territory of the EU, then that is not an export of goods. So the special zero-rating for charity exports does not apply. Giving away aid goods for free within the territory of the EU is likely to be a non-business activity, so any VAT incurred on the aid goods is irrecoverable.

There is a special import VAT exemption for goods imported by a relevant organisation for distribution or loan, free of charge, to victims of a disaster affecting the territory of one or more member states. However, the EC has to make a decision authorising importation of the goods. See 9.5.6 'Import VAT exemptions'

357

9.6.18   Intrastat Return

Intrastat is an EU system for gathering statistics on the level of trade in goods (arrivals and removals) between EU states. Unregistered businesses and organisations moving goods for non-business purposes are exempt from the Intrastat requirements, as are businesses below the Intrastat reporting thresholds of:

• dispatches: £0.25 million;
• arrivals: from 1 January 2014: £1.2 million, from 1 January 2015: £1.5 million.

Where the total level of dispatches or arrivals exceeds these thresholds, then an Intrastat Supplementary Declaration (SD) must be submitted in respect of dispatches or arrivals or both.

At the time of writing, the EU plans to further reduce the level of Intrastat reporting including possibly abolition of the acquisitions threshold (HMRC 2013, *Intrastat: Revised Arrivals Exemption Threshold*, July).

Delivery terms threshold

From 1 January 2014: £24 million; before: £16 million. The same threshold for delivery terms applies to arrivals and dispatches. If your annual EU trade is above the delivery terms threshold you are required to supply additional information relating to delivery terms on your SDs.

Services

Intrastat only applies to intra-EU supplies of goods, it does not apply to intra-EU supplies of services, unless they are an integral part of a contract for the supply of goods (for instance, freight and insurance charges directly related to a particular supply), when they are included in the price of the supply.

Low-value consignment threshold

Low-value transactions can be aggregated and classified to a single commodity code (9950 0000), provided these transactions have a value of £180 or less.

The threshold test

The threshold applies on a calendar year basis (January to December). Once you have exceeded the threshold you must submit SDs until the end of the calendar year and for the next calendar year. If you exceed the threshold for arrivals but not for dispatches, you only have to complete SDs for arrivals and vice versa.

9.6.19 **Triangulation**

Triangulation refers to the situation where an intermediary supplier (I) in an EU state purchases goods from a supplier (S) in another EU state and sells them on to a customer (C) in a third EU state, but the goods are sent directly from S to C.

Under the basic place of supply of goods rules I would have to register for VAT in either S or C's state; however, an optional simplification procedure called triangulation operates to avoid this. This works as follows (assuming I is in the UK):

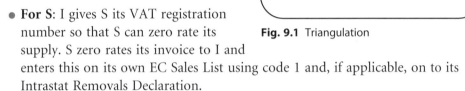

Fig. 9.1 Triangulation

- **For S**: I gives S its VAT registration number so that S can zero rate its supply. S zero rates its invoice to I and enters this on its own EC Sales List using code 1 and, if applicable, on to its Intrastat Removals Declaration.
- **For I**: C provides I with its VAT registration number. I zero rates its supply to C and enters on to its EC Sales List with code 2. I does not account for acquisition VAT and it does not include the sale in boxes 2, 6 or 8 of the UK VAT return, nor does it does it include it on any Intrastat Declaration.
- **For C**: C self-accounts for acquisition VAT and completes any required Intrastat Declaration.

9.6.20 **Consignment and call-off stock**

Consignment stocks

Consignment stocks are goods you transfer between member states to meet future supplies to be made by you, or on your behalf, in the member state of arrival. The movement of the goods occurs before a customer has been found for them. Consignment stocks are treated as a transfer of business goods (see 9.6.16 'Transfers of own goods') and reported when transferred.

Call-off stocks

Call-off stocks are goods transferred by the supplier to another EU State, to be held for an individual customer in the EU State of arrival pending 'call-off' for use by the customer as needed. Title and ownership of the goods remains with the supplier. In cases where the goods are destined for a single identified VAT-registered customer either for consumption within their business, or with which to make onward supplies to their own customers, then the supplier can treat the supply of the goods as a zero-rated removal, provided the customer provides a valid VAT number and the normal zero-rating conditions are met. This avoids the need for a supplier to register for VAT in the customer's EU state. A customer receiving call-off stock treats it as an acquisition. Call-off goods delivered to storage facilities operated by the supplier, rather than the customer, should be treated as consignment stocks, unless the customer is aware of the details of deliveries into storage.

Variation across EU

Not all EU states permit this special call-off stock treatment and those that do subject it to specific requirements. The UK does permit inward call-off stock arrangements. You should check each individual state's requirements.

9.6.21 Installed and assembled goods

A supply of installed or assembled goods occurs when you supply goods and there is a contractual obligation for you to install or assemble the goods for your customer on their premises. For example, a supplier of studio recording equipment where the supply involves installation at the customer's studio. The place of supply of installed or assembled goods is where the installation or assembly of the goods is carried out. The movement of the goods between EU States as part of a supply of installed or assembled goods is not treated as a supply of own goods on removal and is not treated as an acquisition in the EU State of installation or assembly.

Simplified procedure

The supplier of the goods is liable to register for VAT in any EU State in which it supplies installed or assembled goods. However, some EU States operate a simplified procedure which permits the VAT-registered customer to account for the VAT due as acquisition VAT with you zero-rating the removal. You are not required to register in an EU State which has this facility. The UK uses the simplified procedure. This applies when:

- the customer is registered for VAT in the UK;
- the supplier is registered for VAT in another member state; and
- the supplier is not required to be registered here for any other reason.

Only a limited number of EU states permit the simplified procedure (or local versions thereof).

9.6.22   EC proposals for reform

The special rules for intra-EU transfers of goods were introduced in 1992 and have always been regarded as a temporary measure. They are problematic in that they are susceptible to fraud and complicated to operate. In October 2014 the EC set out options for changes to the way intra-EU transfers of goods are dealt with, the objectives being to subject cross-border supplies of goods to VAT in the EU state of consumption whilst at the same time making doing business across the EU as simple and as secure as engaging in purely domestic activities. Options under consideration include:

- requiring the supplier to charge the customer state's VAT and account for this to the customer's state, via a one-stop-shop-type VAT return (see 9.9 'The Mini One Stop Shop (MOSS)'); the EC has now proposed implementing this for distance sales (see 9.6.15 'Distance-selling');
- introducing a **B2B** (business to business) reverse charge-type mechanism, see 9.8 'Place of supply of services rules';
- simplifying the existing rules.

9.7   CROSS-BORDER SERVICES INTRODUCTION

The cross-border supply of services rules may affect you if you supply services to a customer who belongs outside the UK or purchase services from a supplier who belongs outside the UK. Please note the following:

- **Goods**: the rules are different for supplies of goods. See 9.3 'Cross-border goods introduction'.
- **Privileged persons**: supplies of services to privileged persons in other EU states attract special VAT treatment in the same way as do supplies of goods to **privileged persons** (see 9.6 'Intra-EU transfers of goods').

Privileged persons include diplomatic missions, the institutions of the EU, international treaty organisations, and NATO armed forces in particular circumstances. For the special VAT rules for privileged persons see 6.4.11 'Privileged persons in other EU states'. Unless otherwise stated, references to HMRC guidance in this section are to *VAT Notice 741A*.

9.7.1 Meaning of place of supply of services

A supply of services is deemed to take place at a particular location (its **place of supply**) at a particular time (its **time of supply**). That place of supply is where, if it is due, the output VAT is due to an EU VAT authority:

1. If the place of supply is the UK, then the UK VAT rules apply and any output VAT due is due to HMRC. UK input VAT incurred in making the supply is recoverable under the UK's VAT recovery rules.
2. If the place of supply is another EU state, then that state's VAT rules apply and any output VAT due is that state's output VAT due to that state's VAT authority. UK input VAT incurred in making the supply can be recovered in the UK VAT return if the input VAT would have been recoverable had the place of supply been the UK.
3. If the place of supply is outside the EU, the supply is outside the scope of UK and EU VAT, though UK input VAT incurred in making the supply can be recovered in the UK VAT return if the input VAT would have been recoverable had the place of supply been the UK.

The reverse charge

It is normally the supplier that must charge, collect and account for output VAT to the relevant EU VAT authority; however, to avoid the need for a supplier who is not established in an EU state to have to register for VAT in that EU state, and to help ensure collection of VAT, for some supplies of services a locally established customer is required to self-account for output VAT to their local VAT authority, under what is referred to as the **reverse charge**.

This is explained further in 9.7.4 'Reverse charge'.

9.7.2 Place of supply steps

To determine the place of supply of a service:

1. First check that the transaction is a business supply. The principles involved are explained in Chapter 4 'Business and non-business activities'.
2. If the transaction is a business supply, determine the **service type**. There are various specific types ('services related to land', etc.) and if a service does not fall into one of the specific types, a catch-all **general rule** service type. See 9.8 'Place of supply of services rules' for a listing and explanation of the service types. From the service type you can then determine the place of supply.
3. If the place of supply is the UK or another EU state, check if the supply is VAT exempt or subject to the 'reverse charge'. The applicable VAT exemption and reverse charge rules are those of the EU state of supply.

9.7.3 **B2B and B2C**

Some of the place of supply rules (including the general rule) depend on whether the supply is B2B (business to business) or B2C (business to customer or business to consumer).

B2B (Business to business) supply

This is a supply to a customer who has some level of business activity (exempt or taxable). It will normally include supplies to customers who are registered for VAT in any EU state or who are registered for a similar sales tax outside the EU. However, if a business customer purchases services wholly for the private use of the business's owners or its staff, then the supply is treated as B2C.

B2B supplies include supplies to businesses that are not registered for VAT because they make only VAT-exempt supplies and supplies to businesses which make taxable supplies below their local VAT registration threshold. However, if a customer has no business activities and is not VAT-registered then the supply is B2C.

If the customer has mixed business and non-business activities, the supply does not have to be for the purposes of the customer's business activity in order to be B2B. The CJEU case C-291/07 *Kollektivavtalsstiftelsen TRR Trygghetsrådet* v. *Skatteverket* [2008] ECR I-08255 established that for the B2B treatment it is enough that the customer has some level of business activity.

B2C (Business to customer or business to consumer) supplies

These are supplies to customers who do not have any business activities at all. For example, supplies to individuals acting in a private capacity, and supplies to charities, voluntary organisations and public bodies with no business activities. They also include supplies to businesses wholly for the private use of the business's owners or its staff.

B2B evidence

It is generally preferable from the customer's perspective to receive B2B treatment. So, if you supply services to a foreign customer, you must take steps to check that your customer qualifies for B2B treatment and retain this evidence in case of HMRC query. If you are a customer, you may have to provide a foreign supplier with evidence of your business status in order to establish B2B status for a supply.

HMRC provides the following guidance on establishing B2B customer status (*VAT Notice 741A*, section 2.7):

> To satisfy yourself that B2B status applies you should obtain commercial evidence showing that your customer belongs outside the UK and does not receive your supply for a wholly private purpose.
>
> For some supplies of services it will be clear that the supply would not be purchased by anyone for a wholly private purpose.
>
> VAT registration numbers are the best evidence that the supply is not received for a wholly private purpose and should be requested. If your customer is unable to provide a VAT number, you can accept alternative evidence. This includes certificates from fiscal authorities, business letterheads or other commercial documents indicating the nature of the customer's activities. Such evidence should be kept as part of your records. Where VAT numbers are available, they should be shown on your invoice.

HMRC imposes extra evidence requirements for the following supplies:

- a B2B reverse charge supply of electronically supplied services – see 9.8 'Place of supply of services rules';
- B2C intra-EU supplies of digital services (electronic, TV or broadcasting services) – see 9.9 'The Mini One Stop Shop (MOSS)'.

9.7.4 Reverse charge

Under the reverse charge (or 'tax shift'), the liability for paying the output VAT due on a supply of services is moved from the supplier to the customer. This avoids the need for the supplier to register for VAT in the customer's EU state. The reverse charge can affect UK-based establishments in two ways:

1. As a customer

If the place of supply is the UK, a UK VAT-registered customer must self-account for any UK output VAT due to HMRC under the UK reverse charge. The customer is seen as making the supply to themselves in the UK. They charge themselves UK output VAT at the applicable UK rate of VAT. This is added to box 1 on the UK VAT return. The customer is also seen as receiving the supply from themselves. The UK output VAT charged can be recovered as UK input VAT subject to the normal UK VAT recovery rules.

The UK reverse charge applies to a UK customer if all of the following conditions are met (summarised from *VAT Notice 741A*, section 18):

1. The place of supply is the UK.
2. The customer **belongs** in the UK for the purposes of receiving the supply.
3. The supplier does not belong in the UK for the purposes of making the supply.
4. The supply is not VAT exempt and would not be exempt but for an option to tax.
5. The **supply type** is any of:
   (i)   B2B general rule;
   (ii)   B2B services relating to land;
   (iii) B2B event admissions;
   (iv)   B2B passenger transport;
   (v)   B2B services covered by the additional rules (use & enjoyment override) for hired goods (including hired means of transport), telecommunications services, radio and television broadcasting services and electronically supplied services.

If the supply type is any of (5)(ii)–(5)(iv), the UK customer must also be UK VAT-registered. If the supply type is B2B general rule and the customer is not registered for VAT, the supply counts towards the customer's UK VAT registration threshold.

For the meaning of 'belongs' see 9.7.5 'Place of belonging', and for the supply types see 9.8 'Place of supply of services rules'.

2. As a supplier

If the place of supply is another EU state and the reverse charge applies, the customer must self-account for any output VAT due to their local tax authority under their local EU reverse charge. This avoids the need for the UK supplier to register for VAT in the customer's state. A UK VAT-registered supplier must record the sale on its 'EC Sales List' and state 'subject to the reverse charge' (or equivalent) on its VAT invoice to the customer.

The reverse charge applies to a supply by a UK supplier if all of the following conditions are met:

1. The place of supply is another EU state.
2. The customer belongs in that state for the purposes of receiving the supply.
3. The supplier does not belong in that state for the purposes of making the supply.
4. The supply is not VAT exempt under that state's rules.
5. The supply type is B2B general rule, or the state concerned applies the reverse charge to the supply. Most EU states extend the reverse charge to other supplies, though treatments vary. See 14.4 'VAT in other EU states'.

EC Sales List

If a UK VAT-registered supplier makes a B2B reverse charge supply of services to a VAT-registered customer who belongs in another EU state, then the UK supplier must report that sale to HMRC on form VAT 101, the 'EC Sales List'. However, B2B reverse charge sales to unregistered customers in other EU states should be omitted from the EC Sales List. See 12.7 'The EC Sales List' for guidance on how to complete the EC Sales List. Any errors or omissions must be reported on form *VAT101B EC*.

Zero-rated supplies

If you receive a reverse charge supply in the UK that is zero-rated under the UK rules, for example a French business supplies advertising services to a UK charity, the reverse charge does not apply (*VAT Notice 741A*, section 18.10.2). Or it can be seen as applying, but at a zero rate.

VAT recovery

The deemed supply by the customer to themselves is ignored when calculating taxable turnover for partial exemption and business/non-business apportionment calculations.

9.7.5   **Place of belonging**

Some of the place of supply rules depend on where the customer or supplier 'belongs'. To determine where a customer or supplier belongs you must first establish if they are a business, a legal entity with no business activities, or a private individual acting as a private individual.

1. Business

The place of belonging of a business supplier or business customer is determined as follows.

Business establishment

By default a business belongs in the state where its **business establishment** is located. A business can have only one business establishment. The business establishment is the place where the functions of the business's central administration are carried out. In order to determine this, account must be taken of:

- the place where essential decisions concerning the general management of the business are taken;
- the place where the registered office of the business is located; and
- the place where management meets.

Where these criteria do not allow the place of establishment of a business to be determined with certainty, the place where essential decisions concerning the general management of the business are taken takes precedence. This will normally be where the business's head office is located. The mere presence of a postal address may not be taken to be the place of establishment of a business.

Fixed establishment

For a particular supply, however, the place of belonging of a business customer or supplier can switch to a **fixed establishment**.

- **For a business supplier**: if the supplier's services are provided from a fixed establishment of the supplier located in a different state, the place of belonging of the supplier for that supply switches to the state where that fixed establishment is located. For a supplier a fixed establishment is any establishment of the supplier, other than its business establishment, characterised by a sufficient degree of permanence and a suitable structure in terms of human and technical resources to enable it to provide the services which it supplies.
- **For a business customer**: if the services are provided to a fixed establishment of the customer located in a different state, the place of belonging of the customer for that supply switches to where that fixed establishment is located. For a customer a fixed establishment is any establishment of the customer, other than its business establishment, characterised by a sufficient degree of permanence and a suitable structure in terms of human and technical resources to enable it to receive and use the services supplied to it for its own needs.

Permanent address or residence

In the absence of any business establishment or fixed establishment, a business belongs where it has its permanent address or where it usually resides.

2. Non-business entities

To determine the place of belonging of a non-business legal entity such as a charity with wholly non-business activities, follow the rules for businesses adapting as required.

3. Individuals

If an individual is acting in a business capacity, for example, as a self-employed person, follow the rules for business entities. An individual acting as a private person or in a personal capacity is deemed to belong where they have their permanent address or where they usually reside.

HMRC provides the following guidance on determining the place of belonging of individuals and asylum seekers (*VAT Notice 741A*, section 3.5):

> **Individuals** receiving supplies in a private capacity are treated as belonging in the country where they have their usual place of residence. An individual has only one usual place of residence at any point in time. Individuals are normally resident in the country where they have set up home with their family and are in full-time employment. They are not resident in a country they are only visiting as a tourist.

> **Asylum seekers**. For VAT purposes, persons who have not been granted a right or permission to remain in the UK should be treated as belonging in their country of origin. This will apply to, for example, asylum seekers and those entering the UK without permission. In these circumstances, the country in which individuals have their usual or permanent place of residence can only reasonably be seen to be their country of origin unless and until they are granted the right to remain in the UK. Once an individual has been granted leave or permission to remain in the UK, they belong in the UK.

Business v. fixed establishment

The business establishment is the default and the place of belonging only switches away from that if services are actually supplied to or used at a fixed establishment located in a different state. In cases of doubt, the business establishment takes priority. HMRC provides the following guidance (*VAT Notice 741A*, section 3.6):

> For each supply of services, you are regarded as belonging in the country where the establishment most directly connected with that particular supply is located.

To decide which establishment is most directly connected with the supply, you should consider all the facts, including:

● for suppliers, from which establishment the services are actually provided;
● for recipients, at which establishment the services are actually consumed, effectively used or enjoyed;
● which establishment appears on the contracts, correspondence and invoices;
● where the directors or others who entered into the contract are permanently based; and
● at which establishment decisions are taken and controls are exercised over the performance of the contracts.

Normally it is the establishment actually providing or receiving the supply of services which is the establishment most directly connected with the supply, even if the contractual position is different.

Meaning of fixed establishment

For a fixed establishment to exist, a business must have control over both human and technical resources at that place and it must be a permanent establishment.

In *Munster Inns* v. *Revenue & Customs* [2014] UKFTT 563 (TC), a Guernsey-based builder set up an office in England whilst carrying out reconstruction work on a pub. The office had a desk, computer, storage space and phone connection. The First-tier Tribunal decided that the establishment the builder had in England was one with the necessary structure in terms of human and technical resources to provide the service. However, it did not regard that establishment as sufficiently permanent. The contract was likely to last for seven months with the possibility of extension to two years. However, had new contracts been made for further work to be managed from that office that would have indicated a degree of permanence.

Fixed establishment established by agents

The fixed establishments of a business can include the fixed establishments of an agent. An agent is a separate entity that acts under the direction of and on behalf of the business concerned.

Branches and subsidiaries

A branch is a fixed establishment that is a part of a legal entity. It does not act independently of the legal entity. Internal recharges for services provided between an entity and its branches are in principle not supplies for consideration because a supply requires two independent parties to transact. If a branch is independently established, for example as a separately registered company, and is not in a VAT group with its parent, then supplies can take place between the parent and subsidiary company as they are separate legal entities. However, they may be subject to special anti-avoidance measures, as transactions between connected persons, for example see 4.2.4 'Sales to connected parties'.

9.7.6 Cross-border VAT groups

The Principal VAT Directive allows EU states to regard as a single taxable person any persons established within the territory of that state who, whilst legally independent, are closely bound to one another by financial, economic and organisational links.

As explained in 2.2.7 'Future of VAT grouping', the EC's view is that only business establishments and fixed establishments present in a VAT group's state can join the VAT group. Business or fixed establishments located outside the state must be excluded. At the time of writing, HMRC's position (*VGROUPS02400*) is that, when a UK fixed establishment of an overseas company is included in a UK VAT group, it is that overseas company in its entirety which is included in the group, not just the UK fixed establishment, with the result that intra-group transfers between the overseas company and UK fixed establishment are ignored for VAT.

In the case C-7/13 *Skandia America Corp. (USA) filial Sverige* v. *Skatteverket* [2014], the CJEU decided that recharges for IT services between the supplier SAC and its Swedish branch Skandia Sverige were taxable supplies by SAC to the Swedish VAT group of which Skandia Sverige was a member, on the basis that SAC's supplies are to the VAT group which is an independently identified entity for VAT purposes.

Following this case, in *Revenue & Customs Brief 2/15*, HMRC distinguished the UK's VAT grouping rules from Sweden's, on the basis that, under the Swedish rules, only fixed or business establishments physically located in Sweden can join a Swedish VAT group. HMRC's revised position is that an overseas establishment of a UK-established entity is part of a separate taxable person if the overseas establishment is VAT-grouped in a member state that operates similar 'establishment only' grouping provisions to Sweden. HMRC will confirm which states do this and this will be the case whether or not the entity in the UK is part of a UK VAT group. With effect for supplies on or after 1 January 2016, businesses must treat intra-entity services provided to or by such establishments as supplies made to or by another taxable person.

Intra-group reverse charge

An intra-group supply of services is not ignored (that is, it is seen as being within the scope of VAT) in the following circumstances:

- a foreign member of a VAT group (**the foreign supplier**) makes an intra-group supply of services to a **UK member** of the same group and the place of supply of those services is the UK;
- that intra-group supply is not VAT exempt;
- the foreign supplier has itself been supplied with reverse charge services from outside the group;
- those services received by the supplier were not VAT exempt;
- the foreign supplier received the supplies at an overseas establishment; and
- the foreign supplier used the supplies in making the intra-group supply to the UK member

For valuation purposes, the supply is treated as a supply to a connected person and valued at open market value (see 4.2.4 'Sales to connected parties'). However, at September 2014 HMRC accepts, by concession, that the value of the intra-group supply is limited to the value of bought-in supply from outside the group (or the value of all such supplies), provided that the group is in a position to provide evidence in the UK of the value of those services, and that those services have not been undervalued. This concession is due to be enacted.

HMRC also accepts (*VGROUPS01400*) that the intra-group reverse charge will not become due if the supplier makes a supply of services to a fellow member of the same group entirely out of its own resources, or the supply by the supplier to the UK member would be exempt if it were made in the UK.

HMRC accepts (*Revenue & Customs Brief 2/15*) that the intra-group reverse charge does not apply where a supply is from a group member who is a member of an EU VAT group in a state that adopts Sweden-like VAT grouping rules (see above).

9.7.7 **Exempt supplies**

If the place of a supply of services is within the EU, to determine if the supply is VAT exempt, the VAT-exemption rules that must be considered are those of the EU state of the place of supply.

For example, if a UK charity puts on an educational conference in Germany, then B2C admissions are supplied in Germany. It is the German VAT-exemption rules that must be used to see if the supply is exempt.

HMRC provides the following guidance on determining the VAT-exemption rules in other EU states (*VAT Notice 725*, section 17.26):

The law requires that businesses report supplies of services that are taxable in the customer's Member State (from 1 January 2010) and the onus is on businesses to comply with the law. If reasonable attempts, which may include discussing with the customer, or the customer's tax authority, have failed to ascertain what the VAT treatment is in the other Member State(s), businesses may wish to assume that the UK VAT treatment will apply to those supplies. This is on the basis that it should be consistent with the EC Principal VAT Directive and therefore with the law in other Member States. If subsequently it becomes clear that a supply categorised and reported as taxable is in fact exempt, or vice versa, the business must submit a VAT 101B ESL Correction sheet.

As the exemptions are meant to have the same meanings throughout the EU (see the introduction to Chapter 5 'Exempt activities'), the presumption must be that, for example, what is understood to be education is the same throughout the EU. However, states have some discretion in specifying which bodies are able to make such supplies VAT exempt. So the fact that you are an eligible body in the UK does not necessarily mean you will be eligible in another EU state, and vice versa. There is some (limited) guidance on the different VAT-exemption regimes throughout the EU on the EC's website and most EU states have some information on their VAT regimes in English. See 14.4 'VAT in other EU states'.

UK VAT recovery

Under UK law, UK input VAT incurred in making supplies that take place outside the UK is only recoverable if:

- the supply would be taxable if had taken place in the UK; or
- is an exempt supply of insurance or certain financial services supplied to a person who belongs outside the EU.

9.7.8 Use and enjoyment overrides

EU member states may override the normal place of supply rules to treat certain services as supplied within their territory if the place of supply is outside the EU but the services are effectively used and enjoyed within their territory and as supplied outside the EU if the place of supply is their territory but the services are effectively used and enjoyed outside the EU. This is referred to as a 'use and enjoyment override'. The place where a service is effectively used and enjoyed is where it is consumed. The UK has applied the use and enjoyment override to:

- B2B electronically supplied services (see rule 6 below);
- TV, broadcasting and telecoms services (see rule 7 below);
- hire of means of transport (see rules 10 and 11 below);
- hire of other goods (see rule 12 below).

Though see the rules below as some of the implementations are partial.

9.8 PLACE OF SUPPLY OF SERVICES RULES

These rules are for cross-border services as at June 2015. Check *VAT Notice 741A* at the time of your situation as the rules are subject to change and changes of interpretation. The **general rule** applies unless one of the other more specific rules applies:

Place of supply rules – cross-border services		B2B supplies	B2C supplies
1	General rule	Where the customer belongs subject to (a)	Where the supplier belongs
2	Services related to land	Where the land is subject to (b)	Where the land is
3	Services in respect of admission to cultural, artistic, sporting, scientific, educational, entertainment or similar events, such as fairs and exhibitions	Where event takes place subject to (b)	Where event takes place
4	Services relating to cultural, artistic, sporting, scientific, educational, entertainment or similar activities such as fairs and exhibitions	General rule	Where performance takes place
5	Intellectual property rights, advertising, consultancy and professional services, data processing, supply of information, financial services, supply of staff	General rule	Where the supplier belongs subject to (c)
6	Electronically supplied services	General rule subject to (e)	General rule, subject to (c), (f) and (g)
7	TV, broadcasting and telecoms services	General rule subject to (e)	General rule, subject to (c), (d) and (g)

Cont.

Place of supply rules – cross-border services		B2B supplies	B2C supplies
8	Passenger transport (excluding supplies under Tour Operators' Margin Scheme (TOMS))	Where the transport takes place subject to (b) and (j)	Where the transport takes place subject to (j)
9	Transport of goods	General rule subject to (k)	Where the transport takes place subject to (j) and (l)
10	Short-term hire of means of transport	Where put at the disposal of the customer, subject to (e)	Where put at the disposal of the customer, subject to (d)
11	Long-term hire of means of transport	General rule subject to (e)	Where the customer belongs, subject to (d) and (i)
12	Hire of goods excluding means of transport	General rule subject to (e)	General rule subject to (c) and (d)
13	Works on goods	General rule	Where physically performed
14	Restaurant and catering services	Where physically carried out subject to (h)	Where physically carried out subject to (h)
15	Intermediary services	General rule	The place of supply of the underlying service
16	Tour Operators' Margin Scheme (TOMS)	Where supplier belongs subject to (m)	Where supplier belongs subject to (m)

(a) Reverse charge applies if the customer belongs in the EU.

(b) UK reverse charge applies if the supplier belongs outside the UK, the place of supply is the UK, the customer belongs in the UK and the customer is UK VAT-registered. Local reverse charges may also apply to supplies in other EU states as well, seek country specific guidance.

(c) If the customer belongs outside the EU, the place of supply is outside the EU.

(d) Use and enjoyment override:

(i) if the place of supply is the UK but the supply is to any extent effectively used and enjoyed outside the EU, then the place of supply is to that extent outside the EU;

(ii) if the place of supply is outside the EU but the supply is to any extent effectively used and enjoyed in the UK, then the place of supply is to that extent the UK.

(e) As for (d). Under rule (ii), if the customer belongs in the UK and is registered for VAT in the UK, the reverse charge applies.

(f) To 31 December 2014 only. If the supplier belongs outside the EU and the customer belongs inside the EU, the place of supply is where the customer belongs. Non-EU suppliers can opt to use a Special Scheme for non-EU businesses to register in just one EU state. With effect from 1 January 2015 this is replaced by (g) below.

(g) From 1 January 2015, if the customer belongs in the EU, the place of supply is where the customer belongs. There is a nil registration threshold for such supplies. EU and non-EU suppliers can opt to register for MOSS to submit a pan-EU VAT return. See 9.9 'The Mini One Stop Shop (MOSS)'.

(h) If the restaurant and catering services are supplied on a ship, aircraft or train for the transportation of passengers on an intra-EU journey the place of supply is the member state of departure.

(i) The long-term hire of a pleasure boat which is put at the disposal of the customer at the supplier's business establishment, or at some other fixed establishment of the supplier, is to be treated as supplied where the pleasure boat is put at the disposal of the customer.

(j) If the transport takes place in more than one country, it is treated as supplied in each country in proportion to the distance covered in that country.

(k) If the transport takes place wholly outside the EU, the place of supply is outside the EU.

(l) If the transport is intra-EU (from one EU state to another) the place of supply is where the transportation begins.

(m) For the TOMS see 10.2 'Tour Operators' Margin Scheme (TOMS)'.

Rule priority

In *RCI Europe* case C-37/08 *RCI Europe* v. *Revenue & Customs* [2009] ECR I-07533, the CJEU held that the underlying logic of the place of supply rules requires that goods and services are taxed as far as possible in the place of consumption. So if a supply is eligible for more than one of the specific rules, the rule that most closely approximates to taxation in the place of consumption takes priority.

9.8.1 **General rule**

General rule	B2B	Where the customer belongs subject to (a)
	B2C	Where the supplier belongs

(a)   Reverse charge applies if customer belongs in the EU.

The **general rule** applies to a cross-border supply of services if none of the more specific rules (2)–(16) below applies.

History

Before 1 January 2010 the general rule was that the place of supply is where the supplier belongs (B2B and B2C).

9.8.2 **Services related to land**

Services related to land	B2B	Where the land is subject to (b)
	B2C	Where the land is

(b)   UK reverse charge applies if:

- the supplier belongs outside the UK;
- the place of supply is the UK;
- the customer belongs in the UK; and
- the customer is UK VAT-registered.

The UK reverse charge does not apply if the underlying supply is VAT exempt or would be VAT exempt but for an option to tax. If a foreign business opts to tax UK land, it must register for VAT in the UK and charge UK VAT on all of its supplies of that land, for both B2B and B2C.

Local reverse charges may also apply to land-related supplies in EU states as well. Seek country-specific guidance.

Services related to land include the following:

- supplies of freeholds, leases and licences to occupy land or any other contractual right exercisable over or in relation to land, including the provision of holiday accommodation, seasonal pitches for caravans, facilities at caravan parks for persons for whom such pitches are provided, and pitches for tents;
- the provision in an hotel, inn, boarding house or similar establishment of sleeping accommodation or of accommodation in rooms which are provided in conjunction with sleeping accommodation or for a supply of catering;
- any works of construction, demolition, conversion, reconstruction, alteration, enlargement, repair or maintenance of a building or civil engineering work;
- services such as are supplied by estate agents, auctioneers, architects, surveyors, engineers and others involved in matters relating to land.

Exclusions

The following supplies are excluded from this rule:

- the legal administration of a deceased person's estate;
- advice or information relating to land or property markets;
- insurance of property;
- the hiring out of civil engineering plant;
- feasibility studies assessing the potential of particular businesses or business potential in a particular geographic area;
- provision of a recording studio where technicians are included;
- repair and maintenance of free-standing machinery;
- intermediary services for booking hotel or similar accommodation;
- the drawing up of plans for a building if not designated for a particular site.

CJEU case law

In case C-166/05 *Heger Rudi GmbH* v. *Finanzamt Graz-Stadt* [2006] ECR I-07749, the CJEU decided that there must be a 'sufficiently direct connection' between the supply of services and the immovable property concerned, on the ground that it would be contrary to the general scheme of the rule to include every supply of services provided that it has a connection, even a very tenuous one, with immovable property, since a large number of services are connected in one way or another with immovable property.

9.8.3 **B2B Event admissions**

Services in respect of admission to cultural, artistic, sporting, scientific, educational, entertainment or similar events, such as fairs and exhibitions, including **ancillary services** (defined under 'Ancillary services' below) relating to admission to such events	B2B	Where event takes place subject to (b)
	B2C	Where event takes place (via rule 4)

(**b**) UK reverse charge applies if the supplier belongs outside the UK, the place of supply is the UK, the customer belongs in the UK and the customer is UK VAT-registered. Local reverse charges may also apply to supplies in other EU states as well; seek country-specific guidance.

This rule strictly only applies to B2B supplies. However, for B2C supplies of event admissions, the broader rule 4 (B2C services relating to events) makes the supply where the event occurs.

This rule treats B2B services in respect of admission to cultural, artistic, sporting, scientific, educational, entertainment or similar events, such as fairs and exhibitions, as supplied where the event takes place. The rule includes ancillary services relating to admission to such events. Event admissions include the supply of services of which the essential characteristics are the granting of the right of admission to an event in exchange for a ticket or payment, payment in the form of a subscription, a season ticket or a periodic fee, including:

- the right of admission to shows, theatrical performances, circus performances, fairs, amusement parks, concerts, exhibitions, and other similar cultural events;
- the right of admission to sporting events such as matches or competitions;
- the right of admission to educational and scientific events such as conferences and seminars.

Exclusions

The right to use of facilities such as gymnastics halls and similar, in exchange for a fee.

Meaning of event

HMRC's position (*VATPOSS08256*) is that short-duration educational activities such as conferences are events, but events that are only a small or minor part of the supply may be considered to be incidental or ancillary to the main element. For example, an education course may consist of extensive reading materials, marked assignments and examinations, along with a number of classroom sessions. In this case the classroom session, which could potentially otherwise be seen as an event, would represent a non-dominant part of the overall supply of education.

Meaning of admission

HMRC draws a distinction between a supply of admission to an event and a supply of the event itself (*VATPOSS08254*), for example where an organisation pays a third party to host and organise a conference for its staff. This is not a supply of event admissions by the third-party organiser, but comes under the general rule if B2B and rule 4 below if B2C. If event admission is provided as a part of a package of goods and/or services, the normal rules for determining single and multiple supplies apply, see 11.3 'Single and multiple supplies'

Ancillary services

Ancillary services include services which are directly related to admission to such events and which are supplied separately for a consideration to a person attending an event. Such ancillary services include the use of cloakrooms or sanitary facilities but do not include mere intermediary services relating to the sale of tickets (i.e. ticket agents).

Conference stands and packages

HMRC policy on the supply of sites at exhibitions and conferences is (*Revenue & Customs Brief 22/12*):

> Currently HMRC regards the supply of specific stand space at an exhibition or conference as a supply of land. This policy will continue where the service is restricted to the mere supply of space without any accompanying services. However, where stand space is provided with accompanying services as a package, this package (stand and services) will no longer be seen as a supply of land with land related services but will be taxed under the general place of supply rule

(customer location) when supplied to business customers. Accompanying services provided as part of a package includes such things as the design and erection of a temporary stand, security, power, telecommunications, hire of machinery or publicity material.

History

See 'History' under 9.8.4.

9.8.4 **B2C services relating to cultural, artistic, sporting, scientific, educational, entertainment or similar activities**

	B2B	General rule (but see also rule 3)
Services relating to cultural, artistic, sporting, scientific, educational, entertainment or similar activities	B2C	Where activity takes place

With effect from 1 January 2011 this rule only applies to B2C supplies. However, B2B supplies of event admissions are caught by rule 3 (B2B event admissions).

> These are B2C services relating to cultural, artistic, sporting, scientific, educational, entertainment or similar activities, such as fairs and exhibitions, and ancillary services relating to such activities (including services of organisers of such activities). They include B2C admissions to cultural, artistic, sporting, scientific, educational, entertainment or similar events.

Scientific services

HMRC provides the following guidance (*VATPOSS08400*): B2C scientific services within this section are those which involve the extraction of data for a non-business customer. Where a scientific service is supplied as part of a service of research or a professional advice, then this will normally be viewed as a consultancy service and fall under the general rule (9.8.1) or services of consultants (9.8.5). The services of technicians carrying out tests to obtain data are included within this section. Tests carried out outside the UK where the results are compiled in the UK will not make the supply classed as having been performed in the UK. Scientific services which involve oil/gas/mineral exploration or exploitation relate to land and fall within the land-related services rule (9.8.2).

Educational services

HMRC regards educational services within this section as being those where the teacher and the pupil are in the same place at the same time when the supply of education is made, for example in a classroom (*VATPOSS08500*).

Entertainment services

HMRC's view is that entertainment services within this section usually consist of the services of an artist or performer before a live audience, for example, the services of a DJ or musician at a party (*VATPOSS08550*).

History

Before 1 January 2011 the place of supply of B2B and B2C where performed services was where the activities were physically carried out. This was a single place of supply rule that applied to all supplies within the current rules 3 and 4. This single rule was split with effect from 1 January 2011 into rules 3 and 4.

9.8.5   B2C IP rights, advertising, consultancy, etc.

Intellectual property rights, advertising, consultancy and professional services, data processing, information, financial services, supply of staff	B2B	General rule
	B2C	Where the supplier belongs subject to (c)

(c)   If the customer belongs outside the EU, the place of supply is outside the EU.

Intellectual property rights

These are transfers and assignments of copyright, patents, licences, trademarks and similar rights, and the acceptance of any obligation to refrain from pursuing or exercising (in whole or in part) any business activity or any such rights.

Advertising services

In case C-68/92 *European Commission* v. *France* [1993] ECR I-05881, the CJEU defined advertising services as follows:

> The concept of advertising necessarily entails the dissemination of a message intended to inform consumers of the existence and the qualities of a product or service, with a view to increasing sales. Although that message is usually spread, by means of spoken or printed words and/or pictures, by the press, radio and/or television, this can also be done by the partial or exclusive use of other means...

It is... sufficient that a promotional activity, such as the sale of goods at reduced prices, the handing-out to consumers of goods sold to the person distributing them by an advertising agency, the supply of services at reduced prices or free of charge, or the organisation of a cocktail party or banquet, involves the dissemination of a message intended to inform the public of the existence and the qualities of the product or service which is the subject-matter of the activity, with a view to increasing the sales of that product or service, for the activity to be characterised as an advertising service. The same applies to any activity which forms an inseparable part of an advertising campaign and which thereby contributes to conveying the advertising message. This is the case with regard to the production of aids used for a particular advertisement.

Consultancy and professional services

These are services of consultants, engineers, consultancy bureaux, lawyers, accountants, and similar services. HMRC regards these as including (*VATPOSS13250*): market research; research and development; advisory services; written translation services (see 9.8.4 for B2C translation services supplied at a live event); computer software maintenance (consisting of technical back-up and problem-solving services to correct problems with existing software, including file reconstruction/retrieval). Other similar services include: design services, for example the design of clothes or furniture (but not design services directly related to land, such as those of an architect); services of surveyors providing opinions on matters which do not relate to land; services of specialists or technicians which are essentially creative or artistic in nature.

Data processing

Data processing involves the performing of mathematical and logical operations on data according to programmed instructions in order to obtain required information.

Provision of information

HMRC regards this as including (*VATPOSS13250*): provision of tourist information; information supplied by a private enquiry agent; online information services where the subscriber receives the information and not simply the right to access the system or network; telephone helpdesk services for providing computer software support and similar advice.

Financial services

These are banking, financial and insurance services (including reinsurance), other than the provision of safe deposit facilities.

Supply of staff

This involves putting staff under the direction and control of the customer. See 11.1 'Supplies of staff'.

History

Before 1 January 2010, intra-EU B2B supplies were subject to the reverse charge if the customer received the supply for business purposes. B2B supplies to customers outside the EU were supplied where the customer belongs.

9.8.6 Electronically supplied services

Electronically supplied services	B2B	General rule, subject to (e)
	B2C	General rule, subject to (c) (f) and (g)

(c) If the customer belongs outside the EU, the place of supply is outside the EU.

(e) Use and enjoyment override:
  (i) if the place of supply is the UK but the supply is to any extent effectively used and enjoyed outside the EU, then the place of supply is to that extent outside the EU;
  (ii) if the place of supply is outside the EU but the supply is to any extent effectively used and enjoyed in the UK, then the place of supply is to that extent the UK. If the customer belongs in the UK and is registered for VAT in the UK, the reverse charge applies.

(f) To 31 December 2014 only: if the supplier belongs outside the EU and the customer belongs inside the EU, the place of supply is where the customer belongs. Non-EU suppliers can opt to use a Special Scheme for non-EU businesses to register in just one EU state. With effect from 1 January 2015 this is replaced by (g) below.

(g) From 1 January 2015, if the customer belongs in the EU, the place of supply is where the customer belongs. There is a nil registration threshold for such supplies. EU and non-EU suppliers can opt to register for MOSS to submit a pan-EU VAT return. See 9.9 'The Mini One Stop Shop (MOSS)'.

Electronically supplied services are services which are delivered over the Internet or other electronic network the nature of which renders their supply essentially automated and involving minimal human intervention, and would be impossible to ensure in the absence of information technology. This includes:

- website supply, web-hosting and distance maintenance of programmes and equipment;
- the supply of software and the updating of software;
- the supply of images, text and information, and the making available of databases;
- the supply of music, films and games (including games of chance and gambling games);
- the supply of political, cultural, artistic, sporting, scientific, educational or entertainment broadcasts (including broadcasts of events); and
- the supply of distance teaching but excluding teaching services, where the course content is delivered by a teacher over the Internet or an electronic network.

Determining customer status and location

See 9.9.4 'Determining the status of your customer'.

B2B evidence requirements

VAT Notice 741A, section 19.2 states:

> Under normal trading practices you will often know your business customers. Therefore, in such cases, you will not need to routinely check all VAT numbers quoted, provided that the numbers conform to the correct country format. However, where a relationship has not been established with a business customer the VAT number should be checked when: (i) the VAT involved exceeds £500 on a single transaction, *or* (ii) the cumulative VAT on transactions for electronically supplied services to a single customer in a VAT quarter exceeds £500.

> Similarly, if you supply downloaded music, games, films and so on of a kind normally supplied to a private consumer, you would not expect a VAT number to be quoted in such circumstances. However, where a VAT number is quoted in what is clearly a supply to a private consumer the use of that number should be challenged.

Full verification should be undertaken in *all* cases where you have any reason to believe that a VAT number quoted by a customer is false or is being used incorrectly.

See 14.3 'Checking VAT numbers' for guidance on how to check a foreign VAT registration number. See 9.9.4 'Determining the status of your consumer' for further guidance on determining customer status and location for electronically supplied services.

HMRC example

A UK business purchases downloaded information from another UK business for use both in its UK headquarters and its Canadian branch. Although the supply is received in the UK, to the extent it is used in Canada, it is outside the scope of UK VAT. UK VAT is due only to the extent of use by the UK headquarters.

VATPOSS15500

History

Before 1 January 2010 the place of supply of B2B and B2C electronically supplied services was:

- outside the EU if the customer belonged outside the EU;
- subject to the reverse charge if B2B intra-EU;
- if B2C and the customer belonged in another EU state the place of supply was where the supplier belonged, unless (with effect from 1 July 2003) the supplier belonged outside the EU, in which case the place of supply was where the customer belonged.

9.8.7 Broadcasting and telecoms services

TV, broadcasting and telecoms services	B2B	General rule, subject to (e)
	B2C	General rule, subject to (c), (d) and (g)

(c) If the customer belongs outside the EU, the place of supply is outside the EU.

(d) Use and enjoyment override. There are two rules.
  (i) If the place of supply is the UK but the supply is to any extent effectively used and enjoyed outside the EU, then the place of supply is to that extent outside the EU.
  (ii) If the place of supply is outside the EU but the supply is to any extent effectively used and enjoyed in the UK, then the place of supply is to that extent the UK.

(e) As for (d). Under rule (ii), if the customer belongs in the UK and is registered for VAT in the UK, the reverse charge applies.

(g) From 1 January 2015, if the customer belongs in the EU, the place of supply is where the customer belongs. There is a nil registration threshold for such supplies. EU and non-EU suppliers can opt to register for MOSS to submit a pan-EU VAT return. See 9.9 'The Mini One Stop Shop (MOSS)'.

> **Telecommunications** services are services relating to the transmission or reception of signals, writing, images and sounds or information of any nature by radio, optical or other electromagnetic systems, for example the right to use capacity for such transmission, and the provision of access to global information networks.
>
> **Broadcasting services** comprise the supply of audio and audio-visual content for simultaneous listening or viewing by the general public on the basis of a programme schedule by a person that has editorial responsibility. This includes live streaming via the internet if broadcast at the same time as transmission via radio or television.

Determining customer status and location

See 9.9.4 'Determining the status of your customer'.

9.8.8 Passenger transport

Passenger transport (excluding supplies under TOMS)	B2B	Where the transport takes place subject to (b) and (j)
	B2C	Where the transport takes place subject to (j)

(b) UK reverse charge applies if the supplier belongs outside the UK, the place of supply is the UK, the customer belongs in the UK and the customer is

UK VAT-registered. Local reverse charges may also apply to supplies in EU states as well. Seek country-specific guidance.

(j) If the transport takes place in more than one country, it is treated as supplied in each country in proportion to the distance covered in that country.

> **Passenger transport services** include ancillary services such as the transportation of baggage or motor vehicles accompanying the passenger. It includes pleasure cruises and educational or training cruises. A journey which goes outside the territory of a country but (except in an emergency or involuntarily) does not stop outside that country is treated as made wholly in that country.

TOMS

If bought-in passenger transport is supplied as a part of a package with accommodation or other **travel facilities** (see 10.2.1 'Definitions'), then the mandatory TOMS may apply and override rule 8. See 10.2 'Tour Operators' Margin Scheme (TOMS)' for more on the TOMS.

9.8.9 Transport of goods

Transport of goods	B2B	General rule subject to (k)
	B2C	Where the transport takes place subject to (j) and (l)

(j) If the transport takes place in more than one country, it is treated as supplied in each country in proportion to the distance covered in that country.

(k) If the transport takes place wholly outside the EU, the place of supply is outside the EU.

(l) If the transport is intra-EU (from one EU state to another) the place of supply is where the transportation begins.

Zero-rating

To the extent that freight transport services are supplied in the UK, they qualify for zero-rating if they are connected with an export of the goods to a destination outside the EU or an import of goods from a place of origin outside the EU. See 6.4.7 'Freight transport services' for details.

History

Point (k) above was implemented in UK legislation with effect for supplies on or after 20 December 2012. However, HMRC implemented an 'administrative easement' on 15 March 2010 (*Revenue & Customs Brief 13/10*) as a temporary measure to treat B2B supplies of freight transport services enjoyed outside the EU as supplied outside the EU.

9.8.10 Hire of means of transport

Short-term hire of means of transport	B2B	Where put at the disposal of the customer, subject to (e)
	B2C	Where put at the disposal of the customer, subject to (d)
Long-term hire of means of transport	B2B	General rule subject to (e)
	B2C	Where the customer belongs, subject to (d) and (i)

Short-term means continuous possession or use of the means of transport throughout a period of not more than 30 days and in the case of vessels, not more than 90 days.

(d) Use and enjoyment override. There are two rules.
  (i) If the place of supply is the UK but the supply is to any extent effectively used and enjoyed outside the EU, then the place of supply is to that extent outside the EU.
  (ii) If the place of supply is outside the EU but the supply is to any extent effectively used and enjoyed in the UK, then the place of supply is to that extent the UK.

(e) As for (d). Under rule (ii), if the customer belongs in the UK and is registered for VAT in the UK, the reverse charge applies.

(i) The long-term hire of a pleasure boat which is put at the disposal of the customer at the supplier's business establishment, or at some other fixed establishment of the supplier, is to be treated as supplied where the pleasure boat is put at the disposal of the customer.

Means of transport includes vehicles, whether motorised or not, and other equipment and devices designed to transport persons or objects from one place to another, which might be pulled, drawn or pushed by vehicles and which are normally designed to be used and actually capable of being used for transport.

The place where the means of transport is put at the disposal of the customer is the place where the customer or a third party acting on their behalf takes physical possession of it.

Term of hire

The duration of the continuous possession or use of a means of transport which is the subject of hiring shall be determined on the basis of the contract between the parties involved. The contract shall serve as a presumption which may be rebutted by any means in fact or law in order to establish the actual duration of the continuous possession or use.

The fact that the contractual period of short-term hiring is exceeded on grounds of *force majeure* has no bearing on the determination of the duration of the continuous possession or use of the means of transport. Where hiring of one and the same means of transport is covered by consecutive contracts between the same parties, the duration is that of the continuous possession or use of the means of transport provided for under the contracts as a whole.

9.8.11 Hire of goods excluding means of transport

Hire of other goods (excluding means of transport)	B2B	General rule subject to (e)
	B2C	General rule subject to (c) and (d)

(c) If the customer belongs outside the EU, the place of supply is outside the EU.

(d) Use and enjoyment override. There are two rules.

  (i) If the place of supply is the UK but the supply is to any extent effectively used and enjoyed outside the EU, then the place of supply is to that extent outside the EU.

  (ii) If the place of supply is outside the EU but the supply is to any extent effectively used and enjoyed in the UK, then the place of supply is to that extent the UK.

(e) As for (d). Under rule (ii), if the customer belongs and is registered for VAT in the UK, the reverse charge applies.

> **Goods** include all forms of moveable property but exclude land and property or equipment and machinery installed as a fixture and also exclude means of transport (for which see 9.8.10 'Hire of means of transport').

Exclusion

This rule does not cover supplies of the hire or leasing of goods where the services of an operator or technician are included. In such cases the place of supply of such services depends on the nature of the services provided. For the hire of exhibition stands, see 9.8.2 'Services related to land'.

HMRC example

A company belonging in Switzerland hires fax machines from a supplier in the USA. The fax machines are partly used and enjoyed at the Swiss company's London branch. The place of supply is the UK to the extent that the machines are used at the London branch. This is because the goods are used and enjoyed in the UK and the place of supply would otherwise have been outside the EU.

VAT Notice 741A, section 16.6.1

9.8.12 **Works on goods**

Works on goods	B2B	General rule
	B2C	Where physically performed

Goods here comprise tangible moveable property and exclude immoveable property such as land and buildings. For works on and valuation of land and buildings see 9.8.2 'Services related to land'.

Works on goods include: processing, manufacturing or assembling goods, repairs, cleaning or restoration of goods, alterations, calibrations, insulating, lacquering, painting, polishing, resetting (of jewellery), sharpening, varnishing, waterproofing, etc. Note that works on goods for export are zero-rated when supplied in the UK. See 6.3.1 'Export of goods by a charity'.

9.8.13   Restaurant and catering services

Restaurant and catering services	B2B	Where physically carried out subject to (h)
	B2C	Where physically carried out subject to (h)

(h)   If the restaurant and catering services are supplied on a ship, aircraft or train for the transportation of passengers on an intra-EU journey the place of supply is the member state of departure.

Restaurant and catering services mean services consisting of the supply of prepared or unprepared food or beverages or both, for human consumption, accompanied by sufficient support services allowing for the immediate consumption thereof. The provision of food or beverages or both is only one component of the whole in which services shall predominate. Restaurant services are the supply of such services on the premises of the supplier, and catering services are the supply of such services off the premises of the supplier.

Exclusions

The supply of prepared or unprepared food or beverages or both, whether or not including transport but without any other support services, shall not be considered restaurant or catering services.

9.8.14   Intermediary services

Intermediary services	B2B	General rule
	B2C	The place of supply of the underlying service

Intermediary services are the services of persons:

- acting in the name and on behalf of the recipient of the service procured; and
- the services performed by persons acting in the name and on behalf of the provider of the services procured.

Zero-rating

If the place of supply is the UK, then the supply of services consisting of the making of arrangements for any supply of services which is made outside the EU is zero-rated, though this excludes services consisting of the making of arrangements for exempt insurance and financial services. See 6.4.5 'Export-related services'.

If you act as the initial intermediary in arranging zero-rated passenger transport, such as: (i) scheduled flights; (ii) journeys from a place within to a place outside the UK and vice versa; or (iii) most UK transport in vehicles with a carrying capacity of not less than ten people; then your services of arranging it are also zero-rated (*VAT Notice 709/6*, section 3.6). However, if you act as a sub-agent (an intermediary acting for another intermediary), then such services, when supplied in the UK, are standard-rated and see 10.2 'Tour Operators' Margin Scheme (TOMS)' if passenger transport is bought in and resold as a principal or undisclosed agent and without material alteration or processing.

Exemption

Certain insurance-related intermediary services are exempt, see 5.10 'Insurance services'. A supply of arranging travel insurance is exempt if the place of supply is the UK and the insurance is supplied:

- in isolation of any travel;
- in relation to a supply of a travel service on which no UK VAT is payable;
- in relation to the sale of a travel service which bears UK VAT, provided that you notify the traveller, in writing, of the price of the insurance as due under the contract of insurance and any fee related to that insurance charged over and above the premium (*VAT Notice 709/6*, section 3.4).

History

Before 1 January 2010 the default place of supply of intermediary services was the place of supply of the underlying service (B2B or B2C). However there were many exceptions.

9.9 **THE MINI ONE STOP SHOP (MOSS)**

MOSS is a special optional VAT reporting and payment scheme that was introduced with effect from 1 January 2015. On that date the place of supply of certain services (intra-EU B2C digital services, defined below) switched to where the customer belongs. The result is that UK businesses making such supplies to customers in other EU states must now charge the VAT of the customer's EU state and pay that VAT to the VAT authority of the customer's state. For example, a UK business selling a downloaded computer game to a private individual in France must charge French VAT and pay this to the French VAT authority. The MOSS scheme is a simplified way of doing this.

With effect from 1 January 2015 the place of supply of the following B2C intra-EU services became where the customer belongs:

- electronically supplied services;
- broadcasting services;
- telecoms services.

These are referred to collectively as **digital services**. See 9.8.6 and 9.8.7 for the meanings of electronically supplied services, broadcasting services and telecoms services.

- **B2C** means business to consumer, as opposed to B2B which means business to business. See 9.7.3 'B2B and B2C').
- **intra-EU** means supplied from a business or fixed establishment in one EU state to a consumer who belongs in a different EU state. See 9.7.5 'Place of belonging'.

The supplier must account for output VAT, under the VAT rules of each customer's EU state, to each of the VAT authorities of those EU states.

At the time of writing there is a nil VAT registration threshold for B2C intra-EU digital supplies. So any level of B2C intra-EU supply of digital services can create a liability to be registered for VAT in the other EU state. However, in May 2015 the EC announced that it will make legislative proposals in 2016 to introduce a common EU-wide VAT threshold to help small start-up e-commerce businesses.

The MOSS returns are submitted to the VAT authority of the business' local VAT state of registration (HMRC for UK-registered businesses). This scheme is a simplification measure and conditions apply. Otherwise a business must register for VAT in each EU state to which it makes B2C digital supplies and submit separate returns and payments to each state's VAT authority under that state's rules.

The MOSS scheme can only be used to report and pay the output VAT due. It cannot be used to reclaim EU input VAT incurred in making the supplies (for how to recover this, see 9.2 'Recovering foreign VAT').

At the time of writing the MOSS scheme is limited to B2C intra-EU digital services. However, it is envisaged that if MOSS proves successful it will be extended first to B2C distance sales of goods (see 9.6.15 'Distance-selling') and then potentially to other intra-EU supplies.

9.9.1 MOSS scheme principles

There are two versions of the MOSS scheme:

- The **Union Scheme**: this is for businesses that have a business or fixed establishment in an EU state. See 9.7.5 'Place of belonging' for the meanings of business establishment and fixed establishment.
- The **Non-Union Scheme**: this is for businesses that do not have a business or fixed establishment anywhere in the EU, and where the business is not registered or otherwise required to be registered for VAT anywhere within the EU.

Member State of Identification (MSI)

The MSI is the EU state in which the business registers for MOSS. Under the Union Scheme, the MSI must be the state of the business's business establishment, if it has a business establishment within the EU. So UK entities with their head office in the UK must register for MOSS with HMRC.

If the business has no business establishment in the EU but has one fixed establishment within the EU, the business must register for MOSS in the state of that fixed establishment. If the business has no business establishment in the EU but has fixed establishments in several EU states, it can choose which of the fixed establishment states to register in. Under the Non-Union Scheme a business is free to choose its MSI.

Member State of Consumption (MSC)

The MSC is the EU state in which the digital services are consumed. However, under the Union Scheme an MSC cannot be a state where the business has a business or fixed establishment. Under the Union Scheme digital supplies to customers in states where the supplier has a business or fixed establishment are reported on the local VAT return.

Supplies of B2C digital services to persons in EU states where the business does not have any business or fixed establishments are reported and paid for under a single MOSS return. These are referred to as **reportable supplies**. Under the

Non-Union Scheme an MSC can be any EU state including the MSI, so under the Non-Union Scheme, all B2C digital supplies to EU customers are MOSS reportable.

However, if a UK supplier just has a **non-established taxable person** (NETP) VAT registration in a member state (for instance, to account for the VAT on distance sales of goods), the UK supplier can use MOSS to declare and account for the VAT due on digital B2C supplies to consumers in that member state (HMRC 2014, *Place of supply of digital services and VAT Mini One Stop Shop (MOSS) guidance*, section 2.2.1). See 9.9.9 'MOSS and VAT groups', for a complication where the supplier is in a VAT group.

Supplies via agents

The normal agency rules (for which see 11.2 'Agency supplies') are suspended for supplies of:

- electronically supplied services;
- telecommunications services.

which are supplied through an agent. Such supplies are treated both as a supply to the agent and as a supply by the agent (VAT Act 1994, s. 47(4)).

If you supply electronic services to EU consumers via a third-party-run marketplace (such as Amazon, iTunes or eBay), the marketplace is seen as making the B2C consumer supply, and as such responsible for accounting for the associated output VAT. You are seen as making a B2B supply of electronic services to the marketplace. However, if you run an online market place, selling third-party-supplied electronic services to EU non-business consumers, then you will be responsible for any output VAT due and have to register for MOSS or register directly with the EU states of your customers.

HMRC provides the following guidance on supplies via digital portals, platforms, gateways and marketplaces.

> If you supply e-services to consumers through an internet portal, gateway or marketplace, you need to determine whether you are making the supply to the consumer or to the platform operator. If the platform operator identifies you as the seller but sets the general terms and conditions, or authorises payment, or handles delivery/download of the digital service, the platform is considered to be supplying the consumer. They are therefore responsible for accounting for the VAT payment that is charged to the consumer.
>
> HMRC 2014, *VAT: supplying digital services to private consumers*

9.9.2 UK registration

If you are already registered for VAT in the UK, then you use the same VAT registration number for the MOSS return.

If you are not already registered, then HMRC requires you to also register for VAT in the UK to obtain a UK registration number, though you do not have to charge VAT on UK taxable supplies until the UK VAT Registration Threshold is exceeded and you can submit nil UK VAT returns until that point (*Revenue & Customs Brief 46/14*).

You must register for MOSS by the 10th of the calendar month following your first MOSS digital supply, though HMRC may be prepared to accept a belated registration. Your MOSS registration is backdated to the date of your first MOSS digital supply.

9.9.3 MOSS return

This is a quarterly electronic VAT return sent to the MSI detailing all B2C supplies of digital services to customers in other EU States along with the VAT due in each EU State. These returns, along with the VAT paid, are then transmitted by the MSI to the corresponding MSCs.

The business is required to submit a MOSS VAT return for each calendar quarter (three months ending 31 March, 30 June, 30 September and 31 December), whether or not it has actually supplied digital services in that quarter. Where no supplies have been carried out a 'nil return' must be submitted. The MOSS VAT return and accompanying payment must be submitted within 20 days of the end of the period covered by the return.

9.9.4 Determining the status of your customer

You must retain evidence to support your decision as to the customer's status (B2B or B2C).

If the customer provides a VAT registration number, then you should check that the number conforms to the EU state's VAT number format (see 14.3 'Checking VAT numbers'). If it does you can accept that the supply is B2B, unless you supply downloaded music, games, films and so on of a kind normally supplied to a private consumer, in which case HMRC advises that the use of the VAT number should be questioned (*VAT Notice 741A*, section 19.2).

If the customer provides a VAT registration number, the supply is of electronic services and, if the total value of electronic supplies to this customer exceeds £500 in a VAT quarter, you should check the validity of the VAT number by ringing the HMRC VAT helpline or by using the online VIES checking system (see 14.3 'Checking VAT numbers').

If the customer is not VAT-registered you can accept alternative evidence of business status such as evidence from the customer's website, audited accounts, etc. However, in the absence of a valid VAT registration number, a customer cannot insist on B2B treatment and the decision as to whether the supply is B2B or B2C rests with the supplier.

You should retain a record setting out details of the check carried out and results. In the absence of any evidence of business status, the supply should be treated as B2C.

Evidence of customer status should be retained for at least ten years (see 9.9.8 'MOSS records').

9.9.5 Determining customer location

To support MOSS decision-making, HMRC will expect you to obtain evidence of customer location.

HMRC provides guidance on determining customer location as follows (HMRC 2014, *Place of supply of digital services and VAT Mini One Stop Shop (MOSS) guidance*, section 1.5):

- Digital supplies through a telephone box, a telephone kiosk, a Wi-Fi hot spot, an internet café, a restaurant or a hotel lobby, can be presumed to be made to where the phone box/kiosk, etc. is located.
- Digital supplies through a mobile phone can be presumed to be made to the country code of the SIM card.
- Supplies through a decoder can be presumed to be made to the postal address where the decoder is sent or installed.
- Digital supplies on board transport travelling between different EU states can be presumed to be made at the place of departure.

Where one of the presumptions applies, you are only required to retain evidence showing the relevant place. However, if you choose to, you may rebut the presumption with three pieces of non-contradictory commercial evidence. If you are providing digital services in circumstances not listed above, you will need to support your decision by providing two pieces of non-contradictory commercial evidence.

Examples of acceptable commercial evidence include:

- the billing address of the customer;
- the Internet Protocol (IP) address of the device used by the customer;

- the location of the bank;
- the country code of the SIM card used by the customer;
- the location of the customer's fixed land line through which the service is supplied to them;
- other commercially relevant information (for instance, product coding information which electronically links the sale to a particular jurisdiction).

Once you have two pieces of non-contradictory evidence that is all you need and you do not need to collect any further supporting evidence. This is the case even if, for example, you obtain a third piece of evidence which happens to contradict the other two pieces of information.

Micro-businesses

HMRC accepts that UK micro-businesses, that are below the UK VAT registration threshold and are registered for MOSS, may base their customer location, VAT taxation and accounting decisions on information provided to them by their payment service provider (HMRC 2014, *VAT: supplying digital services to private consumers*).

9.9.6 **VAT rates and invoices**

When you invoice a consumer in a currency other than the one used by the Member State of Registration (MSR), your VAT MOSS return will need to show the billed currency amount converted into the currency of the MSR using the rate published by the European Central Bank (ECB) on the last working day of the calendar quarter. You will need to raise and issue VAT invoices in accordance with the requirements of each member state where your consumer is located. The EC website provides guidance on these rules.

9.9.7 **Exclusion from MOSS**

A business will be excluded from the MOSS if reminders have been sent for three immediately preceding calendar quarters, and the VAT return has not been submitted for each return within ten days of the reminder or if the full amount has not been paid within ten days of receiving each of these reminders, unless the outstanding amount for each return is less than €100. Once a business has been excluded on these grounds it cannot re-join the MOSS scheme for a quarantine period of eight calendar quarters.

9.9.8 **MOSS records**

MOSS records must be kept for a minimum of ten years from the end of the year in which the transaction was made. These records have to be made electronically available, on request, to the MSR or any MSC without delay. A failure to make these records available within a month of receiving a reminder from the MSR will be regarded as persistent failure to comply with the rules relating to the scheme and will result in exclusion from the scheme.

9.9.9   MOSS and VAT groups

The *EC Guide to the VAT mini One Stop Shop* (EC 2013), part 1a states:

9) How is a VAT group treated?

Whilst it is acknowledged that Member States legislate for VAT groups domestically in different ways, as a practical solution for the particular circumstances of the mini One Stop Shop, a VAT group shall be treated in the following way:

- A VAT group can use the mini One Stop Shop, but when it registers, it must indicate that it is a VAT group using Box 20 of the registration information;
- A VAT group registers under the VAT identification number with which it is registered for its domestic supplies; where separate numbers are given at a domestic level to group members, a single number should be allocated to the VAT group at least to be used for the mini One Stop Shop registration.
- If a member of the VAT group has, or will have, a fixed establishment in another Member State, the ties with that fixed establishment are broken for mini One Stop Shop registration purposes, and the supplies from that fixed establishment cannot be declared on the mini One Stop Shop VAT return of the VAT group.
- Similarly, supplies from the VAT group to the Member State of that fixed establishment shall be declared via the mini One Stop Shop VAT return, and not via the domestic VAT return of that fixed establishment.
- Therefore a VAT group cannot include any fixed establishments in other Member States in its mini One Stop Shop registration.

The Commission is aware that there are cases outstanding before the Court of Justice of the European Union relating to VAT groups, and as such this guidance may be revised in light of the judgment of the Court.

However, you can continue to use your existing VAT registrations to account for the VAT on other types of B2C supply (for instance, for Distance Sales, B2B reverse charge supplies of services, etc.).

10 VAT special schemes

The VAT schemes considered in this chapter are:

- 10.1 Capital Goods Scheme
- 10.2 Tour Operators' Margin Scheme (TOMS)
- 10.3 Public bodies
- 10.4 Museums and Galleries Refund Scheme
- 10.5 Academy and free schools
- 10.6 Charity VAT refund scheme
- 10.7 Listed Places of Worship Grant Scheme
- 10.8 Memorials Refund Scheme
- 10.9 Cash Accounting Scheme
- 10.10 Annual Accounting Scheme
- 10.11 Retail schemes
- 10.12 Flat Rate Scheme for small businesses
- 10.13 Margin schemes
- 10.14 Abusive schemes
- 10.15 Listed and hallmarked schemes

10.1 CAPITAL GOODS SCHEME

Residual purchases are purchases that are used for a mix of taxable and non-taxable (exempt or non-business) activities. For most residual purchases the VAT is recovered on a provisional basis in the VAT period of the purchase and this provisional VAT recovery is then corrected in the **annual adjustment** (see 3.1.10 'The annual adjustment') at the end of the VAT year (longer period). The annual adjustment determines the percentage of the VAT incurred on the asset that is recoverable (its **overall recovery rate**) and that is normally the end of the matter as far as VAT recovery is concerned.

However, for purchases that create, improve or acquire certain capital assets (**capital items**) you must carry on adjusting the initial VAT recovery for changes in the relative levels of taxable use and non-taxable (exempt plus non-business) use of the capital item over its **adjustment period**.

The adjustment period is a total of ten **adjustment intervals** for land and buildings and five adjustment intervals for other assets (aircraft, ships, boats and computers). This adjustment process is called the **Capital Goods Scheme (CGS)**.

An adjustment interval is normally a complete VAT year (longer period); however, the first adjustment interval runs from the date of first use of the capital item until the end of the longer period of first use.

The scheme works on a capital item by capital item basis. So if you create, improve or acquire a capital item caught by the CGS, you will need to set up a calculation (normally a spreadsheet) for that capital item and, if you have multiple capital items, you will need to set up multiple calculations.

For each capital item you begin by determining an initial level of use for taxable activities in the first adjustment interval (the **baseline percentage**) and then, for each of the subsequent adjustment intervals, you pay or recover 1/10th (land and buildings) or 1/5th (other assets) of the VAT incurred on the asset multiplied by the change in the level of use from the baseline percentage:

$$\text{VAT adjustment} = \frac{\text{VAT incurred}}{10 \text{ or } 5} \times \left(\begin{array}{c} \text{Current} \\ \text{level of use} \\ (\%) \end{array} - \begin{array}{c} \text{Baseline} \\ \text{percentage} \\ (\%) \end{array} \right)$$

If the VAT adjustment is positive, the adjustment amount is recovered from HMRC. If the VAT adjustment is negative, the adjustment amount must be paid to HMRC. If it is zero, no adjustment need be made.

Example: CGS

Charity T has taxable and exempt activities. It purchases a new head office building for £1 million plus VAT of £200,000 on 1 July 2015. It starts to use the building on 31 July 2015 with the new building being put to mixed/residual use. Its VAT year end is 31 March.

Its overall residual recovery percentages as calculated in the annual adjustments for each of the first four VAT years of use are – 2015/16: 80%, 2016/17: 50%, 2017/18: 90%, and 2018/19: 80%.

1. In the VAT year of first use (2015/16) charity T can recover: 80% × £200,000 = £160,000

   T's baseline recovery rate is $\frac{£160,000}{£200,000} \times 100\% = 80\%$

2. In 2016/17 T's taxable use drops to 50%.

   T must pay to HMRC $\frac{£200,000}{10} \times (80\% - 50\%) = £20,000 \times 30\% = £6,000$

3. In 2017/18 taxable use increases to 90%

   T can recover from HMRC:

   $\frac{£200,000}{10} \times (90\% - 80\%) = £20,000 \times 10\% = 22,000$

4. In 2018/19 T's taxable use returns to 80%

   The adjustment is nil as $\frac{£200,000}{10} \times (80\% - 80\%) = £0$

The main HMRC guidance on the CGS is in *VAT Notice 706/2*. References to HMRC guidance below are to the October 2011 edition of this notice unless otherwise stated.

10.1.1 New and old CGSs

Before 1 January 2011, the CGS applied only to input VAT incurred on capital items. Input VAT is the purchase VAT that is directly attributed and apportioned to business (taxable and exempt) activities. It excludes VAT directly attributed and apportioned to non-business activities.

With effect from 1 January 2011, VAT incurred on non-business activities is included in the CGS. Several other changes to the scheme took place on 1 January 2011, including changes to the definition of a capital item and the changes to the point at which the first adjustment interval starts.

If all capital expenditure on a capital item occurred before 1 January 2011 and the adjustment period for the capital item had begun before 1 January 2011, then you carry on applying VAT recovery adjustments for the capital item under the old scheme rules until the scheme terminates.

If all capital expenditure on a capital item is incurred on or after 1 January 2011 then the capital item is covered by the new scheme rules.

The transitional problem is where capital expenditure was incurred before 1 January 2011, the adjustment period had not commenced by 1 January 2011and the capital item is first used on or after 1 January 2011. In such a situation you have what HMRC refers to as a 'split capital item'. Input VAT incurred up to 31 December 2010 must be reviewed in light of any change in the mix of taxable and exempt use, and VAT incurred on or after 1 January 2011 must be reviewed in light of any changes in the relative levels of taxable and non-taxable use (non-taxable is exempt or non-business).

10.1.2 Scope of the CGS

The CGS only applies if **VAT-bearing capital expenditure** of £250,000 or more (land and buildings) or £50,000 or more (airplanes, ships, boats and computers) is incurred on a **capital item** by its **owner**.

10.1.3 Capital items

Capital items are, with effect from 1 January 2011:

1. land on whose acquisition its owner incurs VAT-bearing capital expenditure of £250,000 or more;

2. a building or a civil engineering work, or a part of a building or a part of a civil engineering work, on whose acquisition, construction, refurbishment, fitting out, alteration or extension (including construction of an annexe) its owner incurs VAT-bearing capital expenditure of £250,000 or more;

3. an aircraft, a ship, a boat or other vessel on whose acquisition, construction, manufacture, refurbishment, fitting out, alteration or extension its owner incurs VAT-bearing capital expenditure of £50,000 or more;

4. an individual computer or item of computer equipment on whose acquisition its owner incurs VAT-bearing capital expenditure of £50,000 or more.

A purchased computer or item of computer equipment is covered by the scheme only if it costs £50,000 or more on its own. The scheme does not apply to networks or bulk purchases where the total cost exceeds £50,000 but no individual item exceeds £50,000. Nor does it apply to computerised equipment such as telephone exchanges, software and equipment acquired for resale or sold before it is used.

Before 1 January 2011:

- Alterations, extensions and annexes to buildings were capital items only if they increased the existing floor space by 10% or more. The 10% test was removed with effect from 1 January 2011.
- The value of a refurbishment or fitting out excluded the value of any goods that were not affixed to the building. From 1 January 2011 goods that are capitalised but not affixed to the building are included. Possible examples of goods capitalised but not affixed are carpets and furniture.
- Aircraft, ships, boats and other vessels were wholly excluded from the scheme.
- Only the acquisition or construction of a civil engineering work was caught.

10.1.4 Owners

An owner is a person who has an interest in the capital item. This could, for example, include a tenant of a building who carries out a capital refurbishment on that building. However, if the owner's interest will last for less than three years, the scheme may not apply – see 10.1.7 'Short life assets'.

The owner is deemed to include:

(i) A person to whom a capital item is transferred under the transfer of a business as a going concern (TOGC) rules (see 11.5 'Transfer of a business as a going concern'). The new owner must carry on any CGS adjustments. The new owner is treated as having done everything the original owner has done in respect of the capital item. See 10.1.14 'TOGC disposal of a capital item'.

(ii) The representative member of a VAT group if the capital item is owned by a group member. As the representative member is deemed to make and receive all supplies for the group, it is also deemed to be the owner of any capital items held within the VAT group.

10.1.5 Non-business assets

If you have non-business activities and you acquire or create a capital item you can choose to retain it partly or wholly within your non-business assets. If all or part of an asset is excluded from your business assets because you hold it as a non-business asset, the costs and related VAT are also excluded from the VAT system. Expenditure relating to the element that has been excluded from your business does not count towards the CGS threshold, but the related VAT is always **non-deductible** (see 5.11) and will not benefit from adjustment if the taxable use increases.

HMRC accepts this principle and states (*VAT Notice 706/2*, section 5.2):

> The choice to exclude any part of an asset from your business's assets must be made at the time when the relevant expenditure is incurred and should be recorded to avoid the risk of future disputes. Evidence might include minutes of a board meeting, a note in your VAT file or similar contemporaneous material to evidence your decision.

10.1.6 VAT-bearing capital expenditure

Only VAT-bearing capital expenditure counts towards the £250,000/£50,000 threshold. The costs must bear VAT (either standard-rated or reduced-rated), so this excludes costs that did not bear VAT because they were zero-rated, exempt or **outside the scope** of VAT or where the supplier was not registered for VAT. When adding up costs to check if the threshold is exceeded, you exclude any VAT charged.

The costs must be capital expenditure. HMRC accepts that this means costs that are capitalised in any statutory accounts in accordance with applicable UK GAAP (Generally Accepted Accounting Practice in the UK) principles and HMRC will normally accept the organisation's capitalisation policy, though HMRC states (*VAT Notice 706/02*, section 4.1):

> In some cases charities may incur expenditure of a capital nature on land and property which is not capitalised in their accounts (e.g. certain heritage buildings, churches etc.). This is generally because the charity does not have unfettered freedom to exploit or dispose of the land or property concerned. This will not prevent expenditure that is essentially capital in nature from being adjusted under the Capital Goods Scheme.

Costs incurred before 1 January 2011 exclude any non-business use element.

HMRC's approach to capital expenditure is set out in *VAT Notice 706/2*, section 4) and is summarised as follows:

- **Purchased land and buildings**: these only include the value of the interest in the land and/or building supplied to you, if the supply was taxable and not zero-rated. Do not include any associated costs such as legal or estate agency fees. In calculating the value of the interest supplied to you in the land and/or building, you do not need to include the value of any rent or service charges unless: it has been paid or is payable more than 12 months in advance; or is invoiced by the supplier for a period of more than 12 months. In that case, you should include the value of rent/service charges when calculating the value of the capital item.
- **Construction of buildings**: you should include all the costs involved in making the building ready, such as (all if VAT-bearing only): land, construction services, professional and managerial services including architects, surveyors and site management; demolition and site clearance; building and civil engineering contractors' services; materials used in the construction; security; equipment hire; haulage; landscaping; and fitting out, including the value of any fixtures.
- **Refurbishment and fitting out**: from 1 January 2011 you should include all the costs involved in making the refurbished or fitted out building ready. Before 1 January 2011 you should only include the value of capital expenditure on VAT-bearing supplies of services and of goods affixed to the building or civil engineering work supplied to you for or in connection with the refurbishment or fit out.
- **Phased refurbishments**: if a refurbishment is carried out in phases it may be difficult to determine if there is one refurbishment or several. Normally there is more than one refurbishment when each phase of work is completed before work on the next phase starts and either (i) there are separate contracts for each phase of the work; or (ii) a contract where each phase is a separate option which can be selected.
- **Civil engineering works**: civil engineering work should be given its everyday meaning. It includes such items as roads, bridges, golf courses, running tracks and installation of pipes for connection to mains services.

10.1.7 Short life assets

HMRC states (*VAT Notice 706/2*, section 6.3):

> If your interest in an asset is for fewer than three adjustment intervals then the asset does not fall within the CGS. This is because the CGS only deals with capital expenditure, which is generally expenditure that will be used by a business for a minimum of two years and this normally equates to three intervals under the CGS.

If your interest will last for more than three adjustment intervals but, at the time of first use, either:

- for land, buildings and civil engineering works, the number of complete years your interest in the capital item has left to run is less than nine; or
- for other assets, the number of complete years your interest in the capital item has left to run is less than four.

Then the number of adjustment intervals is reduced to one plus the number of complete years the interest has to run, but subject to a minimum of three. The denominator in the VAT adjustment formula is also adjusted; for example, for a seven-year adjustment period, divide the VAT by 7 not 10.

10.1.8 **Pre-registration capital items**

If you acquire a capital item before you register for VAT, then the VAT incurred on the capital item would have been wholly irrecoverable at the time since you were not registered for VAT. However, if you later register for VAT you may be able to recover some of the VAT incurred under the CGS.

The CGS mechanism for achieving this is to lose one adjustment interval for every complete year between first use of the capital item and VAT registration. There is then one adjustment interval to the day before the start of the first VAT year (registration period), and the remaining adjustment intervals are the subsequent VAT years/longer periods. The baseline recovery percentage is nil (as none of the VAT was recovered initially).

10.1.9 **Later costs**

If VAT is incurred after the end of the first adjustment interval, then the VAT incurred is recovered subject to the annual adjustment at the end of the longer period concerned. The CGS calculation is then amended at the end of the following period. There are two HMRC-approved ways of doing this:

- The combined adjustment method involves re-calculating the baseline percentage and using the revised baseline percentage in the remaining adjustment periods.
- The parallel adjustment method involves carrying out separate calculations for each component for the remaining adjustment periods.

See *VAT Notice 706/2*, section 7.8 for worked examples.

10.1.10 Lost, stolen or destroyed capital items

If a capital item is lost, stolen or destroyed, then no adjustment need be made for remaining complete adjustment periods.

10.1.11 Disposal of a capital item

If a capital item is wholly disposed of before the end of the adjustment period (including a deemed disposal as a result of VAT deregistration) then, unless the disposal is a part of a TOGC (for which, see 10.1.14 'TOGC disposal of a capital item'), at the end of the adjustment interval of disposal a final adjustment must be carried out.

This has two or three components:

1. A normal CGS adjustment is carried out in respect of use during the adjustment interval of disposal. This is calculated as if the item had been in use throughout the adjustment interval based on the overall residual recovery rate for that interval.
2. Adjustments must also be calculated for any remaining complete adjustment intervals. For any remaining complete adjustment intervals use is assumed to be 100% taxable if the disposal was a **taxable supply** (see 1.2.2) and 100% exempt if the disposal was an exempt supply.
3. If the total VAT recovered on the capital item (initially, via the CGS adjustments and for remaining periods as calculated above) is greater than the **output VAT** (see 1.1) chargeable on the disposal, then HMRC is entitled to recover the difference. This is referred to as the **disposal test** (see 10.1.12 'Disposal test' for more information).

For part disposals (with effect from 1 January 2011), the capital item is split into two. A final adjustment is carried out for the part disposed of. Adjustments carry on for the remaining part for the rest of the adjustment period. The VAT **attributable** (see 3.1.3) to the part disposal should be calculated on a fair and reasonable basis. For a part disposal of a building, HMRC accepts that this can be determined by reference to the amount of the floor space disposed of as a proportion of the total floor space of the building (*VAT Notice 706/2*, section 10.2).

10.1.12 Disposal test

HMRC will only apply the disposal test if you benefit from an unjustified tax advantage because of the early sale. HMRC states (*VAT Notice 706/2*, section 11.2):

> The disposal test will only apply if you sell a capital item before the end of the adjustment period and benefit from an unjustified tax advantage because of the early sale. An unjustified tax advantage is normally one arising from an avoidance

scheme where the owner seeks to secure an amount of input VAT that would still be subject to adjustment under the CGS, were it not for the sale of the item, less any output tax due on the sale. We have the discretion to exclude certain disposals from the test and therefore from any disposal test adjustment. For example, it will not be applied:

- to sales of computer equipment
- where an owner disposes of an item at a loss due to market conditions (such as a general downturn in property prices)
- where the value of the item has depreciated
- where the value of the item is reduced for other legitimate reasons (such as accepting a lower price to effect a quick sale)
- where the amount of output VAT on disposal is less than the total input VAT claimed only due to a reduction in the VAT rate; and
- where the item is used only for taxable (including zero-rated) purposes throughout the adjustment period (which includes the final disposal).

10.1.13 Disposal of capital items used for fully taxable purposes

The final adjustment can have an unexpected consequence for fully taxable businesses. If a new non-qualifying building (standard-rated – see 8.6.3 'Qualifying and non-qualifying buildings') is purchased and used for fully taxable activities but its freehold is disposed of after three years (with no option to tax in place, so the disposal is exempt) but before the expiry of the last adjustment interval, then use during the remaining adjustment intervals is deemed to be exempt.

For example, if the building is disposed of at the end of the fifth adjustment interval, half of the VAT recovered on the purchase must be repaid.

The seller can avoid this by opting to tax the building before it is disposed of (though you may require HMRC's permission to opt to tax – see 8.5.2 'Permission to opt to tax'). If the purchaser cannot **disapply** the **option to tax** (see 8.1), this makes the sale standard-rated, and no CGS adjustment need be made (subject to the disposal test).

10.1.14 TOGC disposal of a capital item

If a capital item is disposed of as part of a TOGC, then it is not treated as a disposal by the seller as above. The seller should provide the new owner with details of any active capital items and the new owner should ask for such.

If the purchaser takes over the seller's VAT registration the adjustment interval during which the business is transferred continues without a break. The seller does not need to make any adjustments for that interval. The new owner is responsible for any adjustments as if it had owned the capital item for the whole of the adjustment interval of transfer and for any remaining adjustment intervals in the normal way.

If the purchaser does not take over the seller's VAT registration, then the seller should make a normal adjustment in the adjustment interval of transfer. The new owner then takes over responsibility for the remaining adjustments, the remaining adjustment intervals ending on the anniversary of the date of transfer. If these adjustment intervals do not match the new owner's VAT years, then HMRC advises that the new owner will need to agree a way of calculating subsequent intervals with HMRC.

10.1.15 Change of use of a qualifying building

As explained at 8.3 'Property VAT reliefs', voluntary organisations may be able to zero rate the first purchase or construction of a new building or a part of a new building that is intended for 'qualifying use'. Qualifying use is use for a **relevant charitable purpose** or use for a relevant **residential purpose** (or use for both) (see the definitions of these terms at 8.6.7 and 8.6.9). However, if a new building or a part of a new building is zero-rated in this way, but the use of that building or part changes to non-qualifying within ten years of completion, then a VAT adjustment has to be made under the 'change of use' rules.

The building or part is deemed to be supplied by the organisation to itself. That supply is VAT standard-rated. The organisation must account for output VAT to HMRC on the **deemed supply** but it can recover that output VAT as purchase VAT subject to the normal VAT recovery rules. Those normal VAT recovery rules include the CGS. So if the value of the deemed supply is £250,000 or more, then it is a capital item for the purposes of the CGS. However:

- If, at the date of transfer, 84 or more complete months have passed since the date of completion, then the deemed acquisition is excluded from the CGS.
- The number of adjustment intervals is $\frac{120-Z}{12}$ rounded up to the next whole number, where Z is the number of complete months between completion and date of change of use. The VAT chargeable is divided by this number (not 10) in the VAT adjustment calculation.

10.1.16   **Other considerations**

Adjustments made under the CGS should be ignored when calculating whether exempt activity is *de minimis* (see 3.1 'VAT recovery principles'). If a capital item is not put to any use for a period of time, the use during that period is deemed to be the same as it was before it went out of use.

10.2   **TOUR OPERATORS' MARGIN SCHEME (TOMS)**

Despite its name, the TOMS is not limited to commercial tour operators. Any organisation supplying, in its own name, a taxable package of services that includes passenger transport or overnight accommodation that is bought in and resupplied without material alteration is likely to be acting as a **tour operator** (broadly is a person who buys in and resupplies unchanged travel or accommodation) and may have to apply the mandatory TOMS scheme. The TOMS has two purposes:

- As an EU-wide simplification measure, allowing tour operators to avoid having to register for VAT in every EU state they operate in. However, it also applies to supplies that are enjoyed entirely within the UK and to supplies that are enjoyed entirely outside the EU.
- To ensure that, for travel across the EU, VAT revenue is distributed fairly between the member states of consumption and the member state of the tour operator. The VAT on services such as catering, travel and accommodation is paid in the state of consumption, whereas the tour operator's margin and any services the tour operator adds themselves (**in-house supplies** – see 10.2.1) are subject to VAT in the tour operator's state.

EC v. *Spain*

At the time of writing the CJEU has delivered a judgment (case C-189/11 *European Commission* v. *Spain*) which suggests that the UK's implementation of the TOMS is wrong in some significant respects. However, the EC is reviewing the TOMS with a view to introducing changes and HMRC has decided that it would be too disruptive to make two sets of changes. All changes will be made in one, though businesses can invoke the *EC* v. *Spain* decision by **direct effect** if they wish to (for the definition see 'Direct effect' in the introduction to Chapter 5). The current UK scheme is explained below, though you should check *VAT Notice 709/5* for the latest position. See 10.2.8 '*EC* v. *Spain* case'.

10.2.1 **Definitions**

Travel facilities

Travel facilities are any of the following when supplied to a traveller:

- accommodation;
- passenger transport;
- hire of a means of transport;
- trips or excursions;
- services of tour guides;
- use of special lounges at airports.

Designated travel services

Designated travel services are **travel facilities** that are bought in and resupplied by a **tour operator for the direct benefit of a traveller** and without material alteration. They also include:

- catering;
- admission tickets;
- sports facilities

if such supplies are bought in and sold on without material alteration, for the direct benefit of a traveller, and provided as part of a package with one or more of the travel facilities listed above.

For the direct benefit of a traveller means that the travel facility is used by an individual who is travelling. In the UK, designated travel services are not currently regarded as including supplies of travel facilities that are bought in and resold to a business which itself resells them to a final consumer (**wholesale supplies**, see 10.2.2), though in *EC* v. *Spain* (see 10.2.8) the CJEU has said explicitly that TOMS does cover wholesale supplies. However, under the current UK rules the TOMS does include supplies of travel facilities that are bought in and resold without material alteration to a business for its own consumption, for example for its staff, trustees, directors or volunteers.

In-house supplies

These are supplies made from a tour operator's own resources, or from goods or services a tour operator has bought in but materially altered or further processed, so that what is eventually supplied is different from what was purchased.

Agency supplies

Agency supplies are supplies that a tour operator provides as a **disclosed agent**, that is where the contract for the service is direct between the service provider and traveller. The tour operator will normally receive a commission from the service provider. (See also 7.8.2 'Third-party organiser' for the definition of disclosed agent.)

A margin scheme package

This is a bundle of goods and/or services that includes one or more designated travel services. A margin scheme package can include a mix of designated travel services, in-house supplies and/or agency supplies.

A tour operator

A tour operator is any business that makes margin scheme supplies.

10.2.2 Scope of the TOMS

The TOMS applies when a business supplies a **margin scheme package** (see above).

The TOMS does not apply to:

- **Wholly in-house supplies**: supplies of travel facilities made entirely from a business's own resources and/or supplies of travel facilities that have been bought in but subjected to material alteration by the tour operator.
- **Wholesale supplies**: supplies of travel facilities to a business for resale by that business. However, the TOMS does apply if a margin scheme package is supplied to a business for its own consumption.
- **Wholly agency supplies**: travel-related supplies provided entirely as a disclosed **agent** of a **principal**. This means the business acts in the name of and on behalf of a principal in selling travel facilities to travellers. Charity challenge events organised through commercial event organisers are usually arranged so that the charity acts as a disclosed agent of the event organiser. If you act as a disclosed agent your commission is subject to VAT. See 7.8 'Challenge events' for more on challenge events and 11.2 'Agency supplies' for more on the principal/agent distinction.
- **Exempt supplies**: the TOMS does not apply to exempt supplies, for example supplies of travel ancillary to an exempt educational supply or exempt sporting service. The TOMS only applies where the supply is taxable.

- **Hotel bill back arrangements**: for events and conferences, the conference organiser can handle hotel bookings as agent of the hotel, so the conference does not fall within the TOMS. See 10.2.7 'Hotel bill back'.

10.2.3 VAT status of supplies under the TOMS

The supply of the package is treated as a single supply. It is subject to VAT on its margin, not on the full amount of the consideration. See 10.2.5 'Calculating the margin – UK rules' for more on how to calculate the margin. VAT incurred in supplying the designated travel services is not recoverable or refundable.

Place of supply

The place of supply of this single supply (where it is subject to VAT) is the state in which the tour operator is established or has a fixed establishment from which the tour operator provides the supply. This means that if a business supplies a margin scheme package from a fixed establishment in the UK, the place of supply will be the UK wherever the traveller journeys to.

VAT status

The VAT status of this single supply is:

- **VAT standard-rated** if the package is entirely enjoyed within the EU;
- **VAT zero-rated** if the package is entirely enjoyed outside the EU.

If the package is enjoyed both within and outside the EU, an apportionment is required between standard-rated and zero-rated. HMRC's position on where a package is enjoyed and EU/non-EU packages is as follows:

> If a journey begins or ends outside the EC, it may be treated as being enjoyed wholly outside the EC. Temporary stops for refuelling or 'comfort' breaks are not regarded as stops, providing that passengers are not able to break their journey at these times. The return trip is treated the same way unless any material difference occurs between the two legs, such as a stop.
>
> Generally where a journey involves travel in both EC and non-EC countries, which involve a stop or stops, within the EC, the journey cannot be regarded as either being enjoyed wholly inside or outside of the EC. In order to account for this type of journey within the TOMS, it is necessary to apportion between the EC and non-EC elements of the journey. There are several ways of doing this (for example, using a mileage based split or a nights spent in/out of the EC split), but whatever the method used it should produce a fair and reasonable result.
>
> *VAT Notice 709/5*, section 4

10.2.4 *De minimis* **designated travel services**

Where a business supplies a designated travel service other than transport or accommodation, the business may treat that supply as not being a designated travel service, if it reasonably believes that the total gross value of all such supplies in the next 12 months will not exceed 1% of the total gross value of all supplies.

10.2.5 **Calculating the margin – UK rules**

See sections 8–13 of *VAT Notice 709/5* for detailed rules on how to calculate the margin and output VAT due. These sections are tertiary legislation with statutory force. The broad approach is that an annual calculation must be carried out for all margin scheme packages supplied on a worldwide basis, much like the VAT partial exemption calculation. The TOMS calculation determines an average gross margin for all of the organisation's margin scheme supplies (excluding income and costs attributable to in-house and agency elements) based on the previous VAT year, and then applies this provisionally to the margin scheme supplies in the next year, subject to correction in a year end annual adjustment. The annual adjustment is carried out in the first VAT return of the next VAT year. As an alternative and with HMRC agreement, separate margins can be determined for EU and non-EU sales, with the provisional margin each applying to the respective sales in the next year.

Example: TOMS annual adjustment

A challenge event company puts on a large number of TOMS challenge events as principal. Its results for 2015/16 are:

	EU (£m)	Non-EU (£m)	Total (£m)
Sales	4	8	12
Costs	2	6	8
Margins	2	2	4

Worldwide basis: The gross margin of £4 million is apportioned between zero-rated non-EU sales and standard-rated EU sales on the basis of cost:

EU margin = (2/8) × £4 million = £1 million

VAT due = £1 million × (20/120) = £166,667

Standard-rated margin/total sales = £1 million/£12 million = 8.33%

> In the next year, on a provisional basis 8.33% of all gross proceeds is treated as subject to VAT. For example if total sales in quarter 1 are £4 million, then
>
> Standard-rated margin = 8.33% × £4 million = £333,200
>
> VAT due = £333,200 × (1/6) = £55,533
>
> (**Note:** with VAT at 20%, to calculate the VAT included in a gross price, multiply the gross price by 1/6. This is referred to as the VAT fraction. See 12.1 'VAT fractions and VAT rounding'.)
>
> **EU sales only**: EU margin = £2 million
>
> VAT due = £2 million × (1/6) = £333,333
>
> Standard-rated margin/EU sales = 2/4 = 50%
>
> In the next year, on a provisional basis 50% of all gross proceeds from EU sales is treated as subject to VAT. If total EU sales in quarter 1 are £2 million, then
>
> Standard-rated margin = 50% × £2 million = £500,000
>
> VAT due = £500,000 × (1/6) = £83,333

As can be seen from the above example, using a worldwide basis calculation will usually be better if the margin on non-EU sales is lower than the margin on EU sales, and an EU-only calculation will usually be better if the margin on EU sales is lower than the margin on non-EU sales.

You can only switch to separate calculations (or revert to a single calculation) at the start of your financial year, that is, no later than the due date of your first VAT return for that financial year. Permission to do this must be requested, in writing and in advance of the financial year in question, from HMRC. Permission will not be granted retrospectively. Permission to switch to separate calculations will only be granted if HMRC is satisfied that your records for direct costs and sales are adequate to calculate accurate but separate sets of margins.

Mixed supplies

If a package includes margin scheme supplies sold together with in-house supplies and/or agency supplies, then an apportionment of the package price must be carried out, with:

1. In-house supplies being subject to the normal VAT rules. That is, VAT is due on the full selling price and input VAT incurred on attributable costs is recoverable.
2. Agency supplies being treated separately. Customer payments received as agent must be excluded from the package price if the agency commission is readily identifiable, as must the direct costs of agency supplies. The difference is the agency commission. However, if an agency commission is not readily identifiable the agency supply is included within the TOMS.

10.2.6 Tax point of margin scheme supplies

You must use one of the two methods detailed below to work out the tax point for your margin scheme supplies and any in-house supplies sold within a margin scheme package. You cannot change from one tax point method to another without written permission from HMRC. A change of method will be allowed only in exceptional circumstances, and will not normally be allowed mid-way through a financial year.

1. The tax point is the date of departure of the traveller, or the first date on which the traveller occupies any accommodation, whichever happens first.
2. The tax point is the same as method one, or the date of receipt of payment of a certain size, whichever happens first (the date of receipt of money includes receipt by a travel agent on your behalf). Each time you receive a payment exceeding 20% of the selling price, a tax point for that amount is created. A tax point is also created each time the payments you have received to date (and not already accounted for) exceed 20% when added together. Any amount left outstanding at the time of departure of the traveller or the first date the traveller occupies any accommodation must be accounted for on the earlier of these dates.

Cash and Annual Accounting Schemes

The Cash Accounting Scheme cannot be used for any supplies falling within the TOMS, though the Annual Accounting Scheme can. You should include the figures from your annual TOMS calculation on the VAT return for the VAT year in which the supplies were made.

10.2.7 **Hotel bill back**

Under the **hotel bill back** arrangement, hotel bookings can be made as agent of a business client and not accounted for via the TOMS but paid for via the agent. The hotel issues a VAT invoice for the accommodation to the booking agent, who recovers the VAT charged and then issues a VAT invoice to the business traveller, charging VAT on both the accommodation and their commission. In *Revenue & Customs Brief 21/10* HMRC announced an agreement with the Hotel Booking Agents Association and the Guild of Travel Management Companies that the following arrangements are available generally to all businesses that wish to adopt them:

> Invoices from hotels will be addressed c/o the hotel booking agent for payment. (This is to indicate that the invoice has been issued to the hotel booking agent in its capacity as an agent.) The booking field on the hotel invoice will identify the hotel guest, their employer and will ideally carry a unique reference number. (Until hotels can address their invoices directly to their business customers, it may be necessary for hotel booking agents to enter an employer identification number on the invoice.)

> The hotel booking agent will arrange for payment of the invoice(s) but will not recover the input tax thereon. The hotel booking agent will send the customer a payment request/statement of the expenditure incurred by the hotel booking agent on its behalf, separately identifying the value of its supplies, VAT, etc.

> The payment request/statement should say something along the lines of 'The VAT shown is your input tax which can be reclaimed subject to the normal rules'. The customer will use the payment request/statement as a basis for their input tax reclaim. The hotel booking agent will retain the original hotel invoices and these will be made available if evidence of entitlement is required by HMRC VAT staff.

> The hotel booking agent will send a VAT invoice for its own services, plus the VAT. This may be consolidated with the statement of hotel charges, or it can be a separate document. The hotel booking agent will charge its client the exact amount charged by the bill back supplier, as a disbursement.

10.2.8 *EC* v. *Spain* case

In case C-189/11 *European Commission* v. *Spain*, the CJEU decided that:

- wholesale supplies should be included in the TOMS;
- the margin should be calculated on a transaction-by-transaction basis and not on an annual basis as currently required in the UK.

On 31 January 2014 HMRC issued *Revenue & Customs Brief 05/14* stating:

> These decisions are binding on all Member States. However, after careful consideration, we have decided that there will be no changes to the operation of

TOMS in the UK at this stage, and that businesses should continue to follow existing guidance. This is because:

- the EU Commission has indicated an intention to carry out a review of TOMS, which may result in significant changes to the scheme in future
- making changes now, which may be modified or reversed in future, would be particularly disruptive and costly for business

We will review this after a year.

It is open for any business to apply **direct effect** and operate the TOMS in accordance with the Court's decisions. For example, it is possible that some tour operators may gain a benefit from including wholesale supplies within the TOMS, in which case they may choose to do so if they wish.

Direct effect means invoking EU law (and case law) to override UK law (see the introduction to Chapter 5). Businesses can thus opt to calculate the margin and any output VAT due on an individual transaction basis if they wish.

10.3 PUBLIC BODIES

As explained at 4.1.8 'Public bodies', activities and transactions engaged in as a public authority by states, regional and local government authorities and other bodies 'governed by public law' are regarded as non-business, even where they collect dues, fees, charges, etc. and would otherwise be regarded as business activities.

10.3.1 Section 33 refund bodies

Certain public bodies such as local authorities can claim a refund for the VAT they incur in their non-business activities under section 33 VAT Act 1994. These include the activities they engage in as public authorities, as explained above.

Section 33 refund bodies include local authorities, transport authorities, port health authorities, police authorities (and similar), development corporations, the BBC, the National Rivers Authority; the Environment Agency; national park authorities, fire authorities; the Broads Authority; the Greater London Authority; and Transport for London. Local authorities include county councils, county borough councils, district councils, London boroughs, parish councils, Welsh community councils, Scottish regional, islands or district councils, the City of London, the Council of the Isles of Scilly, and any joint committee or joint board established by two or more of these.

10.3.2 **Government departments and health authorities**

Government departments, regional governments and health authorities can recover some of the VAT they incur in their non-business activities under section 41 of the VAT Act 1994. HM Treasury sets the rules as to what supplies VAT can and cannot be recovered on via Treasury Directions published in the London, Edinburgh and Belfast *Gazettes*.

Government departments and health authorities must register for VAT regardless of the value of the taxable supplies they make. Supplies to government departments and health authorities are subject to the normal VAT rules and so are generally treated the same as a supply to any other customer.

The government of Northern Ireland recovers VAT incurred on non-business activities under section 99 of the VAT Act 1994.

10.4 **MUSEUMS AND GALLERIES REFUND SCHEME**

Certain museums and galleries that offer free public access can recover any VAT incurred in connection with the free admission of the public that is otherwise irrecoverable. To be eligible an organisation:

1. must be a museum or gallery that has been approved by HM Treasury. Certain libraries have also been approved. *VAT Notice 998* contains a list of the approved bodies and the date they are approved from. Other national museums and galleries can request approval (see the address in *VAT Notice 998*). HMRC states that to be successful an applicant must be a national and not local institution and should normally be sponsored by the relevant government department such as the Department for Culture, Media & Sport.
2. must offer free admission to see a collection or collections. Only VAT attributable to the free admissions can be claimed under the scheme and if VAT is attributable to both free and pay admissions, an apportionment must be carried out. Where the public is charged to see special exhibitions this will not bar eligibility; however, the VAT attributable and apportioned to the fee-paying exhibitions cannot be recovered under this scheme.

Only VAT incurred on goods or services received after the date of approval can be recovered. The goods and services must be attributable to the collections for which there is free admission. This includes the costs of acquiring and maintaining the exhibitions, the construction, renovation and maintenance of buildings or parts of buildings used to house them, the costs of advertising and promoting the collections, and the provision of free information about the collections including printed literature, websites and lectures. However, any VAT attributable to business activities cannot be recovered under the scheme. Examples include shops and fee-generating educational activities.

VAT-registered organisations make the claim in their VAT return. Organisations that are not registered must make a written claim to HMRC. Where an organisation starts using the scheme, any input VAT already recovered on related fixed assets and stock that is still on hand at the start of the scheme is not repayable by extra-statutory concession.

Any claim must be made within four years of the supply concerned.

See *VAT Notice 998* for full details.

10.5   ACADEMY AND FREE SCHOOLS

English academies and free schools (referred to collectively in this section as academies) are not part of the local authority and as a result cannot use the section 33 refund scheme. Up to 1 April 2011, the Young People's Learning Agency provided grant funding intended to compensate academies for this. With effect from 1 April 2011, the law was amended to allow academies to obtain a refund for the VAT they incur in their non-business activities. They do it under a scheme set out in section 33b to the VAT Act 1994. This scheme is similar to the section 33 scheme for local authority schools, though with important differences; for example, academies must make the VAT claims themselves rather than via their local authority.

Claims time limit

A section 33b claim must be made within four years of the supply date. For example, if the supply tax point is 3 June 2015, the claim for the VAT on that supply must be made before 3 June 2019.

Claim procedure

VAT-registered academies make a section 33b claim by including the refund amount in box 4 on the VAT return. Academies that are not VAT-registered must contact HMRC and make arrangements for claiming refunds. Claims must be made on form VAT 126. This requires listing the supplier invoices in respect of which a claim is being made, including each supplier's VAT registration number. VAT 126 claims cannot be made more frequently than once per month and must cover a period ending at the end of a calendar month.

If an academy is VAT-registered, it may be advantageous from a cash flow perspective to opt for monthly VAT returns as VAT-registered academies are likely to receive VAT refunds from HMRC. Against this must be offset the extra work of submitting monthly VAT returns.

Supplies to pupils

The broad HMRC policy (*VATEDU70000*) is that sales to academy pupils that meet all of the following conditions are non-business (by analogy with the rule for supplies closely related to exempt education, for which see 5.1.5):

1. The sale is by the academy and not by a trading subsidiary or another body.
2. The sale is at or below cost. Cost can be determined on a full cost recovery basis.
3. The sale is closely related to the non-business provision of free education. See below for items that HMRC considers to be closely related.
4. The goods or services are for the direct use of a pupil receiving free education.

Where a sale meets all of these conditions no VAT is chargeable but any VAT incurred in making the sale can be reclaimed under section 33b.

HMRC accepts that, for academies, the following meet the closely related condition (condition 3 above):

- catering for pupils;
- charges for accommodation at boarding schools;
- charges for breakfast and after school clubs;
- the sale or hire of musical instruments for use in lessons or school orchestras.

HMRC accepts that the following meet the closely related condition for local authority schools:

- school trips;
- transport provided in connection with the provision of free education, for example charges for school buses and minibuses;
- all sales of food and drink, including for example sales in school shops and vending machines.

However, HMRC does not accept that the non-business treatment can apply to:

- sales to staff;
- the sale of school photographs; and
- sales of school uniforms.

Academy sponsorship

HMRC provides the following guidance (*VATEDU70000*).

> It is unlikely that the funding academies receive from sponsors either in the commercial or voluntary sectors will be consideration for any supply. All that sponsors derive in return for their backing is some influence over the appointment of governors and, perhaps, their contribution reflected in the

school's name. However, once appointed, governors are under a legal duty to act in the interests of the school alone, not the sponsors.

CGS

At the time of writing it is not clear if HMRC requires academies to make adjustments for VAT reclaimed under section 33b of the VAT Act 1994 on capital items (see 10.1.3 'Capital items' for the definition of capital items). However, HMRC does require CGS adjustments under the similar section 33 scheme for local authorities, so it seems likely that they will be required under section 33b also.

10.6   **CHARITY VAT REFUND SCHEME**

With effect from 1 April 2015 a VAT refund scheme for VAT incurred in the non-business activities of certain eligible charities was introduced via new sections 33c and 33d of the VAT Act 1994. It applies for purchases made on or after 1 April 2015. This refund scheme is referred to as section 33c below.

At the time of writing the scheme applies to six categories of charity:

1. Palliative care charities

Palliative care charity means a charity the main purpose of which is the provision of palliative care at the direction of, or under the supervision of, a medical professional to persons who are in need of such care as a result of having a terminal illness. Medical professional means a registered medical practitioner, or a registered nurse.

2. Air ambulance charities

An air ambulance charity is a charity the main purpose of which is to provide an air ambulance service in pursuance of arrangements made by, or at the request of, a relevant NHS body.

Relevant NHS body means a body the main purpose of which is to provide ambulance services and which is an NHS foundation trust in England, an NHS trust in Wales, a Special Health Board constituted under section 2 of the National Health Service (Scotland) Act 1978, or a Health and Social Care trust established under the Health and Personal Social Services (Northern Ireland) Order 1991.

3. Search and rescue charities

Search and rescue charity means a charity whose main purpose is to carry out coordinated search and rescue activities in the UK or the UK marine area. Search and rescue activities mean searching for, and rescuing, persons who are, or may be, at risk of death or serious injury.

The search and rescue activities carried out by the charity must be coordinated by a relevant authority. Relevant authority means: the Secretary of State; a police force; the Scottish Fire and Rescue Service; or any other person or body specified by an order made by the Treasury.

UK marine area has the meaning given by section 42(1) of the Marine and Coastal Access Act 2009, which is (broadly) the UK territorial seas, the UK exclusive economic zone, and the UK sector of the continental shelf.

4. Search and rescue support charities

These are charities whose main purpose is to support, develop and promote the activities of a search and rescue charity.

5. Medical courier charities

Medical courier charity means a charity whose main purpose is to provide services for the transportation of **items** intended for use for medical purposes, including in particular: blood; medicines and other medical supplies; and items relating to people who are undergoing medical treatment. **Item** includes any substance.

6. Medical courier support charities

These are charities whose main purpose is to support, develop and promote the activities of a medical courier charity.

For the meaning of charity, see 6.1.1 'Meaning of charity'.

10.6.1　Establishing the main purpose

To establish the main purpose, the charitable purposes or objectives set out in the governing documents must be considered in the light of the actual activities undertaken (for case law on determining the main purpose, see 5.5.5 'Associations for the advancement of knowledge or the fostering of professional expertise').

If the only or the main purpose meets any of the categories above and the charity operates within its objects and powers, then the charity should qualify for the section 33c refund scheme. If there are multiple different purposes, some of which are not related to or ancillary to any of the above, the main purpose must be established.

If the main purpose does not fit into any of the six categories above, then options for obtaining eligibility for refunds for non-business activities include:

- transferring eligible activities into a separate charity, which has as its main purpose the provision of qualifying services;
- ceasing, reducing or transferring non-qualifying services and/or increasing qualifying services, including changing the objects as required.

10.6.2 Section 33c claim deadline

Strictly all claims should be made within four years of the date of supply, import or acquisition.

However, HMRC accepts a VAT 126 claim can be made within four years of the end of the month on which the supply was received (*VAT Notice 1001*, section 4.3). For instance, for a supply of goods in July 2015, you must submit your claim by 31 July 2019.

For a VAT-registered charity, HMRC says you must make your claim within four years of the due date of your return for the VAT period (VAT quarter/month) in which the VAT became chargeable (*VAT Notice 1001*, section 3.4).

10.6.3 Section 33c claim procedure

VAT-registered charities make a section 33c claim by including the refund amount in box 4 on the VAT return. If a charity is VAT-registered and will normally receive VAT refunds from HMRC, it may be advantageous from a cash flow perspective to opt for monthly VAT returns. Against this must be offset the extra work of submitting monthly VAT returns.

If the charity is not registered for VAT, refund claims must be made on form VAT 126. This is available on the HMRC website. It must be completed online, printed out and then posted to the address specified on the website. When your first claim has been approved HMRC will send you a claimer reference number which should be quoted on all future claims. A VAT 126 claim must relate to a period of at least one calendar month, or at least 12 months if it is for less than £100. The period you choose must end on the last day of a calendar month.

10.6.4 Section 33c record-keeping

For both VAT-registered and unregistered charities, you must keep the purchase invoices and other records to support your claims for at least six years, unless you have applied in writing, and HMRC has agreed to your keeping them for a shorter period. All purchase invoices must normally be bona fide VAT invoices, though there are a few situations in which HMRC will accept alternative evidence; see 12.5 'Claiming input VAT'.

10.7 LISTED PLACES OF WORSHIP GRANT SCHEME

This is a grant scheme to refund VAT incurred on eligible repairs and maintenance to listed places of worship. It is funded by the Department for Culture Media & Sport (DCMS). The scheme operates its own website (www.lpwscheme.org.uk) which should be checked for up-to-date details of what claims can be made.

The scheme allows eligible listed places of worship of all religions and faith groups to reclaim the VAT incurred on works carried out to repair, maintain or alter the fabric of an existing listed building where:

- the building's sole or main use must be as a public place of worship. It must be available to the general public for at least six religious services a year and that availability must be publicised and not by invitation only;
- it is a place of worship used by monasteries, nunneries or other similar establishments; or
- it is owned by or vested in a number of DCMS-approved organisations which look after redundant places of worship. The DCMS will consider applications from religious or charitable groups caring for redundant places of worship. These groups would need to demonstrate that their principal or primary purpose is to conserve, repair and maintain redundant listed places of worship which are not in private ownership.

The building must be included on the public registers of listed buildings kept for England, Scotland, Wales and Northern Ireland.

10.7.1 Eligible works

Only works carried out to repair, maintain or alter the fabric of an existing listed building are eligible. The fabric of the building includes foundations, walls, roofs, rainwater goods, drainage, plumbing, fitted kitchens, electrical wiring, fixed internal surfaces, floors, stairs, landings, lightning conductors and all doors and windows. A list of eligible and ineligible works is set out in the Eligibility Checklist page of the Listed Place of Worship Scheme website.

10.7.2 Claims

Claims must be made in arrears but all invoices must be claimed within 12 months of the invoice date. Copy invoices must be sent with the claim.

The minimum value of eligible work that can be put on a single claim to the scheme is £1,000 (excluding VAT). From 1 October 2013, each listed place of worship has also been allowed to submit one claim in respect of works with a value of less than £1000, but more than £500 (excluding the VAT paid) in any 12-month period.

10.8 **MEMORIALS REFUND SCHEME**

This scheme returns in grant aid VAT incurred in the construction, renovation and maintenance of memorials on or after 16 March 2005. The scheme is funded by the Department for Culture Media & Sport with a fixed annual budget. See www.memorialgrant.org.uk for full details.

The scheme is restricted to registered charities and religious groups exempted from registering as charities. The memorial must be a structure. Structures include traditional memorials such as stone crosses, monoliths and statues, as well as plaques fixed to buildings, but exclude any memorial that does not require construction (such as a book or portrait), or is intangible (such as a theatrical or musical event).

Structures that have a dual purpose are not eligible under the scheme, for example a memorial bench or a playground, though by exception stained glass windows are eligible. Also excluded from the scheme are memorial gardens and trees as these are not considered to be structures capable of construction or renovation. However, minor landscaping and planting undertaken in the course of memorial construction will generally be eligible.

All memorials must bear a commemorative inscription or plaque. There is no subject matter restriction beyond a requirement that the memorial commemorates a person or people, an animal or an event.

The memorial must have a minimum 30 hours per week public access, though the access need not be free. If a key must be obtained to access the memorial, the key-holder must be reasonably accessible. If a memorial is constructed in the UK to be erected overseas, any UK VAT incurred on the memorial can be recovered under the scheme.

From 1 April 2012 the Memorial Grant scheme has operated with quarterly fixed budgets (calculated as a quarter of the total annual budget). Payments are made once per quarter and the payable rate depends on the value of the eligible claims received in that quarter, with each claim attracting a fair pro rata payment. If the total funding is not used in any quarter, it is carried forward to the following quarter, but not transferable between financial years.

Claims must be accompanied by original VAT invoices. The invoice must be for works already completed, and must be fully settled prior to submission under the scheme. Payments will be made around the middle of July, October, January and April. In order for an eligible claim to be included in one of the quarterly payment runs applications must be received by the last working day of the preceding month. It is recommended that you obtain proof of posting for all submissions to the scheme.

Any queries on your application must be resolved by the period deadline (see website for deadlines). If your query cannot be resolved within this time, your application will roll forward into the next quarter, and that quarter's payable rate will apply.

10.9 CASH ACCOUNTING SCHEME

By default output VAT is accounted for on an 'accruals basis' under the tax point rules explained in Chapter 12 'Operational Aspects'. These rules are broadly that:

- output VAT becomes due to HMRC at the earlier of when a sales invoice is issued or when it is paid; and
- input VAT is recoverable from HMRC at the earlier of when a purchase invoice is received or paid.

> Under the Cash Accounting Scheme:
>
> - output VAT becomes due to HMRC when it is received from your customer (or if later, the date of any post-dated cheque); and
> - input VAT is recoverable when the purchase invoice is paid (or if later, the date of any post-dated cheque).
>
> To join the scheme you must expect the value of your taxable supplies in the next year will be £1,350,000 or less and certain **relevant supplies** are excluded from the scheme.

10.9.1 Advantages

The Cash Accounting Scheme has three main advantages:

1. **Simplicity**: you can use a basic receipts and payments accounts system to record and account for VAT on financial transactions.
2. **Cash flow**: if you make credit sales the scheme delays the payment of output VAT to HMRC until you receive it from your customer. However, the recovery of input VAT is delayed from the point at which a purchase invoice is received until the point at which it is paid.
3. **Automatic bad debt relief**: as you only pay over output VAT when you receive a payment from the customer, you avoid having to pay over to HMRC output VAT on sales you invoice but have to write off. Under accruals accounting, you must wait six months before being able to reclaim any output VAT paid on a bad debt.

10.9.2 **Joining the scheme**

You may only join the Cash Accounting Scheme if you meet all of the following conditions:

1. You expect the value of your taxable supplies (net of any VAT) in the next 12 months to be less than £1.35 million. When calculating the value of your taxable supplies you should include the net value of any standard-rated, reduced-rated and zero-rated sales but exclude any expected income from the sale of fixed assets.
2. You have made all VAT returns you are required to make.
3. You have paid all VAT due to HMRC or made an arrangement with HMRC for that VAT to be paid in instalments over a specific period.
4. in the previous 12 months you have not been convicted of any offence involving VAT or been assessed to a penalty for VAT evasion involving dishonesty or made any payment subject to compound proceedings in respect of VAT.
5. HMRC has not written to you withdrawing use of the scheme during the last year.
6. HMRC has not written to you and denied you access to the scheme.

There is no need to apply or inform HMRC that you are starting to use the Cash Accounting Scheme, and you may start using the scheme from registration, though you may only switch to the scheme once registered at the start of a VAT period.

10.9.3 **Leaving the scheme**

You may leave the scheme voluntarily at the end of a VAT period, but you must stop using the scheme if any of the following conditions are met:

1. at the end of a VAT period, your taxable turnover in the last 12 months has exceeded £1.6 million; or
2. you are convicted of a VAT offence or penalised for VAT evasion involving dishonesty; or
3. HMRC instructs you to leave the scheme.

10.9.4 **Accounting for transactions**

Output VAT is due to HMRC whenever the customer makes a payment towards a standard-rated or reduced-rated sale. Purchase VAT is incurred when you make a VAT-bearing purchase:

	Cash receipt date	Cash payment date
Cash, coins	date received	date paid
Cheque	the date you receive the cheque, or the date on the cheque, whichever is later. If the cheque is not honoured, then you do not have to account for the VAT. If you have already accounted for the VAT you can adjust your VAT account, or make a refund claim.	the date you sent the cheque, or the date on the cheque, whichever is later. If your cheque is not honoured, you cannot reclaim the VAT. If you have already accounted for the VAT you should adjust your VAT account, or make a voluntary disclosure
Giro, standing order or direct debit	the date your bank account is credited with such a payment	the date your bank account is debited with such a payment
Credit or debit card	the date you make out a sales voucher for the payment (not when you actually receive payment from the card provider)	the date a sales voucher is made out for the payment

10.9.5 **Excluded transactions**

The Cash Accounting Scheme does not apply to the following transactions, which should be accounted for under the normal accruals-basis rules:

- goods purchased or sold under lease purchase, hire purchase, conditional sale or credit sale agreements;
- goods imported or acquired from another EU state;
- supplies where you issue a VAT invoice and payment of that invoice is not due in full within six months of the date it was issued;
- supplies of goods or services where you issue a VAT invoice in advance of making the supply or providing the goods;
- supplies in respect of which it is for the recipient, on the supplier's behalf, to account for and pay the VAT.

If you regularly make any of these types of transaction then you will have to consider how practical it is to run two different schemes at the same time.

10.9.6 **Other factors**

Part payment

If you make or receive payments which:

- are a partial payment of an invoice; or
- cover more than one invoice; or
- relate to an invoice for supplies at different rates of tax,

you must allocate the payment to the invoices in the order in which you issue or receive them. Where you make or receive partial payment of an invoice and VAT is not identified separately you must treat the payment as VAT-inclusive. Where you make or receive payments which relate to an invoice for supplies at different rates of tax you must apportion the amount paid or received between the different rates and treat the amounts on which VAT is due at the standard or lower rate as VAT-inclusive.

Partial exemption

Where an organisation has a mix of non-business, exempt and taxable activities any business/non-business or partial exemption calculations based on levels of income or expenditure should be based on income received or payments made.

Deposits

If you receive or pay a deposit which serves as an advance payment, you must account for it as explained above. However, VAT does not apply to deposits taken as a security to ensure the safe return of goods, whether you refund it upon return of the goods or retain it to compensate you for loss or damage.

10.10 **ANNUAL ACCOUNTING SCHEME**

The Annual Accounting Scheme simplifies the administrative burden of calculating and submitting regular VAT returns. Normally you must submit a VAT return every three months. The Annual Accounting Scheme allows you to submit just one annual VAT return. However, you must still pay regular instalments of VAT over to HMRC. You can choose to make three quarterly or nine monthly instalments.

Payment must be made by direct debit, standing order or other electronic means. At the end of the year you submit a VAT return for the whole year, together with any balancing payment due. You have two months in which to submit the return (compared with one month for the usual quarterly returns). If you have overpaid VAT in the instalments HMRC will refund the difference.

If you register for monthly payments each payment will be calculated as 10% of your previous year's liability. If you register for quarterly payments each payment will be calculated as 25% of your previous year's liability. If you have been registered for 12 months or fewer, HMRC will estimate your annual liability.

10.10.1 Joining the scheme

To join the scheme you must:

- expect to make taxable supplies of under £1.35 million in the next 12 months; in calculating the value of your taxable supplies, standard-rated, reduced-rated and zero-rated sales are included net of VAT, but income from the disposal of fixed assets is excluded;
- not have stopped using the scheme in the last 12 months;
- not be part of a VAT group or divisional registration;
- not have a VAT debt that is getting bigger; if you have a small debt and have agreed proposals with HMRC to clear it, you may be allowed to use the scheme;
- not be insolvent;
- apply to HMRC for permission to join the scheme.

The form for applications is HMRC form VAT600AA or if you want to use the Annual Accounting Scheme in conjunction with the Flat Rate Scheme, you must use the joint application form VAT 600AA/FRS.

10.10.2 Whilst in the scheme

You must inform HMRC:

- if your VAT liability increases by 10% or more since the last time your instalments were calculated. HMRC will amend the interim payments;
- if you realise that the value of your taxable supplies will rise above £1,600,000 for the current year, or it has already gone over £1,600,000.

10.10.3 Leaving the scheme

You can choose to leave the scheme voluntarily by writing to HMRC.

You must leave the scheme if your taxable supplies exceeded £1.6 million in a VAT year. You will usually have to revert to submitting regular VAT returns at the start of the next VAT year, though in certain situations HMRC may make you leave the scheme at an earlier date.

10.10.4 **Other factors**

End of year

If you have a significant level of taxable activity, then having to submit quarterly returns is burdensome, but it does help ensure your VAT affairs are kept up to date. If you join the Annual Accounting Scheme you must make sure that you do not leave it all until the last minute to sort out. Even though you have two months after the end of the year in which to submit the annual VAT return, you will have a year's worth of transactions to sort out.

Other schemes

The scheme can be used with the following schemes; Cash Accounting, retail schemes, margin schemes, CGS and TOMS.

10.11 **RETAIL SCHEMES**

The retail schemes are for use by businesses that make retail sales to unregistered customers where it is impractical to record the VAT due for every individual item sold. Typically, this will be shops that make large numbers of cash sales and that do not possess sophisticated till systems. The retail schemes are used to calculate the output VAT due by the retailer. They can be used in conjunction with normal VAT accounting for other types of activity, such as internet sales.

VAT-registered businesses must be provided with proper VAT invoices or VAT receipts (see 12.4 'VAT invoices'), so retailers with a significant number of VAT-registered customers must have some way of issuing correct VAT invoices to customers on demand. This usually means either accounting for VAT on an item-by-item basis or splitting their sales and only using a retail scheme for sales to unregistered customers. However, occasional cash sales to registered businesses are allowed within a retail scheme, for example a garage supplying petrol to a VAT-registered customer or a retail DIY store supplying building materials to a VAT-registered builder.

There are five standard schemes. If your sales exceed £100 million, then you cannot use one of the standard schemes and must use a bespoke scheme that is agreed individually with HMRC. See *VAT Notice 727* for full details of the schemes.

10.12 **FLAT RATE SCHEME FOR SMALL BUSINESSES**

The Flat Rate Scheme is designed to simplify VAT administration for very small businesses. Under the scheme you calculate the VAT due to HMRC as a percentage of your 'flat rate turnover'. The flat rate you use depends on the business sector that your activity belongs in. See *VAT Notice 733* for a list of business sectors and the applicable rates.

The Flat Rate Scheme is really designed for small businesses making wholly or mainly standard-rated supplies. If zero-rated or exempt sales are a significant proportion of income, then the Flat Rate Scheme is likely to be disadvantageous financially and you should check the likely effect before joining.

You still need to calculate output VAT due under the normal rules and issue VAT invoices to VAT-registered customers. However, you do not have to pay HMRC the output VAT charged to VAT-registered customers.

You cannot recover any input VAT charged on purchases. This means that you do not have to monitor input VAT charged by your suppliers, though in practice certain transactions such as the purchase of fixed assets are excluded from the scheme, and you will need to monitor input VAT for these.

Your flat rate turnover includes zero-rated sales, the gross value of any reduced-rate and standard-rated sales and exempt income but excludes non-business income such as bank interest, grants and donations.

10.12.1 Joining the scheme

To join the scheme an organisation must meet all of the following conditions:

1. There are reasonable grounds for believing that taxable income (net of VAT and excluding any sales of fixed assets) in the next 12 months will be at most £150,000.
2. It is not eligible and was not eligible in the previous two years to join a VAT group. Broadly this means that the organisation is not a parent or subsidiary entity and is not under common control with another organisation.
3. The organisation is not associated with another organisation. This means that it is not controlled by another organisation and is not closely bound to another organisation by financial, economic and organisational links.
4. The organisation is not using the Second-Hand Goods Scheme, TOMS or CGS.
5. The organisation has not used the Flat Rate Scheme in the last 12 months.
6. The organisation must not have been convicted for an offence involving VAT, have accepted a compound penalty offer or been assessed for a penalty for conduct involving dishonesty.

To join the scheme you must apply to HMRC by downloading form VAT600FRS from the HMRC website, completing the form and either posting or emailing it to HMRC.

10.12.2 Leaving the scheme

You can leave the scheme at any time but must notify HMRC.

You must leave the scheme if your flat rate turnover (including VAT and exempt income) exceeds £230,000 or is expected to exceed £230,000 in the next 30 days, or if you become ineligible under any of the other conditions above.

10.12.3 Other factors

Joining reduction

You get a 1% reduction on the flat rate applicable to your business sector in your first year of registration.

Mixed sectors

If your business fits into two or more sectors, then you must apply the flat rate applicable to the main activity based on level of turnover. If the balance between activities changes you must continue to apply the same rate until the anniversary of joining the scheme, and then apply the new rate.

Capital expenditure

If you purchase 'capital expenditure goods', you can reclaim the VAT you have been charged on a single purchase of capital expenditure goods where the amount of the purchase, including VAT, is £2,000 or more. Capital expenditure goods are fixed assets such as computers, vans and furniture. However, if such goods are sold, output VAT must be accounted for on the sale of such goods.

If you purchase capital expenditure goods that are covered by the CGS (for instance, a building costing over £250,000 plus VAT), then you must leave the Flat Rate Scheme.

10.13 MARGIN SCHEMES

VAT is normally due on the full selling price of goods sold. However, where **eligible goods** are sold in **eligible circumstances** then output VAT is only due on the margin.

- Eligible goods are: (i) antiques; (ii) works of art; (iii) collector's items; (iv) and second-hand goods. See below for the definitions.
- Eligible circumstances are that no VAT was chargeable on the supply or the goods were themselves purchased as a margin scheme supply.

Example: Margin scheme

	£
Selling price	100
Purchase price	70
Margin	30
VAT due on margin = 1/6 × £30	5
Net selling price = £100 − £5	95

Note: with VAT at 20%, to calculate the VAT included in a gross price, multiply the gross price by 1/6. This is referred to as the VAT fraction. See 12.1 'VAT fractions and VAT rounding'.

10.13.1   Purpose and advantages

Businesses selling second-hand goods may be at a commercial disadvantage compared with a business selling similar new goods where input VAT has been paid. To rectify this discrepancy the margin scheme allows VAT to be calculated only on the margin (selling price less purchase price) providing the qualifying conditions are met. It is the margin that counts towards your taxable turnover and that is entered into box 6 on the VAT return. If the margin is negative, no VAT is due.

It is only the direct purchase cost that is included in the margin calculation. Costs of repairing the goods and of running the business are excluded, but associated input VAT is recoverable to the extent that it is attributable to the taxable business activity of selling second-hand goods.

The scheme is optional but will usually be advantageous if you are selling eligible goods that are not zero-rated to unregistered customers. You can operate the scheme for individual items, classes of eligible items or all eligible items and in conjunction with normal VAT procedures for other items you sell. You do not need to apply to use the scheme, obtain permission from HMRC or inform HMRC.

10.13.2 **Qualifying conditions**

For the scheme to apply, all of the following conditions must be met:

1. Eligible goods must be sold.
2. The eligible goods must have been acquired in eligible circumstances.
3. You must meet the record-keeping requirements.
4. You must not issue an invoice that shows VAT separately. This means the customer cannot recover the VAT charged on the margin.

10.13.3 **Eligible goods**

The scheme only applies to the following goods:

Antiques, Works of art and Collector's items

See the definitions in 6.5.7 'Imported works of art, antiques and collector's items'.

Second-hand goods

These are goods which are suitable for further use as they are, or after repair. HMRC accepts that in most cases, goods which are second-hand in the ordinary usage of the term will be eligible for the margin schemes (*VAT Notice 718*, section 2.7).

10.13.4 **Eligible circumstances**

The eligible goods must have been obtained without VAT being charged (for instance, from a private individual or unregistered business) or obtained under the margin scheme from another margin scheme supplier. There are, however, two optional exceptions:

1. Where a work of art is purchased from the work's creator or the creator's heirs then it does not matter if the supplier charges VAT. Any input VAT, import VAT or **acquisition VAT** (see 9.6.1 'Acquisitions') cannot be recovered and is included in the purchase price for margin scheme calculations.
2. Where works of art, antiques and collector's items are imported from outside the EU. This import VAT is irrecoverable and is included in the purchase price in margin scheme calculations.

To use either of the two exceptions:

- you must inform the HMRC VAT Written Enquiries Team in writing that you are going to take-up the option, and you must specify the date from which you will be applying it;
- you must exercise the option for a period of at least two years, after which you must inform the HMRC VAT Written Enquiries Team in writing as and when you wish to stop using the scheme;
- you must use the scheme in respect of all transactions and goods comprised in the exceptions; and
- if, having exercised the option, you decide to sell any goods covered by the option outside the scheme (for example, if you export the goods), you are not entitled to recover any input tax on those goods until the period in which you account for VAT on their sale.

10.13.5   Record-keeping requirements

You must either keep detailed records of all goods purchased and sold under the scheme or use 'global accounting' (see 10.13.6 'Global accounting'). Keeping detailed records means obtaining a purchase invoice from the supplier (or completing one yourself if the supplier does not provide one), keeping a stock register detailing all qualifying purchases and sales, and providing a sales invoice with the goods that includes the wording Margin Scheme – second-hand goods, or Margin Scheme – works of art or Margin Scheme – collector's items and antiques, as appropriate.

10.13.6   Global accounting

Under global accounting you can account for VAT, every VAT return period, on your total margin for the period. You can include most of the items which would be eligible for sale under the Margin Scheme as long as they have a purchase price of £500 or less per item. The exceptions to this are any of the following goods (regardless of their purchase price): aircraft; boats and outboard motors; caravans and motor caravans; horses and ponies, and motor vehicles, including motorcycles (except motor vehicles broken up for scrap).

Bulk collections

These can be included in global accounting if the combined purchase price is over £500 but the individual purchase price of each individual item is at most £500. If any individual item has a purchase value of over £500, you must not sell it on under Global Accounting.

Collections

If you purchase an eligible item for £500 or more, and the item is made up of several components valued at less than £500, and you sell the component items individually, then you can use Global Accounting.

10.13.7 **Transfer of a business as a going concern**

If you obtain goods under a TOGC, no VAT will be chargeable on the transfer. But this does not necessarily mean that you will be able to sell the goods on under a margin scheme. You will only be able to use the scheme if the last person to obtain the goods – other than by way of a TOGC or an assignment of rights – would have been entitled to use a margin scheme to sell them. Where there has been a succession of TOGCs or assignments, or a mixture of both, it is the first person in that chain who must have been entitled to use the margin scheme

See *VAT Notice 718* for full details of the margin scheme.

10.14 **ABUSIVE SCHEMES**

The CJEU has developed a principle of **abuse of rights** that applies to taxpayers in respect of VAT. This principle blocks transactions, or series of transactions (**schemes**), that, whilst entirely legal and adhering to the letter of VAT law, are considered an abuse of the 'purposes' of the VAT system that must be rendered ineffective. Such schemes are referred to as **abusive schemes**. The way they are rendered ineffective is by being **redefined**. This means the VAT position reverts to what it would have been in the absence of the scheme. However, no penalty is due as each step was (by definition) legal.

The UK's General Anti-Abuse Rule (GAAR), introduced in Finance Act 2013, does not apply to VAT. The CJEU's doctrine of abuse of rights applies instead.

The abuse principle generally applies to artificial schemes set up solely to gain a VAT advantage. However, it is not artificial to set up an arrangement that saves VAT but is on an 'arm's length' basis, for example:

- In the *Halifax* case (see below), a wholly artificial scheme to improve VAT recovery on construction costs of residual use buildings from 5% to 100% was blocked

- In the *Weald Leasing* case (see 10.14.2) an in-house asset-leasing scheme, set up to defer irrecoverable VAT, would in principle have been acceptable if the assets had been leased on arm's length terms.

10.14.1 The *Halifax* case

In case C-255/02 *Halifax plc Leeds Permanent Development Services Ltd* v. *Customs & Excise* [2006] ECR I-01609, the Halifax Group made mainly VAT-exempt supplies. It constructed a number of call centres via a complicated and artificial scheme, under which, if successful, it would have been able to recover all of the VAT incurred on construction. If they had been constructed directly by the Halifax VAT group, the VAT would have been recoverable at the group's residual recovery rate of 5%.

HMRC rejected the scheme's claim for VAT recovery (partly) on the basis that this was an abuse of rights. Halifax did not dispute that the sole aim of the scheme was to gain a VAT advantage. The CJEU found for HMRC, accepting that the principle of abuse of rights, already established in other areas of EU law, applies to VAT as well. It then formulated the following approach for dealing with **abusive practices**:

1. VAT law must be interpreted as precluding any VAT advantage to be gained from an abusive practice.
2. An abusive practice can be found to exist only if both of the following conditions are met:
   - The transactions concerned, despite formal application of VAT law, result in the accrual of a VAT advantage the grant of which would be contrary to the purpose of VAT law.
   - It must be apparent from a number of objective factors that the essential aim of the transactions concerned is to obtain a VAT advantage. The prohibition of abuse is not relevant where the business activity carried out may have some explanation other than the mere attainment of tax advantages.
3. Where an abusive practice has been found to exist, the transactions involved must be redefined so as to re-establish the situation that would have prevailed in the absence of the transactions constituting that abusive practice.
4. A finding of abusive practice must not lead to a penalty, for which a clear and unambiguous legal basis would be necessary, but rather to an obligation to repay, simply as a consequence of that finding, the VAT advantage.

The CJEU also emphasised that:

- businesses need legal certainty when organising their affairs and so any finding of abusive practice must be based on objective and not subjective criteria;
- a business's choice between exempt transactions and taxable transactions may be based on a range of factors, including VAT considerations. VAT law does not require the business to choose the one which involves paying the highest amount of VAT.

Following the CJEU ruling, the Halifax Group withdrew its appeal against HMRC's refusal to repay the input VAT.

10.14.2 **Contrary to the purposes of VAT law**

For a scheme to be artificial the grant of the VAT advantage must be contrary to the purpose of VAT law. The case C-103/09 *Revenue & Customs* v. *Weald Leasing Ltd* [2010] EWCA Civ ECR I-13589 concerned the Churchill Group of insurance companies and an asset-leasing scheme. The group made mainly VAT-exempt supplies with a residual recovery rate of around 1%. The group arranged to lease equipment and other VAT-bearing assets via a dedicated asset-leasing company (Weald Leasing), held outside the Churchill VAT group, so that Weald could recover the VAT incurred on each asset upfront with the VAT group then paying it back as irrecoverable output VAT over the asset's lease period. HMRC saw this as abusive in that it spread what would otherwise be upfront irrecoverable VAT.

The CJEU observed that the leasing transactions are within the scope of VAT and governed by specific VAT rules, and therefore any tax advantage that arises through leasing transactions carried out within those rules cannot in itself be a VAT advantage the grant of which would be contrary to the purpose of VAT law.

The CJEU held that the VAT advantage accruing from an undertaking's recourse to asset-leasing transactions instead of the outright purchase of those assets, does not constitute a VAT advantage the grant of which would be contrary to the purpose of VAT law, provided that the contractual terms of those transactions, particularly those concerned with setting the level of rentals, correspond to arm's length terms and that the involvement of an intermediate third party in those transactions is not such as to preclude the application of those provisions. The fact that the undertaking does not engage in leasing transactions in the context of its normal commercial operations is irrelevant in that regard.

10.14.3 **Essential aim**

In case C-425/06 *Ministero dell'Economia e delle Finanze* v. *Part Service Srl* [2008] ECR I-00897, the CJEU ruled there can be a finding of an abusive scheme when the accrual of a tax advantage constitutes the principal aim of the transaction or transactions at issue. To determine this the real substance and significance of the transactions must be examined. Account may be taken of the purely artificial nature of the transactions and the links of a legal, economic and/or personal nature between the operators involved in the scheme, those aspects being such as to demonstrate that the accrual of a tax advantage constitutes the principal aim pursued, despite the possible existence, in addition, of economic objectives arising from, for example, marketing, organisation or guarantee considerations.

10.15 **LISTED AND HALLMARKED SCHEMES**

> The use of certain listed and hallmarked schemes must be disclosed to HMRC in particular circumstances. Failure to disclose a notifiable scheme may incur a penalty. Some of these schemes are of relevance to voluntary organisations, in particular listed scheme number 8.

You do not have to notify use of a scheme if you are not VAT-registered or not liable to be registered (see Chapter 2 'Registration and deregistration'). Organisations with business income below £600,000 will generally be exempted from all notification requirements, and organisations with business income below £10 million will generally be exempted from the hallmark scheme disclosure requirements. If the organisation is a member of a group the limits apply to the whole group.

See *VAT Notice 700/8* for full details and for information on reporting schemes.

10.15.1 **Listed schemes**

At the time of writing there are ten listed schemes, as set out below, though new ones may be added in future. The key schemes likely to affect voluntary organisations are schemes 1, 4, 7 and 8. You must notify your involvement in a listed scheme when all the following five conditions are met:

1. You are registered for VAT or liable to be registered for VAT.
2. You are a party to a **notifiable listed scheme** (see 10.15.2 below). This means you are knowingly involved in a notifiable listed scheme. Even if there are other parties to the scheme that have notified HMRC, you must also notify HMRC, although you can make a joint notification with the other parties. If you are unwittingly involved in any of the steps of a notifiable scheme, that is,

you have no knowledge of either the existence of the scheme or the role you play in it, or you act purely in an advisory capacity, then there is no requirement to notify.

3. Your taxable plus exempt income exceeded £600,000 in the year immediately prior to the VAT period of the relevant event or £150,000 in the VAT quarter immediately prior to the VAT period of the relevant event for quarterly VAT returns, or £50,000 in the VAT month immediately prior to the VAT period of the relevant event for monthly VAT returns. If you are a member of a Companies Act group the turnover threshold applies to the whole group, including intra-group transactions but excluding any intra-VAT group transactions.

4. A relevant event occurs. A relevant event is any of the following:
   (a) You show in a VAT return, in respect of any VAT accounting period starting on or after 1 August 2004, a higher or lower net amount of VAT than would be the case but for the listed scheme. You must notify HMRC within 30 days of the due date of the VAT return.
   (b) You make a claim in respect of any VAT accounting period starting on or after 1 August 2004 for which a VAT return has been submitted, for the repayment of output tax over-declared or input tax credit under-claimed that is greater than would be the case but for the listed scheme. You must notify HMRC within 30 days of making the claim.
   (c) The amount of non-deductible VAT you incur, in respect of any VAT accounting period starting on or after 1 August 2005, would have been higher but for the listed scheme. You must notify HMRC within 30 days of the due date for making a return in respect of that accounting period.

5. You have not previously notified your involvement in the scheme.

10.15.2 Notifiable listed schemes

The notifiable listed schemes are:

1. The first grant of a major interest in a building

This is where the first grant of a major interest in a building is zero-rated, made to a connected person and the following input tax is attributed to the grant: (a) input tax in respect of a service charge relating to the building; or (b) input tax in connection with any extension, enlargement, repair, maintenance or refurbishment of the building (other than for remedying defects in the original construction). This scheme will capture a zero-rated first grant of a major interest by a design and build subsidiary if the grant includes any of the supplies described in (a) or (b) above.

Example 1

A housing landlord may seek to use this scheme to recover input tax on the renovation of houses that they had constructed several years earlier. Having decided that some of the houses require major refurbishment, the landlord leases or sells them to a subsidiary in such a way that they attribute to that zero-rated disposal the VAT on the refurbishment, which may be undertaken either before or after the grant. The subsidiary may then simply lease the houses back to the landlord so that they can then let them on again to tenants.

Example 2

The builder of new halls of residence may try to recover future input tax on repairs and maintenance of the buildings, even though the income from the property at that time will be exempt, by building into the initial zero-rated lease or sale a payment for, and agreement to provide, repairs and maintenance in the future.

2. Payment handling services

These are schemes that aim to reduce the VAT due on the advertised price of retail goods or services by transforming an element of the price into an exempt payment handling service such as credit/debit card or cash handling.

3. Value shifting

This is a scheme that comprises or includes the following features: (a) a standard-rated retail supply of goods or services; (b) a linked zero-rated or exempt supply by any person to the same customer; (c) the linked supply is treated as a separate supply under the terms of an agreement made by the customer; (d) the terms of the agreement attribute part of the consideration for the retail supply and linked supply to the linked supply; and (e) the total consideration due for the retail supply and linked supply is no different, or not significantly different, from what it would be for the retail supply alone.

Example of arrangements included in the listed scheme

A retail customer making a large purchase may find that, at the point of sale, they are offered an insurance product with the goods. Rather than paying an additional amount for this cover, the customer will be informed that the ticket price has now been apportioned to cover both the goods and the insurance. If the customer then says they do not want the insurance, there is no reduction of the ticket price to reflect this. The overall price paid by the customer remains the same whether they take the insurance or not.

Examples of arrangements not included in the listed scheme

Notification is not required when the linked goods or services are supplied free, with no part of the price being attributed to that supply. Additionally notification is not required for normal business-promotion arrangements. For example: a retailer offers a 'meal deal' where customers can buy a sandwich, a soft drink and packet of crisps for a single price that is lower than the normal combined price of the three items. When apportioning the cost between the zero-rated and standard-rated items the retailer spreads the discount across all the goods supplied. These arrangements are unlikely to be notifiable as each linked supply would not normally be subject to a separate agreement with the customer; and the total amount payable is likely to be significantly different from what it would be for the standard-rated element alone.

4. Leaseback agreements

This scheme comprises or includes the following features: (a) a person (the 'relevant person') receives a supply of goods, or the leasing or letting on hire of goods (for the purposes of this scheme, goods do not include land transactions); (b) the relevant person uses the goods in their business, but is not entitled to full input tax credit for the VAT on the supply to them; (c) the supply to them is made by a person connected with them; (d) the supplier, or a person connected with them, is entitled to full input tax credit on the purchase of the goods; and (e) the relevant person (or a person connected with them) funds (directly or indirectly) more than 90% of the cost of the goods.

Examples of arrangements included in the listed scheme

A partly exempt trader, such as a bank, requires new computer equipment. The decision is taken that the bank's corporate group will purchase the equipment outright. However, in order to reduce or remove the VAT effect of the irrecoverable input tax, the group acquires the computers in a subsidiary, which then leases them to the bank. Depending on the values and length of the lease, the intention is to spread the irrecoverable VAT cost, or to avoid a proportion of it altogether.

Example of arrangements not included in the listed scheme

Notification is not required for leasing arrangements that are between unconnected parties.

5. Extended approval period

This scheme comprises or includes the following features: (a) a retail supply of goods where the goods are sent or taken on approval, sale or return, or similar terms; (b) a requirement that the customer pays in full before any approval, return or similar period expires; and (c) for the purposes of accounting for VAT, the supplier treats the goods as supplied on a date after the date on which payment is received in full.

6. Groups: third-party suppliers

These are schemes that aim to reduce or remove the VAT incurred on bought-in taxable services (including outsourced services) by a user that cannot recover all of the input tax charged to it for those services. The scheme description is linked to legislation that took effect from 1 August 2004 and which only applies to businesses that are in VAT groups or intend to join a VAT group where the VAT group concerned has a business turnover exceeding £10 million a year. See *VAT Information Sheet 07/04.*

Example of arrangements included in the listed scheme

A partly exempt business, say company A, an insurance company, wants to buy in computer services from third-party company B, but would like to reduce the irrecoverable VAT cost of doing this. Companies A and B establish company C, in which A owns 51% of C's shares. Company A includes C in its VAT Group. Company B owns the remaining shares in C, but these shares confer rights to 99% of the dividends declared by C and 99% of the assets on winding up.

Company C holds the contract to provide the computer services required by company A from company B and employs the staff to provide the service. Besides the dividends, B also receives benefits from C in the form of a management charge for managing C's activity of providing computer services. As a result, almost all of the benefits of company C's activity accrue to company B. Thus company B has access to the profits and benefits of the computer service activity, and company A hopes to avoid a large VAT cost as there will be no VAT charged within the VAT Group.

7. Education and training by a non-profit-making body

This scheme comprises or includes the following features:

1. a non-profit-making body within the VAT Act 1994, Schedule 9, Group 6, Note (1)(e) but not otherwise within note 1 conducts a business whose activities consist wholly or mainly of the supply of VAT-exempt education or vocational training to persons who are not taxable persons;
2. it receives any of the following 'key supplies', for use in that business, from a connected taxable person who is not eligible for the exemption:
    - a capital item (including leasing or letting on hire of a capital item);
    - staff;
    - management services;
    - administration services; or
    - accountancy services; and
3. in any one VAT return accounting period the value of those key supplies comprises 20% or more of the non-profit-making body's costs.

8. Education and training by a non-eligible body

This scheme comprises or includes the following features:

1. a body that is not an **eligible body** for the purposes of the education exemption is connected to a body that is an eligible body; and

2. the non-eligible body conducts a business whose activities consist wholly or mainly of the taxable supply of education or vocational training. In addition, either:

    - the non-eligible body benefits or intends to benefit the eligible body by way of gift, dividend or otherwise; or both:
    - the eligible body makes to the non-eligible body, for use in the non-eligible body's business, any supply (including the leasing or letting on hire) of any of the following 'key supplies': a capital item (including the leasing or letting on hire of a capital item); staff; management services; administration services; or accountancy services; and
    - in any one VAT return accounting period the value of those key supplies comprises 20% or more of the non-eligible body's costs.

See section 5.1.1 'Eligible body' for a list of eligible bodies for the purposes of the education exemption.

> ### Example of education and training by a non-eligible body
>
> An institution, such as a university, has a contract to provide training to employees of a NHS Trust. Normally, the training would be exempt from VAT and thus the VAT on costs involved in providing it would not be recoverable. In order to provide this training, the university needs to build a new facility, but would like to reduce the cost of the irrecoverable VAT on the building. The university may establish a subsidiary that is expressly allowed to distribute its profits, claiming exemption for its training supplies. The subsidiary may have few or no resources, so will need to be provided with those resources by the university under various contracts and agreements. It is also likely that the university would want to access any profits from this activity and may choose to do this by having the subsidiary gift those profits to it under the Gift Aid relief. Thus the university may hope to transform the training into a fully taxable activity and recover the input tax on the new facility in the subsidiary, together with other taxable costs.

9. Cross-border face-value vouchers

This scheme comprises or includes the following features: (a) the supply of a 'relevant service' from a UK supplier (S) to someone (A) in another EU member state; (b) a person (B) in another member state B, who may be the same person as A or a different person, uses S's service to supply a 'relevant service' to a customer in the UK (the 'retail supply'); (c) S (the UK supplier) and B (the person making the retail supply) are connected persons; (d) the customer is not a taxable person and uses a face-value voucher issued by a non-UK person (C), who may be the same person as B or a different person, to obtain the supply; (e) B (the person making the retail supply) does not account for VAT on that supply in the UK or any other EU member state.

Example of cross-border face-value voucher scheme

A company, UK Supplier Ltd, contracts to supply telecommunication services to a related company, Redeemer Ltd, in another EU member state, such as Ireland.

A second related Irish company, Issuer Ltd, issues phone cards and sells them to UK retailers. The retailers sell the cards to UK customers, who use them to obtain telecommunication services from Redeemer Ltd. The cards say that, when they are used, Redeemer Ltd will provide the telecommunication services. Redeemer Ltd does this by buying in the services under its contract with UK Supplier Ltd.

Redeemer Ltd and Issuer Ltd argue that no VAT is due in Ireland or the UK.

---

10. Surrender of a relevant lease

This scheme comprises or includes the following features:

(a) an occupier of a building (or part of a building) agrees with the landlord to the surrender or other early termination of their lease, tenancy or licence to occupy a building;

(b) the building is a capital item within the meaning of the CGS (whether or not the adjustment period has expired);

(c) the occupier, or any person connected with them, is a person who: is a landlord of the building, owns it for the purposes of the CGS, and has elected to waive exemption (also known as 'opting to tax') in relation to it;

(d) before the surrender: the occupier paid VAT on the rent of the building (or part of the building), and was unable to recover this VAT in full; and

(e) following the surrender: the occupier continues to occupy at least 80% of the area previously occupied, and pays no VAT on the rent, or pays less than 50% of the amount of VAT previously paid (comparing similar rental periods).

Examples of arrangements included in the listed scheme

- The occupier surrenders or terminates a taxable lease early and, despite the existence of an option to tax, the connected landlord makes a grant of a new lease that is exempt from VAT by reason of the option to tax disapplication rules.
- The occupier surrenders or terminates a taxable lease early and, despite the existence of an option to tax, the connected landlord sells the building to the occupier as exempt from VAT by reason of the option to tax disapplication rules.
- The occupier, who is also a landlord further back in a chain of leases, arranges for all of the leases to be surrendered, leaving the occupier with the building (possibly paying a small amount of taxable ground rent to the ultimate freeholder).

10.15.3 Hallmarked schemes

The hallmarked scheme reporting requirements only apply if business turnover exceeds £10 million and as such need not concern most charities and voluntary organisations. You must notify a 'hallmarked scheme' if all the following conditions are met:

1. You are registered for VAT or liable to be registered for VAT in the UK.
2. Your business turnover exceeds £10 million in the year immediately prior to the VAT return period that includes the relevant event (see below), or the appropriate proportion of £10 million in the VAT return period immediately prior to the VAT return period that includes the relevant event. If you are a member of a group (for Companies Act purposes) the turnover test is applied to the whole group and includes intra-group transactions but excludes any intra-VAT group transactions.
3. You are a party to a scheme. You are a party to a scheme if you knowingly take part in it. You are not a party to a scheme if you: (a) are unwittingly involved in any of the steps of the scheme (you have no knowledge of either the existence of the scheme or the role you play in it); or (b) act purely in an advisory capacity.
4. That scheme is not a listed scheme.
5. The main purpose, or one of the main purposes, of the scheme is for any person to obtain a tax advantage. The main purpose test is similar to that outlined in 10.14.1 'The *Halifax* case'.

6. A relevant event occurs. A relevant event occurs (broadly) when you show in a VAT return or make a claim for a higher or lower net amount of VAT than would be the case but for the scheme. The scheme must be notified within 30 days of the due date of the return.
7. The scheme contains one or more hallmarks of avoidance. See below.
8. You have not already notified HMRC that you are using the scheme or you have not been provided with a scheme number by someone who has registered the scheme with HMRC.

The hallmarks are:

- **Confidentiality condition agreements**: there is an agreement that prevents or limits a person from giving others details of how a scheme gives rise to a tax advantage.
- **Agreements to share a tax advantage**: there is an agreement that the tax advantage accruing from the scheme be shared, to any extent, between the person to whom it accrues and the promoter or any other person who is a party to the scheme.
- **Contingent fee agreements**: there is an agreement that payment to a promoter of a scheme is partly or wholly contingent on the tax advantage accruing from use of the scheme.
- **Prepayments between connected parties**: the operation of a scheme involves a prepayment being made for supplies between connected persons.
- **Funding by loans, share subscriptions or subscriptions in securities**: this hallmark applies when a supply of goods or services made between two connected persons is funded (in whole or in part): by a loan between connected persons; by one person subscribing for shares in another with whom they are connected; or by one person subscribing in securities issued by another with whom they are connected.
- **Offshore loops**: this hallmark applies when certain exported services (which allow the exporter to recover related input tax) are used to provide other services to UK persons, and these 'imported' services are not subject to VAT.
- **Property transactions between connected persons**: this hallmark applies when: (a) a grant, which is not a zero-rated grant, is made of: any interest in, right over or licence to occupy land, or in relation to land in Scotland, any personal right to call for or be granted any such interest or right; (b) the grantor or grantee of the interest or right is a person who cannot recover input tax in full; (c) a work of any construction, alteration, demolition, repair, maintenance or civil engineering has been or is to be carried out on the land; and (d) the grant is made to a person connected with the grantor.

- **The issue of face-value vouchers**: this hallmark applies when: (a) face-value vouchers are issued for consideration; and (b) either the issuer does not expect at least 75% of the vouchers to be redeemed within three years of their being issued, or whatever the expected redemption rate, the vouchers are issued to a connected person outside any VAT group to which the issuer belongs. A 'promoter' is anyone who, in the course of their trade, profession or business of providing taxation services, designs or sells the arrangements entered into.

11 Other topics

This chapter considers various miscellaneous topics:

- 11.1 Supplies of staff
- 11.2 Agency supplies
- 11.3 Single and multiple supplies
- 11.4 Membership subscriptions
- 11.5 Transfer of a business as a going concern (TOGC)

11.1 SUPPLIES OF STAFF

A supply of staff takes place where one entity (A) puts one of its employees under the direction and control of another entity (B) in return for consideration. If the employee remains under the direction and control of their employer (A) then A is supplying the services performed by the employee to B, not staff.

The VAT implications of supplying staff between organisations can be complicated and this is an area of developing case law.

11.1.1 Employment agencies

An employment agency is a business that locates permanent employees for a customer (though the placement may be for a fixed period). Once recruited, the person becomes an employee of the customer. The agency will normally charge a commission to the customer which is standard-rated for VAT.

11.1.2 Employment businesses

An employment business supplies its own employees to customers on a temporary basis, placing them under the direction and control of the customer. There is an employment relationship between the employment business and worker but no employment relationship between the worker and customer. The persons provided are commonly referred to as temps or agency staff. Special Income Tax rules (Income Tax (Earnings and Pensions) Act 2003 Part 2

Chapter 3) act to treat workers supplied by employment businesses as employees of the employment business.

HMRC's position is that (apart from the nursing agency concession, for which see below) VAT is due on the whole amount paid by the customer to the employment business, including on any salary element and on the employment business's commission. This used to be mitigated by a concession (the **staff hire concession**) which allowed the salary element to be ignored for VAT; however, this concession was withdrawn with effect from 1 April 2009.

However, HMRC's position is the subject of dispute. In the High Court case *Reed Personnel Services Ltd* [1995] STC 588, Reed Nurse provided temporary nurses to hospitals. The VAT Tribunal found that the nursing services were supplied by the nurses and not by Reed and that Reed supplied its administrative services as **agent** (see 11.2), the consideration for these supplies being the commission Reed received. This decision was upheld in the High Court on the basis that the nature of the supplies was a matter of fact for the Tribunal.

But in *Hays Personnel Services Ltd* [1995] VTD 14882 and in *Eyears Ltd* [2007] VTD 20167 the VAT Tribunal found that the employment business was not supplying staff as agent but as principal and as such VAT was due on the whole customer payment.

The case *Reed Employment Ltd* v. *Revenue & Customs* [2011] UKFTT 200 (TC) concerned an historic VAT claim by relating to periods up to 31 December 1993. Reed provided temporary staff to business customers, the customer paying an hourly rate calculated as the temp's salary and on costs plus Reed's commission. HMRC argued that Reed was supplying staff to its customers with VAT due on the whole amount paid to Reed. The First-tier Tribunal rejected this. In the Tribunal's view, the making of a supply of staff must, at the least, connote a passing of control of staff from the supplier to the person receiving the supply. However, at no time did Reed exercise control over its temporary workers, such that control could be ceded by Reed to its clients. The obligations owed by a temporary worker to Reed did not amount to an ability of Reed to exercise control over the temporary worker, and in any event those obligations commenced only after the temporary worker had accepted the assignment, and accordingly had come under the control of the client. The Tribunal found that Reed made a taxable supply of introductory services to the customer, for which its consideration was the commission. The salary paid to the temporary worker by Reed was not a cost component of Reed's own supply and was paid as agent for the customer. Accordingly VAT was only due on the commission.

Following this case HMRC issued *Revenue & Customs Brief 32/11* which states:

> As a judgment of the FTT Reed is only binding on the parties to the appeal. It was decided on its specific facts which involved an historic claim and concerned tax

periods up to 1996. The Reed decision differs from the earlier judgment of the tribunal in Hays Personnel Services Ltd (LON/95/2610) in which the Tribunal determined that Hays was a principal and VAT was due on the whole consideration received. HMRC therefore do not regard Reed as having any wider impact, particularly in relation to the VAT treatment that should apply to employment bureaux operating in the current market conditions and regulatory regime.

At the time of writing a test case supported by the Charity Tax Group is to be brought, it is hoped, to clarify the position (Adecco). The decision is expected in autumn 2015.

11.1.3 No supply or non-business

If the staff are provided for no consideration or if the supply of staff does not amount to a business activity, it is outside the scope of VAT. See Chapter 4 'Business and non-business activities' for how to determine if a supply exists and if an activity is business. If there is no consideration but staff are supplied as part of a broader arrangement there may be non-monetary consideration, bringing the activity within the scope of VAT.

11.1.4 Public sector secondments

HMRC accepts (*VAT Notice 700/34*, section 2.2) that secondments between and by government departments and local authorities are outside the scope of VAT in some situations.

HMRC accepts that the following supplies of staff are outside the scope of VAT:

1. secondments between and by government departments which require specialist knowledge that cannot be obtained from the private sector;
2. secondments between National Health bodies; and
3. some secondments between local authorities and by local authorities where they have a statutory obligation or monopoly.

For (1) HMRC (2015, *Guidance notes on completing the Notice of Appeal*, July) provides an aide memoire for government departments to determine the VAT treatment of supplies of staff:

(a) Determine if the customer is a government department. If yes, go to (b). If no, go to (c).
(b) If the secondee could be obtained only from a government department and not from private practice or the private sector, then it is outside the scope of VAT. If the secondee could be appointed from the private sector – the supply is standard-rated unless the secondment concession applies (for which see below).

(c) If the customer is not a government department, the supply is most likely to be standard-rated unless the secondment concession applies. In exceptional cases the supply may be treated as outside the scope if the only possible source of the secondee is from within government.

11.1.5 Joint contract of employment

Where staff are employed under a joint contract with two or more employers, HMRC accepts that salary payment transfers between employers can be ignored for VAT purposes.

HMRC provides the following guidance (*VAT Notice 700/34*, section 3.2):

> Where staff are jointly employed there is no supply for VAT purposes between the joint employers. Staff are jointly employed if their contracts of employment or letters of appointment make it clear that they have more than one employer. The contract must expressly specify who the employers are for example 'Company A, Company B and Company C', or 'Company A and its subsidiaries'.

Staff are not jointly employed if their contracts are with a single company or person, even if it requires them to work for others. There is no joint employment where for example there is a contract with one employer:

- which lays down that the employee's duties include assisting others
- that the employee will work full-time for another
- where the job title shows that the employee works for a group of associated companies (such as a group accountant)

Joint contracts can, however, present legal difficulties, for example if the employee needs to be disciplined or dismissed.

11.1.6 VAT group

If the supplier and customer are members of the same VAT group, supplies of staff between the two are ignored for (most) VAT purposes and no VAT is due on any salary recharge or commission. See 2.2 'VAT groups'.

11.1.7 Non-business activities concession

HMRC provides the following concession for cost-basis supplies of staff between non-business activities of non-profit organisations (*VAT Notice 701/1*, section 5.17)

> In some circumstances the income from the hire or loan of staff from one charity or voluntary organisation to another can be treated as non-business and outside the scope of VAT. This is subject to the following conditions:
>
> - the employee has been engaged only in the non-business activities of the lending charity/organisation and is being seconded to assist in the non-business activities of the borrowing charity/organisation

- the payment for the supply of the employee's services does not exceed the employee's normal remuneration

A 'voluntary organisation' is a body that operates otherwise than for profit, but does not include any public or local authority. 'Normal remuneration' means the total costs incurred by the lending charity/organisation in employing the member of staff including National Insurance and pension scheme contributions, etc.

11.1.8 Secondment concession

By concession (*VAT Notice 700/34*, Appendix B) HMRC accepts that if a secondment is not by an employment business and the secondee is in effect put on the recipient's payroll, so that the recipient pays the secondee's salary directly to the secondee, any Income Tax or NICs directly to HMRC, any pension contribution directly to the pension provider, etc., then the payments by the recipient are not consideration for a supply.

B. Secondment of staff by businesses other than employment businesses

... 2. The secondment by an employer (other than an employment business within the meaning of the Employment Agencies Act 1973) of a member of its staff (the employee) to another business which:

(a) exercises exclusive control over the allocation and performance of the employee's duties during the period of secondment;
(b) is responsible for paying the employee's remuneration directly to the employee, and/or
(c) discharges the employer's obligations to pay to any third party PAYE, NICs, pension contributions and similar payments relating to the employee, then,
    to the extent that any such payments as are mentioned in paragraphs (b) and (c) above form the consideration or part of the consideration for the secondment of the employee to the other business, they shall be disregarded in determining the value of seconding the employee.

3. For the purposes of paragraph 2 above, an employer shall not be treated as seconding an employee to another business, if the placing of the employee with that other business is done with a view to the employer's (or any other person associated with him) deriving any financial gain from:

(a) the placing of the employee with the other business; or
(b) any other arrangements or understandings (whether or not contractually binding and whether or not for any consideration) between the employer (or any other person associated with him) and the other business (or any person associated with it) with which the employee is placed.

When this concession was introduced in 1997 the then VAT Notice included the following additional guidance on the operation of this concession and in particular the meaning of 'discharges' in bullet point (c):

> The Statement is effective from 1 April 1997. It replaces an earlier informal concession. There are three sections to the Statement. They all have the effect of excluding staff remuneration, PAYE, NICs, pension contributions and similar costs from the taxable consideration for staff secondments if these costs are paid by the recipient businesses directly to the staff and third parties and if other conditions in the sections are met...

> Section B is the principal part of the Statement. If the recipient pays the relevant costs directly to the staff and third parties, you may exclude these amounts from the taxable consideration for your supplies of staff provided:

> - the recipient business exercises exclusive control over the allocation and performance of the employee's duties during the period of secondment; and
> - your business does not derive any financial gain from the secondment, whether this comes directly from the secondment or through any other arrangements you may have with the recipient business – for example, from a management services agreement relating to the seconded staff. Any such arrangement involving an associate of your business, or an associate of the recipient business, will also preclude the supply from the Section B easement.

> It is important to remember that the amounts in question may only be disregarded from determining the consideration and value of the secondment when they are paid directly to the individual and/or third parties. If these amounts are received by you, they cannot be so disregarded and will be taken to be part of the consideration and value of the supply.

11.1.9 Placement of disabled workers concession

By concession (*VAT Notice 700/34*, Appendix, section C) HMRC accepts that, where the sponsor of a disabled worker places the worker with a host company under the Sheltered Placement Scheme (or any similar scheme) and the host company:

(a) is responsible for paying the worker's remuneration directly to the worker; and/or

(b) discharges the sponsor's obligations to pay to any third party PAYE, NICs, pension contributions and similar payments relating to the worker,

then, to the extent that any such payments as are mentioned in paragraphs (a) and (b) above form the consideration or part of the consideration for the placing of the worker with the host company, they shall be disregarded in determining the value of placing the worker with the host company.

See 11.1.8 'Secondment concession' for further guidance on the interpretation of this concession.

11.1.10 **Nursing agencies concession**

By concession (*VAT Notice 701/57*, section 6.5) HMRC accepts that supplies of nurses, nursing auxiliaries and care assistants by state-regulated agencies may be treated as exempt supplies if the supply is of:

- a person registered in the register of qualified nurses and midwives maintained under article 5 of the Nursing and Midwifery Order 2001 providing medical care to the final patient;
- an unregistered nursing auxiliary who is 'directly supervised' by one of the above; or
- an unregistered nursing auxiliary, whose services are supplied to a hospital (NHS or private), hospice, care home with nursing under item 4 of Group 7, Schedule 9 VAT Act 1994 and form part of the care made to the patient.

A nursing auxiliary (also known as a healthcare assistant) is an individual who is not enrolled on any register of medical or health professionals but whose duties must include the provision of medical, as well as personal, care to patients.

The institution to which staff are supplied may be operated by a local authority, NHS body, charity or other organisation operating in the public or private sector.

For the supply of nursing auxiliaries or care assistants to benefit from the concession, they must undertake some direct form of medical care, such as administering drugs or taking blood pressures, for the final patient. The concession does not apply to supplies of general care assistants who are:

- only involved in providing personal care such as catering, washing or dressing the patients;
- working in care homes without nursing where they do not require supervision by health professionals to provide their services.

11.1.11 **Supplies closely related to education**

As explained at 5.1.1 'Eligible body' a supply of education by an **eligible body** is VAT exempt. The exemption extends to goods or services that are 'closely related' to a supply of education, and closely related supplies may include supplies of staff between eligible bodies.

In the *Horizon College* case the CJEU held that a supply of teachers from one eligible body to another is capable of being VAT exempt on the basis that the supply is closely related to a supply of education if all of the following three conditions are satisfied:

1. The supply of staff is ancillary to a principal supply of VAT-exempt education. This means that the supply of staff does not constitute an end in itself, but is a means by which the students may better enjoy the supply of education. However, in order for the students to better enjoy the education provided by the host establishment, it is not necessary for the staff to be supplied directly to those students.
2. The supply of staff must be essential to the exempt supply of education by the host establishment. This means that the supply of staff should be of a nature and quality such that, without recourse to such a service, there could be no assurance that the education provided by the host establishment and, consequently, the education from which its students benefit, would have an equivalent value.
3. The supply must not be intended, essentially, to obtain additional income by carrying out a transaction in direct competition with commercial enterprises liable for VAT, such as commercial placement agencies. The fact that the consideration is on a cost reimbursement basis is not, in itself, sufficient to establish that the transaction is not intended to obtain additional income.

HMRC accepts (*VATEDU53600*) that supplies of teaching staff, teaching assistants and staff for catering or accommodation can be exempt on this basis but not the supply of staff for administration and other services not qualifying as closely related such as ground maintenance.

11.1.12 Supplies closely linked to welfare

Supplies of staff may be VAT exempt on the basis that they are 'closely linked' to welfare or social security work.

As explained in 5.3 'Health and welfare', a supply of welfare services by a charity or state-regulated private welfare institution or public body is VAT exempt.

In the case C-415/04 *Staatssecretaris van Financiën* v. *Stichting Kinderopvang Enschede* [2006] ECR I-01385, the CJEU held that a charity supplying child-minders to parents was capable of being a VAT-exempt supply closely linked to welfare work if:

1. the childcare meets the conditions for VAT exemption;
2. the childcare service is of such a nature or quality that parents could not be assured of obtaining a service of the same value without the assistance of such an intermediary service; and
3. the basic purpose of the intermediary services is not to obtain additional income for the service provider by carrying out transactions which are in direct competition with those of commercial enterprises liable for VAT.

11.1.13 **Paymaster services**

Where each of a number of associated organisations employs its own staff, but one (the paymaster) organisation pays all salaries, taxes and pension contributions on behalf of the others, then recovery of monies paid out by the paymaster is not subject to VAT as it is a disbursement. If a charge is also made for the paymaster's services, this charge is standard-rated unless the charge is between two members of a VAT group.

11.2 **AGENCY SUPPLIES**

An **agent** (or **intermediary**) is someone who acts on behalf of another person (the **principal**) in arranging a supply. A **selling agent** sells the principal's goods or services and a **buying agent** acquires goods or services for the principal.

A business will, as a broad rule, be acting as agent of a principal when all the following conditions are met:

1. There is some form of agreement that the agent will act on behalf of the principal. The agreement need not be in writing.
2. For a supply of goods, the agent does not own the goods but buys or sells them in the name of the principal.
3. For a supply of services, the agent does not provide the services from its own resources.
4. The agent does not materially alter the nature of the goods or services provided.

Examples of agency supplies are:

- A charity acts as agent of a travel company in promoting and selling a challenge event to its supporters.
- A charity, or a charity's trading subsidiary, sells second-hand goods as agent of the owner under the Retail Gift Aid Scheme.
- A charity arranges an insurance contract for a client and receives a commission from the insurance company.

See 11.2.3 'Tests of agency' for case law tests for determining whether supplies are made as agent or principal. See 11.2.2 'VAT status of agency services' for the VAT treatment of supplies of agency services.

11.2.1 **VAT treatment of agency supplies**

The VAT position depends on whether the principal is **disclosed** or **undisclosed**.

Disclosed principal

> A principal is **disclosed** where the customer understands that the agent is acting on behalf of the principal. The sales contract will usually be in the principal's name with a separate agency agreement between the principal or customer and agent.

For VAT purposes there are two supplies:

- a supply of the goods or services concerned directly between the principal and customer;
- a separate supply of agency services by the agent to the principal for which the agent receives a commission.

Only the agent's supply of agency services counts as the agent's taxable turnover for VAT registration and partial exemption purposes.

However, with effect from 1 January 2015, supplies of electronically supplied services and telecommunications services that are made through an agent must be treated as supplied to and by the agent. See 9.8.6–9.8.7 for more on electronically supplied services and broadcasting.

Undisclosed principal

> A principal is undisclosed when the agent acts in their own name in making the supply to the customer. Here the sales contract with the end customer is usually the agent's name with a separate agreement between the principal and agent.

Where the principal is undisclosed there are two possible approaches in the UK:

1. **Concessionaire treatment**: the supply is seen as being made to and by the agent.
2. **Domestic treatment**:
   (a) where goods are acquired from another EU state or imported from outside the EU by an unregistered person and a VAT-registered business acts as agent, the goods are seen as supplied to and by the agent;

(b) where goods are supplied via an agent which acts in its own name, the goods are treated as supplied to and by the agent;

(c) with effect from 1 January 2015, where electronically supplied services or telecommunication services are supplied through an agent, they are treated as supplied to and by the agent;

(d) where services are supplied through an agent who acts in their own name, HMRC may treat the supply as to and by the agent. HMRC provides the following guidance (*VAT Notice 700*, section 22.6):

> If both you and the supplier are registered for VAT, and the supplies are taxable, you may treat yourself as both receiving and supplying those services.
>
> However you must not reclaim input tax under this procedure before you have accounted for the relevant output tax, and you must include the value of the supply in your VAT account and on your VAT return as a supply both made, and received, by you.

(e) any other supply is treated as a supply between the principal and customer with a separate supply of agency services by the agent to the principal.

11.2.2 VAT status of agency services

By default a business supply of agency services is VAT standard-rated; however, exceptions include:

- services performed by insurance brokers and agents are VAT exempt (see 5.10 'Insurance services');
- the provision of services by financial intermediaries is VAT exempt;
- the making of arrangements for an export of goods, for a supply of services which is made outside the EU or for a supply of works on goods for export is zero-rated, see 6.4 'General zero-rated supplies'.

11.2.3 Tests of agency

In *Vehicle Control Services* v. *Revenue & Customs* [2013] EWCA 186, the Court of Appeal held that a car park operator (VCS) was not providing parking to motorists as agent of the landowner, citing the following factors as being significant:

- VCS had the right to determine (and alter) the parking charges.
- VCS had the right to decide what kind of enforcement action to take.
- VCS had no obligation to account to the landowner which is a fundamental feature of agency.
- VCS was pursuing its own commercial objectives in taking enforcement action, whereas an agent is in a fiduciary relation with their principal.

- The landowner does not in fact receive any money.
- The landowner does not know how much money VCS has recovered.
- The landowner has no control over the amount of money that VCS recovers.
- The landowner has no right to know.
- No money passes from the landowner to VCS which is **attributable** (see 3.1.3) to parking charges.

For how HMRC determines if a charity is acting as a disclosed agent of a challenge event company, see 7.8.2 'Third-party organiser'.

11.2.4 Disbursements

In accounting terms, costs incurred as agent for a principal are not expenditure but should be recorded as a debtor on the balance sheet and then cleared when reimbursed by the customer. Such amounts are referred to as disbursements when billed to a customer and can be ignored for VAT purposes.

HMRC permits recharged costs to be treated as disbursements in the following circumstances (*VAT Notice 700*, section 25.1):

You may treat a payment to a third party as a disbursement for VAT purposes if all the following conditions are met:

- you acted as the agent of your client when you paid the third party
- your client actually received and used the goods or services provided by the third party (this condition usually prevents the agent's own travelling and subsistence expenses, phone bills, postage, and other costs being treated as disbursements for VAT purposes)
- your client was responsible for paying the third party (examples include estate duty and stamp duty payable by your client on a contract to be made by the client)
- your client authorised you to make the payment on their behalf
- your client knew that the goods or services you paid for would be provided by a third party
- your outlay will be separately itemised when you invoice your client
- you recover only the exact amount which you paid to the third party, and
- the goods or services, which you paid for, are clearly additional to the supplies which you make to your client on your own account

If you treat a payment as a disbursement for VAT purposes you must keep evidence (such as an order form or a copy invoice) to allow you to show that you were entitled to exclude the payment from the value of your own supply to your principal. You must also be able to show that you did not reclaim input tax on the supply by the third party.

11.3 SINGLE AND MULTIPLE SUPPLIES

Where separately identifiable goods or services (**elements**), with different individual VAT statuses if supplied alone, are supplied together you will need to decide if there is:

■ a multiple supply, where the provision of the different elements is seen as several independent supplies, each subject to separate VAT assessment;
■ a single supply, where the provision of all the elements together is seen as not being independent and attracts a single VAT status.

The supply of the various connected elements is referred to as a **composite supply**. Examples are membership subscriptions providing a range of benefits of differing VAT types; letting property with services such as utilities, cleaning, catering, care, etc.; and supplying printed literature together with electronically supplied literature.

11.3.1 General approach to composite supplies

The general approach to determining the VAT status of a composite supply is:

1. Clearly incidental elements can be ignored

The sale of honey in a glass jar is accepted as being a single zero-rated supply of honey and not as a zero-rated supply of honey and a standard-rated supply of a glass jar. In this case the supply of the glass jar is said to be incidental to the supply of honey. The sale of honey in a special jar, where more value attaches to the jar than to the honey, would likely be an exception. Packaging is usually seen as incidental to and following the VAT treatment of the goods concerned. Delivery charges for a supply of delivered goods (where delivery is a part of the purchase agreement) are also usually seen as incidental to and following the VAT treatment of the goods concerned. However, if delivery is an optional extra, then it is usually seen as a separate standard-rated supply.

2. Independent supplies

A supermarket shopper who purchases a basket of food items, some of which are zero-rated and others standard-rated, is making separate independent decisions when purchasing the items concerned, so the basket of goods is not a single standard-rated or zero-rated supply of goods even though the goods are purchased and paid for as a single transaction. The ability of the customer to choose whether or not to be supplied with an element is an important factor in determining whether there is a single supply or several independent supplies, although it is not decisive. For the supplies to be independent there must be a genuine freedom to choose which reflects economic reality.

3. Concessionary treatment

There are several HMRC concessions that allow a particular treatment to be adopted (single supply or multiple supply). These include:

- **Extra-statutory concession 3.35**: this allows a non-profit-making membership body to treat the consideration it receives for a single supply of membership benefits as if it was a multiple supply of those benefits. See 11.4.1 'Extra Statutory Concession 3.35'.
- The **package tests** for mixed packages of zero- and standard-rated printed matter, including a special package test for charities. There is also an HMRC concession for standard-rated promotional items provided with zero-rated magazines. See 6.4.1 'Books and printed matter'.

4. Closely related supplies

Several of the public interest VAT exemptions extend to supplies that are closely linked to or closely related to the main exempt supply (care, education, sports, and cultural services). Closely linked or related supplies can include supplies that would, if provided by an independent third party, be seen as independent supplies, for example supplies of lunches to school pupils who purchase them optionally and individually. See Chapter 5 'Exempt activities'.

5. Single/multiple supply tests

If none of the above approaches deal with the issue, then the single/multiple supply tests must be applied to determine if the supply concerned is a single supply taking on a single VAT status (though see the next point below) or several independent supplies each taking on their own independently assessed VAT statuses. See 11.3.2 'Single/multiple supply tests'.

6. Split single supplies

A split single supply occurs where a single supply (as determined by the single/multiple supply tests above) is subject to two or more different rates of VAT. In effect, the single supply is converted back into a multiple supply. This can occur for a variety of reasons:

- Sometimes the law specifies that an apportionment of the purchase price must be made between elements eligible for some special treatment and elements which are not. For example the reduced-rating for domestic fuel specifies that if at least 60% of the fuel is for 'qualifying use', the whole supply is treated as reduced-rated and in other cases an apportionment must be made between the reduced-rated part and the standard-rated part. See 'Reduced-rated carve outs' below.

- Sometimes parts of a single supply that would be zero-rated or reduced-rated under the single/multiple supply tests are specifically excluded from zero- or reduced-rating by the legislation, for example the supply of certain types of caravans is zero-rated but the zero-rating excludes any removable contents. See 11.3.5 'Single zero-rated supplies'.

11.3.2 Single/multiple supply tests

These tests have arisen from case law, primarily cases in the CJEU. They were summarised as follows in the case C-42/14 *Minister Finansów* v. *Wojskowa Agencja Mieszkaniowa w Warszawie* [2015]:

> ... for VAT purposes every supply must normally be regarded as distinct and independent. Nevertheless, in accordance with settled case-law of the Court, in certain circumstances, several formally distinct services, which could be supplied separately and thus give rise in turn to taxation or exemption, must be considered to be a single transaction when they are not independent.
>
> - There is a single supply where two or more elements or acts supplied by the taxable person to the customer are so closely linked that they form, objectively, a single, indivisible economic supply, which it would be artificial to split.
> - Such is also the case where one or several services constitute the principal service, and where the other service or services constitute one or several ancillary services which share the tax treatment of the principal service. In particular, a supply must be regarded as ancillary to a principal supply if it does not constitute for customers an end in itself but a means of better enjoying the principal service supplied.
>
> In order to determine whether the services supplied constitute independent services or a single service it is necessary to examine the characteristic elements of the transaction concerned.

11.3.3 Single/multiple supply case law

The CJEU case C-231/94 *Faaborg-Gelting Linien A/S* v. *Finanzamt Flensburg* [1996] ECR I-02395 concerned the supply of meals in a ferry's restaurant, the dispute being (partly) whether this was a supply of goods (food and drink) or of services (preparation, serving, etc.) or a mix of the two.

The CJEU held that regard must be had to all the circumstances in which the transaction takes place in order to identify its characteristic features. The supply of prepared food and drink for immediate consumption is the outcome of a series of services ranging from the cooking of the food to its physical service to a recipient, whilst at the same time an infrastructure is placed at the customer's disposal, including a dining room with appurtenances (cloak rooms, etc.), furniture and crockery. People will have to perform such tasks as laying the table, advising the customer and explaining the food and drink on the menu, serving at table and clearing the table after the food has been eaten. Consequently, restaurant transactions are characterised by a cluster of features and acts, of which the provision of food is only one component and in which services largely predominate. The CJEU concluded that as the services largely predominate, such transactions must be regarded as a single supply of services. The CJEU commented that the situation is different where the transaction relates to takeaway food and is not coupled with services designed to enhance consumption on the spot in an appropriate setting.

The CJEU case C-349/96 *Card Protection Plan Ltd (CPP)* v. *Customs & Excise* [1999] ECR I-00973 considered the VAT status of a plan designed to protect against financial loss and inconvenience resulting from the loss or theft of personal credit/debit cards and of certain other items such as car keys, passports and insurance documents. The plan included what would, in isolation, be a standard-rated supply of 'card/key/passport/document management services' and an exempt supply of insurance services. The UK courts could not agree on the VAT treatment. The House of Lords referred the issue to the CJEU, which held that the following principles apply:

1. Every supply of a service must normally be regarded as distinct and independent.
2. A supply which comprises a single service from an economic point of view should not be artificially split, so as not to distort the functioning of the VAT system.
3. The essential features of the transaction must be ascertained in order to determine whether the business is supplying the customer, being a typical consumer, with several distinct principal services or with a single service.
4. There is a single supply in particular in cases where one or more elements are to be regarded as constituting the principal service, whilst one or more elements are to be regarded, by contrast, as ancillary services which share the VAT treatment of the principal service. A service must be regarded as ancillary to a principal service if it does not constitute for customers an aim in itself, but a means of better enjoying the principal service supplied.
5. In these circumstances, the fact that a single price is charged is not decisive, though a single price may suggest that there is a single service. However, if circumstances indicated that the customers intended to purchase several distinct services, then it would be necessary to identify the part of the single price which related to the each distinct service. The simplest possible method of calculation or assessment should be used for this.

The CJEU case C-41/04 *Levob Verzekeringen BV* v. *Staatssecretaris van Financiën* [2005] ECR I-09433 concerned a supply to an insurance company of off-the-shelf software for $713,000 and a supply of customisation, installation and training services for the software of at least $779,000, the dispute being whether this comprised separate supplies of off-the-shelf software (goods) and customisation/installation/training services (as claimed by Levob) or whether it was a single supply of software services (as claimed by the tax authorities).

The CJEU held that there is a single supply in particular in cases where two or more elements or acts supplied by the business to the customer, being a typical consumer, are so closely linked that they form, objectively, a single, indivisible economic supply, which it would be artificial to split.

It was apparent to the CJEU that the economic purpose of the transaction was the supply of functional software specifically customised to the consumer's requirements. It would be entirely artificial to take the view that such a consumer purchased, from the same supplier, first, pre-existing software which was of no use for the purposes of its economic activity, and only subsequently the customisation, which alone made that software useful to it.

The CJEU held that the fact that separate prices were contractually stipulated for the supply of the basic software and for its customisation is not of itself decisive. Such a fact cannot affect the close link which has been shown to exist between the software and its customisation nor the fact that they form part of a single economic transaction. It follows that the software and its customisation are, in principle, to be regarded as forming a single supply for VAT purposes.

In *Revenue & Customs* v. *Honourable Society of Middle Temple* [2013] UKUT 250 (TCC), the Upper Tribunal provided its summary of the principles to be applied in determining whether there was one supply or several as follows.

The key principles for determining whether a particular transaction should be regarded as a single composite supply or as several independent supplies may be summarised as follows:

1. Every supply must normally be regarded as distinct and independent, although a supply which comprises a single transaction from an economic point of view should not be artificially split.
2. The essential features or characteristic elements of the transaction must be examined in order to determine whether, from the point of view of a typical consumer, the supplies constitute several distinct principal supplies or a single economic supply.
3. There is no absolute rule and all the circumstances must be considered in every transaction.

4. Formally distinct services, which could be supplied separately, must be considered to be a single transaction if they are not independent.

5. There is a single supply where two or more elements are so closely linked that they form a single, indivisible economic supply which it would be artificial to split.

6. In order for different elements to form a single economic supply which it would be artificial to split, they must, from the point of view of a typical consumer, be equally inseparable and indispensable.

7. The fact that, in other circumstances, the different elements can be or are supplied separately by a third party is irrelevant.

8. There is also a single supply where one or more elements are to be regarded as constituting the principal services, while one or more elements are to be regarded as ancillary services which share the tax treatment of the principal element.

9. A service must be regarded as ancillary if it does not constitute for the customer an aim in itself, but is a means of better enjoying the principal service supplied.

10. The ability of the customer to choose whether or not to be supplied with an element is an important factor in determining whether there is a single supply or several independent supplies, although it is not decisive, and there must be a genuine freedom to choose which reflects the economic reality of the arrangements between the parties.

11. Separate invoicing and pricing, if it reflects the interests of the parties, supports the view that the elements are independent supplies, without being decisive.

12. A single supply consisting of several elements is not automatically similar to the supply of those elements separately, and so different tax treatment does not necessarily offend the principle of fiscal neutrality.

11.3.4 Reduced-rated carve outs

As explained in Chapter 6 'Zero and reduced rates', the Principal VAT Directive permits member states to apply up to two reduced rates (each of not less than 5%) to specific types of supply, including supplies of natural gas, electricity, district heating and supplies listed in Annex III to the Directive. Case law has established that EU states may limit such reduced rates to concrete and specific aspects of eligible supplies, provided there is no risk of distortion of competition (case C-94/09 *European Commission* v. *France* [2010] ECR I-04261 (2010), aka the *French Undertakers'* case).

The case *AN Checker & Service Engineers* v. *Revenue & Customs* [2013] UKFTT 506 (TC) concerned the reduced-rating for energy-saving materials, in this case lagging, controls and valves installed as a part of a wider supply of a full central heating system installation. The First-tier Tribunal was of the view that the *French Undertakers'* case relates to the reduced-rating of a part only of what would otherwise be a supply falling within the Principal VAT Directive list of supplies eligible for reduced-rating. As the entire heating system does not fall within the list of eligible items, the entire system would be standard-rated, so no reduced-rating is possible. However, the Tribunal found it unnecessary to decide on this point. UK law (VAT Act 1994 (VATA), s. 29(A)) charges VAT at the reduced rate on 'any supply that is of a description for the time being specified in VATA Schedule 7A'. The Tribunal held that to read this as applying the reduced rate applied to components of an entire heating system would be to depart from the unambiguous meaning of the words used.

11.3.5 **Single zero-rated supplies**

In *Talacre Beach Caravan Sales Ltd* v. *Customs & Excise* [2006], Talacre sold fitted caravans. UK law zero rates the sale of the caravan but excludes from zero-rating any removable contents sold with the caravan. Talacre argued that the removable contents were ancillary to the caravan and so shared its zero-rated treatment (on the basis of the CJEU decision in *Card Protection Plan* (see 11.3.3)). The CJEU held that, because the UK's zero-rating reliefs are a derogation from the Principal VAT Directive and are strictly limited by the Directive to the reliefs in place on 1 January 1991, the Single Supply Rules do not apply to override the UK legislation in force on 1 January 1991. The content of the national legislation in force on 1 January 1991 is decisive in ascertaining the scope of the supplies in respect of which the Principal VAT Directive allows zero-rating to be maintained. In this case the legislation as at 1 January 1991 specifically precluded the removable contents from zero-rating, so these elements were correctly treated as standard-rated.

11.3.6 **Apportioning consideration**

Where a multiple supply is provided for a single price or where a single supply is to be apportioned, the consideration amount must be apportioned between the different types of supply. See 11.4.2 'Apportioning membership subscriptions' for a discussion of the possible approaches.

11.4 **MEMBERSHIP SUBSCRIPTIONS**

Subscriptions and membership can take many forms, so it important to look at what benefits the members actually receive for their subscriptions.

1. **No benefits**: if nothing at all is provided, so that the subscription is in reality a donation, then the membership subscription will be outside the scope of VAT.

2. **Nil benefits**: membership organisations sometimes claim to provide their members with benefits that are not really member benefits at all; for example, an electronic newsletter that anyone can subscribe to via the organisation's website.
3. **Nominal benefits**: if only minor or insubstantial benefits are provided, then it may be possible to argue that the subscription is in substance a donation. HMRC accepts that benefits of nominal value can be ignored, such as simple acknowledgements of support in the form of membership badges, flags or stickers, and listing of names in a programme or on a theatre seat or entrance. However, HMRC considers the following benefits always to be substantive regardless of whether there is any cost to your organisation in supplying them and what that cost might be: priority booking rights, guaranteed seats, discounts on admission charges, and items with a resale value (*VAT Notice 701/45*, section 5.1.2).
4. **Constitutional benefits**: in many situations it should also be possible to ignore formal constitutional benefits for members of the organisation, such as the right to attend the AGM and the right to receive an annual report.
5. **Extra-statutory concession**: by extra-statutory concession (*VAT Notice 48*, section 3.35), HMRC permits non-profit-making membership bodies to apportion their subscriptions between the benefits provided, even if, under the single/multiple supply rules, the subscription would take on a single VAT status. See 11.4.1 'Extra Statutory Concession 3.35'.
6. **Subscriptions to public interest bodies**: the provision by an eligible public interest body to its members of benefits which are referable only to its aims and are available without further payment are VAT exempt, though there are several exclusions. Eligible public interest bodies include trades unions, professional associations, learned societies, representational trade associations, patriotic, political, religious, philosophical, philanthropic and civic bodies. See 5.6 'Subscriptions to public interest bodies'.
7. **Substantial benefits**: where a package of substantial benefits is provided, then, by default, the single/multiple supply rules must be applied to determine the VAT status of the package. See 11.3 'Single and multiple supplies' for an explanation of the single/multiple supply rules. If the package of benefits is a single supply, the whole subscription takes a single VAT status. If the package of benefits is a multiple supply, the subscription must be apportioned between the supplies concerned. See 11.4.2 'Apportioning membership subscriptions'.

11.4.1 Extra-statutory concession 3.35

Under extra-statutory concession 3.35, some non-profit-making membership bodies are permitted to in effect treat their membership subscriptions as separate supplies of the individual benefits concerned (a multiple supply), even where, under the single/multiple supply rules, the subscription should correctly be treated as consideration for a single supply (*VAT Notice 48*, section 3.35).

> Where a membership body supplies, in return for its membership subscription, a principal benefit, together with one or more ancillary benefits, it will normally have to treat the subscription as being in return for that principal benefit. This means that the body will have to ignore the liability to the VAT of the ancillary benefits and account for VAT on the whole subscription based on the liability to VAT of that principal benefit. However bodies that are non-profit making and supply a mixture of zero rated, exempt and/or standard-rated benefits to their members in return for their subscriptions, may apportion such subscriptions to reflect the value and VAT liability of those individual benefits, without regard to whether there is one principal benefit. This concession may not be used for the purpose of tax avoidance.

This can be advantageous, for example where the membership benefits include zero-rated printed matter such as newsletters, magazines, periodicals and journals. It can also be simpler, in that there is no need to apply the sometimes difficult single/multiple supply rules to what is often a changing package of member benefits.

However, note the following:

- If extra-statutory concession 3.35 is applied, it must be applied to all types and elements of subscriptions – you cannot 'pick and choose' (*VAT Notice 701/5*, section 5.1.1).
- HMRC will not accept claims for overpaid VAT on the basis of retrospective application of extra-statutory concession 3.35 (*Revenue & Customs Brief 06/09*). This concession can only be applied going forward in time.
- HMRC policy appears to be to only accept that the concession applies to bona fide membership organisations, where the members have some degree of control over the organisation. HMRC does not accept that it applies to the patron/supporter schemes of arts organisations. See 7.25 'Supporter schemes'.

Mixed consideration/donation

HMRC accepts (*VAT Notice 701/5*, section 5.3) that a subscription can be apportioned between consideration for the benefits provided and an outside-the-scope-of-VAT donation, provided:

- all the substantive benefits provided are available to non-members at no charge or more cheaply than the subscription; you should ignore any nominal benefits (see above); or
- some or all of the substantive benefits are exclusive to members and you are able to demonstrate that the amount paid is higher than the amount that the subscriber would normally have to pay for similar goods or services.

Third-party discounts

HMRC's position on third-party discounts used to be to accept that they could be ignored if they incurred little or no cost to the membership organisation (*V1–37 Control Notes*, section 4.2). However, V1–37 is now withdrawn and the fate of this policy is unknown (to the authors).

> Intangible benefits can be more difficult to apportion on either a cost or value basis. If the benefits are provided by third parties e.g. discounts at selected retail outlets and the provision of such benefits incurs little or no cost to the membership organisation. Whilst we would still regard them as benefits, we would not to apportion them within the membership apportionment method.

Priority booking rights

HMRC provides the following guidance at *VBNB60420*:

> Members of bodies which support theatres often enjoy priority booking rights for performances. If this is the case, no part of the subscription can be a donation. The subscription should be treated in the same way as non-exclusive benefits with any residual part allocated to the priority booking right.

> Organisations may argue that the priority booking right has no value; or the right only has a value when it enables a member to book for an event or performance that will be highly popular or oversubscribed. HMRC will not normally accept either of these arguments. Firstly, we are concerned with whether there has been a supply for which consideration was provided, not whether the supply can be regarded as worth the consideration that was given.

> In this case, the priority booking right has been supplied. The consideration given is what remains of the subscription after all the other elements have been allocated. Hypothetical value is not the test by which a supply is identified in the first place. The question of whether an event is likely to be fully attended, partially attended or not attended at all has no relevance to whether or not members of a body have obtained a right to secure their own attendance in preference to non-members.

However, for Gift Aid, draft HMRC guidance issued in July 2014 suggests that HMRC is prepared to accept that a priority booking right is a nil benefit, provided the donor pays the normal ticket price and cannot benefit from onward sale of the ticket.

11.4.2 Apportioning membership subscriptions

Where a subscription must be apportioned between the benefits provided, a fair and reasonable approach must be used. In addition, the guidance of the CJEU is that the simplest possible method of apportionment should be used (see the CPP case above). Possible apportionment bases include:

- **Market value** – using the market values of the benefits. The problem with this approach is usually that at least some of the member benefits have no reliable market value, though it may be appropriate to use prices for clearly similar commercial products.
- **Cost basis** – using the cost to the organisation of providing each benefit. This will often be the most straightforward basis to use.
- **Other bases** – possibilities include cost plus a markup where some benefits have a market value but others do not. The commercial benefits could be valued at their normal retail price, whilst the non-commercial benefits could be valued at cost plus a markup in order to ensure the valuation bases are equivalent. However, determining a realistic markup is likely to be a problem.

HMRC accepts that a cost basis apportionment is usually acceptable. HMRC states (*VAT Notice 701/5*, section 5.10):

> It is usually acceptable for a club to apportion its total subscription income to reflect the relative cost of providing the different supplies to its members. You can base your calculations for the current financial year on your accounts for the previous financial year, provided you apply this method consistently. You must keep your calculations for inspection by our VAT Assurance staff.

Life subscriptions

Life subscriptions will have to be apportioned on a basis that is reasonable. HMRC (2013, *Charities: detailed guidance notes*, chapter 3, s. 3.31.6) accepts a ten-year basis for Gift Aid, calculated as the benefits receivable in the first ten years of membership. HMRC would hopefully accept the same basis for VAT.

Different types of membership

Different rates of membership and different membership packages may have to be calculated separately.

Overseas subscriptions

Overseas members may not be able to access some benefits such as attendance at events, so it may be appropriate to carry out a different apportionment for overseas members. The place of supply rules must then be taken into consideration (for which see Chapter 9 'International aspects of VAT').

Example: apportioning a membership subscription

The subscription to a non-profit organisation (not a public interest body) is £100 per year and there are 400 members. Substantial membership benefits and costs last year were:

- a free printed magazine four times a year (zero-rated benefit), cost £7,000;
- a free invite to a member only event (standard-rated benefit), cost £2,000;
- free member online resources (standard-rated benefit), cost £1,000;
- free member training courses (exempt benefit), cost £10,000.

A cost-basis apportionment would be calculated as follows:

Benefit	Cost per year	Percentage of cost	
Magazines	£7,000	35%	Zero-rated
Member-only event + online resources	£2,000 + £1,000 = £3,000	15%	Standard-rated
Training courses	£10,000	50%	Exempt
Total	£20,000	100%	

The amount of the £100 subscription treated as standard-rated is thus 15% × £100 = £15. This includes VAT, so the VAT fraction must be applied to determine the output VAT component. The output VAT due per member is thus £15/6 = £2.50 (see 12.1 'VAT fractions and VAT rounding').

11.5 TRANSFER OF A BUSINESS AS A GOING CONCERN

Where a collection of business assets sufficient to constitute a 'going concern' is supplied as a package, a special set of VAT rules may apply to treat the supply as 'neither a supply of goods nor a supply of services' and as such outside the scope of VAT. These rules are referred to as the **transfer of a business as a going concern** or **TOGC** rules. When the TOGC rules apply, no VAT is charged by the person disposing of the business assets and there is no input VAT to be recovered by the person acquiring the business assets.

The business being transferred does not actually have to be a going concern in the accounting or financial sense, it merely has to be capable of operation as such.

Business assets can include tangible assets such as the freehold of or a long lease in land or buildings, other fixed assets such as motor vehicles, computers, plant and machinery, equipment, trading stock, and intangible assets such as debtors, intellectual property rights and goodwill (the difference between the amount paid and the fair values of the identifiable assets and liabilities acquired).

Business transfers can include where:

- all of the assets of a business are purchased by another person and the existing business activity ceases;
- a viable part of an existing business is sold to another person;
- businesses (such as charities) merge without payment;
- all of a business's assets are transferred to a new legal entity.

11.5.1 **TOGC conditions**

For the supply of business assets to qualify as 'neither a supply of goods nor a supply of services' all the following seven conditions must be met:

1. The effect of the transfer must be to put the buyer in possession of a business which can be operated as such to make business supplies. If only part of the business is being transferred, that part must be able to operate alone. It does not matter whether it will be operated separately from any other businesses the new owner carries on.

2. The business, or part business, must be a going concern at the time of the transfer. It can still be a going concern even though it is unprofitable, or is trading under the control of a liquidator or administrative receiver, or a trustee in bankruptcy, or an administrator appointed under the Insolvency Act 1986.

3. The assets transferred must be intended for use by the buyer in carrying on the same kind of business as the old owner. HMRC provides guidance on what are and are not the same kinds of business (*VAT Notice 700/9*, section 7). For example, the sale of an Italian restaurant to become a Mexican restaurant is the same kind of business because it is still a restaurant. For this condition to be met, the buyer need only intend to carry on the same kind of business for a short period. If the buyer intends to carry on the same kind of business for a short period and then restructure the business into a different kind, then this condition is met.

4. There must not be a series of immediately consecutive transfers of the business. Where A sells its assets to B who immediately sells those assets on to C, the TOGC provisions do not apply to any of the transactions because B has not carried on the business.

5. If the seller is registered for VAT, the buyer must:
   - be registered for VAT at the date of transfer; or
   - be required to be registered for VAT at the date of transfer because all of the conditions for compulsory registration are met. For VAT registration purposes, if the seller is registered for VAT (or should be registered for VAT), the buyer is treated as having carried on the seller's transferred business up to the date of the transfer; or
   - have been accepted for voluntary registration at the date of the transfer.
6. There must be no significant break in the normal trading pattern before or immediately after the transfer. A short period of closure that does not significantly disrupt the existing trading pattern, for example for redecoration, will not prevent the business from being transferred as a going concern.
7. If the business being transferred includes a new **non-qualifying building** (see 8.6 'Property terms') or land or buildings on which the seller has exercised an option to tax, then the transfer of the land or buildings is excluded from the TOGC treatment unless the buyer satisfies all of the following conditions:
   (a) The buyer has opted to tax the land or buildings with effect on or before the date of the transfer.
   (b) The buyer has notified HMRC of its option to tax on or before the date of the transfer (see 8.5.7 'Notification requirements'). If notification is by post, the notification must have been correctly addressed and posted on or before the date of the transfer; however, it does not have to have been received by HMRC by then.
   (c) The buyer must, on or before the date of transfer, have notified the seller that the following conditions do not both apply:
      - The opted to tax property, if treated as a taxable supply by the seller, would become a capital item for the buyer. See 10.1 'Capital Goods Scheme' for the definition of a capital item. This condition is broadly met if the value of the opted to tax property being transferred is £250,000 or more.
      - The buyer's **option to tax** on that property will not be **disapplied** as a result of the option to tax anti-avoidance rules. See 8.5.1 'Disapplications' for an explanation of these rules.

The two conditions in (c) above are in SI 1995/1268 VAT Special Provisions Order 1995 article 5(2B) and can be referred to as such.

Where the buyer fails to satisfy all of the above three requirements of TOGC condition (7), the transfer of the opted to tax property will fall outside the TOGC rules and be a taxable supply (unless the buyer disapplies the seller's option to tax; in which case it will be an exempt supply). However, the transfer of other business assets may still qualify to be treated as a TOGC.

11.5.2 **TOGC consequences**

Where a business or a part of a business satisfies the TOGC conditions:

1. No VAT is chargeable on the sale or transfer of the business assets and there is no VAT to be recovered by the purchaser. If VAT is mistakenly charged by the seller, then the buyer has no right to recover the VAT charged, as it is not correctly an input tax. However, where HMRC is wholly satisfied that the amount of VAT on the sale has been both declared and paid to HMRC by the seller, HMRC may allow the buyer to recover it as if it were an input tax (*VTOGC4200*).
2. If the seller transfers a capital item within the Capital Goods Scheme (CGS), the buyer takes over responsibility for making adjustments under the CGS for the remainder of the capital item's adjustment period. A buyer should therefore confirm with the seller whether any property, ships, aircraft or computers being transferred are capital items within their adjustment period, and if so obtain all the information required to complete the adjustments.
3. The buyer becomes responsible for any payback/clawback adjustments on assets transferred. See 3.3.7 'Payback/clawback rules' for more on these.

11.5.3 **Transfer of VAT registration number**

By default the seller's VAT registration number is not transferred to the buyer; however, it can be transferred to the buyer if all of the following conditions are met (summarised from *VATREG30100*):

1. The seller is VAT-registered up to the date of transfer.
2. The seller's VAT registration will be cancelled with effect from the date of transfer. If the seller will still be required to be registered for VAT after the transfer, then this condition is not met.
3. The buyer is not already registered for VAT.
4. The buyer intends to make taxable supplies after the transfer.
5. The buyer and seller agree to the transfer of the VAT registration number.
6. An application is made to HMRC jointly by the buyer and seller. Applications can be made using HMRC form VAT 68 or online. The buyer must also complete HMRC form VAT 1 Application for registration.
7. HMRC agrees to the transfer. HMRC policy is to broadly reject requests where a group registration is involved, or where any assessment, penalty or interest due by the seller is outstanding.

If the VAT registration number is transferred, then the buyer is treated as having carried on the seller's business before the transfer. The buyer takes over responsibility for any VAT returns outstanding and any VAT due or recoverable from before the transfer, including as a result of an error. The seller remains liable for their conduct during periods before the transfer and may be assessed for any penalties arising from their conduct during those periods which come to light after the transfer. However, any tax assessment and related interest will be assessed against the buyer.

Special conditions attaching to the seller's registration do not transfer and must be applied for or notified by the buyer. These include options to tax, special partial exemption methods, and use of special schemes such as annual accounting.

11.5.4 Business records

The seller of a business (or part business) sold as a TOGC retains the business records, unless the VAT registration number is also transferred. However, the seller must make available to the buyer the information necessary for the buyer to comply with its VAT duties. If the buyer is unable to obtain this information from the seller, then HMRC can disclose to the buyer the information HMRC holds that is necessary for the buyer to comply with its duties under VAT law. HMRC will advise the seller of its intention to disclose information to the buyer, thereby providing the opportunity to identify any confidentiality issues.

11.5.5 Transfer of a property rental business

The sale of a building with sitting tenants is capable of being a TOGC even if the building is only partly occupied by tenants. However, if all tenancies and licences will cease on or before the transfer date, then this will not be a TOGC as there is no business activity being transferred. There is no clear *de minimis* limit below which sub-lettings can create a TOGC and the letting of single rooms, spaces for advertising hoardings, or car parking spaces can all potentially create a TOGC.

Before November 2012, HMRC's interpretation of the law was that, for there to be the transfer of a property rental or property development business as a going concern, the interest in land being transferred by the seller must be the same interest as that used by the seller in its business. So if, for example, a freeholder grants a 999-year lease with the benefit of a sublease, the freeholder's business is not transferred as a going concern because of the interest retained.

However, the First-tier Tribunal rejected this view in the case *Robinson Family Ltd* v. *Revenue & Customs* [2012] UKFTT 360 (TC). In that case a business with a 125-year lease of property sold a lease in the property for 125 years less 3 days with the benefit of a sublease. The Tribunal found that, although the seller retained the head lease, that distant interest in a 3-day reversion and the small economic interest which it represented did not alter the substance of the transaction, which was to put the buyer in a position where it was able to continue the previous lettings business of the seller. Following this case, HMRC announced (*Revenue & Customs Brief 30/12*) that it accepts that a reversion retained by the seller is sufficiently small for TOGC treatment to be capable of applying if the value of the interest retained is no more than 1% of the value of the property immediately before the transfer (disregarding any mortgage or charge). Where more than one property is transferred at one time, this test should be applied on a property-by-property basis rather than for the entire portfolio. If the interest retained by the seller represents more than 1% of the value of the property, HMRC will regard that as strongly indicative that the transaction is too complex to be a TOGC.

11.5.6 **Transfer costs**

For the buyer, disposal costs are treated as incurred in the activity being transferred, so if the activity is fully taxable, VAT incurred on the disposal costs is recoverable in full, and if the activity is mixed taxable and VAT exempt, the transfer costs are residual and VAT can be recovered in accordance with the buyer's partial exemption method. If the existing partial exemption method does not produce a fair and reasonable result, you can ask HMRC to agree a special partial exemption method for the transfer costs.

HMRC used to dispute that the seller could recover VAT on transfer costs, as those costs are directly attributable to a transaction which is outside the scope of VAT. However, in case C-408/98 *Abbey National plc* v. *Customs & Excise* [2001] ECR I-01361, the CJEU held that, though the seller's transfer costs were not directly attributable to any taxable supply, they are in principle overheads of the business and as such the VAT incurred is residual. However, if the transferred business is wholly taxable, the CJEU held that the transfer costs are overheads of that part of the business, and as such the VAT incurred is wholly recoverable.

HMRC now accepts (*VAT Notice 700/9*, section 2.6.2) that, where the transferred business made only taxable supplies, then the seller can deduct VAT incurred on the transfer costs. Where the transferred business made only exempt supplies the VAT is not **deductible**, unless *de minimis* (see sections 3.1 and 3.1.11). Where the transferred business made mixed taxable and exempt supplies, then the VAT is residual VAT and is recoverable by reference to the seller's partial exemption method.

11.5.7 **Transfers into a partly exempt VAT group**

Where business assets are transferred under the TOGC rules into (but not within) a partly exempt VAT group, special rules apply. The group must account for output VAT on certain of the assets transferred (as a **deemed supply**). This output VAT can then be recovered in accordance with the group's partial exemption method, treating the affected assets as if they had been purchased in the normal way. If all the assets transferred will be used entirely for taxable activities this rule will have no net effect. But these rules do not apply to the following assets (*VAT Notice 700/9*, section 5.2.1):

- any assets which were assets of the previous owner more than three years before the date of the transfer;
- goodwill such as unidentifiable goodwill, use of a trademark or trading name and the sole right to trade in a particular area;
- any assets which are zero-rated or exempt (for example zero-rated or exempt freehold or leasehold interests in land);
- items which fall within the Capital Goods Scheme.

If the affected assets were transferred below market value, then the output VAT charge must be calculated on the open market value. Where the transferor is unconnected, the price paid will normally be assumed to be the open market value. If separate prices were not specified for affected assets, the consideration must be apportioned.

HMRC may be prepared to accept that no output VAT is due in certain circumstances (*VAT Notice 700/9*, section 5.4):

- HMRC can reduce the VAT chargeable in relation to the self-supply if you can produce satisfactory evidence to show that the previous owner did not recover all of the input tax incurred on the original purchase (for example, if he was partly exempt or the input tax was 'blocked', for instance, on the purchase of a car).
- In a case where the seller's partial exemption recovery rate (during the partial exemption tax year in which the assets were purchased) is equal to or less than the purchaser's recovery rate (during the partial exemption tax year in which the assets were acquired) the VAT charge will be reduced to nil, although no tax will be refunded.
- If you consider that you have evidence to show that the tax due should be reduced you should consult the HMRC advice service.

11.5.8 Transfers of non-business and exempt assets

The TOGC rules are not relevant where the assets transferred are non-business assets. The supply of a non-business asset is outside the scope of VAT. See 4.1.7 'Sale of non-business assets'.

If a wholly exempt business is transferred, then assuming no VAT has been recovered on any tangible assets transferred, their supply will be VAT exempt unless the asset transferred is property that the seller has opted to tax (see 5.11 'Sale of business goods on which VAT was wholly irrecoverable'). However, HMRC takes the view (*VTOGC4500*) that if a payment is made for goodwill this is a taxable supply of services.

12 Operational aspects

This chapter covers the following operational aspects of VAT:

- 12.1 VAT fractions and VAT rounding
- 12.2 Record-keeping
- 12.3 Time of supply
- 12.4 VAT invoices
- 12.5 Claiming input VAT
- 12.6 The VAT return
- 12.7 The EC sales list
- 12.8 Dealing with HMRC
- 12.9 VAT penalties and interest
- 12.10 Blocked input VAT
- 12.11 Sage 50 T-codes

12.1 VAT FRACTIONS AND VAT ROUNDING

A VAT fraction is the proportion of the gross (VAT-inclusive) price that is represented by **output VAT** (see 1.1). The formula for calculating the VAT fraction depends on the applicable rate of VAT:

$$\text{VAT fraction} = \frac{\text{Rate of VAT}\,(\%)}{100\% + \text{Rate of VAT}\,(\%)}$$

- For standard-rated VAT at **20%**, the VAT fraction is **1/6**
- For reduced-rated VAT at **5%** the VAT fraction is **1/21**
- When the standard rate of VAT was 17.5%, the VAT fraction was 7/47
- When the standard rate of VAT was 15% the VAT fraction was 3/23

The appropriate VAT fraction is then multiplied by the gross price to calculate the VAT included:

$$\text{VAT included}\,(£) = \text{VAT fraction}\,(\%) \times \text{Gross price}\,(£)$$

The VAT included figure is rounded down to the nearest penny.

Example: VAT fraction

Gross amount	Applicable rate of VAT	VAT fraction	Amount of VAT included in gross	Net = Gross – VAT
£120	20%	1/6	(1/6) × £120 = £20	£120 – £20 = £100
£105	5%	1/21	(1/21) × £105 = £5	£105 – £5 = £100

12.1.1 VAT rounding

As VAT is charged as a percentage of the net selling price, it sometimes does not work out to be an exact amount of pounds and pence. For example if the net selling price is £1.33, 20% of £1.33 is 26.6p. The VAT rounding rules specify how the VAT charge should be calculated in such circumstances.

When calculating the VAT due on an entire invoice, the VAT should be rounded down to the nearest penny.

Example: invoice rounding

The net price of a 20% standard-rated item is £1.33

The VAT is £1.33 × 20% = 26.6p

This is rounded down to the nearest penny: 26p

The gross selling price is £1.33 + £0.26 = £1.59

If an invoice contains multiple line items then if all line items are at the same rate of VAT, the net prices can be added up and VAT calculated on a whole invoice basis as above. However, if different rates of VAT apply to different line items, it may be necessary to calculate the VAT for each line item separately, add the VAT on each line item and then round as above.

The rules for rounding line items on invoices are that the VAT can be rounded in any of three ways:

● rounded down to the nearest 0.1p, for example 25.57p is rounded to 25.5p; or
● rounded to the nearest 0.5p or 1p using arithmetic rounding – under arithmetic rounding to the nearest 1p, 25.5p goes up to 26p whereas 25.49p goes down to 25p;

- the VAT on the entire invoice is then rounded down to the nearest penny.
- Whatever line item rounding approach is chosen, it must be applied consistently to all line items and to all invoices.

Example: line item invoice rounding

An invoice contains one 20% standard-rated line item costing £1.33 net and one 5% reduced-rated line item costing £1.45 net.

Net price (£)	VAT rate (%)	Exact VAT (p)	round down to 0.1p (£)	round to nearest 0.5p (£)	round to nearest 1p (£)
1.33	20%	26.60	26.60	26.50	27.00
1.45	5%	7.25	7.20	7.50	7.00
Totals		33.85	33.80	34.00	34.00
Round invoice to nearest penny			33.00	34.00	34.00

12.2 RECORD-KEEPING

For VAT purposes you must keep detailed accounting records to support the VAT return for a minimum of six years (ten years for the MOSS return) and in a readily accessible manner. In some situations, for example if you opt to tax a building or you enter into a written agreement with HMRC, you will need to keep associated documentation for as long as the option or agreement is subject to assessment.

The documents that must be kept are:

1. The accounting records, including, where relevant, statutory accounts, cash books, nominal ledgers, sales and purchase ledgers, day books and petty cash records.
2. Transaction records such as till rolls, bank statements and paying-in slips.
3. Sales documentation including copy sales invoices, credit and debit notes, orders, delivery notes, packing notes and related correspondence.
4. Purchases documentation, including original purchase invoices, credit and debit notes, orders, delivery notes and related correspondence.
5. Documentation relating to imports, exports, acquisitions and removals from the UK. See Chapter 9: 'International aspects of VAT' for the types of document you must retain.

6. A listing of transactions to the VAT account, copy VAT returns with supporting documentation and computations.
7. VAT-related correspondence with HMRC, HMRC written agreements, copy zero-rating certificates and similar. If you have opted to tax any property you should keep the election notification to HMRC and HMRC acknowledgement and associated documents until at least six years after the option has expired.

If you are partially exempt or have a mix of business and non-business activities, then your records must cover your exempt and non-business activities as well. If keeping records for six years presents storage problems or will cause undue expense, then you may apply to HMRC for agreement to reduce the length of time some of the records must be kept for.

Paper records may be transferred to microfilm or scanned and stored electronically with prior agreement from HMRC. It is acceptable to store accounting records in electronic form (for example as backups of the accounts system), provided they are readily accessible and convertible into a legible form.

12.3 TIME OF SUPPLY

The **time of supply** rules determine when a supply takes place for VAT purposes, and hence the VAT return in which the related output VAT or input VAT is to be recorded. The time of a supply is also known as the **tax point** of the supply.

12.3.1 Basic tax point

Every supply has a **basic tax point**. This is the date on which the transaction is regarded as actually taking place.

1. For a supply of services, it is when the services are fully performed.
2. For a supply of goods, it is:
   - if the goods are sent to or taken away by the customer: the date they are sent or taken away;
   - if the goods are not moved: when they are made available to the customer;
   - if the goods are supplied on sale or return or on approval: the date the goods are adopted by the customer, or 12 months after they are given to the customer if this is earlier.

12.3.2 Actual tax point

The basic tax point can, however, be superseded (wholly or partly) by an **actual tax point**:
- If the supplier, before the basic tax point, issues a VAT invoice or receives payment, this creates an actual tax point at the invoice date or payment date.

- If the supplier both issues a VAT invoice and receives payment before the basic tax point, the actual tax point is the earlier of the two.
- If the invoice and payment are for only a part of the total due, they create an actual tax point for the part concerned, but the basic tax point remains for the balance.
- If the supplier issues an invoice within 14 days after the basic tax point, the tax point is the invoice date unless the supplier notifies HMRC it has elected to ignore this rule, in which case it remains the basic tax point. Suppliers can ask HMRC to extend the 14-day period if it is not practical to issue a VAT invoice within 14 days, for example because the supplier needs to wait for invoices from its own subcontractors.

To issue VAT invoices, you must send or give them to your customers for them to keep. A tax point cannot be created simply by preparing an invoice.

Example: tax point

A business carries out a piece of consultancy work for £10,000 + VAT. It charges a non-refundable part payment of £4,000 + VAT to cover expenses which it receives by electronic transfer on 1 June. The balance of £6,000 + VAT is payable on completion. On 10 June the business completes the work. On 12 June it issues a VAT invoice showing £6,000 + VAT as due. It receives full settlement by electronic transfer on 20 June.

- **Basic tax point**: the basic tax point is when the work is completed – 10 June.
- **Actual tax point**: the receipt of the non-refundable part payment of £4,000 + VAT creates an actual tax point for this part of the payment on 1 June. However, for the balance of £6,000 + VAT, the basic tax point (10 June) remains.
- **Invoice adjustment**: the basic tax point for the remaining £6,000 + VAT (10 June) is adjusted to the invoice date (12 June) if the invoice is issued within 14 days. The invoice is issued within 14 days, so the tax point for the balance becomes 12 June. The tax points are:

1 June: £4,000 + VAT

12 June £6,000 + VAT

12.3.3 **Accommodation tax points**

A business can ask HMRC to agree to a different basis for determining the tax point of a particular class or classes of transactions. Such tax points are referred to as 'accommodation tax points'. This approach is sometimes used for:

- making the tax point the end of the calendar month in which the supply takes place;
- making the tax point the date a VAT invoice is issued.

This approach can be helpful where a business invoices customers who hold accounts for all supplies in a month at the end of the month or shortly after the end of the month. HMRC policy on accommodation points for monthly invoicing (VATTOS6200) is as follows.

> Many suppliers invoice their sales periodically. Typically this will involve the issue of a single invoice to each customer detailing the supplies made during the preceding monthly or 4/5 week commercial accounting period. So long as this represents the supplier's normal accounting practice an accommodation tax point may be allowed without the need to demonstrate that the normal tax point rules cannot be met. Applications should normally be in writing, stating whether the accommodation tax point is to be linked to the last day of the period covered by the invoice or the date of issue of the invoice. In the latter case this should not normally be permitted to exceed 14 days from the end of the commercial accounting period.

12.3.4 **Exceptions**

There are many exceptions to these basic time of supply rules. Some exceptions are:

Deposits

Where a deposit is taken, this creates an actual tax point if the deposit is part payment towards the total due. If the deposit is normally returned complete then no actual tax point is created, even if the deposit is forfeited.

Cash Accounting Scheme

Under the Cash Accounting Scheme (see Chapter 11 'Other topics') output VAT is recognised when payment is received from the customer and input VAT is recognised when a payment is made to a supplier.

Retentions

Where a retention is held (for example, under a construction contract) the tax point for the retention element is delayed until the retention is invoiced or paid.

Continuous supplies

For a continuous supply (such as renting property) a tax point is created whenever an invoice is issued or payment made, though if the supplier issues an annual invoice in advance showing the payments due in the year the tax points are the earlier of when the payments are due or paid.

Land and buildings

For a supply of a freehold of land or buildings, the basic tax point is completion. If a deposit is paid at exchange then a tax point is created if it is payable to the vendor or to a solicitor acting as the vendor's **agent** (see 11.2). However, if the deposit is paid to a stakeholder who holds the payment on behalf of both parties pending satisfactory performance of the contract, this does not create a tax point until payment is released to the vendor. If the total **consideration** (everything that is paid to the supplier in return for making the supply of goods or services) cannot be determined at completion – for example, when the vendor is entitled to a further payment if the purchaser obtains planning permission – then the tax point for any further payment is the earlier of invoice or receipt of the further payment.

Continuous supplies between connected parties

If there is a continuous supply of:

1. a long lease in land or buildings which is taxable, for example the lease of a car park or of holiday accommodation, but excluding an exempt lease or a lease which is taxable only because the supplier has opted to tax the property;
2. gas, electricity, water, heating, power, refrigeration or ventilation;
3. any other continuous supply (excluding a long lease which is exempt or taxable only because it is opted to tax), for example a continuous supply of management services, leasing of equipment or hire of staff.

And if all of the following conditions are met:

(a) The supplier and customer are connected or are part of the same corporate group (but excluding where they are part of the same VAT group).
(b) The customer cannot recover all of the VAT chargeable on the supply.
(c) No VAT invoice has been issued for the supply within a period of 12 months after the supply commenced or a subsequent period of 12 months.
(d) No payment for the supply has been received within that period.

Then a tax point is created at the end of the 12-month period. However, if a VAT invoice is issued or payment received for the 12-month period within 6 months of the end of the period, the supply is treated as made when the invoice is issued or payment received.

EU supplies of goods

If goods are supplied to a customer in another EU state, then, if the customer is not VAT-registered, the tax point is determined under the basic rules above. If the customer is VAT-registered, the tax point is the earlier of the date of issue of a VAT invoice and the 15th of the month following the month of removal from the UK.

Reverse charge supplies of services

Where a supply of services is subject to VAT in the UK under the UK reverse charge, the tax point of the deemed self-supply by the customer for a single supply of services is the date of completion of the services or, to the extent a payment for the services is made before completion, the date of payment. The tax point for continuous supplies of services subject to the reverse charge is the end of each periodic billing or payment period (or payment where this is earlier), with a compulsory tax point on 31 December each year in cases where a billing/payment period or payment has not arisen in the calendar year.

Digital services

With effect from 1 January 2015 the place of supply of intra-EU **B2C** (business to customer) digital services is where the customer belongs (see 9.9 'The Mini One Stop Shop (MOSS)'). The time of supply rules that apply are those of the customer's state.

HP agreements

If goods are supplied under an agreement where the supplier retains title to the goods until some specified event and the price is determined at the specified event, then the basic tax point is the date the event occurs.

Tour Operators' Margin Scheme (TOMS)

Under the TOMS, the tax point of a margin scheme supply is the earlier of the traveller's departure or first occupation of accommodation by the traveller. Any payment that exceeds 20% of the total consideration creates an actual tax point for that payment.

12.3.5 Change in VAT rate

Where the applicable rate of VAT changes (for example the increase in the standard rate of VAT from 17.5% to 20% on 4 January 2011), a special rule applies.

By default, the rate of VAT applicable is the rate in force at the tax point of the supply concerned. For example, if a business supplied goods to a customer on 3

January 2011 but invoiced for the goods on 4 January 2011, by default the applicable rate of VAT would be 20% as the (actual) tax point for the supply is when the invoice is issued, 4 January 2011.

But under the special change of rate rules:

1. The business can choose to apply the VAT rate at the basic tax point. In the above example this would be the 17.5% rate applicable when the goods were supplied on 3 January 2011.
2. If you make a continuous supply which spans the rate change, or if you make a single supply which is nevertheless carried out over a period which commences before the date of the rate change but is not completed until after that date you may, if you wish, charge VAT at the old rate on the work done up to the rate change and the new rate on the remainder. You must be able to demonstrate that the apportionment between the two amounts accurately reflects the work done in each period.

If you issue a VAT invoice under the basic rules but wish to change the treatment to options (1) or (2) above, you must issue a credit or debit note for the VAT difference within 45 days of the date the VAT rate changed. The note must state 'Credit note – change of VAT rate'.

12.3.6 Historic rates of VAT

Standard rate	From	To
20%	4 January 2011	
17.5%	1 January 2010	3 January 2011
15%	1 December 2008	31 December 2009
17.5%	1 April 1991	30 November 2008
15%	18 June 1979	31 March 1991
8%	29 July 1974	17 June 1979
10%	1 April 1973	28 July 1974
Reduced rate	**From**	**To**
5%	1 September 1997	
8%	1 April 1994	31 August 1997
Higher rate	**From**	**To**
12.5%	12 April 1976	17 June 1979
25%	18 November 1974	11 April 1976

Higher-rate VAT was introduced in November 1974 to apply to petrol (but not diesel oil). In May 1975 this was extended to cover domestic electrical appliances, radios, TVs, hi-fis, pleasure boats, aircraft, towing caravans, photographic equipment, furs and jewellery. Higher-rate VAT was abolished in June 1979 when the standard rate of VAT was put up to 15%.

12.4   VAT INVOICES

A UK VAT-registered supplier must issue a VAT invoice when it:

(a) makes a standard-rated or reduced-rated supply to a VAT-registered customer in the UK;

(b) makes a supply to a customer in another EU state for the purposes of any business activity carried on by that customer;

(c) receives a payment on account for a supply to a customer in another EU state.

Scenario (b) does not apply if the supply is VAT exempt and the customer's state does not require an invoice to be issued for the supply, or if the supply is of VAT-exempt financial or insurance services.

12.4.1   Contents of a UK VAT invoice

Under the UK rules, a VAT invoice must, subject to the exceptions explained below, contain all of the following:

1. invoice number;
2. tax point and invoice date;
3. supplier details;
4. customer details;
5. supply details;
6. totals: the net amount due, the VAT due and the gross amount due;
7. special scenarios.

See below for more on each.

1. **Invoice number**: a sequential number based on one or more series which uniquely identifies the document.
2. **Tax point and invoice date**: the time of supply (tax point) and, if different, the date the invoice is issued.

3. **Supplier details**: the supplier's business's name, address and VAT registration number. If the customer is in another EU state, the VAT registration number must be prefixed 'GB'. In addition:

   - under company law, a registered company must also state its registered name, registration number, registered office address and the part of the UK in which the company is registered (i.e. England and Wales, or Wales, or Scotland, or Northern Ireland) on any invoice it issues;
   - under section 39 Charities Act 2011, a registered charity with gross income in its last financial year exceeding £10,000 must disclose the fact that it is a registered charity in all its invoices, receipts and letters of credit;
   - under s11 Co-operative and Community Benefit Societies Act 2014 a registered society's registered name must appear in legible characters in all of its business correspondence.

4. **Customer details**: the customer's name and address. If the customer is registered for VAT in another EU state, their VAT registration number and country prefix code must also be shown (see 14.4 'VAT in other EU states' for a list of country prefix codes).

5. **Supply details**: a description sufficient to identity the goods or services supplied. For each description the following details must be provided:

   - the quantity of the goods or extent of the services including any unit price;
   - the amount payable (excluding VAT) in any currency;
   - the rate of UK VAT. If different rates of VAT apply to a description, the different parts must be distinguished and listed separately.

6. **Totals**: the invoice must include all of the following:

   - **net due**: the total payable (for all description lines) excluding VAT, in any currency;
   - **discounts**: details of any cash discount provided;
   - **VAT due**: the total UK VAT chargeable in sterling;
   - **gross amount**: the total amount payable by the customer, including VAT;
   - **gross analysis**: if an invoice contains exempt or zero-rated supplies, the invoice must distinguish between exempt, zero-rated and other supplies and state separately the gross total amount payable in respect of each supply and rate.

7. **Special scenarios**: these include:

   - **reverse-charge supplies of services**: where an intra-EU supply of services is subject to a reverse charge (where the customer has to pay any output VAT due on the supply), in whole or in part, the invoice must include the reference 'reverse charge' or equivalent;

- **UK removals of goods**: if goods are supplied to a locally VAT-registered customer in another EU state, the customer's VAT registration number with country prefix code must be quoted on the invoice in order to zero rate the supply (see 9.6 'Intra-EU transfers of goods');
- **intra-EU exempt and zero-rated supplies**: if the supply is a zero-rated or exempt supply to a business customer in another EU state the invoice must also include the words 'zero-rated' or 'exempt', or reference to the applicable legislation, or some other appropriate indication of such status.

12.4.2   Example VAT invoice

VAT invoice

Invoice to: **From:**

Customer name   Supplier name

Customer address   Supplier address

VAT registration number			123456727	
Invoice number			987654	
Invoice date (tax point)			15/12/15	

Item description	Unit price (£)	Quantity	Net (£)	VAT rate
Type 1 widget	20.00	5	100.00	20%
Type 2 widget	10.00	2	20.00	20%
Widgets manual	5.00	1	5.00	0%
Postage & packing	15.00	1	15.00	20%
		Net due	140.00	
		VAT due	27.00	
		Total due	**167.00**	

Gross payable: **Zero rate   5.00**   **Other rates   162.00**

12.4.3 **Exceptions**

Special schemes

VAT invoices must not be issued for supplies made under the Second-Hand Goods Scheme or under the TOMS. For TOMS the invoice must not show the VAT charged and, if the invoice is to another business, it must state: 'this is a Tour Operators' Margin Scheme supply' or 'this supply falls under the Value Added Tax (Tour Operators) Order 1987' or equivalent wording.

Simplified VAT invoice

There are simplified rules for invoices where the invoice amount is for £250 or less (excluding VAT). A supplier does not have to provide a full VAT invoice for such a supply unless the customer belongs in another EU state. A simplified VAT invoice must include the following:

1. the supplier's name, address and VAT registration number;
2. the time of supply (tax point);
3. a description which identifies the goods or services supplied;
4. and for each VAT rate applicable, the gross amount payable (including VAT) and the VAT rate charged.

This arrangement was originally restricted to retailers, but was extended to all suppliers with effect from 1 January 2013.

Modified VAT invoice

Provided your customer agrees, HMRC accepts (*VAT Notice 700*, section 16.6) that you can issue an invoice showing the following:

1. The VAT-inclusive value of each standard-rated or reduced-rated supply (instead of the VAT-exclusive values).
2. At the foot of the invoice, it must show separately:
   - the total VAT-inclusive value of the standard-rated or reduced-rated supplies;
   - the total VAT payable on those supplies shown in sterling;
   - the total value, excluding VAT, of those supplies;
   - the total value of any zero-rated supplies included on the invoice; and
   - the total value of any exempt supplies included on the invoice.

In all other respects the invoice should show the details required for a full VAT invoice. If you are asked for a VAT invoice, but are unable to use either a simplified invoice or modified VAT invoice, you must issue a full VAT invoice.

12.4.4   **Whose VAT invoicing rules apply?**

By default the VAT invoicing rules of the EU state where a supply of goods or services is deemed to take place apply. However:

- The VAT invoicing rules of the supplier's state apply if the place of supply is another EU state, the supplier is not established in that state (or any fixed establishment of the supplier's in that state does not intervene in the supply), and the supply is subject to the reverse charge. However, if the customer issues invoices under a self-billing arrangement, then the VAT invoice rules of the customer's state apply
- The VAT invoicing rules of the supplier's state apply if the place of supply is outside the EU

For more on the place of supply rules for goods or services, see Chapter 9 'International aspects of VAT'.

12.4.5   **Self-billed invoices**

A customer may issue themselves with a VAT invoice if the conditions below are met. This arrangement is frequently used where only the customer knows the value of the supply, for example under a royalty agreement.

The conditions are:

- The customer and supplier must enter into a self-billing agreement which authorises the customer to produce self-billed invoices for a specified period. The agreement must stipulate that the supplier will not issue VAT invoices for supplies covered by the agreement, that the supplier will accept each self-billed invoice and that the supplier will notify the customer if they cease to be registered for VAT or change their VAT registration number.
- The VAT invoice must contain all the information required on a VAT invoice (see above).
- Each self-billed VAT invoice which includes an amount of output VAT must contain the statement 'The VAT shown is your output tax due to HMRC'.
- The customer keeps copies of all the self-billing agreements it enters into and the names, addresses and VAT registration numbers of the suppliers who have entered into such agreements.

12.4.6   **Pro-forma invoices**

A pro-forma invoice is an invoice which is issued in advance of any supply or customer payment, in order to request a deposit or prepayment or to satisfy some requirement of the customer's before they can initiate a supply. A pro-forma invoice is not a VAT invoice and cannot be used to substitute for one.

Any pro-forma invoices should always be clearly described as such and should be endorsed 'This is not a VAT invoice'.

If the customer then makes a payment or the goods or services are supplied, a tax point will normally be created requiring a VAT invoice to be issued (see 12.3 'Time of supply').

12.4.7 Timing of a VAT invoice

Subject to exceptions as explained below, a VAT invoice must be issued within 30 days of a tax point arising, unless the tax point arose as a result of an invoice being issued. The 30-day limit can be extended if you are awaiting invoices from your own subcontractors or you are newly registered but have not been notified of your VAT registration number.

If goods are supplied to a VAT-registered customer in another EU state, the VAT invoice must be issued by the 15th of the month following the month in which the goods leave the UK.

12.4.8 Credit and debit notes

If you issue a VAT invoice which is incorrect in some way, you cannot simply scrap it and issue a corrected invoice. You must either issue a credit or debit note to correct the original invoice or issue a credit note to completely reverse the original invoice and then issue a new invoice.

Credit and debit notes should use the rates of VAT applicable at the original time of supply. They should be issued within one month of the need for an adjustment being discovered. A credit or debit note should be headed 'credit note' or 'debit note' as appropriate and include, as a minimum, the following:

1. the identifying number and date of issue;
2. the name, address and registration number of the supplier;
3. the name and address of the customer;
4. the reason for its issue – for example, 'returned goods';
5. a description which identifies the goods or services for which credit is being claimed or allowed;
6. the quantity and amount for each description;
7. the total amount credited, excluding VAT;
8. the rate and amount of VAT credited; and
9. the number and date of the original VAT invoice. If you cannot do this (for example, because returned goods cannot be identified with a particular invoice), you must be able to satisfy HMRC by other means that you accounted for VAT on the original supply.

Credits for zero-rated or exempt supplies included in a credit or debit note must be totalled separately and the note must show clearly that no VAT credit has been allowed for them. If credit notes are issued without VAT adjustment, they should state 'This is not a credit note for VAT'.

12.4.9 Bad debts

If a customer fails to pay, then you cannot deal with this by issuing a credit note. Instead, you must claim bad debt relief through your VAT return. You can claim for any output VAT that you have paid to HMRC but not received from the customer.

Before you can claim:

- the goods or services must have been provided to the customer;
- the debt must have remained unpaid for a period of six months after the later of the time payment was due and the date of the supply;
- for supplies made after 30 April 1997, you must claim within four years and six months of the later of when payment is due or the date of supply; and
- the debt must have been written off in your accounts.

You cannot reclaim VAT on a debt that has been sold, factored or assigned. If the supply is partly paid, you can claim for the unpaid part. If goods are sold with reservation of title until the goods are paid for, then this does not prevent bad debt relief being claimed.

To claim a refund you should include the amount of the VAT you are claiming in Box 4 of your VAT return which covers the date when you fulfil the conditions to make a claim.

If you are using the Cash Accounting Scheme you only account for output VAT when the customer pays. If the customer fails to pay then no output VAT will have been accounted for. If, under the Cash Accounting Scheme, the customer pays by cheque but the cheque bounces after you have paid the output VAT to HMRC, you may adjust for this in your next VAT return.

If you have claimed bad debt relief and you later receive a payment for the supply, you must repay to HMRC the VAT element included in the payment. All payments you receive for the supply or supplies must be shown in your bad debt account. When you are repaying all or part of your refund, put the amount you are repaying in Box 1 of your VAT return for the period in which you received the payment.

If you are no longer registered for VAT and therefore do not make VAT returns, you must still repay all or part of the refund. Contact HMRC for guidance.

If you are insured for the VAT-inclusive amount of the debt and your insurer pays you, your bad-debt-relief entitlement is not affected and you may still claim for the full amount.

12.4.10 Discounts

Unconditional discounts

Unconditional discounts such as bulk discounts and customer status discounts that are granted at the time of the supply have the effect of reducing the customer's liability and hence may also reduce any VAT chargeable.

Conditional discounts

If a discount is conditional on some future event, for example a retrospective discount if the customer's total purchases exceed a certain level, then invoices raised before the condition is met should ignore the discount. Any credit note or retrospective discount provided when the condition is met should include an adjustment to the VAT already charged.

Prompt payment discounts

A prompt payment discount is an agreement that the customer can pay a reduced amount if payment is made within a set time. If payment is not made within the time limit, the full invoice amount is due.

The VAT rules for prompt payment discounts (PPDs) changed on 1 April 2015. With effect from 1 April 2015, if a PPD is offered VAT is due on the undiscounted amount, unless and until the discounted amount is paid in accordance with the PPD terms. Suppliers should charge VAT on and issue a VAT invoice for the full undiscounted price and then either issue a VAT credit note if the discount is successfully taken up, or include the following wording on the invoice (*Revenue & Customs Brief 49/14*):

> A discount of X% of the full price applies if payment is made within Y days of the invoice date. No credit note will be issued. Following payment you must ensure you have only recovered the VAT actually paid.

Additionally HMRC suggests that invoices show: (i) the discounted price; (ii) the VAT on the discounted price; and (iii) the total amount due if the PPD is taken up.

Before 1 April 2015, if a PPD was offered, the price charged was taken to be the lower discounted price, whether or not the prompt payment offer was taken up. But if the terms allowed the customer to pay by instalments, the VAT value was based on the amount the customer actually paid.

12.5 CLAIMING INPUT VAT

In order to be able to deduct input VAT, a business must:

1. hold appropriate evidence that the input VAT has been validly incurred by the business wholly or partly for a taxable activity of the business;
2. make a valid claim for that input VAT within the time limits and claim rules. VAT must normally be claimed within four years of the due date for the return for the claim period in which the VAT first became recoverable.

Normally (1) requires possession of a valid VAT invoice from the supplier (including, where applicable, a simplified VAT invoice or modified VAT invoice). Only UK VAT can be recovered in a UK VAT return.

See 12.4 'VAT invoices'. For the requirements of a VAT invoice, see '9.2 Recovering foreign VAT' for details of how to recover VAT incurred in other EU states. See 12.6.8 'The capping rules' for the time limit for claiming input VAT.

12.5.1 Valid VAT invoices

Pro-forma invoices, reminders and statements are not valid VAT invoices, even if they contain all the information required on a VAT invoice. Valid VAT debit and credit notes can be used to support VAT adjustments.

12.5.2 Employee expenses

HMRC accepts that input VAT incurred by employees on business expenses can be recovered (subject always to the VAT recovery rules as explained in Chapter 3 'Recovering VAT') in the following circumstances:

- fuel for vehicles;
- other employee travel and subsistence expenses;
- no VAT invoice provided;
- mobile phones;
- employer paid or refunded removal expenses.

See below for more details on each.

Fuel for vehicles

See 12.10.5 'Fuel payments'.

Other employee travel and subsistence expenses.

VAT incurred on other employee travel and subsistence expenses (including meals and hotel accommodation) can be recovered by the business provided it holds a valid VAT invoice, even if the VAT invoice is made out to an employee. This is subject to the condition that the business refunds the employee for the expense. If the business partially refunds the expense, only a corresponding portion of the VAT can be treated as input VAT (*VAT Notice 700*, section 12.1).

No VAT invoice provided

In some situations it is not possible to obtain a VAT invoice. HMRC accepts (*VAT Notice 700*, section 19.7.5) that input VAT can be recovered without a full and properly completed VAT invoice provided you are sure the supplier is registered for VAT (if in doubt, check with the HMRC VAT Helpline) and the total cost of each **taxable supply** is £25 or less (including VAT). This applies to:

- phone calls from public or private phones
- purchases through coin-operated machines
- car park charges (on-street parking meters are not subject to VAT); and
- a single or return toll charge paid at the tollbooth. However, you need to obtain a VAT invoice, irrespective of the price of each individual toll if:
  - you purchase a book of toll tickets; or
  - you use a tolled road, bridge or crossing under an arrangement where you pay in advance for your journeys, or you are invoiced in arrears for your journeys, or a combination of the two (for example, if you use an electronic tag or if you are an account customer). This excludes tolls charged by the: Cleddau Bridge, Clifton Suspension Bridge, Dartford Bridge, Erskine Bridge, Forth Road Bridge, Humber Bridge, Itchen Bridge, Mersey Tunnel, Tamar Bridge, Tay Bridge, and Tyne Tunnel.

Mobile phone purchases and standing charges

Where a business provides its employees with mobile phones for business use, then, regardless of whether it allows private use, it can treat as input VAT all the VAT it incurs on purchasing a phone and on standing charges for keeping it connected to the network, providing that the charges do not contain any element for calls (*VAT Notice 700*, section 12A).

Mobile phone call charges

The VAT treatment depends on how private calls are handled by the business (from *VAT Notice 700*, section 12A):

- If a business does not allow its employees to make private calls, all of the VAT incurred on the call charges is input VAT. HMRC will accept that this is the case where a business has imposed clear rules prohibiting private use and enforces them. However, HMRC realises that in practice businesses with such a policy often tolerate a small amount of private calls. HMRC is prepared to treat such minimal use as being insignificant for VAT purposes and it will not prevent a business treating all the VAT it incurs on calls as input VAT.

- If a business charges its employees for any private calls they make, then it may treat the VAT incurred on the calls as input VAT, but must account for output VAT on the amounts it charges.
- If a business allows its employees to make private calls without charge, then it must apportion the VAT incurred on the call charges, with the VAT apportioned to private calls being irrecoverable. HMRC does not accept that a business can adopt an alternative treatment of accounting for output VAT on the private use. Businesses can choose any apportionment method that suits their individual circumstances, providing that the method chosen produces a fair and reasonable result. For example, businesses could analyse a sample of bills taken over a reasonable period of time and use the same ratio for future VAT recovery on mobile phone bills.
- Where the phone package allows the business to make a certain quantity of calls for a fixed monthly payment and there is no separate standing charge, then it must apportion the VAT on the total charge for the package. Similarly, where the contract is for the purchase of the phone and the advance purchase of a set amount of call time for a single charge, the apportionment will also apply to the whole charge.

Employer paid or refunded removal expenses

HMRC accepts (*VIT42100*) that a business can treat the VAT incurred as its input VAT if it reimburses employees for these removal expenses:

- estate agents' and solicitors' fees
- storage and removal of household and personal effects; and
- services such as plumbing in washing machines or altering curtains.

If the business pays part of an expense, then only that proportion of the input VAT can be claimed. These rules also apply if the employee is a new employee moving home to take-up a post. However, if a fixed rate allowance is paid there is no input VAT to claim. HMRC will not reject claims out of hand if the relevant invoices are addressed to the employee rather than the business. HMRC will accept alternative evidence, provided that the business provides satisfactory evidence that it has paid for and incurred the VAT on these expenses. When directors, partners or sole proprietors move home they may have a personal rather than a business purpose. If HMRC is satisfied that the move was for a business purpose, HMRC will accept a claim for input VAT. The rules that apply to moves by employees also apply to claims made when directors, partners and sole proprietors move home.

12.5.3 **Subcontractor expenses**

HMRC accepts that an employer can recover VAT incurred on expenses by self-employed subcontractors in the same way as for employees. HMRC provides the following guidance at *VIT13400*:

> A business might pay for subsistence, road fuel or other motoring costs incurred by self-employed people working for it. If it does the tax incurred is input tax of the business provided:
>
> * the individual is engaged on the same basis as an employee; in other words they are paid on a fixed rate basis, being un-associated with the trading profits of the business;
> * the individual incurs the expenditure only in respect of their 'employment' by the business. Where someone like a self-employed salesman represents a number of firms at the same time, their subsistence does not relate to any one 'employer' and none of those firms can treat the VAT incurred as input tax;
> * the individuals receive no payment from the end customer;
> * the business pays them back at cost, including VAT, dealing with the expense in the normal business accounts.
>
> These guidelines also apply to actors, extras and other casual workers engaged in film, TV or similar productions.
>
> Where the individual is registered for VAT in their own capacity the tax should normally be treated as incurred by the individual for the purpose of their business. HMRC may exceptionally allow recovery by the 'employer' only if we are satisfied that the individual has not recovered tax under their own registration.
>
> Sometimes an 'employer' will incur subsistence type expenditure for a number of 'employees' at the same time. For example, a film company on location may block book a hotel. In such circumstances there will be a single tax invoice from hotel to 'employer'. The 'employer' can claim input tax on the expenditure even if some of the individuals are VAT registered.

12.5.4 **Missing VAT invoices**

Where VAT invoices are not present, HMRC officers have discretion in what they can accept as appropriate evidence to support recovery of input VAT. HMRC officers must exercise their discretion and consider whether suitable alternative evidence exists. They should look for evidence that the transaction did actually occur as described, on normal commercial terms, for business purposes and between validly UK-registered businesses.

Supplies not subject to widespread fraud and abuse

See below for a list of supplies that are subject to widespread fraud and abuse as defined. HMRC will ask the following questions in the absence of a valid VAT invoice (*VIT31200*):

1. Do you have alternative documentary evidence other than an invoice (e.g. supplier statement)?
2. Do you have evidence of receipt of a taxable supply on which VAT has been charged?
3. Do you have evidence of payment?
4. Do you have evidence of how the goods/services have been consumed within your business or their onward supply?
5. How did you know that the supplier existed?
6. How was your relationship with the supplier established? For example: How was contact made? Do you know where the supplier operates from (have you been there)?
7. How do you contact them? How do you know they can supply the goods or services? If goods, how do you know the goods are not stolen? How do you return faulty supplies?

If you do not possess a valid VAT invoice and are unable to obtain one, then, provided you can satisfactorily answer most of the above questions, you may deduct the input VAT subject to review by HMRC at your next VAT inspection. A refusal by HMRC to accept alternative evidence can be challenged at the tax tribunal (First-tier Tribunal and Upper Tribunal).

Supplies of goods subject to widespread fraud and abuse

For supplies of the following goods, in order to deduct the input VAT without a valid VAT invoice, you must be able to satisfactorily answer all or nearly all of the above questions and HMRC may ask additional questions to test whether you took reasonable care in respect of transactions to ensure that the supplier and the supply were bona fide:

1. computers and any other equipment, including parts, accessories and software, made or adapted for use in connection with computers or computer systems;
2. telephones and any other equipment, including parts and accessories, made or adapted for use in connection with telephones or telecommunications;
3. alcoholic drinks liable to excise duty;
4. all oils that are **held out for sale** as road fuel (i.e. advertising and otherwise describing the product at its point of sale as fuel or firewood, with packaging and wrapping that is consistent with this).

12.5.5 **No supply**

If you have been defrauded by a supplier sending you a VAT invoice which you have paid but the associated goods and services are not supplied, then the input VAT is not recoverable as no supply has taken place. If you have already recovered the input VAT when it becomes clear that you have been defrauded, then you must correct this in the next VAT return.

12.5.6 **Unpaid supplier invoices**

If you receive supplies and claim input VAT on those supplies but have not paid for them by six months after the payment became due, then you must repay the input VAT to HMRC in your next VAT return.

The payment is regarded as being due on the later of:

- the date of the supply; or
- the date when the consideration for the supply became due (normally the invoice date).

If you have part paid, then you need only repay the unpaid proportion.

If you are in dispute with the supplier and the supplier agrees to extend the due date, the six-month period runs from the revised due date.

You should make a negative entry in the VAT allowable part of your VAT account, and account for the repayment on your return covering the date when repayment became due. The repayment is recorded as a negative entry in box 4 on the VAT return.

If you later pay the supplier, then you can reclaim any input VAT that was repaid. You reclaim the input VAT by including it in box 4 of the VAT return for the period in which the payment is made.

12.5.7 **Invoices made out to third parties**

If a VAT invoice is made out to another person then the input VAT may not be **deductible** (see 3.1). If the invoice is made out to another person by mistake, then the supplier should be asked to correct this. No VAT should be deducted until the corrected invoice is received.

If a third party pays for supplies made to another person, the third party cannot normally deduct the input VAT. However, HMRC accepts that an employer can recover VAT on a VAT invoice made out to an employee or subcontractor in some situations, see 12.5.2 'Employee expenses' and 12.5.3 'Subcontractor expenses'. See also 3.3.10 for VAT recovery on the costs of setting up and running a funded pension scheme.

12.6 **THE VAT RETURN**

All VAT-registered businesses must complete a periodic VAT return detailing output VAT charged in the return period, input VAT recovered in the period, the net amount of VAT due to or claimed from HMRC for the period, the net value of sales and purchases in the period and various other figures. This must normally be accompanied by payment of any amount due. If a net amount is being claimed from HMRC, then the return serves as your claim to this.

12.6.1 **VAT return boxes**

The standard UK VAT return (form VAT 100 or its online equivalent) has nine numeric boxes for completion. You should enter numbers in each box, using 0.00 for zero. For negative numbers you must use a minus sign for the online return, for example -7.00, but brackets for a paper return, for example (7.00). Terms in bold are explained in the Glossary.

Box 1: VAT due in this period on sales and other outputs

- *Include*: all UK **output VAT** charged in the period; UK VAT charged on **distance sales** of goods to unregistered customers in other EU states; UK VAT charged on supplies of services where the **place of supply** is the UK; UK VAT due on **reverse charge** purchases of services; VAT due on the sale of assets; VAT on **fuel scale charges**; VAT on private use of business assets; estimates and **annual adjustments** under the **TOMS**.
- *Exclude*: foreign (non-UK) VAT charged; assessments raised by HMRC.
- *Deduct*: VAT on credit notes issued to customers.
- *Cash Accounting Scheme*: enter output VAT when received, not when charged.

Box 2: VAT due in this period on acquisitions from other EU member states

- *Include*: **acquisition VAT** (see 9.6.1 'Acquisitions') on goods acquired from suppliers in other **EU states**.
- *Exclude*: VAT on supplies of services, VAT on **reverse charge supplies**.
- *Cash Accounting Scheme*: this scheme does not apply to **acquisitions of goods**; these must be reported on a receivable basis.

Box 3: Total VAT due

This is the sum of boxes 1 and 2. In the online VAT return, this box is calculated automatically.

Box 4: VAT reclaimed in this period on purchases and other inputs (including acquisitions from the EU)

- *Include*: **recoverable input VAT** for the period; recoverable **acquisition VAT** for the period; recoverable **import VAT** for the period; bad debt relief claimed in the period, recoverable VAT charged on **reverse charge** purchases of services from abroad; any **annual adjustment** or adjustment under the Capital Goods Scheme.
- *Exclude*: foreign (non-UK) input VAT; **irrecoverable VAT** such as VAT that is **attributable** to non-business or exempt activities (unless *de minimis*); input VAT on supplies where proper VAT documentation is not held; **blocked input VAT**; input VAT on goods and services purchased under a **margin scheme** or under the **TOMS**.

See the Glossary for definitions of all terms in bold.

- *Deduct*: VAT on credit notes issued by suppliers to the extent that the associated input VAT was recovered.
- *Cash Accounting Scheme*: base input VAT claim on payments made, not invoices received.

Box 5: Net VAT to be paid to Customs or reclaimed by you

This is the difference between boxes 3 and 4. In the online VAT return, this box is calculated automatically.

- *Annual Accounting Scheme*: do not deduct any instalments you have paid during the period when calculating the figure to put into this box. However, the end-of-the-year payment you send with your annual return should be the box 5 figure minus any instalments you have already made for the period.

Box 6: Total value of sales and all other outputs excluding any VAT

- *Include*: the net value of all taxable supplies (including zero-rated supplies) and all exempt supplies; EU sales of goods included in box 8; exports of goods; supplies of services whose place of supply is outside the UK; the net value of reverse charge purchases of services from abroad; the net margin on margin scheme supplies or supplies under the TOMS.
- *Exclude*: non-business income such as block grants, public donations, insurance claims, bank interest and investment income.
- *Deduct*: net amount of any sales refunds.
- *Cash Accounting Scheme*: base sales on amounts received, not invoices issued.

Box 7: Total value of purchases and all other inputs excluding any VAT

- *Include*: purchases attributable to taxable and exempt activities (net of any input VAT); **outside the scope** supplies with the right of recovery; **reverse charge** purchases of services, **acquisitions of goods** from EU suppliers entered into box 9.
- *Exclude*: purchases **attributable** to **non-business activities**; irrecoverable VAT; taxes (PAYE and national insurance, business rates, Insurance Premium Tax); wages and salaries; MOT certificates; motor vehicle licence duty; purchases of margin scheme supplies and purchases under the TOMS.
- *Cash Accounting Scheme*: base purchases on payments made, not invoices received.

Box 8: Total value of all supplies of goods and related costs, excluding any VAT, to other EU member states

- *Include*: the net value of sales of goods to VAT-registered businesses in other EU states; directly related charges such as freight and insurance; **distance sales** to customers in other EU states above the respective states' **distance-selling thresholds**; dispatches of own goods to a branch in another EU state for business purposes.
- *Exclude*: sales of goods to unregistered customers in other EU states below the respective states' **distance-selling thresholds**; sales of services to customers in other EU states.
- *Cash Accounting Scheme:* sales must be reported at the normal tax point for intra-EU supplies of goods, not on a cash-received basis.
- *EC Sales List*: if you make entries in Box 8 then you must also complete an EC sales list – see 12.7 'The EC sales list'.

Box 9: Total value of all acquisitions of goods and related costs, excluding any VAT, from other EU member states

- *Include*: the value of goods purchased from suppliers in other EU states; directly related charges such as freight and insurance.
- *Exclude*: supplies of services received from suppliers in other EU states. Goods received from suppliers outside the EU (**imports**).

12.6.2   Submission of VAT returns and payment of VAT

Most VAT returns must now be completed online via the Government Gateway. You must first obtain a Government Gateway Account. This provides you with a login and password to access and submit your VAT returns. You must then pay any VAT due electronically, to clear into HMRC's account by the due date of the return.

The return and VAT are, by default, due no later than the last day of the next month. However, if you submit and pay online then you are granted an extra 7 days.

Example: due date for online return and payment

VAT period end	Due date
31 March 2016	7 May 2016
30 June 2016	7 August 2016
30 September 2016	7 November 2016
31 December 2016	7 February 2017

However, your deadlines for the return or payment (or both) will be different if you:

- use the VAT Annual Accounting Scheme: the deadline is two calendar months after the end of your VAT period;
- you come within the scope of the payments on account (POA) scheme. See 12.6.3 'Payments on account scheme'.

The deadline for when your electronic payment should clear into HMRC's bank account is usually the same as the deadline for your return. You should check with your bank how long it will take your payment to clear into HMRC's bank account as some methods of payment do not operate over the weekend or on a bank holiday.

If you pay by online direct debit, HMRC provides an extra three days. If you pay by online direct debit, and you submit your return on or before the due date, HMRC will collect payment from your nominated bank account a further three bank working days after the due date for your return.

If you submit paper VAT returns and post cheques, the return must be sent to arrive by the due date shown on the VAT return. With effect from 1 April 2010, any cheque payment must have cleared in HMRC's bank account by the due date of the return – a cheque is regarded as clearing on the second business day after the date of receipt. If posting a return close to the deadline, it is recommended that you obtain a certificate of posting in case the return is delayed in the postal system.

12.6.3 Payments on account scheme

Every VAT-registered business not making monthly VAT returns is required to make POA if its annual VAT liability exceeds £2.3 million. Each affected business must make interim payments at the end of the second and third months of each VAT quarter. These interim payments are POA of the quarterly VAT liability. A balancing payment for the quarter is then made with the quarterly VAT return.

HMRC will notify affected businesses when they must join POA and of the interim payment amounts and due dates. The POA and the balancing payments must be made electronically, and cleared funds must be in HMRC's bank account by close of business on the due date.

12.6.4 Late VAT returns and payments

If the VAT return or payment is late, then this is referred to as a **default**. If no return is sent in, then HMRC will estimate the VAT due. If a payment bounces, HMRC will not re-present it; so you should make sure you have sufficient cleared funds in the relevant account. If you do not have the funds or can make only a part payment, you should contact HMRC and explain the situation.

The first time you default, HMRC will send you a warning (referred to as a Surcharge Liability Notice). This warns you that if you default again within 12 months of the date of the notice, you become liable for a penalty, referred to as a Default Surcharge. If you default again within this period, then you will have to pay the Default Surcharge and you will receive a Surcharge Liability Notice Extension, extending the defaulting period by a further 12 months.

The Default Surcharge is calculated as a percentage of the VAT that is outstanding, so if no VAT was actually outstanding, the Default Surcharge is zero. The percentage increases each time you are late. The first time a Surcharge is payable, it is 2%. The Surcharge is 5% the second time it is payable, then it increases by 5% each time you are late. There is a minimum of £30 and a maximum rate of 15%. If the Surcharge at the 2% or 5% rate is less than £400, HMRC will waive the penalty, though you will be issued with a Surcharge Liability Notice Extension, and the rate for the next default will go up. Small businesses (turnover below £150,000) will also be let off their very first default and just issued with a warning instead.

12.6.5 Reasonable excuse

You may be able to avoid liability for a Surcharge if you had a reasonable excuse for not paying on time. An excuse is reasonable if a conscientious person, having due regard for the law and exercising reasonable foresight and due diligence, would have been unable to avoid the default in the same circumstances and at the same time. However, you must also have dealt with the problem as quickly as the conscientious person would have done.

HMRC has provided some guidance on what it considers might be reasonable excuses. They include computer breakdown, theft or destruction of key records, sudden illness or loss of key personnel and an unexpected cash crisis. However, the key test is that a reasonable person would have been unable to avoid the default.

Illness or loss of key personnel is less likely to be considered reasonable in larger organisations. Planned holiday will never be a reasonable excuse. Lack of funds is not in itself a reasonable excuse, though if the lack was genuinely unexpected and caused by fraud, act of God or sudden non-payment by a normally reliable customer or funder, then it may have a reasonable cause.

A reasonable person will be expected to have contacted HMRC and informed them of any problem as soon as possible. If you know that you are going to be in default, you should contact HMRC and explain the problem. If you are having problems with accounting, such as a computer breakdown, or if the person who normally prepares the return is unavailable, you can request permission to submit an estimated return. If you do not have enough funds to pay, then you should contact HMRC and try to arrange a payment schedule.

If you cannot pay, then HMRC has an extensive range of powers to recover the debt, including the power to enter your premises and seize your goods without the need for a court order.

12.6.6 **Errors and mistakes**

If, after you have submitted a VAT return, you discover it contained errors or omissions, you must follow a set procedure to correct the return. Errors can arise in many ways, for example:

- the accounting system produces incorrect figures
- data is entered incorrectly into the accounting system
- you misunderstood the VAT status of one or more transactions
- court cases have since established that a treatment you applied was incorrect.

There is no need to correct errors that are more than four years old (unless they were deliberate – in which case the time limit for correction is 20 years – see 12.6.8 'The capping rules'). Generally, you cannot reclaim overpaid VAT and do not have to pay underpaid VAT if it relates to a VAT period that ended more than four years after you discovered the error. However, you must deal with an error when you discover it, otherwise it becomes deliberate. It is recommended that you keep a record of the error, the date it was discovered, the date it was dealt with and details of how it was dealt with.

You can correct one or more errors by making an adjustment on the VAT return for the period when the errors were discovered if:

- the net value of the errors is at most £10,000; or
- the net value of the errors is less than £50,000 and is less than 1% of the box 6 turnover figure for the return.

The net value of the error is the net amount of output VAT and input VAT owing to or recoverable from HMRC. If these limits are exceeded you must notify HMRC in writing of the error.

You may also notify HMRC of errors below the above thresholds. HMRC provides form VAT 652 'Notification of Errors in VAT Returns' that can be used to notify errors, though use of the form is not mandatory.

HMRC can charge penalties for errors in VAT returns that have resulted in an underpayment to HMRC, see 12.9 'VAT penalties'.

12.6.7 Unjust enrichment

If, by making a refund of overpaid output VAT, a claimant would be **unjustly enriched** as a result of the error, HMRC may deny or reduce the claim to what it thinks is fair. The burden of proof is on HMRC. HMRC must show that someone other than the claimant bore the economic burden of the overcharged VAT.

Overcharged output VAT is normally paid by the customer, so at first sight the customer bears the economic burden. However, the fact that the customer paid the VAT is not sufficient in itself to establish who bore the economic burden of the VAT. For example, the supplier may have had to absorb the VAT by reducing its margins in order to remain competitive in a price-sensitive market. If the buyer was trading before VAT registration and kept its gross price the same upon VAT registration, that suggests that it is the supplier that is bearing the economic burden.

HMRC will generally take the following factors into account when deciding who bore the economic burden of the wrongly charged output VAT (*VR4300*):

- **Substitute products**: if a product competes with products that are at lower or nil rates of VAT, this indicates that the supplier bore the economic burden of the VAT, as the supplier will have had to absorb the VAT cost in order to remain competitive
- **Addictiveness and necessity**: HMRC's view is that customers are less price-sensitive where addictive goods (such as cigarettes) or necessities (such as bread) are concerned; so the economic burden of the VAT is more likely to be borne by the customer.

- **Market position**: the market position of the supplier must be considered. For example, a supplier with a near monopoly is less likely to bear the economic burden of the VAT
- **Historic prices**: if the price went up when the product was first subject to VAT or when the VAT rate increased on 4 January 2011, and if the price decreased when the VAT rate decreased on 1 December 2008, that indicates that the customer bore the economic burden of the VAT.
- **Decline in profits**: if profits declined when VAT was added, that may indicate that the business bore the economic burden of the VAT.
- **VAT-registered customers**: if the majority of the claimant's customers are registered for VAT, it is far more likely that VAT has been passed on. Fully taxable VAT-registered traders are not VAT-sensitive and, as a result, it is likely that the claimant will have taken this into account when setting their prices.

If the supplier accepts (or HMRC proves) that they would be unjustly enriched, then HMRC will only refund the output VAT if the supplier enters into an agreement with HMRC to refund the VAT to its customers. The supplier must:

1. sign an undertaking in the format set out in section 10 of *VAT Notice 700/45*;
2. make all refunds to customers within 90 days;
3. repay any residual amounts not returned to customers after 90 days to HMRC within 14 days;
4. pass any statutory interest paid with the refunds to customers; this is subject to the same terms and conditions as the refund;
5. keep the following records: (i) names and addresses of those customers it intends to reimburse; (ii) the total amount of money paid to each customer; (iii) the amount of interest, if applicable, paid to each customer; and (iv) the date it refunded the money.

12.6.8   The capping rules

The capping rules act to limit your ability to make retrospective claims for overpayments made to HMRC. The capping rules work both ways, preventing you from reclaiming over-declared output VAT and under-claimed input VAT and preventing HMRC from assessing for underpaid output VAT or over-claimed input VAT. If the error arose despite taking reasonable care or as a result of a careless error, the capping rules from the taxpayer's perspective are as follows:

1. **Output VAT errors**: output VAT errors (over- or under-payment) cannot be corrected more than four years after the end of the VAT period in which the output VAT was accounted for.
2. **Under-claimed input VAT**: under-claimed input VAT cannot be claimed more than four years after the due date of the return for the period in which the VAT was chargeable, though if you could not claim at that time because

you did not hold an appropriate VAT invoice, the four-year time limit runs from the due date of the return in which the VAT invoice was received.

3. **Over-claimed input VAT**: errors resulting in an over-claim of input VAT cannot be corrected more than four years after the end of the VAT period in which the input VAT was over-claimed.

4. **Errors in a voluntary disclosure**: if you overpaid output VAT as a result of an erroneous voluntary disclosure, or as a result of an assessment based on an erroneous voluntary disclosure, the time limit is four years after the end of the VAT period in which the disclosure was made.

5. **Errors in HMRC assessments**: if you have overpaid output VAT as a result of an assessment (other than an assessment based on an erroneous voluntary disclosure), the time limit is four years after the end of the VAT period in which the assessment was made.

Deliberate errors

If the error was deliberate, the four-year limit above is replaced with 20 years.

Exceptions

The four-year cap does not apply in various situations including:

- the first return made following compulsory backdated registration;
- where the consideration for a supply is not fixed until four years after the supply took place, for example due to a belated discount;
- where a late VAT invoice is received from a supplier as a result of the supplier's backdated registration for VAT;
- penalties paid but which are shown not to be due;
- claims under the DIY house-builder scheme. These must be made within three months of completion; see 8.3.5 'DIY builders and convertors VAT refund scheme'.

Annual adjustment

HMRC explains the calculations required where the VAT period of the partial exemption annual adjustment is not capped but parts of the longer period concerned are capped (*PE4160*) as follows:

- Carry out the partial exemption calculations the business should have made (use the correct figures in the method in place at that time). Make adjustments for those periods which are not capped.
- Carry out the correct longer period adjustment as it should have made including, if applicable, any required re-attribution and *de minimis* calculations (in doing this you should use the corrected quarterly figures, even where corrections could not be assessed/repaid due to capping).

- Compare the correct longer-period adjustment with the correct partial exemption calculations for all the periods within the longer period. Any difference is your corrected annual adjustment.

12.7   THE EC SALES LIST

In addition to the VAT return (VAT 100) form, a UK VAT-registered business must complete an EC Sales List (VAT 101) for all of the following:

1. A supply of goods to a VAT-registered business in another EU state. This applies even if you didn't invoice for them – unless they count as samples under the VAT rules.
2. Removal of any of your own goods to a VAT-registered branch, office or subsidiary company that you own in another EU state.
3. If you give a VAT-registered customer in another EU state a credit note for goods – even if you didn't supply them with any goods in this period.
4. A supply of services to a VAT-registered EU business, where the place of supply is the customer's state and the supply is subject to the reverse charge in that state.

For each VAT-registered EU customer, you must list the following on the EC Sales List:

- The EU country code of the business (AU = Austria, etc., see 14.4 'VAT in other EU states' for a list).
- The VAT registration number of the customer. This should exclude the country code of the customer, or any spaces, dashes or commas.
- The total value of sales to this customer in the return period, expressed in sterling and rounded down to the nearest whole pound.
- The sale-type code as follows: 0 means a sale of goods, 2 means a triangulated sale in which you acted as an intermediate supplier (see 9.6.19 'Triangulation'), 3 means a reverse charge supply of services. If you make more than one type of sale to the same customer, you must list each type separately on the EC Sales List.

12.7.1   Simplified EC Sales List

If your business only makes a low level of supply of goods to VAT-registered customers in another EU country you may not need to fill in the full EC Sales List.

You can contact HMRC and ask for permission to submit a simplified annual EC Sales List, if all of these conditions are met:

- The value of your total taxable turnover in a year is not more than the VAT registration threshold plus £25,500.

- Your supplies to customers in other EU countries are not more than £11,000 a year.
- Your sales do not include **new means of transport**.

If HMRC agrees that you can use the simplified EC Sales List it means that you:

- never need to fill in the actual value of your supplies to each customer – instead you enter a nominal value of £1;
- only have to complete the form once a year – you agree with HMRC when you're going to send it in.

12.7.2 EC Sales List period

The EC Sales List can normally be submitted quarterly, though if you supply in excess of £35,000 of goods to VAT-registered EU customers you must submit monthly EC Sales Lists and you can request monthly returns.

If you make annual VAT returns you can contact HMRC to apply for approval to submit your EC Sales List once a year, provided you meet all of the following conditions:

1. your total annual taxable turnover does not exceed £145,000,
2. the annual value of your supplies to other EU countries is not more than £11,000, and
3. your sales do not include new means of transport.

Quarterly EC Sales Lists must be submitted for calendar quarters (three months to 31 March, 30 June, 30 September and 31 December), so the reporting periods may not coincide with your VAT return quarters. You can apply to HMRC to change your VAT return periods to coincide with your calendar quarterly EC Sales List period.

12.7.3 Return format

At the time of writing EC Sales Lists can be submitted using an online form, via uploading a data-file in one of various permitted formats (including csv or xml), or via a paper return.

12.7.4 Return deadline

If a paper return is submitted the deadline for receipt by HMRC is 14 days after the due date. If you submit electronically the deadline is 21 days.

12.7.5 **Errors in the EC Sales List**

You must tell HMRC about all errors and omissions on an EC Sales List where the total errors exceed £100, an incorrect VAT registration number has been quoted, or you have used the wrong transaction type indicator when completing the EC Sales List (or ESL).

You can download a form VAT 101B (ESL Corrections) from the HMRC website to notify of any errors made.

If you submit your EC Sales List online using the ECSL service, any errors are highlighted onscreen as you complete the form, allowing you to correct them prior to submission. If you choose to submit the EC Sales List with some errors still remaining, you will be able to correct these errors online, up to 21 days after the date of submission. After that date, the facility will no longer be available and any outstanding errors will be notified to you in writing, as explained below.

If you submit by CSV or XML you can still use the online correction service to correct error lines identified at the time of submission. Alternatively, if you decide to submit a new file, you must delete the error lines from your original submission within 21 days, using the 'Correct declaration errors' page on the ECSL Online Service, to avoid receiving correspondence on this subject.

12.7.6 **EC Sales List penalties**

If a supplier has failed to submit an EC Sales List, then HMRC may serve notice on the supplier, stating that they are in default in relation to the particular statement; and that (subject to below) no action will be taken if the default is remedied before the end of the period of 14 days beginning with the day after the notice date. If the person fails to remedy within 14 days then they become liable for a penalty. This is calculated on a daily rate as explained below. The person then becomes liable for a penalty without notice if they default again within 12 months.

The penalty rates are: £5 per day late if the first default, £10 per day if the second default and £15 per day if the third default, each subject to a cap of 100 days. There is a minimum penalty of £50.

If a supplier submits an EC Sales List containing a material inaccuracy, HMRC may, within six months of discovering the inaccuracy, issue the supplier with a written warning that future inaccurate returns might result in the serving of a notice under section 65 VAT Act 1994. If there is then a second inaccurate return made within two years of the day after the date of the warning, HMRC has six months from discovering the second inaccuracy in which to issue a notice stating that any future inaccuracies will attract a penalty. If there is then another inaccurate return and the due date is within two years of the penalty notice, then that return is subject to a £100 penalty.

However, the following are not regarded as material inaccuracies:

- where there is a reasonable excuse for the inaccuracy (see 12.6.5 'Reasonable excuse' for more on reasonable excuses);
- where the supplier corrects the inaccuracies at a time when they had no reason to believe that enquiries were being made by HMRC into the supplier's affairs;
- where the person is convicted of an offence by reason of submitting a statement containing a material inaccuracy by any person.

If a warning notice relates only to statements that contain immaterial inaccuracies, then it is deemed not to have been served.

12.8 DEALING WITH HMRC

It is always better to enquire whether or not a particular activity is going to be taxable, if there is any doubt at all. There are many activities undertaken by voluntary organisations which fall into 'grey areas'.

For general queries concerning charities phone the Charities helpline, and for other general queries phone the General VAT helpline (see 14.1 'Contacting HMRC' for phone numbers and addresses).

However, it may be risky to rely on telephone advice for significant issues or if significant amounts are involved. In such situations it may be preferable to get HMRC's advice in writing by making a written enquiry (including by email). Written enquiries concerning charities should be sent to HMRC charities office in Bootle, and there are also specialist offices for international supplies, the option to tax, registration and deregistration and VAT grouping. All other written enquiries should be addressed to the general enquiries service. The general enquiry service will pass your query on to the relevant office if it cannot deal with it itself.

When obtaining advice it is important that you disclose all potentially relevant information. If you fail to do this, HMRC may disregard its advice and assess you for any underpayment of VAT. If you have relied on written advice provided by HMRC that was based upon full disclosure of the facts, then, if that advice turns out to be incorrect, HMRC will generally not raise a backdated assessment.

12.8.1 HMRC assessments

If HMRC discovers a mistake in a VAT return or if you fail to submit a VAT return, they may raise an assessment for the VAT due. HMRC may estimate the amount due. It may therefore be to your advantage if you can agree with HMRC that you will perform any calculations involved and have them checked and confirmed by HMRC.

From 1 April 2009, HMRC must issue an assessment before the later of:

- two years after the end of the VAT return period; and
- one year after evidence of facts, sufficient in the opinion of HMRC to justify the making of an assessment, comes to their knowledge.

However, this is subject to an overall cap as follows:

- For cases involving deliberate under-declaration, fraud, failure to notify an obligation to register for VAT or loss due to use of a notifiable scheme which the taxpayer has failed to notify to HMRC (see 10.15 'Listed and hallmarked schemes'), the time limit is 20 years from the end of the relevant VAT period.
- For assessments relating to failure to submit a VAT return, failure to pay the full amount shown as due on the return, or for submission of an incorrect VAT return, the deadline is four years after the end of the VAT period concerned.
- If the assessment is made on an individual who has died, it must be made within four years of death.

12.8.2 **HMRC review**

Most decisions and assessments made by HMRC can be appealed to the tax tribunal (see 12.8.3 'The tax tribunal'). If a decision is appealable to the tax tribunal, then HMRC must offer a review of that decision and that offer must be made by notice given at the same time as the decision. HMRC (2010), *How to appeal against an HMRC decision – indirect tax*, states that it will offer you an opportunity to have the decision reviewed by an officer who was not previously involved in the original decision.

You then have 30 days, from the date of the document containing notification of the offer, to accept that offer, though HMRC can also issue a notice extending the deadline. However, you cannot accept an offer of review if you have already appealed to the tax tribunal.

The HMRC reviewer can decide to uphold the decision, vary it or cancel it. The HMRC reviewer must issue their decision within 45 days of HMRC receiving acceptance of the offer, though the parties can agree to extend this deadline. If HMRC does not complete its review within the 45 days (or longer agreed period) it will write to you explaining that the review is upheld. You will then have 30 days to send your appeal to the tax tribunal, if you wish to do so.

If you disagree with the decision reached by the review officer you can appeal to the tax tribunal. You need to do this within 30 days of the review conclusion letter (or the letter telling you that the review conclusion is treated as upholding the original decision). The tax tribunal can alter the decision if it thinks it is wrong.

12.8.3 **The tax tribunal**

A wide range of HMRC decisions can be appealed to the tax tribunal (which includes both the First-tier Tribunal and Upper Tribunal). These include: the amount of output VAT due, the amount of input VAT that can be recovered, and registration or cancellation of registration. However, notable exceptions are appeals relating to VAT refund schemes (s. 33, s. 33a, etc. of the VAT Act 1994). In addition, the role of the tax tribunal in relation to **legitimate expectation** (reliance on HMRC guidance or instructions) is limited, see 12.8.5 'Legitimate expectation'. The guidance below is taken from the Ministry of Justice guidance notes on completing the T241 TS-TaxApG1 form (HM Courts & Tribunals Service 2015).

Appeal deadline

If you have not accepted the offer of a review of HMRC's decision, or requested a review, you must appeal to the tribunal within 30 days of the date of the HMRC letter notifying you of the decision.

If you accepted the offer of a review, or requested a review, you must appeal within 30 days of the date of the HMRC letter notifying you of the conclusion of the review, or the notification from HMRC that the review is to be treated as having concluded that the decision is upheld, or (if you requested a late review) the date of HMRC's refusal of that request.

If you are not the person to whom the notice is addressed, but nevertheless have a right of appeal, you must appeal within 30 days of when you become aware of the decision.

Where a review is undertaken, you may not appeal to the tribunal until the earlier of the following:

- the date of the document notifying the conclusions of the review;
- if HMRC has undertaken a review, and the period of 45 days (or longer if agreed) has expired, the date of the document notifying you of the conclusion which the review is treated as having reached;
- if you requested a review out of time, and a review is not undertaken, the date on which HMRC decided not to undertake a review.

Late appeals

If you have been unable to make your appeal to the tribunal within the appropriate time limit, you can ask the tribunal for permission to appeal late. You must provide the reasons for the delay and why the tribunal should give you permission to appeal late. The tribunal will consider whether you have good reasons for making an appeal late and may or may not grant your request.

Payment of VAT

If the VAT in dispute has not been paid to HMRC, it needs to be paid or secured before the appeal can proceed, unless HMRC agrees that your appeal may proceed without payment because payment would cause you hardship. If HMRC does not agree, you may apply to the tribunal to make a direction that your appeal can proceed without payment. If HMRC has not granted a hardship application, your case cannot proceed before the tribunal until you either pay the tax in dispute or a direction to proceed is granted.

Costs

In most tax cases each side will pay its own costs. In certain circumstances, the tribunal may order one side to pay costs to the other. Those circumstances can include the case where one side has behaved unreasonably in the way it has carried out the case. Costs awards in those circumstances are quite rare. For appeals started before 1 April 2009, the tribunal has discretion to order that they continue to be covered by the rules which applied before 1 April 2009. If costs are granted against a party, that party cannot reclaim any of the VAT incurred by the other (see 3.3.9 'Who can reclaim input VAT').

Complex cases

There is a special rule that additionally applies to cases categorised by the tribunal as 'complex', where the winning party can ask for the losing party to pay its costs. However, you can choose to opt out of this rule, so that each party pays its own costs except where one side has behaved unreasonably. If your appeal is categorised as complex, you will be notified of this as soon as it has been categorised and given information about the implications, including your right to opt out of the complex costs rule. Applications for costs should be requested in writing no later than 28 days after the date on which the tribunal sends the decision notice or notice of withdrawal, and should be accompanied by a schedule of the costs and expenses claimed.

Appeal process

To make an appeal to the tax tribunal, you complete a notice of appeal form (T240 TS-TaxAp1), which can be downloaded from the Ministry of Justice website. This should be sent together with the disputed decision by post or by email to the HM Courts & Tribunals Service First-tier Tribunal (Tax) address, as shown on the form.

Fees for appeals to the First-tier Tribunal (Tax)

At the time of writing the government is proposing to introduce separate fees for both application to the First-tier Tribunal and for the actual hearing.

12.8.4 **The higher courts**

First-tier Tribunal decisions can be appealed on a point of law to the Upper-tier Tribunal (Tax) and then on up through the chain of courts all the way to the Supreme Court. However, the initial tribunal's findings on the facts of a case are usually final. Tribunals and courts can also refer questions to the CJEU, though such referrals can only be made by the tribunal or court and not by the parties.

The VAT Tribunal

Under the Tribunals, Courts and Enforcement Act 2007 all tribunals (tax and non-tax) were unified into a single structure with effect from 1 April 2009. Before then VAT cases were heard by the VAT and Duties Tribunal.

12.8.5 **Legitimate expectation**

> If you have clear guidance from HMRC that you should or can act in some way that later turns out to be wrong, then you may be able to reply on that guidance and avoid a retrospective VAT liability under the principle of **legitimate expectation**.

This can arise because, for example:

- HMRC staff instructed you to apply some VAT treatment that turns out to be wrong;
- you agreed with HMRC that you could apply some VAT treatment that turns out to be wrong;
- the HMRC guidance at the time clearly indicated that this treatment was applicable or acceptable.

This principle of **legitimate expectation** was explained as follows in the Court of Appeal case *R* v. *North and East Devon Health Authority* [1999] EWCA Civ 1871:

> Where the court considers that a lawful promise or practice has induced a legitimate expectation of a benefit which is substantive, not simply procedural, authority now establishes that . . . the court will in a proper case decide whether to frustrate the expectation is so unfair that to take a new and different course will amount to an abuse of power. Here, once the legitimacy of the expectation is

established, the court will have the task of weighing the requirements of fairness against any overriding interest relied upon for the change of policy.

In *Oxfam* v. *Revenue & Customs* [2009] EWHC 3078 (Ch), the High Court found that the First-tier Tribunal has jurisdiction in some cases to consider legitimate expectations arising out of the lawful exercise of its powers by HMRC (in accepting a business/non-business method). However, in *Revenue & Customs* v. *Noor* [2013] UKUT 71 (TCC), the Upper Tribunal decided that jurisdiction does not extend to a situation where HMRC acts beyond its powers, such as by giving a misdirection. Where HMRC acts beyond its powers, jurisdiction rests with the Upper-tier Tribunal, High Court (England & Wales) or Court of Sessions (Scotland).

12.9 VAT PENALTIES

HMRC can issue penalties for a wide range of VAT-related actions or inactions, including for:

- **errors in a VAT return**: see 12.9.2 'Penalties for an error in a VAT return';
- **failure to register for VAT on time**, see 12.9.3 'Penalties for failure to register for VAT on time';
- **failure to submit a VAT return on time or pay VAT on time**: these penalties are (at the time of writing) charged via the 'default surcharge' regime, see 12.6.4 'Late VAT returns and payments';
- **failures relating to the EC Sales List**: see 12.7.6 'EC Sales List penalties';
- **issuing an incorrect zero-rating certificate**, see 8.3.8 'Certificates';
- **failure to notify use of a 'listed' or 'hallmarked' VAT scheme**, see 10.15 'Listed and hallmarked schemes';
- **failure of assorted regulatory provisions** such as the failure to notify HMRC of the cessation of taxable supplies or of an intention to make taxable supplies after registration;
- **fraudulent VAT evasion** – this can attract penalties and/or prison sentences.

With VAT penalties it is important to check the up-to-date HMRC guidance at the time of your query, as the regime may have changed from the one described here. At the time of writing the entire tax penalties regime (for VAT and other taxes) is up for discussion via an HMRC (2015) paper (*HMRC Penalties: a Discussion Document*). This envisages moving towards a more automated digital penalty system to reflect changes in the way HMRC works. For example, in respect of the behavioural penalties (see 12.9.1 'Behavioural penalties') the document states:

> Many of these penalties were designed at a time when most tax enquiries were undertaken with our customers in person. With new digital ways of working increasingly making it quicker and easier for customers to deal with us online, we want to ensure our system adapts to this new way of working.

12.9.1 **Behavioural penalties**

The penalty regime for errors in a VAT return and failure to register for VAT on time are 'behavioural' penalties, introduced with effect from 1 April 2009 for errors in VAT returns and extended to failure to register for VAT on time with effect from 1 April 2010. The same regime also covers inaccuracies in a variety of other tax returns.

Article 6 rights

The behavioural penalties are designed to change behaviour and are deliberately punitive. HMRC accepts (*CH300200*) that, where penalties have a maximum rate of at least 70% (i.e. for deliberate errors but not for careless errors), such penalties are classed as criminal for the purposes of the European Convention on Human Rights (ECHR) Article 6. However, in *Jussila v. Finland* 73053/01 [2006] ECHR 996, the appellant was subjected to VAT surcharges equivalent to 10% of the under-assessed VAT with a maximum rate of 20%. The ECHR held that the surcharges were not intended as pecuniary compensation for damage but as a punishment to deter re-offending. It concluded that, without more evidence, this establishes the criminal nature of the offence.

Article 6 ECHR gives a person subject to a criminal charge the following rights:

- to a fair and public hearing within a reasonable time by an independent and impartial tribunal established by law;
- a presumption of innocence until proved guilty by the law. This means the burden of proof rests on HMRC, though the standard of proof is civil (balance of probabilities) not criminal;
- to be informed promptly, in a language which the person understands and in detail, of the nature and cause of the accusation;
- to have adequate time and facilities for the preparation of any defence;
- to defend in person or through legal assistance of the person's own choosing or, if the person has not sufficient means to pay for legal assistance, to be given it free when the interests of justice so require;
- to examine witnesses against and to obtain the attendance and examination of witnesses for under the same conditions;
- to have the free assistance of an interpreter if the person cannot understand or speak the language used in court.

12.9.2 **Penalties for errors in a VAT return**

The VAT penalty regime for inaccuracies in a VAT return changed with effect from 1 April 2009. The level of penalty depends on the taxpayer's behaviour and is expressed as a percentage of the net VAT due to HMRC. If the error results in a net amount due from HMRC or a nil amount due to HMRC there is no penalty. If the error results in a net amount due to HMRC the penalties are:

Type of behaviour	Maximum penalty rate	Minimum penalty rate	
		Unprompted disclosure	Prompted disclosure
Error despite reasonable care	No penalty	–	–
Careless error	30%	0%	15%
Deliberate but not concealed error	70%	20%	35%
Deliberate and concealed error	100%	30%	50%

However, if the error is a timing error, resulting in VAT being paid to HMRC later than it should have been, the penalty is 5% of the net VAT due to HMRC for each year of delay.

Reasonable care

If the error occurred despite taking reasonable care, then no penalty is due. The test refers to what a reasonable taxpayer, exercising reasonable diligence in the completion and submission of the return, would have done in the circumstances.

HMRC accepts that the level of care that is reasonable depends on the circumstances (*CH81120*):

Every person must take reasonable care, but 'reasonable care' cannot be identified without consideration of the particular person's abilities and circumstances. HMRC recognises the wide range of abilities and circumstances of those persons completing returns or claims.

So whilst each person has a responsibility to take reasonable care, what is necessary for each person to discharge that responsibility has to be viewed in the light of that person's abilities and circumstances.

For example, we do not expect the same level of knowledge or expertise from a self-employed un-represented individual as we do from a large multinational company. We would expect a higher degree of care to be taken over large and complex matters than simple straightforward ones.

HMRC expects each person to make and preserve sufficient records for them to make a correct and complete return. A person with simple, straightforward tax affairs needs only a simple regime provided they follow it carefully. But a person with larger and more complex tax affairs will need to put in place more sophisticated systems and follow them equally carefully.

In HMRC's view it is reasonable to expect a person who encounters a transaction or other event with which they are not familiar to take care to find out about the correct tax treatment or to seek appropriate advice. If after that the person is still unsure they should draw attention to the entry and the uncertainty when they send the return or document to us. In these circumstances the person will have taken reasonable care to draw our attention to the point and if they are wrong they will not have been carelessly so.

Examples: reasonable care

HMRC accepts that the following are capable of being errors despite reasonable care (*CH81130*)

- a reasonably arguable view of situations that is subsequently not upheld
- an arithmetical or transposition inaccuracy that is not so large, either in absolute terms or relative to overall liability, as to produce an obviously odd result or be picked up by a quality check
- following advice from HMRC that later proves to be wrong, provided that all the details and circumstances were given when the advice was sought
- acting on advice from a competent adviser which proves to be wrong despite the fact that the adviser was given a full set of accurate facts
- accepting and using information from another person where it is not possible to check that the information is accurate and complete

---

Insignificant processing or coding errors

HMRC staff are instructed (CH 81130) to treat a person as taking reasonable care if:

- arrangements or systems (such as comprehensive internal accounting systems and controls with specific reference to tax-sensitive areas) exist that, if followed, could reasonably be expected to produce an accurate basis for the calculation of tax due by the internal tax department, or external agent, and
- despite the above, inaccuracies arise in processing or coding items through the person's accounting system which result in a mis-statement of tax liability, and
- the effect of the inaccuracies is not significant in relation to the person's overall tax liability for the relevant tax period.

Careless, deliberate and concealed errors

A careless error is one that is due to a failure to take reasonable care, but is not deliberate or concealed. An error in a return which was neither careless nor deliberate when the return was submitted, is treated as careless if the taxpayer discovered the inaccuracy at some later time, and did not take reasonable steps to inform HMRC.

A deliberate but not concealed error occurs if the inaccuracy is deliberate but the taxpayer does not make arrangements to conceal it.

Disclosure

A person discloses an inaccuracy by: telling HMRC about it; giving HMRC reasonable help in quantifying the inaccuracy; and allowing HMRC access to records for the purpose of ensuring that the inaccuracy is fully corrected.

Disclosure is unprompted if made at a time when the person making it has no reason to believe that HMRC has discovered or is about to discover the inaccuracy.

Penalty reductions

HMRC will give a penalty reduction depending on the quality of the disclosure and the assistance and access it receives in calculating the error as follows. The percentage below is the percentage of the maximum reduction available (*CH82442, CH82450* and *CH82460*):

Up to	For:
30%	telling HMRC about the error. Telling includes: admitting that the document was inaccurate or that there was an under-assessment, disclosing the inaccuracy in full, explaining how and why the inaccuracy arose.
40%	helping HMRC. This includes: giving reasonable help in quantifying the inaccuracy or under-assessment, positive assistance as opposed to passive acceptance or obstruction, actively engaging in the work to accurately quantify the inaccuracies, and volunteering any information relevant to the disclosure.
30%	giving HMRC access. This includes a person responding positively to HMRC requests for information and documents and allowing access to their business and other records and other relevant documents.

Special circumstances

If HMRC thinks it right because of 'special circumstances', HMRC may reduce a penalty below the minimum, stay a penalty or agree a compromise in relation to proceedings for a penalty. However, special circumstances do not include the ability to pay or the fact that a potential loss of revenue from one taxpayer is balanced by a potential over-payment by the other.

For circumstances to be special they must be exceptional, abnormal or unusual (decided in *Bluu Solutions Ltd* v. *Revenue & Customs* [2015] UKFTT 95 (TC)). HMRC also accepts that it includes where a result is produced that is contrary to the clear compliance intention of the penalty law (*CH170600*).

Suspended penalties

HMRC may also suspend a part or the whole of a careless error penalty for up to two years if compliance with a condition of suspension would help the taxpayer to avoid becoming liable to further careless error penalties. This includes careless errors for other taxes such as Income Tax and Corporation Tax.

A condition of suspension may specify action to be taken, and a period within which it must be taken. On the expiry of the period of suspension, if the taxpayer satisfies HMRC that the conditions of suspension have been complied with, the suspended penalty or part is cancelled. Otherwise the suspended penalty or part becomes payable. However, if, during the period of suspension, the taxpayer becomes liable for another careless error penalty (including for Income Tax, Corporation Tax, etc.), the suspended penalty or part becomes payable.

Suspension conditions

HMRC provides the following guidance to their staff on setting conditions (*CH83154*):

> Where inaccuracies arose because existing systems or record-keeping processes were not good enough to ensure a correct return, you may set a suspension condition requiring the person to introduce or improve a system or process

> Where inaccuracies arose because staff were not using existing systems or record-keeping processes correctly, you may set a condition that the person provides additional training for the staff. But providing the training is only part of the answer. You also need to be sure that the training is effective. You therefore need to consider another condition that focuses on the business taking appropriate steps to control the risk of the error recurring. If this can be demonstrated, the person will have met this condition.

In *Fane* v. *Revenue & Customs* [2011] UKFTT 210 (TC), the First-tier Tribunal stated that a condition of suspension must contain something more than just a basic requirement that tax returns should be free from careless inaccuracies. The condition of suspension must contain a more practical and measurable condition (such as improvement to systems) which would help the taxpayer to achieve the statutory objective, i.e. the tax returns should be free from errors caused by a failure to exercise reasonable care. In *Boughey* v. *Revenue & Customs* [2012] UKFTT 398 (TC), the taxpayer made a one-off error in relation to Income Tax on a redundancy payment and HMRC argued that it had to set a condition specific to redundancy payments and it was unable to do so as they were unlikely to recur. However, the Tribunal rejected this. HMRC had proceeded on the erroneous legal basis that any condition of suspension must be designed to ensure that, in the future, the taxpayer correctly declared the receipt of any redundancy payments. However, the condition must help prevent all careless error penalties (for all relevant taxes), so it need not be specific to the type of error or even tax involved. The First-tier Tribunal accepted that the taxpayer's proposal to have his Income Tax return prepared by a qualified accountant was designed to or would assist in the submitting of accurate Income Tax returns and suspended the penalty for two years.

12.9.3 Penalties for failure to register for VAT on time

If you should have registered for VAT at some point in the past, then you are treated as having been registered for VAT from that point and having to account for output VAT on taxable supplies and being able to recover input VAT on attributable purchases. This is explained in more detail at 2.1.12 'Late registration'.

If late VAT registration results in a net amount of VAT due to HMRC, then a penalty may be due to HMRC as follows:

Type of behaviour	Maximum penalty rate	Minimum penalty rate	
		Unprompted disclosure	Prompted disclosure
Occurred despite reasonable care	No penalty	–	–
Careless	30%	0%	15%
Deliberate but not concealed	70%	20%	35%
Deliberate and concealed	100%	30%	50%

The penalty structure and regime are similar to that for errors in VAT returns (see 12.9.2 'Penalties for errors in a VAT return') and the same concepts of reasonable care, deliberate, concealed, prompted and unprompted disclosure apply.

Reasonable excuse

There is no penalty if the failure to register for VAT is not deliberate and there is a reasonable excuse. See 12.6.5 'Reasonable excuse'. However:

- an insufficiency of funds is never a reasonable excuse, unless attributable to events outside the business's control;
- where the business relies on another person to do anything, that is not a reasonable excuse unless the business took reasonable care to avoid the failure;
- where the business had a reasonable excuse, but that excuse has ceased, the business is treated as having continued having the excuse if the failure is remedied without unreasonable delay after the excuse ceased.

12.10   BLOCKED INPUT VAT

There are two key areas where input VAT recovery is blocked by special rules: **business entertaining** and motor vehicles. Each of these areas is considered below.

12.10.1   Business entertaining

Input VAT incurred on most types of **business entertaining** is 'blocked' – this means it cannot be recovered, even if it is attributable to a taxable activity.

> **Business entertainment** means the provision, in the course of a business activity, of free entertainment to people who are not employees. Entertainment includes food, drink, accommodation and entrance to events. If entertainment is incidentally supplied to employees then the associated input VAT is also blocked, for example a restaurant meal for customers at which staff are present.

Input VAT is not blocked if it relates to the following:

1. Entertainment for overseas customers if it is reasonable in scale and character. Overseas customer means any customer not ordinarily resident or carrying on a business in the UK, including the Isle of Man.
2. Subsistence expenses paid to employees while travelling for business purposes.
3. Staff entertainment such as annual parties, team-building exercises and outings, though if attendance at the event is restricted to the directors or partners of a business the input VAT may be blocked.
4. Entertainment provided by clubs and associations which is available to all eligible members without specific charge. This is considered to be part of the benefits received in return for payment of the appropriate membership subscription.
5. Free drinks given to customers paying for meals at a restaurant or similar establishment.
6. Entertainment provided by local authorities at civic functions.
7. Entertainment of a non-personal nature provided freely by a store, or similar establishment, to members of the general public to attract custom or to advertise a trader's premises. This includes hiring circus performers, musicians, or other entertainers but does not apply to promotional events where customers attend by invitation only.
8. VAT on necessary meals and accommodation provided by recognised representative sporting bodies to amateur sports persons chosen to represent that body in a competition (*VAT Notice 48*, section 3.10).

12.10.2 Purchasing cars

Where an organisation buys cars for use by its employees, recovery of input VAT on the purchase of the car is completely blocked if the car is intended to be available for private use. The test is not whether the car is actually put to private use, but whether it is available for private use. To avoid being available for private use there must be physical or legal barriers that prevent it, the barriers must be enforced and they must be effective. Though it is possible to make a car unavailable for private use, the many tribunal and court cases on this subject demonstrate that this is far from easy. HMRC accepts (*VIT52700*) that pool cars are not available for private use provided the car is:

- usually kept at the principal place of business;
- not allocated to an individual; and
- not kept at an employee's home.

Even if the car is unavailable for private use, input VAT recovery may be restricted by the normal VAT rules if there is any use for exempt or non-business activities.

Input VAT is also blocked on optional accessories bought at the same time as the car, though if bought afterwards the input VAT is not automatically blocked. However, even when input VAT on purchase costs is blocked, input VAT on maintenance costs is recoverable subject to the normal recovery rules.

If a car on which input VAT was blocked is sold, no output VAT should be charged on the sale. If no input VAT was charged when purchasing the car, for example, if it was bought second-hand from an unregistered person, then the car can be sold under the second-hand margin scheme (see 10.13 'Margin schemes').

12.10.3 Leasing cars

If an organisation leases a car for 10 days or fewer, then VAT on the leasing cost is not blocked. If the lease is for a longer period and the car is available for private use, then 50% of the VAT is blocked. Charges for maintenance and excess mileage by the leasing company may avoid the 50% block if they are identified separately on the invoice.

Where VAT on a leased car is blocked and the car is partly used for non-business or exempt activities, then the VAT should be attributed in the following order:

- first, apportion the VAT between business and non-business use
- 50% of the VAT attributable to business use is then blocked
- apportion the unblocked VAT between exempt and taxable use.

12.10.4 Private use of company cars

If input VAT was blocked on the purchase or lease of a company car, then the organisation does not have to charge itself output VAT on the private usage. However, if input VAT on the purchase or lease of a car was not blocked and the car is actually put to private use, there is a taxable supply by the organisation to the private user.

Even if the organisation makes no actual charge to the private user, it must account for output VAT on the supply. HMRC states (*VAT Notice 700/64*, section 6.4) that the output VAT should be based either on the organisation's costs incurred in making the vehicle available for private use (such as depreciation, repairs and running costs) or on one of the HMRC agreements with the motor trade set out in *VAT Notice 700/57*.

12.10.5 Fuel payments

If an employer pays for fuel used by its employees and recovers the VAT on that fuel, then if any of that fuel is put to private use by any employee, there is a **deemed supply** of the fuel by the employer to the employee on which the employer must account for output VAT to HMRC.

The car may be owned by the organisation or by the employee and the employer may pay for fuel directly, for example by providing staff with company credit cards or company fuel cards, or it may refund employees for the fuel they purchase personally.

If the employer refunds the employee, then, irrespective of the way in which the employee is refunded, the employee must obtain a VAT invoice for the fuel and give this to the employer in order for the employer to be able to deduct any input VAT. HMRC accepts (*VAT Notice 700/64*, section 8.9) that in practice fuel invoices are unlikely to match the amounts claimed, but suggests that employers instruct employees who make fuel claims to obtain VAT invoices for all fuel purchases. The total amount on the invoices must equal or exceed the amount claimed and the invoices should predate the claim.

Possible fuel payment scenarios are:

1. All fuel is used for the employer's activities. There is no private use of the fuel by the employee. The employer can recover VAT on the fuel subject to the normal VAT recovery rules.
2. The employee makes private use of some of the fuel. The employer can:
   - recover all of the VAT incurred on the fuel and apply the **Fuel Scale Charge** (see 12.10.7 'Fuel Scale Charge' for more on the Fuel Scale Charge); or
   - apportion the fuel between the employee's private use and use for the employer's activities by keeping mileage records. The VAT on the fuel apportioned to private use is irrecoverable. The VAT on the fuel apportioned to employer activities is recoverable subject to the normal VAT recovery rules; there is no need to apply the Fuel Scale Charge;
   - claim none of the VAT incurred on the fuel; there is then no need to keep mileage records or apply the Fuel Scale Charge.

12.10.6　Advisory fuel rates

HMRC publishes advisory fuel rates which can be used to calculate the fuel component of a mileage allowance. The rates are based on engine size and fuel type (petrol, diesel or LPG) and change regularly. You should check the HMRC website for the latest rates.

Example: advisory fuel rates

Medical Assistance Charity pays an employee a mileage allowance of 45p per mile for 200 miles business travel in the employee's car which has a 1400cc petrol engine. The advisory fuel rate for a 1400cc petrol engine at the date of the claim is 14p per mile.

The deemed fuel component of the allowance is 14p × 200 = £28

This includes VAT, so the associated input VAT is (assuming a standard rate of VAT of 20%) 1/6 × £28 = £4.67

Medical Assistance Charity may treat this as purchase VAT and recover subject to the normal VAT recovery rules, as long as the employee provides one or more VAT invoices dated on or before the date of the claim to cover the fuel (totalling at least £28 including VAT).

12.10.7 Fuel Scale Charge

The Fuel Scale Charge can be used to determine the VAT-inclusive value of the deemed supply that is made when fuel is put to private use. The organisation can recover all the VAT charged on the fuel as input VAT. However, the organisation must charge itself the fuel scale charge as output VAT.

This avoids the need to keep mileage records, though if private use is small it is likely to be more expensive than exact apportionment.

One of the main problems with the Fuel Scale Charge is that, where the business is partly exempt and cannot recover all of the input VAT it incurs on road fuel, this can lead to results that are unfair – output VAT is payable in full on the private use of road fuel when input VAT was only partly deductible when the assets were acquired. Up to 1 January 2014 an HMRC concession (*PE4450*) addressed this, allowing the output VAT charge to be apportioned using the partial exemption recovery rate. With effect from then this concession is removed and HMRC has provided the following advice (HMRC 2012, *HMRC VAT: Road Fuel Scale Charges* (summary of responses)):

Possible ways of continuing to enjoy a fair and reasonable level of VAT recovery

Road Fuel Scale Charges are optional and taxpayers have the options of either not claiming any VAT on road fuel or keeping mileage records to establish what fuel is incurred on business journeys instead.

Claiming no input tax is only likely to give an acceptable answer where taxpayers have very low partial exemption recovery rates. This is because it leaves taxpayers getting no deduction of input tax in relation to business journeys.

Keeping mileage records will allow road fuel to only be included in business assets to the extent that it is used in business journeys. As no business road fuel will be used in private journeys no scale charges will arise.

Some taxpayers may find that keeping mileage records will impose an administrative burden disproportionate to the VAT they will be able to recover, particularly taxpayers with low partial exemption recovery rates. In such cases a solution that operates via their partial exemption method may be preferable.

Most partly exempt businesses with low recovery rates and significant input tax on road fuel will have special methods for partial exemption. HMRC will consider requests for inclusion of a road fuel scale charge sector in such special methods. The sector would accept only a portion of road fuel input tax, and would fully recover that input tax. That portion of input tax would reflect the use of road fuel in private journeys. HMRC accepts that in the majority of cases the input tax incurred on private journey road fuel will be equal to the scale charges payable.

Fuel Scale charge history

Since 1 May 2007 the fuel scale charge has been based on the car's CO_2 rating. Before 1 May 2007 it was based on the car's engine capacity and type of fuel. For new cars the CO_2 rating is shown on the registration certificate issued by the DVLA. Alternatively, you can search by make and model at: carfueldata.direct.gov.uk. For very old cars that do not have an official CO_2 rating, the scale charge is based on the engine's capacity. See *VAT Notice 700/64* for up-to-date details of scale charge rates.

HMRC provides three tables of scale charges – one for use with monthly VAT returns, one for use with quarterly VAT returns and one for use with annual VAT returns. If an employee starts or stops using a car in a return period or changes car you can apportion the scale charge.

12.11 SAGE 50 T-CODES

Many small and medium-sized voluntary organisations use Sage 50 Accounts (previously called Sage Line 50) to manage their finances. Sage 50 is primarily designed for commercial businesses; however, it can be adapted to the needs of organisations that have a mix of non-business, exempt and taxable activities.

12.11.1 Default T-codes

Sage 50 manages VAT by using 'T-codes'. There are 100 T-codes available (T0–T99). Every transaction is assigned a T-code, and the T-code determines the transaction's VAT treatment. By default, Sage 50's T-codes are as follows:

Tax code	Description: SR = standard-rated, RR = reduced-rated, ZR = zero-rated	Rate of VAT	In use	Rev chg	EC
T0	Zero-rated transactions (ZR)	0%	Y	N	N
T1	Standard-rated transactions (SR)	20%	Y	N	N
T2	Exempt transactions	0%	Y	N	N
T4	Sale of goods to VAT-registered EC customers	0%	Y	N	SG
T5	Reduced-rated transactions (RR)	5%	Y	N	N
T7	ZR purchases of goods from EC suppliers	T0	Y	N	PG
T8	SR purchases of goods from EC suppliers	T1	Y	N	PG
T9	Non-VATable transactions	0%	N	N	N
T20	Reverse charge	T1	Y	Y	N
T22	Sales of services to VAT-registered EC customers	0%	Y	N	SS
T23	ZR purchases of services from EC suppliers	T0	Y	N	PS
T24	SR purchases of services from EC suppliers	T1	Y	N	PS
T25	Flat Rate Capital Asset	20%	Y	N	N

- **Rate, In use, Rev chg** and **EC** are the T-code settings, accessed by double clicking on the T-code's entry on the Tax Codes tab of Sage's Configuration Editor. This brings up the **Edit Tax Code** dialog box (a pop up window that allows you to change each of these settings).
- **Rate of VAT**: this determines how Sage 50 calculates the associated VAT. Use of another T-code indicates that the T-code's rate is linked to the other T-code's rate.
- **In use flag**: this determines whether or not associated transactions are included in the VAT return. When you activate Sage's VAT routine, it will analyse the postings to the Purchase and Sales Tax Control accounts and compile the VAT return. It will ignore transactions coded to T9 (In use = 'N'), but include transactions coded to the other T-codes where In use = 'Y'.
- **Rev chg**: this indicates that the code is used for the intra-UK reverse charge on bulk transactions in computer chips, mobile phones, etc.
- For **EC settings** and codes T4, T7, T8, T22, T23 and T24 see 12.11.4 'Cross-border T-codes'

12.11.2   Problems with the default T-code structure

In preparing the VAT return Sage 50 assumes that all input VAT posted to the purchase tax control account is recoverable. If you have non-business or exempt activities this is unlikely to be the case. You will need to know the input VAT attributable to exempt and non-business activities and also, if you are using a 'standard' income-based non-business method or partial exemption method (see Chapter 3 'Recovering VAT'), the income (excluding VAT) attributable to non-business and exempt activities.

Sage's default T-code structure will not necessarily provide you with this information. However, the T-codes can be adapted to do so. The following is an example of a T-code structure that could be used to provide this information for an organisation with a mix of taxable, exempt and non-business activities and that uses the 'standard' income-based methods to apportion residual VAT.

12.11.3 Example T-codes for mixed activities

Tax code	Description: ZR = zero-rated, RR = reduced-rated, SR = standard-rated	Rate of VAT	In use	Rev chg	EC
T0	Zero-rated income (ZR)	0%	Y	N	N
T1	Standard-rated income (SR)	20%	Y	N	N
T2	Exempt income	0%	Y	N	N
T3	Non-business income	0%	Y	N	N
T4	Omitted non-business income	0%	Y	N	N
T5	SR purchases directly attributable to taxable activities	20%	Y	N	N
T6	SR purchases directly attributable to exempt activities	20%	Y	N	N
T7	SR purchases directly attributable to non-business activities	20%	Y	N	N
T8	SR residual purchases & overheads	20%	Y	N	N
T9	Non-VATable transactions	0%	N	N	N
T10	RR residual purchases & overheads	5%	Y	N	N
T11	Standard-rated sales of capital assets	20%	Y	N	N
T12	Reportable non-VAT-bearing purchases	0%	Y	N	N

T0–T4 and T11 income codes

These codes are used to identify the different types of income. Only income coded to T1 or T11 should generate any output VAT. The net income coded to T0, T1, T2 and T11 is entered into box 6 on the VAT return. As the level of non-business income is required for the business/non-business split, it is coded to T3 rather than T9. As T3 is in use, this ensures that the level of non-business income is recorded in the Sage VAT reports. Code T4 is used to record non-business income that can be omitted from any business/non-business apportionment such as bank interest (see 3.1 'VAT recovery principles' for more on this). T11 is used for standard-rated sales of capital assets that must be omitted from the business/non-business method and standard partial exemption method (see 3.2.4 'Excluded supplies').

T5–T10 and T12 purchase codes

T5–T10 and T12 purchase codes are used to identify the different types of purchase. VAT on purchases that relate directly to taxable activities is recoverable. By coding standard-rated purchases that relate directly to taxable activities to a separate code (T5), the related recoverable VAT can be easily identified. If the organisation has exempt activities a separate code is created for standard-rated purchases directly attributable to exempt activities (T6). The VAT posted to T6 will feed into the *de minimis* computation. Standard-rated purchases directly attributable to non-business activities are coded to T7. The VAT posted to T7 will not normally be recoverable (that is unless a section 33 VAT recovery scheme applies, for which see Chapter 10).

For overheads and other types of expense that include VAT but which cannot be directly attributed to a particular type of activity there are two codes: T8 for standard-rated costs and T10 for reduced-rated fuel and power (if applicable, see 6.5.5 'Fuel and power'). If any reduced-rated costs are directly attributable to a particular type of activity you will need to create a separate T-code for these. T12 is used for expenditure on which no VAT is incurred and which needs to be reported in box 7 of the VAT return (for example a purchase of zero-rated printed matter for a business activity).

T9

Code T9 is used for other transactions that do not have any associated VAT and that do not need to be reported. Examples include salaries, PAYE, National Insurance payments and business rates.

12.11.4 **Cross-border T-codes**

By default Sage 50 includes the codes set out below to deal with cross-border supplies. As T4, T7 and T8 are used for other purposes in the example structure above, their functions would have to be assigned to unused codes.

Code	Description (SR = standard rate, ZR = zero rate)	Rate	In use	Rev chg	EC
T4	Sale of goods to VAT-registered EU customers	0%	Y	N	SG
T7	ZR purchases of goods from EU suppliers	T0	Y	N	PG
T8	SR purchases of goods from EU suppliers	T1	Y	N	PG
T22	Sales of services to EC customers	0%	Y	N	SS
T23	ZR purchases of services from EC suppliers	T0	Y	N	PS
T24	SR purchases of services from EC suppliers	T1	Y	N	PS

- **EC:** this flag indicates a T-code used for intra-EU supplies, though T23 and T24 can also be used for purchases from outside the EU that are subject to the UK reverse charge. To enable cross-border functionality, check the tick box 'Enable EC code' in the code's Edit Tax Code dialog box. SS = sales of services, PS = purchase of services, SG = sales of goods, PG = purchases of goods.
- **T4** (amended as required): use this code for sales of goods to EU customers that are locally registered for VAT. Updates VAT return box 8 (sales of goods to VAT-registered businesses in other EU states) and box 6 (total sales). If the customer is assigned an EC VAT number, the sale is added to the EC Sales List.
- **T7** (amended as required): use this code for purchases of goods from VAT-registered EU suppliers that are zero-rated in the UK (such as printed books and children's clothes). Updates VAT return box 9 (acquisitions of goods from other EU states) and box 7 (total purchases).
- **T8** (amended as required): use this code for purchases of goods from VAT-registered EU suppliers that are standard-rated in the UK (i.e. excluding printed books, children's clothes, etc.). Updates VAT return box 2 (acquisition VAT due) using the tax rate applied to T1, box 4 (input VAT claimed), box 9 (acquisitions of goods from other EU states) and box 7 (total purchases).

- **T22**: use this code for sales of services to customers in other EU states that are subject to VAT in the customer's state under the reverse charge. Updates VAT return box 6 (total sales). If the customer is assigned an EC VAT number, the sale is listed in the EC Sales List. If the customer is not assigned an EC VAT number, the sale is not listed in the EC Sales List.
- **T23**: use this code for purchases of services from non-UK suppliers that are subject to zero-rated VAT in the UK under the UK reverse charge (for example a purchase of advertising services by a UK charity). Updates VAT return box 6 (total sales) and box 7 (total purchases).
- **T24**: use this code for purchases of services from non-UK suppliers that are subject to standard-rated VAT in the UK under the UK reverse charge. Note that the reverse charge applies to purchases from non-EU suppliers as well as EU suppliers. Updates VAT return box 1 (output VAT due), box 4 (input VAT claimed), box 6 (total sales) and box 7 (total purchases).

13 Cases

13.1 *APPLE AND PEAR DEVELOPMENT COUNCIL*

The Apple and Pear Development Council was a statutory body set up to promote and improve the quality of apples and pears grown in England and Wales. It charged a mandatory levy to apple and pear growers, based on their acreage under cultivation. UK Customs claimed the levy was **consideration** (everything that is paid to the supplier in return for making the supply of goods or services) for promotional services to the growers by the Council. The CJEU held that the concept of a supply of goods or services effected 'for consideration' presupposes the existence of a direct link between the goods or services provided and the consideration received. In case C-102/86 *Apple and Pear Development Council* v. *Customs & Excise* [1988] UKHL ECR 1443, the CJEU decided that in the Council's case there was a weight of factors which indicated that there was no direct link between the levy and promotional services:

- the benefits deriving from the services accrued to the whole industry and any benefits derived by individual growers derived indirectly from those accruing to the industry as a whole
- there was no relationship between the level of the benefits individual growers obtained from the services and the amount of the mandatory charges
- the charges were imposed by virtue of a statutory, and not a contractual, obligation and were recoverable from each individual grower whether or not a given service of the Council conferred a benefit on the grower.

This was in contrast to the voluntary Kingdom Scheme run by the Council, which promoted the sale of top quality apples. Apart from an initial government grant, the Kingdom Scheme was self-financing and growers voluntarily paid for services directed to their specific products. The English courts had already found this to be a supply for consideration and the Kingdom Scheme was not referred to the CJEU.

13.2 *ARMBRECHT*

In the *Armbrecht* case (C-291/92 *Finanzamt Uelzen* v. *Dieter Armbrecht* [1995] ECR I-02775), Mr Armbrecht, a hotelier, owned a hotel building comprising a guesthouse, a restaurant and a private **dwelling** (see 8.3.1 'Terminology'). He opted to tax the building (with the result that its sale would become taxable rather than exempt). When he sold the business he charged VAT on the sale of the guesthouse and restaurant but treated the sale of the dwelling as **outside the scope** of VAT. The tax authorities claimed for VAT on the sale of the dwelling as well.

The CJEU held that it is clear from the Principal VAT Directive that a taxable person must act 'as such' for a transaction to be subject to VAT. A taxable person performing a transaction in a private capacity does not act as a taxable person. The transaction is not, therefore, subject to VAT. Nor is a taxable person precluded from retaining part of an item of property amongst their private assets and excluding it from the VAT system. The taxable person must, however, throughout their period of ownership of the property in question, demonstrate an intention to retain it amongst their private assets. This makes it possible for a taxable person to choose whether or not to integrate into their business part of an asset which is given over to their private use.

The CJEU also held that, as far as VAT recovery on an apportioned asset is concerned, any apportionment between the part allocated to the taxable person's business activities and the part retained for private use must be based on the proportions of private and business use in the year of acquisition and not on a geographical division.

13.3 *AUTO LEASE HOLLAND*

In case C-185/01 *Auto Lease Holland BV* v. *Bundesamt für Finanzen* [2003] ECR I-01317, a car leasing company offered lessees a fuel card which enabled them to purchase fuel in Auto Lease's name. The fuel suppliers invoiced Auto Lease for the fuel and Auto Lease invoiced its lessees. The dispute was whether the fuel was supplied to Auto Lease or to the lessees. The CJEU held that, in order to decide this, it was necessary to determine who actually has the right to dispose of the fuel as owner. The CJEU decided that this was the lessee. They obtained the fuel directly at filling stations and Auto Lease did not at any time have the right to decide in what way the fuel must be used or to what end. The lessee also bore the full cost of the fuel. The fuel-card agreement was not for a supply of fuel, but rather a contract to finance its purchase. Auto Lease did not purchase the fuel in order subsequently to resell it to the lessee; the lessee purchased the fuel, having a free choice as to its quality and quantity, as well as the time of purchase. Auto Lease acted as a supplier of credit vis-à-vis the lessee.

However, in *Minister Finansów* v. *Wojskowa Agencja Mieszkaniowa w Warszawie* [2015], the CJEU distinguished the situation where a landlord contracts with utility providers to provide water, gas, electricity, etc. to supply utilities which the landlord then resupplies to tenants. Even though the tenants ultimately consume the utilities, it is the landlord who determines and is directly liable for the quantity, quality and timing of the utility company supplies. So the goods are supplied by the utility companies to the landlord and then resupplied by the landlord to the tenants.

13.4   *BATH FESTIVALS TRUST*

In the case *Bath Festivals Trust* [2008] VTD 20840, a charity entered into a service level agreement with a district authority under which it was required to put on a variety of cultural events in return for what was expressed to be a consideration. The requirements included the provision of box office services for third-party-organised cultural events in the area. HMRC argued that the funding was an outside-the-scope-of-VAT grant, the Trust argued that it was consideration for a business supply. The agreement set out the number and nature of the events to be put on and set targets to be achieved such as increasing the number of people aged up to 25 attending events to 20% of total attendees. The VAT Tribunal considered the key issue to be the provisions in the service level agreements which did not permit the Trust a completely free hand. For example, it would not, if it were simply in receipt of a grant, be under an obligation to attract 20% of under-25-year-olds to its performances. Nor would it have to incur the expense of providing box office facilities to all other cultural events in the area. The Tribunal found the Trust to be making a business supply of services to the district authority.

13.5   *DONALDSON'S COLLEGE*

In *Donaldson's College* [2005] VTD 19258, a charity operated a school for deaf and hearing-impaired children. It was funded 35% by fees charged to each child's local authority and 65% by a block grant from the Scottish government. The decision as to the split was made by the Scottish government and the amount charged to the local authority bore no relation to the cost of education. No fee was ever charged directly to a parent (except in exceptional circumstances) and there was no competition or any likelihood of it and no prospect or expectation of financial independence. The VAT Tribunal found that Donaldson's was not predominantly concerned with the making of taxable supplies for a consideration. It was instead predominantly concerned with providing a service which is required to be provided by the State, that is to say, the provision of education to deaf or partially hearing children and children with communication difficulties. It decided that the services are not provided to the local authority, the entire exercise being for all practical purposes controlled by central government.

13.6 *DUTCH POTATO* CASE

In case C-154/80 *Staatssecretaris van Financiën* v. *Association coopérative 'Coöperatieve Aardappelenbewaarplaats GA'* [1981] ECR 445, known as the *Dutch potato* case, a Dutch agricultural cooperative provided potato storage facilities for its members. The members normally paid a standard-rated fee to use the facilities, but one year the cooperative provided storage up to a certain weight of potatoes for free. The Dutch tax authorities claimed that the consequent reduction in the value of the members' shares in the cooperative was consideration for the supply of storage for the year. The CJEU held that any consideration for the provision of a service that is not in money must be capable of being expressed in money; otherwise there is nothing to apply the rate of VAT to. The CJEU held that, as a consequence, a provision of services for which no definite subjective consideration is received does not constitute a provision of services against payment and is therefore not a supply.

13.7 *EC V. FINLAND*

In case C-246/08 *European Commission* v. *Finland* [2009] ECR I-10605, the Finnish government extended its legal aid scheme from persons with no income to persons with low levels of income. Such persons had to part pay for legal services supplied by public offices, the percentage payable being on a sliding scale from 20% to 75% depending on the level of the person's income and savings. The balance was funded by general block grants to the public offices. The part payments accounted for approximately 23% of the costs of providing the part-fee-funded legal services.

The dispute was whether the part payments were consideration for the supply of legal services. The CJEU observed that, although the part payment represents a portion of the fees, its amount is not calculated solely on the basis of those fees, but also depends upon the recipient's income and assets. Thus, it is the level of the latter and not, for example, the number of hours worked by the public offices or the complexity of the case concerned which determines the portion of the fees for which the recipient remains responsible. It follows that the part payment depends only in part on the actual value of the services provided; the more modest the recipient's income and assets, the less strong the link with that value will be.

The CJEU considered that this was borne out by the fact that the part payments made in 2007 by recipients of legal aid services provided by the public offices (which relate to only one-third of all the services provided by public offices) amounted to €1.9 million, whilst the gross operating costs of those offices were €24.5 million. Even if that included legal aid services provided other than in court proceedings, such a difference suggests that the part payment borne by recipients must be regarded more as a fee, receipt of which does not, per se, mean that a given activity is economic in nature, than as consideration in the strict sense.

The CJEU held that it does not appear that the link between the legal aid services provided by public offices and the payment to be made by the recipients is sufficiently direct for that payment to be regarded as consideration for those services and, accordingly, for those services to be regarded as economic activities. The Advocate General's view was that there is a certain link between the service and part payment, since the part payment is calculated as a percentage of the value of the service, but that the link is neither direct nor does it have the intensity required in order to identify a service effected for consideration, because it is contaminated by taking account of the client's income and assets. The more modest the person's income, the less direct the link will be.

13.8 *EC V. FRENCH REPUBLIC*

In case C-50/87 *European Commission* v. *France* [1988] ECR I-04797, the French government introduced new legislation under which undertakings letting immovable property which they had purchased or built could deduct only a fraction of the VAT charged on the purchase or construction where the annual income from the letting was less than one-fifteenth (6.7%) of the property's value. The legislation related to leases at below market rates granted by certain undertakings to their subsidiaries or by certain local authorities to sports or cultural associations for social reasons or to undertakings in order to help them to establish themselves.

The CJEU first rejected the French approach of restricting input VAT recovery on the basis that this would be a fundamental breach of the principle of VAT. The CJEU accepted that legislation is necessary in order to deal with lettings at low rents granted by local authorities to associations with social objects or to undertakings which have come to their areas in order to establish themselves. Without such, the result of such practices would be to allow local authorities to make subsidies which would in part be borne by the state if the principle of total and immediate deduction were upheld.

However, in order to deal with such situations the Principal VAT Directive already provides for a system of adjustment. The CJEU held that where, because of the amount of the rent, the lease must necessarily be regarded as involving a concession and not as constituting an economic activity, the deduction initially made is adjusted and the time limit for that adjustment may be extended up to ten years.

13.9 *EC V. NETHERLANDS*

In case C-235/85 *European Commission* v. *Netherlands* [1987] ECR 1471, the CJEU held that by defining a taxable person as any person who independently carries out an economic activity, whatever the purpose or results of that activity, the Principal VAT Directive attributes to VAT a very wide scope. Economic activities include all activities of producers, traders and persons supplying services, including the activities of the professions. Those definitions show that the scope of the term 'economic activities' is very wide, and that the term is objective in character, in the sense that the activity is considered per se and without regard to its purpose or results.

13.10 *FANFIELD LTD AND THEXTON TRAINING LTD*

The case *Fanfield Ltd & Thexton Training Ltd* v. *Revenue & Customs* [2011] UKFTT 42 (TC) considered the situation where a business earns interest on 'realised profits' in the same way as a private investor. The First-tier Tribunal held that the deposits made by Fanfield and Thexton were the results of decisions as to the investments of profits after they had been earned. The activity that actually earns the interest for Fanfield and Thexton is the decision to leave the money on account for long enough to earn interest, and that is not in itself a business activity nor is it in any sense a direct and permanent extension of a business activity. Interest earned in this way is therefore outside the scope of VAT.

13.11 *FLORIDIENNE*

In case C-142/99 *Floridienne SA and Berginvest SA* v. *Belgian State* [2000] ECR I-09567, the CJEU held that, where a holding company makes capital available to its subsidiaries in return for interest, that activity may of itself be considered an economic activity, consisting in exploiting that capital with a view to obtaining income by way of interest therefrom on a continuing basis, provided that it is not carried out merely on an occasional basis, is not confined to managing an investment portfolio in the same way as a private investor and is carried out with a business or commercial purpose characterised by, in particular, a concern to maximise returns on capital investment.

13.12 *GÖTZ*

In case C-408/06 *Landesanstalt für Landwirtschaft* v. *Franz Götz* [2007] ECR I-11295, the issue at dispute was the sale of milk quotas by a statutory body. The CJEU explained that the requirement for a permanent activity which generates income on a continuing basis is necessary under both limbs of the definition of economic activity. Economic activity is defined as including all activities of producers, traders and persons supplying services, *inter alia* the exploitation of tangible or intangible property for the purpose of obtaining income therefrom on a continuing basis. The latter criteria, relating to the permanent nature of the activity and the income which is obtained from it, have been treated by the case law as applying not only to the exploitation of property, but to all of the activities referred to. An activity is thus, generally, categorised as economic where it is permanent and is carried out in return for remuneration which is received by the person carrying out the activity. Where an activity is capable of being carried out by economic operators it will be for the national court to determine whether the activity at issue is permanent and is carried out in return for remuneration. It is also for that national court to establish, if necessary, whether the activity is carried out for the purpose of receiving that remuneration, while taking account of the fact that the receipt of a payment does not, per se, mean that a given activity is economic in nature.

13.13 *HILLINGDON LEGAL RESOURCE CENTRE*

In *Hillingdon Legal Resource Centre* [1991] VTD 5210 a charity operated a citizens' advice centre and received grant funding from a local authority. The Centre argued that the grant payment was consideration for a supply on the basis that the grant conditions required a detailed report and that accounts be submitted to the local authority to show that the grant was being used as originally intended. The VAT Tribunal ruled that the conditions were simply good housekeeping to ensure the correct use of the payment and did not make the payment consideration for a supply. This decision was followed in *Wolverhampton Citizens Advice Bureau* [2000] VTD 16411 where there was a service level agreement with the local authority.

13.14 *HONG-KONG TRADE DEVELOPMENT COUNCIL*

If there is no consideration, there is no supply. In case C-89/81 *Staatssecretaris van Financiën* v. *Hong-Kong Trade Development Council* [1982] ECR 1277, the CJEU held that the provision of goods and services for free is not a supply.

13.15 *HUTCHISON 3G*

The case C-369/04 *Hutchison 3G UK Ltd* v. *Customs & Excise* [2007] ECR I-05247 concerned the granting of government licences to mobile phone operators by way of auction and whether or not this was an economic activity. The licences granted the operators the right to use specific bands of the electromagnetic spectrum. The CJEU held that, in issuing 3G licences, the UK government was carrying out its duty under community law (Directive 2002/21/EC). Such a duty can only be undertaken in the UK by the UK government. It is not an activity that can be carried out by economic operators and is therefore not an activity of producers, traders, etc. In addition, the UK government carries out this activity exclusively for the purposes of carrying out its regulatory duties and not for the purpose of generating income on a continuing basis. It is therefore not an economic activity. The fact that the issuing of licences gives rise to a payment cannot affect that decision.

13.16 *KRETZTECHNIK*

In *Kretztechnik C-465/03 Kretztechnik AG v. Finanzamt Linz* [2005] ECR I-04357, the CJEU held that the issue by a company of shares for the purpose of raising capital was neither a supply of goods nor a supply of services. A company that issues new shares is increasing its assets by acquiring additional capital, whilst granting the new shareholders a right of ownership of part of the capital. From the issuing company's point of view, the aim is to raise capital and not to provide services. As far as the shareholder is concerned, the payment is not a payment of consideration but an investment or an employment of capital.

13.17 *KUWAIT PETROLEUM*

In case C-48/97 *Kuwait Petroleum (GB) Ltd v. Customs & Excise* [1999] ECR I-02323, a business operated a sales promotion scheme, in which customers were offered a voucher with every 12 litres of fuel purchased. The price of the fuel was the same whether or not the customer accepted the vouchers. When a customer had collected enough vouchers, they were entitled to redeem them for goods chosen from a gift catalogue. Kuwait Petroleum sought to reclaim VAT incurred on the gift goods by arguing that they were supplied to customers in return for a part of the customer's payment.

The CJEU rejected this. Kuwait Petroleum could not argue that the parties had agreed that a part of the consideration was for the vouchers or gift goods, as customers paid the same whether or not they took the vouchers. The CJEU held that it is necessary to enquire whether, at the time of purchasing the fuel, the customers and Kuwait Petroleum had agreed that part of the price paid for the fuel, whether identifiable or not, would constitute the value given in return for the vouchers or the redemption goods. That was clearly not the case here. However, the CJEU went on to find that, as Kuwait Petroleum had deducted the VAT on the gift goods, disposal of them for free was a **deemed supply** of goods on which **output VAT** was due (see 4.2 'Exceptions').

13.18 *LANDBODEN-AGRARDIENSTE*

In case C-384/95 *Landboden-Agrardienste GmbH & Co. KG v. Finanzamt Calau* [1997] ECR I-07387, a farmer was given compensation under a national scheme for agreeing not to harvest at least 20% of his potato crop. The dispute was, as in the *Mohr* case (see 13.21 '*Mohr*'), whether the compensation was consideration for a supply of services. The tax authority argued that the *Mohr* decision should be ignored on the basis that the fact that VAT is a general tax on consumption should not be used as a basis for determining whether there is a supply of services. The CJEU rejected this. The tax authority had failed to recognise that VAT is not a tax on income but a tax on consumption. A taxable person's income is relevant for VAT purposes only if it constitutes the consideration for a supply of goods or services to a consumer. If there is no consumption, then there should be no VAT.

The Advocate General explained that it is necessary to distinguish between supplies of goods and services. A supply of goods by a taxable person always entails consumption regardless of the use, if any, to which the goods are put. Consumption of goods does not mean actual use but merely the acquisition of the right to dispose of the goods as owner. The position regarding services is more complex. The acquisition of a service is more difficult to verify. Any payment, except perhaps a gift, will have conditions attached to it whose performance might, by creative use of language, be described as a service. The Advocate General then stated that, in order to determine whether a service has been provided, it is necessary to examine the transaction in the light of the aims and characteristics of the VAT system. These comprise the application to goods and services of a general tax on consumption. Compensation for not harvesting potatoes does not fit in with that definition as there is nothing consumed. Also the concept of a supply of services does not depend on the use made of a service by the person who pays for it. Only the nature of the undertaking given is to be taken into consideration, but for such an undertaking to be within the scope of VAT it must imply consumption. The CJEU held that, since the farmer does not provide services to an identifiable consumer or any benefit capable of being regarded as a cost component of the activity of another person in the commercial chain, there is no consumption.

13.19   *LONGRIDGE ON THAMES*

In *Longridge on the Thames* v. *Revenue & Customs* [2013] UKFTT 158 (TC), fees were charged for water-based sports courses (canoeing, kayaking, etc.) on a break-even basis taking into account grants and donations. The courses were also heavily subsidised by the use of volunteers. The Tribunal decided that this was a non-business activity on the basis that the charges were set with a view to a range of factors balancing the desire to provide the activities at the lowest cost possible with the need to maintain long-term viability. It decided that the following are the most significant of those factors: charges are set with a view to their affordability for the young people the charity wishes to benefit; charges are set with a view to covering operational expenses after taking account of donated income and also of the contributions of volunteers; discretion is given to permit reducing or waiving charges in particular cases where pursuit of the charitable objects is especially desirable; and all capital projects (with the exception of the original acquisition of the site, which was partly funded by borrowing) are financed by donations and grants, so that no part of the charges is directly or indirectly expended on the acquisition or funding of capital assets.

In the FTT's view those were not factors which are indicative of a business, even if certain of those factors may demonstrate a degree of financial care and prudence aimed at ensuring that the charity can continue to carry out its activities. On appeal by HMRC, the Upper-tier Tribunal agreed stating, after reviewing the case law:

> These cases show that there is a dividing line to be drawn between a situation akin to that in Morrison's Academy where the activities do amount to the furtherance of a business even though the activities are not aimed at making a profit and a situation akin to that in Finland where the activity is not conducted as a business even though payment is made by the recipient for the services provided. In my judgment, it is also clear it is for the FTT to decide, on the basis of all the facts before it, on which side of the line the instant case falls. The FTT here considered the scale of the payments made, the way they were calculated and the way the finances of Longridge were dealt with in terms of donations and the use of volunteers. There is nothing in their discussion of the test to be applied or in their application of that test to the facts found that shows any error of law.

At the time of writing HMRC has been granted permission to appeal this decision to the Court of Appeal.

13.20 *LORD FISHER*

In the High Court case *Customs & Excise* v. *Lord Fisher* [1981] STC 238, the organiser of a shoot for friends and relations sought substantial contributions from those participating towards the expenses involved. Lord Fisher was assessed on the basis that the financial contributions made were consideration for a taxable supply of services made in the course of a business.

The judge rejected this. In regard to 'business', on earlier authority (*Morrison's Academy*, see 13.22) business is or may be in particular contexts a word of very wide meaning, but the ordinary meaning of the word business excludes any activity which is no more than an activity for pleasure and social enjoyment, though the fact that the pursuit of profit or earnings was not the motive did not prevent an activity from being a business if in other respects it plainly was. The judge referred to the six indicia listed by HMRC as being derived from the case law as the test as to whether an activity was a business – was it (a) a 'serious undertaking earnestly pursued'; (b) pursued with reasonable continuity; (c) substantial in amount; (d) conducted regularly on sound and recognised business principles; (e) predominantly concerned with the making of taxable supplies to consumers for a consideration; (f) such as consisted of taxable supplies of a kind commonly made by those who seek to make profit from them?

On the facts as found by the Tribunal the judge was satisfied that the shoot was organised for the enjoyment of Lord Fisher's friends and not as a commercial enterprise. The contributions to expenses were no more than that. The arrangements lacked an economic content.

13.21 *MOHR*

In case C-215/94 *Jürgen Mohr* v. *Finanzamt Bad Segeberg* [1996] ECR I-00959, a dairy farmer was given EC compensation for permanently ceasing milk production. The tax authority demanded output VAT on the compensation on the basis that it was consideration for a supply of services. The CJEU rejected this stating:

> It should be recalled that VAT is a general tax on the consumption of goods and services. In a case such as the present one, there is no consumption as envisaged in the Community VAT system. By compensating farmers who undertake to cease their milk production, the Community does not acquire goods or services for its own use but acts in the common interest of promoting the proper functioning of the Community milk market. In those circumstances, the undertaking given by a farmer that he will discontinue his milk production does not entail either for the Community or for the competent national authorities any benefit which would enable them to be considered consumers of a service. The undertaking in question does not therefore constitute a supply of services.

13.22 *MORRISON'S ACADEMY*

In *Customs & Excise* v. *Morrison's Academy Boarding Houses Association* [1978] STC 1, the Court of Session was considering a charity which in promotion of its charitable objects owned and operated six boarding houses in which, during school terms, pupils of the Academy, with which it was associated, were accommodated. The company charged fees so that neither profit nor loss was incurred. The charity claimed that the services supplied were not supplied 'in the course of a business carried on' by the Association. The Court, in a multi-judge decision, rejecting this concluded that the services were subject to VAT.

Lord Emslie stated:

> In my opinion it will never be possible or desirable to define exhaustively 'business' within the meaning of [VAT law]. What one must do is to discover what are the activities of the taxable person in the course of which taxable

supplies are made. If these activities are, as in this case, predominantly concerned with the making of taxable supplies to consumers for a consideration, it seems to me to require no straining of the language of [VAT law] to enable one to conclude that the taxable person is in the 'business' of making taxable supplies, and that taxable supplies which he makes are supplies made in the course of carrying on that business, especially if, as in this case, the supplies are of a kind which, subject to differences of detail, are made commercially by those who seek to profit by them.

For my part I consider that there is no justification in this case for holding that the activities deliberately and continuously pursued by the association in a business like way are not a 'business' for VAT purposes merely because the underlying motive is to assist Morrisons' Academy. Further I see no possible justification for there being any 'commercial element' in these activities to bring the association's supplies within the scope of the tax. I am not at all clear what is meant by a 'commercial element' if it is something different from the pursuit of profit, but if there is a difference it appears to me that all activities customarily carried on by persons actively pursuing an occupation, profession or vocation will normally possess it in the sense that what is done is done for such a return that the operation will not be conducted at a loss.

Lord Cameron said:

If the making of a profit or gain is irrelevant to the issue of liability to this tax, then it seems to me absence of such a purpose is equally irrelevant to the issue of whether the potential taxpayer carries on a 'business' in making the taxable supplies. What has to be looked at is the activity itself and so regarding the matter I think it is impossible to resist the conclusion that in pursuing the objects for which the association was formed and is carried on the association are engaged in the carrying on of a business, that of providing boarding house accommodation and facilities for a particular section of the public who are invited to take advantage of the facilities provided, namely the parents of pupils of Morrison's Academy. If the question is put another way, how would this activity be properly described, without any reference to the issues of tax liability? I think the answer would be that it is essentially a business activity of a very usual and normal kind. It has every mark of a business activity: it is regular, conducted on sound and recognised business principles, with a structure which can be recognised as providing a familiar constitutional mechanism for carrying on a commercial undertaking, and it has as its declared purpose the provision of goods and services which are of a type provided and exchanged in course of everyday life and commerce. Not only so, but to some extent the association is necessarily competing in the market with other persons and concerns offering precisely similar services to the same clients or customers, i.e. the parents of pupils of Morrison's Academy who may seek or require residential and boarding accommodation.

13.23 *POLYSAR INVESTMENTS*

In case C-60/90 *Polysar Investments Netherlands BV* v. *Inspecteur der Invoerrechten en Accijnzen* [1991] ECR I-03111, the CJEU held that the mere acquisition and holding of shares in a company is not to be regarded as an economic activity, conferring on the holder the status of a taxable person. The mere acquisition of financial holdings in other undertakings does not amount to the exploitation of property for the purpose of obtaining income therefrom on a continuing basis, because any dividend yielded by that holding is merely the result of ownership of the property. However, it is otherwise where the holding is accompanied by direct or indirect involvement in the management of the companies in which the holding has been acquired.

13.24 *RĒDLIHS*

In the *Rēdlihs* case (C-263/11 *Ainārs Rēdlihs* v. *Valsts ieņēmumu dienests* [2012]), Mr Rēdlihs purchased a forest for his personal use. He did not claim any VAT related to the purchase. A storm subsequently blew down some of the trees. Mr Rēdlihs sold the fallen trees, making 37 separate supplies of timber over a period of 9 months. He did not account for output VAT on the sales. The Latvian VAT authority assessed Mr Rēdlihs for VAT on the sales. The dispute was whether or not the timber sales were an economic activity. The CJEU analysed the situation as follows (abbreviated):

> the sale of the fruits of tangible property, such as the sale of timber from a private forest, must be regarded as 'exploitation' of that property. It follows that such transactions must be regarded as 'economic activity' if they are effected for the purpose of obtaining income therefrom on a continuing basis.

> The issue of whether the activity at issue, namely the exploitation of a private forest, is designed to obtain income on a continuing basis is an issue of fact which must be assessed having regard to all the circumstances of the case, which include, inter alia, the nature of the property concerned.

> That criterion must make it possible to determine whether an individual has used property in such a way that his activity is to be regarded as economic activity. The fact that property is suitable only for economic exploitation will normally be sufficient for a finding that its owner is exploiting it for the purposes of economic activities and, consequently, for the purpose of obtaining income on a continuing basis. On the other hand, if, by reason of its nature, property is capable of being used for both economic and private purposes, all the circumstances in which it is used will have to be examined in order to determine whether it is actually being used for the purpose of obtaining income on a continuing basis.

> In the latter case, comparing the circumstances in which the person concerned actually uses the property with the circumstances in which the corresponding economic activity is usually carried out may be one way of ascertaining whether

the activity concerned is carried on for the purpose of obtaining income on a continuing basis. Thus, where the person concerned takes active steps in forestry management by mobilising resources similar to those deployed by a producer, a trader or a person supplying services, the activity at issue must be regarded as an 'economic activity'.

Furthermore, the fact that the supplies of timber were effected with a view to alleviating the consequences of a case of *force majeure* cannot, in itself, lead to the conclusion that those supplies were made on an occasional basis and not 'for the purposes of obtaining income therefrom on a continuing basis'. Such supplies may fall within the scope of continuous exploitation of tangible property.

The fruits of tangible property, such as timber from a forest, may, by their very nature and depending on their characteristics and, in particular, their age, not be suitable for immediate economic exploitation, as a certain period of time may be objectively necessary before those fruits can become amenable to economic exploitation. Nevertheless, that does not mean that the supplies of timber which have taken place in the meantime, as a result of alleged *force majeure*, do not come within the scope of exploitation of tangible property for the purposes of obtaining income therefrom on a continuing basis.

Although criteria based on the results of the activity in question cannot in themselves make it possible to determine whether the activity is carried on for the purpose of obtaining income on a continuing basis, the actual length of the period over which the supplies took place, the number of customers and the amount of earnings are also factors which, forming part of the circumstances of the case as a whole, may be taken into account, with others, when that question is under consideration.

The fact that person acquired the tangible property to meet his own personal needs, does not preclude that property from being subsequently used for the purposes of the exercise of an 'economic activity'. The question as to whether an individual has acquired property for the needs of his economic activities or for his own needs arises when that individual requests the right to deduct the input VAT paid.

Having regard to the foregoing, the answer is that supplies of timber made by a natural person for the purpose of alleviating the consequences of a case of *force majeure* come within the scope of the exploitation of tangible property, which must be regarded as an 'economic activity', where those supplies are carried out for the purposes of obtaining income therefrom on a continuing basis. It is for the national court to carry out an assessment of all the circumstances of the case in order to determine whether the exploitation of tangible property, such as a forest, is carried out for the purposes of obtaining income therefrom on a continuing basis.

13.25 *RIVERSIDE HOUSING ASSOCIATION* AND *CARDIFF COMMUNITY HOUSING ASSOCIATION*

In the case *Riverside Housing Association* v. *Revenue & Customs* [2006] EWHC 2383 (Ch), the High Court found that the Association's activities of letting properties on assured tenancies to residential occupiers, selling properties to tenants under right-to-buy provisions, and selling properties which were surplus to requirements were all business activities. This contrasts with an earlier VAT Tribunal decision in *Cardiff Community Housing Association* [2000] VTD 16841 in which a charitable community housing association's activities were considered to be non-business.

13.26 *R. J. TOLSMA*

In case C-16/93 *R. J. Tolsma* v. *Inspecteur der Omzetbelasting Leeuwarden* [1994] ECR I-00743, Mr Tolsma solicited donations by playing a barrel organ on the streets of the Netherlands. The Dutch tax authority claimed that the donations from passers-by were consideration for a supply of musical entertainment. The CJEU held that a supply is effected 'for consideration' only if there is a legal relationship between the provider of the service and the recipient pursuant to which there is reciprocal performance, the remuneration received by the provider of the service constituting the value actually given in return for the service supplied to the recipient. The CJEU decided that in Mr Tolsma's case there was no supply. First, there was no agreement between the parties, since the passers-by voluntarily made donations, whose amount they determined as they wished. Secondly, there was no necessary link between the musical service and the payments. The passers-by did not request music to be played for them; moreover, they paid sums which depended not on the musical service but on subjective motives. Some persons placed money, sometimes a considerable sum, in the musician's collecting tin without lingering, whereas others listened to the music for some time without making any donation at all.

13.27 *ROMPELMAN* AND *GABALFRISA*

In case C-268/83 *Rompelman* v. *Minister van Financiën* [1985] ECR 655, the CJEU held that the acts preparatory to an economic activity, such as the acquisition of assets and the purchase of immovable property, must themselves be treated as constituting a part of the economic activity. And in case C-110/98 *Gabalfrisa SL* v. *Agencia Estatal de Administración Tributaria (AEAT)* [2000] ECR I-01577, the Advocate General held that economic activity encompasses acts ancillary to the pursuit of a commercial or professional activity.

13.28 *SOCIÉTÉ THERMALE D'EUGÉNIE-LES-BAINS*

In case C-277/05 *Société Thermale d'Eugénie-les-Bains* v. *Ministère de l'Économie des Finances et de l'Industrie* [2007] ECR I-06415, the French tax authorities tried to claim that forfeited non-returnable booking deposits held by a hotel were consideration for the supply of a reservation service. The CJEU held that the payment of a deposit and the reservation could not constitute reciprocal performance as the reservation arises directly from the contract for accommodation (the contract cannot be honoured without it), not from the payment of the deposit. The fact that the deposit is applied towards the price of the reserved room, if the client takes up occupancy, confirms that the deposit cannot constitute the consideration for the supply of an independent and identifiable reservation service. The CJEU held that the retention of the deposit by the hotel, following the client's cancellation, is intended to provide fixed compensation to offset the consequences of non-performance of the contract and as such is not consideration for any supply.

13.29 *ST PAUL'S COMMUNITY PROJECT*

A similar decision to *Yarburgh Children's Trust* (see 13.33 'Yarburgh Children's Trust') was reached in the High Court case *St Paul's Community Project* (2004), where a charity provided a nursery for social reasons, to support disadvantaged families. It had an admissions policy skewed in favour of disadvantaged and problem children. The nursery charged fees of £85–£95 per place per week. The cost of providing a place was £130 and fees were subsidised by a grant. The fees charged were significantly lower than those charged by commercial nurseries, despite St Paul's paying higher salaries and using a higher proportion of staff trained to a higher level of expertise than would normally be required. The fees were pitched at levels designed only to cover the costs of the nursery after grants and donations.

13.30 *UNIVERSITY OF SOUTHAMPTON*

In *University of Southampton* v. *Revenue & Customs* [2006] EWHC 528 (Ch), the University argued that its publicly funded research (PFR) was a part of its overall business activity and as such VAT incurred on PFR was partly recoverable. The High Court rejected this. It found that PFR in its own right was an important aspect of the University's activities. PFR was no more carried out for the benefit of commercial research than vice versa; and research generally was no more carried out for the benefit of education than vice versa. All activities are relevant and important to the University as an institution and to its reputation. It is artificial to regard one activity as standing in such a relation to another activity, that the costs incurred on the one are to be viewed as overhead costs of the other. The High Court concluded that the PFR in question was a separate non-business activity, though it did not reject the possibility that a particular piece of PFR might be business.

13.31 *VAN TIEM*

In case C-186/89 *W. M. van Tiem* v. *Staatssecretaris van Financiën* [1990] ECR I-04363, the CJEU held that the term 'exploitation' refers to all transactions, whatever may be their legal form, by which it is sought to obtain income from the property in question on a continuing basis. In the case the court decided that a grant of a licence to occupy land was exploitation of the right over land.

13.32 *WELLCOME TRUST*

In case C-155/94 *Wellcome Trust Ltd* v. *Customs & Excise* [1996] VATTR ECR I-03013, the CJEU held that buying and selling shares, bonds and other financial instruments may fall within the scope of VAT, for example as a part of a commercial share-trading activity or where shares are purchased in order to secure a direct or indirect involvement in the management of the companies concerned. However, the Trust was forbidden from such activities by its terms. Consequently, and irrespective of whether the activities in question are similar to those of an investment trust or a pension fund, the conclusion must be that a trust in such a position must be regarded as confining its activities to managing an investment portfolio in the same way as a private investor.

The CJEU held that the concept of economic activities does not include an activity consisting in the purchase and sale of shares and other securities by a trustee in the course of the management of the assets of a charitable trust. The CJEU added that, while the principle of fiscal neutrality requires that all economic activities should be treated in the same way, it also assumes that the activity in question can be classified as an economic activity.

13.33 *YARBURGH CHILDREN'S TRUST*

The High Court case *Customs & Excise* v. *Yarburgh Children's Trust* [2001] EWHC 2201 (Ch) concerned a cooperative playgroup run by trained staff with the benefit of help provided by parents under the control of a committee on which parents predominated. The playgroup was not profit-led and struggled to maintain the balance between remaining affordable and meeting its operating costs. Playgroup fees were fixed on this basis. The court held that the operation of the playgroup was not a business activity.

The court considered this to be a very different arrangement from a commercial playgroup run for a profit. The court held that an intention to trade at a profit is not an essential feature of a business, but it is relevant to the consideration of whether the playgroup can seriously be regarded as doing anything more than the carrying out of its charitable functions. The court also stated that the transaction looked at in isolation will not usually be enough to decide whether it was carried out in the course or furtherance of a business or a supply by a taxable person acting as such, and the question of the correct VAT treatment cannot be answered by reference to the fact that a service was provided at a price: that is the beginning not the end of the enquiry.

14 Further information

This chapter is divided into the following sections:

- 14.1 Contacting HM Revenue & Customs (HMRC)
- 14.2 The HMRC website
- 14.3 Checking VAT numbers
- 14.4 VAT in other EU states
- 14.5 Other useful websites and sources

14.1 CONTACTING HM REVENUE & CUSTOMS (HMRC)

The following contact information is correct at the time of writing.

- **VAT registration**: this can be done online or by downloading forms, filling them in and sending them to the address on the form. Currently some types of registration can only be done via forms (group registration in particular), though this may change with time. See www.gov.uk/vat-registration/how-to-register.
- **General VAT helpline**: 0300 200 3700 (8am–6pm, Mon–Fri excluding bank holidays) with textphone at 0300 200 3719. For calls from abroad ring 44 2920 501 261.
- **Charities helpline**: 0300 123 1073 – open from 8am–5pm, Mon–Fri excluding bank holidays. Use for charity specific queries. Also deals with charity-related direct tax and Gift Aid queries and VAT reliefs for disabled and elderly persons.
- **Charity written enquiries**:
  - Email: there is a special web form to use for charities (Charities and VAT – Enquiry form for Charities).
  - Post: HM Revenue & Customs, Charities Correspondence S0708, PO Box 205, Bootle L69 9AZ.
- **General written enquiries** should be sent to: HM Revenue & Customs, VAT Written Enquiries Team, 4th Floor, Alexander House, Victoria Avenue, Southend-On-Sea, Essex SS99 1BD.

- **Option to tax notifications:**
  - Email: optiontotaxnationalunit@hmrc.gsi.gov.uk.
  - Post: HM Revenue & Customs, Option to Tax Unit, Cotton House, 7 Cochrane Street, Glasgow G1 1GY.
- **VAT schemes:** notification of listed and hallmarked VAT schemes can be made by post or email. By email to: vat.avoidance.disclosures.bst@hmrc.gsi.gov.uk and by post to: HM Revenue & Customs, CTIAA Intelligence S0528, PO Box 194, Bootle, L69 9AA.
- **National Import Reliefs Unit:** the address is: National Import Reliefs Unit, HM Revenue and Customs, Abbey House, Head Street, Enniskillen, County Fermanagh Northern Ireland BT74 7JL. Telephone: 02866 344 557; fax: 0286 344 571; email: niru@hmrc.gov.uk.

14.2   HMRC WEBSITE

At the time of writing the HMRC website is being migrated to www.gov.uk and web addresses are not provided as they are subject to change. However, the following are the key HMRC online VAT resources:

- **Government Gateway:** access your online account to complete UK and Mini One Stop Shop VAT returns and make VAT payments.
- **VAT rates and thresholds:** including historic rates and VAT registration and deregistration thresholds.
- **Forms:** access the various HMRC VAT forms.
- **VAT Notices:** HMRC produces an extensive range of VAT Notices covering most aspects of VAT in detail. The VAT Notices are key sources of guidance on VAT and HMRC's views on areas of uncertainty. They also contain the text of many HMRC concessions and some have statutory force (tertiary legislation).
- **Revenue and Customs Briefs:** these announce changes in HMRC policy, often following changes in legislation or court cases. Before 2007 the Revenue & Customs Briefs were referred to as 'Business Briefs'.
- **VAT Information Sheets:** these are new or updated guidance in more detail than the Revenue and Customs Briefs.
- **HMRC Internal Guidance:** you can access much of the HMRC internal guidance on VAT, written for the use of HMRC staff. However, key parts are sometimes blanked out.
- **What's new?:** listing of changes to the website including Budget changes, press releases, recent changes to legislation and new developments.

14.3 **CHECKING VAT NUMBERS**

- **EU VAT Information Exchange System (VIES)**: see ec.europa.eu/taxation_ customs/vies/. The VIES system only allows you to check the validity of a VAT number, not its association with a particular business name or address. In addition the VIES system can take time to be updated by EU states. You must identify yourself by entering your own VAT registration number. You should keep a record of the date and time that the enquiry was made and the result.
- **HMRC National Advice Service** You can ring 0300 200 3700 to check a customer's VAT registration number (including EU customers) and to verify that the name and address is correct. Keep a record of the date, time and result.

14.3.1 **UK VAT number formats**

Most UK VAT numbers have a particular format which is nine digits long. This is split into groups of three, four and two digits, for example 123 4567 89. The last two digits are check digits, as explained below.

Where a business operates in divisions the above number is appended by three digits, for example: 123 4567 89 003. Government departments have the letters GD then three digits from 000 to 499 (for example, GD123). Health authorities have the letters HA then three digits from 500 to 999 (for example, HA567)

Check digits. UK VAT numbers follow a particular type of internal integrity check – a 'modulus check'. HMRC ran out of numbers for the first type of integrity check (modulus 97) in 2010 and so started a new series with the new type (modulus 9755) from then on.

You can check the integrity of a nine-digit UK VAT number as follows:

1. List the first seven digits of the number. Multiply the first number by 8, the second by 7, the third by 6, the fourth by 5, the fifth by 4, the sixth by 3 and the seventh by 2. Add up all those numbers (say $\sum$).
2. Under the modulus 9755 system, add 55 to $\sum$. Under the modulus 97 system do not add to $\sum$.
3. From the result, keep subtracting 97 until the number becomes zero or negative. The positive value of that number should be the last two digits of the VAT number.

Example: *(modulus 97)* VAT Number 234–5678-47

2	×	8	=	16
3	×	7	=	21
4	×	6	=	24
5	×	5	=	25
6	×	4	=	24
7	×	3	=	21
8	×	2	=	16
4		T =		147
7				−97
		=		50
				−97
47	←	=		−47

14.3.2 EU VAT number formats

See below for VAT number formats for each EU state

14.4 VAT IN OTHER EU STATES

14.4.1 AT Austria

- **Joined the EU**: 1 January 1995
- **VAT name**: Mehrwertsteuer / Umsatzsteuer (MWST, UST)
- **VAT no. format**: U12345678 (Chars = 9) First character is always U
- **Territory**: Austria includes Jungholtz and Mittelberg

14.4.2 BE Belgium

- **Joined the EU**: 1 January 1957
- **VAT name**: Belasting over de toegevoegde waarde or taxe sur la valeur ajoutée (BTW, TVA)
- **VAT no. format**: 0123456789 (Chars = 10) Nine digits prior to 1 April 2005. Prefix any nine-digit numbers with '0'

14.4.3 BG Bulgaria

- **Joined the EU**: 1 January 2007
- **VAT name**: Данък добавена стойност (ДДС)
- **VAT no. format**: 012345678 or 0123456789 (Chars = 9 or 10)

14.4.4 **HR Croatia**

- **Joined the EU**: 1 July 2013
- **VAT name**: Porez na dodanu vrijednost (PDV)
- **VAT no. format**: 12345678901 (Chars = 11)

14.4.5 **CY Cyprus**

- **Joined the EU**: 1 May 2004
- **VAT name**: Φόρος Προστιθέμενης Αξίας (ΦΠΑ)
- **VAT no. format**: 12345678X (Chars = 9) Last character must be a letter
- **Territory**: Cyprus includes the British Overseas Territory Sovereign Base Areas (Akrotiri and Dhekelia) but excludes the Turkish controlled parts of Northern Cyprus (which is outside the EU). Supplies to UK armed forces stationed in Cyprus can be zero-rated in certain circumstances, see Section 6.4.11 'Privileged persons in other EU states'

14.4.6 **CZ Czech Republic**

- **Joined the EU**: 1 May 2004
- **VAT name**: Daň z přidané hodnoty (DPH)
- **VAT no. format**: 12345678 or 123456789 or 1234567890 (Chars = 8, 9 or 10). Where 11, 12 or 13 numbers are quoted – delete the first three as these are a tax code

14.4.7 **DK Denmark**

- **Joined the EU**: 1 January 1973
- **VAT name**: Meromsætningsafgift (MOMS)
- **VAT no. format**: 12345678 (Chars = 8)
- **Territory**: Denmark excludes the Faroe Islands and Greenland (both outside the EU)

14.4.8 **EE Estonia**

- **Joined the EU**: 1 May 2004
- **VAT name**: käibemaks (KM)
- **VAT no. format**: 123456789 (Chars = 9)

14.4.9 **FI Finland**

- **Joined the EU**: 1 January 1995
- **VAT name**: Arvonlisävero (ALV)
- **VAT no. format**: 12345678 (Chars = 8)
- **Territory**: Finland excludes the Åland Islands. The Åland Islands are not part of the VAT and excise areas of the EU but are in its Customs Union Area

14.4.10 FR France

- **Joined the EU**: 1 January 1957
- **VAT name:** taxe sur la valeur ajoutée (TVA)
- **VAT no. format**: 12345678901 or X1234567890 or 1X123456789 or XX123456789 (Chars = 11) May include alpha character(s), either first, second or first and second. All alpha characters except I and O are valid. Must be the 11 alpha numeric TVA number, not the 14 digit SERIT (système d'identification du répertoire des entreprises) number
- **Territory**: France includes Monaco and Corsica but excludes the French territories of French Guiana, Guadeloupe, Martinique, Reunion and St Pierre and Miquelon (all outside the EU)

14.4.11 DE Germany

- **Joined the EU**: 1 January 1957
- **VAT name:** Mehrwertsteuer or Umsatzsteuer (MWST, UST)
- **VAT no. format**: 123456789 (Chars = 9) Must be the nine character Umsatzsteuer Identifikationsnummer (ust – Id Nr) not the ten character Umsatzsteuer nummer
- **Territory**: Germany excludes Busingen and the Isle of Heligoland (both outside the EU)

14.4.12 GR Greece

- **Joined the EU**: 1 January 1981
- **VAT name:** Φόρος Προστιθέμενης Αξίας (ΦΠΑ)
- **VAT no. format**: 012345678 (Chars = 9)
- **Territory**: Greece excludes Mount Athos for VAT purposes. Mount Athos is, however, in the EU's Customs Union Area

14.4.13 HU Hungary

- **Joined the EU**: 1 May 2004
- **VAT name:** Általános forgalmi adó (ÁFA)
- **VAT no. format**: 12345678 (Chars = 8)

14.4.14 IE Ireland

- **Joined the EU**: 1 January 1973
- **VAT name:** Cáin Bhreisluacha (CBL)
- **VAT no. format**: 1234567X or 1X23456X or 1234567XX (Chars = 8 or 9) Includes one or two alpha characters – either last, or second and last. Second character can also be '+' or '*'

14.4.15   IT Italy

- **Joined the EU**: 1 January 1957
- **VAT name**: Imposta sul Valore Aggiunto (IVA)
- **VAT no. format**: 12345678901 (Chars = 11)
- **Territory**: Italy excludes the communes of Livigno and Campione d'Italia and the Italian waters of Lake Lugano which are outside the EU

14.4.16   LV Latvia

- **Joined the EU**: 1 May 2004
- **VAT name**: Pievienotās vērtības nodoklis (PVN)
- **VAT no.** format: 12345678901 (Chars = 11)

14.4.17   LT Lithuania

- **Joined the EU**: 1 May 2004
- **VAT name**: Pridėtinės vertės mokestis (PVM)
- **VAT no. format**: 123456789 or 123456789012 (Chars = 9 or 12)

14.4.18   LU Luxembourg

- **Joined the EU**: 1 January 1957
- **VAT name**: taxe sur la valeur ajoutée (TVA)
- **VAT no. format**: 12345678 (Chars = 8)

14.4.19   MT Malta

- **Joined the EU**: 1 May 2004
- **VAT name**: Taxxa tal-Valur Miżjud (VAT)
- **VAT no. format**: 12345678 (Chars = 8)

14.4.20   NL Netherlands

- **Joined the EU**: 1 January 1957
- **VAT name**: Belasting over de toegevoegde waarde (BTW)
- **VAT no. format**: 123456789B01 (Chars = 12) The tenth digit is always B. Three digit suffixes will always be in the range B01 to B99

14.4.21   PL Poland

- **Joined the EU**: 1 May 2004
- **VAT name**: Podatek od towarów i usług (PTU)
- **VAT no. format**: 1234567890 (Chars = 10)

14.4.22 **PT Portugal**

- **Joined the EU**: 1 January 1986
- **VAT name**: Imposto sobre o Valor Acrescentado (IVA)
- **VAT no. format**: 123456789 (Chars = 9)
- **Territory**: Portugal includes the Azores and Madeira

14.4.23 **RO Romania**

- **Joined the EU**: 1 January 2007
- **VAT name**: Taxa pe valoarea adăugată (TVA)
- **VAT no. format**: 1234567890 (Chars = 2 to 10 digits)

14.4.24 **SK Slovakia**

- **Joined the EU**: 1 May 2004
- **VAT name**: Daň z pridanej hodnoty (DPH)
- **VAT no. format**: 1234567890 (Chars = 10)

14.4.25 **SI Slovenia**

- **Joined the EU**: 1 May 2004
- **VAT name**: Davek na dodano vrednost (DDV)
- **VAT no. format**: 12345678 (Chars = 8)

14.4.26 **ES Spain**

- **Joined the EU**: 1 January 1986
- **VAT name**: Impuesto sobre el Valor Añadido (IVA)
- **VAT no. format**: X12345678 or 12345678X or X1234567X (Chars = 9)
  Includes one or two alpha characters – first or last, or first and last
- **Territory**: Spain includes the Balearic Islands but excludes Ceuta, Melilla and the Canary Islands, though the Canary Islands are in the EU's Customs Union Area

14.4.27 **SE Sweden**

- **Joined the EU**: 1 January 1995
- **VAT name**: Mervärdesskatt (MOMS)
- **VAT no. format**: 123456789001 (Chars = 12)

EU candidate countries: at June 2015 EU candidate countries are: Iceland, the former Yugoslav Republic of Macedonia, Montenegro, Serbia and Turkey

14.5 OTHER USEFUL WEBSITES AND SOURCES

- **www.lpwscheme.org.uk** – listed places of worship scheme
- **www.memorialgrant.org.uk** – memorial grants scheme
- **www.legislation.gov.uk** – original and updated primary legislation; however, much of the legislation is not fully updated
- **www.bailii.org** – extensive case law database
- **ec.europa.eu/taxation_customs/taxation/vat/traders/vat_community/ index_en.htm** – VAT legislation and information on VAT regulations in other EU member states: follow the link for relevant country

14.5.1 Sayer Vincent website: www.sayervincent.co.uk

Specifically for charities and not-for-profit organisations, the Sayer Vincent website has a section on VAT where latest news and developments are covered as well as detailed guidance on aspects of VAT relevant to charities. It also has sections on other areas of finance, management, governance and fundraising for charities. Details of update seminars and training are also available.

14.5.2 Other publications by Sayer Vincent

A Practical Guide to Financial Management for Charities and Voluntary Organisations, Kate Sayer (3rd edition, Directory of Social Change, 2007)

A Practical Guide to Managing in a Downturn: Staying Solvent and Surviving Well, Kate Sayer (ed.), Margaret Bennett, Tony Elischer, Stephen Lloyd, Ian Oakley-Smith (Directory of Social Change, 2009)

References

GENERAL

Charity Commission (2007), *CC35 Trustees, Trading and Tax: How charities may lawfully trade*, April 2007, section D19 'Can a charity guarantee the liabilities of a trading subsidiary?'

OUP (2015), 'invalid, n', www.oxforddictionaries.com, Oxford Dictionaries online, accessed 21 September 2015

RICS (2015), *RICS Property Measurement*, Royal Institution of Chartered Surveyors [Members can download this from www.rics.org/uk; *RICS Property Measurement* updates the RICS Code of Measuring Practice, 6th edition and incorporates International Property Measurement Standards (IPMS)]

Royal Mail (2015), 'Information on VAT and postal services' [web page] www.royalmail.com/information-vat-and-postal-services, accessed 25 October 2015

States of Jersey (2015), 'Overseas businesses and GST refunds', gov.je, accessed 5 November 2015

EUROPEAN COMMISSION

EC (2009), *Communication from the Commission to the Council and the European Parliament on the VAT Group Option Provided for in Article 11 of Council Directive 2006/112/EC on the Common System of Value Added Tax*, Brussels, Commission of the European Communities, 2 July, COM(2009) 325

EC (2013), *Guide to the VAT Mini One Stop Shop*, European Commission, 23 October 2013, available as a PDF from ec.europa.eu

EC (2015), *Communication from the Commission to the European Parliament, the Council, the European Economic and Social Committee and the Committee of the Regions: A digital single market strategy for Europe*, Brussels, European Commission, 6 May, COM(2015) 192

HMRC PUBLICATIONS
General guidance

HMRC (2010), *How to Appeal Against an HMRC Decision: Indirect tax*, available at webarchive.nationalarchives.gov.uk

HMRC (2011), *Fundraising Events: Exemption for charities and other qualifying bodies*, HM Revenue and Customs, available at www.gov.uk/government/publications

HMRC (2012), *HMRC VAT: Road Fuel Scale Charges: Changing UK law to comply with EU law and streamlining the scheme; technical note* (summary of responses), HM Revenue and Customs, December, available at webarchive.nationalarchives.gov.uk

HMRC (2013), *Intrastat: Revised arrivals exemption threshold*, HM Revenue and Customs, 31 July 2013 (within document, 24 July 2013), available at www.gov.uk/government/publications

HMRC (2014), *Economic Operator Registration and Identification Scheme: Supporting guidance*, HM Revenue and Customs, 4 December 2014, last updated 18 February 2015, available at www.gov.uk/guidance/eori-supporting-guidance

HMRC (2014), *Place of Supply of Digital Services and VAT Mini One Stop Shop (MOSS) Guidance*, HM Revenue and Customs, not accessible online at the time of writing

HMRC (2014), *VAT Relief on Substantially and Permanently Adapted Motor Vehicles for Disabled Wheelchair Users: Summary of responses*, HM Revenue and Customs, 30 June 2014, last updated 17 December 2014, available at www.gov.uk/government/consultations

HMRC (2014), *VAT: Supplying Digital Services to Private Consumers*, HM Revenue and Customs, 19 December 2014, last updated 24 March 2015, available at www.gov.uk/government/publications

HMRC (2014), *Withdrawal of Extra Statutory Concessions: Technical note and call for evidence*, HM Revenue and Customs, 31 January 2014, not accessible online at the time of writing

HMRC (2015), Chapter 3: 'Gift Aid' in *Charities: Detailed guidance notes*, HM Revenue and Customs, 17 September 2013, last updated 22 September 2015, available at www.gov.uk/government/publications

HMRC (2015), *Guidance Notes on Completing the Notice of Appeal*, HM Revenue and Customs, 19 July

HMRC (2015), *HMRC Penalties: A discussion document*, HM Revenue and Customs and David Gauke MP, 2 February 2015, last updated 17 September 2015, available at www.gov.uk/government/consultations

Office of Public Service (2015), *Public Bodies*, not accessible at the time of writing

Business Briefs

Business Briefs can be accessed via the National Archives: webarchive.nationalarchives.gov.uk.

Business Brief 17/94, HM Customs and Excise, n.d., unavailable

Business Brief 03/96, HM Customs and Excise, n.d., unavailable

Business Brief 02/05, HM Customs and Excise, 9 February 2005

Business Brief 19/05, HM Revenue and Customs, 10 October 2005

Business Brief 22/05, HM Revenue and Customs, 2 December 2005

Business Brief 23/06, HM Revenue and Customs, 22 December 2006

Forms

C18, 'Post clearance demand note – goods imported from outside the EU or intra-EU movement not in free circulation', unpublished

C88, 'Import and export: Single Administrative Document full 8 part set (C88 (1–8)', 4 April 2014, available at www.gov.uk/government/collections/import-and-export-forms

C160, customs declaration forms, available at www.gov.uk/government/collections/import-and-export-forms

C285, 'Import and export: Application for repayment/remission', 23 September 2014, last updated 21 December 2014, available at www.gov.uk/government/collections/import-and-export-forms

C1201, 'Import and export: Guarantee deferment of payment to HMRC', 4 April 2014, last updated 16 April 2015, available at www.gov.uk/government/collections/import-and-export-forms

CN22, customs declaration form, available at www.royalmail.com/business/help/sending/customs

CN23, customs declaration form, available at www.royalmail.com/business/help/sending/customs

VAT101B, 'VAT: EC sales list correction sheet', HM Revenue and Customs, 1 May 2013, available at www.gov.uk/government/publications/vat-ec-sales-list-correction-sheet-vat101b

VAT1614F, 'Opting to tax land and buildings: New buildings – exclusion from an option to tax', available at www.gov.uk/government/uploads/system/uploads/attachment_data/file/461552/VAT1614F.pdf

The following three forms are available at www.gov.uk/government/ collections/vat-forms

VAT1615A, 'Declaration for zero-rated VAT supply of adapted vehicles and services', available within *VAT1615: Purchasing zero-rated adapted vehicles (guidance for customers)*

VAT600AA&FRS, 'Application to join the Annual Accounting Scheme and Flat Rate Scheme', 5 September 2014

VAT600AA, 'Application to join the Annual Accounting Scheme', 8 September 2014, last updated 16 April 2015

HM Courts and Tribunals Service

This form and guidance can be found at hmctsformfinder.justice.gov.uk.

HM Courts & Tribunals Service (2015), T241 TS-TaxApG1, *Guidance Notes on Completing the Notice of Appeal*, HM Courts & Tribunals Service First-tier Tribunal (Tax)

HM Courts & Tribunals Service (2015), T240 TS-TaxAp1, *Notice of Appeal*, HM Courts & Tribunals Service First-tier Tribunal (Tax)

Information sheets

VAT information sheets can be found at www.gov.uk/government/collections/ vat-information-sheets or, if archived, at webarchive.nationalarchives.gov.uk.

Information Sheet 07/08: VAT: Partial exemption – VAT adjustments when house builders let their dwellings before selling them

VAT Information Sheet 08/98: Charities: Supply, repair and maintenance of relevant goods (including adapted motor vehicles)

VAT Information Sheet 07/04: Eligibility rules for VAT grouping

VAT Information Sheet 08/09: Changes to the zero-rate for buildings used for a relevant charitable use, not available at the time of writing

VAT Information Sheet 03/10: Guidelines for the treatment of university trading companies, not available at the time of writing

VAT Information Sheet 13/10: Calculating qualifying use for a charitable or a communal residential building, 21 June 2010, archived

VAT Information Sheet 07/12: Guidance on the cost sharing exemption – from 17 Jul 2012, archived

VAT Information Sheet 10/13: Provision of storage facilities, 8 August 2013

VAT Information Sheet 11/13: Supplies of research between eligible bodies, 10 July 2014

VAT Information Sheet 02/14: Buildings that are dwellings and used for a relevant residential purpose, 30 January 2014

Manuals

HMRC manuals can be found at www.hmrc.gov.uk/thelibrary/manuals.htm.

CH – Compliance Handbook

CH81120 – Penalties for inaccuracies: Types of inaccuracy: What is reasonable care

CH81130 – Penalties for inaccuracies: Types of inaccuracy: Inaccuracy despite taking reasonable care

CH82442 – Penalties for inaccuracies: Calculating the penalty: Penalty reductions for quality of disclosure: Telling: Introduction

CH82450 – Penalties for inaccuracies: Calculating the penalty: Penalty reductions for quality of disclosure: Helping

CH82460 – Penalties for inaccuracies: Calculating the penalty: Penalty reductions for quality of disclosure: Giving access

CH83154 – Penalties for inaccuracies: How to process the penalty: Suspension of a penalty: suspension conditions: Specific suspension conditions

CH170600 – Special reduction: What are special circumstances

CH300200 – The Human Rights Act and penalties: HMRC penalties

EXPP – Export Procedures

EXPP8250 – Guidance on other procedures: Disaster relief/humanitarian aid

PE – Partial Exemption Guidance

PE1450 – Partial exemption basics and the standard method: The standard method override

PE3110 – Partial exemption special methods: Backdating approval

PE4160 – Other partial exemption issues: Longer period adjustment: What longer period adjustments cannot be used for

PE4450 – Other partial exemption issues: Petrol scale charges

VATEDU – VAT Education Manual

VATEDU37000 – Group 6 Item 1 Education, research and vocational training provided by eligible bodies: Research

VATEDU39700 – Group 6 Item 1 Education, research and vocational training provided by eligible bodies: Eligible bodies: Other organisations

VATEDU40200 – Group 6 Item 2 Private tuition and tutorial colleges: Scope of the private tuition exemption

VATEDU51600 – Group 6 Item 4 Closely related supplies: Goods and services that are not 'closely related' to supplies of education

VATEDU52000 – Group 6 Item 4 Closely related supplies: Tuck shops and vending machines

VATEDU53200 – Group 6 Item 4 Closely related supplies: Goods and services sold to the pupils etc. of other eligible bodies

VATEDU53600 – Group 6 Item 4 Closely related supplies: Special treatment for staff between eligible bodies

VATEDU70000 – Academies

VATGPB – VAT Government and Public Bodies

VATGPB8520 – Other local authority activities: Contracted out leisure services: memorandum of understanding paragraphs 1 & 2

VATLP – VAT Land and Property

VATLP06130 – Single supplies: Where leasing or letting is just one element of a contract: case law about single supplies comprising a bundle of elements

VATLP11400 – Hotels and similar establishments (Item 1d): Homeless people and asylum seekers

VATLP19300 – Letting of sports facilities (item 1m): Intervals between sessions

VATLP19400 – Letting of sports facilities (item 1m): The recipient of the supply

VATLP22320 – Option to tax: Supplies not affected by an option: buildings to be used solely for relevant charitable purpose

VATPOSS – Place of Supply of Services

VATPOSS08254 – Where performed services: Supplies of admission to relevant business customers: meaning of 'admission'

VATPOSS08256 – Where performed services: Supplies of admission to relevant business customers: meaning of 'event'

VATPOSS08400 – Where performed services: Scientific services

VATPOSS08500 – Where performed services: Education services

VATPOSS08550 – Where performed services: Entertainment services

VATPOSS13250 – Other services to non-EU customers (B2C): Services of consultants, engineers, lawyers, accountants, similar services, data processing, and the provision of information

VATPOSS15500 – Use and enjoyment: Electronically supplied services

VATREG – VAT Registration

VATREG19150 – Exception from registration: Retrospective applications

VATREG30100 – Transfers of going concerns (TOGCS): Reallocation of VAT registration number (VAT 68 Action): Conditions of reallocation

VATSM – VAT Single Market

VATSM4320 – Transfers of own goods: Goods sent from the UK: Supply position

VATTOS6000 – Accommodation tax points

VATTOS6200 – Accommodation tax points: Monthly invoicing

VBNB – VAT Business/Non-Business Manual

VBNB31000 – Apportionment of tax: Methods of apportionment

VBNB33000 – Apportionment of tax: Methods for apportionment of tax

VBNB60420 – Clubs and associations: Have the members given a subscription or other consideration?

VCHAR – VAT Charities

VCHAR3400 – Business and non-business: Charitable activities: When is a donation not a donation?

VCHAR3520 – Business and non-business: Charitable activities: Treatment of welfare services supplied below cost: Origins of the relief

VCHAR3540 – Business and non-business: Charitable Activities: Treatment of welfare services supplied below cost: How does the relief work?

VCHAR3580 – Business and non-business: Charitable activities: Treatment of welfare services supplied below cost: Valuing the supply

VCHAR3600 – Business and non-business: Charitable activities: Treatment of welfare services supplied below cost: Is the welfare service available to all distressed people equally?

VCHAR6000 – Ambulance services

VCHAR9200 – Fund-raising: Donations

VCHAR9300 – Fund-raising: Exempt charity fund-raising events

VCHAR9400 – Fund-Raising: Fund-raising events and a charity's trading subsidiary

VCHAR10000 – Grant funding

VCHAR14950 – Medical and scientific equipment ('relevant goods'): Funding for the purchase of qualifying equipment

VCONST – Construction Manual

VCONST15130 – 'Relevant residential purpose' – interpretation of terms: Relevant residential purpose – background: Differences between 'residential accommodation' and 'home or institution'

VCONST15300 – 'Relevant residential purpose' – Interpretation of terms: Category (c) – hospices

VGROUPS – Groups

VGROUPS01400 – General principles of VAT group treatment: When is an intra group reverse charge not due?

VGROUPS01550 – General principles of VAT group treatment: Other matters

VGROUPS02400 – Eligibility for VAT group treatment: 'Established' and 'fixed establishment'

VIT – VAT Input Tax

VIT13400 – VAT input tax basics: When input tax can be claimed by the business on supplies to employees

VIT31200 – How to treat input tax: Alternative evidence for claiming input tax

VIT32000 – How to treat input tax: Pre-registration, pre-incorporation and post-deregistration claims to input tax under regulation 111

VIT42100 – Specific issues: Removal expenses

VR4300 – Unjust Enrichment: Some Items to Consider: Contents Page

VRDP – VAT Relief for Disabled People

VRDP06500 – Adjustable beds [item 2(b)]: what features make a bed eligible for vat relief?

VRDP13000 – Chair lifts and stair lifts [item 2(d)]

VRDP19000 – Hoists and lifters [item 2(e)]

VRDP29300 – Motor vehicles [items 2(f) and 2a]: What does 'substantially and permanently adapted' mean under item 2(f) for a vehicle adapted to carry a person seated in a wheelchair or lying on a stretcher?

VRDP33000 – Sanitary devices [item 2(c)]

VRDP39000 – Parts and accessories [item 2(h)]

VTAXPER – VAT Taxable Person Manual

VTAXPER72000 – Particular trades: School photographers

VTOGC – Transfer of a Going Concern

VTOGC4200 – Common areas of difficulty: Tax incorrectly charged

VTOGC4500 – Common areas of difficulty: Transfer of a wholly exempt business

VTUPB – Trade Unions and Professional Bodies

VTUPB1300 – Trade unions and professional bodies: Background and law: UK law – history of the exemption group

VTUPB4300 – Trade unions and professional bodies: Item 1(b) professional associations: restriction to individuals

VTUPB7000 – Apportionment; retrospective registration claims

Manuals (archived – inaccessible)

V1–9 Charities

V1–37 Control notes

Notices

VAT Notices can be found at www.gov.uk/government/collections/vat-notices-numerical-order.

Notice 236: Returned goods relief, 29 April 2014

Notice 252: Valuation of imported goods for customs purposes, VAT and trade statistics, 1 July 2013

VAT Notice 48: Extra statutory concessions, 19 May 2015, last updated 21 May 2015

VAT Notice 317: Imports by charities free of duty and VAT, 28 February 2006

VAT Notice 700: The VAT guide, 17 December 2014, last updated 1 April 2015

VAT Notice 700/1: Should I be registered for VAT?, 25 February 2014

VAT Notice 700/2: Group and divisional registration, 6 August 2014, last updated 8 August 2014

VAT Notice 700/8: Disclosure of VAT avoidance schemes, 30 October 2013

VAT Notice 700/9: Transfer of a business as a going concern, 6 December 2012

VAT Notice 700/17: Funded pension schemes, 28 December 2012

VAT Notice 700/24: Postage, delivery charges and direct marketing, 1 April 2003, last updated 9 June 2015

VAT Notice 700/34: Staff, 6 June 2012

VAT Notice 700/57: Administrative agreements entered into with trade bodies, 9 August 2004, last updated 6 August 2014

VAT Notice 700/64: Motoring expenses, 13 February 2014

VAT Notice 701/1: Charities, 28 October 2014

VAT Notice 701/2: Welfare, 5 July 2011

VAT Notice 701/5: Clubs and associations, 16 October 2013

VAT Notice 701/6: Supplements, 1 April 1997

VAT Notice 701/7: VAT reliefs for disabled and older people, 18 December 2014, last updated 18 December 2014

VAT Notice 701/10: Zero-rating of books and other forms of printed matter, 13 December 2011, last updated 9 June 2015

VAT Notice 701/29: Betting, gaming and lotteries, 25 February 2013

VAT Notice 701/30: Education and vocational training, 25 February 2014

VAT Notice 701/31: Health institutions, 22 August 2014

VAT Notice 701/35: Youth clubs, 28 June 2011

VAT Notice 701/36: Insurance, 12 February 2013

VAT Notice 701/41: Sponsorship, 1 March 2002

VAT Notice 701/45: Sport, 2 August 2011

VAT Notice 701/47: Culture, 1 September 2011

VAT Notice 701/57: Health professionals and pharmaceutical products, 28 July 2014, last updated 31 July 2014

VAT Notice 701/58: Charity advertising and goods connected with collecting donations, 1 March 2002

VAT Notice 702: Imports, 20 October 2014, last updated 20 October 2014

VAT Notice 702/9: VAT – import customs procedures, 15 October 2012

VAT Notice 703: Export of goods from the UK, 28 March 2014

VAT Notice 704: VAT retail exports, 2 November 2004, last updated 6 August 2014

VAT Notice 706: Partial exemption, 16 June 2011

VAT Notice 706/2: Capital goods scheme, 19 October 2011

VAT Notice 708: Buildings and construction, 13 August 2014, last updated 14 August 2014

VAT Notice 709/1: Catering and take-away food, 7 October 2013

VAT Notice 709/3: Hotels and holiday accommodation, 8 June 2013

VAT Notice 709/5: Tour operators margin scheme, 14 December 2009

VAT Notice 709/6: Travel agents and tour operators, 1 March 2002

VAT Notice 714: Zero rating young children's clothing and footwear, 23 March 2015, last updated 24 March 2015

VAT Notice 718: The VAT Margin Scheme and global accounting, 7 April 2011

VAT Notice 725: The single market, 3 January 2014

VAT Notice 727: Retail schemes, 10 May 2012

VAT Notice 733: Flat Rate Scheme for small businesses, 3 May 2013

VAT Notice 741A: Place of supply of services, 24 February 2010

VAT Notice 742: Land and property, 29 May 2012

VAT Notice 742A: Opting to tax land and buildings, 16 April 2014

VAT Notice 744C: Ships, aircraft and associated services, 20 July 2011

VAT Notice 998: VAT refund scheme for national museums and galleries, 9 May 2013

VAT Notice 1001: VAT refund scheme for certain charities, 28 April 2015, last updated 22 September 2015

Revenue and Customs Briefs (archived)

Revenue and Customs Briefs can be accessed via the National Archives: webarchive.nationalarchives.gov.uk.

Revenue and Customs Brief 29/07: Charities – Extra Statutory Concession 3.29 – VAT: 'charitable' buildings – the 'change of use' charge, 27 March 2007

Revenue and Customs Brief 57/08: VAT – Excess charges in non-local authority car parks, 8 December 2008

Revenue and Customs Brief 06/09: Claims for retrospective application of Extra-Statutory Concession (ESC) 3.35, 20 February 2009

Revenue and Customs Brief 02/10: Lennartz accounting – new policy following ECJ case, 22 January 2010

Revenue and Customs Brief 13/10: Place of supply of freight transport and associated services – used and enjoyed outside the EU, 17 March 2010

Revenue and Customs Brief 15/10: Changes to implement ECJ decision in Canterbury Hockey Clubs C-253/07 mainly affecting affiliation fees, 29 March 2010

Revenue and Customs Brief 21/10: Tour Operators' Margin Scheme and the treatment of 'hotel billback' transactions, 21 May 2010

Revenue and Customs brief 25/10: Pay-per-click charity advertisements, 7 June 2010

Revenue and Customs Brief 31/10: HM Revenue & Customs position following the Court of Appeal Judgment in Insurancewide and Trader Media Group, 3 August 2010

Revenue and Customs Brief 32/11: HMRC's position following the First-Tier Tribunal decision in the case of Reed Employment Limited, 24 August 2011

Revenue and Customs Brief 47/11: VAT – zero rate – 'extra care accommodation', 30 December 2011

Revenue and Customs Brief 22/12: The place of supply of services connected to land, 2 August 2012

Revenue and Customs Brief 26/12: Withdrawal of the reduced rate of VAT for energy saving materials installed in buildings used for a relevant charitable purpose – infringement proceedings by the European Commission, 20 Aug 2012

Revenue and Customs Brief 30/12: A change in HM Revenue & Customs' (HMRC's) position following the decision of the Tax Tribunal in the case of Robinson Family Limited ([2012] UKFTT 360 (TC), TC02046), 16 November 2012

Revenue and Customs Briefs

Revenue and Customs Briefs can be found at www.gov.uk/government/collections/revenue-and-customs-briefs.

Revenue and Customs Brief 10 (2013): Withdrawal of the VAT exemption for supplies of research, 25 April 2013

Revenue and Customs Brief 5 (2014): Tour Operator Margin Schemes, 31 January 2014

Revenue and Customs Brief 14 (2014): Withdrawal of concessions for student accommodation and dining halls, 7 April 2014

Revenue and Customs Brief 39 (2014): VAT – liability catering and other services linked to education, 10 November 2014

Revenue and Customs Brief 43 (2014): VAT on pension fund management costs, 25 November 2014

Revenue and Customs Brief 46 (2014): VAT rule change and the VAT Mini One Stop Shop – additional guidance, 10 December 2014

Revenue and Customs Brief 49 (2014): VAT – prompt payment discounts, 22 December 2014

Revenue and Customs Brief 2 (2015): VAT grouping rules and the Skandia judgment, 10 February 2015

Revenue and Customs Brief 8 (2015): Deduction of VAT on pension fund management costs, 26 March 2015

Revenue and Customs Brief 13 (2015): Reduced rate of VAT for the installation of energy saving materials, 31 July 2015, updated 18 August 2015

Glossary

Terms highlighted in bold are included elsewhere within the Glossary.

Term	Meaning	See Chapter
Acquisition	**Goods** brought into the **UK** from another **EU** state.	9
Acquisition VAT	VAT due on certain **acquisitions** from VAT-registered suppliers in other **EU** states. Instead of the supplier charging **output VAT** the customer must self-account for acquisition VAT. The acquisition VAT must be paid over to **HMRC** like output VAT. Acquisition VAT can be treated like **input VAT** and is potentially **recoverable**.	9
Activity	A set of actions through which resources are mobilised to produce specific outputs.	4
Actual tax point	An actual tax point is created for a **supply** if, before the **basic tax point**, a **VAT invoice** is issued or payment is received for the supply. The actual tax point is the earlier of the invoice being issued and payment being received.	12
Agent	An agent is a legal person that is authorised to act on behalf of a **principal**. An agent can be **disclosed** or **undisclosed**.	11
Annexe	A building that is distinct from but ancillary to another building or buildings. In certain circumstances the construction of an annexe can be **zero-rated**.	8
Annual Accounting Scheme	The annual accounting scheme allows you to submit just one annual **VAT return**. However, you must still pay regular instalments of VAT over to **HMRC**.	10.10
Annual adjustment	Organisations with a mix of **exempt** and **taxable activities** must usually perform a periodic calculation of **input VAT attributable** to taxable activities on an annual basis in the annual adjustment.	3
Attributable	Purchases and their associated **VAT** are attributable to a **supply** or **activity** if they have a direct and immediate link with the supply or activity. Generally the attributable costs of an activity are, for VAT purposes, its **direct costs**, and a portion of the **residual costs** of the organisation.	3

Term	Meaning	See Chapter
B2B	B2B (Business to business) **supply**. This is a supply to a customer who is registered for VAT or who has some level of **business activity** (exempt or taxable). However, if a business customer purchases **services** wholly for the private use of the business's owners or its staff, then the supply is treated as **B2C**.	9
B2C	B2C (Business to customer or business to consumer) **supplies**. These are supplies to customers who are not registered for VAT and who do not have any **business activities** at all. They also include supplies to businesses wholly for the private use of the business's owners or its staff.	9
Barter transaction	A **supply** (say from A to B) where **consideration** is paid in the form of another supply (from B to A). For VAT purposes there are two supplies (A to B and B to A) with the consideration for each being offset.	7
Basic tax point	The basic tax point is: for a **supply of goods**, when the customer takes possession of the **goods**, and for a **supply of services**, when the **service** is complete.	12
Blocked VAT	VAT incurred on certain purchases is always **irrecoverable**. Blocked VAT includes VAT on business entertaining and cars available for private use.	12
Business activities	For an **activity** to be business it must meet the **business tests**.	4
Business tests	**UK** case law has established various tests to determine whether or not an **activity** is a **business activity**. The business tests are: 1. Is the activity a serious undertaking earnestly pursued? 2. Is the activity an occupation or function, which is actively pursued with reasonable or recognisable continuity? 3. Does the activity have a certain measure of substance in terms of the quarterly or annual value of taxable supplies made? 4. Is the activity conducted in a regular manner and on sound and recognised business principles? 5. Is the activity predominantly concerned with the making of **taxable supplies** for a **consideration**? 6. Are the taxable supplies that are being made of a kind which, subject to differences of detail, are commonly made by those who seek to profit from them?	4

Term	Meaning	See Chapter
Capital Goods Scheme	A special VAT scheme applicable to the purchase, construction, alteration or renovation of **capital items** that are put to mixed **taxable** and **exempt** or **non-business** use.	10
Capital item	Land, buildings or civil engineering works whose VAT-bearing cost is £250,000 or more or an item of computer equipment, aircraft, ship, boat or other vessel whose VAT-bearing cost is £50,000 or more.	10
Cash Accounting Scheme	Under the Cash Accounting Scheme: ■ **output VAT** becomes due to **HMRC** when it is received from your customer (or if later, the date of any post-dated cheque); and ■ **input VAT** is recoverable when the purchase invoice is paid (or if later, the date of any post-dated cheque).	10.9
Charity	For tax purposes (including for VAT purposes) a charity is a body that: 1. is established for charitable purposes only; 2. is subject to the control of a **UK** court in the exercise of its jurisdiction with respect to charities, or any other court in the exercise of a corresponding jurisdiction under the law of a relevant territory. Relevant territories were originally the member states of the **EU**, Iceland and Norway, but Lichtenstein was added with effect from 31 July 2014; 3. has complied with any requirement to be registered with a charity regulator; 4. has managers who are fit and proper persons to be managers of the body.	6
Consideration	Everything received in return for making a **supply**. Includes **barter supplies**, part exchange, granting of rights and acceptance of constraints or limitations. Consideration must be capable of being expressed in money and there must be a direct link between the supply and the consideration. Indirect links, possible links and contaminated links are not enough.	4
Cost sharing group (CSG)	In certain circumstances independent entities with **non-business** or **exempt activities** can set up a separate entity (a cost sharing group) in order for that entity to supply them with **services** for use in their non-business or exempt activities. If the qualifying conditions are met, those supplies are VAT exempt whatever their nature.	5

587

Term	Meaning	See Chapter
Deductible, deducting VAT	**Input VAT** is said to be deductible if it can be recovered, or netted off against any **output VAT** due, in the **VAT return**. Input VAT is only deductible if it is **attributable** to a **taxable activity**, is attributable to an **exempt activity** and the level of exempt activity is *de minimis*, or is deductible under some other legislative provision.	3
Deemed supplies	Certain transactions are deemed to be **supplies** even if there is no **consideration.** These include: ■ the permanent transfer or disposal of business assets; ■ the temporary use of business assets for non-business purposes; ■ retention of business assets on deregistration.	4
De minimis, the de minimis test	The *de minimis* test comprises three conditions. If one or more of the conditions is satisfied, then you are *de minimis* for the period concerned and can recover all the **exempt input VAT** for that period. A period is a VAT month, quarter or longer period: ■ *Condition 1*: total **input VAT** is less than or equal to £1,875* and the turnover on **exempt supplies** is less than or equal to the turnover on **taxable supplies**; ■ *Condition 2*: total input VAT less input VAT directly **attributable** to **taxable activities** is less than or equal to £1,875* and the turnover on exempt supplies is less than or equal to the turnover on taxable supplies; ■ *Condition 3*: exempt input VAT is less than or equal to £1,875* and less than or equal to 50% of total input VAT. * If **VAT returns** are submitted monthly, the figure of £1,875 above is replaced with £625, and for a 12-month longer period annual adjustment, it is replaced with £7,500. For a longer period that is less than 12 months, the figure to use is £625 multiplied by the number of whole or part months in the longer period.	3
Deregistration threshold	The level of **taxable supplies** below which a business can de-register for VAT. The deregistration threshold is normally £2,000 less than the **registration threshold**.	2
Direct costs, directly attributable	The costs that are incurred by the **activity** and for no other purpose.	3
Disapply, disapplication	Stopping an **option to tax** from having effect for a particular **supply**.	8

Term	Meaning	See Chapter
Disbursement	Costs incurred as **agent** for a **principal** and held in a suspense account on the balance sheet.	11
Disclosed agent	An **agent** that routinely discloses the identity of its **principal** to the third party.	11
Dispatch	**Goods** sent to a destination in another **EU** state.	9
Distance sales, distance-selling thresholds	Distance sales are sales of **goods**, made in the course of a taxable **business activity**, to unregistered customers in other **EU** states where the supplier or an **agent** of the supplier is responsible for the delivery of the goods. When the total annual VAT-exclusive value of sales to customers in any particular EU state reaches that state's Distance-Selling Threshold the **UK** supplier must register for VAT in that state and then charge local VAT on those sales and complete a local **VAT return**.	9.6.15
Dwelling	Self-contained living accommodation that has no internal access to any other dwelling (apart from emergency-use-only doors). Its separate use or disposal must not be prohibited by a covenant or planning consent or similar. Statutory planning consent must have been granted (if applicable) and the building must have been constructed or altered in accordance with that consent.	8
EC Sales List	Report due to **HMRC** of sales of **goods** and certain sales of **services** to VAT-registered **EU** customers.	9, 12
Economic activity	Synonymous with **business activity**. The **Principal VAT Directive** defines an economic **activity** as: ■ all activities of producers, traders and persons supplying **services** including mining and agricultural activities and activities of professions; ■ the exploitation of tangible or intangible property for the purposes of obtaining income therefrom on a continuing basis is in particular regarded as an economic activity.	4
Education	A course, class or lesson of instruction or study in any subject, regardless of when and where it takes place.	5
European Union (EU)	At the time of writing, and for VAT purposes, the EU comprises 28 member states: Austria, Belgium, Bulgaria, Croatia, Cyprus, Czech Republic, Denmark, Estonia, Finland, France, Germany, Greece, Hungary, Ireland, Italy, Latvia, Lithuania, Luxembourg, Malta, Netherlands, Poland, Portugal, Romania, Slovakia, Slovenia, Spain, Sweden, and the **UK**.	14

Term	Meaning	See Chapter
Examination services	The setting and marking of examinations, the setting of educational or training standards, the making of assessments and other **services** provided with a view to ensuring educational and training standards are maintained.	5
Exempt input VAT	The VAT on purchases **directly attributed** and apportioned to **exempt activities**.	3
Exempt supply, exempt activities	Certain **business supplies** do not carry any VAT because they are specifically exempted by **VAT legislation**. Examples include certain health, welfare, educational, cultural and sporting supplies.	5, 8
Export	**Goods** sent to a destination outside the **EU**. The goods may either be sent by the supplier to a destination outside the EU (direct exports) or collected by the customer and taken outside the EU (indirect exports).	9
Extra statutory concession (ESC)	A relaxation which gives taxpayers a reduction in tax liability to which they would not be entitled under the strict letter of the law.	Various
Fuel Scale Charge	The Fuel Scale Charge can be used to determine the VAT-inclusive value of the **deemed supply** that is made when business fuel is put to private use.	12.10.7
Fundraising event (qualifying)	Events which are organised by a **charity**, charities or other qualifying bodies, whose purpose is to raise funds for the organiser(s) and which are promoted as such, and which meet various other conditions. Supplies of **goods** or **services** by the organiser(s) in connection with a qualifying fundraising event are VAT **exempt**.	5, 7
Goods (supply of)	Goods are tangible objects. A supply of goods is the transfer of the right to dispose of goods as owner.	4
HM Revenue & Customs (HMRC)	The **UK** government body responsible for the administration and collection of UK VAT.	14
Import	**Goods** brought into the **UK** from outside the **EU**.	9
Import VAT	VAT due on certain **goods imported** from countries outside the **EU**. Import VAT is normally payable at the point of importation along with any Customs Duties that may be due.	9
Input VAT	VAT incurred on purchases that are **attributable** to **business activities**.	3

Term	Meaning	See Chapter
Irrecoverable VAT	VAT that is incurred on a purchase but cannot be **recovered**. This normally includes: **blocked VAT**, VAT **attributable** to **non-business activities** and VAT attributable to **exempt activities** where the level of exempt activity is not *de minimis.*	3
Lennartz mechanism	Where an asset is purchased, acquired or constructed and the asset will be put to mixed **business** and **private** use, the asset may be assigned as a business asset. This permits full recovery of any VAT **attributable** to the **taxable** use of the asset. **Output VAT** is then due on any private use of the asset. This is known as the Lennartz mechanism.	3
Margin scheme, margin scheme supply	**Supplies** ordinarily made by tour operators or travel agents that are bought in and re-supplied as **principal** or **undisclosed agent** without material alteration or further processing. For example, supplies of accommodation and passenger transport.	10
Methods	The formula or process for calculating how much **residual VAT** can be **recovered**. Methods are usually sub-divided into: ■ business/non-business methods which apportion residual VAT between **business** and **non-business** activities; ■ **partial exemption** methods which apportion residual VAT between **taxable** and **exempt** activities. However, combined methods are also possible.	3
Mini One Stop Shop (MOSS)	A special VAT registration scheme for reporting and accounting for VAT due to other **EU** states on certain supplies of **services** to customers in those states.	9
Non-business activity	An **activity** which is not **business**. Activities funded entirely by grants or donations are normally non-business. The activity of generating income from financial investments is normally, in the hands of a **charity**, considered to be non-business.	4
Non-business VAT	The VAT on purchases **directly attributed** and **apportioned** to **non-business activities**.	4
Option to tax	A formal declaration made by a business in relation to one or more specific properties (land, buildings, or civil engineering works) that henceforth that business's **supplies** of that property will, by default, be VAT **standard-rated** rather than VAT exempt.	8

Term	Meaning	See Chapter
Output VAT	The VAT you charge on sales and which you have to collect from customers. You then pay this over to **HMRC** after deducting **input VAT** you have paid out on **attributable** purchases.	1
Outside the scope (of VAT)	Transactions which are not covered by the VAT regime.	4
Partial exemption, partially exempt	Used to describe the situation where a business makes **taxable** and **exempt supplies**. The business must apportion its **residual VAT** between the taxable and **exempt activities** using a partial exemption **method**.	3
Place of supply	The place where a **supply** takes place. The place of supply normally determines which country's VAT rules (if any) apply to the supply. If both the customer and supplier are in the **UK**, the place of supply will normally be the UK. If either the customer or supplier is outside the UK, then the place of supply may be outside the UK.	9
Principal	You are principal when you **supply** your own **goods** or **services** to a third party.	10
Principal VAT Directive	The main source of **VAT legislation** in the **EU**. At the time of writing this is Council Directive 2006/112/EC.	4, 5, 9
Rate of VAT	VAT is applied as a specified percentage of the selling price. The percentage used is the 'rate of VAT'. At the time of writing the UK has three rates of VAT: ■ the **standard rate**: for 15/16 this is 20%; ■ the **reduced rate**: for 15/16 this is 5%; ■ the **zero rate**: the rate of VAT applicable is zero per cent. The standard and reduced rates are subject to change over time.	2, 12
Recovering VAT	The process of deducting **input VAT** from the **output VAT** due to **HMRC**. Input VAT **attributable** to **taxable supplies** is recoverable, as is input VAT attributable to **exempt supplies** if the level of exempt activity is *de minimis*.	3
Reduced rate	Certain **taxable supplies** are eligible for a reduced **rate of VAT**, currently 5%.	6
Registration threshold	The level of **taxable supplies** above which a business must register for VAT. The VAT registration threshold is normally uprated each year in the government's annual budget.	2

Term	Meaning	See Chapter
Relevant charitable purpose	Use by a **charity** in either or both of the following ways: ■ otherwise than in the course or furtherance of **business;** ■ as a **village hall** or similarly in providing social or recreational facilities for a local community.	8
Relevant residential purpose	Use as one or more of the following: ■ a home or other institution providing residential accommodation for children; ■ a home or other institution providing residential accommodation with personal care for persons in need of personal care by reason of old age, disablement, past or present dependence on alcohol or drugs or past or present mental disorder; ■ a hospice; ■ residential accommodation for students or school pupils; ■ residential accommodation for members of any of the armed forces; ■ a monastery, nunnery or similar establishment; or ■ an institution which is the sole or main residence of at least 90% of its residents. But excludes use as a hospital or similar institution, prison or similar institution, or hotel, inn or similar establishment.	8
Removal	**Goods** supplied to an organisation or individual in another **EU** state.	9
Residual expenses/costs	Costs that cannot be **directly attributed** to one type of activity: **non-business**, **exempt** or **taxable**. Typically residual expenses include the overheads and central function costs of an organisation.	3
Residual VAT	VAT incurred on **residual expenses**.	3
Reverse charge	In certain situations the customer must charge themselves **output VAT** and pay this to **HMRC**, as opposed to the supplier charging the customer output VAT and paying this to HMRC. Such scenarios include where a **UK** VAT-registered customer receives certain supplies of **services** from a non-UK supplier.	9

593

Term	Meaning	See Chapter
Self-supply	Where an organisation must charge itself **output VAT**. Self-supplies can arise in a variety of ways including: ■ using business assets for **non-business** or private purposes – see Chapter 4; ■ constructing a building from your own resources – see Chapter 8; ■ using motor vehicles for private purposes – see Chapter 12.	4, 8, 12
Services (supply of)	Any **supply** which does not constitute a supply of **goods**.	4
Single/multiple supply tests (CPP/Levob tests)	The single/multiple supply tests arising from the Card Protection Plan and Levob cases: ■ Every supply of a **service** must normally be regarded as distinct and independent. ■ A **supply** which comprises a single service from an economic point of view should not be artificially split, so as to distort the functioning of the VAT system. ■ The essential features of the transaction must be ascertained in order to determine whether the taxable person is supplying a typical consumer with several distinct principal services or with a single service. ■ There is a single supply where one or more elements are to be regarded as constituting the principal service, with the remainder regarded as ancillary services which share the tax treatment of the principal service. ■ A service is ancillary to a principal service if it does not constitute for customers an aim in itself, but a means of better enjoying the principal service supplied. ■ Where two or more elements supplied by a taxable person to a typical customer, are so closely linked that they form objectively, from an economic point of view, a whole transaction, which it would be artificial to split, then all those elements or acts constitute a single supply.	11, 13
Standard Rate of VAT	The standard rate of VAT was 17.5% between 1 April 1991 and 30 November 2008, 15% from 1 December 2008 to 31 December 2009, 17.5% from 1 January 2010 to 3 January 2011, and 20% from 4 January 2011.	12
Standard-rated supply	A **taxable supply** which is not eligible for **zero** or **reduced rating**.	1

Term	Meaning	See Chapter
Supply	Certain transactions are always deemed to be a **supply** (see **deemed supplies**). Otherwise there is a supply when **goods** or **services** are provided in return for **consideration**. For the supply to be made in return for the consideration there must be a direct link between the supply and consideration.	4
Tax point	The point in time when a **supply** is regarded as taking place. The tax point of a supply is the **basic tax point** unless there is an earlier **actual tax point**, in which case it is the actual tax point, or a **VAT invoice** is issued for the supply within two weeks of the basic tax point, in which case it is the invoice date. This rule is modified for certain special types of supply.	12
Taxable supply, taxable activity	All **business supplies** which are not **exempt** are taxable. The **UK** currently applies three different **rates of VAT** to taxable supplies; the **zero rate** (0%) and **reduced rate** apply to certain specific categories of **goods** and **services**, and the **standard rate** to all others.	6
Time of supply	The point in time when a **supply** is regarded as taking place. See **tax point**.	12
Tour Operators' Margin Scheme (TOMS)	Special VAT scheme that applies where a package of travel and/or accommodation is provided to a traveller by an entity acting as **principal** or **undisclosed agent**. Voluntary organisations most commonly encounter TOMS in connection with challenge events.	7, 10
Transfer of a going concern	Where the assets of a **business** are transferred as a going concern and the purchaser intends carrying on the business, then special VAT rules apply to the assets transferred.	11
Undisclosed agent	An **agent** that does not routinely disclose the identity of the **principal** to third parties.	11
United Kingdom (UK)	The VAT territory of the UK. For VAT purposes this includes England, Wales, Scotland, Northern Ireland and the Isle of Man but excludes the Channel Islands and Gibraltar.	9
VAT fraction	The proportion of the gross amount (net + VAT) that is VAT. For VAT at 20% the VAT fraction is 1/6. For VAT at 5% the VAT fraction is 1/21.	1

Term	Meaning	See Chapter
VAT group	Under certain circumstances entities may form a VAT group, or join a VAT group with the VAT group being treated as a single entity for (most) VAT purposes.	2
VAT invoice	An invoice that contains specific information such as the VAT registration number of the supplier and the VAT charged.	12
VAT law, VAT legislation	VAT is an **EU**-wide tax that is implemented nationally and is the subject of various EU directives. Each EU state must implement these directives into its national legislation. In the **UK** the principal legislation is in the VAT Act 1994.	12
VAT refund schemes	Certain types of entity can obtain a refund for the VAT incurred in particular activities. Eligible entities include: local authorities, academy and free schools, national museums and galleries, hospices, search and rescue organisations, listed places of worship.	10
VAT return	A periodic return which must be made to **HMRC**. Normally VAT returns must be submitted electronically every three months, though returns can also be submitted monthly or annually under certain circumstances.	12
Village hall	A building which is used to provide social or recreational activities for a local community. There must be a high degree of community and voluntary involvement in the running of the building, a desire to promote the use of the facilities by members of the community, a great emphasis on the needs of and benefits to the local community, and any charges should not be set commercially.	8
Vocational training	Training, re-training or the provision of work experience for: 1. any trade, profession or employment; or 2. any voluntary work connected with: • education, health, safety, or welfare; or • the carrying out of activities of a charitable nature.	5
Within the scope of VAT	An activity is within the scope of VAT if it is covered by **VAT law**. See also **business activity**.	4
Zero-rated	Certain **business supplies** are **taxable**, but carry VAT at zero rate.	6

Index

Index entries refer to page numbers. Entries are in word-by-word alphabetical order. Legal cases are in italics.